SALVATORE
ZECCHINI
Editor

LESSONS FROM THE ECONOMIC TRANSITION

Central and Eastern Europe in the 1990s

KLUWER ACADEMIC PUBLISHERS
Dordrecht / Boston / London

Distributors for North America:
Kluwer Academic Publishers
101 Philip Drive
Assinippi Park
Norwell, Massachusetts 02061 USA

Distributors for all other countries:
Kluwer Academic Publishers Group
Distribution Centre
Post Office Box 322
3300 AH Dordrecht, THE NETHERLANDS

Library of Congress Cataloging-in-Publication Data

Lessons from the economic transition : Central and Eastern Europe in the 1990s / Salvatore Zecchini, editor.

p. cm.

ISBN 0-7923-9852-1. -- ISBN 0-7923-9857-2 (pbk.)

1. Europe, Central--Economic policy. 2. Europe, Eastern--Economic policy--1989- 3. Europe, Central--Economic conditions. 4. Europe, Eastern--Economic conditions--1989- I. Zecchini, Salvatore.

HC244.L455 1997

338.943--dc21 96-49917

CIP

Printed on acid-free paper.

Printed in the United States of America

LESSONS FROM THE ECONOMIC TRANSITION

Central and Eastern Europe in the 1990s

Contents

Part II — Enterprise restructuring and private sector development

Part III — Unemployment and the reform of social policies

Preface

An attentive reader embarking on this book might wonder what "the" economic transition to which the title refers might be. In this century almost all countries have gone through periods of economic transition; but which period of economic history can claim to embody the notion or to represent the era of "the" transition? Definitely, no country or group of countries has experienced anything comparable to the economic upheavals that the fall of communism has brought about in a large portion of the world in just three years (1989 to 1991). No other "transition" to date has prompted more interest and more studies among economists, academics and policy-makers than has the transformation of centrally planned economies into market-based systems. It is this transformation that has come to define "the" transition.

Early in the transformation process (in November 1990), with the support of the Centre for Co-operation with the Economies in Transition (CCET), I launched a conference to examine the challenges faced by these countries. About six years have gone by and a new economic landscape has emerged in that part of the world. The difficulties in transforming these economies have exceeded all expectations, and economic performances have varied considerably across countries. The time has come, therefore, to make a first evaluation of progress and problems, with a view to extracting useful policy lessons to guide policy-makers in successfully completing the transition in the near future.

To this end, a number of major experts, policy-makers and academics, from reforming countries and from the OECD area, were recently invited to examine the main issues and policy controversies, and, from this basis, to suggest improvements to current transition strategies and their implementation. Not all the invitees accepted, which came as no surprise, since the task is very challenging, demanding painstaking analysis of an economic reality still in a state of flux. Eventually, twenty-two analytical contributions were prepared, addressing a large range of problematic aspects of the transition experience to date, bringing to light new evidence and evaluating the validity of information now available on the transition economies. Whereas the subject of the book is the transition in all post-communist countries, the focus of the contributions is primarily on the Visegrad countries, Bulgaria, Romania and Russia. These contributions constituted the basis for the debate over a wider range of transition issues which took place in a colloquium held in May 1996 in the framework of the CCET programme. The debate involved a larger number of experts than the original contributors, which added evidence and provided a broader perspective in assessing the findings of the studies and in evaluating both viability and feasibility of proposed policy improvements.

This book is not, however, a collection of proceedings of the colloquium. Rather, it is a coherent presentation of the analyses and views expressed by prominent experts about the main shortcomings and pitfalls in transition policies applied so far, as well as being an attempt to point the way forward to push the transition through. It is a merit of this book to highlight the complex interrelation between the requirements of the economics of the transition and the social and political constraints faced by the Central and Eastern European countries (CEECs).

As regards the book's structure, the list of all contributors is followed by an introduction that serves to explain the interconnections between the different contributions and to highlight the most policy-relevant findings. In essence, the introduction guides the reader in approaching the long series of complex issues, and in focusing on the main points of interest. From a substantive point of view, the true introduction to the issues is contained in the opening contribution of the book. The book is organised following what is considered an order of urgency of the problems to be addressed by CEECs' policy-makers in the current stage of the transition. The various inputs are arranged in such a manner as to complement each other, or to bring out contrasting analyses or viewpoints.

A number of comments are also included. These relate more to the thematic issues than to the specific features of the contributions in the various chapters. In many respects, the comments are an important addition to understanding the policy challenges. In the same light, the reports on the debates do not summarise all the interventions but aim at giving a balanced presentation of conflicting views on central policy questions. Following such a diversity of issues and points of view, the policy conclusions neither represent a summary of the findings, nor seek to reach a consensus on policy recommendations. Rather, they reflect the editor's own reading of contributions, comments and debates, and, it is hoped, provide a succinct set of policy suggestions that could receive wide support among experts. Instead of looking backward to list successes and failures of past or on-going policies, the conclusions are forward-looking, to help policy-makers to extract, from that diversity of views, a few clear messages about the direction in which policies for the next stage of the transition should be oriented. To experts and researchers, the book also offers many insights and hints on new areas and approaches to be explored for policy analysis and policy development.

All contributions have required some editorial intervention prior to their publication. In the case of authors' contributions, editing was very limited, and confined to points of accuracy, though a few, for reasons of clarity, necessitated more extensive interventions to improve the linguistic presentation. The comments had, however, to be extensively edited, in order to maintain the focus on the specific issues presented in each Part, and to fit them in the limited space available.

An editor's role is not to pass judgement on the essays and views he includes in his book. In accordance with this principle, it is left to the reader of this book to form his or her own view about the threads of analysis or conclusion to be followed or rejected. The editor's overriding concern has been to present as varied a range of evidence, analysis and opinion from all sides *(West and East)* as necessary to bear testimony to the gaps or shortcomings in transition policies, as well as to the "cultural" differences still remaining in evaluating them and the transition as a whole. This is not to imply that the transition is a divisive issue. On the contrary, it is notable in the CEECs that even the staunchest opponents of the reforms of the 1990s no longer advocate a return to the past regime but argue for improvements in the new regime.

It would not have been possible to prepare this book without the assistance of a team of highly skilled and dedicated collaborators. I am deeply indebted to them and grateful for their unstinting support of my endeavour to complete this book in just three months. A special word of appreciation must go to Nils Bjorksten, with whom I have discussed several parts of the book, and who assisted me in preparing reports on the debates, in revising some of the texts, and in reviewing corrections. I am also grateful to C. Marshall Mills for helping me in organising the work, improving the presentation of the book, reviewing the amended texts, and co-ordinating the preparation of the text for printing. For the latter task, I also wish to thank Catherine Findlay and Jane Hamilton for their patient and attentive contribution to the publication of the book. Other members of the team helped me to revise the texts from a language point of view, to type and to collate them. To all, I wish to express my appreciation for their valuable inputs.

Notwithstanding all this support, the responsibility for any remaining mistakes, as well as for the overall editorial work, remains with me. Each author or discussant evidently takes responsibility for the contents of his contribution. Accordingly, this book does not express the views of the OECD or any other institution with which the contributors might be affiliated.

Salvatore Zecchini

Paris, September 1996

Contributors

Philippe Aghion
Deputy Chief Economist
EBRD
London, United Kingdom
and Professor
Nuffield College
Oxford, United Kingdom

Leszek Balcerowicz
Professor
President of Advisory Council
Foundation for Economic Education
Warsaw, Poland

Amit Bhaduri
Professor
Jawaharlal Nehru University
New Delhi, India

Tito Boeri
OECD Directorate for Education, Employment, Labour and Social Affairs
Paris, France

Jozef Brhel
State Secretary
Ministry of the Economy
Bratislava, Slovak Republic

Octavian V. Cãrare
Private Ownership Fund
Transylvania, Romania

Wendy Carlin
Professor
University College
London, United Kingdom

Simon Commander
The World Bank
Washington DC, USA

Richard N. Cooper
Professor
Harvard University
Cambridge, MA, USA

Fabrizio Coricelli
Professor
Faculty of Economics
University of Siena
Siena, Italy

Lászlo Csaba
Senior Economist
Kopint-Datorg Economic Research
and Professor,
College of Foreign Trade
Budapest, Hungary

Daniel Daianu
Chief Economist
National Bank of Romania
Bucharest, Romania

Rumen Dobrinsky
President
Centre for Economic and Strategic Research
Sofia, Bulgaria

Zdenek Drabek
World Trade Organisation
Geneva, Switzerland

Michael Ellman
Professor
University of Amsterdam
Amsterdam, Netherlands

Randall K. Filer
Professor
Hunter College, CUNY
New York, USA
CERGE-EI
Prague, Czech Republic

Stanley Fischer
IMF
Washington DC, USA
Research Associate, NBER
On leave from MIT
Cambridge, MA, USA

Roman Frydman
Professor
New York University
New York, USA

János Gács
IIASA
Economic Transition and
Integration Project
Laxenburg, Austria

Alan Gelb
The World Bank
Washington DC, USA

Stanislaw Gomulka
Professor
London School of Economics
London, United Kingdom

Marek Góra
Professor
Warsaw School of Economics
Warsaw, Poland

Daniel Gros
Professor
CEPS
Brussels, Belgium

Peter Havlik
Deputy Director
WIIW
Vienna, Austria

Eduard Hochreiter
Senior Adviser and Head Economics
Studies Division
Austrian National Bank
Vienna, Austria

Miroslav Hrncir
Director
Institute of Economics
Czech National Bank
Prague, Czech Republic

Gabor Hunya
WIIW
Vienna, Austria

András Inotai
Director
Institute for World Economics
of the Hungarian Academy of
Sciences
Budapest, Hungary

Richard Jackman
Professor
London School of Economics
Centre for Economic
Performance
London, United Kingdom

Vincent Koen
OECD Economics Department
Paris, France

János Kornai
Professor
Harvard University
Cambridge, MA, USA
Permanent Fellow
Institute for Advanced Study
Collegium Budapest
Budapest, Hungary

Hans-Peter Lankes
EBRD
London, United Kingdom

Kazimierz Laski
Professor
Director of WIIW
Vienna, Austria

Edward Leamer
Professor
Anderson Graduate School of Management/UCLA
Los Angeles, USA

John Litwack
OECD Economics Department
Paris, France

Silvana Malle
OECD Economics Department
Paris, France

Martha de Melo
The World Bank
Washington DC, USA

Misu Negritoiu
Chief Economic Advisor to the President of the Republic of Romania
Bucharest, Romania

Krzysztof J. Ners
Director
Policy Education Centre on Transition
Warsaw, Poland

David Newbery
Professor
University of Cambridge
Cambridge, United Kingdom

Joaquim Oliveira-Martins
OECD Economics Department
Paris, France

Catalin Pauna
Queen Mary and Westfield College
London, United Kingdom

Enrico Perotti
Professor
University of Amsterdam
Amsterdam, Netherlands

Andrzej Rapaczynski
Professor
Columbia University School of Law
New York, USA

Gérard Roland
Professor
ECARE
Free University of Brussels
Brussels, Belgium

Jim Rollo
Chief Economic Adviser
Foreign and Commonwealth Office
London, United Kingdom

Dariusz Rosati
Minister of Foreign Affairs
Warsaw, Poland,
formerly with UN/ECE,
Geneva, Switzerland

Jacek Rostowski
Professor
Central European University
Budapest, Hungary

Ratna Sahay
IMF
Washington DC, USA

Stefano Scarpetta
OECD Economics Department
Paris, France

Nicholas Stern
Chief Economist
EBRD and Professor
London School of Economics
London, United Kingdom

Jan Svejnar
Professor
University of Pittsburgh
Pittsburgh, USA and
CERGE-EI
Prague, Czech Republic

Andrei Tolstopiatenko
Professor
Moscow State University
Moscow, Russian Federation

Carlos A. Végh
Professor
UCLA
Los Angeles, USA
On leave from the IMF
Washington, DC

A. J. Venables
Professor
London School of Economics
London, United Kingdom

Heinrich Vogel
Director
Bundesinstitut für
Ostwissenschaftliche und
Internationale Studien
Cologne, Germany

Georg Winckler
Professor
University of Vienna
Vienna, Austria

Salvatore Zecchini
OECD Deputy Secretary-General
Director, Centre for
Co-operation with the
Economies in Transition
Paris, France

Other participants in the discussions:

Hans Blommestein
OECD Directorate for Financial,
Fiscal and Enterprise Affairs
Paris, France

Béla Kadar
Chairman of Parliamentary
Committee for Budget and Finance
Budapest, Hungary

Stilpon Nestor
OECD Directorate for Financial,
Fiscal and Entrerprise Affairs
Paris, France

Thomas Nowotny
OECD Centre for Co-operation with
the Economies in Transition
Paris, France

Andreas Wörgötter
Economics Department
Institute for Advanced Studies
Vienna, Austria

Abbreviations

ASP 1995	Adjustment and Stabilization programme of 1995 in Hungary
b.o.p.	Balance of payments
CAP	Common Agricultural Policy of the EU
CCET	Centre for Co-operation with the Economies in Transition, OECD
CEE	Central and Eastern Europe
CEECs	All post-communist countries in Central and Eastern Europe and former Soviet Union, unless otherwise defined
CEFTA	Central European Free Trade Agreement
CEPS	Centre for European Policy Studies
CERGE-EI	Centre for Economic Research and Graduate Education, Charles University - Economics Institute, The Academy of Sciences of the Czech Republic
CIS	Commonwealth of Independent States
CMEA	Council for Mutual Economic Assistance
Comecon	See CMEA
CPI	Consumer Price Index
CSA	Central Statistical Agency
CUNY	City University of New York
DOEs	Domestically-owned enterprises
EBRD	European Bank for Reconstruction and Development
ECARE	European Centre for Advanced Research in Economics
EEA	European Economic Area
EFTA	European Free Trade Association
EMU	European Monetary Union
EPU	European Payments Union
ERDI	Exchange Rate Deviation Index
EU	European Union
FCs	Foreign-owned companies
FDI	Foreign Direct Investment
FIE	Foreign Investment Enterprise
FRG	Federal Republic of Germany
FSU	Former Soviet Union
GCS	Global compensation scheme in Romania, 1991
GDP	Gross Domestic Product
GDR	German Democratic Republic
GFI	Gross Fixed Investment
GFI-E	Gross Fixed Investment in Equipment
GI	Gross Investment
GNP	Gross National Product

Goskomstat	Russian central statistical agency
HBS	Household Budget Survey
IBRD	International Bank for Reconstruction and Development
IFI	International Financial Institutions
IGC	EU intergovernmental conference
IIASA	International Institute for Applied Systems Analysis
IMF	International Monetary Fund
IPF	Investment Privatisation Funds
JV	Joint Venture
LFS	Labour force survey
LTU	Long term unemployment
M&E	Machinery and Equipment
MEBOs	Management-employee buyouts
MFN	Most Favoured Nation trade classification
MIT	Massachusetts Institute of Technology
NAFTA	North American Free Trade Agreement
NBER	National Bureau of Economic Research
NBR	National Bank of Romania
NIC	New Industrial Countries
NIF	National Investment Funds
NIS	New Independent States of the former Soviet Union
OECD	Organisation for Economic Co-operation and Development
OEEC	Organisation for European Economic Co-operation
POF	Private ownership funds in Romania
PPI	Producer Price Index
PPP	Purchasing Power Parity
R&D	Research and development
RCs	Reforming Countries
SITC	Standard international trade classification
SOEs	State-owned enterprises
TFP	Total factor productivity
TVEs	Township and Village Enterprises
UCLA	University of California, Los Angeles
UN/ECE	United Nations/Economic Commission for Europe
Uruguay Round	The last multilateral trade negotiations round under GATT, concluded in 1993.
VAT	Value-added tax
Visegrad Countries	Czech Republic, Hungary, Poland and Slovak Republic only
WIIW	The Vienna Institute for Comparative Economic Studies
WTO	World Trade Organisation

Introduction

Salvatore Zecchini

What have we learned from CEECs' economic transition to a market-based system during the current decade? Are there any lessons that can provide reliable guidance to these countries to improve their policies for the rest of this decade? These are the central questions that are addressed in this book, drawing on the analyses and comments of a number of major experts in the field.

The question as to whether there are any lessons is less rhetorical than might appear because there are good reasons to cast doubts on the possibility of arriving at significant and uncontroversial policy conclusions that can be applied across the region. The time period since the beginning of the transition spans too few years — from four to six years depending on the country — to allow experts to gather comprehensive evidence on the impact and shortcomings of transition policies. Contrary to some views, extending the period of reference backward to include previous reforms would not help since those reforms were only limited attempts to improve small portions of an economic system that remained firmly anchored to central planning and extensive public interference in enterprise decisions. Only in this decade did former communist countries abandon that system and aim directly at building a market-based system.

Wide differences existed at the beginning of the transition among these countries in terms of socio-political conditions, economic imbalances and human and physical resource endowments. This explains in part why policy outcomes differ widely across countries even though their strategies were broadly similar, as they included essentially the same components, namely price and trade liberalisation, macroeconomic stabilization, creation of market institutions and privatisation. Of course, other factors have to be added, particularly the differences in the combination and sequencing of measures and in policy implementation. Some countries have shown more determination than others in introducing radical changes and in maintaining the reform momentum, mostly by taking maximum advantage of the window of opportunity that the political upheaval offered them initially.

To answer the original questions, it is also necessary to overcome problems in the availability and accuracy of data at both macro and micro levels. For instance, while GDP and employment figures were probably overstated in the pre-transition period, they were likely under-reported in the following years, making it difficult to evaluate the turning points in output recovery and the changes in social welfare conditions over time.

Nevertheless, after allowing for all these factors and caveats, it is possible to identify, on the basis of the experience to date, some patterns in the transition process that are common to all CEECs and some policy factors that have led either to success (i.e. rapid output recovery) or to failure (i.e. prolonged economic decline). The proof that this is possible is given by the analyses presented in this book. There is nothing deterministic in the successes or failures experienced by the CEECs. Policies have, instead, been the determining factor, and their historical record in this decade points to the need for some policy adjustments and calls authorities' attention to some policy lessons.

Assessing this experience implies dealing with a host of questions, issues and sectors, since no part of these economies is left untouched in the process of changing the economic system. Political, social and governmental institutions had to be adjusted in order to interact properly with the new environment of liberalisation of economic initiatives, competition in the marketplace and market outcomes. As one book cannot cover all this ground meaningfully, four subject areas were selected for this book, in view of their critical importance in explaining the results achieved to date, and assisting policy-making for a successful transformation of these economies and the subsequent period. The four themes, which are addressed in the four parts of this book, concern the overall framework of the transition strategy, the restructuring and development of the enterprise sector, the unemployment problem and social policies, and the integration of CEECs into the world economy.

The policy framework for each transition economy has had strong and weak points; after examining these points, can the main ingredients of a successful transition model be identified? The goal of macroeconomic stabilization has proved to be more elusive than expected: have prerequisites been missing? Social and political constraints have reduced the scope for implementing a coherent reform strategy: how should these be dealt with? As the supply side of the economy has responded with unexpectedly long lags to market liberalisation, what structural impediments should be removed as a matter of priority? The slow restructuring of public firms has certainly contributed to this situation. Is rapid privatisation the answer? The evidence shows that even after privatisation, restructuring has been slow in many cases, since corporate governance and management quality have not improved adequately. To this end, what contribution has been given by the banking system and the equity market? New entrepreneurs seem to find it difficult to compete for capital to launch new initiatives or to participate in the enterprise restructuring process.

The latter process has also brought to light the problems of hidden unemployment and labour reallocation towards the expanding sectors or firms. Regardless of whether rising unemployment is a temporary consequence of the success of the transition or a long-term phenomenon, it poses a threat to further progress in economic transformation because it hardens social resistance. Social policies and transfer payments for pensions and health care have helped to cushion to some extent the impact of higher unemployment and falling living standards but at such a cost for public budgets that their financial sustainability is in doubt. How can the social welfare system be made more effective under the existing budget constraints?

Rapid output growth can ease several of these problems. Thus far, one of the main sources of growth has been foreign demand in a context of easier market access to the OECD area than was the case in the pre-transition period. What lessons can be drawn from the recent experience of regional trade integration after the disintegration of the Comecon area? What policy implications derive from the prospects of a full customs union with the EU countries? Currency convertibility and exchange rate depreciation have helped the CEECs to gain market share abroad. What orientation should be given to exchange rate policy in the face of the conflicting goals of curbing inflation and keeping current account deficits at sustainable levels? While foreign capital has to supplement domestic saving in bolstering fixed investment, foreign investors seem wary of investing in some CEECs: how can obstacles and disincentives be overcome?

This brief summary of the main transition issues suffices to explain the reasons for selecting the four themes as the main focuses around which the various contributions are organised. Each theme is addressed from different angles and through such a range of viewpoints as to put the issues into perspective and not to lead to an unqualified acceptance of simplistic explanations for or solutions to complex socio-economic problems.

The first part deals with the main successes and failures of the overall strategy and consists of two critical overviews of transition approaches and their results, a series of *ex post* tests of the policy recipes recommended by the Bretton Woods institutions, a case study focusing on Hungary and two discussions of the political constraints faced by governments in reforming the economic system. The overviews are presented by **Zecchini** and **Stern**.

The first author identifies the building blocks of the transition strategies applied in Russia and six CEECs and highlights how similar their policy frameworks were. Differences lie mainly in the order of priority assigned to conflicting goals, the timing of measures, the continuity of reform efforts, and the degree to which the authorities buffered the impact of market signals or opportunities. A number of flaws are singled out in policy implementation with respect to the interconnection between macroeconomic management and structural reform, the promotion of entrepreneurship, the development of the payments and financial systems and the functioning of the labour market. In contrast, external trade liberalisation and foreign exchange policy seem broadly in line with the objective of expanding participation in world markets.

Stern broadens the scope of the overview to all transition economies, applies a set of qualitative indicators to assess progress in reform, dwells upon privatisation and restructuring of financial institutions, and discusses problems related to development of physical infrastructure inherited from the old regime. His conclusions reinforce those reached in the preceding overview and underscore some policy recommendations. He presents statistical evidence to show that those reforming countries which applied macroeconomic discipline and reform in higher doses have experienced smaller output declines and quicker recoveries. It is important, according to the author, that the state restrict its role to defining and enforcing the basic rules of a decentralised economy, while resisting pressures to interfere with market competition. Resumption of output growth and fixed investment requires stability in a broad sense and a deepening of structural reforms. The physical infrastructure must be reoriented towards the needs of the newly-established market system.

De Melo and **Gelb** add new evidence to support some of the points raised in the overviews. They widen the list of countries under consideration to include some that cannot be defined as post-communist economies, such as Vietnam, China or Slovenia. They also construct indices of economic liberalisation and explore the correlations of these indices with output growth and inflation. By ranking reforming countries according to these indices, they find a confirmation for the thesis that reforms help achieve inflation control and growth recovery. Furthermore, through a time series analysis centred on the year of regime switching, they provide econometric evidence that failure to reform does not preserve initial economic conditions, but leads to a prolonged output decline. In contrast, intensive reforms are followed by lower inflation and higher growth over a seven year time horizon. Interestingly, the authors also argue that, depending on the initial pattern of distortions and repression across sectors, liberalisation triggered different processes of economy-wide adjustment, giving rise to virtuous circles in some countries and vicious circles in others. To illustrate this point, Russia's reform experience is contrasted to that of China.

Additional support for De Melo and Gelb's findings is given by the quantitative analysis of **Fischer**, **Sahay** and **Vegh**. They examine the output and inflation profiles of different groups of reforming countries in order to identify the determinants of these variables during the transition and to shed light on the long-term growth prospects of these countries. While the results of their econometric tests confirm the existence of typical output and inflation profiles for a period centred around the time of macroeconomic stabilization, with real output rebounds following inflation stabilization, these results also indicate that lower fiscal deficits and a pegged exchange rate regime (i.e. a strong nominal anchor) have a significantly positive impact on both inflation (i.e. quickly reducing high inflation) and growth. As regards the determinants of long-term growth, their econometric exercise, based on both neo-classical and endogenous growth models, points out the benefits that can stem from policies aimed at promoting fixed investment but also from enhancing human capital and improving capital efficiency.

Laski and **Bhaduri** challenge the rationale behind demand management policies followed by a number of CEECs and eventually reject the appropriateness of conventional views on financial stabilization for the transition economies. In observing an excessive compression of domestic demand with otherwise avoidable losses in output and employment, they highlight some flaws in policy design. In particular, governments have overlooked the demand reducing implications of supply shocks due to the transition. If these effects had been allowed for, an expansionary policy stance might have been warranted, instead of demand-restricting measures. Nor were the latter always justified, in the authors' view, to check inflation, since the persistence of inflation was not demand-related. In the presence of a cost-push type of inflationary pressure due to low industrial capacity utilisation, restrictive monetary and fiscal policies have paradoxically ended up making the inflation problem worse. According to the authors, another weakness of the transition strategy rests with the misinterpretation of the state's role and responsibility in the new system. An active industrial policy is advocated, especially to prepare viable firms for privatisation.

The case of Hungary's latest stabilization programme is used by **Kornai** to show the risks of macroeconomic mismanagement during the transition and the benefits of a carefully balanced approach, such as the one applied by Hungary in 1995-96. This has been directed towards redressing imbalances while not damaging growth. The key to this outcome is seen in the adoption of a well diversified range of macro and structural measures, including, among others, a significant devaluation, an incomes policy, cuts in welfare entitlements and an acceleration of privatisation. Of course, it is too early to judge the durability of the results of this programme at the macroeconomic level, although on the supply side the continuing improvement in productivity bodes well for Hungary's long-term growth prospects.

The contributions by **Balcerowicz** and **Roland** offer intriguing insights into the political economy of radical reform. The first author presents a categorisation of the attitudes of voters and politicians in CEECs with respect to economic change before and after the political breakthrough. Political consensus to carry out the reform programme has depended, among other factors, on voters' perceptions of positive or negative linkages between reform policies and non-economic events or issues. For example, the prospect of joining the EU has been seen as a positive linkage in the Visegrad countries, while the loss of a hegemonic position in the region was considered a negative linkage in Russia. The inherited economic conditions are also viewed as having had a major impact on the leeway that governments have had in accelerating or delaying the transformation process, as well as in making appropriate decisions concerning the policy mix. By inheriting an improving economy after the first round of reforms carried out by its predecessor, the new government is not forced to introduce new painful measures and is therefore in a better position to be re-elected.

This aspect of the political cycle is extensively elaborated by **Roland**. After examining the role of various *ex ante* and *ex post* political constraints in the transition period, he highlights a link between the choice of a gradualist or "big bang" approach and the government's perception of the probability of re-election. When the latter is considered exogenous, fast and extensive reform are likely, with the result of restricting the successor government's latitude for policy reversal, since this becomes too costly. On the basis of this constraint, the author explains the absence of policy reversals which is observed throughout the region after political backlashes. However, given the generalised backlash against a supposedly generalised "big bang" approach to the transition, he has doubts about the exogeneity of re-election probabilities in the reforming countries to date. Policy continuity is also attributed to a geopolitical factor, since the economic transition was seen by Central European and Baltic countries as a means to free themselves from the Soviet (not to say Russian) influence and to become tightly anchored in the "West". In assessing the impact of political constraints, privatisation is regarded as being the area most affected, as both its pace and methods have closely reflected the government's concerns with building large constituencies in support of continuing progress in reform.

Privatisation and the unrelated diffusion of new private enterprises are two primary factors to spur the restructuring of these economies. How far has restructuring progressed and how should it be further promoted? Part II deals with these two questions by exploring, first, the behaviour of fixed investment in a number of CEECs (Rostowski), then examining the effects of changes in ownership patterns on corporate governance (Aghion and Carlin; Frydman and Rapaczynski) as well as the contribution of foreign investors to enterprise restructuring (Hunya), and finally, providing evidence on the role of banks in this process, with reference to Romania's experience (Carare and Perotti).

Contrary to widespread convictions that structural adjustment has been modest to date, **Rostowski** argues on the basis of official statistics that in some transition economies, such as Poland and Hungary, gross capital formation fell by much smaller proportions than GDP and to a much smaller extent relative to market economies during the Great Depression (1929-1933). Such resilience of investment, which he calls "the central paradox of the Great Transition Depression", suggests two conclusions. First, a considerable amount of restructuring has already taken place in the face of large output declines; further, restructuring is not just of a "defensive" nature, in the sense of involving a mere down-sizing of firms. Second, the fall in output can be traced back to supply-side adjustments, following shifts in demand, rather than to aggregate demand compression.

Drawing on evidence supplied by surveys of enterprises, **Aghion** and **Carlin** are more restrained in assessing the possibility of reaching robust conclusions as to the speed of restructuring and the pattern of corporate governance that will prevail. On the first point, after observing how effective hard budget constraints have been in prompting insiders, i.e. managers and employees, to implement survival-oriented adjustment plans, the authors analyse the impact of different initial ownership structures on micro-economic reorganisation. They conclude by recommending that privatisation schemes that give preference to insiders, particularly workers, should include measures aimed at avoiding collusion in the resale of shares against outside ownership. As regards the second point, corporate governance structures are evolving in different directions among CEECs. In the Czech Republic, there are examples of ownership concentration along the lines of the German model of industrial holding companies, while in Poland the Anglo-Saxon model, which is centred on the role of the stock market, also has many followers.

Frydman and **Rapaczynski** take a more pessimistic view of insiders' role in enterprise restructuring and call for a reassessment of the ability of the privatisation methods followed to date to attain this goal. If the firms to be privatised are not expected to become viable under market conditions, privatisation is unlikely to eliminate rent-seeking behaviour and might bolster political opposition to reforms. In the opposite case, privatisation can lead to improvements in performance, depending on the weight of insiders in the ownership structure. Conferring a controlling stake to insiders would not help in promoting restructuring, since they tend to oppose reforms, as indicated by recent surveys of their attitudes.

A large amount of empirical evidence is used by **Hunya** to examine the impact of privatisation and FDI on restructuring in the most advanced transition economies. The conclusions that he reaches depart to some extent from those of the preceding authors. Looking at a number of indicators of restructuring, Hunya finds that privatised and foreign-owned companies (FCs) have been more likely to engage in a major overhaul than state-owned firms, although the difference between the two groups is not very large in this respect. Furthermore, the process of reorganisation has been much more rapid in FCs than in domestically-owned enterprises (DOEs). As a result of the larger FDI penetration in Hungary, its manufacturing industry has been undergoing a faster adjustment than has been the case in the other Visegrad countries. The faster reorganisation observed in general among FCs is not, however, a guarantee for their longer-term development, because they are subject to the global strategy of multinational enterprises. The slower pace of DOEs' restructuring is partly attributed to the inefficiencies of the domestic financial sector, inefficiencies which the FCs are less affected by.

Evidence on the implications of such financial constraints is provided by **Carare** and **Perotti** with respect to Romania. To evaluate the contribution of the banking system to enterprise restructuring, they perform econometric tests on data derived from a sample of Romanian state-owned enterprises. The results show that in allocating credit, banks tend to give preference, on average, to the larger and less profitable firms, that also have sizeable trade or debt arrears. As a consequence, bank credit appears to have become a replacement for the discontinued public subsidies to SOEs. At the same time, such bank inefficiency deprives "better" firms of the financing that is necessary for their restructuring and development. Freeing bank management from political interference is seen as an important component of any programme directed at improving credit allocation.

Enterprise restructuring necessarily implies shedding excess labour as well as reallocating labour towards expanding firms. In this process, unemployment might emerge, but it would be a mistake to attribute primarily to these two factors the high unemployment rates which, with few exceptions, have persisted in the CEECs during the entire transition. The complex nature of the unemployment problem in these economies, and some of its solutions, are analysed from various angles in Part III. Commander and Tolstopiatenko examine the labour market impact of public transfer payments to both the unemployed and enterprises; Ellman scrutinises characteristics and causes of the demographic crisis that has compounded social strains; Gora, Jackman and Pauna focus on the performance of the new labour markets; and Newbery deals with the financing of social policies.

Given the divergence of unemployment trends between Central and Eastern Europe, on the one hand, and the former Soviet Union, on the other, **Commander** and **Tolstopiatenko** aim at evaluating the various factors that can account for this difference. Among these factors, they underscore the role of the unemployment benefits system: while in the former group of countries, this system has been so generous as to create rigidities in labour market and stickiness in unemployment, in the latter group, it has generated incentives for workers to remain in firms, due to the low level of benefits. In fact, FSU countries' tight benefit policy has continued to limit open unemployment (thereby following an orientation similar to that of the old regime) and it has contributed to raising the degree of wage flexibility. Evidently, this policy approach has been made possible by a number of implicit subsidies to employment in the form of soft financing of enterprises through non-payment of tax and social-security liabilities, easy access to bank credit, and inter-enterprise and wage arrears. After testing econometrically the relative weight of these factors through a stylised model, the authors conclude that if these subsidised workers were transferred into unemployment and were granted benefits equivalent to those implicit subsidies, unemployment would not increase significantly but would last longer, similarly to what can be observed in Central and Eastern Europe.

In all transition economies, wage declines and joblessness have been closely associated with the spreading of poverty and a generalised demographic crisis. Evidence of these conditions is provided by **Ellman** in analysing the sharp fall in natality rates, the rise in mortality and the large flows of international migration. In no other region are these trends more evident than in the FSU. Whether or not specific measures (as opposed to general policies aimed at improving economic performance) are required to ease the situation is a matter for debate in these countries, but the implications of present conditions for socio-economic development cannot be overlooked, due in part to their consequences for social policies and the public budget. The intensity of international migration is a sign of an unsettled economic situation and persistent social hardship several years after the beginning of the transition. Migration is hardly evident in the most advanced transition economies, namely the Visegrad countries, while it is considerable in the others.

Have social hardship and high unemployment hampered enterprise restructuring and the reallocation of labour towards expanding sectors? By another token, has restructuring led to rising unemployment, due to market failures in labour reallocation? To answer these questions, **Jackman** and **Pauna** use a set of comparators and correlation indices. On this basis, they reject the traditional view that unemployment during the transition was the necessary consequence of progress in resource reallocation. Unemployment is, instead, believed to be the result of economy-wide shocks leading to employment losses across sectors, whereas no correlation is found between the rate of new job creation (which is considered a better indicator of successful restructuring than others frequently used) and labour shedding in the sectors with excess employment. Current policies directed to accelerating the latter process, therefore, seem inappropriate because they subsidise job destruction at high social as well as budgetary cost, and ultimately prolong unemployment. As an alternative, the authors suggest a series of changes in the unemployment benefits regime. Barring a Russian approach, which involves low and limited benefits, because of the consequent rise in social hardship, a "workfare" conditionality could be applied in granting these benefits. For instance, the unemployed could be required to carry out socially valuable work, or to accept a temporary job or training as a condition for receiving the benefits; this would also discourage their participation in the shadow economy. Such an "active" labour market policy has already been successfully tried in the Czech Republic, although it is not a solution to the problem of an overall shortage of jobs.

To explain international differences in unemployment rates, even within the group of Visegrad countries, **Gora** emphasises dissimilarities in policy approaches and divergent adjustment patterns across countries on both sides, labour demand and supply. Adjustment, on the demand side, has been mostly driven by private sector development, and it seems poorly correlated with GDP evolution, as Poland, the fastest growing economy, also has the highest unemployment rate. On the supply side, Hungary and Poland represent two extreme cases, with the former experiencing a considerable fall in the labour force participation rate, while in the latter there has been no significant change in the labour force. In this context, differences in labour market performances also seem to reflect particular institutional structures and policies with respect to the unemployed. As long as unemployment support measures are used as a social policy instrument, rather than being geared to labour market problems, as is the case in Poland, the author doubts that output expansion will suffice to lower the current unemployment rate.

The analysis of social benefits, together with the tax system, is developed by **Newbery** from the perspective of the economic viability and cost effectiveness of these systems. After examining the experience of the Visegrad countries, the author recommends a series of changes to improve targeting of social expenditure and to reduce distortions and inefficiencies in the tax regime. Reforming the pension system appears to pose more difficulties than improving unemployment insurance. Several reasons, including the need to lower the high marginal taxes on labour income and excessive redistribution in the case of Hungary, militate in favour of closely linking pension payments to the levels of accumulated contributions. This could have, however, far-reaching implications on intergenerational income redistribution and incentives for private saving. Reform of the tax structure seems inevitable since with the passage to a market economy, profit tax will provide a much smaller share of total revenue than under the old regime. Shifting the fiscal burden more towards taxing individual incomes seems possible, and will raise pressure for public expenditure cuts and for higher efficiency in taxation. In this endeavour, the revenue gains from simplifying the tax system and minimising its administrative cost should outstrip, according to the author, their costs in distributional terms. Difficult issues have, nevertheless, to be solved, especially in balancing direct taxes with indirect ones, and in introducing local taxation and taxes on property and capital income. Unfortunately, in several of these areas, such as fiscal deficits, pensions and capital taxation, the OECD countries' experience does not always offer satisfactory models.

Any success the CEECs have achieved to date in renovating their economies and spurring output recovery, owes a great deal to their external policy choices, notably with respect to trade liberalisation and exchange rates. Such choices affected almost all sectors of the economy, and had a major impact on market conditions and the pace of macroeconomic stabilization. An assessment of these policies is presented in Part IV through the analysis of external currency convertibility (Cooper), the implications of the exchange rate regime (Rosati), the long-term trends in foreign trade (Leamer), the process of sub-regional economic integration (Inotai), and the problems faced by foreign investors (Lankes and Venables).

In drawing an interesting comparison between OEEC countries' experience in the 1950s and the CEECs during the transition, **Cooper** finds several factors that can justify CEECs' relatively rapid move to declare current account convertibility, according to art. VIII of IMF rules. At the same time, many of the feared consequences of currency convertibility and the ensuing depreciation (especially capital flight, prolonged fall in real consumption and a worsening income distribution) appear to have been quite manageable for these countries in a context of fast export penetration into OECD markets, prudent macroeconomic management and economic liberalisation. Such an experience in attaining convertibility, after allowing for some special circumstances, is seen by the author as a lesson for developing countries that still maintain exchange controls hampering current account payments.

Achieving and sustaining convertibility hinge upon pursuing appropriate exchange rate policies. The selection of an optimal exchange rate regime during the transition is examined by **Rosati**. After the initial devaluation that has to accompany the first strides towards convertibility, the author advocates a fixed exchange rate regime as a means of lowering inflationary expectations and to reduce uncertainty in the business environment. Once these objectives are attained, a tendency for the currency to appreciate in real terms usually sets in. As this trend might lead to deviations from the targeted path towards the equilibrium rate, it is suggested that CEECs gradually move to a flexible exchange regime by, first, introducing a crawling peg and, eventually, a flexible system with a pre-determined fluctuation band. Such flexibility is also useful to partly absorb the impact of sizeable capital flows, whenever they threaten monetary stability. Additional monetary measures are, however, needed should capital movements lead to currency misalignments or excessive exchange rate volatility.

Apart from a proper currency management, high work effort leading to fast labour productivity growth and access to the developed West European markets are considered by **Leamer** to be the two major factors which would enable these economies to catch up with the high *per capita* income countries. On both fronts, the author explores some of the risks faced by the CEECs. The structure of transition economies may develop into a dichotomy between high-productivity, high-wage (capital-intensive) sectors and low-wage (labour-intensive) sectors. Depending on which sector group will prevail over the medium-term, each economy's comparative advantage in trade could evolve in different directions. This evolution would also reflect the significant locational advantages that are related to the short distance of CEECs from rich Western markets. The effective distance might, however, be increased by the presence of barriers to access into these markets.

In **Inotai**'s view, instead, accession into the EU is currently more important for Central European countries than the market distance factor, for the purpose of stimulating trade and growth. This equally applies to trade within the same group of countries. Accession to EU would actually provide the framework for intensifying all economic relationships at the sub-regional level, and to launch big projects for regional infrastructural works. In this process, sub-regional trade would acquire the same intra-industry pattern as that prevailing in intra-regional EU trade. Until the accession, sub-regional co-operation would remain, according to the author, limited and dominated by "defensive" considerations vis-à-vis EU exports.

Why has foreign investment driven the economic recovery of these countries to such a limited extent as compared to trade? **Lankes** and **Venables** find a number of important answers in the results of an investor survey which was conducted for the EBRD in 1995. The survey findings tend to debunk a series of conventional explanations about the motivating or deterring factors for foreign investment in these economies. For the majority of investors in the region, the most relevant inducement comes from the comparatively low level of unit labour costs, due to the availability of <u>skilled</u> workers with relatively low wages and a productivity level not far below that of the home-country. In contrast, tax incentives are of minor importance, on average, while the stability of the tax regime is considered at least as valuable as tax privileges. Export barriers in foreign markets are viewed as a problem only by a minority of investors in some CEECs; interestingly, considerable obstacles are found in trade between transition economies. The presence of tariffs on imports, particularly from the EU area, is a more significant problem. On the whole, foreign investment is highly responsive to the progress made by the country on all fronts of the transition process.

The studies included in this book cover a wide range of fundamental transition issues, but evidently, neither exhaust the evaluation of this field, nor aim at offering definitive answers on every issue. The evidence itself, that is presented here, leaves room for alternative interpretations and further testing of policy impact. Nevertheless, the authors have the merit of both clarifying the complex inter-relationships between different factors (belonging to the political, social, and economic realms), different policy measures and different economic results, and pointing to significant improvements that can be introduced in the CEECs' policy-making. They also suggest new avenues or new areas for exploration. Their contributions are complemented and enriched by the evidence and analyses provided in the comments by the discussants, and the debate, which is reported here, adds perspective to them. To take full account of all these elements, a set of policy-oriented conclusions is presented at the end of each part.

Part I

Main successes and failures in the transition strategy

1

Transition approaches in retrospect

Salvatore Zecchini

Introduction: The transition framework

Four years after the 1917 Russian revolution, V.I. Lenin warned his fellow communists that to complete the transition to a centrally planned economy would take "at least a century". If this was deemed appropriate for a transition that basically involved centralisation of ownership of all production assets and the creation of one central command structure presiding over the entire economic activity of a country, then the reverse process of transferring the economy's assets and responsibility for economic decisions to a universe of individual economic agents that have to interact with each other in a completely new, competitive market context should require at least an equal amount of time for its successful completion. Assuming this perspective, it is surprising to find that the general expectation among the population in the reforming countries (RCs) of Central and Eastern Europe and the former Soviet Union at the beginning of the transition was that through a liberalisation of economic activity, it would be possible to bring about a rapid transformation of the economic system and, hence, a rapid improvement in living standards.

Six years after the transition to a market-based system began in the RCs[1], this process is still far from being achieved; the Czech and Slovak republics, Hungary and Poland have reached a second stage at which the authorities are taking stock f the reform measures already adopted before moving to the next round of adjustment of reforms and their completion. In the other RCs, the transition still seems to be in the phase in which a minimum of reform is still in the process of being introduced. Overall, however, the expectations for a speedy completion of the transition remain unfulfilled, and in some countries, widespread disappointment with the present economic situation has made progress more arduous than ever before.

In none of these countries has the progression from a command economy to one based on competitive markets been a smooth and linear advance towards a predetermined model of a market economy. Rather, it has evolved out of a series of

An earlier version of this essay was published in MOST, Economic Policy in Transitional Economies, 5: 1-44, 1995, Kluwer Academic Publishers. The author wishes to thank Nils Bjorksten for collaborating in the preparation of the table and the figure. The views presented in this essay are the sole responsibility of the author and do not necessarily reflect those of any institutions with which the author is associated.

'swings' between, on the one hand, the launch of bold reforms in certain limited areas, and on the other, delays in their completion or in moving ahead with further reform. These 'swings' have arisen in response to the different problems and difficulties encountered by the RCs, in particular those of a political, technical and economic nature. Initially, all the countries espoused the transition as their main objective, even if they had a very vague notion of what it meant, of what market model to pursue and its implications. It did not appear clear to the political leadership that transition consists essentially of transforming economic agents' behaviour through a radical change of the institutional framework that determines economic rewards and penalties. This would result not just from the enactment of a few laws on market liberalisation, but from a multitude of sectoral and macroeconomic policy measures, institutional arrangements, operational regulations related to market structures and their participants, and constraints on government intervention in the economy.

Although the authorities of all RCs assumed the transition as an objective in itself, they neither aimed at this target with firm determination over the entire period, nor put it on the top of their policy priorities, the only exception being perhaps the Czech Republic. On the one hand, the focus of their policy strategy often shifted towards pursuing the elusive objective of macroeconomic balance. Macroeconomic stabilization is a target distinct from the transition goal, since it is required and can be pursued regardless of the type of economic system in place. In fact, in their attempts to redress macroeconomic imbalances, most RCs resorted to direct intervention in the economy along lines typical of the old economic system, rather than relying on the new market mechanisms.

On the other hand, the transition was seen by the authorities as an instrument to achieve other objectives, namely political and economic ones. From a political point of view, liberalising economic activity and creating a vast class of property owners was considered as a means to underpin the emerging, liberal democracy and to bring the RCs into closer co-operation with Western Europe and other OECD countries. From an economic vantage point, it was expected that the transition would unleash domestic market forces and foreign support to such an extent as to lead to a rapid expansion of national income. Hence, the transition was considered as an instrument for reaching the ultimate objective: strong economic development. Undoubtedly, if the social costs of the transition were to exceed its economic benefits in terms of output growth and welfare gains, or if economic recovery did not materialise in a short period, confidence in the transition itself would be undermined and political support would wane. Unfortunately, this is exactly what has happened in several RCs, as 'transition fatigue' has set in during 1994-95.

Also contributing to this situation were the unprecedented technical difficulties of the transition itself and its co-ordination with the policy requirements of macroeconomic stabilization and economic development. At the centre of these difficulties lies the fourfold problem of deciding the speed of implementation of institutional changes, the sequence of reforms in the various sectors, their relation to demand management measures and the depth of the reforms themselves. The solution to this problem was also subject to the constraint of having to redress the inherited macroeconomic imbalances.

In the face of so many difficulties, the disappointing progress in the transition and total and *per capita* income levels that are, in general, significantly below those at the beginning of this decade, can the transition approaches followed by the RCs be considered appropriate? What were their major weaknesses and strengths? What policy lessons can be drawn in order to improve the current strategies and increase the chances of a rapid transition? These questions are addressed in this overview of transition approaches. In this endeavour, no attempt is made to give an account of the vast, albeit somewhat repetitive, literature on the analysis of the transition, literature that has sprung up since 1990 at a pace exceeding that of the transition itself. Rather, this evaluation is based on the analytical work, policy dialogue and policy assistance that the OECD has carried out in this decade in the context of the programme of co-operation managed by its Centre for Co-operation with the Economies in Transition (CCET). While this programme has covered all segments of economic reform and macro-stabilization, and has been oriented towards all RCs, for reasons of practicality in the context of this relatively short essay, the focus will be limited to a group of countries (Russia, Poland, Hungary, Czech and Slovak republics, Bulgaria and Romania) and to the main areas of policy intervention.

After discussing some of the statistical problems that are faced in policy analysis and policy-making, the subsequent sections of the paper aim to clarify the initial conditions of these economies, to identify the priority issues with which these countries were confronted in the early 1990s and to characterise the transition approaches followed by these countries on the basis of their main features. A comparative evaluation follows concerning the results and weaknesses of these strategies from a general point of view, as well as with respect to the main problem areas. The final section is devoted to a summary of the principal adjustments to transition strategies which can be recommended in light of the experience accumulated so far. In addressing such complex issues while, at the same time, using a statistical basis that does not provide adequate information to construct comprehensive quantitative indicators of structural reforms, that lacks sufficient reliability and that does not capture a number of variables relevant to policy-making and policy evaluation, it is necessary to be cautious about drawing definitive conclusions. Most, if not all, critical lessons presented here must be interpreted as preliminary findings that are derived from the available evidence and that need further tests, once more information and analysis is provided. However imperfect and tentative these conclusions might be, they are still a useful source of reflection for those countries which remain in the midst of the upheaval of changing their socio-economic system and which cannot wait for the perfect answer before dealing with their future.

1. The information gaps

At the beginning of the transition, the general view among policy-makers in the RCs, and even more so among those in the international community working to support the RCs, was that the information tools available were inadequate to help design the transition policies, monitor policy effects and identify, at an early stage, areas for policy adjustment. It was assumed that the major problems would be technical in nature, especially the need to master the intricacies of the System of National Accounts which had to replace the Material Product System, since the latter did not measure the full flow of national product (particularly the service sector's output). Other gaps were also evident in the recording of balance of payments flows, in the measurement of price movements and in tracing business trends. After a history of governmental manipulation of statistics, a new culture also needed to be built in the statistical services for the purpose of obtaining an accurate and objective record of relevant economic phenomena.

The accumulated experience of the 1990s indicates that, although the aforementioned concerns should be addressed, major problems also exist in other areas. First of all, the existing statistical services are not prepared to measure economic facts which are not directly observable in all their detail. The traditional approach of precisely and meticulously quantifying facts related to the implementation of the central plan was suited to an era in which the economy was dominated by relatively few large firms over which the government held strong control through the bookkeeping system. However, in the newly emerging economy, made up of many private firms with much less rigorous bookkeeping, this approach is insufficient. Therefore, there is a need to complement this approach with reliable techniques to estimate the correct figure for a given aggregate, since a proper estimate is more useful than incomplete data. So far, it has been very difficult to introduce this improvement, with the result being that income and trade data suffer from substantial gaps.

Another reason for incomplete data is given by the rapid development of a hidden or underground economy in all RCs, particularly in the service sector. In a pilot study sponsored by the OECD, it is estimated that in 1992 the size of the unrecorded economy in Hungary amounted to more than 20 per cent of recorded GNP. Under-recording mainly affects the activities of the private sector and does not allow a clear picture to be drawn of the evolution of the private enterprise sector, its investment, its labour demand and labour costs. These shortcomings could be partly overcome by carrying out business surveys or by using sampling techniques to construct indicators of business trends, both of which are areas where the OECD has provided technical assistance.

External trade and balance of payments data also show deficiencies and inconsistencies, which can be attributed to the blurring of national customs boundaries, especially for trade within the former Soviet Union, the failure to record small-scale cross-border trade as well as capital flight, and the weaknesses in recording methodologies. For instance, significant inconsistencies emerge in trade with OECD countries between the figures reported by the RCs and those recorded by the OECD trade partners.

Other problems concern the role and usefulness of statistical information in helping the authorities manage the transition; these problems have a strong 'cultural' dimension that is difficult to change. Statistics often continue to be produced following old methodologies because the main users in government do not know what use to make of statistics oriented towards a market economy. Thus, there is a tendency to produce 'new-methodology' figures for the international organisations and 'old-methodology' figures for internal use within the government. Furthermore, it is often the case that compilers of statistics have skills which are too limited to enable them to analyse, in economic terms, the figures for which they are responsible, with the result being that the quality of data is not sufficiently tested.

Time-series analysis is seriously affected by insufficient consistency of data over time. Although the declared objective is to adopt 'international standards', RC authorities have not yet fully realised that the application of a constant methodology is essential if comparisons over time, as well as across countries, are to be made. This also reflects a traditional attitude held by policy-makers to pay scant attention to the analysis of past trends as an indicator of how to improve policy design. The same attitude is evident in the preference given by statistical offices to speed in the trade-off between timeliness of data and accuracy. Data are usually compiled with a very short time lag vis-à-vis their time reference; however, this is done at the expense of the data's accuracy. Moreover, no systematic effort is generally made to revise the data once more detailed or complete information becomes available.

From this experience a few conclusions can be drawn. The statistical base related to the evolution of these economies during the transition is still partial, with an underlying bias towards capturing the public sector's economic activities, while leaving gaps in the measurement of the most dynamic economic sector (i.e. private enterprises). The assistance provided by the OECD and other institutions has helped refine the compilation of statistical aggregates and the integration of different sets of aggregates, but has not yet led to improvements in the underlying statistical base. To reach such a target, more time is required to establish a new system for collecting data, filling gaps and developing a new 'culture' in the RCs' national statistical services. The major incentive to rapid progress in this direction should come from the demands of policy-makers — those who must find new methods to deal with the emerging reality of market forces which can no longer be controlled through direct interventions by the State. To this effect, programmes for a major overhaul of statistical services need to be launched and their implementation should be supported by external assistance.

While several statistics produced by the RCs are now comparable with those of some OECD countries, in general, comparability is subject to a considerable margin of error, due to weaknesses in data gathering and the statistical methods used in the RCs. This is the case, for instance, for price indices whose limited reliability affects the quality of price deflators and consequently the calculation of 'real' variables. Comparability of some macroeconomic aggregates, such as real GDP and total demand, over the transition period is also affected by the sizeable variations in relative prices and sectoral composition of national output. However, some of the problems faced by the RCs are somewhat similar to those encountered by OECD countries (e.g. the measurement of the underground economy or comparability of GDP data over time). The OECD countries' statistical assistance to the RCs could provide both sides with a good opportunity to explore new approaches to these common problems and to find solutions that could set new international standards.

2. Initial conditions and policy challenges

One striking feature of the transition is that in only a few years, RC economies, whose evolutions under central planning had been tightly intertwined due to structural and systemic factors, have not followed similar patterns of performance. These instead have diverged significantly from country to country. Such divergences are not just the result of differences in transition strategies, but are to a considerable extent due to certain differences in the initial economic conditions and structures. As regards the macroeconomic situation, available statistical evidence indicates that the RCs, with few exceptions, had imbalances that needed adjustment. Of the group of RCs under consideration, Russia, Poland and Bulgaria were more severely affected than the others by inflationary pressures, external current account deficits and budget deficits (see the table). By contrast, Czechoslovakia and Romania were in better shape, as their only major imbalance was concentrated in public accounts. However, Romania's macroeconomic situation was more precarious than that of Czechoslovakia, because it was already associated with a reduction of national product and a tendency towards economic stagnation.

Apart from the scant statistical evidence available on macroeconomic conditions, authorities in the RCs were aware of the existence of hidden imbalances in their economies, although they were unable to estimate their quantitative dimensions. Excess demand, accumulated over several years in the household sector and among enterprises, was thought to be a characteristic of all RCs, as evidenced not by inflation, but rather by the widespread shortages of both consumer and investment goods and by the considerable holdings in both sectors of financial saving that was scarcely remunerated and in rather liquid form. Unemployment, which was officially non-existent, was hidden through labour hoarding among enterprises, leading to relatively low labour productivity. The presence of tight management of import and export quantities, together with subsidisation of exports, indicates that the exchange rate was at a level far from that capable of ensuring balanced external trade.

On systemic and structural grounds, differences across countries were also substantial. In previous decades, Hungary and Poland had already begun to loosen the grip of public direct control over the economy by giving some autonomy to public enterprises and by permitting the emergence of a limited private sector. The distance of the other RCs from a market-oriented economy was far greater, despite timid attempts to inject market-type incentives into the management of public enterprises in the second half of the 1980s. Notwithstanding these modest reforms, in all RCs, the system of relative prices greatly departed from one based on world market prices, due to the standard objective of RC governments to obtain extensive cross-sectoral subsidisation through the price system, particularly with regard to energy. Consequently, the passage to a system of prices determined in markets open to domestic and external competition would have implied a major shock for both the supply and demand sides of the economy.

Additional structural difficulties had to be faced by some RCs. Countries such as Bulgaria had a relatively narrow production base and were overly dependent on the demand of the quasi-captive Comecon market. In most RCs, production structures were heavily distorted in favour of industrial activities, regardless of their industries' economic efficiency and competitiveness in a free-market context. Although most RCs belong to the group of middle-income countries, some, such as Romania, had to deal with serious problems of economic under-development.

In such a diversified set of situations, the policy challenges in the transition period vary from country to country and cannot be merely summarised in the four terms of macro-stabilization, liberalisation, privatisation and enterprise restructuring. As all RCs shared the task of having to transform their economic system, all of them were expected to act on the four main dimensions of a market system:

- to put in place market structures;
- to develop market participants by freeing enterprises and households in their decisions to produce, invest, consume and price their resources;
- to establish a new payments system for the economy and develop a new financial system to muster savings and allocate financial capital;
- to reduce the size of the public sector in the production of goods and services, while developing indirect tools for economic management (as opposed to the old system of direct intervention).

As one dimension is no substitute for the other, progress is necessary in parallel on all four dimensions; otherwise distortions, perverse effects and even failure of the market system could result.

In addition to this common task, countries such as Russia, Poland and Bulgaria had to curb strong inflationary pressures by draining the excess liquidity in their economies. Furthermore, Poland and Bulgaria had to reduce domestic absorption of resources and generate a trade surplus in order to be able to service the huge debt which they had accumulated in the 1980s. For Czechoslovakia, Hungary and Romania, the main macroeconomic task was instead to prevent losing control of domestic demand expansion once they relinquished direct control over wages and income formation, as well as over credit creation. This was particularly critical for Hungary since, in the presence of a considerable foreign debt, it aimed at maintaining a sustainable current balance position, (i.e. an excess of investment over national savings, to an extent that could be covered by potential inflows of private capital). Such a diversity of tasks also concerned the RCs outside the group under consideration. Most of the new independent states of the former Soviet Union, for instance, were confronted with the shock of having to drastically curtail domestic demand, as they were losing the subsidies that they had been receiving from Russia, in particular through the distorted price system. Furthermore, all RCs which were net energy importers were hit by the increase of the energy prices to world market levels.

Besides macroeconomic tasks, there were tasks related to the need for an economic development strategy or a higher output growth strategy than had existed in the 1980s. All RCs recognised that a reorientation of development should result from the new incentives and penalties offered by competition in an open market. Nevertheless, among RC authorities, doubts existed regarding the autonomous capacity of domestic economic forces to trigger a strong output recovery in the short-term once these forces were allowed to operate in a free market environment. Foreign inputs of capital and technology were considered essential to achieve this end, and therefore structural conditions had to be established to attract foreign enterprises. Some indirect form of government support to the enterprise sector was also thought to be inevitable. Furthermore, with the collapse of the Comecon market, and especially the Russian market, it was deemed urgent to overcome the inadequacy of the domestic market size by gaining access to rich countries' markets. Eventually, the policy approach of each RC reflected the relative importance which it attached to the three goals of transition, stabilization and development. This, in turn, led to different combinations of policy priorities.

3. Adopted policy approaches

The 'optimal' transition approach is a notion dear to academics and in principle useful for policy-makers, not as a guide for their actions (since we do not live in an optimal world), but as a benchmark against which to compare the transition path which is actually followed. No comprehensive optimal approach, however, has been developed so far in economic literature due to the complexity of the interrelationships and interactions between structural, systemic and macroeconomic variables. Only some limited criteria have been proposed for partial optimisation through an appropriate sequencing of some reform measures. In the absence of optimal models, practical guidance rules or a history of transition experiences from which to draw lessons, the RCs had to consider their policy approaches in the first transition phase as an experimentation of techniques for socio-economic transformation, rather than as a blueprint for constructing a new economy. They had to search for second-or third-best solutions, to monitor progress very closely, being ready to adjust or reverse measures as long as experience was being gained, and to compare their experience with those of other transition countries in order to benefit from their successes or failures.

These aspects of complexity and experimentation make it difficult to categorise each RC approach. The RCs' reforms cannot be characterised on the basis of summary quantitative indicators because institutional, structural and systemic measures, as well as their effects, escape accurate quantification. Hence in this essay, RC policy approaches are characterised on the basis of sectors or institutions to which groups of measures were addressed, the particular mix of policy priorities of each country, the timing of policy implementation and the depth of policy impact.

3.1 Common characteristics

In spite of significant differences between the RCs, their policies during the transition shared a number of common features which are worth highlighting at the outset. Once liberal, democratic systems were installed in the RCs, there was no alternative but to abandon central planning, since, as the antinomy of democracy, centrally planned systems deprive citizens of one of their main liberties (economic freedom) and tend to impose, from the top down, choices concerning the demand side or the supply side of the economy. Not even a democratically elected government could replace, by means of central planning, the individual in economic choices affecting his or her economic well-being. By another token, it was rightly thought that a hybrid system (such as the one in place in China) with two coexisting components, one managed by central planners and another based on private initiative and competitive markets, raises problems of internal consistency and management which far exceed the possible benefits. Consequently, central planning was abandoned abruptly and systemic transformation was launched almost overnight.

The first implication was that all RCs were forced to liberalise price formation almost at once; more than two-thirds of prices as a ratio to total production or consumption were set free. A degree of price control was, however, retained by excluding energy products, public utilities and rents from liberalisation, with the aim of cushioning the impact of liberalisation for the few main products and services over which enterprises and households did not have any significant market power in price determination and to which they could not adjust, except gradually, due to the structural rigidity of their demand. Price liberalisation in closed economies such as the RCs, which were dominated by a few large-scale suppliers, would have led to rising profit margins and limited incentives to improve cost efficiency and competitiveness. It was necessary to complement free pricing by opening up the economy to external competition. This was carried out by all RCs along three lines:

- first, government-managed trade was eliminated and a new customs tariff system was applied with a relatively low average rate and few tariff spikes;
- second, a bridge was established between domestic and foreign markets by introducing, *de facto*, a high degree of external convertibility into the currency. Convertibility concerned almost all current account payments made by enterprises, while limitations were placed on household purchases of convertible currencies for tourism and restrictions remained on capital account convertibility for residents. Current account convertibility was more a *de facto* condition than a *de jure* engagement, because it was not founded on transparent foreign exchange markets it coexisted with multiple exchange rate practices, and it did not limit government freedom to add new convertibility restrictions when needed. Fulfilling these three conditions would have implied full current account convertibility according to the definition of the IMF (Article VIII of its rules), but this commitment has been taken only by few RCs[2], starting from the second quarter of 1995;
- third, the new integration of domestic markets with the world economy had to be supported by a sizeable devaluation of the exchange rate, as the initial rate was clearly overvalued and would have triggered a balance-of-payments crisis once the economy was opened. No one knew or could make a reliable estimation of the degree of currency over-evaluation; nor was there a representative foreign exchange market to signal a level at which the currency would settle; nor did the RCs have enough foreign reserves to defend a given rate. Under these conditions, and also taking into account the need to avoid frequent devaluations, all RCs devalued their currencies considerably.

Another common element in the transition strategy was what can be called a 'legislative shock'. Dozens of new laws and law-decrees were rapidly issued in order to establish private ownership and market institutions, and to allow and regulate all economic activities which were forbidden under central planning. In the rush to avoid a legislative vacuum following the abolition of communist rules, old (pre-communist era) laws were revived or foreign legislative models were followed. The speed of the enactment of law at this time prevented the adoption of a comprehensive legislation programme which would have coherently dealt with the various parts of the economy. Instead, various pieces of legislation were enacted separately, in an almost uncoordinated fashion and at different moments, leaving the task of reorganising the legislative system to a later stage. Furthermore, the 'legislative shock' did not exert its full impact on the reality of the economy since law implementation (through operational regulations) and law enforcement were seriously inadequate.

Since the beginning of the transition process, a major concern for the RCs was to drain excess liquidity from the economy and to curb domestic demand expansion in order to both stem the secondary inflationary waves following the initial price liberalisation and balance the external current account. Macroeconomic stabilization was a major component of the RCs' policy strategy and was pursued irrespective of progress made in systemic transformation; in reality, it was carried out mainly through direct intervention in credit creation and allocation and in the public budget deficit, rather than through market-oriented instruments.

Common to all the RCs were a number of other policy attitudes notably characterised by either an inadequate or a complete lack of action on the part of the authorities. One of these, public enterprise restructuring, has in every instance been a relatively slow process which even today is still far from being achieved. The delays can be attributed to two main factors:

- the difficulties in establishing an effective social and labour market policy which would provide some income protection to redundant workers expelled from

- restructured firms and help them to find new jobs;

- a lack of skills and financial means in the public sector to reorganise loss-making firms.

None of the major instruments available for extensive enterprise restructuring (i.e. privatisation, bankruptcy or liquidation and financial reform to impose financial discipline) was used with enough determination to push restructuring through.

Although privatisation of small enterprises and individual small-scale assets was completed by all RCs in about two and a half years, the transfer of medium and large enterprises to private hands was delayed in most countries; only in the Czech Republic and Russia did such privatisation begin, and it has yet to be completed. Bankruptcy laws were enacted with delays and have been applied only rarely. Hungary alone has attempted to enforce bankruptcy procedures, but it was forced to mitigate this policy once it became evident that such action was having a 'domino' effect, leading to the closure of large portions of its enterprise sector.

Financial restructuring of enterprises and bank balance sheets, as well as financial reform, have lagged behind. Governments were caught in a dilemma. On the one hand, taking over firms' bad debts was creating a 'moral hazard problem', to the extent that it did not prevent the continuation of irresponsible lending. On the other hand, enforcing financial discipline standards could lead to enterprises' failures and with it to the closing of many banks and a destabilization of the entire banking system. As for the structure of the commercial banking system, the RCs have been slow to apply the new regulatory and institutional measures to deal with the problems of concentration of bank intermediation, inadequate competition and deficiencies in bank management and supervision. Even less attention has generally been devoted to regulating non-bank financial intermediaries and financial markets. Common to all RCs has been the separation of central banking from other banking institutions, the development of monetary and exchange rate policy management, the creation of banking supervision services and a substantial liberalisation of interest rate determination by banks.

Delays in restructuring public firms and enforcing financial discipline obliged all RCs to introduce policies aimed at limiting the rise of public wages. To this effect, penalties were imposed on public firms through taxation, but their impact has been uneven as substantial arrears in tax payments have also emerged.

As regards the medium-term development of these economies, none of the RCs have devised a development strategy or policy aimed at boosting its comparative advantages in international trade by channelling resources towards predetermined sectors or projects. No serious attempts were generally made to select promising economic sectors for development through protection or special support, since there was no clear vision of what the 'winning' sectors would be in the medium-term under competitive market conditions. Old practices, with the government selecting 'winning' sectors, were no longer trusted. Support was, however, given through finance and trade measures to some firms or sectors on a transitory basis, but this essentially reflected the need to deal with sectoral crises or enterprise insolvencies. In fact, the constraints of crisis management prevailed over any intention to pursue a new industrial policy different from that of the old system.

Overall, even initially when there was a clear policy design for the first phase of the transition policy, implementation did not aim at searching for an 'optimal' sequencing of measures but rather was pragmatic and subject to frequent adjustments. Policy action followed a pattern dictated by the pressure of deteriorating economic conditions, the extent of political support for reforms in the country, the need to contain social hardship due to reforms and the management capacity of an administration that was trained to operate the old economic system. Once the effects of a given set of measures were evident, policies often focused on minimising disruptions and social costs. As a consequence, the structure of prices, incentives, rewards and penalties, whose radical change was intended to alter economic agents' behaviour fundamentally, actually changed only gradually, because countervailing measures were taken on different fronts to moderate their impact.

3.2 Policy differences

With so many important elements in common across the RCs, it is not possible to say that a fundamental difference exists between RC policy approaches: they all had the same components and goals and were subject to broadly similar domestic economic constraints. Policy differences, instead, lie in the relative priority assigned to different goals, in the speed, depth and timing of the various reforms, in the extent to which market-based incentives were offset or blunted by other government interventions and in the determination shown in redressing macroeconomic imbalances. All these aspects concern policy implementation more than policy design.

Poland, Czechoslovakia and Russia front-loaded their strategy with strong measures to reduce domestic aggregate demand, lower inflation and stabilize the external value of their currencies after their devaluation, while liberalising trade and banking. This was necessary to reverse inflationary expectations and to introduce a measure of financial discipline into the enterprise sector. Nevertheless, in the face of a sharp reduction of real income and standards of living and the slow response of the production system to new market opportunities, Poland and Russia could not sustain the tightening of financial policies; after about 2-3 quarters they had to ease their policy stance and give some financial respite to the most affected sectors. Afterwards, progress in structural reform was gradual, accompanied by relatively short cycles of financial tightening (for approximately 2-3 quarters) followed by an easing (1-2 quarters). In the same period, as the need to support domestic industries prevailed over the need for more competition in the domestic market, both countries backtracked somewhat on trade liberalisation by raising the average level of external tariffs. Financial system reform and public enterprise restructuring clearly lagged behind other reforms and was reflected in the slow pace of macroeconomic stabilization.

Czechoslovakia showed greater determination in bringing about macroeconomic stability and in building a constituency in support of reforms. By accelerating the transfer of public firms ownership into private hands through mass privatisation, it expanded the share of its population which had a direct economic interest in the reforms. Since, at the beginning of the transition, Czechoslovakia was free from the severe macroeconomic imbalances that affected other RCs, and therefore was supported by a higher degree of social consensus, it could retain certain anchors for monetary discipline, such as a stable exchange rate. This helped to create a relatively stable macroeconomic environment which facilitated structural reforms and the economic recovery. At the same time, accelerated privatisation made an increasing number of enterprises accountable for their own successes and failures, even though it did not lead to a rapid move towards enterprise restructuring.

After repeated attempts to curb inflation and excess demand with little success, Russia's policy focus shifted to accelerating privatisation along lines similar to Czechoslovakia's model, with expectations of widening the support for market reforms among the population and freeing the public sector from its responsibility to bail out public firms. As in Czechoslovakia, accelerated privatisation did not lead to swift enterprise restructuring. In these countries and, indeed, in all the RCs, such restructuring, as well as the expansion of the private enterprise sector, has been hampered by several factors: the weaknesses and distortions in the financial system, the embryonic state of market infrastructures and the gaps in the legal framework of economic activity.

Bulgaria's initial policy balance instead focused more on the liberalisation of economic activity than on privatisation and restructuring, and included a limited degree of macrostabilization. However, public enterprises have adjusted slowly to the new incentives for competition in the marketplace, while they have continued to receive indirect protection vis-à-vis competitors and creditors from the public authorities. Such a slow response to reforms by enterprises contributed significantly to continuing real output reductions and persistently high inflation, with the final result being that macroeconomic discipline became un-sustainable and structural reforms lost momentum. Thus, by 1994 (the fourth year of the transition), the transition process stalled and a new government was voted in on the expectation of a new, decisive policy approach. This has not yet materialised while the country has faced a new financial crisis. Overall, public enterprise restructuring, enterprise privatisation and bank rehabilitation have been progressing more slowly as compared to the approach of the three countries previously mentioned.

Romania and Hungary give two clear examples of a step-by-step approach in implementing price and trade liberalisation, privatisation, enterprise reform and financial restructuring as well as price stabilization. As Hungary in 1990 was more advanced than other RCs in the transition, there was no sense of urgency among its authorities to launch widespread and far-reaching reforms. Only by 1992 had this country, by and large, completed price and trade liberalisation, while, as regards the other reforms, no rapid advances in implementation were made in the first three years of transition, with the exception of a legal and institutional framework which was put in place. Actually, the slow restructuring of public enterprises and banking institutions, together with lags in privatisation, have hampered decisive progress towards price stability, while considerable fiscal imbalances have resulted from the rise in social expenditures and in general from high public expenditure as a ratio to GDP. While Hungary's economic liberalisation and institutional reforms, coupled with generous tax breaks, spurred the largest FDI inflows among the RCs, the over-riding concerns held by its authorities to limit the social costs of economic transformation mitigated the incentive to make adjustments in labour and capital allocation, thereby contributing to the slow output recovery. When the authorities eventually began to enforce bankruptcy law and financial discipline (between late 1993 and early 1994) in order to accelerate the pace of firms' restructuring and macroeconomic stabilization, the widespread rigidities still characterising the economy's supply side made it impossible to sustain this policy stance for more than a very short period. A decisive approach to macroeconomic stabilization and reform had eventually to be launched in 1995, involving cuts in social welfare expenditure and privatisation of large firms.

Romania's approach was even more gradual, although a large number of reform laws establishing a market economy were introduced in the initial phase of the transition (a nominal 'legislative shock' not matched by an actual one in the economy). Market mechanisms were allowed to actually work to a limited extent; in comparison with the other RCs under consideration, price and external trade were liberalised over a longer period, and government influence over management of an enterprise sector that is still largely in public hands remained significant. The initial policy strategy coupled a gradual price and trade liberalisation with small-scale privatisation and a tightening of credit expansion. As the new financial discipline was followed by sizeable output declines for a prolonged period (see the table), the authorities' strategy turned to support the enterprise sector mainly by providing

Table. Macroeconomic Stabilization.

	Year	GDP[1]		Consumer prices[1]		Current balances[3]		General govt balance[4]	
		Outcome	Dev.[2]	Outcome	Dev.[2]	Outcome	Dev.[3]	Outcome	Dev.
Bulgaria	1989	-0.4		6.4		-1.3			
	1990	-9.0		26		-1.2		-9.0	
	1991	-17.0	-6.0	490[5]	256	-0.9	1.1	-3.6	-3.7
	1992	-8.0	-4.0	82-79[5]	14	-0.7	0.7	-6.9	-2.4
	1993	-4.2		64[5]		-1.4		-11.4	
	1994	1.4		125	95	0.1	-0.3	-5.6	-0.2
	1995	2.5		33		0.3		-6.8	
	1996[12]	-4.0		150		0.0		-6.5	
Czechoslovakia	1989	1.0		1.4		0.3		-2.4	
	1990	-0.4		19		-1.1		0.7	
	1991	-16.0	-11.0	54	24	0.4	2.9	-1.0	-1.8
	1992	-5.0		12		-0.5			
Czech Republic	1993	-0.5	-1.5	21	3	0.1	-0.5	0.6	0.6
	1994	2.6		10.7		0.0		-2.0	
	1995	4.8		9.1		-1.9		-1.5	
	1996[12]	5.6		8.4		-2.4		-0.8	
Slovak Republic	1993	-4.1	4.9	23	-2.6	-0.7	1.8	-7.5	0.9
	1994	4.9	4.9	11.7	-3.3	0.7		-1.2[10]	0.8
	1995	7.4		7.2		0.5		0.7[10]	
	1996[12]	5.0		7		0.0		-1.5[10]	
Hungary	1989	-0.2		17.1		-1.4			
	1990	-3.3		28		0.1		0.2[8]	
	1991	-11.9	-8.9	35	-2	0.3	1.5	3.9[8]	5.4
	1992	-5.0	0.0	23	2	0.5	1.15	-7.0[8]	-6.5
	1993	-0.8	-0.8	21	4	-3.5	-8.9	-6.0	0
	1994	3.0		21		-3.9		-8.3	-0.3
	1995	1.5		28		-2.5		-6.5	
	1996[12]	2.0		22		-2.0		-4.0	
Poland	1989	0.0		251.1		-1.2			
	1990	-12.0	-9.0	586	492	0.7	3.7	0.5[7,8]	1.5
	1991	-8.0	11[6]	70	34	-2.2	0.5	-5.9[7,8]	-3.4
	1992	1.5	1.5[6]	43	7	-0.3	0.0	-6[7,8]	-1.0
	1993	3.8	-0.2	35	0	-2.3	0.3	-2.9[7,8]	2.4
	1994	5.2	0.5	29	9	-0.9[9]	1.6	-2.7	0.3
	1995	7.0	2.0	22	1.9	-2.1[9]	-0.2	-2.9	-0.3
	1996[12]	5.5		19		-2.9[9]		-2.8	
Romania	1989	-4.0		0.9		2.9			
	1990	-7.4		5.1		-1.7		1.0	
	1991	-14.0	-9.0	166	3	-1.4	1.0	-0.8	1.6
	1992	-13.5	-13.5	210.4	-59.6	-1.7	-0.1	-4.6	-2.6
	1993	1.3		295		-1.2		-0.7	
	1994	3.5	3.5	62	-13	-0.4		-1.0	2.0
	1995	6.9		28		-1.5		-3.6	
	1996[12]	4.0		25		-1.5		-2.5	
USSR/Russia	1989	2.4		2					
	1990	-4.0		5		-5.1			
	1991	-17.0		91		2.3			
	1992	-19.0		1500		-5.7		-18.8	
	1993	-12.0		840		2.6		-9.5	
	1994	-15.0[11]	-5.0	226	-173	0.0	12.2	-10.1	-6.5
	1995	-4.0	5.1	131	-12	7.0	8.2	-4.0	-3.2
	1996[12]	-2.0		30		2.5		-4.0	

[1] Percentage change; [2] Deviation of the outcome from the projection; algebraic difference in percentage points between outcome figures and figures related to IMF programme objectives or projections (outcome - projection); [3] In billions of US dollars; [4] Percentage of GDP. In this case, adding the deviation to the outcome gives the target; [5] December-on-December; [6] Deviations from Polish government projections; [7] Cash basis; excludes accrued interest on foreign debt; [8] State budget excluding local authorities, including extra-budgetary funds; [9] Excluding (large) unrecorded cross-border trade flows; [10] Exclude principal payments on public debt and clearing account transactions; [11] An alternative 1994 GDP figure of -12.6 was presented by the World Bank and Goskomstat in *Report on the National Accounts*, Washington DC and Moscow, October 1995; [12] Projections by the OECD Secretariat.

Data sources: OECD, IMF and national sources.

guarantees on bank loans or by assuming banks' bad debt. This blunted many of the incentives for enterprise restructuring that can arise as a result of market competition and led to the re-emergence of the bad loans problem and to a rather loose financial policy stance. In the last three years, the policy strategy has not aimed at accelerating structural adjustment and enterprise reorganisation through privatisation, but has focused on dealing on a piecemeal basis with various sectoral and enterprise crises, raising problems of consistency between fragmentary measures. Such a piecemeal and loose approach is making both the transition and the restoration of macroeconomic balance distant objectives to achieve.

4. Main results and lessons

4.1 General overview

The results of RCs' policies have generally fallen short of authorities' expectations on three fronts: putting in place a functioning market system, redressing macroeconomic imbalances and engineering a strong output recovery. The only exceptions are possibly represented by the Czech Republic, Poland and Hungary which have come closer than the other RCs to the three objectives.

Systemic changes have taken root in all RCs' economies but are not pervasive enough. Most of these economies must still complete market infrastructures, develop the distribution system, raise the level of market competition, liberalise some prices (such as energy prices). Legislation needed to support market activities, such as contract and company laws, must still be enacted or should be revised. The public sector still accounts for a large portion of national output (estimated at about two-fifths in the most advanced RCs) and, in spite of some progress in restructuring, there is no clear evidence that public-owned enterprises can presently sustain market competition and become viable without further government support. The banking system is still burdened by sizeable bad debts, and other financial institutions and markets are too flimsy to fulfil their role of mobilising savings and improving credit allocation.

Price stability has not yet been achieved by any RC, with inflation (except in the Czech and Slovak republics) running at rates between 19 per cent and 150 per cent per annum at consumer level (see the table). Rising deficits have also emerged in external current accounts, and their trend is not in a downward direction. In expanding economies, such deficits could be justified if they stand against a strong investment trend which raises the economy's output potential over the medium-term. However, fixed investment has picked up only recently and in few RCs, and therefore external current deficits largely reflect national saving shortfalls.

Output has fully recovered only in Poland and the Czech Republic under the impulse of the private sector's expansion. In other RCs, only in 1994 has it been possible to reverse the declining trend of the 1990s; nevertheless, growth in these cases appears to be founded on a fragile basis, as it is accompanied by macroeconomic imbalances.

All these failures are also the result of external factors, such as the collapse of intraregional trade, tensions in the Balkan region and the weak economic conjuncture in Western Europe in the early years of this decade. Nevertheless, the major responsibility lies with the conduct of domestic policies and social resistance to drastic changes in the RCs themselves. Several considerations can be drawn in general from these experiences.

Frequent discontinuities in policy implementation, which have been common to all RCs, made it more difficult to achieve both reform targets and macrostabilization, since they adversely affected enterprise and household expectations. Such 'stop-and-go' policies have not created strong expectations about the continuity of reforms and consequently have not adequately contributed to behavioural changes among economic agents so as to accelerate adjustment to structural reforms. Even worse, the many policy reversals, as well as the policy exceptions for particular cases and sectors, especially in the countries lagging behind, have cast doubts about the depth of reforms and have fed expectations of a bail-out by the government vis-à-vis the market pressures to restructure and adjust.

A particularly damaging form of policy instability has been the level of unpredictability related to the use of the newly established policy levers by authorities. For instance, tax rates, external tariffs and trade barriers, foreign direct investment (FDI) support measures and financial and trade regulations have been changed frequently and to a sizeable extent. Of course, these policies have to respond to changing circumstances and need to be mended once experience has been gained; indeed, a large number of imperfections cannot be avoided during the initial phase of the transition, as several reforms have to be introduced in a very short time and without sufficient skills for their preparation. Nevertheless, policy changes in the course of the transition were often abrupt, were discriminatory between economic sectors and within the same sector, did not fit with the initially stated policy intentions and raised doubts about the actual policy priorities over the short-term.

Such policy instability bears a great deal of responsibility for the dismal evolution of domestic investment, FDI and private sector development. Credibility of policy strategy has yet to be built in most RCs, and this requires coherence of measures over time, clear announcement of the different policy stages well in advance of their implementation, continuity of implementation and open explanations of reasons for policy deviations. The one or two RCs which have most heavily invested in building such credibility are now well ahead of the others in the transition process.

If the so-called 'shock therapy' is defined as a drastic policy-induced compression of domestic demand, coupled with full liberalisation of prices and trade and with a strong pressure for enterprise restructuring, even without government support, then none of the reforming economies can be said to have actually suffered under shock therapy, because in no country was it truly applied. All RCs have instead introduced reforms and tightened demand in a staggered approach, have cushioned the most severe impact of their measures and have applied 'gradualism', albeit in different degrees. Initial policies in some RCs might have appeared as a shock but this was due to the fact that the RCs could not afford to accommodate excess demand over the medium-term, or even the short-term, due to a lack of means to cover external deficits. At the same time, they wanted to give unequivocal signals that they were not aiming at a gradual exit from a centrally planned economic system along lines previously tried by some RCs in the 1980s. The abandonment of the old system was not only a political necessity but the very cornerstone of the transition strategy.

With the benefit of hindsight, it is evident that there was an initial under-estimation of the behavioural inertia that had been built in among economic agents by the old system, as well as an under-estimation of the structural rigidities in the reallocation of capital and labour towards the most competitive sectors. Given these economic parameters, it does not seem that a critical mass of structural and macroeconomic measures was initially introduced in order to obtain rapid economic restructuring through changes in rewards and penalties for production factors, although it is hard to define, even in general terms, what the 'critical mass' must include, since it is a function of the initial imbalances of each RC and its degree of structural rigidity, whose measure is largely unknown. The system of relative prices changed swiftly year after year, but the general environment of persistently high inflation and various government measures aimed at mitigating the impact of reforms dampened the role of these changes.

If not from shock therapy, then the RCs have suffered from some policy inconsistency across the spectrum of reform and macroeconomic measures. At both stages of design and implementation, the interlinkages between measures for market development, enterprise restructuring and aggregate demand management have been weak. For instance, synergies between external trade liberalisation, sharp depreciation of the real exchange rate and enterprise restructuring have been limited. It was initially thought by the RCs that price and trade liberalisation, together with a disinflationary policy, would suffice to generate, in the short-term, opportunities for output expansion and consequently provide an incentive for structural adjustment. The latter had to be reinforced at a later stage by more time-consuming privatisation. In fact, public enterprises adjusted slowly to new trade opportunities and the overall decline in demand increased social resistance to structural adjustment. When this became evident, some RCs gave impetus to privatisation and structural adjustment through various means, including income support measures; others just bailed out enterprises and mitigated financial discipline.

However, in both country groups, determinant factors for accelerating the transition and obtaining a strong recovery in output are the simultaneous development of a competitive private enterprise sector and a good environment for conducting business. On both grounds the policies of the two country groups have been inadequate because structural impediments to business development remain widespread and pervasive. Because of these impediments, even in countries where privatisation has been rapid, a strong drive towards good corporate governance and investment in fixed capital has not yet been produced. The blossoming of the underground economy can also be attributed in part to these obstacles. The growth potential of all these economies could be rapidly increased if the authorities would now focus their policies on easing these structural impediments. For example, the financial system is burdened by distortions in bank credit allocation, fragility of the banking structures and the vulnerability of financial markets. Other impediments include excessive regulations inherited from the old system, inadequate enforcement of commercial laws and the still ample margin of government interference in market competition through selective support measures.

During the past two years, a 'wait-and-see' policy attitude has developed in a number of RCs, under which the authorities wait for more results to come from the measures initially adopted, rather than completing the reforms and continuing the progress towards macroeconomic stability. Some even believe that a 'muddling-through' approach, involving only marginal adjustments to the reforms already enacted, is sufficient to make progress in the transition. The comparative results so far obtained by these RCs do not seem to support these approaches: countries that have continued with reform measures halve achieved comparatively higher GDP growth and have made greater progress towards lower inflation.

In general, policy strategies have not been constrained by political instability since all the new democracies have had rather stable governments. Nevertheless, the political cycle of parliamentary elections in some RCs has led to a decisively short-term orientation in the policies followed over the past two years. In anticipation of approaching elections, governments have searched for rapid and partial improvements of economic and social conditions at the expense of deviating from original policy intents, leading to distortions and delays in reforms. This experience, which is not unusual in Western democracies, underlines the importance of an early launch of radical reform measures. Front-loading the policy strategy in the early phase of the political cycle presents the twin advantages of sending strong signals on the expected changes in the economy and of making it more costly to reverse policies if, at the end of the political cycle, the electorate votes to change the government.

4.2 Macroeconomic stabilisation

Since the beginning of the transition process, macroeconomic stabilization has been at the core of the policy strategy of all RCs. It is therefore striking that macroeconomic stability has not yet been achieved in any of the RCs. Among the many questions that this disappointing outcome raises, three seem of particular interest:

- is macrostabilization a necessary prerequisite if the reform process is to advance?
- what can explain this outcome?
- how can this objective be achieved?

As regards the first question, the historical experience of the RCs, as well as of developing countries, indicates that it is possible to reform and transform the economy even in the face of significant macroeconomic imbalances. Poland has managed to establish a market economy that is growing at around 5 per cent per year, despite an annual inflation rate hovering around 20 per cent. Russia created a market system and privatised most of its enterprises while inflation was running in the three-digit range on an annual basis. Nevertheless, such experiences also show that a reformed market economy cannot reach a sustained growth path in the presence of a rising trend in macro-imbalances. Even if these countries have not achieved price stability and external balance, they have however consistently progressed in this direction. In periods when excess domestic demand was driving inflation and external deficits much higher, economic activity in these countries tended to stagnate because of the high uncertainty about future price and cost levels (in absolute and relative terms) and about the availability of balance of payments financing (see the figure). Furthermore, rising public sector dissaving tended to crowd out private investment. Hence, continuing progress towards macrobalance appears a requirement, if not a precondition, that must accompany economic liberalisation and the establishment of a market system.

As to the causes for the limited success of macrostabilization policies, attention has focused on the possibility that compression of domestic demand was excessive

Figure. Price Stabilisation and output performance.

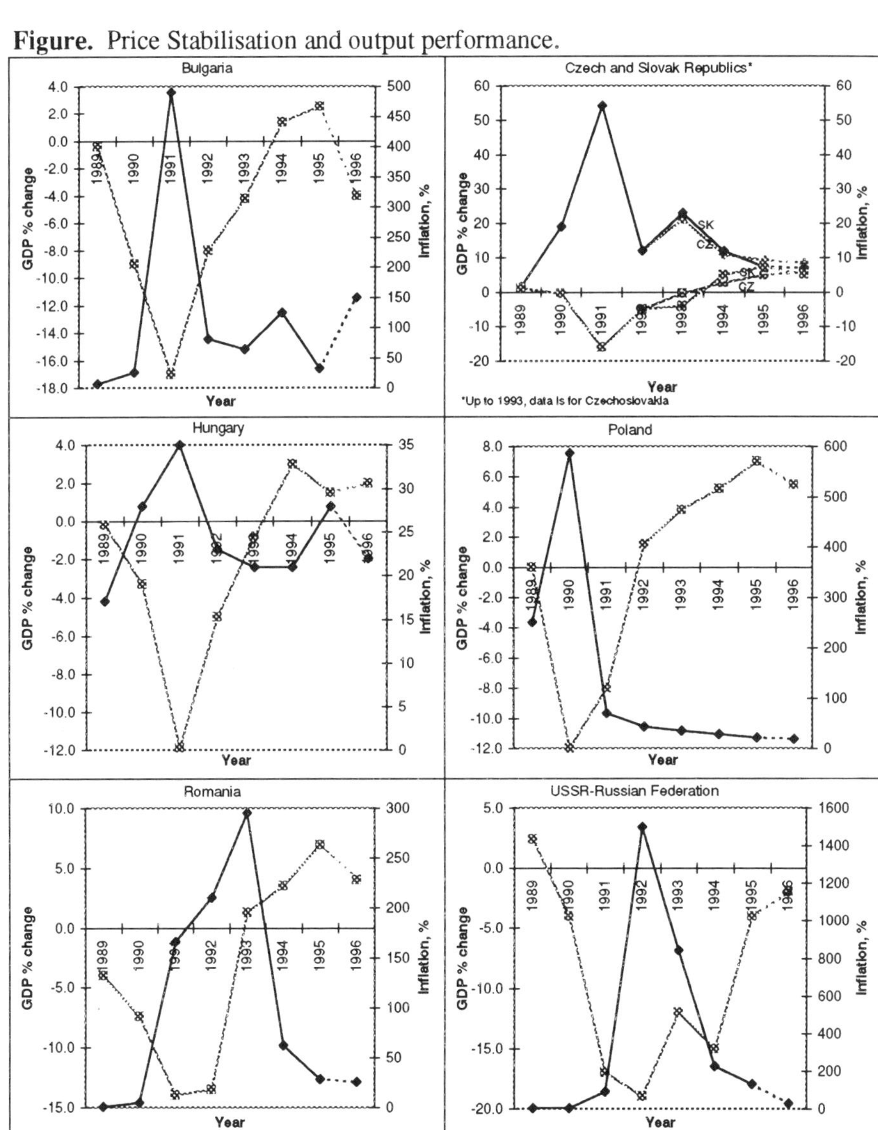

Key: Real GDP growth; Inflation

Data source: OECD. Data for 1996 represent OECD Secretariat projections.

and therefore not socially or politically sustainable. In particular, drastic attempts to lower inflation rapidly, namely in a few quarters rather than a few years, were believed to have deepened output reduction and made enterprise restructuring more difficult. Output decline was actually due to a combination of external factors (the fall in trade between the RCs and the low economic juncture in Western Europe), supply side factors (the phasing out of productions that have become un-competitive under the new price system while the expansion of competitive productions lags behind) and demand factors (monetary and fiscal tightening together with sharp exchange rate depreciation). With the liberalisation of prices, it was necessary to drain excess liquidity out of the economy and in addition to inject a measure of financial discipline into enterprises and households. Even when over short periods some overshooting in policy tightening occurred, this was corrected within a few quarters. The persistence of high inflation bears witness to the relatively accommodating stance of monetary and fiscal policies.

Furthermore, there is not enough evidence to indicate that progress towards lower inflation has compromised output recovery. The chart shows the relationship between inflation and GDP growth for the six RCs under consideration. From this it can be inferred that a significant inverse correlation exists between the five variables, whereby GDP recovers following reductions in inflation.

Among the reasons for the limited success in macrostabilization, it is necessary to explore whether the instruments which were used to this end were up to the task. The RCs have put emphasis on limiting net credit expansion of the banking system, on curtailing credit to Government and on increasing policy-controlled interest rates. The interrelationship between these monetary targets and structural changes, however, has been rather loose and not sufficiently emphasized in the policy strategy. This has led to either a low degree of effectiveness in policy action to the extent that macroeconomic balance was not reached even though the credit targets were achieved or it has brought about perverse effects. For instance, interest rate increases did not make a sufficient dent in the credit demand of public enterprises that were not subject to financial discipline, while credit tightening tended to ration credit to private enterprises more than to public ones. The rapid increase of inter-enterprise arrears is another signal of the limited effect of credit tightening in an environment that has not yet adjusted to financial discipline.

To some extent, the persistence of high inflation reflected the difficulty in forcing changes into the system of relative prices. In an environment of downward price rigidity and widespread market imperfections, and with enterprises still learning pricing policies in a competitive environment, continuing inflation was a way to gradually push relative prices towards a new structure. However, such an accommodating monetary policy stance vis-à-vis sectoral inflationary pressures seems to have lasted too long, thereby contributing to a degree of instability in the price structure.

How can the chances of success in macrostabilization during the next phase of the transition be increased? Recent experience suggests three main answers to this question. First, close co-ordination must be established between the restructuring of the enterprise sector and the rehabilitation of the banking system. An enterprise sector more responsive to financial constraints and a banking system freed from the burden of bad debt and which is able to improve credit allocation, would greatly enhance the effectiveness of monetary policy. Second, in order to contain fiscal imbalances, it is crucial to restructure social expenditures and bring them into line with available fiscal resources. Third, in parallel with gaining control over domestic sources of inflationary pressures, it is advisable to slow down the exchange rate depreciation with a view to stabilizing inflation expectations. Of course, a nominal exchange rate anchor would be premature in the face of still high inflation, since it would lead to rapid declines in competitiveness. But in the context of a strong disinflationary policy, an early shift towards fixed, albeit adjustable, exchange rates seems warranted.

4.3 Enterprise restructuring and privatisation

In the current stage of the transition, there is anecdotal evidence that a certain amount of operational and financial restructuring of the enterprise sector has already taken place, although there are no clear indicators showing how far profitability and competitiveness have been restored, particularly in the manufacturing sector. Most of the progress in restructuring was made after the first two or three years of the transition, particularly in the most advanced RCs, but even in these countries the bulk of the restructuring must still be completed. The authorities have generally adopted a multi-track approach that has relied upon several instruments: corporatisation of public firms, privatisation, wage norms for public firms, cuts in subsidies, preferential allocation of credit or credit guarantees (possibly on favourable terms), liquidation and bankruptcy enforcement. These instruments have been applied in an uneven manner, with special support being granted to deal with individual industrial crises, but with no general strategy applied across the entire industry, apart from macroeconomic measures, such as monetary tightening and exchange rate depreciation.

The underlying idea has generally been that a decentralised approach based on market mechanisms is the only feasible policy, since governments lack skills and resources to select and restructure potentially viable firms. Although this approach is in principle fully justified, in reality it leads to delays, distortions and risks of high social tensions and of an overly rapid contraction of the country's production base. In the RCs, market mechanisms are not yet functioning in such a way as to provide support to the potentially most viable firms and to penalise the less viable ones. Since financial discipline is not adequate, there is room for perverse incentives for the less competitive enterprises to survive. Hence, within the general framework of a decentralised approach to restructuring, a set of general, sectoral and microeconomic-oriented policies has to be implemented in order to facilitate the market-led restructuring.

Privatisation has been considered an important tool to this end. It has become evident that delays in privatisation are not a long-term solution to the restructuring problem because of the eventual high costs involved, especially in terms of pressure on public expenditure and difficulties in restoring macroeconomic balance. If privatisation needs to be accelerated, then the RCs should focus on a rapid transfer of ownership, rather than on trying to pursue a multitude of goals that often conflict with one another, such as to search at the same time for the best sale price, strategic investors, an equal distribution of assets among the population and social and investment guarantees. As shown by the experiences of the Czech Republic and Russia, mass privatisation is the best tool for rapid ownership transfer, but it does not guarantee an equally rapid restructuring of enterprises.

In general, privatisation alone is not a sufficient condition for rapidly encouraging firms to operate more efficiently. Surveys of privatised firms indicate that in the majority of cases, management has not changed after privatisation; in the few cases where management has changed, the new managers have come from within the firm. When employees have gained ownership control over the privatised firm, the managers' task of reorganising the firm has been constrained by employee resistance to radical restructuring. By contrast, the transfer of firms to foreign owners has generally been followed by rapid reorganisation, rising sales and exports, and capital investment. However, foreign owners have been interested mainly in firms which command substantial market power, and they have aimed at reinforcing their dominant position in the market, even by asking the government to introduce barriers to market access.

Therefore, in order to promote enterprise restructuring, privatisation must be coupled with mechanisms to improve corporate governance, to make credit allocation less inefficient, to diversify firms' financial sources, to develop labour market and social policies and to enforce demonopolisation and more open market access.

Corporate governance can be strengthened through capital markets, investment funds, banks and strategic investors. New equity markets have emerged and have allowed some ownership reshuffling and concentration after privatisation. In order for these markets to be useful instruments to enforce good corporate governance, they must overcome several weaknesses, such as low liquidity, significant information asymmetries, weak regulatory frameworks and insufficient transparency of market transactions. Investment funds have come to control the largest portion of privatised companies in several RCs, but it is questionable whether they have the necessary skills to control company management or the capacity to influence management on the basis of minority shares that are constrained to modest percentages due to laws against asset concentration risk. Banks are still the main source of capital for privatised firms and, as such, they influence corporate governance. Nevertheless, their capacity to assess the credit-worthiness of firms still seems limited, and the expansion of their equity holdings appears incompatible with the need to safeguard depositors' interests, especially given the relatively high risk profile that already characterises their portfolio because of the relatively large proportion of dubious loans. Shortcomings in the use of these various instruments can and should be corrected without the need for RCs to favour a particular model for enhancing corporate governance. Regardless of whether an RC relies on a widely dispersed corporate ownership and efficient stock markets or on dominant investors, rules have to be tightened to enforce management accountability and corporate accounting transparency.

The restructuring and development of privatised firms remains difficult due to social and financial constraints. To become competitive, privatised firms have to shed excess labour, to abandon responsibility for social services and to be financially supported in the retraining of their labour force. Moreover, they need better commercial banking services and possibilities to diversify their financial sources outside bank borrowing. This interconnection between restructuring, on the one hand, and labour market and social policies and financial reform, on the other, has not been adequately addressed by the RCs, despite the fact that it could be a powerful method to promote enterprise rehabilitation and expansion.

To this end, there has also been a shortfall of market-based competitive pressures. De-monopolisation has not always taken place before privatisation, and foreign trade liberalisation has generally not succeeded in breaking the market power of firms that used to be the main suppliers under the old system. To the extent that major sectors are still dominated by a few enterprises, the cost of their inefficiencies is borne by other enterprises or consumers in the form of higher prices. Competition laws were issued in all RCs; however, this has not yet ensured a competitive environment in several markets. Action is therefore required, particularly in two directions. First, these laws should be properly enforced, because action taken thus far against non-competitive practices has been weak and sometimes has fostered distortions, inasmuch as it has aimed at imposing ceilings on profit margins through direct government intervention. Second, in several sectors, market structures should be scrutinised and, if monopolistic or oligopolistic structures are not justifiable, various measures should be used in order to actively promote new entries into the market.

An incentive to restructuring could stem from the application of bankruptcy laws. Insolvency procedures have seldom been applied, not only because of creditor passivity but also because of a feared ‘domino’ effect due to their liquidation bias. For most of the transition period, the RCs have only viewed bankruptcy law as a mechanism for debt-collection, and have not seen its alternative importance as a tool to trigger a decentralised process of public firm restructuring and privatisation. Only in 1994 did this latter orientation begin to emerge. Such action should continue to be pursued, particularly in light of the encouraging results which have recently been produced. In Poland, ‘conciliation’ procedures have been led by creditor banks vis-à-vis public firms, with the double effect of forcing these firms to launch a restructuring plan and spurring them to seek privatisation assistance, while at the same time settling the bad debt problem. In Russia, responsibility for restructuring or liquidating has been assigned to a public institution specialised in this task.

With respect to the restructuring objective, prior experience with tax-based controls on wage increases has been disappointing since wage dynamics have repeatedly exceeded the norm. Moreover, wage limits have not discouraged labour hoarding, but rather have hindered the development of a better link between pay levels and job productivity. It is advisable to phase out these wage controls and to resort to other instruments for those enterprises that will not be privatised. Among these tools, prominence should be given to setting tight accounting standards to monitor public firms’ performance. Consideration should also be given to making managers accountable for generating enough resources to cover capital depreciation allowances and to remunerate equity capital.

4.4 Financial development

Financial development has been one of the weakest points in the transition strategy for most RCs. Early in the transition process there were four major problem areas:

- payment system;
- bank rehabilitation;
- banking system structure and supervision;
- financial market development.

Progress in these four areas, made relatively late in the transition, has been rather uneven. The RCs' approach has generally been slowly implemented and has not been well co-ordinated with other reforms.

In spite of many improvements in the payments system, in the most advanced RCs there is still a need to improve the national clearing system in order to reduce the duration of the debit float of banks. Payment settlement procedures must also be made more rapid and efficient so as to reduce settlement risks and, consequently, excess liquidity holdings. In other RCs, such as Russia, the payments system is still largely inefficient and cumbersome, representing an impediment to business development. Clearly, there are no major issues preventing rapid improvements in this field, but there is the question of assigning a higher priority to this area in the government's agenda.

The solution to the bad loan problem of RC banks has been hampered by a number of difficult issues. Despite its importance, this problem has not been addressed as a major policy priority and, in general, not enough incentives have been created for banks and enterprises to deflate this problem, with the possible exception of Poland, where a bank-led debt restructuring plan was introduced in 1994. The initial stock of bad loans stemming from the old centrally-planned system was largely nullified by high inflation. The problem, however, reproduced itself and grew as public banks generally behaved as passive lenders, often rolling over their loans and capitalising matured interest. Passivity was not just the result of having an inadequate technical capacity to engage in the analysis of creditworthiness, but was also a reflection of a number of additional conditions: insufficient accountability of banks vis-à-vis the public owner, under-capitalisation with the resulting incentive to lend to public firms embodying an implicit public guarantee, relatively lax financial discipline on a macroeconomic scale, ineffective insolvency procedures for enterprises and inadequate bank supervision.

While most RCs have not acted on the problem, some (Poland and Hungary, in particular) have taken partial approaches; these, however, do not assure that the problem will not reproduce itself. One method has involved shifting bad loans to a government institution in exchange for a capital injection by the government. This raises a 'moral hazard problem', to the extent that such a method can lead to a systematic bail-out of banks with little incentive for performance improvement. Another method (used in Poland) gives banks the responsibility of cleaning up their own portfolios; it provides an incentive (in the form of limited and conditional recapitalisation) to the banks that force the debtor to settle or service its non-performing debt in the context of a financial restructuring plan. However, there are some drawbacks with this method. For banks that are undercapitalised and lack reserves, the cost of the 'clean-up' will weigh heavily on their intermediation costs, leaving ample spreads between borrowing and lending rates. To the extent that a bank accepts debt/equity conversions, it is doubtful whether the risk profile of the bank's assets would improve, as there is no certainty about the future profitability of the firm whose shares are now in the bank's hands. Furthermore, the 'moral hazard problem' is reduced, but not eliminated by this method. It is interesting to note that bank privatisation has very seldom been used as a tool to promote bank efficiency. The justification has been that an ownership transfer would not bring about the expected improvements since it takes place in a structural environment, which does not provide enough incentives for better performance. Such a justification does not appear to generally hold valid for the RCs.

Regardless of which method of recapitalisation is used, it is clear that these approaches are insufficient and must be complemented by accompanying policies. In essence, RCs should create the necessary overall conditions to turn passive lenders, namely the banks, into institutions capable of promoting an efficient allocation of credit (i.e. to select their debtors on the basis of their creditworthiness in a competitive market context). This involves a series of structural changes in the banking system, changes which, thus far, have not been squarely addressed.

First, with respect to the legal framework of the banking system, accounting standards need to be tightened and enforced together with reporting requirements and capital adequacy ratios. Competition in the banking industry is too limited given the segmentation of the market and banks' regional concentration or specialisation in sectoral lending. Opening up the banking industry to foreign banks (with an excellent business record, preferably) could ease some of these shortcomings.

Second, good bank governance can also be induced by modifying the ownership structure of the banking system. The RCs have generally neglected or under-estimated the importance of this aspect. It is not solely a question of privatising a significant portion of the banking industry by overcoming the resistance of those pressure groups that have been benefiting in terms of credit allocation preferences. There is also a problem of 'captive banking', under which borrowing firms control the ownership of their bank lender. The result is a confusion between business risk and lending risk, to the detriment of efficient credit allocation and protection of depositors' savings. Ownership and lending interrelationships between banks and non-financial enterprises should be regulated more effectively than they are at present.

Third, the spread between lending and borrowing rates is generally too large and penalising for the economy's development. This is the consequence of both a high incidence of non-performing assets in banks' portfolios and operating cost/asset ratios that are high in comparison with international standards. If market competition is not expected to improve in the short-term to the point of spurring banks to reduce these spreads, then the RCs should consider whether temporary regulations are needed in order to induce banks to strengthen their reserves and to narrow their relative operating costs.

In the field of bank supervision, the RCs have generally made progress in setting out a legal and institutional framework, but they have not yet succeeded in enforcing it. As the shortage of skilled staff continues to be a major impediment to effective supervision, it cannot be expected that rapid progress will be made in the near future. So long as bank supervision is more nominal than actual, the banking system will most likely continue to be subject to a high risk of instability, even in the face of appropriate prudential regulations and comprehensive reporting requirements for the banks.

With respect to the development of equity and bond markets and non-bank financial institutions, the RCs have generally followed a rather liberal approach, limiting their intervention to the issuance of basic regulations and leaving ample room for private initiative. This approach seems justified by the need to diversify enterprises' financial sources outside the banking system, to support the ownership reshuffle after privatisation, to reduce the role of banks in financing the public budget deficit and to promote new investment opportunities in order to mobilise private savings in the direction of funding enterprise restructuring and expansion plans. In an environment which is largely unregulated, capital markets have developed with unexpected rapidity and with some positive results. Stock exchanges in Budapest, Prague and Warsaw have established good operational standards and have reached a minimum of liquidity. Government debt instruments are now traded in significant amounts in markets which are becoming a new gauge of changing liquidity conditions in the economy. At the present stage of financial development, however, capital markets have not yet become a major source of funds for enterprises, mainly because the surrounding environment has not been favourable enough to market-participation. Information on the economic situation of the user of funds is inadequate; the market infrastructure is still undergoing development; the range of investors is limited in spite of the proliferation of investment funds; government securities tend to crowd out other financial instruments in investors' preferences; and macroeconomic conditions are generally perceived as unstable.

Overall, it appears that the RCs' opportunities for economic recovery, enterprise restructuring and expansion of the private enterprise sector have been constrained by the inadequate attention paid by governments to the development of a sound financial system. Although it is true that the more advanced RCs in this regard are also those which have made greater gains in macroeconomic adjustment and privatisation, the latter policies alone are not sufficient for the financial sector to develop. Recapitalisation of banks and structural issues related to bank and non-bank intermediaries, as well as financial markets, need to be addressed urgently and with far-reaching measures, if the financial system is to sustain the incipient economic recovery. Moreover, the gap that has arisen between financial liberalisation and the effective application of prudential regulations must be filled by developing a capacity to supervise all financial institutions. In its absence, the financial system will most likely remain highly vulnerable to financial crises that can undermine the economy's growth prospects.

4.5 Labour market and social policies

Labour market and social policies have received a great deal of attention from the authorities since the beginning of the transition, and the action programmes in these areas have been rapidly implemented. In such a process of radical economic transformation, the rise in unemployment was an inevitable phenomenon, resulting from both the exposure of pre-existing hidden unemployment (particularly in the form of labour hoarding by firms), and the lack of symmetry between job destruction due to structural adjustment and job creation in new business initiatives. The unemployment rates themselves do not offer a full picture of the labour market conditions that characterise the transition period in all the RCs. Unemployment appears as a rather stagnant pool, with a low rate of reintegration of job-seekers into work. In many cases the lack of job opportunities has resulted in job-seekers leaving the labour market altogether, an aspect which is not captured by the unemployment rate but instead by the decline in participation rates. Nevertheless, an amount of labour reallocation has taken place between sectors and enterprises, mostly in the form of direct job-to-job shifts, in particular towards the private enterprise sector. Like recent unemployment experiences in the OECD's European countries, unemployment in the RCs is unevenly spread among social groups and regions. It has disproportionately struck young, unskilled and older workers, together with some ethnic, minorities. It is also heavily concentrated in rural areas and mono-cultural industrial regions, while it is much lower in large urban areas, thereby indicating a low labour mobility.

To address these aspects of the labour market problem and to deal with the underlying rising trend of unemployment, the RCs have quickly adopted multi-pronged labour market programmes. The general strategy has been to gradually shift the thrust of public intervention from generalised subsidisation of labour hoarding in loss-making public enterprises to a selective approach aimed at favouring labour mobility, bringing labour supply in line with the evolving characteristics of labour demand and, to a limited extent, to raise labour demand itself. The policy instruments have included unemployment benefits, training, employment subsidies and measures to reduce labour supply pressure on the market through social security benefits. Overall, these policies have succeeded in limiting the potential for social tensions and social resistance to reforms, in creating some of the labour market's foundations which did not exist under the old regime and in facilitating labour reallocation. Consequently, they have managed to contain the unemployment problem and, accordingly, stabilize its level[3]. It is however questionable whether they have provided viable, long-term solutions.

The effectiveness of this strategy is weakened by three groups of problems:

- the insufficient co-ordination of labour market policies with other policies, especially those aimed at supporting job creation through the development of the private enterprise sector, as well as through the promotion of labour intensive sectors, such as the services sector;
- the targeting of measures;
- the financial viability of these policies.

As to the first group, the transition experience so far suggests that the opening line of attack on unemployment must focus on creating conditions that foster the expansion of the most dynamic (i.e. competitive) sectors of the economy. As private enterprises, especially those operating in competitive domestic markets or competing in export markets, represent the driving force of the economy's recovery, policies which support the growth of these enterprises ultimately support new job creation. If government policies do not ease structural constraints hindering these sectors, such as the underdeveloped infrastructure of product markets, the difficulty of tapping financial sources and the slow pace of enterprise privatisation and economic deregulation, the possibilities of job creation will be constrained or will increase mostly in the underground economy. The second line of attack must be directed towards helping to shift excess labour from declining sectors, or enterprises in the process of being restructured, towards expanding sectors through the so-called active labour market policies. Although these policies have been applied by the RCs, they have only met with modest success because thus far, the expansion of private enterprises has not been great enough to make a dent in unemployment and because the restructuring of public enterprises, with the consequent release of labour resources, has generally advanced quite slowly. For instance, job placement services, vocational training and retraining are most effective for the reintegration into work when they operate in a context of rising labour demand and close co-operation with the enterprise sector, conditions that have seldom been met in the transition period. Instead, it has often been the case that training and retraining have been carried out in an 'economic vacuum', namely in regions with very few job vacancies and very dim job prospects, with the consequence that employment results have been disappointing. Moreover, housing market policies have not worked to encourage labour mobility towards regions with excess labour demand.

The most controversial measures to fight unemployment are those which aim to reduce the supply of labour, since they suppress the unemployment problem rather than solving it, and involve high costs for the economy and society. Nonetheless, the RCs have made great use of these measures, above all during the early stages of the transition. These are stop-gap measures that involve conflicts between the short-run objective of relieving social tensions and long-term goals such as balancing public finances, reducing the non-wage component of labour costs (social security contributions) and enhancing the contribution of available labour resources to the development of the economy. For example, promoting early retirement of workers ends up by increasing the fiscal burden of an ageing society or raising the price of labour, i.e. the price of the production factor that is in excess supply.

A general problem that has arisen with the full range of labour market and social policies is their effectiveness in dealing with the specific characteristics of the unemployment problem. In several of the RCs, there is evidence that the long-term unemployed (those out of work for more than 6 to 12 months, depending on the country) receive less public assistance in job placement and counselling than do other unemployed. Unemployment benefits have been managed with lax eligibility criteria and little attention has been paid to promote the return of the unemployed to work. Active labour market measures, such as vocational training and retraining programmes, instead need to be expanded into areas where job vacancies co-exist with unemployment (labour mismatch). In contrast, in areas where there is a stagnant or falling demand for labour, it seems more appropriate to focus public resources on direct job creation schemes or unemployment benefits, as has been successfully done in the Czech and Slovak republics.

Another problem is related to the new laws governing collective dismissals; they tend to delay the enterprise restructuring process by limiting labour force adjustment at the enterprise level. Moreover, by raising the dismissal costs, they affect the propensity to hire workers and end up lengthening the average duration of unemployment spells.

As regards social policies, the health-care and social-security systems which were adopted in the transition period have proven too generous to be affordable by the RCs in the current phase of their economic development. While public expenditures for pensions have grown rapidly, adding new tensions to the budget, pension benefits are generally low and many pensioners live in poverty. In the trade-off between effectiveness of social protection and its extension, the RCs have generally leaned towards the latter by adopting low retirement ages and lax disability criteria, with the result of being able to ensure only low benefit levels, which are weakly linked to workers' previous earnings. Such an approach needs to be rebalanced in the direction of restricting extension (for example, through higher retirement ages and more means testing in deciding the level of social protection) while increasing the average benefit level.

The financial viability of the current system of social protection also seems generally questionable. On the one hand, in several RCs, a wide wedge already exists between the cost of labour and take-home pay, with social security contributions accounting for about one-third of total labour costs (for instance in the Visegrad countries). On the other hand, social security contributions do not sufficiently cover social security expenditures and must be complemented by general tax revenue, with the ultimate result being a trend towards higher fiscal deficits. Under these conditions, it appears that the RCs have little room to deal with this funding problem; either they widen the labour cost wedge or they increase general taxation. Most likely, part of the adjustment must be carried out by downscaling or placing limits on social expenditures. This makes it even more necessary to improve expenditure effectiveness in order to contain social discontent resulting from the adjustments.

Overall, the weaknesses of the RCs' labour and social policies do not seem to differ significantly from those that are currently encountered in several OECD countries. This is not surprising, given that the RCs have shaped their policies following OECD countries' models, particularly those of Western Europe. However, they have apparently under-estimated the importance of having a proper infrastructure in place in order to manage these policies effectively; even worse, they have not drawn enough on the experience of the OECD countries in order to avoid the same shortcomings. Consequently, they are now faced with the bigger challenge of having to make unpopular corrections against the backdrop of an already high level of social discontent.

Conclusions

Looking back at the transition approaches followed during the first phase of the transition, a number of general conclusions can be drawn that can serve as lessons for planning the policies to complete the transition. These lessons are built on the premise that the RCs' approaches have not represented a continuation of the gradual reforms undertaken under the centrally planned system, reforms which introduced market incentives into a system still dominated by state intervention. Rather, they have reflected the decision to move to a new economic system, a decision that was seen as the necessary corollary to the fundamental choice to change the political regime to a liberal democracy.

The overriding objective of policy-makers has been to smooth the path to a new period of sustained economic growth. Several RCs holding this perspective have often considered market mechanisms as instruments to be applied only to the extent that they deliver the targeted growth results; if costs in the short-run far exceed the benefits expected over the medium-term, then the impact of these mechanisms, it is felt, must be restrained.

To date, the transition approaches have had limited success in achieving robust, economic recovery and in implanting market mechanisms. This outcome must be ascribed to the economic legacy of the old regime and to the RC policies themselves more than to exogenous factors (for example, the collapse of traditional export markets or the economic embargo in the Balkan region), although, at times, these latter factors have had a substantial impact on these economies. The policy approaches have been rather similar in their conception throughout the RCs, but they have also been implemented very unevenly, both across countries and across the range of measures which were initially envisaged. If the pace of the transition has not been as rapid as initially expected and if some RCs continue to lag behind others, it is not because of the policy choice made by each RC between adopting a 'shock approach' or following gradual policies. For the past transition period as a whole, the magnitude of the policy-induced shocks has not differed significantly among these RCs, although there were differences over very short periods. With the possible exception of one or two small economies, the tightening of monetary conditions by the RCs or reductions in their domestic absorption of resources have not been carried out to such a degree and duration as to prevent fiscal deficit and double-digit inflation from persisting. The limited cases of overshooting in macroeconomic stabilization were short-lived enough not to be representative of the overall policy stance. All RCs have enacted reforms and structural changes with a measure of gradualism and have been ready to cushion, or even offset in various ways, their impact in order to limit social hardship.

Gradualism was a matter of necessity for all RCs since it is not technically possible all at once to liberalise prices and trade, to build the legal and institutional foundations of the market-economy, to stabilize prices and to relaunch output growth. Instead, other factors have had a determinant influence on the limited progress made by the RCs in achieving their transition goals, in particular the coherence and parallelism that have been applied in implementing the major components of RCs policy strategies and the consistency of policy implementation over time.

On the grounds of policy coherence, there have been a number of flaws which more concerned the implementation stage than the strategy design. In shaping their policies, the RCs were initially convinced that, in order to push their economies towards a path of reform and growth, it would be sufficient to introduce a number of laws and institutions establishing the market system, to liberalise a high proportion of prices and trade and to control aggregate demand through credit levers. In particular, it was thought that macroeconomic discipline would force structural change. In reality, the experience of the RCs has shown that:

- the new market-oriented institutions have not functioned properly and have generated distortions;
- enterprises and households have been adjusting to a competitive market environment slowly due to a 'built-in' behavioural inertia which had developed under the old regime;
- tight financial discipline could not be sustained in the face of such slow adjustment.

Two factors together can explain the sluggishness in the response of the economy's supply side to the reforms: the incentives, rewards and penalties deriving from the new market system were not strong enough, while, at the same time, the economy's structural rigidities were too strong. Incentives and penalties were partially blunted by market imperfections (for example, insufficient competition together with little enforcement of contractual obligations and insolvency procedures) and government intervention to support particular sections of the economy, while the reallocation of capital and labour was made more difficult by the inadequacy of the two main reallocation instruments besides the market: private enterprise and the financial system. The RCs policy focus, therefore, must be rebalanced in the latter two directions.

It was a major policy flaw not to have supported both private entrepreneurship and the general expansion of the private enterprise sector with greater determination and by means of a wide set of well-aimed measures. It is not just a question of accelerating privatisation and restructuring public enterprises. Even more importantly, an environment must be created which is conducive to new business initiatives and trade- and market-based competition, and which supports the diffusion of small- and medium-sized enterprises (SMEs), especially those in long-neglected production sectors such as services. The evidence indicates that, on the supply side of the economy, the revival of economic growth originated in the private enterprise sector (specifically in the SMEs) and in the export-oriented firms, rather than in the industrial giants created by the old regime. Hence, in order to foster overall economic revival, greater attention must be devoted to creating better conditions for the development of private enterprises.

Another major flaw is represented by the slow pace at which the payments and financial systems are being reconstructed. RC policies have so far focused mainly on dealing with bank crises and the clean-up of bad loans; they have not yet, however, succeeded in preventing the recurrence of this problem. To date, these countries have not comprehensively addressed two major requirements for economic development:

- the establishment of a payments system that can promote rather than hinder trade;
- the creation of a financial system, composed of banks and other financial intermediaries, that can both mobilise savings and finance the expansion of the private enterprise sector on the basis of balanced capital structures.

By addressing aspects related to the structure, ownership, competition and supervision in the banking industry, as well as among other financial institutions, the RCs are more likely to achieve a lasting solution to the bad loan problem than they would if they continue to focus their policies on periodically removing bad loans from banks' balance sheets.

One fault of policy implementation in some countries concerns the timing of their reforms. In those RCs where the bulk of the reforms was not concentrated in the early stages of transition, it became difficult to push reform through at later stages since social and political resistance to change had hardened considerably. Furthermore, discontinuities or even temporary reversals in policy implementation tend to create confusion among economic agents regarding the direction of the entire reform process and, consequently, cause delays in the needed adjustments of economic agents' behaviour. The evidence suggests that, in view of enhancing policy viability, the RCs should invest more heavily in the credibility of their policies and better synchronise the timing of their measures with their political cycle.

Even though it cannot be viewed as a fault of the transition approaches, it is evident that part of their inadequacy stemmed from insufficient knowledge of the size of the initial imbalances and structural rigidities. In addition, the policy instruments and the skills initially available to the policy-makers fell short of the policy challenges they faced. While in the past few years these constraints have somewhat eased, there remains a large need to upgrade the capacity to manage the new economic system. This applies as much to public administration as to management of private enterprises.

No major policy flaws can be found in the external trade liberalisation and foreign exchange policies of the RCs. Overall, these countries have carefully managed external tariff reductions, combining a low measure of trade protection with an exchange rate policy aimed at preserving competitiveness, following the initial exchange rate adjustments[4]. The collapse of inter-regional (i.e. CMEA area) trade cannot be viewed as a policy flaw because it was the inevitable consequence of the passage to a system of trade and pricing based on market forces. Nor can we recommend the creation of a regional payments union as a valid means to sustain inter-regional trade, because the fall in inter-regional trade is due to problems that a mere payments union alone cannot solve: first, the changing pattern of the RCs comparative advantage once world market prices were applied and, second, the lack of long-term funding for structural trade deficits.

If not a flaw, certainly a weakness of the transition strategies was the fact that, at least initially, they relied on excessive expectations of external assistance, including private and official capital flows and technical assistance from advanced industrial countries and multilateral institutions. In reality, the role of foreign capital in supporting the transition has been relatively modest, although not insignificant. According to OECD calculations, in the period 1990-94, the total of net resource flows to all RCs amounted to US$107 billion, which corresponds on annual average to just about 0.1 per cent of the OECD countries' total GNP. By comparison, the aid provided by the United States under the Marshall Plan in the period 1948-51 amounted to about 1.5 per cent of its GDP. In terms of the RCs' GNP[5] for 1992, net resource inflows in 1992 were estimated to have reached on average 1.2 per cent, but with a wide dispersion among the different RCs; in some of the medium-sized economies[6] they attained more than 3 per cent, while in the large economies[7] they remained around 1 per cent. Most of the resource flow was in the form of loans at market terms, while grants and soft loans represented about 29 per cent of the total flow. Foreign direct investment flows were disappointingly low at about US$12 billion, with heavy concentration in very few RCs. This tends to support anecdotal evidence that, despite the large tax holidays granted by the RCs, foreign investors do not generally find business conditions in these countries attractive enough. Technical assistance by advanced industrial countries and international institutions has been considerable; however, it is difficult to measure its impact on the transition process since it involves qualitative considerations more than quantitative ones related to the amount of expenditure.

At present, it seems that the RCs have scaled down their expectations of external assistance and are aware that success in the transition depends essentially on the soundness of their policies in mobilising domestic resources. The question could nevertheless be raised whether a larger net flow of foreign resources and technical assistance would have helped the RCs' transition approaches to be more effective and consequently would have accelerated the pace of the transition. The answer basically depends on the conditionality that accompanies capital flows and technical assistance and on their timing. Leaving aside private foreign investment (because it obeys business considerations), official funding during the transition has responded to a variety of goals which were not always fully consistent among themselves. If unconditional funding runs the risk of fostering delays in reforms and structural adjustment, inappropriate conditionality might create distortions and make the transition more difficult. The experience of the RCs reveals a number of cases in which RC policies were deflected in the direction of particular objectives pursued by the donor, in which there was not consistency between the measures recommended by the different providers of financing, or in which financing delays attributable to donors compromised RC policy implementation. Better co-ordination is therefore needed, and the beneficiary RC can greatly contribute to this goal by ensuring that resources are channelled towards appropriate policies.

In conclusion, notwithstanding imperfect policy approaches and discontinuous policy implementation, the RCs have managed to advance in the transition and to avoid generally backtracking in the face of social difficulties or following political reversals stemming from recent parliamentary elections. If progress is to continue over the next five years, what is most necessary at present is to adjust priorities somewhat and to show greater determination when implementing these policies. Such goals seem feasible, given that the RCs have better instruments at their disposal than they had at the start of this decade. To believe that a 'muddling-through' approach will be enough to accomplish the transition is illusory, since this has already proven to be the longest and most costly way.

Notes

[1] For some countries in the area, the transition has been underway for a shorter period.
[2] By mid-1996, ten RCs from Europe, FSU and former Yugoslavia as well as Mongolia had accepted art. VIII obligations.
[3] Russia is a notable exception.
[4] This conclusion does not apply to Russia, where an intricate system of export quotas and trade licenses has remained in place until very recently.
[5] For the seven RCs under consideration.
[6] In Hungary: 3.8 per cent; and in Romania: 3.3 per cent.
[7] In Russia: 0.9 per cent; and in Poland: 1.2 per cent.

References

Kirkpatrick, G., 1994, *Transition experiences compared: Lessons from Central and Eastern Europe's reforms*, OECD, [mimeo].

Marrer, P., Zecchini, S., (eds.), 1991, *The transition to a market economy*, vol. 1, OECD.

OECD/CCET, 1994, 1995, 1996, *Aid and other resource flows to the Central and Eastern European Countries and New Independent states of the former Soviet Union*, [mimeo].

OECD/CCET, 1992, *Bulgaria - An economic assessment.*

OECD/CCET, 1992, 1994, Economic surveys: *Poland.*

OECD/CCET, 1991, 1993, 1994, 1995, *Economic surveys: Hungary.*

OECD/CCET, 1991, 1994, *Economic surveys: Czech and Slovak Republics.*

OECD/CCET, 1995, *Economic surveys: The Russian Federation.*

OECD/CCET, 1994, *Foreign Direct Investment in Central and Eastern European Countries and NIS.*

OECD/CCET, 1993, *The labour market in Poland.*

OECD/CCET, 1995, *Mass privatisation - An initial assessment.*

OECD/CCET, 1995, *Review of the Labour Market in the Czech Republic.*

OECD/CCET, 1993, *Romania - An economic assessment.*

OECD/CCET, 1992, 1995, *Short-term economic indicators - Transition economies.*

OECD/CCET, 1995, *Social and Labour Market Policies in Hungary.*

OECD/CCET, 1996, *Trade Policy and the Transition Process.*

OECD/CCET, 1993, *Transformation of the banking system: portfolio restructuring, privatisation and the payment system.*

OECD/CCET, *Trends and policies in privatisation*, vol. 1-2.

OECD/CCET, 1994, *Unemployment in transition countries: transient or persistent?.*

OECD/CCET and ILO, 1993, *Structural changes in Central and Eastern Europe: labour market and social policy implications.*

OECD, *Economic outlook*. vol. 53-56.

Zecchini, S., 1994, "Financial development in economies in transition", in *IMF-WB, Building sound finance in emerging market economies.*

Zecchini, S., 1994, "Problems and prospects for privatisation in post-communist countries", in *Privatisation in NACC countries*, NATO.

Zecchini, S., 1995, "The role of international financial institutions in the transition process", in *Journal of Comparative Economics*, February.

2

The transition in Eastern Europe and the former Soviet Union: some strategic lessons from the experience of 25 countries over six years

Nicholas Stern

1. Introduction

The second half of 1989, with the fall of the Berlin wall and of a number of communist governments, brought dramatic developments in the process of collapse of the communist system in Eastern Europe and the Soviet Union. The economic transition from the command to the market economy began in earnest in the late 1980s with the Balcerowicz reforms in Poland and the gradual market reforms in Hungary. The end of the Soviet bloc as an integrated economic unit was marked by the historic meeting of the Council for Mutual Economic Assistance (CMEA or Comecon) in Sofia in January 1990 and its decision that trade should be conducted in hard currency and based on world prices. The Soviet Union itself collapsed as an entity following the unsuccessful coup attempt of August 1991 (by the end of that year Gorbachev had resigned as President and the Soviet Union ceased to exist) and in October 1991 the President of Russia, Yeltsin, announced a drastic economic reform programme, under the Gaidar team. Thus the momentous events of these extraordinary two years embodied four inter-related and fundamental elements: the arrival of political democracy; the disintegration of an empire; the collapse[1] of an economic bloc; and the launch of the transition. Any attempt to understand the economic aspects of transition in the region must clearly take account of this broader context and the interrelation of these elements.[2] It must also take account of the

I am very grateful for the guidance and contributions of my colleagues at the EBRD, Kasper Bartholdy, Andrea Minton Beddoes, Julian Exeter, Steven Fries, Vanessa Glasmacher, Ricardo Lago, Andrea Minton Beddoes, Tanya Normak, Ivan Szegvari and Andrew Tyrie, and for the comments of the participants at the Elisha Pazner Memorial Lecture at the University of Tel Aviv, 13 May 1996 and at the OECD/CCET Colloquium, "Economic Transformation and Development of Central and Eastern Europe: What Lessons from the 1990s?", Paris, 29-30 May 1996. The views expressed are not necessarily those of the EBRD.

the different countries and the differences in the nature and timing of the reform and stabilization programmes.

The purpose of this paper is to draw strategic lessons from the experience of the economic transition. It will be based on the experience since 1990 of the 25 countries of operations of the European Bank for Reconstruction and Development (EBRD).[3] The purpose is not to attempt to answer the hypothetical question of what a ruler (with or without extensive powers) might have done if given the opportunity to start again. It is rather to use the cross-country experience built up over these six years to draw lessons for policy in economic reform and to identify the key issues for the next years. There is no doubt that these next years, like the last few years, will be decisive for the region: institutions will be developed, defined and consolidated; major political uncertainties affecting the future of the transition will be resolved; the basic codes of economic and political behaviour will be affirmed or established; crucial aspects of the growth and structure of the economies will be determined; basic issues concerning the relationships of the countries with Europe and the rest of the world will be presented for examination, discussion and decisions.

The experience of the last six years puts us in a much stronger analytical position than at the start of the transition. At that time there was little theory or experience to guide the fundamental change from command to market. Most theoretical and empirical study of comparative systems was concerned with precisely that — comparing the functioning of different systems — and not with the transition process itself. It is true that there had been some relevant historical experience of profound systemic change in economies, but that was mostly from market to command, such as in the Soviet economy in the 1920s and 1930s and the UK economy at the beginning of the second World War.[4] And the great changes in China had started ten years earlier than the onset of transition in Eastern Europe and the former Soviet Union. But for the first few years in China (1979-83) these reforms were confined to agriculture and at the end of the 1980s analytical work on the consequences of the reforms in industry, launched in the mid-1980s, was limited. It must also be recognised that the profound political upheavals that occurred in 1989 and the early 1990s in Eastern Europe and the former Soviet Union did not apply to China. Indeed, it is interesting that in October 1992, when Russia was undergoing the traumas of its first year of economic reform and Gaidar was about to be replaced by Chernomyrdin, the important 14th Congress of the Communist Party of China was both reaffirming its commitment to the market economy *and* its firm political control.

The rest of the paper is organised as follows. In Section 2 we set out the evidence from the 25 countries of operations of the EBRD since 1990 on growth and inflation, linking the developments to the economic reforms, and we present indicators for various aspects of the reforms themselves on a number of dimensions of the transition to the market economy. Some problems in building the institutions of the market economy are analysed in Section 3, particularly concerning questions of privatisation, restructuring and corporate governance, and the building of financial institutions. We also discuss briefly the interrelationships between the political and economic systems and their reform. In Section 4 we consider the physical legacy which transition economies have to overcome in infrastructure and the environment. In each of Sections 2, 3 and 4 we bring out some key lessons for economic policy and reform which arise from the experience of the last few years. These lessons are gathered together in the final section.

2. The experience of 25 countries since 1990

Macroeconomic indicators for the 25 countries for the 1990s are presented in Table 1, on inflation, and Table 2, on growth in GDP.[5] We consider inflation first and look at general patterns in the table before examining some individual country experiences. From 1991 to 1993 inflation was high and rising in most of the region. This arose from the loss of macroeconomic control at the same time as prices were liberalised. This loss of macroeconomic control resulted largely from the collapse of the tax base, without a corresponding reduction in expenditure. The tax base had been, under the old regime, essentially the profits and turnover of the large state enterprises. The taxes on enterprises were fairly easy to administer since payments were channelled through the monobank system. With the general disruption of the economy, including the collapse of the CMEA, and the beginning of competition, output and profits fell sharply. At the same time, incentives to evade taxes increased strongly and the ability to monitor them through the banking system deteriorated sharply. Together the implications for overall revenue collections were disastrous, with falls of the order of 15-20 per cent of GDP in two years.[6] Macroeconomic control began to be asserted in much of the region in 1993 and 1994, in many cases with the help of IMF programmes, and impressive falls in inflation took place in 1994 and 1995. By 1995 most countries had inflation below 50 per cent *per annum*, and in six cases inflation *per annum* had come down to single digits.

It is clear that inflation can be, and in many cases was, arrested remarkably quickly with strong fiscal and monetary policies. In this respect, as in a number of others, the inflation experience of the western part of the region, notably the Czech and Slovak republics, Hungary, and Poland (the Visegrad countries), where inflation was being held to 60 per cent or less even in 1991, was less extreme than the experience of the CIS where inflation reached levels of around 10 000 per cent (for example, in 1993 in Armenia, Turkmenistan and the Ukraine).

At the same time that inflation rose in the early years of the transition in most countries, output fell sharply. There were a number of reasons for this, important among them being the breakdown of a cumbersome economic system which was highly integrated across the former command economies. Payment mechanisms switched suddenly to hard currency with prices moving towards world levels. Crucial inputs became unavailable or unaffordable.[7] At the same time competition, including from imports, intensified with many enterprises being ill-equipped to compete in these unfamiliar circumstances. Orders for the defence industry dropped dramatically. Thus the fall came both from supply and demand factors.[8] The fall was smaller and the recovery was quicker in Eastern Europe and the Baltics. Albania, Poland, Romania, and Slovenia showed positive growth in 1993 and 12 countries showed positive growth in 1994. Indeed, Poland had started to grow again in 1992 and by now has surpassed the output levels recorded in 1989. A number of countries in the western part of the region now seem to be set on paths of sustained

Table 1. Inflation in Eastern Europe, the Baltics and the CIS[1].

	Retail/consumer prices (end-year)					
	1991	1992	1993	1994	1995 Estimate	1996 Projection
	(Percentage change)					
Albania	104	237	31	16	6	6
Armenia	25	1341	10996	1885	25	20
Azerbaijan	126	1395	1294	1788	86	30
Belarus	93	1558	1994	1957	340	80
Bulgaria	339	79	64	122	33	30
Croatia	149	937	1150	-3	4	5
Czech Republic	52	13	18	10	8	7
Estonia	304	954	36	42	29	22
FYR Macedonia	115	1935	230	55	9	6
Georgia	131	1176	7488	8279	25	20
Hungary	32	22	21	21	28	22
Kazakstan	150	2567	2169	1160	60	30
Kyrgyzstan	170	1771	1366	87	32	25
Latvia	262	958	35	26	23	20
Lithuania	345	1175	189	45	36	30
Moldova	151	2198	837	116	24	16
Poland	60	44	38	29	22	19
Romania	223	199	296	62	28	20
Russia	144	2318	841	203	131	45
Slovak Republic	58	9	25	12	7	7
Slovenia	247	93	23	18	9	6
Tajikistan	204	1364	7344	5	1350	500
Turkmenistan	155	644	9750	1330	770	500
Ukraine	161	2000	10155	401	180	60
Uzbekistan	169	910	885	1281	115	40
Eastern Europe, the Baltics and the CIS	131	1379	1043	227	88	34
Eastern Europe and the Baltic countries[2]	111	176	127	30	20	16
The Commonwealth of Independent States[3]	145	2245	1703	369	138	48

Notes:

1. Data for 1989-94 represents the most recent official estimates of outturns as reflected in publications from the national authorities, the IMF, the World Bank, the OECD, PlanEcon and the Institute of International Finance. Data for 1995 are preliminary actuals, mostly official government estimates. Data for 1996 represent EBRD projections.
2. Estimates for real GDP represent weighted averages for Albania, Bulgaria, Croatia, the Czech Republic, Estonia, FYR Macedonia, Hungary, Latvia, Lithuania, Poland, Romania, the Slovak Republic and Slovenia. The weights used were EBRD estimates of nominal dollar-GDP for 1995.
3. Here taken to include all countries of the former Soviet Union, except Estonia, Latvia and Lithuania. Estimates for real GDP represent weighted averages. The weights used were EBRD estimates of nominal dollar-GDP for 1995.

growth at levels of 5 per cent or so, while some CIS countries are now returning to positive growth at 1-3 per cent.

It must, however, also be remembered that, for a number of reasons, outputs in the transition period have probably been under-estimated relative to the preceding period. As a result, the resumption of growth may have been quicker than the official statistics imply. The reasons for under-estimation include (i) an incentive to under-report outputs and revenues for tax reasons now, whereas previously the planning system encouraged over-reporting, (ii) weaker statistical coverage of new enterprises, (iii) old price indices which under-valued newer products, (iv) higher

Table 2. Growth in Eastern Europe, the Baltics and the CIS[1].

	1990	1991	1992	Real GDP 1993	1994	1995 Estimate	1996 Projection	Estimated level of real GDP in 95
	(Percentage change)							(1989=100)
Albania	- 10	- 28	-10	11	7	6	5	74
Armenia	- 7	- 11	- 52	-15	5	7	7	38
Azerbaijan	- 12	- 1	- 23	- 23	- 21	- 17	- 7	34
Belarus	- 3	- 1	- 10	- 12	- 20	- 12	- 5	54
Bulgaria	- 9	- 12	- 7	- 2	1	3	3	75
Croatia	- 9	- 14	- 9	- 3	1	2	5	71
Czech Republic	0	- 14	- 6	- 1	3	5	6	86
Estonia	- 8	- 11	- 14	- 7	- 3	4	6	66
FYR Macedonia	- 10	- 12	- 21	- 8	- 4	- 4	3	53
Georgia	- 12	- 14	- 40	- 39	- 35	- 5	5	17
Hungary	- 4	- 12	- 3	- 1	3	2	2	86
Kazakstan	0	- 13	- 13	- 12	- 25	- 9	1	45
Kyrgyzstan	3	- 5	- 25	- 16	- 27	- 6	1	42
Latvia	3	- 8	- 35	- 15	2	1	1	54
Lithuania	- 5	- 13	- 38	- 24	2	3	3	41
Moldova	- 2	- 18	- 29	- 1	- 31	2	2	40
Poland	- 12	- 7	3	4	6	7	6	99
Romania	- 6	- 13	- 9	1	4	7	4	84
Russia	- 4	- 13	- 15	- 9	- 13	- 4	3	55
Slovak Republic	0	- 15	- 6	- 4	5	7	6	85
Slovenia	- 5	- 8	- 5	1	6	5	5	93
Tajikistan	- 2	- 7	- 29	- 11	- 21	- 12	- 8	40
Turkmenistan	2	- 5	- 5	- 10	- 19	- 14	0	58
Ukraine	- 3	- 12	- 17	- 17	- 23	- 12	- 2	40
Uzbekistan	2	- 1	- 11	- 2	- 4	- 2	- 3	83
Eastern Europe, the Baltics and the CIS	- 5	- 12	- 11	- 5	- 5	0	4	68
Eastern Europe and the Baltic countries[2]	- 7	- 11	- 4	0	4	5	5	88
The Commonwealth of Independent States[3]	- 4	- 12	- 15	- 10	- 14	- 5	2	53

Notes:

1. Data for 1989-94 represents the most recent official estimates of outturns as reflected in publications from the national authorities, the IMF, the World Bank, the OECD, PlanEcon and the Institute of International Finance. Data for 1995 are preliminary actuals, mostly official government estimates. Data for 1996 represent EBRD projections.
2. Estimates for real GDP represent weighted averages for Albania, Bulgaria, Croatia, the Czech Republic, Estonia, FYR Macedonia, Hungary, Latvia, Lithuania, Poland, Romania, the Slovak Republic and Slovenia. The weights used were EBRD estimates of nominal dollar-GDP for 1995.
3. Here taken to include all countries of the former Soviet Union, except Estonia, Latvia and Lithuania. Estimates for real GDP represent weighted averages. The weights used were EBRD estimates of nominal dollar-GDP for 1995.

quality, (v) better matching of outputs and demand. From this perspective the output recovery looks even more impressive. These reservations about the data are substantial and thus any interpretations of the history based on output should pay attention more to broad trends than to detail on particular figures. There are a number of other indicators (for example, electricity consumption and living conditions), which, whilst they have their own difficulties, tell broadly similar stories. For further discussion see *Transition Reports* 1994 and 1995.

The resumption of growth must be seen as fairly rapid in historical perspective. For example, in the period 1945-1947, GDP in the US economy fell by around 20 per cent, with the adjustment from a war to a peace economy and did not recover 1945 levels until the early 1950s. The shock to, and the required adjustment in, the economies of the region have surely been larger than that to the post-war US economy. For much of the region there are grounds for suggesting that growth at levels of 5 per cent or so can be sustained if the right policies are upheld over a long period. Indeed, many of the features underpinning the East Asia 'miracle' are present in much of the region today: an educated labour force; an open economy; macroeconomic stability; nearby markets; strategic investors with strong interests and so on.

This moderately optimistic picture for the future in much of the region should not conceal recognition of the great social costs of change, particularly in the CIS. Deep stresses have been reflected, for example, in a dramatic fall (five or six years) in male life expectancy in Russia. Some part of this fall may be due to a decline in public health, but the causes of death strongly suggest a rise in stress.[9] These rises in death rates have generally not been present in those countries which pressed ahead more strongly in reform. Broadly, their social indicators have continued their pre-reform trend.

From the cross-country comparisons it is clear that recovery took place sooner and most strongly where reform began earlier and was pursued most firmly, and where macroeconomic control was maintained most successfully. One must not immediately jump to the conclusion that the causation runs from policy to recovery. The reasons for difficulties with formulating and implementing policy are also reasons for poor economic performance. For example, the disintegration of the administrative system appears to have been more severe in the CIS. Further, the political atmosphere for many in the CIS was closer to disaffection and disillusion than that of liberation, the feeling experienced in much of the eastern Europe and the Baltics. In such circumstances the willingness and confidence to take hard economic and political decisions was probably stronger in the western part of the region. In this sense the initial period of "extraordinary politics", emphasized by Balcerowicz, represented a much stronger opportunity in Eastern Europe and the Baltics than in the CIS (Balcerowicz, 1995).

One must also take account of the many other differences across countries at the start of the transition in understanding their differential performance: some had industrial and economic structures which were "more difficult" to reform (heavy dependence on a completely uncompetitive capital goods industry, or large-scale collectivised agriculture); some had heavy debts, others very little; some are mineral resource rich, others are not; some had experimented with reform or already had extensive private sectors; some only had 40 years of the command economy, others had 70 years; some have close geographical proximity to Western developed market economies, others do not; and so on. Nevertheless, many of the countries that have performed relatively well were in weak positions with respect to a number of the issues indicated above, for example, few mineral resources, "difficult" industrial structures and substantial debt.

Nevertheless, whilst acknowledging these issues, the timing of recovery suggests strongly that it was good policy that led to good performance. In most countries

Table 3. Progress in transition in Eastern Europe, the Baltics and the CIS[1, 2].

Countries	Private sector share of GDP in %. mid-95 (rough EBRD estimate)	Large-scale privatisation	Small-scale privatisation	Enterprise restructuring	Price liberalisation	Trade & foreign exchange system	Competition policy	Banking reform & interest rate liberalisation	Securities markets & non-bank financial institutions	Extensiveness & effectiveness of legal rules on investment
Albania	60	2	4	2	3	4	1	2	1	2
Armenia	45	2	3	2	3	3	1	2	1	2
Azerbaijan	25	1	1	2	3	2	1	2	1	1
Belarus	15	2	2	2	3	2	2	2	2	2
Bulgaria	45	2	3	2	3	4	2	2	2	3
Croatia	45	3	4*	2	3	4	1	3	2	3
Czech Rep.	70	4	4*	3	3	4*	3	3	3	4
Estonia	65	4	4	3	3	4	3	3	2	3
FYROM	40	2	4	2	3	4	1	3	1	2
Georgia	30	2	3	2	3	2	1	2	1	2
Hungary	60	4	4*	3	3	4*	3	3	3	4
Kazakstan	25	2	2	1	3	3	2	2	2	2
Kyrgyzstan	40	4	4	2	3	4	2	2	2	2
Latvia	60	2	4	2	3	4	2	3	2	2
Lithuania	55	3	4	2	3	4	2	3	2	2
Moldova	30	3	3	2	3	4	2	2	2	2
Poland	60	3	4*	3	3	4*	3	3	3	4
Romania	40	2	3	2	3	4*	1	3	2	2
Russian Fed.	55	3	4	2	3	3	2	2	2	2
Slovak Rep.	60	3	4*	3	3	4*	3	3	3	3
Slovenia	45	3	4*	3	3	4*	2	3	3	3
Tajikistan	15	2	2	1	3	2	1	1	1	1
Turkmenistan	15	1	1	1	2	1	1	1	1	1
Ukraine	35	2	2	2	3	3	2	2	2	2
Uzbekistan	30	3	3	2	3	2	2	2	2	2

Notes:

1. Most advanced industrial economies would qualify for the 4* rating for almost all the transition indicators. Table 2.1 assesses the status rather than the pace of change. For instance, Slovenia's score of 4* on small-scale privatisation, despite the absence of a comprehensive privatisation programme, reflects the fact that small-scale activity in Slovenia was largely private before transition began.
2. The scoring runs from 1 for least advanced or little progress through 4 for comprehensive or advanced reform to 4* for the standard of most advanced industrial economies. For more details on scoring methods, please refer to the notes for Table 2.1 of the *Transition Report* for 1995.

fixed investment fell sharply in the late 1980s and early 1990s both in real terms and as a share of GDP. In many cases the investment share began to rise within a year from price liberalisation and stabilization and the growth in GDP soon after. Further, if one examines the pattern of foreign direct investment (FDI), we see that FDI is much stronger in countries with macroeconomic stability and strong reforms. And if one examines investment intentions it is clear, as one might expect, that stability and economic reform are very strong determinants of investment, see Chart 1 and Chart 2. For further discussion of these issues see Chapters 3 and 4 of the *Transition Report 1995* and Lankes (1996).

The overall conclusion must be that there were real choices at the beginning of reform, and that good policy, in terms of macroeconomic stability and economic reforms, was a key factor in good performance. Further, the results came impressively quickly. It must be recognised also, however, that the political circumstances and difficulties surrounding those choices varied greatly across countries.

Chart 1. Relation between inflation and foreign direct investment
25 countries in transition

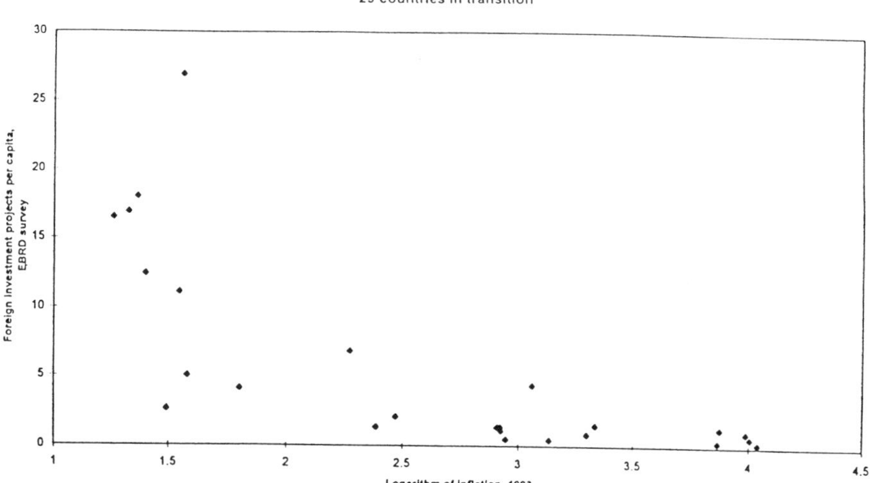

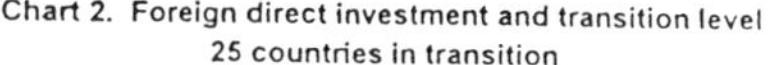
Chart 2. Foreign direct investment and transition level
25 countries in transition

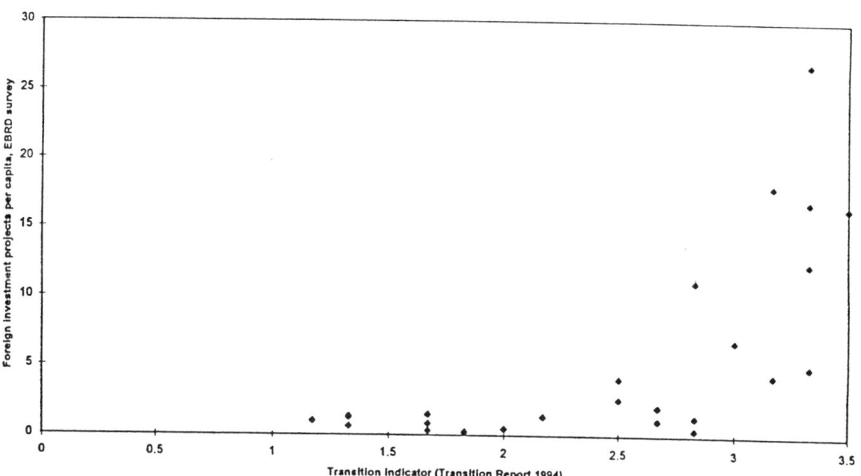

We turn now to a brief discussion of some more detailed aspects of reform. In the *Transition Reports* of 1994 and 1995 the Office of the Chief Economist of the EBRD has presented simple scorings to indicate the state of progress on various dimensions of the transition to the market economy — Table 2.1 from the 1995 *Report* is reproduced here as Table 3. This is not the place to discuss the table in detail (see *Transition Report*, 1994 and 1995) and we draw attention only to some broad features of the approach and results. But before going into the detail of the scoring, let us note the high proportion of output coming from the private sector — seven countries with 60 per cent or more, and more than half the countries with 45 per cent or more. This transformation has been remarkably rapid. In contrast, in 1924, seven years after the Bolshevik revolution, only 35 per cent of the output of the USSR came from the public sector.

The approach to transition indicators which we adopted involves specifying central elements or dimensions of the market economy and examining how far an economy has moved from the old system to the market economy. The key elements identified were: the basic "atom" on the production side, the private enterprise; market structures where economic agents interact; financial institutions as central determinants of how transactions occur, budget constraints are enforced and present and future are linked; and legal underpinnings of the systems of contract and investment. Within these four broad headings a number of sub-dimensions were introduced, as set out in Table 3. The scoring methods are described briefly in a note to Table 3 (for more detail, please refer to the *Transition Report* for 1995, Table 2.1).

This simple approach, of course, leaves out much that is important. In particular there are many aspects of the way in which the state is structured and performs which are fundamental to the functioning of the market economy. Indeed, one can argue that the definition and functioning of the state is at the heart of the economic performance of a market economy both in transition economies and elsewhere.[10] It is vital that the tasks allocated to the state should not be over-ambitious in the sense that they strain fiscal balances and administrative capability, that they curtail incentives excessively or that they allocate discretionary power in a way that generates rent-seeking and corruption. At the same time the state powers must be sufficiently strong and well administered that they can deliver basic legal, defence, health, education and social security services on the one hand, and well-regulated and competitive markets and financial services on the other. That is a challenging set of tasks for any state. To establish these services and methods of functioning, starting from the very different and heavy structures of the old system, must be a lengthy and difficult process. Much has been achieved but there is far to go. These over-arching and basic considerations are reflected only in a limited way in the indicators of Table 3.

Our brief discussion of Table 3 highlights only some broad lessons. We begin with the columns. There are some dimensions, such as trade and price liberalisation[11] and small-scale privatisation which involve limited or simple institutional development, where progress has been substantial across the region. These are reforms which can be, and were, introduced quickly. The more challenging market reforms which involve major institutional change are the ones which take time. These include large-scale privatisation, enterprise restructuring, financial sector reform and the introduction of effective competition policy and legal structures.

The pattern described is most easily understandable in terms of the time required to do different types of activity, rather than in terms of any priorities for "sequencing" of reforms. The building of institutions takes time. Clear examples are the financial and legal institutions. Banks depend on special skills including accounting, credit analysis, and the like. These depend on the establishment of relationships, track records and working methods. Legal systems have to be first established and then implemented. The analysis (Chapter 6) of the *Transition Report* for 1995 shows that implementation has been much weaker than the setting of legal structures themselves. Similar considerations apply to competition policy and, more generally, to the changing role of the state discussed briefly above.

For enterprises, effective corporate governance will take time to establish. It involves reliability and transparency in codes of behaviour, information, relationships between managers, owners and the government, and so on. The form of corporate governance will influence the decision-making for restructuring in a basic way.

Restructuring itself will be a major and fundamental task involving investment, hard decisions and dislocation. It will be much less painful if economic growth, effective corporate governance, and well-functioning "safety nets" are established.

Having emphasized that the observed pattern of reforms reflects the time which is inherently involved in particular tasks it is important to recognise that there are key elements which do have to be introduced quickly if institutions are to develop successfully. These are price and trade liberalisation, macroeconomic stability and hard budget constraints. Liberalised prices without hard budget constraints and competition can simply lead to inflation. Taken together, however, these key elements provide the necessary market pressure for the further institution building and investment which will follow.

This brief examination of the progress of transition on its different dimensions leads quickly to an indication of the challenges that lie ahead. But it also provides some understanding of the nature of these challenges. This is the topic of the next section.

3. Building institutions

In this and the next section we focus on four key areas of fundamental importance to all transition economies, however far advanced: corporate governance and restructuring; financial institutions; infrastructure and the environment. We examine the first two as central examples of institution building and the latter two under the heading of the physical legacy of the old regime.

The brief analysis of the experience of the transition of the last six years has emphasized the importance of building or rebuilding institutions, including the private enterprise itself, financial and legal institutions, and those of the state. We concentrate on just two areas where investment depends closely on related institutions. As an investor focused on the private sector, the EBRD has special interests here. These are: first, privatisation, restructuring and corporate governance; and, second, financial institutions. At the end of this section we comment briefly on the role of the political process in relation to the building of the economic and other institutions supporting a market economy.

Privatisation, restructuring and corporate governance

Large-scale privatisation in the transition countries is either very recent, still under way, or has not yet begun. Nevertheless evidence is beginning to emerge which does point the way to certain strategic lessons for the transition. We draw broadly on three major and differing examples: the Czech Republic, Poland and Russia. The evidence is discussed in more detail in Chapter 8 of the *Transition Report* of 1995.[12]

Broadly speaking we may characterise these experiences as follows. The Czech Republic had two waves of mass privatisation based on vouchers. The first was launched (when the Czech and Slovak republics were together) in mid-1992 and was completed by mid-1993. It created 8.5 million shareholders in a combined Czech and Slovak population of 15.5 million (the republics separated on 1 January 1993). The second wave was launched in the spring of 1994 and completed in the spring of 1995. Approximately 70 per cent of the vouchers were placed with investment funds which used them to purchase shares. These investment funds were private entities, established by banks, among others. The main structures resulting from the mass privatisation programme in the Czech Republic are outside ownership of firms dispersed among private voucher holders or outside ownership more concentrated with investment funds (IPFs) and the National Property Fund. The process of privatisation, however, was not only through voucher-based mass methods but also through direct cash sales which indeed, accounted for two-thirds of the book value of the assets privatised.

In the face of strong pressures from enterprise insiders, successive Polish governments opted for a multi-track and more drawn out approaches to privatisation. The first approach involved privatisation of enterprises by sale or transfer (either by selling the assets of state-owned enterprises or through their conversion into a joint-stock company and selling shares). By the end of 1995 some 25 per cent (more than 2 000) of the enterprises owned by the state had been privatised in this way. In 1995 a long delayed voucher-based mass privatisation system got under way. An important vehicle was the establishment of 15 National Investment Funds (NIFs) to which more than 500 firms were allocated in the second half of 1995. Thus we essentially have one track of cash privatisation and a second track of mass privatisation, but after a delay during which some restructuring took place and with established NIFs which can deal directly with the management of firms assigned to them.[13]

The Russian mass privatisation was, in turn, very different from the Czech and Polish cases. About 15 000 medium and large-scale enterprises, employing some 70 per cent of the industrial workforce, had been privatised under a voucher programme by the summer of 1994. This mass privatisation strongly favoured workers and management and resulted in a high degree of insider ownership. On average, workers retained 50 per cent of the shares (although part of that was non-voting), managers 10 per cent, and only 20 per cent of equity was held by outside investors while another 20 per cent remained in state hands. The management with a relatively modest direct shareholding (which has increased to about 20 per cent) has had almost unlimited control over most of the enterprises as (i) through various devices senior management effectively represent the workers-owners (and some of the shares held by workers are non-voting), (ii) the single largest outside shareholder, the state is typically passive in exercising its ownership rights, and (iii) the remaining outside ownership is widely dispersed.

A second, cash-based, wave of privatisation was initiated in mid-1994, but has been proceeding very slowly. Attempts to take this forward in late 1995 proved problematic (with complaints of rigged auctions and the granting of special privileges under shares-for-loans deals) and have been suspended.

The Hungarian approach to privatisation was rather different and was based largely on direct sales to domestic and foreign investors. This approach was associated with major inflows of foreign direct investment into the country. We concentrate on the first three cases for the purposes of this discussion.

The different approaches to mass privatisation have, in a sense, provided a laboratory from which some strategic lessons can be drawn. While the experience is in its early stages, there are some important patterns emerging. The form of privatisation has strong consequences for corporate governance which, in turn, has important implications for restructuring decisions. Both dispersed outsider ownership (as in the Czech example) and insider ownership (as in the Russian example) leave great power in the hands of managers and workers. This may imply reluctance to proceed with the kind of deep or strategic restructuring which is necessary, and which involves substantial investment, but which can impose significant costs and dislocation on insiders (for further detail of the argument see Chapter 8 of the *Transition Report*, 1995).

We distinguish in this analysis between reactive restructuring, on the one hand, and deep or strategic restructuring on the other. By the former we mean the basic attention to cost control which comes from a hardening of budget constraints (for example, through labour-shedding, wage reductions or plant closures). By the latter, we mean substantial change in product lines and methods of production associated with a radical reorientation of the firm and its activities of the kind that can deliver large improvements in enterprise performance and growth over the long run. This type of restructuring involves strong and creative managers. It will often require a change of management from those who were managing under the old system with its different priorities and incentives. It will require some mechanism for forcing a change of management where the incumbent is not willing or able to adjust to the new circumstances. This type of restructuring will generally require some concentrated outsider ownership. The evidence set out in Chapter 8 of the *Transition Report* for 1995, on the reform of different types of firm, provides some support for this line of reasoning.

Given that successful restructuring of activities, itself a fundamental part of the transition process, would seem to require some concentrated outsider ownership, one should then ask how this can come about. The Czech approach to mass privatisation was to provide voucher-based privatisation and then to let the markets generate investment funds, and other vehicles, to improve share value by improving performance. The Polish experience has been to delay mass-privatisation but to tighten budget constraints and generate some commercialisation prior to privatisation. Indeed, managers of firms which were to-be-privatised, but were still state-owned, seem to have provided some quite strong improvements in productivity.[14] Under the mass-privatisation scheme currently under way, the concentrated outside ownership is provided by the National Investment Funds which have been designed and engineered by the government.

In the Russian case, concentrated outsider ownership has yet to appear strongly. The further development of capital markets will, it is to be hoped, play an important part in this process. The government will also have a role to play in requiring proper and transparent reporting and accounting. Outside finance will itself promote improved corporate governance, since outside lenders or equity holders will require to be convinced that their money is in safe, productive and accountable hands before making extensive commitments.

Competition and hard budget constraints will force restructuring in the coming years. The capital stock and product range inherited from the old system are ill-suited to the open market economy. For example, at unification between half and two-thirds of the East German capital stock became subject to write-off under West German accountancy rules.[15] We have emphasized the importance of strategic investment in this process. Such investment and its finance will both require and bring improved corporate governance.

The experience of the transition is demonstrating the importance of corporate governance for restructuring. The task of restructuring is enormous and in most cases in its early phases. It will be for government and for the markets together to deliver the kind of corporate governance which is necessary to support restructuring. While one can expect that hard budget constraints and competition will eventually force restructuring, the development of policies and institutions will have a major influence on the path, costs and outcome of the process. The government should ensure that the conditions are set for the market to play its proper role in the restructuring process. In this context, the participation of international financial institutions in investments in the private sector can make an important contribution to the setting of standards.

Financial institutions

Financial institutions are both central to a market economy and were almost entirely absent under the old regime. They are in many respects the most novel and important aspects of the transition. Their functions are absolutely fundamental to the market economy, including: the enforcement of hard budget constraints; allowing convenient transactions; providing liquidity; linking savings and investment efficiently; transforming maturities and so on. But their construction will take time. These institutions depend particularly strongly on track records, relationships, experience, special skills and procedures for regulation.

The structure and role of banks under the old regime created a problematic ***inheritance***. A central aspect of the creation of viable and reliable banks is adequate treatment of the non-performing loans. In other words, the "cleaning up" of the balance sheet. At the same time it is crucial to prevent the circumstances which allowed the bad loans to recur. We discuss the problems briefly in turn — both involve some strategic lessons.

Two approaches to the problem of recapitalisation to deal with bad loans may be identified: "carve-out" and "work-out". Under carve-out, the bad loans are identified and removed from the bank to another institution, "the hospital bank".

The latter institution does not make new loans but concentrates on dealing with the old, non-performing, loans. It collects as much as possible of outstanding obligations, rescheduling and writing-off as necessary.[16] At some point its tasks would be completed.

Under "work-out", the lending institution itself attempts to deal with the non-performing loans while carrying on its business. The government will have to guarantee loans or to provide it with new capital, for example, in the form of government bonds, so that it can stay liquid and solvent during the process. This recapitalisation would be in relation to the overall quantity and state of the bad loans. In this approach, it is important that the bank retains some incentive, and the means, to recover non-performing loans, for example, through a commitment to bank privatisation and the provision of special debt work-out procedures.

Whatever method is followed there are problems of identifying bad loans, of establishing credibility, and preventing reappearance. In transition economies, governments have only limited experience with the banking supervision necessary to verify loan quality. Bank recapitalisation programmes thus must be designed in a way which encourages the accurate disclosure of loan quality. Moreover, if the government has rescued banks once, the banks might believe that it will happen again.[17] This can lead to carelessness, or worse, in their treatment of new loans. It is also important to recognise that many of the bad loans arose in the first place, from government pressures to provide loans to favoured or sensitive enterprises. The banks were an essential part of the softness of budget constraints. If the non-performing loans are not to reappear via the same route, then such pressures must cease.

One should not under-estimate the political and other pressures behind this process of using banks to succour individuals and enterprises. Such pressures can be intense. They also arise from banking practices which were fairly standard under the old regime — financial performance was secondary to the physical fulfilment of planning targets and the survival of enterprises was not really in question. Changing the practices is a central part of the transition.

In helping build a ***new system,*** both government and outside investors have a role to play in helping to stop these bad loans from reappearing. For the government, establishing and strengthening banking supervision is a vital part of this process. Outside investors will wish to scrutinise bank balance sheets closely before taking equity or granting loans. As with other enterprises, competition and hard budget constraints will impose discipline and it is government and markets which combine together to force hard budget constraints on the banks themselves.

In this regard a strong central bank, with considerable independence from the political system, will be an important part of the enforcement mechanisms on both banks and government. In particular it can require the government to keep its subsidies in the open, and explicitly on budget, rather than concealing them in the banking system.

In all economies the ***regulation*** of financial institutions is an important task for government. In carrying out this task it must balance the advantages of competition, which will involve the penalties of failure for banks which do not perform, and the requirements for safety and confidence in the system which are necessary for it to function effectively, without panics or the threat of systemic collapse. It must also protect against fraud, corruption and money-laundering, which are endemic hazards of any banking system. These are formidable tasks and they are still more formidable when banks themselves, as well as the regulatory institutions, are being constructed from scratch or arise from fundamental reconstructions of the old state institutions. It is not surprising that the process of constructing a banking system has led to the wide-spread need to recapitalise banks and, in some countries, to banking crises (including in Estonia, Latvia, Lithuania, and Russia).

We have argued that financial institutions present an area of activity where the government will have to work together with the market, in ensuring the growth of a new and crucial set of services for the market economy. The area is of particular importance given the magnitude of the investment challenges of the coming years. The investment which will be necessary to underpin the growth required for overcoming the low living standards of the old regime and the costs of reconstruction must, for the most part, be financed domestically. Financial institutions must be central to this process if these savings are to be realised and allocated efficiently.

Relations between the political and economic transition

We have focused in this section on just two examples where the building of new institutions involves critical strategic approaches by government. In each case they involve basic interactions between government and the private sector in enforcing and generating creative and responsible market behaviour. They are key examples but there are many others. They clearly illustrate, as did the history described in Section 2, the crucial interrelationships between political and economic reform. We conclude this section with a brief, but more general focus on these interrelationships.

Having recognised their importance throughout our discussion, let us however, dispose immediately of an over-mechanical or dogmatic approach to these issues. Some are tempted to argue that political liberalism, in the form of democracy, is an essential precondition for economic liberalism. Theoretical arguments are sometimes proposed in terms of political authoritarianism automatically leading to a command economy, or that political and economic freedoms are inseparable; sometimes empirical associations are offered.

This is not the place to go into these arguments in detail but there are sufficiently many, major examples in contradiction to this position to make for great scepticism concerning any inevitability in the relationship. Indeed, both the theoretical and empirical arguments are unconvincing. One can provide examples of political authoritarianism with economic liberalism, democracy with extensive public ownership and direction of the economy, political authoritarianism with a command economy and of democracy with economic liberalism. The last two cases are fairly obviously represented respectively, by the old regime in the communist countries and most current OECD countries. Let us focus on the first two.

There are many important examples of economic liberalisation, and reform in that direction, without multi-party democracy. Recent examples include Pinochet's Chile, Taiwan in the first decades following the establishment of the People's Republic of China, the People's Republic of China itself in the last 17 years, Hong Kong, Spain under Franco post-1959, and so on. Post-independence India provides an example of socialism and close public control of production in a democratic system.[18] These examples (including India and China) are too important to be dismissed as minor aberrations. And, in any case we should ask ourselves the following question. If an alternative econometric specification of the relationship between political and economic variables produced a weaker association, would we become much less enthusiastic in our support for democracy? The arguments for democracy in terms of human rights are surely overwhelming. They are not well served by attempts to lean on dubious empirical "laws" in their support.

Let us return to the transition economies and focus on just two related lessons. The first is the importance of the state in imposing and supporting the basic "rules of the game" in the decentralised economy, and the second is the importance of the state in keeping out detailed decision-making. Several important examples embodying the first have been given above: strong fiscal policies require an effective tax administration; restructuring requires good corporate governance, competition and hard budget constraints; an effective banking system requires both competition and regulation. There are many others. The task of redefining and creating a strong but limited state is fundamental to the transition.

We turn to the second lesson. There will be constant pressures, inherited from the old system but not unique to it, for special favours, support and protection. The most extreme forms of pressure for special favours are corruption, criminality and the mafia. There is no doubt that they have become severe problems in some countries of the region. It is a crucial part of the competitive process that these pressures be resisted. This, too, is vital for respect and support for the new economic system. There is no magic formula for this but constant awareness, vigilance and a high public profile for the issue can make a contribution. These pressures pose basic challenges for the economic and political processes of transition. In this context, however, the openness of many of the societies is encouraging. Democracy and freedom of expression can help the transparency and exposure which can provide some check on those who would want to manipulate the system.

Finally, we must note the importance of the transition and economic performance for democracy. In many countries there were great expectations of the rewards from the market economy. We have argued that, in historical terms, there has indeed been rapid progress. But there have been heavy social costs (for example, the dramatic fall in life expectancy in many CIS countries, see Chapter 2 of the *Transition Report*, 1995). They have been unequally distributed. In many countries there has been considerable disillusionment with the process. Unless transition progresses and economic results are delivered, democracy, in some countries, could be threatened. And, as we have seen, it is resolution and advance in the reforms that produces economic results and reduces social costs, not the reverse.

4. Overcoming the physical legacy

In addition to the problems involved in building effective institutions to support the market economy, the transition economies have to deal with the physical legacy left from the old regime. The emphasis here is on two aspects of particular importance:

infrastructure and the environment. Historical developments in these areas followed from the nature of the previous command system, and overcoming the legacy is a central part of the transition process. This will require substantial investment to reorient activities towards a market economy and modern methods and standards.

The capital stock embodied in infrastructure was heavily influenced by the priorities and methods of the old regime. These involved, for example, scant concern for the preferences of the consumer (few household telephones and weak facilities for the private car), facilities oriented to special priorities for heavy goods production, excessive integration across countries or regions for reasons of political control (transportation of bulky materials over huge distances), limited concern for costs (particularly power and energy), and indifference towards the environment (power and energy and the transport of raw materials). The transformation of infrastructure is a crucial element of the transition.

The investment needs and the strains on government budgets are such that much of the investment for infrastructure must come from the private sector. This private investment will bring with it orientation to the market and control of costs. One of the tasks of government is to provide the right regulatory environment to allow this private infrastructure investment to take place.

It is important to note that the problems in different sectors will be different. In telecommunications, for example, the regulatory environment must provide for the very substantial investments that are necessary to make the system competitive and compatible with outside technologies and practices. Household penetrations were extremely low and the technologies so antiquated that the inherited capital stock has very limited value over the medium-term. Harmonisation of regulatory practices, as well as technologies, with international practice will become increasingly important as telecommunications become more and more a traded good.

On the other hand, in power there was over-investment and great wastefulness. Key problems are raising prices and enforcing collections, metering and the promotion of energy efficiency. In the power industry, the arguments for private ownership and investment are much stronger for some parts of the system (generation) than for others (transmission and distribution). In both telecommunications and power, the ability to enforce revenue collections through disconnections is basic to successful commercialisation.

Throughout infrastructure, and particularly for its private provision, EU standards of provision and regulation will be important for those 11 countries seeking accession to the EU. Taking all these factors together there can be no doubt that overcoming the legacy of the old system in infrastructure presents a major strategic and investment challenge for the next years of the transition.

Environmental degradation was pervasive in the old regime. Its concern with production targets and its focus on heavy industry implied neglect for the environment and an unpleasant and dangerous legacy. The investment programme throughout industry required to overcome this legacy is formidable. It will require improvements across the board in both the production and consumption processes. Much of this can be promoted by pricing for power and energy which takes account of real resource costs and externalities. Elsewhere it will require regulation and monitoring. This will be necessary for factories, water supply, mineral extraction and transportation and so on. There will also be investments to recover from earlier damage. Such investments cannot all be carried out at once, and much of it must be part of the normal replacement cycle for capital goods and structures.

The types and magnitude of the necessary environmental spending will no doubt be under examination by the EU in the preparations for accession. An early study (1993) of six countries (Bulgaria, the Czech Republic, Hungary, Poland, Romania and the Slovak Republic) estimated environmental investments of ECU 91 billion, or 15-20 per cent of GDP, to bring them up to EU standards.[19] Such investments, if they are to be carried out effectively (or at all) would have to be spread over a long period. The process has barely started and there is no doubt that it will present a major challenge in the coming years.

5. Concluding remarks

Our examination of the experience of the transition in 25 countries over the last six years has been oriented to drawing specific strategic lessons for the process of reform and in particular, future strategy. We have avoided abstract reasoning concerning, for example, sequencing and have tried to tie the analysis to the experience itself. We examined first (in Section 2) the overall macroeconomic indicators (inflation and growth) and then basic dimensions of the reform process in terms of the transition indicators developed in the Office of the Chief Economist in the EBRD.

The discussion of the macroeconomic indicators lead to a number of basic conclusions.

- Those countries which had the most firm and speedy approach to stabilization and reform suffered smaller falls in output and saw the most rapid recovery.
- Recovery of investment is an important ingredient in the resumption of growth.
- Investment is promoted by stability (discouraged by instability) and by the advance of market reforms.

We have expressed these historical observations in a form which can readily be translated into the obvious strategic lessons. It is striking that they strongly reflect the lessons from studies of investment and growth in 100 and more developing countries since the second World War.[20]

There was an opportunity for the adoption of firm policies towards stabilization and reform in the early days of political optimism which were present in some countries in 1989 and 1990. Those countries which grasped the opportunity have done particularly well. However, the pressure and degree of such optimism and readiness to make sacrifices for change varied across countries. The political environment, given the difficulties of the 1980s in the USSR, was less favourable in the CIS. If further examples arise in the future the strategic lesson is to act quickly and firmly but such an observation is now of limited usefulness for countries that are already five, six or seven years into the transition.

It does, however, raise question marks over the suggestion that, in the circumstances that existed in 1990, a slower transition would have implied less costs. This does not seem to be consistent with the evidence. The example of China since 1979 does not nullify this argument. China did not experience economic disintegration, it had much more self-sufficient regions, agriculture was still dominant and had experienced only a quarter of a century of collectivisation (so that the "household-responsibility system" could draw on the familiarity of peasant farming), the administrative mechanisms were not breaking down and the central government retained firm political control. In these circumstances, the strategy of experimentation and gradualism was an option that seems to have led to successful growth. It is, of course, quite possible that speedier and more comprehensive reforms would have led to results that were even better. And one must recognise too that the size of agriculture in the Chinese economy, and its employment of many hundreds of millions of people, is such that its transformation in four or five years was itself a dramatic and rapid event to which the term "gradualism" is not very well applied.

The examination of the transition indicators lead to the following broad conclusions:

- Trade and price liberalisation and small-scale privatisation were carried out quickly.
- Large-scale privatisation came more slowly and restructuring, which must be a lengthy process given the nature of the task and the heavy inheritance, is in its early stages.
- Nevertheless the establishment of the private sector has come remarkably quickly in historical terms.
- The building of reliable and effective financial and legal institutions is taking time.

Broadly speaking, these patterns do not reflect a careful strategy of sequencing, but rather the time taken for different activities. Building new institutions and economic restructuring are time- and resource-intensive processes. If a process takes time then it is important to start it quickly. And it is impressive how consistently similar have been the avowed objectives of newly elected leaders in Eastern Europe and most of the FSU, even when the going got tough.

The experiences show that "shock therapy" versus "gradualism" is a false dichotomy and an unhelpful way of presenting the issues. Some things can and should be done quickly, others take longer. Where political and administrative structures have broken down, then gradualism may simply be a euphemism for the prolongation of uncertainty and stress (witness the high mortality rates in the CIS over the last years). The nature of the starting point is crucial.

Market economies must contain and be underpinned by a whole range of institutions which were absent under the old system. In Section 3 we focused on the building of just two: corporate governance (and its relation to privatisation and restructuring) and financial institutions. The conclusions were as follows:

- The form of privatisation has strong implications for corporate governance which itself is influential in restructuring.
- Effective corporate governance and restructuring are promoted by concentrated outside ownership and outside finance. They are hindered by insider ownership or dispersed outsider ownership.
- The promotion of corporate governance can be left to the market or helped by specific institutions or funds.
- Financial institutions are at the heart of a well-functioning market economy. They depend on track records, relationships and skills which must be constructed over time.
- Governments have a responsibility to regulate and to provide a competitive and reliable financial sector.
- Recapitalisation and restructuring of non-performing assets can take place in a number of ways but there are challenges of moral hazard in identifying non-performing assets, of control in preventing their reappearance and of credibility in insisting that rescue packages will not be readily available again.
- The central bank, if it is to be an effective regulator, must have some independence from the government of the day. It should enforce hard budget constraints on banks and prevent the banking system from becoming an instrument of political pressure, subsidy and favouritism.

It must be recognised that these represent difficult tasks for governments at any stage. Indeed they cause real problems in many established market economies. Outside assistance in tackling them will be of great importance for the transition economies. Further, it is crucial to keep procedures as simple as possible and not to overload administrative capabilities which are in the process of being acquired.

In Section 4 we looked more closely at the physical legacy which transition economies have to overcome in infrastructure and the environment. As with the building of effective institutions, these two areas will represent substantial challenges in the next few years. Our conclusions were as follows:

- Infrastructure was neglected and distorted under the old regime. It will require substantial investment to reorient it to a market economy and modern methods. Private investment must play a role.
- The problems in different areas of infrastructure are very different. For example, telecommunications require substantial investment. For power and energy, attention should be focused on pricing, efficiency in use and the environment.

- In all areas, commercialisation in terms of attention to cost control and revenue operation are vital. For the latter enforcement of collection is basic (and will involve the possibility of disconnection).
- Environmental issues were not a priority of the old regime and other priorities — particularly heavy goods production — mitigated against the environment.
- There was an unfortunate coincidence between a wasteful economic system and high mineral resource endowments which encouraged both profligacy and environmental degradation.
- Economic pricing (real resource costs, plus externalities, plus indirect taxes) will make, with metering, a major environmental contribution.
- Investments in new equipment and in reclamation will involve huge resource costs.

The analysis above has shown substantial variations across countries in the progress made in transition. Some countries have made great strides in the establishment of the market economy. There has also been impressive progress toward macroeconomic stability after the early loss of control in most countries. For all countries the next years will be decisive years; and we have identified some of the central strategic challenges.

We focused particularly on four areas that will require substantial institution building and investments; corporate governance and restructuring, financial institutions, infrastructure and the environment. All of these four areas represent major issues for governments in the region in the coming years. They all will be central to the discussions for accession to the EU for many countries in the region. They all represent issues at the heart of the transition in terms of overcoming the legacy of neglect and misplaced incentives of the old regime. They all are areas in which an international financial institution such as the EBRD can play a special role in bringing the required investments to fruition.

An overarching theme in all the discussion has been the need for a strong but limited state. It must deliver on basic responsibilities of government, including macroeconomic stability, a competitive economic system, and basic social and administrative services. And it must resist the temptation and incentives to interfere and protect on behalf of special interests.

In the countries of the region the market economy is here to stay. There are too many who have a clear interest in the new system. The memories of the waste, inefficiencies, pains and humiliations of the old regime are still present. But the dislocations and costs have been large and the reservations have been clearly expressed in the ballot box and elsewhere. In these circumstances the temptation for greater involvement in the details of industry and for impossible populist promises are great. The pleas for protectionist policies for industry and for special privileges for interest groups will be strong. But this type of *dirigisme* leads to manipulation, rent-seeking, corruption and poor performance. It has continually failed elsewhere. The lessons of history should be learned. What is needed from government is a stable economic system with clear and enforced rules, and the creation of the conditions which will provide social protection for, and investment in, its people.

Notes

[1] This was accompanied by severe difficulties in the functioning and establishment of administrative arrangements.
[2] For example, the collapse of the CMEA was an important element in the assertion of independence by some countries from the old Soviet empire.
[3] From April 1996 this number is 26, with the joining of Bosnia-Herzegovina. In fact, at the original foundation of the EBRD in 1991, prior to the dissolution of the USSR, there were eight countries of operations.
[4] Further examples would be associated with the war effort at the outbreak of the second World War.
[5] These tables use data from the national authorities, the IMF, the World Bank, the OECD, PlanEcon, and the Institute of International Finance. They are drawn from the *Transition Report Update*, 1996, prepared by staff of the Office of the Chief Economist of the EBRD.
[6] In the former Czechoslovakia, for example, total revenue fell from 69.5 per cent of GDP in 1989 to 55 per cent of GDP in 1991. In Bulgaria total revenue fell from 59.8 per cent in 1989 to 42.3 per cent in 1991.
[7] Or, if payment was demanded "upfront", they could not be financed.
[8] The evidence suggests that the supply factors were of particular importance. For example, the decline of investment was much less than might be expected from a demand-induced recession (see Rostowski, 1996).
[9] See *Transition Report*, 1995, Chapter 2; and UNICEF-ICDC, 1995, *Central and Eastern Europe in transition. Regional Monitoring Report 3*.
[10] See for example, Stern, 1989, pp. 597-686; Stern, 1991, pp. 241-271; and Buiter, Lago, and Stern, 1996.
[11] On prices, the scoring of 4 has not been used since in all countries there are still very substantial controls and subsidies (implicit or explicit) in energy and housing.
[12] It is also the subject of the papers by Aghion and Carlin, 1996; Hunya, 1996; and Rapaczynski, 1996.
[13] The programme provides for enterprise restructuring through the allocation of lead shareholdings in each enterprise to one NIF, with each of the other NIFs holding a small minority stake. It is expected that the fund managers of the NIFs will concentrate their efforts on those enterprises in which their NIF has lead shareholdings, using their expertise to assist the enterprises in improving their businesses.
[14] See for example, Pinto, Belka, Krayewski, 1993; and Pinto and van Wijnbergen, 1995.
[15] See for example, Sinn and Sinn, 1992, and for further examples from other countries, see Chapter 4 of the *Transition Report*, 1995.
[16] This has been the approach followed with the "Consolidation Bank" established in 1991 in the Czech and Slovak Federal Republic.
[17] In Hungary recapitalisation of some banks has indeed occurred more than once.
[18] Of course, post-independence India always had a large private sector including most of agriculture.
[19] See Chapter 4 of *Transition Report*, 1995, p.80.
[20] See, for example, Little, Cooper, Corden, and Rajapatirana, 1993, or see much of the modern literature on growth, for example, Bruno, 1993, Fischer, 1991, Barro, 1995. Interestingly, the negative relationship between inflation and growth appears to be strong above inflation rates of 20 per cent or so *per annum*, but not below.

References

Aghion, P. and Carlin, W., 1996, "Restructuring outcomes and the evolution of ownership patterns in Central and Eastern Europe", Paper presented at the OECD/CCET Colloquium: "Economic Transformation and Development of Central and Eastern Europe: What Lessons from the 1990s?", Paris, 29-30 May.

Balcerowicz, L., 1995, *Socialism, capitalism, transformation*, Central European University Press, Budapest.

Barro, R., 1995, "Inflation and economic growth", Bank of England Quarterly Review, May, pp. 166-76.

Bruno, M., 1993, *Inflation and growth in recent history and policy: application of an integrated approach*, Hebrew University, mimeo, March.

Buiter, W., Lago, R. and Stern, N., 1996, "Promoting an effective market economy in a changing world: economic institutions and macroeconomic policies", mimeo.

EBRD, *Transition Report*, 1995.

EBRD, *Transition Report Update*, 1996.

Fischer, S., 1991, "Growth, macroeconomics and development", NBER Macroeconomics Annual, pp. 329-364.

Frydman, R. and Rapaczynski, A., 1996, "Corporate governance and the political effects of privatisation", Paper presented at the OECD/CCET Colloquium: "Economic Transformation and Development of Central and Eastern Europe: What Lessons from the 1990s?", Paris, 29-30 May.

Hunya, G., 1996, "Large privatisation, restructuring and foreign direct investment", Paper presented at the OECD/CCET Colloquium: "Economic Transformation and Development of Central and Eastern Europe: What Lessons from the 1990s?", Paris, 29-30 May.

Lankes, H.P., 1996, "Foreign direct investment in eastern Europe and the former Soviet Union: results from a survey of investors", Paper presented at the OECD/CCET Colloquium: "Economic Transformation and Development of Central and Eastern Europe: What Lessons from the 1990s?", Paris, 29-30 May.

Little, I., Cooper, R., Corden, W. and Rajapatirana, S., 1993, *Boom, crisis and adjustment: The macroeconomic experience of developing countries, 1970-1990*, Oxford University Press, December.

Pinto, B., Belka, M. and Krayewski, S., 1993, "Transforming state enterprises in Poland: evidence on adjustment in manufacturing firms", *Brookings Papers on Economic Activity*, Vol. 1, pp. 213-270.

Pinto, B. and van Wijnbergen, S., 1995, "Ownership and corporate control in Poland: why state firms defied the odds", CEPR Discussion Paper No. 1273, December.

Rostowski, J., 1996, "Comparing two Great Depressions: 1929-33 to 1989-93", Paper presented at the OECD/CCET Colloquium: "Economic Transformation and Development of Central and Eastern Europe: What Lessons from the 1990s?", Paris, 29-30 May.

Sinn, G. and Sinn, H.-W., 1992, *Jump-start: The economic unification of Germany*, Massachusetts Institute of Technology, p. 44.

Stern, N., 1989, "The economics of development: a survey", *The Economic Journal*, No. 397, Vol. 99, September, pp. 597-686.

Stern, N., 1991, "Alfred Marshall Lecture: Public policy and the economics of development", *European Economic Review*, 35, pp. 241-271.

UNICEF-ICDC, 1995, *Central and Eastern Europe in transition. Regional Monitoring Report 3.*

3

Transition to date: a comparative overview

Martha de Melo and Alan Gelb

1. Introduction

Experience with the transition from plan to market has varied greatly across the reforming socialist countries. By the start of 1996 transition countries fell into three broad categories — growing, recovering, and lagging (Table 1). In the first category, China and Vietnam have experienced uninterrupted growth in real GDP since the beginning of their reforms in 1978 and 1986, respectively. Poorer and more rural than the socialist countries of Central and Eastern Europe (CEE) and the Newly Independent States (NIS) of the former Soviet Union, they started reforms under very different structural and macroeconomic conditions (see Sachs and Woo, 1994; McKinnon, 1994). In particular, their state sectors were relatively small, household savings were low, and they were under-financialised. This was in sharp contrast to the high household savings that had produced a large money overhang in most CEE and NIS countries at the start of reform. Also, China's trading relations were independent of the planned CMEA system, whose collapse disrupted trade in CEE and NIS, while Vietnam was only partially integrated into this system.

The Baltics, Armenia, Mongolia (which is analysed in the NIS group because of its previous close links with the Soviet economy) and all CEE countries except the former Yugoslav Republic of Macedonia (FYROM) are shown in Table 1 as "recovering". They have all passed through a severe "transformational recession" but have returned to positive growth, in some cases at quite rapid rates. Many of these countries experienced very large maximum declines in recorded GDP since 1989; the least severe was 15 per cent (Poland and Slovenia). On balance, output losses in recovering countries have been less than in the "lagging" countries which comprised other NIS countries plus FYROM. This latter group was still contracting in 1994/95, and many countries continued to suffer from high inflation. The group includes the majority of the countries whose economies have been severely affected

The views expressed in this paper are those of the authors and not necessarily those of the World Bank.

by regional tensions, and in particular by costly blockades or, in some cases, civil wars — Armenia, Croatia, FYROM, Azerbaijan, Georgia and Tajikistan; these countries are indicated by an asterisk in Table 1.

Table 1. Classification of transition economies by recent growth experience.

	Transition Base Year [a]	Index of Lowest Real GDP since 1989 [b]	Average Real GDP Growth since Start of Transition	Average GDP Growth in 1994/95
Growing:				
China	1978	--	9.4	11.0
Vietnam	1986	--	7.1	9.2
Recovering:				
Albania	1990	65	-2.5	7.0
Estonia	1991	68	-1.6	5.5
Slovenia	1991	84	1.7	5.5
Poland	1989	86	-0.6	5.3
Slovak Republic	1989	76	-2.7	4.9
Mongolia	1989	75	-3.0	4.4
Romania	1989	72	-4.0	3.7
Lithuania	1991	43	-11.8	3.5
Czech Republic	1989	79	-2.6	3.3
Armenia*	1991	34	-15.5	2.5
Hungary	1989	80	-2.8	2.5
Bulgaria	1989	73	-4.4	2.2
Latvia	1991	55	-10.4	2.0
Croatia*	1991	69	-2.1	1.9
Lagging:				
Uzbekistan	1991	87	-5.0	-3.3
FYROM*	1991	58	-9.8	-5.1
Georgia*	1991	25	-24.2	-7.5
Kyrgyz Republic	1991	62	-14.1	-7.5
Russia	1991	72	-9.7	-7.8
Turkmenistan	1991	83	-10.1	-12.5
Ukraine	1991	61	-14.8	-14.0
Moldova	1991	56	-17.0	-15.0
Belarus	1991	76	-13.2	-15.8
Azerbaijan*	1991	59	-18.2	-18.5
Kazakstan	1991	65	-15.8	-18.5
Tajikistan*	1991	41	-24.6	-18.5

* Indicates countries affected by regional tensions.

a) This year indicates the beginning of reforms in East Asia, political change in Central and Eastern Europe, and the break-up of the former Soviet Union and the former Yugoslavia.

b) Real GDP did not decline in China and Vietnam.

Organisation of the paper

The purpose of this paper is to provide a broad comparative overview of the experience with transition to date and, in doing so, to try to account for the wide variation in country experience. Following a brief description below of the transition process, Section 2 explores the comparative experience of the vast majority of countries that fall into the "recovering" and "lagging" categories. To do this, we consider the relationship between liberalising reforms on the one hand and broad outcomes — growth and inflation — on the other. A more detailed look at the time path of growth and inflation for reformers and non-reformers takes into account the negative effect of regional tensions and a few important initial conditions as well as the duration and intensity of reform. The analysis covers 26 countries in CEE and the NIS from 1989 through 1995. The section closes with a review of selected adjustment indicators for different reform groups.

In Section 3, we introduce some additional considerations to existing analyses of why the experience of the "growing" and "lagging" countries has differed so dramatically. Specifically, we consider how differences in initial conditions and reforms have interacted to produce very different patterns of relative price and output changes in China and Russia. We conclude that initial conditions are important determinants of the evolution of income distribution, which may affect economic outcomes by stimulating Keynesian leakages and capital outflows during the transition. These issues are not unlike those debated in the Latin American structuralist literature of the 1950s and 1960s (see Seers, 1963). Initial conditions can thus help push countries into vicious or virtuous circles, but the outcome will also depend on the strength of fiscal and financial sector policies, and therefore on the implementation of reforms.

Any analysis of transition is complicated by serious deficiencies in data. Post-reform growth is probably seriously understated in many CEE and NIS countries which have seen a large increase in the share of the informal economy. Typically, the size of the output drop is over-estimated, and where national accounts have been re-estimated, sizeable corrections have resulted. On the other hand, growth is probably slightly overstated in China. Consistent estimates for many variables, including trade data, are simply not available. Under these circumstances, we focus on broad patterns and trends and on averages within country groups, rather than on fine distinctions.

Structural adjustment in transition

We propose a simple model of a planned socialist economy with repressed and overbuilt activities and sectors. An essential dimension of transition is liberalising the economy, allowing the repressed sectors to expand and forcing the overbuilt sectors to adjust. But the process of liberalisation not only introduces new incentives consistent with worldwide supply and demand; it disrupts the old planned regime. Following De Melo, Denizer and Gelb (1996), we distinguish four main characteristics of the centrally planned economy which are affected by liberalisation:

1. The economy was co-ordinated through plans (or, in reality, bureaucratic bargaining). Heavy industry and agriculture were subsidised; services, exports to market economies and light industries were repressed and allocated few resources.
2. Private ownership was severely limited.
3. Prices were administratively fixed and changed rarely; relative prices were heavily distorted. Natural resources were seriously under-priced (the labour theory of value did not recognise natural rent), and high inputs of energy and

other primary goods meant that many firms added negative value at world market prices. Relative to their poor quality, consumer goods were costly; indeed, many products would have remained unsold in a competitive, open market economy.

4. Macroeconomic balance was sustained by direct controls. If wage increases exceeded the value of consumer goods sold at fixed prices, as often happened near the end of the old regimes, goods were rationed and a money overhang in the form of excess household financial assets developed.

Price and trade liberalisation, privatisation, and the encouragement of new private businesses expose such an economy to huge adjustment pressures. The first effect is an increase in the price level, as the money overhang is dissipated. How long inflation persists at high levels depends, however, on monetary policy, and in particular on how long and extensively governments continue to subsidise declining sectors. Overall growth will, at first, suffer from the weaknesses of new, co-ordinating market mechanisms, but will then pick up as repressed sectors and activities expand, in response to the lifting of constraints. Because adjustment processes take time, the number of years that an economy has been exposed to reform — not just the current status of reform — is critical. As the growth of market economies is adversely affected by high inflation (Bruno and Easterly, 1995 place a critical threshold at 40 per cent), we would expect to see a recovery in growth only after initial inflation has been brought down to moderate levels.

Adjustment during transition also has effects on the pattern of income distribution and therefore on demand. The extent to which living standards change in transition is a contentious question, because some of the key gains, such as the end of queuing and the large increase in the quality and variety of goods, are not easily quantifiable. Neither, for that matter, are some of the potential losses such as stresses due to higher economic uncertainty and the rise of organised crime, which has become a serious concern in some countries. Nevertheless, to the extent that repressed sectors are intensive in relatively poor and unskilled labour, reforms will tend to introduce an equalising element into the overall distribution, whereas the reverse will follow if repressed sectors are high-skill or capital- or natural-resource intensive. If different groups have different propensities to import, and also to save in foreign currency, spending leakages will also differ depending on the initial pattern of sectoral repression and the evolution of income distribution.

2. Transition in CEE/FSU: reforms and outcomes

What accounts for the very different experience of recovering and lagging economies? The main factor is found to be government policies during transition. Several indicators of policy change can be used to support the classification of countries according to the extent to which their reforms have progressed. Using one of these indicators, an index of liberalisation, we look at the overall relationship with growth and inflation during transition. As indicated by the simple model above, economic liberalisation facilitates both inflation control and a recovery in growth. Next, we explore the time profile of reform, taking into account a few simple initial and exogenous conditions, such as those associated with regional tensions, as well as the intensity and duration of reform. The experience of different reform groups is consistent with selected indicators of adjustment shown at the end of this section.

Table 2. Indicators of economic & political reform (unweighted averages).

	Cumulative Liberalisation Index, 1995[1]	Composite EBRD Indicator[2], 1995	Political Reform (Gastil)[3], 1989-95	Changes in Private Sector Share, 1990-95
Group 1	6.9	29.8	9.5	43.3
Group 2	4.7	24.0	7.4	41.4
Group 3	3.4	22.5	2.8	30.9
Group 4	2.0	17.5	0.3	14.5

1. Updated index from de Melo, Denizer and Gelb, 1996.
2. Averaged sum of EBRD scores for nine transition indicators.
3. Average of changes in Gastil index between 1989 and 1995.

Note: Group 1: Czech Republic, Hungary, Poland, Slovak Republic and Slovenia.
Group 2: Albania, Bulgaria, Estonia, Latvia, Lithuania, Mongolia and Romania.
Group 3: Kazakstan, Kyrgyz Republic, Moldova and Russia.
Group 4: Belarus, Turkmenistan, Ukraine and Uzbekistan.
RT (regional tensions) countries include: Armenia, Azerbaijan, Croatia, FYROM, Georgia and Tajikistan.

Indicators of reform

The reform groups shown in Table 2 are based on country rankings according to a simple measure of liberalisation that we use as the primary indicator of reform (see De Melo, Denizer and Gelb, 1996 for details on the construction of this index, which has been updated to cover the period 1989-1995). The measure of liberalisation has three components: liberalisation of internal prices and markets; liberalisation of external trade and exchange regime; and liberalisation of entry for private business, including progress with privatisation. Weights on these components are 0.3, 0.3 and 0.4, respectively.[1] CEE/NIS countries not affected by regional tensions are classified into four reform groups according to the cumulative, or equivalently the average, degree of liberalisation over 1989-95. This overall index of liberalisation captures both the duration and intensity of reform. Countries that have suffered from regional tensions are put into a separate group (RT); unlike the other groups, the liberalisation index varies widely from country to country within this group.

Table 2 also shows simple group averages for several other indicators of reform. Rankings are consistent across the groups defined earlier, with advanced reformers in Group 1 showing the highest average score and slow reformers in Group 4 the lowest. The closest relationship is between economic liberalisation and political reform, as measured by the Gastil index of political rights and civil liberties compiled by Freedom House. This suggests that in CEE and NIS, political reforms have driven economic reforms — or at least have allowed space for them, by creating a period of "extraordinary politics" (see De Melo, Denizer and Gelb, 1996; Balcerowicz, 1995). The cross-country Spearman rank correlation between these variables in 1994 was 0.91 for countries in the four reform groups. Figure 1 shows the very close association between political change and economic reform in the Visegrad countries and the Baltics. Parallel developments occurred in Central Asian countries until 1993 but have since diverged, with average economic liberalisation continuing — albeit at a slower pace than in the two other groups — and average political freedom, as measured by the Gastil index, somewhat declining.[2]

Figure 1. Political and economic liberalisation in selected country groups

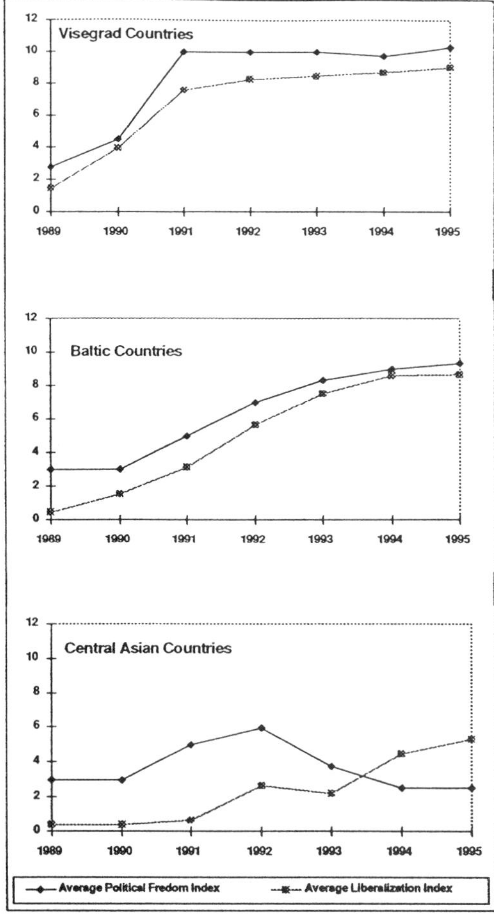

Sources: Cumulative liberalisation index updated from De Melo, Denizer and Gelb, 1996; political index from Freedom House Review, various issues.

Across groups, there is also a correspondence between the liberalisation index and changes in the private sector share in the economy. The private sector was marginally larger on average in Group 1 countries at the beginning of transition, but its share grew rapidly during the period 1989-95. The cumulative liberalisation index also correlates with an indicator of the status of institutional reform in 1995, derived from the sum of the transition indicator rankings in EBRD 1995. These variables are not completely independent, since EBRD data was used to help calibrate the liberalisation index, but the correspondence between the two indicators reflects the time dimension built into the liberalisation measure — institutional as well as behavioural change occurs with some lag — as well as the fact that economic reforms create demand for market-supporting institutional change.

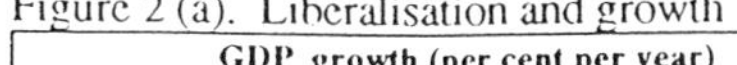
Figure 2 (a). Liberalisation and growth

Figure 2 (b). Liberalisation and inflation

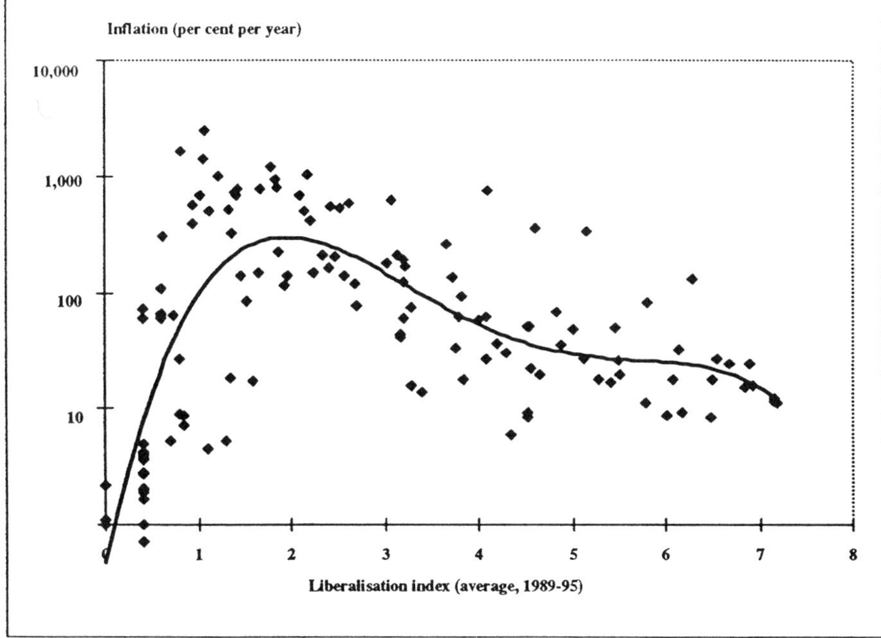

The effect of reform on growth and inflation

Using panel data for 20 countries over 1989-95 (RT countries are excluded), the relationships between cumulative liberalisation and growth and inflation are shown in Figure 2, together with fourth-degree polynomial regression lines. Growth and inflation appear as mirror-images in their relationship to the intensity and duration of reform. As liberalisation gets underway, countries in CEE and NIS experience a drop in output. Greater exposure to liberalised market forces is, however, associated with a return to positive growth. In the case of inflation, the initial stage of reforms is marked by a sharp price spike, but liberalising the economy enables governments to sever links with the enterprise sector, withdraw subsidies (particularly quasi-fiscal transfers effected through cheap credit from the central bank), and bring down inflation. While both growth and inflation are treated as endogenous variables here, there is also a direct linkage between them, as stabilization is essential to a recovery of growth.[3]

Explaining the time path of growth and inflation

How regular over time is the response of transition economies to changes in the economic policy regime? Is the real difference simply that many of the earlier reformers were in CEE rather than in the NIS? To approach such questions, we estimate regime-switching regressions for growth and inflation. A country is considered to be in one of two states — unreformed or reformed — according to the liberalisation index discussed above, and a switch point between these regimes is determined for each country. The years before reform are designated according to the number of periods from 1989 onwards up to the switch point (YB), or after reform as the number of years after the switch (YA). A dummy for regional tensions (RT) is included for every country and year in which economic outcomes were clearly dominated by non-economic factors such as blockades or wars.

It remains to determine the switch point. For countries such as Poland, which initiated a radical reform programme in 1990, this is straightforward, but for more gradual reformers it can be less clear, and any choice is, to an extent, arbitrary. The switch point used in De Melo, Denizer and Gelb, 1996 was based on the cumulative liberalisation index converted to "Poland-equivalent reform years". This procedure, (according to which Russia, for example, has been exposed to market forces about half as much as Poland since 1989) has the benefit of not involving an arbitrary judgement on a threshold level of the index. It is, however, progressively less satisfactory as the post-reform period is extended since small differences in intensity have an increasingly large impact on the switch point.

An alternative procedure, used in this paper, is therefore to set a threshold level for the liberalisation index and to complement this by a measure of reform intensity. The threshold is set at 0.4; any country-year scoring above this level is taken to represent a sufficiently market-based system to be considered as in the reform period.[4] In addition, an intensity variable (INT) is defined for post-reform years, as the average of the liberalisation scores for all years after, but not including, the year of liberalisation. This enables a distinction to be drawn between the impact of

Table 3. Regime-switching regressions for growth and inflation (1989-95).

	Growth			Inflation		
Variables	**1**	**2**	**3**	**4**	**5**	**6**
INTERCEPT	-11.5	-11.0	-11.6	2.5	2.6	2.2
	(1.4)	*(1.4)*	*(1.6)*	*(0.1)*	*(0.1)*	*(0.1)*
YB1	14.0	13.5	14.0	-2.2	-2.3	-2.2
	(2.1)	*(2.1)*	*(2.1)*	*(0.1)*	*(0.1)*	*(0.1)*
YB2	7.8	7.3	7.9	-1.8	-1.9	-1.8
	(2.1)	*(2.1)*	*(2.1)*	*(0.1)*	*(0.1)*	*(0.1)*
YB3	2.3	1.6	2.4	-0.6	-0.6	-0.7
	(2.2)	*(2.2)*	*(2.3)*	*(0.2)*	*(0.1)*	*(0.1)*
YB4	-10.0	-10.9	-9.8	0.3	0.2	0.1
	(2.6)	*(2.6)*	*(2.7)*	*(0.2)*	*(0.2)*	*(0.2)*
YB5	-1.6	-2.7	-1.4	0.5	0.5	0.4
	(2.9)	*(3.0)*	*(3.0)*	*(0.2)*	*(0.2)*	*(0.2)*
YB6	-7.0	-7.9	-6.8	0.5	0.5	0.4
	(3.1)	*(3.1)*	*(3.1)*	*(0.2)*	*(0.2)*	*(0.2)*
YB7	7.3	6.0	7.4	-0.1	-0.1	-0.2
	(5.3)	*(5.3)*	*(5.3)*	*(0.4)*	*(0.4)*	*(0.4)*
YA1	4.8	-7.1	4.7	-0.4	0.5	-0.4
	(2.2)	*(2.0)*	*(2.2)*	*(0.1)*	*(0.1)*	*(0.1)*
YA2	10.0	--	9.9	-0.7	--	-0.7
	(2.2)		*(2.2)*	*(0.2)*		*(0.1)*
YA3	12.8	--	12.7	-0.9	--	-0.8
	(2.3)		*(2.4)*	*(0.2)*		*(0.2)*
YA4	14.3	--	14.1	-0.9	--	-0.7
	(2.8)		*(2.9)*	*(0.2)*		*(0.2)*
YA5	16.6	--	16.4	-1.1	--	-0.9
	(3.5)		*(3.6)*	*(0.2)*		*(0.2)*
YA6	18.9	--	18.7	-1.8	--	-1.6
	(4.5)		*(4.5)*	*(0.3)*		*(0.3)*
RT	-8.6	-7.0	-8.6	0.5	0.4	0.4
	(1.7)	*(1.7)*	*(1.7)*	*(0.1)*	*(0.1)*	*(0.1)*
INTENSITY (YA)	--	16.4	--	--	-1.4	--
		(2.4)			*(0.2)*	
CEE	--	--	0.4	--	--	--
			(1.3)			
MONOV	--	--	--	--	--	1.7
						(0.4)
R2	0.55	0.53	0.55	0.74	0.76	0.77

NB Standard errors are shown in parenthesis.

sustained, yet incomplete, liberalisation, and that of intense, yet more recent, liberalisation.

Figure 3. Growth and inflation profiles

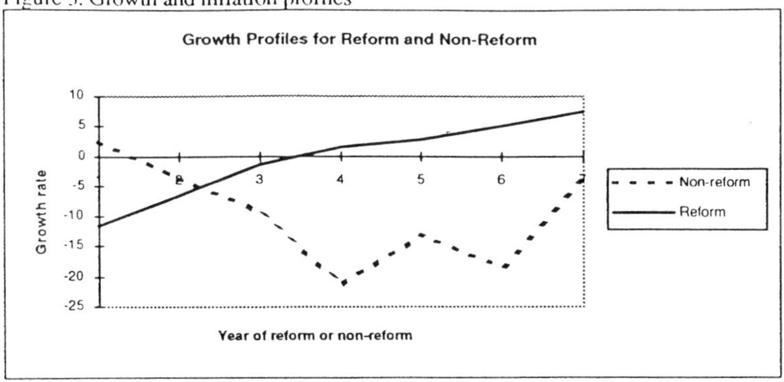

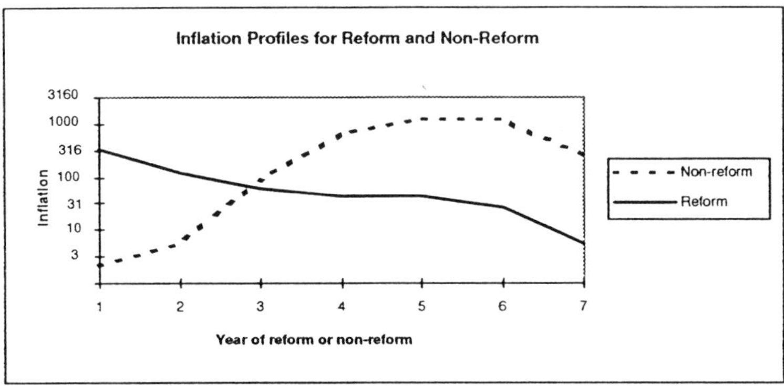

In Table 3, equations 1 and 4 regress growth and the log of inflation rates on all dummy variables representing each of the pre- and post-reform years, as well as a dummy representing the RT country-years. The implied profiles of growth over time for a "non-reforming" country and a "reforming" country are shown in Figure 3. Countries that remain in an unreformed state for an extended period see a progressive decline in growth and an increase in inflation to very high levels. In the initial year of reform, freeing prices leads to a sharp inflationary spike and output contracts by 11.5 per cent. But thereafter, growth begins to recover and inflation comes down; by the third year of reform, aggregate output and inflation are comparable in the two policy states and thereafter the reform profile comes out ahead on both measures of economic performance. Standard errors for coefficients in the growth equation are generally 2-3 per cent except for the extreme observations six or seven years before and after reform, where there are few country cases. The switching regression provides a particularly strong explanator of the inflationary experience of the sample of countries.

The regressions also show the high costs of blockades and wars in the region. Each year of regional tensions involves a loss of over 8 percentage points of measured GDP, and the RT dummy is also highly significant in the inflation equation.

How important is the intensity of liberalisation, given its duration? The result of including intensity as an additional explanatory variable differs as between the growth and inflation equation. In the former, the coefficient is small and insignificant. This is because the intensity variable is highly collinear with the set of post-reform dummies — the coefficients of these dummies in a regression with intensity as the dependent variable are similar to those on the post-reform dummies in the growth regression itself. The impact of intensity on growth therefore cannot be separated out from that of the duration of reforms. In the inflation equation, however, intensity enters with a significant negative coefficient — countries that have advanced further with liberalising reforms (as well as applied them for longer) typically also have lower inflation rates.

Because intensity is collinear with the post-reform dummies, it offers an alternative specification, which is shown in regressions 2 and 5 in Table 3. In this model, INT replaces all post-reform dummies after year two. The mean difference between the average post-reform growth of a comprehensive liberaliser, such as the Czech Republic or Estonia, and a less comprehensive reformer, such as Bulgaria, is on the order of 3 per cent per year.

How important are initial conditions in the outcomes of the different countries? Do the profiles reflect different starting points, rather than different policies? A more comprehensive treatment of initial conditions by De Melo, Denizer, Gelb and Tenev (1996 forthcoming) suggests that composite initial conditions derived from the first two principal components of a number of country characteristics may indeed have significant explanatory power, but that the broad relationships between policy and outcomes still hold.

Here we assess the effect of including three initial conditions in the regressions. In the growth equations, we included:

1. Location in CEE (versus the NIS);
2. The pre-reform share of industry in GDP;

and in the inflation equations, we include:

3. The size of initial monetary overhang relative to GDP (MONOV). Because of the difficulty of specifying an equilibrium demand for money, MONOV is proxied by the percentage change in deflated wages over 1987-89 less the percentage change in real GDP. MONOV ranges from -7 per cent in Hungary and Czechoslovakia to almost 26 per cent in the NIS.

Regression 3 in Table 3 includes the CEE dummy: the coefficient is positive but not significant. Similarly, the share of industry (not shown in Table 3) has a negative coefficient (more industrialisation involves greater restructuring and lower growth) but the coefficient is again not significant. A high initial monetary overhang is, however significantly associated with higher inflation (regression 6) — the effect of the Soviet money overhang is comparable to that of the RT dummy in its effect on average inflation over the period.

Figure 4. Indicators of adjustment across reform groups

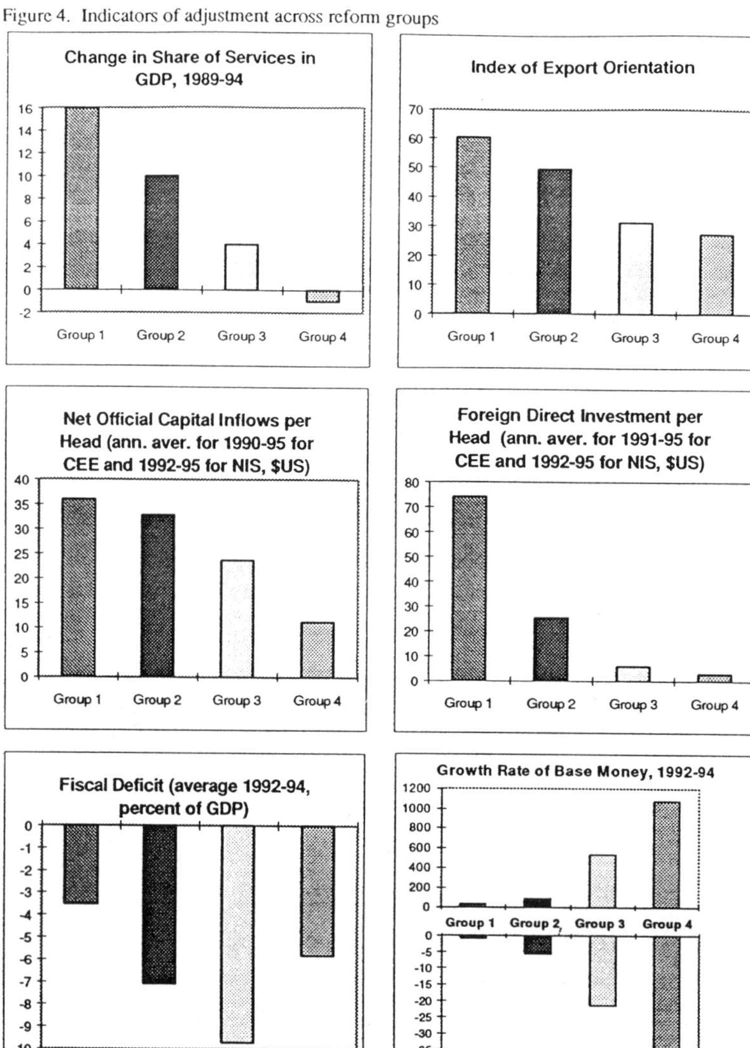

Note: Group 1 represents the most advanced reformers and Group 4 the least advanced reformers.

Selected indicators of adjustment

Selected indicators of adjustment can also help explain the differential experience of the four reform groups. The first two charts in Figure 4 show the sources of recovery for advanced reformers. Most advanced reformers have seen a dramatic increase in the share of their service sector in overall GDP, reflecting both relative price changes and growth in non-government services. They have also been more successful in re-orienting their exports towards market economies.[5]

Recovery has been assisted by net inflows of official development assistance, which has been almost three times higher, on a *per capita* basis, in the most advanced reformers than in the slowest reformers. This suggests that reforms have been rewarded by both bilateral and multilateral lending. Even more striking, and more significant in dollar terms, is the concentration of private direct foreign investment in the advanced reformers. FDI *per capita* has been concentrated in Group 1 countries and was twice as high as net official inflows during 1990-95. Although not shown, average fixed investment levels do not differ too much from one reform group to another, although variation within groups is relatively high; the quality of investment would seem to be more important than the level of investment in explaining growth.

Relative to GDP, fiscal revenues (not shown) have been maintained in the advanced reformers and, in some cases, have increased as a share of GDP, whereas revenues started out lower in slower reformers and have declined dramatically, particularly in intermediate reformers. Real government expenditures (deflated by the GDP deflator) have halved in some of these countries. According to Figure 4, fiscal deficits have tended to be largest in the intermediate reformers, but conventionally measured fiscal deficits do not tell the whole story. Base money growth has been far higher in the slowest reformers, and the difference largely reflects quasi-fiscal losses of central banks, as these have sought to prop up the declining sectors. Such losses have been larger and more persistent in countries slower to liberalise (for estimates of quasi-fiscal deficits, see De Melo, Denizer and Gelb, 1996), and these countries have also seen less growth from structural reallocation. Highly negative real discount rates (see Figure 4) in slow reformers increase the attractiveness of foreign currencies and inhibit the efficient allocation of resources. They thus help to explain both the growth and inflation experience.

3. Vicious versus virtuous circles

Clearly, initial conditions and policies are both important in determining the outcomes of transition, and the former include both structural and macroeconomic factors. We briefly review some important differences between China and Russia (see Sachs and Woo, 1994; McKinnon, 1994), and then turn to their impact on inter-industry linkages and macroeconomic feedback effects.

Table 4. Economic structure in Russia and China.

	Russia		China		
	1990	1994	1978	1985	1994
GDP per capita at PPP ($)	6,960	5,260	1,000	1,600	2,510
State sector employment share (per cent)	90	44	19	19	18
Sectoral employment shares (per cent)					
Agriculture	13	15	71	62	58
Industry	42	38	15	17	18
Services	45	47	14	21	25

Source: World Bank and IMF databases and World Bank staff estimates.

Taking the base year for transition as 1978 in China and 1990 in Russia, Table 4 shows some indicators of initial economic structure and changes through time. Real *per capita* income was several times higher in Russia, and the sectoral structure of employment was very different. The capital-intensity of the Russian economy, as well as the share devoted to military purposes, was much higher. This, together with Russia's deep involvement in CMEA and intra-Soviet trade, were important reasons why transition in Russia has been associated with severe disruptions in the economy and associated output declines. Central planning and the share of the state sector were also far more important in the Russian economy. For China, it was possible to grow around the state enterprises by releasing labour from agriculture; for Russia, the pervasiveness of the state sector (including large state farms) has made it necessary to radically restructure these enterprises.

The patterns of sectoral repression also differed a great deal between Russia and China. In both, state industry was overbuilt and favoured with high relative prices and/or subsidies.[6] In China, the main repressed sector was agriculture, although trade and business service margins were also controlled and repressed. In Russia, agriculture was heavily mechanised, input-intensive and subsidised. Services were repressed; in addition, so was the formidable Russian energy sector — the implicit transfer to energy users due to low prices might have been on the order of 11 per cent of GDP.[7]

These differences imply that liberalisation unleashed different patterns of economy-wide adjustment. Price reform plus the introduction of the household responsibility system in 1978 permitted Chinese farmers to retain a higher proportion of their output and created incentives for efficiency. Value added price deflators for agriculture and industry show a 46 per cent increase in the agricultural terms of trade between 1978 and 1985 and a continuing if smaller increase through the early 1990s. Low agricultural productivity permitted relatively large boosts to output in the first few years of reform, and higher productivity also released cheap labour for non-agricultural employment.

Table 5a. Changes in sectoral composition of Russian GDP: 1990-94 (%).

Sector	Change in Share at Current Prices	Volume Effect	Deflator Effect
Agriculture	**-9**	**2**	**-11**
Industry	**-7**	**-7**	**0**
of which			
Fuel Energy	4	1	3
Other	-11	-7	-4
Services	**27**	**13**	**14**
of which			
Transport & Communications	4	-2	6
Trade	9	3	6

Source: Goskomstat.

Note: The volume affects the change in the constant price share in GDP; the deflator effect is the change in share due to the change in the sector deflator relative to the GDP deflator. To reduce interaction effects, estimates are computed as averages of the effects derived from base and final year weights.

Initially at least, China's reforms reduced income disparities. The Gini coefficient fell from an estimated 0.32 in 1980 to 0.26 in 1984 as the rural sector grew. The incidence of rural poverty dropped from 30 per cent to 8 per cent (Ying, 1996; Gelb, Jefferson and Singh, 1993). Especially during this early period, changes in the distribution of income reinforced demand for basic consumer goods which could be produced domestically — and Chinese households also saved at a high rate.[8] The rapid growth of China's township and village enterprises (TVEs) is suggestive of the strong induced investment effect arising out of the concurrence of strong forward linkages from agriculture and strong backward linkages from rural industry (see Hirschman, 1958). Investment opportunities were clear and resources were available, providing a strong stimulus to growth.

Table 5b. Changes in sectoral composition of China's GDP: 1979-94 (%).

Sector	Change in Share at Current Prices	Volume Effect	Deflator Effect
Agriculture	-10	-17	6
Industry	-0	13	-15
Services	10	5	5

Source: World Bank Data.

In Russia, data on changes in the sectoral composition of output and relative price effects suggest a very different story. Table 5a decomposes changes in sectoral shares in GDP into volume and relative price (deflator) effects, using an average of initial and final-year weighting to reduce cross-terms. The rural/urban terms of trade declined sharply between 1990 and 1994, as farm input prices rose (especially fuel and fertilisers) and partial controls on food prices were maintained. The share of agriculture in GDP plummeted, even though it contracted less than the overall economy in real terms — a very different pattern from that in China, shown in Table 5b. Rural incomes fell sharply in Russia relative to urban incomes. At the same time, certain higher income activities, such as the fuel-energy sector, saw their GDP shares increase due to both price and volume effects. The rest of industry (especially light industry) suffered from both volume and relative price declines. The large increase in the share of the service sector (notable also in China) was, in Russia, mainly due to increased incomes for financial intermediation and business services — government services barely maintained their share, while trade and transport enjoyed relatively modest gains.[9]

These patterns were closely reflected in the profiles of relative wage changes as shown in Figure 5. Relative to the average, wage levels in energy and banking have soared, while wages in agriculture and light industry have fallen behind.[10] Regressions suggest that some 30-40 per cent of the differences in income per head across oblasts may be attributed to such sectoral differences in their economic bases. And, unlike China in its early phase of reform, income differentials in Russia appear to have opened up sharply. Comparable pre- and post-reform data are not available, but the increase may have been between 0.14 and 0.24, with the post-reform Gini coefficient measured at about 0.48, slightly above a typical level for a middle income country.

Figure 5. Evolution of relative wages by sector: Russia 1970 - 1994

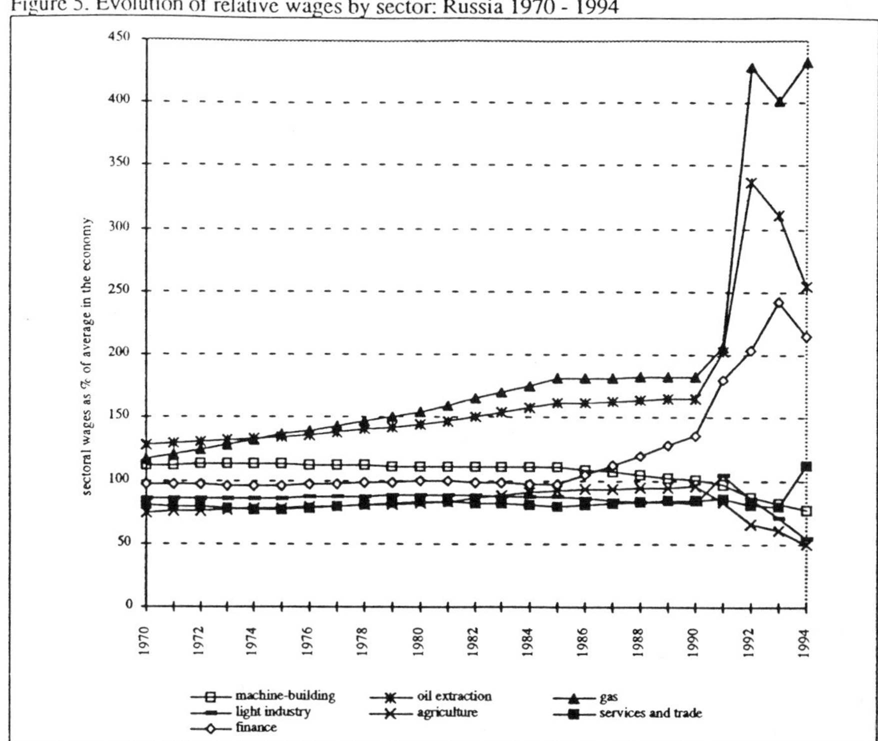

How does increasing income dispersion feed back into macroeconomic aggregates? Table 6 presents survey evidence on the preferences of Russians in different income groups. Those with higher incomes are more in favour of a market economy. They also favour high-quality foreign consumer goods over domestic goods by a wider margin.[11] Consumer imports from the "far abroad" appear to have been considerable; average import penetration ratios in 1993-94 were close to a third for both food processing and light industry, and close to a half for the category of miscellaneous industries. Imports are far more prominent in certain sub-sectors — production of television sets in Russia fell from 4.5 million units in 1991 to fewer than 1 million in 1995, while import penetration rose from about 5 per cent to more than 80 per cent.[12]

The evolution of income distribution may also affect capital flows. Fixed investment levels in Russia are respectable by international standards, but they are far lower than in China. As shown in Table 7, a large part of the difference appears to reflect the combined impact of capital flight and direct foreign investment, which acts as an injection in China but as a large leakage in Russia.[13] Indeed, some estimates show domestic savings before capital flight almost as high in Russia as in China (Halligan and Teplukhin, 1995). A number of factors affect capital flight, including the perceived soundness of the domestic financial system, macroeconomic stability and the accelerator effect of high income growth. All of these are more favourable in China. But from Table 6, higher-income households

Table 6. Preferences by income group: Russia 1995 (%).

	Better Off (in upper 10%)	Income Group Medium (11%-63%)	Worse Off (in lower 63%)
Monthly income by household (000 Roubles)	608	196	107
Type of Economy Favoured			
Goods in shops, even if high prices	62	51	30
Controlled prices, even if shortages	38	49	70
Preferences for western consumer goods, at twice the price of Russian goods			
Japanese TV	85	63	48
Watch	54	32	29
Chocolate	32	13	10
Have Savings	65	30	19
In hard currency	19	5	1

Source: Richard Rose, CSPP, University of Strathclyde, New Russian Barometer, IV, Glasgow. Fieldwork was conducted in March-April 1995.

Table 7. Selected macroeconomic indicators: Russia and China (%).

	Russia Average 1992-94	China Average 1992-94
GDP real growth	-12	13
Inflation	850	14
M2/GDP	17	86
Real Discount rate	-41	-7
Fixed investment/GDP	22	34
FDI net of capital flight/GDP	-6	4

Source: World Bank and IMF databases and World Bank staff estimates.

are also more likely to be accumulating foreign-denominated assets, as are firms with large surpluses — often those in energy or other natural resource-intensive sectors.

4. Conclusions

Countries in CEE and the NIS embarking on transition from plan to market have done so from considerably different starting points. Nevertheless, the transition process shows some strong commonalities, both across countries and over time. These become more apparent when countries are ranked in terms of their overall exposure to liberalising reforms. This measure includes both the level of liberalisation achieved and the duration of reforms.

In analysing the relationships between these reforms and outcomes, this paper updates and extends Denizer, De Melo and Gelb (1995), using an alternative criterion for determining the switching point between non-reformed and reformed states. In CEE and the NIS, the process of economic liberalisation — of domestic markets, foreign trade and new business entry — has closely followed that of political liberalisation. Adjustment to economic liberalisation involves the expansion of previously repressed sectors and activities, and the contraction of overbuilt sectors. The former include trade, finance and other business services and exports to established market economies (in particular, to the OECD). Overbuilt sectors include, in particular, industry, and in parts of CEE and the NIS, agriculture. On average (and based on official data) the expansion of repressed sectors begins to offset the contraction of overbuilt sectors after about three years of reform. Failure to reform does not preserve the *status quo*, but opens up the prospect of a more extended economic decline.

The wide range of recent growth rates reflects both different intensities of reforms and the fact that countries started reforms at different times. The general U-shaped relationship is robust to the inclusion of individual country characteristics, such as a possibly more favourable location in CEE versus in the NIS; the initial conditions included in this paper enter with the expected signs but are not significant. The estimates highlight the cost of non-economic factors — on average, one year of blockade or warfare has cost the countries involved over 8 per cent of GDP. Even allowing for larger under-reporting of output in these countries, the indicated cost is high.

There is also a surprisingly close linkage between exposure to reforms and inflation, which follows a mirror-image of the growth relationship. Even though liberalisation involves a sharp initial price spike, no transition country in the region has brought inflation down to moderate levels without substantial, and sustained, liberalising reforms. This is partly because reforms facilitate the control of fiscal deficits through allowing large cuts in expenditures and, in particular, fiscal subsidies. Deflated expenditures have indeed fallen very sharply for many of the countries, especially those in the intermediate liberalisation categories, where they have often halved over four years. But even more important has been the effect of cutting credit subsidies from central banks, by restricting the growth of base money and sharply raising discount rates towards positive real levels (see De Melo and Denizer (1996) for a more detailed analysis of monetary policy). Like established market economies, transition countries do not resume growth until inflation has been brought down to moderate levels. Net official capital inflows have been larger, on a per head basis, to those countries that have advanced further in reforms, but are already overtaken for the most advanced reformers by inflows of private FDI. But initial macroeconomic conditions are also clearly important — the initial level of the money overhang has a large effect on subsequent inflation, possibly because higher initial inflation results in a smaller base for the inflation tax.

Finally, the paper considers how the initial pattern of repressed sectors can influence the payoff to liberalisation through its effect in encouraging virtuous or vicious circles. This paper focuses on a particular issue: changes in income distribution and leakages into saving abroad and consumer imports. Here, there have been major differences between Russia and China.

China's reforms initially redistributed income towards the poorer rural sector, creating a demand for simple manufactures as well as for industrial investment, that could be financed through rising household savings. Product quality could be upgraded as income rose over time. Initial rural productivity gains therefore fed back into the economy with minimal leakages.

In contrast, reforms in Russia have involved a large shift in the domestic terms of trade against agriculture (which was previously heavily subsidised), and also against light industry, and in favour of oil, gas and financial intermediation. These shifts are mirrored in patterns of wage dispersion and also to some extent on a regional basis, and appear to be one of the reasons for the sharp increase in income dispersion seen in Russia after 1990. With greater preferences for high-quality imported goods and foreign savings at higher incomes, one outcome is higher leakages, especially given the weakness of fiscal and financial sector linkages. Although it is not possible to measure these leakages precisely or to compare them with previous levels, it seems likely that their increase exceeds the direct gain to Russia's energy sector.

Russia does not appear to lack savings — indeed, increased natural resource income usually translates into higher savings in energy-exporting countries. However, a major challenge for the future is to find ways to recycle gains in the previously repressed sectors, and their associated savings, back into Russia's economy. In addition to fiscal and financial sector reforms, as well as improved corporate governance in firms, this will require a sustained period of macroeconomic stability to encourage investment, including in the consumer goods sectors.

Notes

[1] For discussion of sensitivity to weighting, see De Melo, Denizer and Gelb (1996).

[2] Political freedom ratings for NIS countries in earlier years are taken as those of the Soviet Union.

[3] Because growth rates are known to be understated post-reform, some estimates have tried to capture the possible extent of mis-measurement by using electricity indicators (Kaufmann, 1995). De Melo, Denizer and Gelb (1996) reports the results of sensitivity analysis that allow for likely patterns of bias. While this analysis does affect the coefficients of regressions such as developed in this paper, it does not change the overall patterns or conclusions.

[4] Countries at this level of liberalisation typically have taken major steps to free domestic prices and to open international trade, but have not yet consolidated reforms to facilitate a high level of private entry.

[5] The index of export orientation is the sum of four sets of country rankings, by the following criteria: (a) percentage change in dollar value exports, (b) percentage change in CMEA or interrepublican trade shares in total exports, (c) percentage increase in manufactured exports to the OECD, and (d) the ratio of exports to OECD to GDP in 1994. For more details, see Wang, Winters and Kaminski (1996).

[6] Industry was less overbuilt in China, although at distorted prices its share in GDP was high.

[7] World Bank estimate.

[8] The second phase of largely urban reform after 1985 has seen an increase in the Gini index to close to 0.40, and the number of absolutely poor stopped falling although economic growth continued. As demand for more sophisticated goods increased, so production capabilities were upgraded, for example, from black-and-white to colour televisions.

[9] Financial intermediation services, which are considered as intermediates in the national accounts, saw a share increase of 10 per cent, half due to increased volume and half due to higher margins.

[10] Wage arrears show no systematic relationship with sectoral wage levels. They are high in both the gas and agricultural sector, for different reasons.

[11] The survey does not capture the super-rich, who can be expected to have an even higher preference for imports.

[12] The Economist, April 15, pp 57-58.

[13] There was also considerable export of capital through credits to other countries in the FSU, although some of this was used to finance exports from Russia. On average, over 1992-94, these credits may have been some 4 per cent of GDP (Dabrowski, 1995).

References

Balcerowicz, L. and Gelb, A., 1994 "Macropolicies in Transition to a Market Economy: A Three–Year Perspective," prepared for the World Bank Annual Conference on Development Economics, Washington, D.C., April 28-29.

Barro, R.J., 1994, "Democracy and Growth", *NBER Working Paper Series*, n°. 4909, National Bureau of Economic Research, Washington, D.C, October.

Bruno, M., 1993, "Stabilization and the Macroeconomics of Transition: How Different is Eastern Europe?," in *Economics of Transition*, Vol. 1, n°. 1, EBRD, pp. 5-19.

Dabrowski, M., 1995, *Why did the Ruble Area Have to Collapse*?, Center for Economic and Social Research, Warsaw.

de Melo, M. and Denizer, C., 1996, *Monetary Policy During Transition: an Overview*, Policy Research Department, World Bank, Washington, D.C.

de Melo, M., Denizer, C., Gelb, A., 1996, "From Plan to Market: Patterns of Transition" *World Bank Economic Review*, September.

de Melo, M., Denizer, C., Gelb, A. and Tenev, S., 1995, *Explaining Transition: The Role of Initial Conditions in Reforming Socialist Countries*, Policy Research Department, World Bank, Washington, D.C.

Diaz-Alejandro, C.F., 1963, "A Note on the Impact of Devaluation and the Redistributive Effect," in *The Journal of Political Economy*, vol. 71.

EBRD, 1994, *Transition Report*, London.

EBRD, 1995, *Transition Report Update*, London, April.

Gelb, A., Jefferson, G., and Singh, I., 1993, "Can Communist Economies Transform Incrementally? The Experience of China," in Blanchard, O. and Fischer, S. (eds.), *NBER Macroeconomics Annual*, The MIT Press, vol. 8, pp. 87-133.

Halligan, L. and Teplukhin, P., 1995, "Investment Disincentives in Russia,", Russian-European Centre for Economic Policy Working Paper, September.

Hirschman, A. O., 1958, *The Strategy of Economic Development*, Yale University Press, New Haven.

Karatnycky, A., 1995, "Democracies on the Rise, Democracies at Risk," in *Freedom Review*, Freedom House, pp. 5-22, January/February.

Kornai, J., 1993, "Transformational Recession: A General Phenomenon Examined through the Example of Hungary's Development", *Economie Applique*, vol. 46, n°. 2, pp. 181–227.

McKinnon, R.I, 1994, "Financial Growth and Macroeconomic Stability in China, 1978-1992: Implications for Russia and Other Transitional Economies", *Journal of Comparative Economics*, vol. 18, n°. 3, pp. 438-470, June.

Sachs, J. and Woo, W.T., 1994, "Structural Factors in the Economic Reforms of China, Eastern Europe, and the Former Soviet Union", Economic Policy, vol 18, April.

Seers, D., 1963, "A Theory of Inflation and Growth in Under-developed Countries Based on the Experience of Latin America", *Oxford Economic Papers*, June

Wing, T.W., 1994, "The Art of Reforming Centrally Planned Economies: Comparing China, Poland, and Russia", Journal of Comparative Economics, vol. 18, n°. 3, pp. 276-309, June.

Ying, Y., 1996, "Income, Poverty and Inequality in China during Transition to a Market Economy", Research Paper n°. 10 for Research Project on Income Distribution during the Transition, February.

4

From transition to market: evidence and growth prospects

Stanley Fischer, Ratna Sahay and Carlos A. Végh

1. Introduction

It is now over six years since the start of the Polish economic reform programme, and over four years since the break-up of the Soviet Union. *A priori* speculation about the nature of the economic transition can now give way to a discussion of what has happened so far, and to a better informed speculation — though speculation nonetheless — of what may happen in future. The story so far is that the leading reformers of Central and Eastern Europe (CEE) have moved impressively down he road to macroeconomic stability and a market economy, and that most of the remaining countries have taken major strides towards stabilization and reform. The output costs of reform in most economies have probably exceeded expectations,[1] but output declines have stopped in all countries that have stabilized and growth has begun in most of them. The fear that politics would not sustain reform unless progress was rapid has turned out not to be valid in most countries.[2]

In this paper, we take a look at the progress made so far by the transition economies in their journey towards a market economy, and evaluate their long-run prospects for growth. Specifically, the paper first presents data that summarise the behaviour of output and inflation in the transition economies, and then regression evidence that seeks to account for differences in performance among countries. The regressions, which cover the period 1992-1995, update results based on data through 1994 presented in Fischer, Sahay and Vegh (1996a).[3] We then turn to a numerical, but more speculative, exercise to assess the long-run growth potential of the transition economies.

The authors thank Sergey Alexashenko, Laszlo Csaba, Stanislaw Gomulka, Jim Haley, Silvana Malle, John Odling-Smee, Nicholas Stern, Georg Winckler, Jeromin Zettelmeyer and conference participants for helpful comments and discussions; our IMF colleagues for making data available and helping us to interpret them; and Manzoor Gill for excellent research assistance. Views expressed are those of the authors and not necessarily those of the International Monetary Fund.

2. Recent experience in the transition economies

In this section we examine the behaviour of GDP growth and inflation for 26 economies in transition in eastern Europe, the former Soviet Union, and Mongolia. Most of the data used in this paper have been provided by IMF economists working on these countries.[4] It is well known that these data are likely to suffer from serious biases. In particular, the output data are subject to both conceptual and measurement problems. At a conceptual level, prices before the transition were out of line with both costs and world prices, and goods were in any case often not available at those prices. As relative prices change in the transition process and resources move towards sectors whose prices have risen, output declines in base prices are overstated relative to declines measured at world or new prices. The measurement problems are mostly related to the fact that as state-sector output declines and private-sector output rises, an increasing share of output tends not to be recorded given that statistical services — some of which had to be built essentially from scratch — are still rudimentary.

Table 1. Annual Output Growth in Transition Economies, 1989–95

Country	1989	1990	1991	1992	1993	1994	1995	Output growing in 1996?
Albania	9.8	−10.0	−28.0	−7.2	9.6	9.4	8.6	yes
Armenia	14.2	−7.2	−11.8	−52.3	−14.8	5.3	5.0	yes
Azerbaijan	−4.4	−11.7	−0.7	−22.1	−23.1	−21.1	−13.2	no
Belarus	7.9	−3.2	−1.2	−9.6	−10.7	−19.1	−10.2	no
Bulgaria	−0.5	−9.1	−11.7	−7.3	−2.4	1.4	2.5	yes
Croatia	−1.5	−8.5	−20.9	−9.7	−3.7	0.8	−1.5	yes
Czech Republic	1.4	−1.2	−14.2	−6.4	−0.9	2.6	4.8	yes
Estonia	−1.1	−3.6	−11.9	−21.6	−8.4	3.0	4.0	yes
Georgia	−4.8	−12.4	−20.6	−44.8	−25.4	−11.3	−5.0	yes
Hungary	0.7	−3.5	−11.9	−3.0	−0.8	2.9	1.7	yes
Kazakhstan	−0.4	−0.4	−18.8	−13.9	−12.0	−25.0	−8.9	yes
Kyrgyz Republic	3.0	4.0	−5.0	−19.3	−16.1	−26.2	1.3	yes
Latvia	3.0	−2.3	−11.1	−35.2	−14.8	2.0	0.4	yes
Lithuania	1.5	−5.0	−13.4	0.0	−18.4	1.0	3.5	yes
Macedonia	0.9	−9.7	−10.7	−21.1	−8.4	−8.2	−3.0	yes
Moldova	8.8	−1.5	−18.0	−29.1	−1.2	−31.2	−3.1	yes
Mongolia	4.2	−2.0	−9.2	−9.5	−3.0	2.1	6.3	yes
Poland	0.2	−11.6	−7.0	2.6	3.8	6.0	6.5	yes
Romania	−5.8	−7.4	−12.9	−8.8	1.3	3.9	6.9	yes
Russia	3.0	−2.0	−12.9	−19.0	−12.0	−15.0	−4.0	no
Slovak Republic	4.5	−0.4	−15.9	−6.7	−4.7	4.8	7.4	yes
Slovenia	−2.7	−4.7	−8.1	−5.4	1.3	5.5	4.0	yes
Tajikistan	−2.9	−1.6	−7.1	−29.0	−11.0	−21.5	−12.5	no
Turkmenistan	−7.0	−2.3	−4.8	−5.3	−10.2	−20.0	−13.9	no
Ukraine	4.1	−3.6	−11.9	−17.0	−13.0	−21.8	−11.4	no
Uzbekistan	3.7	4.3	−0.9	−11.0	−2.4	−3.5	−1.2	no

Sources: National authorities; International Monetary Fund; The World Bank.

2.1 *Basic macroeconomic indicators*

Tables 1-3 show annual output and inflation data for the 26 transition economies since 1989.[5] Several facts stand out:

- Output declines during the transition have been very large. Table 1 presents annual output growth data for the 26 countries in our sample for the period 1989-1995. As of 1995, the reported average cumulative output decline during the transition process was 41 per cent (Table 3). In several countries, reported output has fallen by around two-thirds, which would indicate a virtual collapse of the economy. While these data are surely exaggerated, output declines have nonetheless been dramatic.[6] The output decline was most severe in the former Soviet Union countries dependent on intra-republican trade and in those that suffered civil war or trade embargoes — Armenia, Georgia, Azerbaijan, Moldova, Tajikistan and Ukraine in the FSU and Croatia and former Yugoslav Republic of Macedonia (FYROM) in CEE (Table 3). To gain some perspective, recall that output in the United States declined by 34 per cent during the Great Depression. Even though there were surely better reform strategies than those actually pursued, the creative destruction of the transition process would have implied large output declines even under the best policies.[7]

- The worst is over in most economies; as of 1995, 14 out of the 26 economies in our sample had begun to grow. Growth began as early as 1993-94 in most CEE and the Baltics, but by 1995 was not yet apparent in the official data for two-thirds of the FSU countries. Expected growth for 1996 is positive in all but seven countries in the sample.

- Inflation rates have been extremely high in the transition process, higher in the former Soviet Union and the former Yugoslavia than in other countries. In only three countries — the Czech Republic, the Slovak Republic and Hungary — did annual inflation remain below triple digits throughout. In two countries — Armenia and Ukraine — it reached more than 10 000 per cent in the year of maximum inflation.[8] All countries in the former Soviet Union (except the Baltics) experienced inflation of more than 1 000 per cent in the year of maximum inflation. Maximum inflation rates were significantly lower in CEE. In most countries, there was an initial jump in inflation, associated with price liberalisation and devaluation. This can be thought of as primarily a price level change (see Sahay and Végh, 1996). In most countries, but less so in CEE, inflation increased in subsequent years, but has declined in virtually all countries since then.

- Inflation stabilization is succeeding. By 1995, the average inflation rate (measured December-to-December) in CEE and the Baltics was only 20 per cent per annum. Although inflation was about 390 per cent in the former Soviet Union and Mongolia, inflation was below half that level in nine of those 12 countries (Table 3). Table 2 also includes expected inflation rates for 1996, which suggest continuing improvements in inflation performance in most of the transition economies.

Table 2. Annual inflation in transition economies, 1989-95 (period average).

Country	1989	1990	1991	1992	1993	1994	1995	Inflation < 50% in 1996
Albania	0.0	0.0	35.5	225.2	85.0	22.6	7.8	yes
Armenia	2.0	5,6	100.3	824.5	3731.9	5273.4	176.8	yes
Azerbaijan	2.0	7.8	61.4	912.6	1129.9	1664.4	411.7	yes
Belarus	1.7	4.5	94.1	969.9	1187.9	2222.1	709.0	no
Bulgaria	6.4	23.9	333.5	82.0	72.8	96.0	62.1	yes
Croatia	1200.0	609.2	122.6	663.3	1516.0	97.5	2.0	yes
Czech Republic	1.4	9.5	56.7	11.1	20.8	10.0	9.1	yes
Estonia	2.0	23.1	212.5	1069.3	89.0	47.7	28.3	yes
Georgia	0.9	3.3	78.5	888.3	3126.3	17246.2	169.0	yes
Hungary	16.9	29.2	34.2	23.0	22.5	18.8	28.2	yes
Kazakstan	2.0	4.2	90.9	1513.7	1662.3	1879.9	176.3	yes
Kyrgyz Republic	2.0	4.2	85.0	853.8	1208.7	278.1	42.8	yes
Latvia	4.7	10.5	124.7	951.1	109.0	35.8	25.1	yes
Lithuania	2.1	8.4	224.7	1020.5	410.4	72.1	36.5	yes
Macedonia	1246.0	608.4	114.9	1692.6	334.5	122.6	17.4	yes
Moldova	4.5	110.0	162.0	1276.4	788.0	329.4	30.2	yes
Mongolia	0.0	0.0	20.2	202.8	268.4	88.3	56.8	yes
Poland	251.1	600.0	76.4	43.0	35.3	32.2	27.8	yes
Romania	0.9	4.7	161.1	210.3	256.0	136.8	32.0	yes
Russia	2.4	5.7	92.7	1353.0	896.0	301.1	190.2	no
Slovak Republic	1.4	10.8	78.3	10.1	23.1	13.4	9.9	yes
Slovenia	1306.0	549.7	117.7	201.3	32.3	19.8	12.8	yes
Tajikistan	2.0	5.6	111.6	1159.8	2194.8	350.4	635.4	no
Turkmenistan	2.0	4.2	102.5	493.3	3102.4	1748.9	1261.5	no
Ukraine	2.0	3.0	94.1	1210.0	4734.9	891.2	376.4	no
Uzbekistan	0.7	4.0	105.0	645.5	534.2	1568.3	304.6	no

Sources: National authorities; International Monetary Fund; The World Bank.

The detailed data presented in Tables 1-3 are summarised in Figures 1-3.[9] Panel (a) in Figure 1 shows the (unweighted) average growth rate of measured real GDP since 1989 — which we take to be the year in which the transformation process began — through 1995. Measured growth has on average been negative in every year (but was close to zero in 1995). The growth rate reached a trough in 1992, reflecting the effects of the break-up of the Soviet Union and the collapse of CMEA trade. The growth rate then increased, but remained negative. The corresponding plot for the level of real GDP in panel (a) in Figure 2 shows that, on average, GDP in 1994 was about 60 per cent of its initial level. The year 1995 saw a virtual stop to the process of output decline.

It is clear from Tables 1 and 3 that the behaviour of output differs between, on the one hand, the CEE and Baltic countries (EEB) and, on the other hand, the countries of the former Soviet Union (excluding the Baltics) and Mongolia (FSUM). We therefore present output profiles in levels and growth rates for these groups of countries in Figures 1 and 2 in panels (b) and (c), respectively. The average level of output reached a minimum in EEB in 1993, and has since begun to grow [Figure 2, panel (b)]. At that point, output had fallen 30 per cent below the 1989 level. In the FSUM countries, output continued to fall through 1995, albeit at a declining rate. The level in 1995 was less than 50 per cent of the 1989 level.

Table 3. Inflation and Output Performance in Transition Economies, 1989–95

Country	Year in which inflation was highest 1/	Maximum annual inflation 1/	Year in which inflation fell below 50% 1/ 2/	Annual inflation in 1995 1/	Year in which output was lowest 3/	Cumulative output decline (1989=100) 3/	Cumulative output growth since lowest level 4/
Albania	1992	236.6	1993	6.1	1992	39.9	30.2
Armenia	1993	10896.2	1995	32.1	1993	66.7	10.5
Azerbaijan	1994	1788.0	--	84.5	1995	64.0	--
Belarus	1993	1994.0	--	244.5	1995	43.9	--
Bulgaria	1991	338.8	1995	32.9	1993	27.4	3.9
Croatia	1993	1149.7	1994	3.7	1993 6/	37.0	--
Czech Republic	1991	52.1	1992	7.5	1993	21.4	7.5
Estonia	1992	946.7	1993	28.8	1993	35.3	7.2
Georgia	1993	7487.9	--	62.3	1995	75.9	--
Hungary	1990	34.6	n.a.	28.5	1993	18.2	4.7
Kazakhstan	1992	2566.6	--	60.4	1995	58.1	--
Kyrgyz Republic	1993	1365.6	1995	31.5	1994	50.6	1.3
Latvia	1992	958.2	1993	23.3	1993	52.0	2.4
Lithuania	1992	1162.6	1994	35.5	1993	32.9	4.5
Macedonia, FYR	1992	1927.3	1995	9.3	1995	48.1	--
Moldova	1992	2198.4	1995	23.8	1995	62.3	--
Mongolia	1992	325.0	--	53.6	1993	21.9	8.6
Poland	1989	639.6	1992	24.2	1991	17.8	20.2
Romania	1993	295.5	1995	27.2	1992	26.4	12.5
Russia	1992	2510.4	--	131.4	1995	50.3	--
Slovak Republic	1991	58.3	1992	17.3	1993	25.5	12.6
Slovenia	1991	246.7	1993	8.6	1992	16.0	9.7
Tajikistan	1993	7343.7	--5/	2131.9	1995	60.3	--
Turkmenistan	1993	9743.0	--	1906.7	1995	45.5	--
Ukraine	1993	10155.0	--	181.4	1995	57.5	--
Uzbekistan	1994	1232.8	--	112.0	1995	14.3	--
All transition economies 7/		2602.1		204.2		41.1	
Eastern Europe and Baltics 7/		619.0		19.5		30.6	
FSU and Mongolia 7/		4585.1		388.9		51.6	

Sources: IMF staff estimates; national authorities.

1/ Inflation calculated from December to December.
2/ A "--" indicates that inflation was above 50% during the transition years, as of 1995. In Hungary's case, this criterion is not applicable because inflation was below 50% even before 1989.
3/ Output decline from 1989 to the year in which output was lowest. For countries in which output has not begun to grow, 1995 is taken as the year of minimum output. GDP measured on an annual average basis.
4/ Lowest level refers to the lowest output level reached during 1989–95. A "--" indicates that no positive growth has been recorded as of 1995.
5/ Although inflation in 1994 was only 1.1 percent, it was a temporary phenomenon caused by a shortage of bank notes.
6/ Output revived marginally (0.8 percent) in 1994 and then declined by 1.5 percent in 1995.
7/ Simple average.

The pattern of inflation since the start of the transition process is presented in Figure 3. Inflation increased dramatically from 1991 to 1994. The process turned around in 1995 when average inflation declined sharply. Separate profiles for the EEB and FSUM countries show that inflation in the EEB remained well below the levels in the FSUM, and turned down sooner.

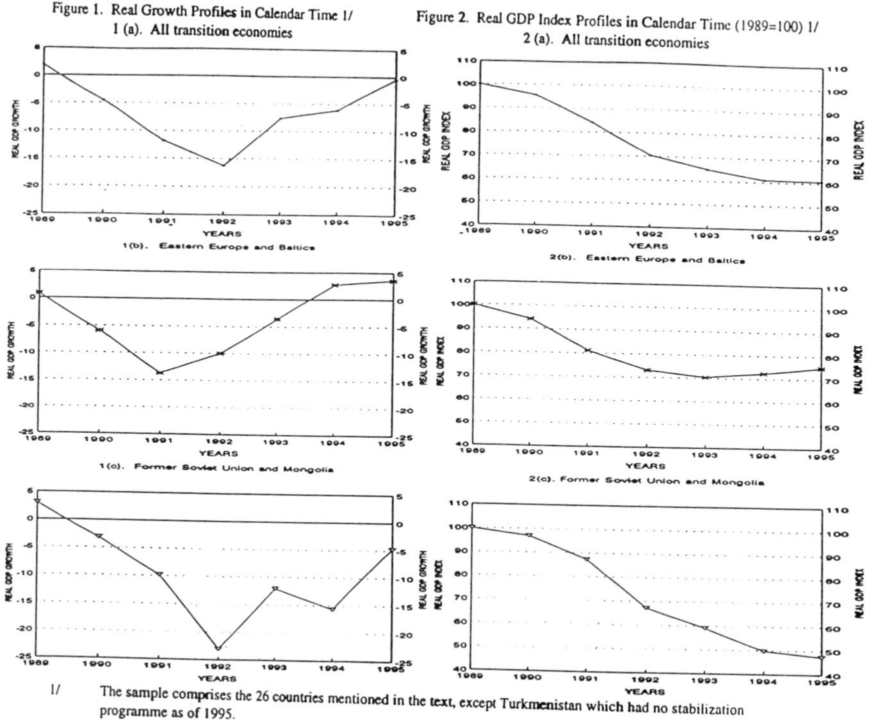

Figure 1. Real Growth Profiles in Calendar Time 1/
1 (a). All transition economies

Figure 2. Real GDP Index Profiles in Calendar Time (1989=100) 1/
2 (a). All transition economies

1/ The sample comprises the 26 countries mentioned in the text, except Turkmenistan which had no stabilization programme as of 1995.

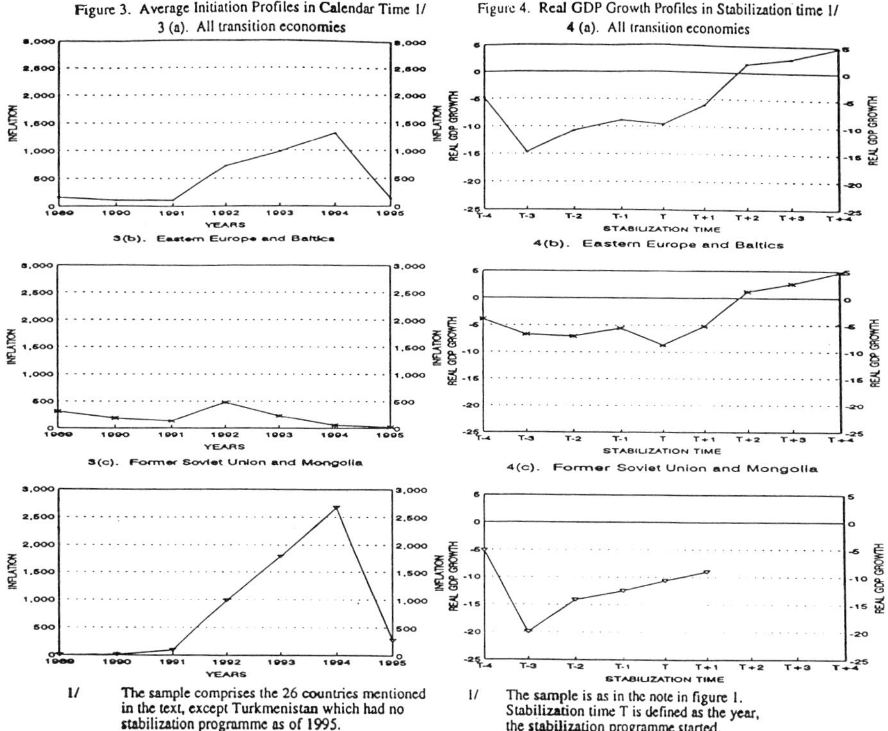

1/ The sample comprises the 26 countries mentioned in the text, except Turkmenistan which had no stabilization programme as of 1995.

1/ The sample is as in the note in figure 1. Stabilization time T is defined as the year, the stabilization programme started.

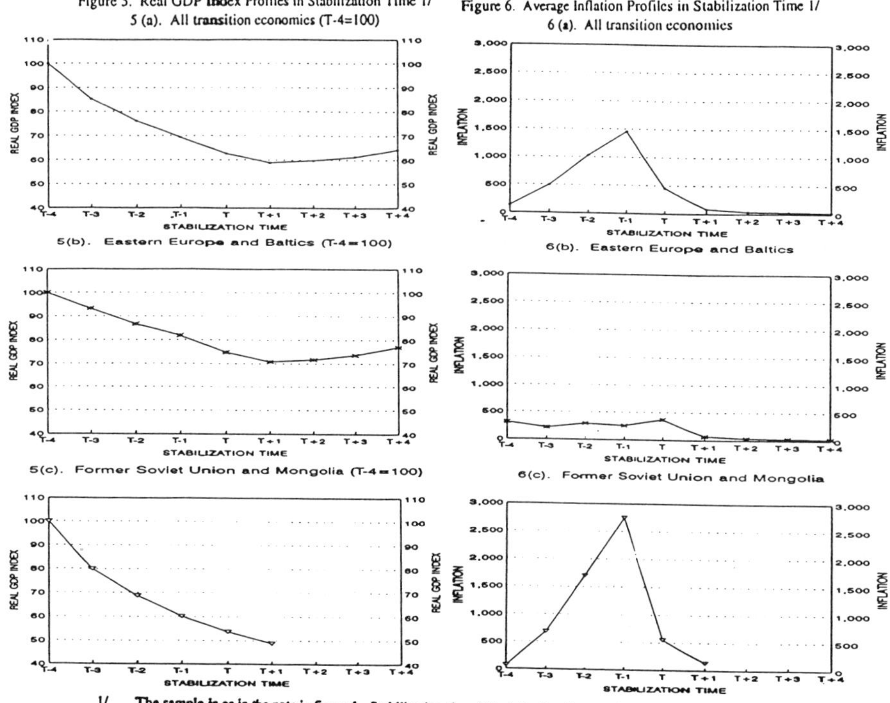

1/ The sample is as in the note in figure 1. Stabilization time T is defined as the year the stabilization programme started.

2.2 Stabilization and growth

Figures 1-3 highlight the differences between the output and inflation profiles of two groups of countries: Eastern Europe and the Baltics, and the former Soviet Union and Mongolia. In this section, we argue that one key difference between the two groups is the date in which countries started their stabilization programmes. In so doing, we will also argue that there is a typical profile of output and inflation that may be expected to develop around the time of stabilization.

As Table 4 documents, countries started their stabilization plans at different dates. According to IMF economists working on those countries, stabilization attempts have been implemented in 25 of the 26 countries, with Turkmenistan being the exception. For each country we list the date on which the stabilization programme was implemented. The date given is the starting date of a country's inflation stabilization programme, and not necessarily the starting date of an IMF programme. When several stabilization attempts have been made (which was the case in six countries), we take the most serious attempt (as of end-1995) as the reference date.[10]

The third column of Table 4 indicates the exchange rate regime adopted during the stabilization programme. Countries that announced an exchange rate peg, including a crawling peg, are classified as having a fixed rate regime. In two cases — Croatia and FYROM — the exchange rate regime is classified as a peg on the basis of the policies actually implemented, even though the authorities did not explicitly announce it as such. Several FSU countries (Armenia, Azerbaijan, Belarus, Georgia, Kazakstan, and the Kyrgyz Republic) that began their stabilization programmes under a flexible exchange rate regime had begun to peg *de facto* their currencies to the US dollar by 1995 and are listed as flexible/fixed. Latvia, Lithuania, and Russia are also listed as flexible/fixed because they had flexible rate regimes at the time of stabilization but later moved to a fixed rate.

Given that countries started their stabilization programmes at different points in chronological time, we have computed output and inflation profiles relative to the date of stabilization; that is, in "stabilization time".[11] Stabilization time is denoted by T+j, where T is the year in which the stabilization programme was implemented and j is the number of years preceding or following the year of stabilization.[12]

The shift from chronological time in Figures 1-3 to stabilization time in Figures 4-6 changes the picture dramatically. Panel (a) in Figure 4 shows large negative rates of GDP growth until the year of stabilization. Output growth then begins to recover, with GDP growth becoming positive two years after stabilization. The corresponding pattern in terms of levels is shown in panel (a) in Figure 5. Panel (a) in Figure 6 shows that inflation, in turn, peaks in the year before stabilization, falls sharply when the stabilization plan is implemented, and remains low thereafter.

Since there were systematic differences in the date of stabilization between the countries of the former Soviet Union and those of eastern Europe, the stabilization time profiles in Figures 4-6 represent a changing population of countries. In particular, the observations for T+3 and T+4 come from Eastern Europe and the Baltics, rather than from the other republics of the former Soviet Union.

We now want to examine whether the time profiles, where they overlap, are essentially similar. In Figures 4 and 5 we present output growth and level profiles in

Figure 7. Fiscal Balance Profiles (Percentage of GDP) 1/

7(a). Calendar time

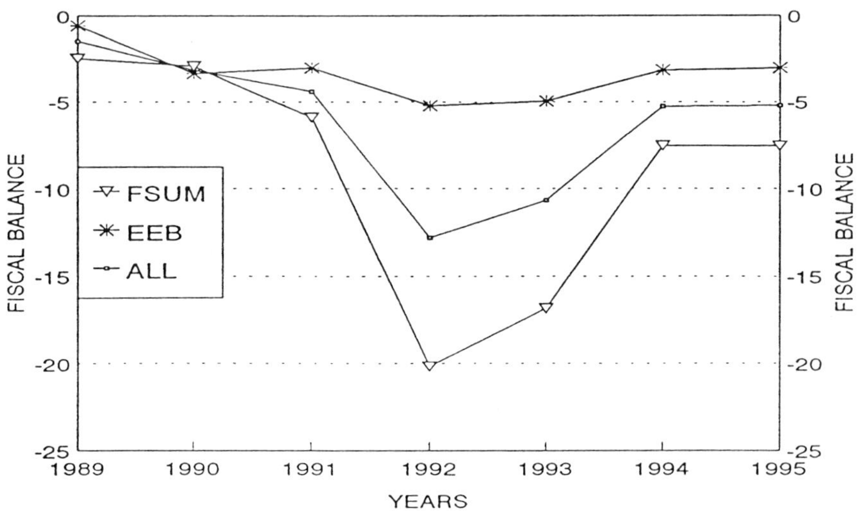

7(b). Stabilization time

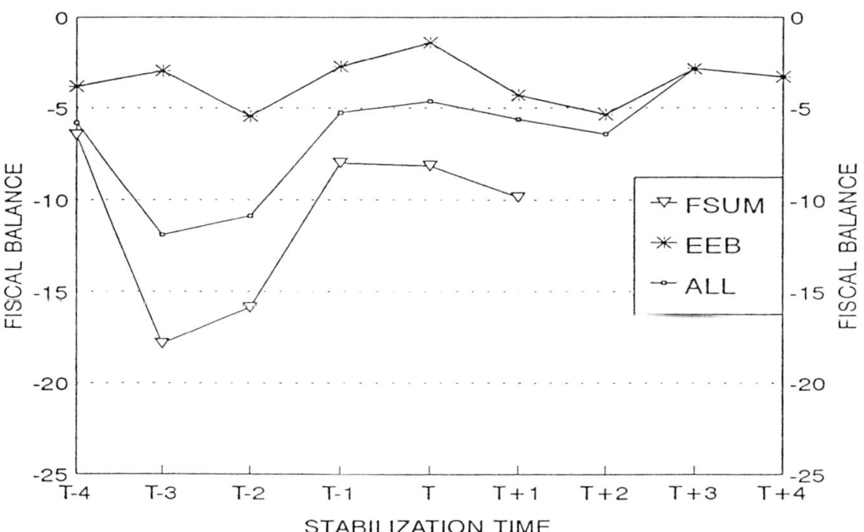

1/ The sample is as in the note in figure 1. Stabilization time T is defined as the year the stabilization programme started.

stabilization time for the two groups of countries. Growth in the EEB countries was negative and declining up to the year of stabilization [Figure 4, panel (b)]. Real GDP growth turned positive two years after stabilization. Indeed, by 1996 output has begun to grow in all these countries. Output levels for EEB are shown in Figure 5 in panel (b). For the FSUM group, panel (c) in Figures 4 and 5 show that the level of output has been declining continuously. The shape of the real GDP index profile is very similar to that for the EEB countries. Of course, average GDP for the EEB countries never fell as low as it did for the FSUM countries.

Inflation profiles in stabilization time are presented in Figure 6. The pattern shown in the different panels is similar, with inflation peaking one year before or in the year of stabilization and then declining sharply. However, inflation in the EEB economies never reached the levels that it did in the former Soviet Union. After stabilization, the average rate of inflation in EEB quickly fell below 100 per cent, and then below 50 per cent, although the scale of the chart makes this difficult to discern.

Underlying the behaviour of output and inflation are significant changes in fiscal policy. These are illustrated in Figure 7. In chronological time, for the whole sample (panel a), the deficit increased markedly until 1992, and improved afterwards. Panel (b) in Figure 7, in stabilization time, shows very large average fiscal deficits early on, followed by a significant improvement in the years leading to stabilization and, with a brief interruption, continued improvement. In stabilization time, the profiles for the two groups of countries are broadly similar, but the fiscal situation in FSUM was on average significantly worse than that in EEB. Overall, the behaviour of fiscal balances roughly mirrors the behaviour of inflation.

The simple — but essential — message that emerges from this section is that real GDP rebounds following inflation stabilization, which in turn appears highly correlated with the improvement in the public finances. We shall now seek to refine the basic story.

3. Determinants of growth and inflation in the transition

In this section we present some simple econometric evidence on the determinants of growth and inflation during the transition process. Regressions were run with the average annual rate of growth of real GDP and the logarithm of annual end-of-period inflation as the dependent variables. As explanatory variables, we included macroeconomic policies (exchange rate and fiscal policy), the extent of structural reforms, and exogenous shocks (the effects of the CMEA collapse in 1991 and the break-up of the Soviet Union in January 1992).[13]

The exchange rate regime (as listed in Table 4) is characterised by a dummy variable which takes on a value of one when the exchange rate is fixed, and zero otherwise. If the exchange rate regime changed during the sample period 1992-95 (as in some former Soviet Union countries), we adopted the procedure of assigning the value of one (zero); if the exchange rate regime was fixed (flexible) for more than six months in that year.

Table 4. Stabilization Programs in Transition Economies, 1989–95

Country	Stabilization program date	Exchange regime adopted	Pre–program inflation (12–month) 1/
Albania	August 1992	Flexible	292.6
Armenia	December 1994	Flexible/Fixed 2/	1884.5
Azerbaijan	January 1995	Flexible/Fixed 2/	1651.0
Belarus	November 1994 3/	Flexible/Fixed 2/	2179.8
Bulgaria	February 1991 3/	Flexible	244.6
Croatia	October 1993	Fixed	1902.8
Czech Republic	January 1991	Fixed	45.5
Estonia	June 1992	Fixed	1085.7
Georgia	September 1994	Flexible/Fixed 2/	56476.2
Hungary	March 1990	Fixed	26.0
Kazakhstan	January 1994	Flexible/Fixed 2/	2315.4
Kyrgyz Republic	May 1993	Flexible/Fixed 2/	934.0
Latvia	June 1992	Flexible/Fixed 4/	817.8
Lithuania	June 1992	Flexible/Fixed 4/	708.7
Macedonia, FYR	January 1994	Fixed	247.7
Moldova	September 1993	Flexible	1089.7
Mongolia	October 1992 3/	Flexible	281.6
Poland	January 1990	Fixed	1096.1
Romania	October 1993 3/	Flexible	314.3
Russia	April 1995 3/	Flexible/Fixed 4/	218.4
Slovak Republic	January 1991	Fixed	45.9
Slovenia	February 1992	Flexible	288.4
Tajikistan	February 1995 3/	Flexible	73.0
Turkmenistan	Not started	Not applicable	1906.7
Ukraine	November 1994	Flexible	645.1
Uzbekistan	November 1994	Flexible	1555.1
All transition economies 5/			840.4
Eastern Europe and Baltics 5/			547.4
FSU and Mongolia 5/			1157.8

Sources: IMF estimates; The World Bank; national authorities; De Melo, Denizer, and Gelb (1995).

1/ Inflation in the twelve months previous to the month of the stabilization program. For Turkmenistan, the figure is for the latest year available (1995).

2/ As of 1995, these countries adopted a de–facto peg to the US dollar.

3/ The date of the most serious stabilization attempt.

4/ The Latvian currency was pegged to the SDR in February 1994; Lithuania adopted a currency board in April 1994. Russia announced an exchange rate corridor in July 1995. All three countries had flexible exchange rate regimes prior to these dates.

5/ Simple averages for all variables; excludes Georgia's extreme inflation value.

The extent of structural reforms in each year was measured as an economic liberalisation index, LIBERAL (as computed by de Melo, Denizer, and Gelb (1995) for the period 1989-95 based on information presented in the 1994 and 1995 *Transition Reports*), where 0 represents an unreformed planned economy and 1 represents a fully reformed economy. This index is a weighted average of three indices: price liberalisation and competition (LII, with a weight of 0.3), trade and foreign exchange regime (LIE, with a weight of 0.3), and privatisation and banking reform (LIP, with a weight of 0.4). On the basis of the yearly liberalisation index, de Melo, Denizer, and Gelb (1995) construct a <u>cumulative</u> liberalisation index (CLI) to capture the speed and depth of reforms over the 1989-95 period. The trade disruptions caused by the break-ups of the CMEA and the Soviet Union in 1992 were summarised by a dummy variable (Y92) which takes a value of 1 for the year 1992 and 0 otherwise.

For the purpose of this econometric exercise, we considered the period 1989-95 period and thus excluded the period 1989-1991. The main reason for excluding the period 1989-1991 is that we found it difficult to characterise macroeconomic policy in more than half the countries before 1992 — namely in the former Soviet Union and Albania. In particular, it makes little sense to use the same definitions for the exchange rate regime of the pre-and post-reform period.

To carry out the econometric analysis, we pooled the cross-section and time series data for all 25 countries for four years, 1992-1995.[14] To capture fixed effects, we allowed the intercept to vary across countries. This formulation enables us to test whether there are differences across countries (presumably reflecting omitted variables), modelled as parametric shifts in the regression function.

The role of the exchange rate regime in stabilization and growth has long been a subject of controversy. A strong case can be made for using the exchange rate as a nominal anchor in reducing inflation in transition economies (Sahay and Vegh, 1996; Hansson and Sachs, 1995). This case is buttressed by the fact that exchange-rate based stabilizations have often been associated with growth rather than recession (Rebelo and Végh, 1995; Easterly, 1995). Our *a priori* expectation, therefore, was that countries with fixed exchange rate regimes would experience a quicker revival of output. We also expected growth to be lower the larger the fiscal deficit and the smaller the extent of market-oriented reforms.

While we will use our regressions for drawing lessons, we should note that causation is in some cases not self-evident. For instance, it is surely the case that growth may feed back into fiscal balances through higher revenues. We find less persuasive the argument that low inflation countries may have chosen a fixed exchange rate. In any event, good instruments are not easy to come by. Our regressions should therefore not be viewed as reflecting deep structural relations but rather as a convenient way of presenting the data. Further qualification is needed given that the data are sparse and preliminary.

Table 5 reports the regression results obtained from the fixed effects model. In all cases, country-specific effects turned out to be highly significant (using a likelihood ratio test), indicating that there were some differences across countries which are not captured by the explanatory variables. The regression results indicate that a pegged exchange rate regime, tighter fiscal policy, and most measures of structural reforms affected growth positively. Thus, we find — not surprisingly — that countries that achieved macroeconomic stabilization (through the use of fixed exchange rates and tight fiscal policy) and undertook deeper reforms are growing faster during the transition. We also found that the break-up of the CMEA and the Soviet Union had a very large negative impact on growth.

The inflation regressions strongly support the notion that a fixed exchange rate regime and lower fiscal deficits helped in quickly stabilizing high inflation. Thus, while there is little doubt that correcting the underlying fiscal imbalances is essential for the success of a stabilization programme, a strong nominal anchor appears to be

Table 5. Fixed Effects Model for 25 Transition Economies, 1992–95
(t–statistics in parenthesis)

	Dependent Variable: GDP growth							Dependent Variable: Log of inflation						
	(1)	(2)	(3)	(4)	(5)	(6)	(7)	(8)	(9)	(10)	(11)	(12)	(13)	(14)
FIXED	11.67	9.09	5.75	7.08	6.43	10.20	8.24	−2.81	−2.61	−1.93	−1.82	−1.64	−2.45	−2.07
	(3.99)	(3.40)	(1.90)	(2.15)	(1.84)	(3.27)	(2.70)	(−6.37)	(−5.90)	(−4.22)	(−3.88)	(−3.29)	(−5.32)	(−4.78)
FISCAL	0.34	0.21	0.26	0.29	0.33	0.31	0.29	−0.07	−0.06	−0.06	−0.06	−0.07	−0.06	−0.06
	(2.89)	(1.91)	(2.44)	(2.60)	(2.93)	(2.61)	(2.60)	(−3.98)	(−3.35)	(−3.63)	(−3.77)	(−4.27)	(−3.61)	(−3.77)
Y92		−8.51							0.67					
		(−4.44)							(2.13)					
CLI			4.99							−0.74				
			(4.07)							(−3.96)				
LIBERAL				30.72							−6.65			
				(2.70)							(−4.09)			
LIE					22.50							−5.01		
					(2.54)							(−3.97)		
LII						13.70							−3.31	
						(1.32)							(−2.15)	
LIP							28.78							−6.16
							(2.80)							(−4.20)
R–squared	0.62	0.70	0.69	0.66	0.65	0.63	0.66	0.74	0.76	0.79	0.79	0.79	0.76	0.79
Adjusted R–squared	0.49	0.59	0.58	0.53	0.52	0.49	0.53	0.65	0.67	0.71	0.71	0.71	0.67	0.72
Likelihood ratio	67.32	78.68	57.64	53.44	53.46	57.54	60.29	79.21	81.36	61.20	59.10	62.18	53.34	77.44
Probability value	0.000	0.000	0.000	0.001	0.001	0.000	0.000	0.000	0.000	0.000	0.000	0.000	0.001	0.000
Number of observations	100	100	100	100	100	100	100	100	100	100	100	100	100	100

an important component as well. Structural reforms have also helped in lowering inflation.

4. Growth prospects in the long-run

The previous section focused on the factors that have affected growth during the transition to a market economy. As the transformation process continues, the forces highlighted in Table 5 are likely to become less important, and will be taken over by the neo-classical determinants of growth. This section is devoted to addressing long-term growth prospects in transition economies. Given the short period of time elapsed since the transition process began, any meaningful estimation of long-term growth parameters for transition economies is precluded. Our methodology will therefore consist of drawing upon past cross-country studies of the determinants of growth to make predictions for the transition economies. Assuming that the structural relationships estimated in previous studies are robust, we predict rates of growth for the transition economies, conditional on initial conditions and various control variables (such as investment ratios and government consumption), which are taken to reflect government policies. While admittedly crude — and subject to obvious and some more subtle criticisms — we view this exercise as providing a very rough idea of the long-term growth potential of these economies.[15]

Table 6 presents information on some long-run determinants of growth for those transition economies for which a full data set was available. Data are presented for the latest available year. Thus, population growth rates are for 1993 (source: World Bank); primary and secondary school ratios are mostly for 1993, otherwise one or two years before 1993 (sources: World Bank and Krajnyak and Zettelmeyer, 1996); gross capital formation is for 1995 (sources: IMF and OECD), exports and government consumption (in per cent of GDP) for 1995 (source: IMF); and initial *per capita* income in US dollars on a purchasing power parity basis is for 1994 (sources: World Bank and IMF).

Given the data available for these countries, we predict future growth prospects using an equation of the form

$$g(t) = f(\underset{-}{Y_0}, \underset{+}{PS_0}, \underset{+}{SS_0}; \underset{+}{INV(t)}, \underset{?}{GOV(t)}, \underset{-}{POP(t)}), \qquad (1)$$

where g(t) is *per capita* growth during the time interval t, Y_0 is the *per capita* income in the starting year, PS_0 is the primary school enrolment rate (in per cent of the total primary school-aged population), SS_0 is the secondary school enrolment rate (in per cent of the total secondary school-aged population), INV(t) is gross capital formation (in per cent of GDP) during the time interval t, GOV(t) is government consumption expenditure (in per cent of GDP) during the time interval t, and POP(t) is the growth rate of the population during the time interval t.

The predicted signs from neo-classical and endogenous growth models are presented below the explanatory variables in equation (1). *Per capita* growth, g(t), is negatively related to Y_0 — this follows from the neo-classical convergence hypothesis that, *ceteris paribus*, poorer countries tend to grow faster than richer

Table 6. Factors Affecting Long-term Growth in Transition Economies

	Population Growth Rate (WB)	Primary School Enrollment (share of school age population) (WB)	Secondary School Enrollment (share of school age population) (WB, KZ)	Gross Capital Formation (share of GDP) in current prices (OECD, WEO)	Per Capita Income in US$ PPP based (WB, IMF)	Export of Goods and Services (share of GDP) in current prices (IMF)	Government Consumption Expenditure (share of GDP) in current prices (IMF)	Inflation in 1995 (period average) (IMF)
1 Albania	1.19	0.96	0.79	0.17	495	0.13	0.12	7.8
2 Azerbaijan	1.28	0.89	0.83	0.24	1720	0.41	0.13	411.7
3 Bulgaria	-0.35	0.86	0.71	0.12	4280	0.50	0.17	62.1
4 Croatia	0.06	0.87	0.80	0.10	3872	0.41	0.30	2.0
5 Czech Rep.	-0.06	0.99	0.89	0.31	7940	0.52	0.20	9.1
6 Estonia	-0.31	0.83	0.92	0.30	6634	0.68	0.21	28.3
7 Hungary	-0.53	0.94	0.81	0.23	7010	0.32	0.10	28.2
8 Latvia	-0.53	0.83	0.92	0.18	5170	0.41	0.20	25.1
9 FYROM	1.12	0.87	0.80	0.38	1604	0.45	0.14	17.4
10 Moldova	0.41	0.77	0.81	0.12	2270	0.44	0.23	30.2
11 Poland	0.20	0.98	0.83	0.16	5480	0.27	0.18	27.8
12 Romania	0.19	0.86	0.80	0.30	2950	0.28	0.14	32.0
13 Russia	0.55	1.07	0.92	0.26	4510	0.22	0.17	190.2
14 Slovak Rep.	0.35	1.01	0.96	0.22	6730	0.65	0.20	9.9
15 Slovenia	0.41	0.97	0.80	0.25	5982	0.54	0.20	12.8
Average	0.26	0.91	0.84	0.22	4443	0.42	0.18	59.6

Sources: International Monetary Fund (IMF), The World Bank (WB), Organisation for Economic Co-operation and Development (OECD), and Krajnyak and Zettelmeyer (KZ, 1996).

ones. The primary and secondary school enrolment ratios represent investment in human capital. Countries investing more in human capital tend to grow faster (see Romer, 1990; Grossman and Helpman, 1991). Higher physical investment ratios also increase the growth rate. There is no consensus in the empirical literature regarding the effects of government consumption on growth (for contrasting results, see Ram, 1986 and Levine and Renelt, 1992). The impact on growth should depend on the type of government spending, as well as on the distortions associated with its financing. Some growth models with endogenous population growth predict that *per capita* income and population growth rates should move inversely because higher population growth rates imply that a larger amount of time is spent in raising children than in other productive activities.

Referring back to the basic data in Table 6, the PPP-based *per capita* income (in US dollars) varies widely across countries, with Albania at the low end of the spectrum and the Czech Republic at the other extreme. In 1994, all countries were well below the OECD country average of US$18 602. The average *per capita* income (US$4 443) is also low from a global perspective — by World Bank (1996) standards these are lower-middle income economies. Given the relatively low initial *per capita* incomes, the convergence hypothesis predicts a relatively faster rate of growth in the future.

The most striking features in Table 6 are the extremely high primary and secondary school enrolment ratios. Other things being equal, these ratios imply a higher growth potential. However, despite the high level of basic education existing in most of the transition economies, further human capital investment is required to provide retraining in market-based institutions, build entrepreneurial skills, and ensure technological innovation and adaptation.[16]

The latest available information on gross capital formation indicates that the average in 1994 stood at 22 per cent of GDP, and that there was a wide variation across countries. While this average figure is comparable to the one prevailing in the industrial countries during the period 1950-73, it is low compared to the average of 30 per cent for the fast growing economies during the period 1985-94.[17]

Government consumption in most countries declined sharply from a level of 50-60 per cent of GDP at the start of the transformation process, to an average level of 18 per cent in 1995.[18] While government consumption at the previous rates was not sustainable and must have affected growth negatively, it is becoming increasingly clear that sharp reductions in expenditures on the scale seen in some of

Table 7. Transition Economies in a Global Perspective

Variable	Fast-growers	Slow-growers	Transition economies in 1995 1/
Primary-school enrollment rate (in 1960)	0.90	0.54	0.91
Secondary-school enrollment rate (in 1960)	0.30	0.10	0.84
Share of investment in GDP (during 1960-89)	0.23	0.17	0.22
Government consumption/GDP (during 1960-89)	0.16	0.12	0.18
Share of exports to GDP (during 1960-89)	0.32	0.23	0.42
Annual inflation rate (during 1960-89)	12.3	31.1	59.6

Source: Levine and Renelt (1992) and Table 6.
1/ Average for 15 transition economies.

Table 8. Forecasting Long-Term Trend Growth (Barro)

	Population Growth Rate (WB)	Primary School Enrollment (share of school age population) (WB)	Secondary School Enrollment (share of school age population) (WB,KZ)	Per Capita Income in US$ PPP based (WB,IMF)	Government Consumption Expenditure (share of GDP) in current prices (IMF)	Forecasted Per Capita Growth Rate	Forecasted Growth Rate
1 Albania	1.19	0.96	0.79	495	0.12	6.91	8.09
2 Azerbaijan	1.28	0.89	0.83	1720	0.13	5.77	7.05
3 Bulgaria	-0.35	0.86	0.71	4280	0.17	4.28	3.93
4 Croatia	0.06	0.87	0.80	3872	0.30	3.08	3.14
5 Czech Republic	-0.06	0.99	0.89	7940	0.20	4.24	4.18
6 Estonia	-0.31	0.83	0.92	6634	0.21	3.98	3.67
7 Hungary	-0.53	0.94	0.81	7010	0.10	5.15	4.62
8 Latvia	-0.53	0.83	0.92	5170	0.20	4.27	3.75
9 Macedonia, FYR	1.12	0.87	0.80	1604	0.14	5.61	6.72
10 Moldova	0.41	0.77	0.81	2270	0.23	4.10	4.51
11 Poland	0.20	0.98	0.83	5480	0.18	4.59	4.79
12 Romania	0.19	0.86	0.80	2950	0.14	5.16	5.35
13 Russia	0.55	1.07	0.92	4510	0.17	5.32	5.87
14 Slovak Republic	0.35	1.01	0.96	6730	0.20	4.66	5.00
15 Slovenia	0.41	0.97	0.80	5982	0.20	4.16	4.57
Averages	0.26	0.91	0.839	4443	0.18	4.75	5.02

Sources: International Monetary Fund (IMF), The World Bank (WB), Organisation for Economic Co-operation and Development (OECD), and Krajnyak and Zettelmeyer (KZ,1996).

the transition economies may be adversely affecting the reform process (see, for example, Haque and Sahay, 1996). Involuntary expenditure compression, sequestration, and a build-up of arrears have often resulted from the sharp revenue declines and the need to reduce budget deficits for various reasons (including stabilization, see Cheasty and Davis, 1996). Indeed, it is likely that growth would be enhanced by more public spending on building market-based institutions, improving the quality of government administration, and setting up a social safety net.[19]

Population growth rates in the transition economies are low, and in many cases negative. As the extensive state support system for dependants, particularly children, is reduced, we would expect a further decline in population growth rates. According to equation (1), this means higher *per capita* growth. However, it is also likely that population growth rates will recover once the economic prospects for individuals in these economies become less uncertain.

Table 7 provides preliminary insights on the growth potential in transition economies by comparing key determinants of growth with past averages for slow and fast-growing countries presented in Levine and Renelt (1992). Again, human capital indicators are extremely favourable and so is the degree of openness of the economies. The inflation rate in 1995 was still quite high (and much higher than the average for both sub-groups) but given current stabilization policies, we can expect the recent trend of rapid decline in inflation rates to continue.[20]

To project long-term growth in transition economies, we used the equations estimated by Barro (1991) and Levine and Renelt (1992).[21] Tables 8, 9, and 10 present our simulation results under alternative specifications. These are:

Barro growth equation:

$$\textit{per capita}\text{ growth} = 0.0302^* - 0.0075^*\, Y_{1960} + 0.025^*\, \text{PRIM} + 0.0305^*\, \text{SEC} - 0.119^*\, \text{GOV} \quad (2)$$

Levine and Renelt growth equation:

$$\text{per capita growth} = -\,0.83 - 0.35^*\, Y_{1960} - 0.38\, \text{POP} + 3.17^*\, \text{SEC} + 17.5^*\, \text{INV} \quad (3)$$

Here Y_{1960} is the initial level of real per capita income at international prices (expressed in logs in the Barro equation and divided by 1000 in the Levine-Renelt equation), POP is the growth rate of population, PRIM is the gross primary school enrolment rate, SEC is the gross secondary school enrolment rate, GOV is the share of government consumption expenditure in GDP, and INV is the share of investment in GDP. (The stars next to the estimated coefficients indicate that they are significant at least at the 5 per cent level.)

The average per capita growth rates forecasted by Barro's and Levine-Renelt's equations are fairly close — between 4 and 5 per cent per annum (Tables 8 and 9). The most optimistic scenario, not surprisingly, is obtained by using the Barro equation (Table 8), which gives a relatively high weight to the human capital variables. The projected average per-capita growth rate is 4.75 per cent, with all countries within the range of 3-7 per cent. In the simulation based on the Levine and Renelt equation (Table 9), the per-capita growth rate falls to about 4 per cent. The relative per-capita growth rates of the countries also change; for example, Albania's growth rate declines from 7 per cent to about 4 per cent, while Estonia's

Table 9. Forecasting long-term trend growth (Levine-Renelt)

	Population Growth Rate	Secondary School Enrollment (share school age population) (WB, KZ)	Gross Capital Formation (share of GDP) in current prices (OECD, WEO)	Per Capita Income in US$ PPP based (WB, IMF)	Forecasted Per Capita Growth Rate	Forecasted Growth Rate
1 Albania	1.19	0.79	0.17	495	4.08	5.27
2 Azerbaijan	1.28	0.83	0.24	1720	4.83	6.10
3 Bulgaria	-0.35	0.71	0.12	4280	2.16	1.80
4 Croatia	0.06	0.80	0.10	3872	1.99	2.06
5 Czech Rep.	-0.06	0.89	0.31	7940	4.66	4.60
6 Estonia	-0.31	0.92	0.30	6634	5.18	4.86
7 Hungary	-0.53	0.81	0.23	7010	3.51	2.98
8 Latvia	-0.53	0.92	0.18	5170	3.63	3.10
9 FYROM	1.12	0.80	0.38	1604	7.28	8.40
10 Moldova	0.41	0.81	0.12	2270	2.94	3.35
11 Poland	0.20	0.83	0.16	5480	2.59	2.79
12 Romania	0.19	0.80	0.30	2950	5.80	5.99
13 Russia	0.55	0.92	0.26	4510	4.83	5.38
14 Slovak Rep.	0.35	0.96	0.22	6730	3.63	3.98
15 Slovenia	0.41	0.80	0.25	5982	3.78	4.19
Average	0.26	0.84	0.22	4443	4.06	4.32

Sources: International Monetary Fund (IMF), The World Bank (WB), Organisation for Economic Co-operation and Development (OECD), and Krajnyak and Zettelmeyer (KZ, 1996).

ranking rises sharply. The main force that brings about this difference is the inclusion of investment in Levine and Renelt but not in Barro.[22]

Based on initial per capita income and the projected growth rates, Table 10 indicates the number of years it would take for each of these economies to reach the current average per-capita income of the OECD. Given initial conditions and current economic policies, it would take on average 35 years using the Barro regression and 45 years according to the Levine and Renelt equation. The best-placed countries appear to be the Czech Republic and Estonia, which would converge in around 20-25 years according to both regressions.

We set out policy implications in Table 10, by asking how the long-term average per capita growth would be affected if investments rates were raised and government consumption reduced in the future. The results suggest that changes in investment ratios would have significant implications for long-term growth. For instance, under the Levine-Renelt specification, the number of years to reach current OECD levels declines from 45 years to 30 years as investment rates rise by eight percentage points from 22 per cent to 30 per cent), on average. The effects of reducing government expenditure by 8 percentage points (from 18 per cent to 10 per cent in the Barro equation) are less noticeable, with the number of years to reach OECD levels declining by only six years.

This simple exercise thus suggests that the key to rapid growth in the transition economies is adopting policies that promote investment. It should be noted, however, that particular attention should be given to the quality of investment.

Table 10. Forecasting GDP convergence to OECD countries

	Per Capita Income in US$ (PPP based) (WB, IMF:1994)	Barro				Levine– Renelt			
		At current government consumption rates		Government consumption =10 percent (in percent of GDP)		At current investment rates		Investment =30 percent (in percent of GDP)	
		Forecasted Per Capita Growth	Number of years to reach current OECD levels	Forecasted Per Capita Growth	Number of years to reach current OECD levels	Forecasted Per Capita Growth	Number of years to reach current OECD levels	Forecasted Per Capita Growth	Number of years to reach current OECD levels
1 Albania	495	6.91	54	7.17	52	4.08	91	6.30	59
2 Azerbaijan	1720	5.77	42	6.18	40	4.83	51	5.96	41
3 Bulgaria	4280	4.28	35	5.06	30	2.16	69	5.31	28
4 Croatia	3872	3.08	52	5.43	30	1.99	80	5.58	29
5 Czech Republic	7940	4.24	20	5.47	16	4.66	19	4.48	19
6 Estonia	6634	3.98	26	5.29	20	5.18	20	5.13	21
7 Hungary	7010	5.15	19	5.19	19	3.51	28	4.74	21
8 Latvia	5170	4.27	31	5.48	24	3.63	36	5.73	23
9 Macedonia, FYR	1604	5.61	45	6.09	41	7.28	35	5.97	42
10 Moldova	2270	4.10	52	5.61	39	2.94	73	6.04	36
11 Poland	5480	4.59	27	5.54	23	2.59	48	5.06	25
12 Romania	2950	5.16	37	5.61	34	5.80	33	5.85	32
13 Russia	4510	5.32	27	6.18	24	4.83	30	5.55	26
14 Slovak Republic	6730	4.66	22	5.85	18	3.63	29	4.98	21
15 Slovenia	5982	4.16	28	5.35	22	3.78	31	4.71	25
Average for transition	4443	4.75	35	5.70	29	4.06	45	5.43	30
OECD average (1994)	18602	Not applicable				Not applicable			

While many of the transition economies have traditionally had high investment ratios, the efficiency of the capital stock has typically been low. Hence, policies should focus not only on increasing the level of investment, but also in improving its efficiency.

Finally, it should be stressed that the projections have abstracted from some potentially very important external, political, and institutional factors. While such factors are hard to assess quantitatively (even in the existing growth literature), they are likely to have an important influence on the growth process.

5. Concluding remarks

This paper has analysed the growth and inflation performance of the transition economies and given a rough idea of their long-term growth potential. While it is clear that the costs of the transition have been high (even adjusting for data problems), the goods news is that the worst appears to be over, and all but seven transition economies in our sample had begun to grow by 1996. While admittedly crude, projections based on standard growth regressions suggest that it will take around 20 years for the faster reformers to reach current OECD per-capita income levels.

Many of the transition economies have moved rapidly on several of the necessary fronts, particularly in liberalising the price, foreign exchange and trade regimes. In most economies, privatisation of state enterprises is still far from complete and the banking system is under severe strain. Under these conditions, benefits from properly directed government spending on reforms and from foreign direct investment in enhancing human and physical capital are potentially large. While not all transition economies are equally well-placed, the starting conditions are favourable in most countries. Policies will make all the difference.

Notes

[1] We believe this to be true even taking account of data imperfections that generally overstate the decline of output.

[2] Aslund, Boone, and Johnson (1996) make a convincing case that reformers have done well at the polls.

[3] To the extent possible, we will make the presentation self-contained, referring to previous results in footnotes.

[4] See Fischer, Sahay, and Végh (1996a) for details on data definitions, sources, and limitations.

[5] Data for China and the Indochinese economies in transition are not included in this study.

[6] Kaufmann and Kaliberda (1995) construct estimates of output that draw, among other variables, on electricity consumption. They conclude that the overall GDP decline during 1989-94 was 17 per cent in CEE and 33.4 per cent in the former Soviet Union.

[7] Sachs (1996) makes the case that a substantial and co-ordinated aid effort in 1992 would have made the Russian reform process much more successful.

[8] Inflation in these countries would have met the classic Cagan definition of hyperinflation, more than 50 per cent per month. Serbia, for which we do not have complete data, also suffered from hyperinflation.

[9] For reasons explained later, Turkmenistan is excluded from the time profiles.

[10] The choice of a particular stabilization date, when there have been multiple attempts, necessarily requires a judgement call. We have tried to make this judgement on the basis of the policy package associated with the stabilization attempt, rather than on *ex post* inflation performance.

[11] Of the 26 countries in the sample, Turkmenistan was excluded in computing profiles in stabilization time because there has been no stabilization attempt as of end-1995.

[12] The number of observations for each year in stabilization time is likely to differ (see Fischer, Sahay, and Vegh (1996a) for details). For the purposes of the time profiles shown in the paper, we report averages only for those years in stabilization time for which there are at least three observations.

[13] See Fischer, Sahay, and Végh (1995a) for details on data definitions and methodology.

[14] To be specific, the estimated equation for the pooled cross-section time-series regressions takes the form:

$$DEPVAR_{it} = \alpha_i + \beta_1 FIXED_{it} + \beta_2 FISCAL_{it} + \beta_3 CLI_{it} \text{ (or } \beta_4 LIBERAL_{it} \text{ or } \beta_5 LIE_{it} \text{ or } \beta_6 LII_{it} \text{ or } \beta_7 LIP_{it}) + \beta_8 Y92_{it} + u_{it},$$

where DEPVAR is GDP growth, as defined above; i (=1,..25) indexes the country; t (=1992, 1993, 1994, 1995) indexes time; and u is an error term assumed to be i.i.d over i and t and uncorrelated with the explanatory variables. FIXED is the exchange rate dummy; FISCAL is the government balance variable (thus, a fiscal deficit takes on a negative value); CLI is the cumulative value of the liberalisation index; LIBERAL is the value of the weighted liberalisation index; LIE is the liberalisation index for trade and foreign exchange regime; LII is the liberalisation index for price and competition; LIP is the liberalisation index for privatisation and banking reform; and Y92 is the time dummy for 1992.

[15] In addition, these rates of growth should be viewed as a long-term average. Based on neo-classical growth theory, one should expect that the initial growth rates would be higher than these averages and then decrease over time as they converge to OECD levels.

[16] Despite consistently high human capital indicators, Easterly and Fischer (1994) show that a leading cause of economic decline in the former Soviet Union was the low elasticity of substitution between capital and labour, which they argue were in part explained by lack of entrepreneurial skills and the slow adaptation to imported technological progress.

[17] This group of countries includes Chile, Hong Kong, Korea (South), Malaysia, Mauritius, Singapore, Taiwan Province of China, and Thailand (based on the IMF's World Economic Outlook database).

[18] We have to repeat the standard warning on data: data on gross capital formation as well as on government consumption are subject to a wide margin of error, primarily because the demand-based UN system of national income accounting is still at a very rudimentary stage in most of these countries.

[19] Keefer and Knack (1995) present empirical evidence from cross-country growth regressions that point to the positive impact on growth of better institutions.

[20] See Fischer (1993) for evidence that inflation is negatively associated with growth.

[21] We chose these equations both because they are widely quoted and because it was relatively straightforward to obtain data for the transition economies matching the right-hand side variables in the Barro (1991) and Levine and Renelt (1992) regressions.

[22] It should be noted that the projections are very sensitive to current policies (in particular investment ratios). Since investment ratios may differ quite a bit from year to year, the scenario below which assumes a uniform rate of investment of 30 per cent of GDP may convey a better, if optimistic, picture.

References

Aslund, Anders, Peter Boone and Simon Johnson, 1996, "How to Stabilize: Lessons from Post-Communist Countries", prepared for the Brookings Panel on Economic Activity, March 28-29.

Barro, Robert J., 1991, "Economic Growth in a Cross-Section of Countries", *Quarterly Journal of Economics*, Vol. 106, pp. 407-443.

Barro, Robert J. and Jong-Wha Lee, 1993, "International Comparisons for Educational Attainment", *Journal of Monetary Economics*, Vol. 32, pp. 363-394.

Cheasty, Adrienne and Jeffrey Davis, 1996, "Fiscal Transition in Countries of the Former Soviet Union: An Interim Assessment", mimeo, International Monetary Fund.

De Melo, Martha, Cevdet Denizer and Alan Gelb, 1996, "From Plan to Market: Patterns of Transition", mimeo, World Bank.

Easterly, William, "When is Stabilization Expansionary?", mimeo, World Bank, 1995, forthcoming in *Economic Policy*.

Easterly, William and Stanley Fischer, 1994, "The Soviet Economic Decline: Historical and Republican Data", mimeo, World Bank, March.

European Bank for Reconstruction and Development, 1994, *Transition Report*, London: EBRD, October.

European Bank for Reconstruction and Development, 1995, *Transition Report Update*, London: EBRD, April.

Fischer, Stanley, 1993, "The Role of Macroeconomic Factors in Growth", *Journal of Monetary Economics*, Vol. 32, pp. 485-512.

Fischer, Stanley, Ratna Sahay and Carlos A. Végh, 1996a, "Stabilization and Growth in Transition Economies: The Early Experience", *Journal of Economic Perspectives*, Vol. 10, Spring 1996, pp. 45-66.

Fischer, Stanley, Ratna Sahay and Carlos A. Végh, 1996b, "Economies in Transition: The Beginnings of Growth", *American Economic Review*, Papers and Proceedings, Vol. 86, pp. 229-233.

Grossman, Gene M. and Elhanan Helpman, 1991, *Innovation and Growth in the Global Economy*, Cambridge, MA, MIT Press.

Haque, Nadeem Ul and Ratna Sahay, "Do Government Wage Cuts Close Budget Deficits? — A Conceptual Framework for Developing Countries and Transition Economies", IMF Working Paper 96/19, forthcoming in *IMF Staff Papers*.

Hansson, Ardo and Jeffrey Sachs, 1994, "Monetary Institutions and Credible Stabilization: A Comparison of Experience in the Baltics," mimeo, Harvard University.

Kaufmann, Daniel and Aleksander Kaliberda, 1995, "Integrating the Unofficial Economy into the Dynamics of Post-Socialist Economies: A Framework of Analysis and Evidence", mimeo, World Bank Kyiv office.

Krajnyak, Kornelia and Jeromin Zettelmeyer, 1996, "Competitiveness in Transition Economies", mimeo, International Monetary Fund.

Levine, Ross and David Renelt, 1992, "A Sensitivity Analysis of Cross-Country Growth Regressions", *American Economic Review*, Vol. 82, pp. 942-63.

OECD/CCET, 1996, *Short-term Economic Indicators: Transition Economies*, 1/1996.

Ram, Rati, 1986, "Wagner's Hypothesis in Time Series and Cross-Section Perspectives: Evidence from 'Real' Data for 155 Countries", *Review of Economics and Statistics*, pp. 194-204.

Rebelo, Sergio and Carlos A. Végh, 1995, "Real Effects of Exchange Rate-Based Stabilization: An Analysis of Competing Theories", *NBER Macroeconomics Annual*, 125-174.

Romer, Paul M., 1990, "Endogenous Technological Change", *Journal of Political Economy*, Vol. 98, pp. S71-S102.

Sachs, Jeffrey, 1996, "It Could Have Been So Much Better", *Moscow Times*, May 6.

Sahay, Ratna and Carlos A. Végh, 1996, "Inflation and Stabilization in Transition Economies: An Analytical Interpretation of the Evidence", *Journal of Policy Reform*, Vol. 1 , pp. 75-108.

World Bank, 1996, *The World Bank Atlas*.

5

Lessons to be drawn from main mistakes in the transition strategy

Kazimierz Laski

in co-operation with
Amit Bhaduri

Indeed there seems to be a certain instant attraction between the old ideologues of the left and the ideologues of the right. Both are driven by religious fervour, not rational analysis. As many of the ideologues have rejected the Marxian ideology, they have adopted the ideology of free markets.

Joseph E. Stiglitz (1994)

Let us start our analysis by asking a simple counter-factual question: would the overall transition strategy be the same if the command economy had happened to collapse 20 years earlier? Nobody knows the answer, but we guess that the strategy would be different from the one followed since 1990. Most probably, it would not be concerned almost exclusively with the supply side and not simply assume that full employment depends basically on the wage level. It would also most probably not assume that prices depend directly on the quantity of money and budget deficits. Last but not least, it would most probably not assume that state failures loom larger than market failures and would therefore not require a minimal role for the state in economic matters. At the beginning of the 1970s, the experience of the successful policy of rebuilding market economies after the second World War in Europe was still fresh in people's minds. Of course, that policy also aimed at getting rid of post-war hyperinflation, but it did not forget that its ultimate goal was to put idle resources to use, and to shift them from less productive to more productive activities. That policy involved government guidance and planning because it did not share the belief that spontaneous market forces alone would take care of post-war reconstruction and of unemployment by creating jobs for everybody.

The overall transition of the 1990s did not correspond to our guesses; it has been moulded by the economic ideas prevailing in the last 20 years. These ideas find perhaps their best expression in the overall principle that by controlling the proper value of some crucial *financial* variables, the government can decisively influence the *real* economic variables. More specifically, the necessary and sufficient elements of a sound macroeconomic policy are a balanced state budget (or at least declining levels of budget deficits on the way to this goal), which is considered the responsibility of fiscal policy, and a low level of inflation as well as a stable level of the exchange rate, which is considered the responsibility of monetary policy. It is explicitly or implicitly assumed that, if only these conditions are respected, full employment with satisfactory economic growth can be ensured in the long run. As a result, economic management is limited to the management of these financial variables. From this perspective, the fact that in the Maastricht criteria there is no explicit mention of the employment level is not a coincidence; it is a direct consequence of the assumed primacy of financial over real economic variables.

We shall argue in this paper that most mistakes in the transition strategy of the 1990s can be traced to such a prevailing economic perspective. Important elements of economic theory have been disregarded only because they have gone out of fashion in this new orthodoxy. Although the transition strategy was more or less uniform in the whole area, we concentrate our analysis on the Central and Eastern European countries (CEECs); we disregard the post-Soviet countries because they are characterised by some special features related to an empire breaking down. We shall argue in Section 1 that the role of aggregate demand in the general transformation strategy has been almost entirely ignored; in the following Section 2, we shall show that the persistent inflation in the transforming countries is of a cost-push rather than of a demand-pull type, with different policy implications. Finally, in Section 3 we reconsider the role of the state in the transformation process.

1. The significance of demand management

We start by repeating some well-known relations regarding how aggregate demand is formed. We assume that investment decisions (made in real terms) precede in time investment undertaken in a given period. Since investment and savings of a given period are *ex post* identical, it follows that investment of a given period, being determined by previous investment decisions, cannot be determined by savings of the same period. Consequently, investment must causally determine savings and not *vice versa*. Nevertheless, savings are of the utmost importance, particularly in the form of retained profits, as a factor influencing future investment, but this fact should not be confused with the causal determination of savings by investment in a given period.

Extending the equality between investment and savings in an open economy with some economic role for the government we get the general equation,

$$SP = IP + D + E \qquad (1)$$

where IP is private (gross) investment of the business sector;

$D = G - T$ is the budget deficit, being the difference between G, government expenditure for goods and services, and T, government revenue from all kinds of taxes including social security payments;

$E = X - M$ is the trade surplus being the difference between exports X and imports M of goods and non-factor services; and

SP is private (gross) savings of individual households plus undistributed profits.

According to (1), it is the sum of private investment plus budget deficit plus trade surplus which determines private savings SP and not *vice versa.* The link between SP and GDP is given by the private propensity to save, defined as the ratio between SP and GDP, i.e. s = SP/GDP so that (1) becomes

$$GDP = (1/s)SP = (1/s)\ [(IP + D + E)]. \qquad (2)$$

If s is a constant in (2), we get

$$\Delta(GDP) = (1/s)\Delta(SP) = [\Delta(IP) + \Delta D + \Delta E] \quad (3)$$

while allowing for changes in s,

$$\Delta(GDP) = (GDP)[g(SP) - gs]/(1 + gs) \qquad (4)$$

where g(SP) and gs denote the rate of growth of SP and s, respectively (i.e. g represents the operator for proportional change of a variable).

From a broad macroeconomic perspective, the command economies were supply-constrained shortage economies, where both the level and the pattern of demand kept continuously ahead of supply. As a result, compression of demand became unavoidable at the initial stages of transition, as these economies struggled to move from the supply-determined logic of central planning to the logic of the demand-determined market-oriented system. Consequently, aggregate demand assumed an important role during the process of transition. And yet, the role of demand was underestimated in almost every case of "shock therapy" in so far as demand contraction was an "overkill" in two respects. The reduction in the *level* of demand went considerably beyond what was necessary. Moreover, it continued for a longer period of *time* than was necessary. The underlying theoretical reasons for this mistake need to be appreciated. They are to be found in the monetarist doctrine that strongly influenced the design of shock therapy. It postulated wrongly that reducing demand through such methods as domestic credit restriction and reduction of government budget deficit affects almost exclusively prices, but not quantities supplied.[1] Thus, inflation all along has been fought by compressing demand, while almost no attention has been paid to the fact that lower aggregate demand would also reduce aggregate supply, i.e. the level of economic activity in the process. Aggregate demand and aggregate supply management are *not* independent variables; indeed, they are highly interdependent, and the designers of the transformation strategy should have recognised this interdependence from the beginning. For instance, a reduction in the "money" supply not only reduces prices, but also quantities, even if the velocity of circulation remains a quasi-constant.

In order to emphasize the practical consequences of this theoretical mistake in policy design, we present in Table 1 the changes in the composition of aggregate output registered during the first five years of the transformation in CEECs. Because of difficulties in obtaining reliable, more detailed, statistical data on the structure of government expenditure, we use a shortened version of equation (1). Taking into account that budget deficit D is equal to the difference between government investment IG and government savings SG (which, in turn, is defined as the difference T – CG, where CG denotes government consumption) we get from (1)

$$SP + SG = IP + IG + E$$

or $\quad SD = ID + E \quad (5)$

where $\quad$ SD = SP + SG denotes domestic savings, and

ID = IP + IG denotes domestic investment (gross capital formation).

From Table 1 we learn that in all transition countries, gross capital formation ID, the largest part of domestic savings, declined strongly. Also GDP showed a strong fall in all countries. However, GDP declined less than in proportion to ID because the domestic savings ratio SD/GDP also declined. As a matter of fact, this decline in savings propensity softened the decline in GDP caused by the sharp reduction of gross capital formation. In other words, had the domestic savings ratio been constant, the depth of the transformational recession would have been even greater. In all the countries considered in Table 1, the decline of ID and GDP hit the bottom of recession around 1991-93 before the process of growth restarted. However, it should be stressed that in the period under consideration, ID and GDP had not yet reached the pre-transformation level. In most cases the reversal in the direction of change in both ID and GDP occurred at the same time, demonstrating the leading role of gross capital formation in determining the size of aggregate demand. As far as the domestic savings ratio is concerned, we observe in most cases some stabilization of this ratio at about the end of the period under consideration, however, at a level below its initial value.

The other component of domestic savings in equation (5), the trade surplus E, behaves in most countries counter-cyclically; indeed, it is partly an endogenous

Table 1. Domestic savings (SD), gross capital formation (ID) and trade surplus (E) in relation to GDP, in %, at current prices, and GDP, gross capital formation (ID) and gross fixed capital formation (IDF) indices, at constant prices.

		SD/GDP	ID/GDP	E/GDP	GDP	ID	IDF
Bulgaria							
	1989	32.9[a]	33.1[a]	-0.2[a]	100.0	100.0	100.0
	1990	26.0	30.4	0.5	90.9	74.9	81.5
	1991	26.9	22.6	4.3	80.3	63.2	65.3
	1992	14.1	19.9	-5.8	74.4	56.2	60.5
	1993	7.7	15.3	-7.6	73.3	44.9	50.0
	1994	12.5	13.1	-0.6	74.6	40.3	50.5
Czech Republic							
	1989	30.6[a]	26.8[a]	3.8[a]	100.0	100.0	100.0
	1990	29.9	28.6	1.3	98.9	103.7	97.9
	1991	36.7	29.9	6.8	84.7	88.2	80.5
	1992	27.4	27.1	0.4	79.3	72.7	87.7
	1993	20.2	18.0	2.2	78.6	71.1	81.0
	1994	20.1	20.5	-0.4	80.6	86.8	95.0
Hungary							
	1989	29.9[a]	26.6[a]	3.3[a]	100.0	100.0	100.0
	1990	28.0	25.4	2.6	96.5	95.8	92.9
	1991	19.5	20.5	-1.0	85.0	75.6	83.2
	1992	15.8	16.1	-0.3	82.4	59.2	80.9
	1993	11.8	20.0	-8.2	81.9	80.2	82.3
	1994	15.7	22.2	-6.5	84.3	93.3	92.3
Poland							
	1989	42.3[a]	38.5[a b]	100.0	100.0	100.0	100.0
	1990	32.8	25.6	7.1	88.4	75.2	89.4
	1991	18.0	19.9	-1.9	82.3	60.1	85.5
	1992	16.7	15.2	1.5	84.4	52.3	87.4
	1993	16.5	15.6	1.0	87.6	59.0	89.9
	1994	16.9	15.9	1.0	92.1	64.3	98.2

Table 1. (cont.)

	SD/GDP	ID/GDP	E/GDP	GDP	ID	IDF
Romania						
1989	29.5	26.8	2.7	100.0	.	100.0
1990	20.8	30.3	-9.5	94.4	.	64.5
1991	24.1	28.0	-3.9	82.2	.	44.1
1992	23.0	31.4	-8.4	75.1	.	48.9
1993	24.0	29.0	-5.0	76.1	.	52.9
1994	24.9	26.9	-2.1	79.1	.	63.5
Slovak Republic						
1989	28.5[a]	29.7[a]	-1.2[a]	100.0	.	
1990	24.2	33.5	-9.2[a]	97.5	.	
1991	28.3	35.1	-6.9[a]	83.4	.	
1992	23.3	26.5	-4.5[e]	77.9	.	100.0[c]
1993	16.4	21.9	-6.0[e]	75.1	.	84.0
1994	19.4	17.1	6.1[e]	78.7	.	80.8
Slovenia						
1989	.	.	.	100.0	.	.
1990	34.0	16.8	15.7[e]	95.3	.	100.0[d]
1991	29.5	15.6	12.2[e]	87.6	.	85.2
1992	27.5	17.1	9.1[e]	82.9	.	72.5
1993	24.1	19.1	3.0[e]	83.9	.	83.4
1994	27.8	20.7	5.0[e]	88.4	.	98.6

a) Estimated; b) Including changes in inventories at the incredible level of 22.1 per cent of GDP; c) Data starting from 1992; d) Data starting from 1990; e) Including statistical error.
Source: WIIW database.

variable that adjusts as a consequence of changes in the level of income and economic activity. Thus, E increases in a slump, because imports decline, and decreases when the process of growth restarts with higher imports. But of course, other factors also influence the trade surplus.

The budget deficit D is, even to a higher degree than the trade surplus E, an endogenous variable. It happens to increase when GDP declines because government revenues decline and government social expenditures increase. For the opposite reasons, the budget deficit tends to decrease when the process of growth restarts. The partly endogenous character of D makes the budget deficit somewhat inappropriate as a major instrument of stabilization policy.

Let us assume that a country is confronted at the same time with a budget deficit D ($D > 0$) and a significant import surplus $-E$ ($E < 0$), which it cannot sustain. In this situation it is often argued that by reducing the internal gap (between government expenditures and revenues), mostly by reducing government consumer expenditure (i.e., by increasing government savings), the external gap (between export revenues and import expenditures) can also be reduced. In other words, increased government savings are expected to replace foreign savings. To emphasize this point, rewrite for example (1) as

$$SP - IP = D + E.$$

It can be seen that given IP and E, a lower budget deficit D may be associated simply with a correspondingly lower level of private savings that results from Keynesian income adjustment through a lower GDP caused by lower aggregate demand. Typically, however, downward income adjustment would also reduce the level of induced import, and thus raise E and prevent SP from falling *pari passu* with D. Because of this factor, the reduction of private savings is smaller than the decrease of government consumer expenditures, and domestic savings SD (being the sum of private and government savings) increase by the amount by which the import surplus declines. The direct cause of this improvement is the fall of GDP and the related fall of imports. This happens in every recession, whatever its direct cause. It is misleading to interpret this result as replacement of foreign savings by government savings achieved in the budget.

The central point of this analysis is that a reduction in the trade deficit brought about by the contraction of aggregate demand and income is unlikely to be a sustainable strategy in the longer run. Because it simply means an unviable strategy of sacrificing the growth potential of the economy indefinitely for a stronger international payment position.

It should be mentioned that the role of aggregate demand restriction as one of the causes of the transformational recession is more widely recognised now. We may quote two representative opinions:

Kornai (1993) writes: "The recession cannot be explained solely in terms of insufficient demand. Even now, only half the firms consider the insufficiency of demand as the obstacle to production. (Nor does inadequate demand become the sole obstacle to production in a mature, developed capitalist economy, even during the downward phase of the trade cycle. The frequency there is at most 70-80 per cent. See Laffont (1985). We currently face a 'half-Keynesian' situation, for whose treatment a doctrinaire Keynesian therapy is not suitable *in itself.* But the other half of the comment must be added immediately: precisely because the situation is already half-Keynesian, demand plays a very marked role in determining output. In a post-socialist transformational recession, the 'brake' has not been applied by central controls on supply, as was the case when investment and production were curbed in the socialist economy. Although we are not faced with a recession produced *exclusively* on the demand side, the demand side has assumed the primary role."

Borenzstein and Ostry, analysing the causes of the recession in Poland, have compared the role of macroeconomic factors on the demand side (restrictive fiscal, monetary and income policies) and on the supply side (increase of administered prices of services and energy together with credit restrictions) and have come to the following conclusion: "... macroeconomic policies accounted for most of the output change; moreover, industry-specific shocks proved statistically insignificant" (see IMF, 1993).

Nevertheless, these views are not unanimously accepted. Many argue that output losses during the transformational recession were caused mainly by the disruption on the supply side and have, therefore, little to do with aggregate demand. This argument is often presented with the help of the aggregate demand (AD) and aggregate supply (AS) model. In this model, it is sought to generalise the Keynesian theory of effective demand by explicitly incorporating the supply side. A falling AD and a rising AS curve intersect in the price-quantity space to determine simultaneously the equilibrium level of price and output.

We wish to emphasize that this is an acceptable approach in the analysis of a specific good, in a partial equilibrium analysis. If the capacity in, say, the mustard industry has shrunk for some reason (for example, a fire), resulting in a leftward shift of the mustard supply curve, we can assume that the demand curve for mustard has not moved simultaneously. Indeed, income losses of mustard producers, caused directly and indirectly by the fire, are insignificant in relation to total income (co-determining demand for mustard) and, therefore, can be ignored. If, however, the partial equilibrium analysis deals with a sufficiently important good (for example, cars), and the related capacity shrinks (because of a fire in a big car factory), provoking a leftward shift of the supply curve concerned, we can no longer, strictly speaking, assume that the respective demand curve remains unchanged. Indeed, the direct and indirect income losses related to the fire in a big car factory are not negligible and therefore that very supply shock would also shift the car demand curve to the left. For this very reason, if we consider the entire economy, we cannot shift the aggregate supply curve without shifting at the same time the aggregate demand curve in a significant way. Although the separation between aggregate demand and aggregate supply is misleading in a macroeconomic context, this construction is used not only in textbooks but also in many empirically oriented research papers (for example Bruno, 1986; Blanchard, 1989; Bernanke, 1994).

In Figure 1 the aggregate demand curve AD_0 cuts the vertical segment of the aggregate supply curve AS_0 in point A_0 (or even above it) symbolising the tendency of the command economy to be as near as possible to the capacity limit as measured by capacity output Y_0. The initial price level P_0 is well below the equilibrium price level P_e, leading to a sellers' market and suppressed inflation as characteristic features of a command economy. If the capacity were adjusted to a market environment and price liberalisation, the transformation would require a small reduction of aggregate demand in order to create the capacity reserves necessary for some flexibility of supply. The market would, then, be cleared at a price level near P_e and an output level near Y_0. Compared to the initial position, the real output and employment would somewhat decline, and the price level would increase, leading at a given money rate w to a considerable fall of the "statistical" real wage rate (from w/P_0 to w/P_e), but only to a marginal decline of its real purchasing power. Judging by the statistical data foreseen for the first years in the stabilization programmes, the authors of these programmes must have had in mind a development of this kind.

In reality, part of the capacity has proved to be non-useable under market conditions. A good example of this phenomenon is the loss of the CMEA markets, especially of the Soviet market, for manufactured goods which could not be sold elsewhere. A related phenomenon are home-produced goods of inferior quality which were crowded out from the internal market by imported goods of higher quality as soon as foreign trade had been liberalised. Hence, a part of existing capacity has practically ceased to exist and the related loss of output can be attributed to a supply shock. This shock is presented in Figure 1 by the shift of the aggregate supply curve from position AS_0 before the transformation to position AS_1 after the transformation, resulting in a new capacity output Y. Thus, capacity output has shrunk by $Y_0 - Y = \Delta E$, where $\Delta E < 0$ measures the combined result of the fall in exports and the increase in imports due to the supply shock. After the CMEA markets had collapsed and after a rapid trade liberalisation had been decided, the loss of output equal to $-\Delta E$ was unavoidable and became one of the constraints facing transformation strategy. Once the firms were expected not only to produce goods but also to sell them on a competitive market, they had to stop the production of goods which could not be sold either abroad or inside the country. More specifically, no expansion of internal aggregate demand could revitalise the capacity lost by the specified supply shock.

This is, however, not the full story. Let us assume — as a mental experiment — that neither IP nor D changed and let us ask, what happens to the AD_0 curve when, for reasons already explained, the trade surplus E changes by ΔE ($\Delta E < 0$)? Assuming a constant private propensity to save s, the aggregate demand curve is shifted according to (3) from position AD_0 to position AD_1 by a distance equal to $\Delta Y = (1/s)\Delta E$. With s at the beginning of the transformation process in the range of about 30 per cent, the shift of aggregate demand would be about three times stronger than the shift of the aggregate supply curve linked to the initial supply shock. The new output Y_1 and the new price level P_1 are determined by the co-ordinates of point E_1 at which the AD curve crosses the AS_1 curve. The resulting loss of output is equal to $Y_0 - Y_1$, of which the part $Y_0 - Y$ is due to the supply shock and the part $Y - Y_1$ is due to the decline of aggregate demand caused by the supply shock. This latter part of lost output needs to be explained exclusively in terms of contraction of aggregate demand.

Figure 1

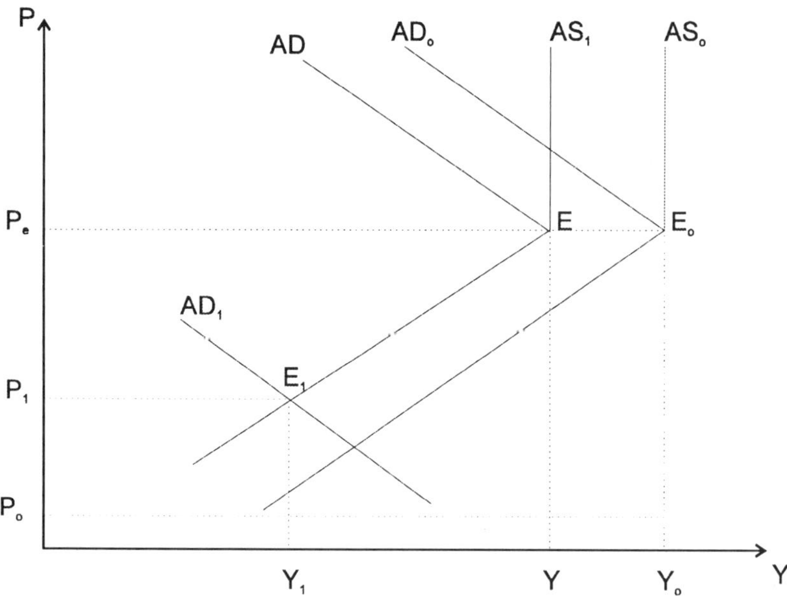

The implication of the above analysis deserves special attention. The fall in supply is justified typically on grounds of "efficiency", for instance by evoking the Schumpeterian image of "creative destruction". It is argued that total import liberalisation would weed out the (internationally) inefficient producers, but would allow the efficient ones to survive. The argument is wrong from a macroeconomic standpoint, because, as long as import liberalisation leads to a larger import surplus (or current account deficit), at any given level of investment, it would shrink the size of the domestic market through the multiplier mechanism discussed above. In this process not only inefficient firms lose out to foreign competitors and go bankrupt, but, as jobs are lost in these firms, it reduces demand for products of even efficient firms in a chain reaction. As a result, not only the inefficient, but also the efficient firms are adversely affected, because the domestic market shrinks all around.

The appropriate policy in the presence of a supply shock would be to estimate the consequent leftward shift of the AD curve and to try to push it partly back to the right in order to come as near as possible to point E in which capacity output Y could be achieved at a price level P_e. These measures could involve, for example, the toleration of an increase in the budget deficit D provoked by the transformational recession or the redistribution of incomes towards groups with a higher propensity to consume, such as wage earners, in order to reduce the average propensity to save (for example, by a less restrictive wage policy preventing excessive reduction of consumption). Of course, *ex ante* nobody knows exactly the position of point E. However, an understanding of the necessary link between aggregate supply and aggregate demand is essential so that the very *direction* of policy becomes clear for limiting the losses to an unavoidable minimum. This was, however, not the case in practice in most instances.[2]

The interdependence between aggregate demand and aggregate supply helps us not only to better understand the past experience of the transforming countries, but can also be used to solve the problems arising now and in the future. We would like to illustrate this point by just two examples.

Almost all CEECs now show quite impressive rates of growth of GDP and industry. It is very often assumed that this high growth will last for a longer time, and bold estimates are made as far as the narrowing of the gap in the GDP *per capita* between these countries and the EU average is concerned. It is possible that these expectations will materialise, but they should not be treated as independent of the policy pursued. What we observe now is mostly a recovery from the transformational recession, and high rates of growth under these conditions are not unusual. They are mostly due to a better utilisation of the capacities inherited from the past, accompanied sometimes by small, very productive modernisation investment. The recovery, however, will very soon come to an end. Once the level of utilisation of capacity cannot be increased further, the continuation of high growth would require a strong expansion of business investment. Also investment in long-neglected capital-intensive areas like infrastructure and residential building would be required to create the general preconditions for further growth. All this would confront the governments concerned with problems that can hardly be solved if efforts are concentrated on balancing the budget and fighting inflation only.

From the point of view presented in this paper, the governments should continuously take care of a satisfying level of aggregate demand, especially at the moment at which the rates of growth may start to decline. Strong incentives to invest for firms, direct government investment in infrastructure, overdue cheap credits for residential building, a wage policy that gives the workers their share in increased productivity, not only because of social justice, but also in order to secure a growing market for consumer goods — these are some examples of the growth-supporting policy we have in mind. Also other policy decisions, not related to a possible slowing-down of growth, should be checked from the point of view of their influence upon aggregate demand. For instance, the reform of the social security system and the creation of special retirement funds may create incentives to increase savings, but these incentives, unless accompanied by higher investment, may negatively influence growth according to the "paradox of thrift".

Our second example is related to the foreign trade balance. We can observe already now a deterioration in the balances of trade and current accounts already now in some transforming countries when they move from recession to recovery. This should be expected because as a rule imports grow faster than exports in countries which expand more quickly than their main trading partner, the EU. Overcoming the foreign trade bottleneck would be one of the most difficult questions to be solved if the CEECs want to succeed in reducing the development gap in relation to the EU.

The proper way to ease the foreign trade bottleneck — disregarding the much-needed and welcomed inflow of foreign capital, especially in the form of direct investment — is to accelerate the growth of exports and decelerate the growth of imports in order to keep the import surplus at a tolerable level. A competitive real exchange rate, together with some other measures, is the most important instrument in achieving this goal in the short run (and, in the longer run, the expansion of export capacity). True, some acceleration of inflation would follow nominal devaluation, and the related fall in real wages would shrink the market for consumer goods and counterbalance the growth stimulus caused by the hoped-for improvement in the foreign trade balance. These consequences are unavoidable but should not be increased by linking the problem of foreign trade difficulties with restrictive fiscal policies. Indeed, when devaluation is supported by a restrictive fiscal policy the losses in output and consumption are magnified without helping substantially (as proved earlier in this paper) to solve the foreign trade problem. This analysis seems applicable to the policy package started in Hungary in 1995, which has combined strong devaluation with quite restrictive fiscal policies (see also Oblath, 1995). The danger exists that this example would also be followed by other transformation countries when budget deficits and foreign trade difficulties occur at the same time.

To sum up, the main lessons of stabilization experience are twofold. First, the "monetarist" assumption that demand contraction would fall mostly on prices to contain the rate of inflation is wrong. Demand contraction also fell largely on output through the magnifying effect of the multiplier mechanism and led to a transformational recession of unnecessarily severe magnitude and duration. This could have been avoided to some extent, if more attention had been paid to the formation of aggregate demand. Second, the macroeconomic dichotomy between a supply shock and a demand shock is false. The two cannot be separated, even in theory. Uncritically accepting such a false separation leads also to misleading policy conclusions (like "creative destruction" for greater efficiency).

2. How to control persistent inflation

While the conventional stabilization programmes failed to anticipate the depth of the recession in the transforming countries, their policy package turned out to be relatively more effective in fighting inflation. An immediate, though partial explanation of this phenomenon would run along the following lines: the measures aimed at curbing credit and the budget deficit and related restrictive monetary and fiscal policies contracted demand. This demand contraction showed up partly in negative output adjustment (see Section 1) resulting in recession, and partly in price adjustment resulting, after an initial jump of price liberalisation, in the slowing-down of inflation. Moreover, the slowdown of inflation was helped further by a nominal wage anchor and by the international price discipline imposed by the newly liberalised foreign trade regime, both of which kept a check on nominal price rises.

This simple explanation, and the strategy of massive demand contraction for the sake of price stabilization, is valid and unavoidable in situations of acute inflation to hyperinflation with an overhang of liquidity with the public. This was indeed the case in most transforming countries in the initial phase of stabilization. In a hyperinflation, domestic currency loses its function as a "store of value", i.e. there is a general reluctance to hold money for *future* purchases. In this flight away from money to physical commodities, money is used almost entirely as an *immediate* medium of exchange for transactions. When money has almost no role as a "store of value" and is only an immediate medium of exchange with the velocity of circulation approaching its maximal institutionally determined value, the quantity theory of money begins to approximate the functioning of the economy. The higher the quantity of money, the higher the price level, while output remains constant or even declines when hyperinflation continues. A reduction in the money supply, especially by reducing the high-powered base money, can be effective in checking hyperinflation. Indeed, there is no alternative to drastic restraint on the money supply and even currency reform in such extreme situations. However, it is an extraordinary folly to treat all inflation as hyperinflation of this kind! It is essential to recognise that the mechanisms fuelling inflationary processes are different in different situations.

Hyperinflation is an extreme case of demand-pull inflation. If — measured in real terms — the sum IP + D + E increases, savings SP have to adjust to this sum. If free capacity exists, we describe this process as *quantity* adjustment, because savings increase *pari passu* with consumption and so does GDP, while the relation between unit variable cost and price remains more or less constant. If free capacity does not exist, we describe this process as *price* adjustment, because with given GDP, savings increase to the detriment of consumption, while the relation between unit variable cost and price increases. When we speak of the relation between unit variable cost and price we mean in reality the mark-up per unit of industrial output. With quantity adjustment the mark-up per unit of industrial output remains constant. Hence, the increase in profits is due to the increase in capacity utilisation in the industrial sector. However, with price adjustment the mark-up per unit of industrial output increases (Bhaduri and Falkinger, 1990). Such price adjustment may become a starting point of demand-pull inflation.

One way to answer the question whether inflationary price adjustment was of the demand-pull type would be to investigate the mark-up ratio and find out whether it increased. We cannot go into details in this paper, but intuitively the answer seems negative as far as the persistent inflation in transforming economies is concerned. First, the increase in the mark-up ratio leads to a redistribution of income from wages to profits, and as the propensity to save out of profits is higher than out of wages, this would also lead to an increase in the overall savings ratios. We have seen that this did not happen: the savings ratio declined everywhere to stabilize at a lower level. Second, if we were really confronted with a demand-pull inflation in both periods we would expect that — assuming a more or less similar rate of growth of unit variable cost — inflation would accelerate in the second period, after the recession hit bottom. This did not happen. Although we are now confronted in most countries with rather high rates of growth of aggregate demand, inflation clearly decelerated. On the contrary, the only country in which inflation accelerated anew in 1995 was Hungary, where aggregate demand had been drastically restricted that year!

Circumstantial evidence, therefore, suggests the current process of inflation in the transforming countries to be rather of a cost-push type. While indiscriminate demand contraction was undoubtedly effective in the early stages of transformation, it is seldom realised that the *persistence* of inflation in some of these economies can no longer be eradicated through further contraction of demand. In most of these countries, a kind of *recessionary inflation* was at work which was aggravated rather than abated by demand contraction. Such an inflationary process arises from two sources. First, attempts to reduce the level of the government budget deficit have often involved raising the administered prices of essential inputs such as electricity, transport etc. They have, in turn, raised the unit variable cost of industrial production which has led to higher mark-up prices. Very high nominal interest rates and the higher cost of imported inputs, after initial radical devaluation, further strengthened this inflationary pressure operating through higher unit costs. Second — and this point is often misunderstood — recession itself has meant lower capacity utilisation in industry, so the recurring overhead costs like managerial personnel salaries, interest payments on debt, etc. of the enterprises were spread over a smaller amount of output produced. Consequently, the unit overhead costs tended to increase as recession led to lower production. With less subsidy from the government, the enterprises have tried to cover their rising *unit* cost of overhead expenditure at lower capacity utilisation by raising prices. In this process of recessionary inflation, the deeper the recession, the stronger would be the pressure on enterprises to raise prices to cover unit overhead costs. Almost paradoxically for standard theory, the more the government tries to combat the recessionary inflation through restrictive fiscal policies like cutting the budget deficit, or restrictive monetary policies like high nominal interest rates, the more likely is inflation to be fuelled — because following these policies would tend to reduce the degree of industrial capacity utilisation even further.

The concept of cost-push inflation presented above explains why the increase in aggregate demand and output observed in the second phase of the transformation has been accompanied by a deceleration, but not an acceleration, of inflation. The increase in administered prices was less pronounced as the budgetary situation mostly improved because of revenue growth linked to economic growth. At the same, time unit overhead costs declined because they are a decreasing function of output.

It should be emphasized that the persistence of inflation in transforming countries is of a "cost-push" type with the important difference that it is not led by exaggerated wage claims and, therefore, has little to do with the tightness of the labour market. It should also be noted that the consumer price index (CPI) in these transforming countries increased as a rule faster than the producer price index (PPI). Indeed, as already mentioned, administered prices of services (like rents, heating, telecommunication etc.) have increased very strongly. Since they have a higher share in the CPI than in the PPI, this contributed to the faster growth of the former. In these circumstances it is possible to observe at the same time a decrease in real wages (measured in CPI) in relation to labour productivity and an increase in real product wages (measured in PPI). As a result, real product wages, being an index of real labour costs, may increase, although at the same time real wages in relation to labour productivity may decrease. This is a particularly unattractive combination, because workers as consumers do not get enough to keep their share in labour productivity intact while real labour costs for the employers also increase.

A restrictive financial policy, as we have seen, is not the proper method to combat a cost-push inflation and can even become counter-productive. The fight against a cost-push inflation should address directly its causes, i.e. unit variable costs under a normal degree of capacity utilisation. Two measures seem here of utmost importance. First, an income policy is required, if possible agreed upon by employees and employers, concerning an acceptable compromise about the share of wages and profits in value added in the whole economy and, in particular, sectors and branches. More specifically, the growth of money wages should prevent unit labour costs from increasing more strongly than prices. Second, in a country with an inflation rate not higher than in its main trading partners, the nominal exchange rate should not increase and prevent the import of inflation. At present, however, the situation is an opposite one. The CEECs have, as a group, higher inflation than the EU. In these circumstances an increase in the real exchange rate is unavoidable and a difficult compromise is necessary between supporting the competitiveness of the CEECs, on the one hand, and slowing down the increase in national prices of imported goods and imported inputs, on the other hand.

3. The transformational role of the state

From the standpoint of general economic theory, the most important role of the state consists in creating "external economies" for the private sector which the latter can internalise or appropriate to increase its profitability. External economies, to be created by the state and appropriated by the private sector, can come either from a reduction in the production costs of the private sector or from its higher revenue. For instance, better public schooling or communication services may increase private profitability by reducing the latter's cost of training or communication. Similarly, the controversial issue of protection of specific industries against foreign competition can be looked upon as a way of creating external economies for these industries by increasing their revenues, rather than decreasing their costs, under protection. Indeed, even demand expansion policies along Keynesian lines can be looked upon as creating revenue-augmenting external economies for the private sector in some circumstances. Nevertheless, the question of which types of "external economies" for the private sector are most beneficial at a particular stage of economic development cannot be settled in general. Nevertheless, the concept of "market friendliness" of the state can be interpreted usefully as consisting of creating such external economies that can be appropriated by the private enterprise. Its implications, however, deserve emphasis, particularly in the context of the transformational role of the state.

To begin with a biological analogy, internationalisation of externalities by the private sector would place it somewhat in the role of a "parasite" on a "host" population represented by the state. This parasitic advantage of benefiting from external economies can continue to grow, as long as the host population — the state in this case — also grows in some sense. A parasite's health and fortune are interlinked with the health of the population which hosts it. Thus, it would be difficult to imagine the private sector expanding vigorously, while the state is decaying during the process of transformation.

Continuing with the biological analogy, there might also exist a kind of "symbiosis" of mutual benefit between the "parasite" and the "host". The state as the "host" gets resources from the "parasite" (the private sector), which are necessary to fulfil its different goals. Some of these goals need not be related directly to the creation of external economies. One of these goals might be the correction of the distribution of income resulting from the market mechanism in the name of social solidarity (for example, the creation of equal opportunities for every child, the care for those who are in need, etc.). However, the expansion of state activities should not go so far as to thwart the private sector by this expansion. In other words, the state cannot continuously increase *relative* to the private sector, or widen its activities in the economic sphere without upsetting the symbiotic balance of mutual advantage.

It should be stressed that the *nature* of the external economies to be created by the state for private appropriation changes continuously and is not context-free. For instance, at some (initial) stage, it may be the usual economic and social infrastructure like education, health and communications or the legal infrastructure for enforcement of contracts in economic transactions which create the most important external economies. At another stage of development, it may be research and development expenditure for selected industries, their temporary protection, and other elements of industrial policy in general. In the legal sphere, proper functioning of stock exchange markets may require enforcement of special rules by the state at some stage of development. Thus, the nature of the external economies to be generated by the state, as well as the ways they are to be appropriated, partially or totally, by the private sector change over time. It is a dynamic process of adaptation by both the state and the market, where it is not so much the size of the state but how it adapts successfully to the requirements for the development of the market that becomes the critical issue.[3]

The dominant role of the authoritarian state in the command economy, together with the formal suppression of private initiative, killed the private and even collective creativity which has always been the driving force behind economic progress. This was the definitive reason for the ossification of this system long before it collapsed. Hence, it was understandable that the transformation from the command to a market economy was accompanied by an overriding tendency to push back the state and to rely in economic matters almost exclusively on the spontaneity of market forces. The fashionable doctrine of a minimal state naturally looked attractive in this context. It was, however, a false start.

Since the economic role of the state depends on the stage of development, and is not context-free in that sense, we need to focus specifically on the context of the transforming economies. In other words, the rather abstract debate between "market failure" and "government failure" is not particularly helpful, and the need is to concentrate on the specific issues of economic change facing these economies. There are at least three issues of outstanding importance that deserve special attention: (1) the problem of price and trade reform; (2) the problem of industrial policy for future growth; and finally, (3) some major institutional changes including the "privatisation" debate.

It should be noted at the outset that price and trade reform have mostly been introduced already in the economies under consideration. These are reforms which have a relatively fast speed of adjustment, i.e. they can be introduced rather quickly by the governments concerned. Although industrial policy can also be announced relatively quickly, its consequences are relatively slowly transmitted through the economy and, in this sense, it is not a fast-moving variable. By their very nature, most institutional changes are even slower-moving variables and this applies with particular force to "privatisation". Indeed, one of the lessons of past transformation experience, specially in the guise of "shock therapy", was that too little attention has been paid to these different speeds of adjustment (see also Tsang, 1996).

Almost every observer agrees that privatisation of the most important sectors of the economy, especially industry, is a necessary pre-condition for an efficient market system, but successful privatisation can be carried out only slowly. It is necessary to differentiate between sectors with low capital intensity, on the one hand, like services, commerce, distribution, handicrafts and even small-scale industry, where privatisation can be accomplished relatively quickly, and capital-intensive sectors, on the other hand. In the former, privatisation is interlinked with the creation of new economic units, with ownership and management concentrated in the hands of the same person or family. It is no accident that everywhere in the transforming countries private firms of this kind have been booming.

The problem of capital-intensive sectors, especially large firms, is quite different. Arrow (1993) identifies three reasons for which a quick privatisation of these firms is not possible or advisable. First, internal savings required for the private domestic purchase of big firms accumulate only slowly; second, the definition by the market of the sales value of the firms requires stable economic conditions which can be achieved only gradually; and finally, the production sector needs to be restructured in many cases before it can be sold. These are arguments that should be given serious consideration.

Internal savings inherited from the command economy were small and additionally decimated by high inflation before, or at the beginning of, the transformation. They severely limited the possibility of selling big firms inside the country. This difficulty did not apply to foreign capital which should be welcome, not only because it provides adequate financial means, but also because it brings with it modern technology and management. But foreign capital is interested only in a relatively small part of the historically inherited capital stock of the former command economies. It should be stressed that even if foreign capital were ready to buy all existing big firms, this arrangement might lead to dangerous conflicts between the internal labour force and foreign owners. Under these conditions, normal social conflicts related to bargaining about wages and working conditions would take on an additional unhealthily nationalistic flavour, as already observed in some countries.

The so-called "voucher privatisation" was intended directly to face the problem of lacking internal savings, and the solution adopted in the Czech Republic is considered the most consistent application of this idea. This is not the proper place to discuss the results of this method. But there are doubts as to whether it has really achieved its main goal. Mertlík (1996) argues that the Czech privatisation means *de facto* the movement from one form of public ownership to another form of public ownership. Large — and also a majority of medium-size — enterprises are, with some exceptions, controlled by Investment Privatisation Funds (IPFs); the IPFs in turn, also with a few exceptions, are controlled by the major Czech banks, which in turn are mostly controlled by IPFs, closing the circle. Mertlík concludes that what the Czechs have after five years of privatisation is a "national financial capitalism" with a central role of the national government as a "core investor" indirectly controlling (via IPFs and through the network of its capital shares) the central nervous system of more or less the whole industrial economy. The most important role in the corporate governance of voucher-privatised firms is played by managers, the principal controllers of the flow of inner information concerning firms. Their position was probably enhanced compared to the situation before privatisation. Mertlík concludes that the voucher privatisation, the main purpose of which was to solve the problem of *absentee ownership* inherited from the command economy, resulted in a large-scale and long-run institutionalisation of the *absentee ownership*. An essential theoretical error, as we have already pointed out, was to believe that "voucher privatisation" would short-circuit the time required for slow-moving institutional change.

If we distrust schemes like that of voucher privatisation for short-circuiting complex institutional change, then the only solution seems to be to accept the fact that large capital-intensive firms have to be owned and controlled by the state for quite a while. They should operate as independent corporate units, exposed to the discipline of the market, with the budget constraint hardening gradually over time. At the final stage of the command economy, the idea of market socialism, with state-owned firms behaving as independent economic units, was quite popular with those who wanted to improve the command economy rather than replace it by a capitalist system. This idea is definitely dead, at least for the time being. It seems, however, that some elements of market socialism in the sense mentioned before, as the most efficient way to prepare large firms for privatisation, are still applicable. The goal consists in finding out the sales value of firms. The sales value is determined not by the cost of equipment but only by the ability to produce and sell with profits goods and services. Hence, only the market practice can provide a basis for evaluating this value. Without this practice the price of a firm would be more or less randomly fixed, opening the way for corruption and irregularities. This market valuation problem is crucially linked to the question of restructuring. Some firms can be restructured easily (for example, when the quality of goods is adequate and only packing and marketing are needed in order to make firms viable). In other cases, changes in the capacity itself are necessary, and this requires financial means and time. Step by step, with progressing market practice, firms should be sold to private owners, domestic or foreign, as soon as their survival seems to be assured.

In several cases, however, no restructuring is possible and the slow phasing-out of existing firms is the only solution. In other words their "market evaluation" is extremely poor. In these cases the goal can be best achieved by the state. As long as a firm produces value added, covering only labour costs — and there is large unemployment — it should be kept alive even though it does not produce profits. If the firm is not able to cover even its labour costs, it is still reasonable both in terms of "opportunity costs" and also from the budgetary point of view, to continue its functioning and subsidise the wage bill to the amount of the unemployment dole and social security payments which would arise in case of liquidation of the firm. Only when this condition is not fulfilled, the firm should be closed down. From a macroeconomic point of view (which should take into account the multiplier effects also) even this condition may be softened if the closing of a large firm would reduce the value added in the economy as a whole. As the employment situation differs according to regions, this policy, especially its sequencing in time, should be closely adjusted to the requirement of the local labour market. Of course, when unemployment decreases this policy should be discontinued.

Thus, the specific role of the state in the transformation process proper is to support the privatisation and the creation of small units by all possible means, especially credit policy. Further, its role is to create conditions for the inflow of FDI linked to privatisation or to green-field projects. Last but not least, its role consists in preparing the bulk of large firms for functioning in a market environment and in restructuring them as a pre-condition for their successful privatisation. As not all firms can be restructured at the same time, an appropriate industrial policy is unavoidable. Part of this policy is the gradual phasing-out of firms which cannot be transformed into viable market units. One of the big mistakes of the transformation strategy has been the "state desertion" (Portes, 1992) which has been observed in many cases. It consisted in a policy of leaving the state-owned enterprises alone and even discriminating against them in comparison with the private sector.

4. Summary

The lessons drawn from the main mistakes in the transition strategy in all sections of this paper can be summarised as follows:

The main topic of Section 1, the central part of the paper, is the false dichotomy between prices and quantities as being independent of each other, present in the overall transition strategy. In reality, when aggregate demand was restricted, not only prices but also quantities were seriously affected. Because aggregate demand was restricted too strongly and for too long, partly avoidable losses in output and employment have occurred.

Related to this idea is the treatment in the transition strategy of aggregate demand and aggregate supply as independent of each other. Especially the supply shock has been analysed without taking into account its influence upon aggregate demand. If this relation were understood, in many cases expansionary measures instead of restrictive ones would be advisable. Also, when the recovery phase of the transformational recession is over, a proper understanding of these two ideas remains important for making future basic macroeconomic decisions.

The methods of fighting inflation adopted in the CEECs were directed at demand-pull inflation. We criticised these methods in Section 2, arguing that, with the exception of the very beginning of the transformation, the countries concerned were confronted rather with cost-push inflation. The proper way to reduce this kind of inflation is a wage policy, being part of the overall income policy, and a careful exchange rate policy, trying to find a compromise between upholding competitiveness on foreign markets, on the one hand, and preventing prices of imported inputs from continuously increasing unit costs, on the other hand. Our analysis in Section 2 has also shown that with quite intensive growth in the recovery phase, i.e. with increasing aggregate demand, inflation decelerated rather than accelerated in the CEECs.

The last section has been devoted to the role of government in a market economy. The main mistake in the transformation strategy, especially at the beginning, was a programmatic absence of the state in economic matters, especially of industrial policy of any kind. The state sector has simply been deserted by the government. We have also criticised big social engineering schemes like the "voucher privatisation" of large state firms. We argued that a steady though slower privatisation pace, combined with restructuring of some firms and phasing-out of others, may in the end yield better results than fashionable *ad hoc* schemes trying to short-circuit the time required for slow-moving institutional change.

Notes

[1] Gomulka (1993), a long-time advisor to the Ministers of Finance in Poland, admits quite frankly that prices rather than quantities were the direct targets of the stabilisation plan for Poland: "The Balcerowicz group and IMF have attached less importance to quantity indexes, which they believed they could influence only marginally, than to the price level which, as it seemed to them, they could control to a great degree." This is a very revealing statement, because it admits that in the transformation strategy quantities were treated in opposition to prices as largely independent of aggregate demand policy.

[2] Gomulka (1992), commenting on a diagram which served partially as a pattern for Figure 1, treats supply shock and demand contraction as completely independent from each other.

[3] In some sense, the transition from the command to the market economy can be compared to such historical events as the transition from the feudal to the capitalist system. Polanyi (1957) stresses in his fundamental work on the origin of the capitalist society the essential role which the state has played in the transition from a protectionist system in medieval towns to a self-regulating market economy.

References

Amsden, A. et al., 1994, *The Market Meets its Match*, Harvard University Press, Cambridge, Mass.

Arrow, K.J., 1993, *Economic Transition: Speed and Scope*, Paper delivered at the Chinese University of Hong Kong, October.

Bhaduri, A., 1986, *Macroeconomics. The Dynamic of Commodity Production*, Macmillan.

Bernanke, B.S., 1994, "The Macroeconomics of the Great Depression: A Comparative Approach", National Bureau of Economic Research, *NBER Working Paper*, No. 4814, August.

Bhaduri, A. and Falkinger, J., 1990, "Optimal price adjustment under incomplete information", *European Economic Review*, Vol. 34, pp. 941-952.

Blanchard, O.J., 1989, "A Traditional Interpretation of Macroeconomic Fluctuations", *American Economic Review*, Vol. 79, pp. 1146-1164.

Bruno, M., 1986, "Aggregate Supply and Demand Factors in OECD Unemployment: An Update", *Economica*, No. 53, pp. 35-52.

Gomulka, S., 1992, "Polish Economic Reform, 1990-91: Principles, Policies and Outcomes", *Cambridge Journal of Economics*, Vol. 16, No. 3, September, pp. 355-72.

Gomulka, S., 1993, "B. Polityka stabilizacyjna w Polsce 1990-93: odpowiedzi na pytania" (Stabilisation policy in Poland 1990-93: answers to questions), *Studia i Materialy*, Institute of Economics, Polish Academy of Sciences, No. 43, Warsaw, pp. 75-81.

IMF, 1993, *IMF Survey*, Vol. 22, No. 9, 3 May.

Kornai, J., 1993, *Transformational Recession. A General Phenomenon Examined through the Example of Hungary's Development*, Francois Perroux Lecture, Collegium Budapest, Institute for Advanced Studies, *Discussion Papers*, No. 1, June.

Mertlík, P., 1996, "Czech Privatisation: From Public Ownership to Public Ownership in Five Years", Paper prepared for the 3rd AGENDA Workshop on Lessons from Transformation, 12-14 April 1996, Vienna (mimeographed).

Oblath, G., 1995, "Economic Growth and Fiscal Crisis in Central and Eastern Europe", *WIIW Research Reports*, No. 218, The Vienna Institute for Comparative Economic Studies, Vienna.

Pasinetti, L., 1988, "Technical Progress and International Trade", *Empirica. Austrian Economic Papers*, Vol. 15, No. 1.

Polanyi, K., 1957, *The Great Transformation. The political and economic origins of our time*, Boston, Beacon Press.

Portes, R., 1992, "The contraction of Eastern Europe's Economies" (Comments on M. Blejer and A. Gelb, IMF–World Bank Conference, 4-5 June 1992), mimeographed.

Stiglitz, J.E., 1994, *Whither Socialism?*, The MIT Press, Cambridge Mass., London, p. 3.

Tsang, S.-K., 1996, "Against big bang in economic transition: normative and positive arguments", *Cambridge Journal of Economics*, Vol. 20, pp. 183-93.

6

Adjustment without recession: a case study of Hungarian stabilization

János Kornai

1. Introduction

On 12 March 1995, Hungary's government and central bank announced a tough programme of adjustment and stabilization. (I will refer to this by the abbreviation ASP 95.[1]) The process of implementing this programme had been taking place for 15 months at the time of this study, which is an attempt to assess and take stock of its results so far.

The terms adjustment and stabilization are applied to economic-policy programmes of many different kinds. Along with other components, they usually include measures to reduce inflation. This, however, was not the case with the Hungarian programme of adjustment and stabilization in 1995, which belongs to a class designed mainly to overcome serious current account and budget disequilibria and avert an external and internal debt crisis.

Fifteen months is a short time. So caution and moderation are called for in applauding the programme's early successes, because they could easily slip from our grasp. Indeed, it would be more accurate to entitle the study "adjustment without recession *so far*."[2] With this warning in mind, it is worthwhile to start assessing the developments up to now.[3] I concentrate mainly on experiences that point beyond the specific case of Hungary and may be instructive elsewhere.

The study has the following structure. Section 2 considers the programme's results so far and the costs and sacrifices entailed in applying it. Section 3 examines the instruments the programme employs and the extent to which they can still be used in the future. Finally, Section 4 assesses the tasks ahead, the threats to what has been achieved so far, and the prospects for Hungary's development.

My research was supported by the Hungarian National Scientific Research Foundation (OTKA). I am most grateful to Mária Kovács for her devoted help in compiling the data and editing the text of the paper, and to Brian McLean for the translation. I am also thankful for the research assistance of Judit Rimler, Ágnes Benedict and Miguel Messmacher. I benefited from consultations with László Csaba, Zsuzsa Dániel, Rudiger Dornbusch, John McHale, Judit Neményi, Gábor Oblath, Jeffrey Sachs, György Surányi, Georg Winckler and Charles Wyplosz; some of these colleagues also read the first draft of this paper. I thank them for their valuable advice. Naturally I alone am responsible for the contents of the paper.

2. Achievements and costs

The main macroeconomic indices appear in Table 1. I will return to these subsequently.

Table 1. Macroeconomic indicators of Hungary, 1993-1995.

Indicators	1993	1994	1995
1. **GDP** (annual growth rate, %)	-0.6	2.9	1.5[a]
2. **GDP per capita**[b] (US dollar)	3,745	4,061	4,300
3. **Household consumption**[c] (annual growth rate, %)	1.3	-0.4	-5.7[a]
4. **Gross fixed investments** (annual growth rate, %)	2.0	12.5	1.2[a]
5. **Exports**[d] (annual volume indices)	-13.1	16.6	8.1
6. **Imports**[d] (annual volume indices)	20.9	14.5	-4.0
7. **Trade balance**[e] (million US dollar)	-3,247	-3,635	-2,442
8. **Balance on current account** (million US dollar)	-3,455	-3,911	-2,480
9. **Net convertible currency debt**[f] (million US dollar)	14,927	18,936	16,817
10. **Convertible currency reserves**[f] (in percentage of annual imports in the current account)	59.4	60.2	79.0
11. **Unemployment rate**[g] **(%)**	12.1	10.4	10.4
12. **Employment**[h] (employees in percentage of population)	42.2	40.2	39.5
13. **Balance of the general government** (GFS balance[i], in percentage of GDP)	-5.2	-7.4	-4.0
14. **Inflation** (annual consumer price indices)	22.5	18.8	28.2
15. **Gross average earnings**[j] (annual growth rate,%)	22.0	24.7	16.8
16. **Net average earnings**[j] (annual growth rate, %)	17.9	27.1	12.6
17. **Real wage per wage-earner** (annual growth rate, %)	-3.8	7.0	-12.2

Notes: a) Preliminary data; b) Converted from Hungarian forints by the annual average of the official commercial exchange rate. c) Actual final consumption of GDP by households; d) The exports and imports data are based on customs statistics. The imports data include 1993 arms imports from Russia in repayment of earlier debt; e) Trade related payments of the current account; f) December 31; g) Registered unemployed at the end of the year in percentage of the active (employed and unemployed) population in the previous year; h) January 1; i) For more detailed fiscal data and explanation see Table 4; j) Gross average earnings of full time employees. 1993-1994: indices are calculated from the data of organisations; with more than 20 employees. 1995: indices are calculated from the data of organisations with more than 10 employees.

Sources: Row 1, 3, and 4: 1993-1994: Central Statistical Office (1996c), 1995: Central Statistical Office 1996a) and direct communication of the Central Statistical Office; Row 2: Central Statistical Office (1996a); Row 5 and Row 6: 1993-1994: Central Statistical Office (1995a, p. 253), 1995: calculation of the National Bank of Hungary on the basis of data from the Central Statistical Office; Row 7 and 8: 1993: National Bank of Hungary (1995, p. 109), 1994-1995: Central Statistical Office (1996b, p. 41); Row 9: 1993: National Bank of Hungary (1995, p. 111), 1994-1995: Central Statistical Office (1996b, p. 41); Row 10: Calculation of the National Bank of Hungary; Row 11: National Bank of Hungary (1996b, p. 57); Row 12: Central Statistical Office (1995c, pp. 4-5); Row 13: National Bank of Hungary (1996c); Row 14: 1993-1994: Central Statistical Office (1995a, p. 286), 1995: Central Statistical Office (1996b, p. 37); Row 15 and Row 16: Central Statistical Office (1996d), 1995: Central Statistical Office (1996b, p. 38); Row 17: 1993-1994: Central Statistical Office (1996d), 1995: Ministry of Finance (1996b, Table 14).

2.1 Avoiding imminent catastrophe

Many favourable developments have occurred in the post-socialist Hungarian economy of the 1990s. To mention some of the most important ones, liberalisation of prices and foreign trade is essentially complete, huge numbers of private firms have been founded, strides have been made in privatising state-owned enterprises, massive structural transformation has occurred in the composition of production and foreign trade has been adjusted to conditions after the collapse of Comecon. In 1994, GDP started to grow again, after the deep transformational recession ensuing from the change of course in 1990.

However, the developments in Hungary had some disquieting features as well. The socialist system had bequeathed the country a dire macroeconomic heritage, above all a very high foreign debt. In this respect, the starting point for the Hungarian economy was worse than for most other post-socialist economies. There were many difficult tasks that the government in office in 1990-94 failed to perform, and the succeeding government, which took office in 1994, vacillated for several months before doing so. By 1993, the current account deficit had already reached 9.0 per cent of GDP. When this recurred in the following year, with a deficit of 9.5 per cent, there was a real danger that the external finances of the country would get in serious trouble. Partly tied up with this, there was a mounting budget deficit, which reached 8.2 per cent of GDP in 1994, according to the national accounts.[4, 5]

The equilibrium problems caused the rise in external and internal debt to accelerate. The growing costs of servicing this debt raised the current account and budget deficits even more, so that further loans had to be raised to cover them. The international financial world, on seeing the unfavourable financial macro indicators, began to lose confidence in Hungary, which had hitherto been a favourite in Eastern Europe for always paying its debts on time. The process I have outlined is well known to be self-propelling. The decline in Hungary's image became manifest in worse credit conditions, which pushed the country even closer to a debt spiral.

I analysed in an earlier study (Kornai, 1996a) the historical, political and social reasons why successive governments wavered and why they protracted and postponed the increasingly inescapable radical measures. I cannot cover these again here. Furthermore, only future historians, looking behind the political scenes, will be able to discover what combination of effects eventually brought to an end the habitual conduct of decades — the policy of "muddling through". A big part in steeling the Hungarian government to take radical action was certainly played by the deterrent lesson of the Mexican crisis. It made oppressive reading to see the guesswork in the international financial press — which country was going to follow Mexico? — and find Hungary named as prime candidate.

What came in Hungary in March 1995 was preventive therapy. Its most important result was to avert a catastrophe that would have ensued if the programme of adjustment and stabilization had not been initiated. This point I try to convey in Table 2, which compares the courses of events in Mexico and Hungary, and Table 3, which features the course of crises in some other countries and shows episodes inherently resembling the situation in Hungary before ASP 95.[6]

I would not like to take the analogy too far. Each country has a history that is individual and strictly speaking unique. Still, there are some major similarities between the developments in Hungary and the episodes in the other countries featured in Tables 2 and 3.[7]

Table 2. Macroeconomic indicators: Hungary versus Mexico, 1994-1995.

Indicators	Mexico		Hungary	
	1994	1995	1994	1995
1. **GDP** (annual growth rate, %)	3.7	-6.6[a]	2.9	1.5[a]
2. **Real private consumption**[b] (annual growth rate, %)	3.7	-12.0[a]	-0.4	-5.7[a]
3. **Industrial production** (annual growth rate, %)	4.1	-7.8[a]	9.6	4.8
4. **Employment in manufacturing**[c] (annual change in the number of employees, %)	1.1	-7.7[a]	-9.1	-5.3
5. **Real earnings**[d] (annual growth rate, %)	3.7	-12.6[a]	7.0	-12.2
6. **Inflation**[e] (annual consumer price indices)	7.1	51.9	18.8	28.2
7. **Balance on current account/GDP**(%)	-7.9	-0.2[a]	-9.5	-5.4[a]
8. **Net external debt/GDP**[f] (%)	32.2	37.6[a]	45.9	38.4

Notes: a) Preliminary data; b) For Hungary actual final consumption of GDP by households; c) December/December for Mexico. For Hungary average number of employees; the Hungarian 1995 figure refers to firms with more than 10 employees. Total national unemployment and employment data for Mexico, statistically comparable to the Hungarian data, are not available. For the Hungarian figures see Table 1, Rows 11 and 12, which show that the increase of manufacturing unemployment was associated with decreases in other sectors since total employment and the national unemployment rate remained almost unchanged. There is no available information about changes across sectors in Mexico; d) For Mexico, real monthly earnings in manufacturing. For Hungary, real wage per wage earner (see Note k in Table 1); e) December/December for Mexico; f) Net external debt for Mexico includes public debt only, for Hungary it includes both public and private foreign debt.

Sources: **Mexico**: The data were collected or calculated by Miguel Messmacher on the basis of the following sources: Row 1, Row 3, and Row 4: 1994: Banco de Mexico (1995, p. f, Table II-16, II-3 and II-9), 1995: Banco de Mexico (1996b); Row 2: OECD (1995, Table 3). Row 5: OECD (1996, pp. 62-63); Row 6: Banco de Mexico (1996a, Table III-1); Row 7: International Monetary Fund (1996b, pp. 394-395) and 1994: Banco de Mexico (1995, Table IV-1b), 1995: Banco de Mexico (1996b); Row 8: Mexican Ministry of Finance (1995). **Hungary**: Row 1: See sources of Row 1 in Table 1; Row 2: See sources of Row 3 in Table 1; Row 3: Central Statistical Office (1996b, p. 8); Row 4: 1994: Central Statistical Office (1995a, p. 143), 1995: National Bank of Hungary (1996b, p. 56). Row 5: See sources of Row 17 in Table 1. Row 6: See sources of Row 14 in Table 1. Row 7 and Row 8: National Bank of Hungary (1996c).

- They are small countries with open economies, in which foreign trade plays a crucial role. Each suffered adverse phenomena in its trade, with imports running away by comparison with exports. Not least, the trade imbalance led to problems on the current account.
- In some countries listed, the situation was worsened by the budget deficit.
- Several analysts believe that one cause of the problems, perhaps the chief one, was the rise in the real exchange rate, and as a result, the overvaluation of the domestic currency.
- The countries had attracted large amounts of credit and investment in various forms; each had long been attractive to lenders and investors, on whose confidence the country's financial situation came greatly to depend.

These are the antecedents I would like to underline. These are the respects in which events in Hungary and the other countries in the tables resemble each other. There the similarity ends, however. For the catastrophe that overtook the others *did not occur* in Hungary.

Though the course of each was different, almost every episode of crisis was typically a cumulative process. These are events similar to fire breaking out in a

Table 3, A-E. Episodes of crisis and adjustment in selected Latin American countries.

Country	Worst year of current account deficit	Year of adjustment	-4	-3	-2	-1	0	1	2	3	4
Table 3A. Annual growth rates of GDP (%) (Growth positive, decline negative).											
Chile	1981	1982	9.9	8.2	8.3	7.8	5.5	-14.1	-0.7	6.4	2.5
Costa Rica	1981	1981	8.9	6.3	4.9	0.8	-2.3	-7.3	2.9	8.0	0.7
Argentina	1981	1981[a]	6.2	-3.3	7.3	1.5	-5.7	-3.1	3.7	1.8	-6.6
Brazil	1982	1983[a]	5.0	6.8	9.1	-4.4	0.6	-2.9	5.4	7.9	7.5
Mexico	1981	1982	3.4	8.3	9.2	8.3	7.9	-0.6	-4.2	3.6	2.6
Table 3B. Current account balance/GDP (%) (Deficit negative, surplus positive).											
Chile	1981	1982	-5.3	7.1	-5.7	-7.1	14.5	-9.5	-5.7	-11.0	8.6
Costa Rica	1981	1981	-7.5	10.3	-13.8	-13.7	-15.6	-10.4	9.9	-6.9	7.4
Argentina	1981	1981[a]	3.2	2.8	-0.5	-2.3	-2.8	-2.8	-2.3	-2.1	-1.1
Brazil	1982	1983[a]	-3.5	-4.8	-5.5	-4.5	-5.9	-3.59	0.0	-0.1	-2.0
Mexico	1981	1982	-2.2	-3.0	-4.0	-5.4	-6.5	-3.4	3.9	2.4	0.4
Table 3C.[1] Real exchange rate growth rate (%) (Appreciation negative, depreciation positive).											
Chile	1981	1982	-10.6	-6.7	-4.2	-16.0	-7.9	81.9	-3.4	27.4	13.6
Costa Rica	1981	1981	2.2	0.9	2.3	-4.1	239.3	-37.5	-16.3	2.6	1.2
Argentina	1981	1981[a]	-16.0	-34.4	-30.8	-30.4	96.2	168.6	11.4	10.3	-39.9
Brazil	1982	1983[a]	1.1	48.2	-4.4	4.7	6.2	66.0	13.8	4.1	-40.9
Mexico	1981	1982	-5.9	-7.4	-6.9	-10.8	-3.3	96.5	-14.8	-12.3	22.2
Table 3D. Inflation rate (%) (Average annual change of the CPI, increase positive).											
Chile	1981	1982	91.1	40.1	33.4	35.1	19.7	9.9	27.3	19.9	30.7
Costa Rica	1981	1981	4.2	6.7	8.7	18.4	36.9	89.4	33.0	11.8	15.1
Argentina	1981	1981[a]	176.0	175.5	159.5	100.8	104.5	164.8	343.8	626.7	672.1
Brazil	1982	1983[a]	38.7	52.7	82.8	105.6	97.8	142.1	197.0	226.9	145.2
Mexico	1981	1982	29.0	16.2	20.0	29.8	28.7	98.8	80.8	59.2	63.7
Table 3E. Annual change in private consumption (%) (Growth positive, decline negative).											
Chile	1981	1982	16.6	9.8	14.2	14.4	15.5	-35.6	-8.1	25.2	-5.6
Costa Rica	1981	1981	11.9	9.1	2.0	-2.5	-3.1	-7.9	3.7	7.5	3.1
Argentina[b]	1981	1981[a]	2.5	-1.4	14.0	8.0	-3.8	-6.2	4.1	3.8	-6.8
Brazil	1982	1983[a]	2.3	9.6	6.6	-4.2	3.9	0.7	5.2	2.7	6.8
Mexico	1981	1982	0.3	9.3	9.9	9.4	8.3	-6.5	-7.0	4.4	4.1

Source: International Monetary Fund (1995, respective country tables).
For Mexico, 1977-1978: The World Bank (1995b, pp. 464-466).
Notes: [(1)] Growth rate of real exchange rates = (1+ rate of change in nominal exchange rate)x(1+US inflation) / (1+domestic inflation); [a] N/A. The table indicates the year of devaluation; [b] In case of Argentina, total consumption.
Year 0 is chosen according to the largest current account deficit during the episode. The calendar year assigned as "year 0" for a given country is indicated in the third column.
The countries are listed in the order of the largest GDP decline. (Chile is #1, because the decline of 14.1 per cent in 1982 was the largest among the selected countries.) The order of countries is identical in all tables.
The table was compiled by Miguel Messmacher.

crowded hall — panic spreads, and everyone rushes for the narrow doorway, meanwhile trampling on each other and blocking the exit (Kindleberger, 1978). In financial crises, people rush in alarm to withdraw their money and try to get rid of their investments, causing a tumultuous capital flight. It is the panic that accelerates and reinforces the process, which is why the collapse is so sudden. This panic is what Hungary managed to avoid.[8]

Where the catastrophe ensues, the most dramatic consequence is the serious fall in production that occurs in a short time, and the concomitant abrupt rise in unemployment (see Tables 2 and 3). This is the brutal process that reduces domestic absorption through a rapid contraction in aggregate demand and rectifies the displacement in the proportion between absorption and production. The preventive ASP 95 allowed (or more cautiously, has so far allowed) Hungary to avoid this calamity of recession. It would have been particularly painful in Hungary's case, because the country has still not recovered from the problems caused by the transformational recession after 1990. If Table 1 is compared with Tables 2 and 3, it can be seen that Hungary's production in 1995, far from sinking, even rose to a modest extent, while unemployment remained basically unchanged instead of making a jump.

Hungarian and foreign economists conversant with the history of crises and stabilization efforts have expressed respect for this achievement, but not the Hungarian public, even though it is the greatest success scored by ASP 95. For the man in the street, there is no sense of accomplishment in having averted a catastrophe outside his experience. Indeed, some have been irresponsible enough to suggest that it would have been better if Hungary had shared Mexico's fate. In the end, runs the argument, the country would have been forgiven its debts and pulled out of the mire, just as the United States, other developed countries and the international financial institutions which rescued Mexico.[9] Apart from the grave doubts about how much help a far more distant Hungary could have expected from the United States, Mexico still paid a dreadful price for the catastrophe, in spite of the help it received.

2.2 *Starting to adjust the macroeconomic proportions*

Apart from having short-term preventive effects, ASP 95 has already begun, in several essential ways, to rectify the adverse macroeconomic proportions that were the deep underlying causes of the situation of potential catastrophe. It can be hoped that this will have beneficial effects in the medium and long term as well. Let me draw attention to the following changes, which are presented numerically in Table 1.

1. The most important is the current-account deficit, which had remained obstinately at a very high level for two years. This was substantially lower in 1995 than in 1994, its proportion of GDP falling by four percentage points. The net debt/GDP ratio shows significant improvement (see Table 2, Rows 7 and 8).[10]

2. The volume of exports, which had already grown substantially in the previous year, rose by a further 8.1 per cent in 1995. Thus, ASP 95 can really count as an export-led adjustment. Meanwhile the volume of imports, having risen appreciably in the previous year, fell by 4.0 per cent (see Table 1).

3. A contraction occurred in domestic absorption but, as I mentioned, without a fall in production, which rose somewhat. This was made possible by the very change in the proportions. On the demand side there was a rise mainly in the proportion of exports and, if only to a small extent, investment, while that of consumption fell. On the supply side, the proportion of domestic production rose and that of imports fell. This is shown in Figures 1 and 2.

4. The budget deficit (GFS balance, in percentage of GDP) has been reduced by 3.4 percentage points.

5. The profitability of the business sector rose, on average from 3.8 per cent to 8.2 per cent.[11] The profits of profitable firms increased and the losses of loss-makers decreased. The state budget's share of total credit placement fell

and the share of business rose. These circumstances all helped to raise the business sector's prospects of growth.

Figure 1. Factors Contributing to the Change of the Volume of Aggregate Demand.

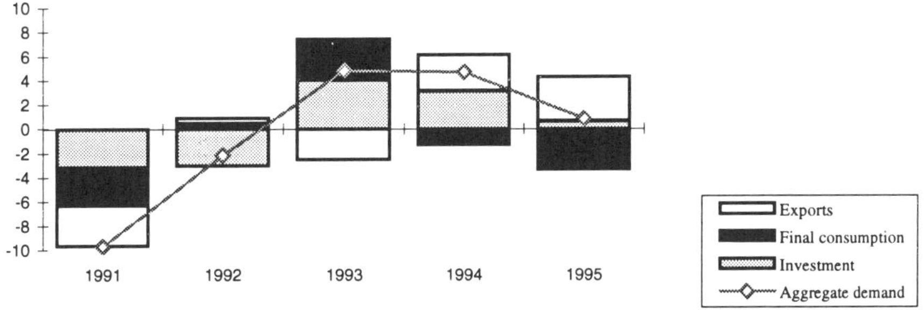

Source: National Bank of Hungary (1996*a*, p. 4).
Note: The underlying figures for 1995 are not consistent with figures in Table 1 and 2 , because they are based on a different preliminary estimate, although the changes point in the same direction.

Figure 2. Factors Contributing to the Change of the Volume of Aggregate Supply.

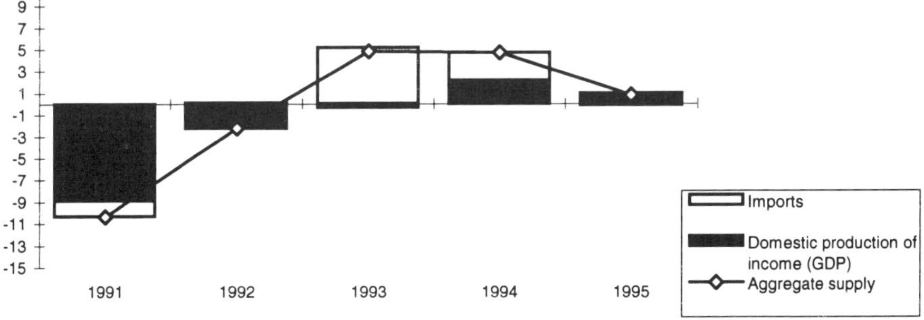

Source: National Bank of Hungary (1996*a*, p. 5).
Note: See note to Figure 1.

ASP 95 increased the financial world's confidence in Hungary. The credit ratings began to rise again, and the barriers to Hungarian borrowing were removed. The papers of consequence in the world and the big banks involved in Eastern European investment and lending gave the programme a positive assessment. A credit agreement was finally reached with the IMF, and Hungary was admitted into the OECD. These two events put an official seal of approval on Hungary's improved scores.

Figure 3. Consumer Price.

Increase of price level, %

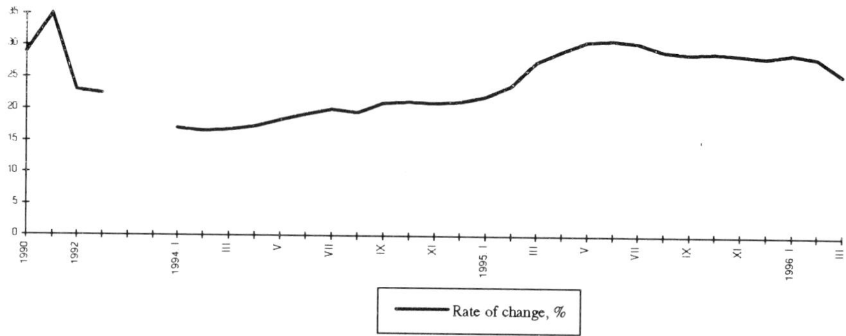

Sources: 1991-1993: Central Statistical Office (1995*a* , p. 286), 1994-1995: National Bank of Hungary (1995*b*, p. 67), 1996: Central Statistical Office (1996*e*, p. 63).

Note: Data for 1990-1993 show growth of the average price level of a given year from the average price level of the earlier year. Data for 1994-1996 show growth of the average price level of a given month from the average price level of the month 12 months earlier.

Figure 4. Real Exchange Rate.

Previous year = 100

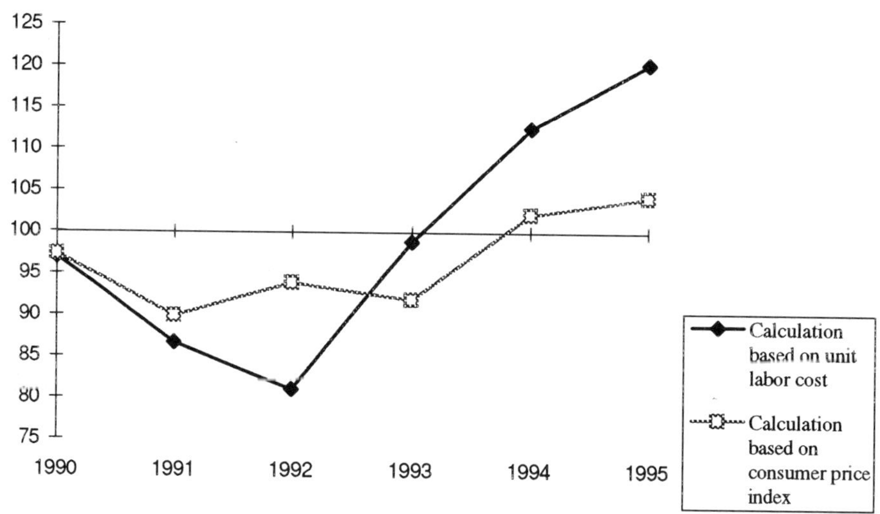

Source: A. Szentgyörgyvári and I. Baár (1996, p. 2).

Note: Index larger than 100 means real depreciation, index smaller than 100 means real appreciation compared to the previous year.

2.3 *The price of adjustment*

A heavy price had to be paid for adjusting the macroeconomic processes.

Figure 3 shows how inflation accelerated after the devaluation and other measures decided prior to the programme (for instance, the increase of energy prices). However, it remained within the range of moderate and controlled inflation, and is now easing again after its post-ASP 95 peak.

The nominal wage rise fell far short of the rise in the price level, causing a drastic cut in real wages. Meanwhile several welfare benefits have been reduced or cut under the tightening of budget spending.

These changes will be discussed in the next section in more detail. Here it is only necessary to note how broad sections of the Hungarian public made major sacrifices for the approach to a healthier macroeconomic equilibrium. Many whose standard of living had already fallen saw it decline further, while social inequality has increased. The sense of security has weakened in much of the population, mainly, of course, among the direct financial losers by the programme. Disillusion and bitterness have taken hold.

3. The instruments of the programme

The choice of instruments for ASP 95 was severely restricted by the fact that Hungary does not have a long history of being a market economy. It is an economy that entered on a post-socialist transformation after several decades of socialism. This difference of history is worth bearing in mind, even though Hungary's situation and problems show close similarities with other countries at a similar level of economic development, including several Latin American countries, for instance.

The government and central bank have used instruments of several kinds simultaneously in applying the programme. The economic policy has been heterodox, with orthodox instruments of financial stabilization augmented by several unorthodox methods. One notable feature of ASP 95 is that it has not followed the dogmatic formula of restoring equilibrium simply by contraction, i.e. indiscriminate narrowing of aggregate demand, which would have brought a serious fall in production. The aim instead has been an adjustment that minimises the albeit inevitable temporary slow-down in growth, and seeks to avoid an absolute fall in production. The approach to the desired macro proportions has been by way of reallocation of production and absorption, not absolute contraction.[12]

A separate problem is that some of the instruments can only be used for a certain time. The most they can give is an initial boost to the adjustment process; they cannot be relied on later. During the survey, I will mention specifically which instruments can only be used temporarily.

3.1 *Exchange rate and foreign trade policy*

During the period prior to ASP 95, the government and central bank had devalued the forint (HUF) from time to time, but retained a fixed exchange rate between devaluations. There were two problems with this exchange rate policy. One was that the real exchange rate of forint was rising in spite of the nominal depreciation. This trend accelerated notably in certain periods, for example in 1991-1992 (see Figure 4, and Halpern, 1996; Oblath, 1995). The other trouble was the unpredictability of the exchange rate policy. No-one knew beforehand when a devaluation would occur or how big it would be. Long overdue exchange rate adjustments would be put off time and again. This made it hard for investors to make considered business calculations. Towards the end, deflationary expectations were mounting and speculative attacks against the forint were emerging.

To overcome these two problems, ASP 95 included the following measures:

As an initial step, the forint was devalued by 9 per cent. A foreign exchange regime with a pre-announced crawling peg was introduced with immediate effect, under which the central bank announces for a longer period (6-12 months) in advance the pace at which it will devalue the forint.[13] This began with a monthly rate of 1.9 per cent, which was reduced gradually in the later stages. The monthly rate of devaluation for 1996 will be 1.2 per cent.

In setting the rate, monetary policy-makers attempt to retain more or less the real exchange rate produced by the initial devaluation, and prevent the real appreciation of the forint. The announced rate of nominal devaluation rests on a careful forecast of the rate difference between domestic and foreign inflation.[14] This entails gauging in advance on the expenditure side what nominal wage increase can be "squeezed in" beneath the planned upper limit of inflation, given the likely trend in Hungarian productivity.

The pre-announced crawling peg needs to be coupled with an appropriate interest-rate policy. If the rate is not high enough, it becomes worthwhile for investors to start converting their forint holdings into foreign exchange on a mass scale and withdrawing them from Hungary. This would cause the exchange rate to collapse.

It is certainly an achievement that the announced exchange rate has been fully adhered to so far. The central bank has allowed itself a band of plus or minus 2.5 per cent around the announced rate. It would intervene if the exchange rate on the inter-bank currency market moves out of this band. In fact, the market rate has never exceeded the intervention band. Rates on the black (or rather grey) currency market in the street, catering for the general public and foreign visitors, do not deviate from the official rates either. In private savings, there is a trend away from savings in foreign exchange, towards savings in forints. Starting 1 January 1996 the Hungarian currency became convertible in current transactions.[15] This combination of circumstances has dampened the speculation in this sphere, and greatly increased confidence in the forint and the credibility of monetary policy.

The initial and subsequent continuous devaluations have caused a very drastic nominal depreciation of the forint. The exchange rate in November 1995 represented a nominal depreciation of 30.6 per cent over the rate 12 months earlier. The real effective exchange rate, as is shown on Figure 4, changed much less, of course, since inflation accelerated. There are several known methods of measuring this. If inflation is measured by the industrial wholesale price index, the real effective exchange rate decreased by 5.5 per cent over the above-mentioned period. Discounting seasonal effects and taking unit labour costs as a basis, the decrease was 17.1 per cent over the first 10 months of 1995 (compared to the same period of

1994).[16] I will leave open here the problems of measurement methodology. Whatever the case, there was a nominal depreciation in excess of inflation, which substantially improved the competitiveness of Hungarian production on export markets.[17]

Apart from the devaluation and the new exchange-rate policy, ASP 95 tried other instruments designed to adjust foreign trade.

An 8 per cent import surcharge was imposed, augmenting the effect of existing tariffs. The programme refrained from restricting imports by such administrative means as further quotas. However, it seemed expedient to curb temporarily (as it is allowed by the international agreements) the runaway import demand with an import surcharge effective for a period of two years. This also yields substantial extra budget revenue.[18]

So to some extent, the programme is asymmetrical: it lays great emphasis on curbing import demand. However, this takes place in a differentiated way, because it seeks mainly to curb the import demand induced by consumption. The import surcharge is refunded to those who use the products imported for investment or for export production. This underlines still more that ASP 95 is designed to encourage investment and export-led growth.

Nonetheless, it must be admitted that the economic policy borders on protectionism in this respect. Special treatment of imports can only be justified by the threat of a balance-of-payments crisis. If the same course were pursued permanently, it would cause distortion of relative prices and slow down the improvement of efficiency. So later, when the results have been consolidated, the country will have to move towards reducing tariffs and opening up even more widely, for this is the road that leads to lasting rapid growth.

There are various debates going on about the exchange rate policy for the future. One issue concerns the connection between exchange rate policy and policy designed to reduce inflation. Hungary, like many other countries, has some people who advocate using real appreciation as an instrument for slowing down inflation.[19] This would be a big mistake, in my view. Inflation is a grave problem, but so long as it is kept under control and within the range of moderate inflation, it remains a bearable problem. On the other hand, if real appreciation of the forint makes the trade and current account balances start to worsen and confidence begins to erode again, the country will be back on the brink of a debt crisis. A tendency to real appreciation, alongside other factors, can be found among the culprits in all the countries where a payments and debt crisis ensued.[20] This is confirmed by Table 3, where every crisis episode was preceded by real appreciation. For Hungary, as for the other small open economies, export-led growth represents the true, lasting escape from the struggles of today. The competitiveness of the economy must be promoted by various instruments, of which more will be said later. However, this is certainly the aspect that the exchange rate policy must promote in the first place.

3.2 Income policy

In the framework of the adjustment, it was unavoidable to have a sharp reduction in consumption. The orthodox recipe is to achieve this by a thoroughly painful course of treatment. There is a serious fall in production, accompanied by a large increase in unemployment, which forces real wages down, through the mechanism of the labour market. This occurs after a long delay, because of the rigidity of wages and the frictions in labour market adjustment. Indeed, a much larger unemployment increment is needed to achieve the wage level necessary in macroeconomic terms than would be the case if there were a mechanism free of friction and delay. Empirical writings of the "wage curve" (particularly Blanchflower and Oswald, 1994) suggest as a rule of thumb that unemployment must double to cause a 10 per cent fall in wages. It is not worth trying to decide how far this empirical regularity, based mainly on observations of regional differences within a particular country, would have applied to Hungary today. However, the figure certainly demonstrates that without state intervention, only a very substantial rise in the already high unemployment rate of over 10 per cent would have led to the new proportions of consumption, investment and exports desirable in macroeconomic terms.

Instead, ASP 95 applied other, non-orthodox means of forcing down real wages, with the help of direct state intervention. Central state wage controls ceased in Hungary in 1992. Year after year there are talks between the employees', the employers' organisations and the government about pay, employment, and other current aspects of economic policy. Even if agreement is reached, it is not binding. Such talks duly took place early in 1995, but they dragged on fruitlessly. The announcement of ASP 95 fell like a thunderbolt. The employers gave reluctant support. The unions took various stances. The reactions in various trades at various times ranged from strong protests, strikes and street demonstrations to relatively resigned acquiescence. The Hungarian heterodox programme, unlike, for example, the Israeli stabilization, does not rest on a declared agreement reached with the unions (see Bruno, 1993).

The government imposed unilateral limits on nominal pay rises in organisations funded by the budget (in public administration, the armed forces, education and health) and in firms still owned predominantly by the state. For brevity's sake, I will not give details here of the differentiated nominal pay increases allowed in the state sector as interpreted in this broader sense; in general, the limit was a 15 per cent nominal wage increase for 1995. Certainly this rise was substantially slower than the sudden increase in the level of consumer prices. The government did not interfere in private sector pay. However, as the state and private sectors largely share a common pool of labour, private employers followed more or less the same wage policy as the state employers.

As Table 1 has shown, real wages fell by more than 12 per cent. This can also be taken to mean that the employed made a big sacrifice in real wages to maintain the existing employment level. There have been cases in the labour market history, on an enterprise or national scale, of the employees voluntarily making such sacrifice out of solidarity. Under ASP 95, this sacrifice was compelled by two factors. One was state intervention, and the other the force of surprise. It is a well-known proposition of macroeconomics that the agents in the economy react differently to inflation depending on whether it is in line with expectations or unanticipated and unawaited. They tailor wage demands to the former in advance, but they cannot adjust to the latter in time, since their scope for action is blocked, or at least impeded by existing wage contracts.[21] This effect too has certainly contributed to the very sudden fall in real income.

It can be stated that income policy intervention, like exchange rate policy, has been one of the keys to ASP 95's efficacy so far.

It is doubtful how long these elements of income policy can be maintained. Certainly the state sector will decline in relative size, which in itself will narrow the scope for applying instruments similar to the 1995 intervention. The chance of increasing resistance to this kind of income policy cannot be ruled out either.

Nor is it just that the scope is narrowing. Thought should also be given to how desirable these instruments are. The criteria of a fair distribution of income speak against them. The incomes "caught" have been the ones easiest to catch, which affronts those who lose by it, and offends others' sense of justice as well.

3.3 Fiscal policy

The budget deficit showed a tendency to increase in the period before ASP 95 (see Table 4). There were fears that the country might enter a debt spiral. On the fiscal side, this would have meant that the deficit grew because of the budget's increasing interest burden, that the interest rate grew because of the crowding-out effect of the growing borrowing requirement of the budget, which would increase the interest burden further, and so on.[22]

ASP 95 has halted this tendency and begun to reverse it. The most important change is that the real value of expenditure in the primary budget has fallen significantly, while the real value of revenue has remained roughly the same. As a consequence, the primary budget deficit has passed into surplus.[23] This provides a

Table 4. Fiscal balance and gross debt of the general government (as percentage of GDP).

Indicators	1992	1993	1994	1995[a]
1. Primary SNA balance of the general government	2.7	-2.0	-2.8	2.0
2. Borrowing requirement of the general government				
SNA-system	-6.9	-5.5	-8.2	-6.5
GFS-system	-6.0	-5.2	-7.4	-4.0
3. Gross debt of general government	79.2	90.0	87.6	87.7
Consolidated gross public debt[b]	65.2	83.4	82.5	86.5
Domestic	12.1	23.2	23.5	24.5
Foreign	53.3	60.2	59.0	62.0
International reserves	15.7	21.9	20.3	33.0

Sources: National Bank of Hungary (1996c) and direct communication by the National Bank of Hungary.

Notes: The general government alongside the central government includes the extra budgetary funds, social security and health insurance funds and local governments. The main differences of the SNA and GFS methods are the following: in the SNA system of the state budget privatisation income and repayment of state loans do not feature as revenues, thus the borrowing requirement is not lessened by their amount, as it is in the GFS system; the SNA system considers foreign borrowing as revenue while the GFS system accounts it as financing.

a) Preliminary data.

b) The consolidated gross public debt includes the total debt (domestic and foreign) of the general government and the foreign debt of the National Bank of Hungary.

Table 5. Consolidated General Government Expenditure: International Comparison (as percentage of GDP).

Country	Year	Consolidated general government: current expenditure	capital	total
Lithuania	1993	22.0	2.6	24.6
Kazakstan	1993			23.5
Estonia	1993	30.2	2.0	32.2
Russia	1993			32.9
US	1992	36.3	2.5	38.8
Romania	1992	37.0	4.4	41.4
United Kingdom	1991	39.7	4.1	43.8
France	1992	46.2	4.6	50.9
Czech Republic	1993	41.4	6.8	48.2
Canada	1991	48.3	2.2	50.5
Germany[a]	1992	45.7	4.9	50.6
Ukraine	1993	50.4	1.7	52.1
Austria	1992	46.8	5.5	52.3
Belgium	1992	50.7	3.1	53.8
Netherlands	1992	52.7	3.8	56.5
Norway	1990	53.2	3.5	56.7
Hungary	1994	55.1	6.7	61.8
Denmark[a]	1993	58.9	2.8	61.8
Sweden	1993	67.6	3.3	71.0

Note: a) Data are provisional or preliminary.
Sources: P. Horváth (1996, p. 11). Primary sources: International Monetary Fund (1994a). For Lithuania and Estonia International Monetary Fund (1994b), for Kazakstan International Monetary Fund (1994c), for Ukraine International Monetary Fund (1994d) and for Russia International Monetary Fund (1994e). For Hungary, calculated on the basis of the publications by the Ministry of Finance of Hungary. Source of GDP in the cases of Germany and Austria: The World Bank (1995b).

source from which the great burden of debt on public finances can be reduced and the self-generating spiral of public debt can be broken.[24]

The changes in the fiscal sphere have included some measures that reduce certain universal welfare entitlements or apply a means test to them.

- Higher education ceased to be free. Although the fees imposed cover only a fraction of tuition costs, they go some way to applying the principle that those who will enjoy a lifetime's higher income thanks to their degree should contribute to the educational investment. Regrettably, a system of loans for students has still not been instituted.

- In line with the principle of need, the sphere of entitlement to maternity benefits and family allowance has been reduced.

- Dental care has ceased to be generally and fully free of charge. The provision remains free for specified exceptional groups (such as children and young people, the elderly, and the needy). The budget subsidy on pharmaceuticals has fallen and become more targeted.

- A start has been made to lengthening the period of active life, by raising the general retiring age. (Hungary has been one of the countries where the retiring age is very low: 55 for women and 60 for men.)

Actually very few practical steps have been taken to reform the welfare sector.[25] It was unfortunate that one or two of the measures were introduced too hastily, without sufficient preparation.[26] Even so, there is symbolic significance in the fact that such measures have occurred at all. The changes over the last three decades had all been in the same direction, creating successive new entitlements year by year that added to the welfare commitments of the state. The system of entitlements at any time was politically taboo. There was no political force willing to tackle painful reforms. It has now been shown that things can be changed, which opens the way to ideas for reform in this field as well. A start has been made to devising and debating proposals for reforming the welfare sector, although, regrettably, the process is still only at the very beginning.[27]

International experience shows that fiscal reforms become lasting if they are based more on reducing expenditure than on increasing revenue (see Alesina and Perotti, 1995; Giavazzi and Pagano, 1990 and 1996). This applies all the more to Hungary, as a country with one of the highest ratios of state spending to GDP in the world (see Table 5). ASP 95 radically took this approach. The decrease in the budget deficit in 1995 was achieved by making spending cuts of HUF 3 for every additional HUF 1 of fiscal revenue.[28]

Most of the fiscal reform is still ahead, including concomitant reassessment of the role of the state. Many functions that the state has hitherto performed by bureaucratic means, at taxpayers' expense, must be transferred — completely or partially — to the market, to for-profit and non-profit bodies, and to the voluntary organisations of a civil society.

3.4 Monetary policy and savings

The financial administration and the central bank, in opting for the exchange rate regime described in Section 3.1, substantially reduced the room for manoeuvre in monetary policy. The chosen regime in effect sets a fixed exchange rate at a given time, or only allows the exchange rate to move within a narrow band around a fixed mean. Although the fixed exchange rate continuously changes in time, this does not alter the fact that the present system belongs to the fixed, not the flexible, floating category of regimes. Furthermore, it means that the central bank has no way of setting quantitative monetary targets for itself. It has to adapt to the conditions of money supply and demand.

Even so, some instruments remain: altering the compulsory reserve rates, changing the rate of interest paid on compulsory or voluntary deposits by commercial banks, open market transactions, etc. Certainly it is worrying to think that the central bank, with its constitutional duty to combat inflation, has lost its leading role in this respect. The front-line battle concerns the budget deficit and the running away of incomes.

Although the monetary policy was tight, ASP 95 set out to reallocate lending, rather than reduce lending overall. Compared with the previous year, 1995 was one in which the budget received relatively fewer resources and the business sector relatively more. This redirection of lending is among the unorthodox features of the programme.

One of the most fortunate occurrences in the monetary sphere was somewhat unexpected. While economic policy reduced household income, household savings increased. Net lending by households rose from HUF 294 billion in 1994 to HUF 391 billion in 1995. Adjusted for inflation the increase of savings was 3 per cent.[29] There were certainly several factors at work. For a while, real interest rates rose enough to encourage saving.[30] There may also have been an inducement to save in the more and more general feeling that the future holds many uncertainties and people can no longer rely on help from a paternalist state. This has been brought home by several changes: from full employment and chronic labour shortage to mass unemployment, hardening of the earlier soft budget constraint and the associated constant threat to business survival, and the reduction in the universal commitments of the welfare state. The idea was put forward by Feldstein (1974) that the spread of state care will reduce private savings. Debate has continued in the West about how far this hypothesis can stand its ground. Now, the laboratory of post-socialist transition provides a new way of testing the hypothesis, with a process in the opposite direction. It is too soon to draw far-reaching conclusions from the Hungarian figures for 1995. Hungarian savings may still fluctuate a great deal in

Figure 5. Premia on Conversion.

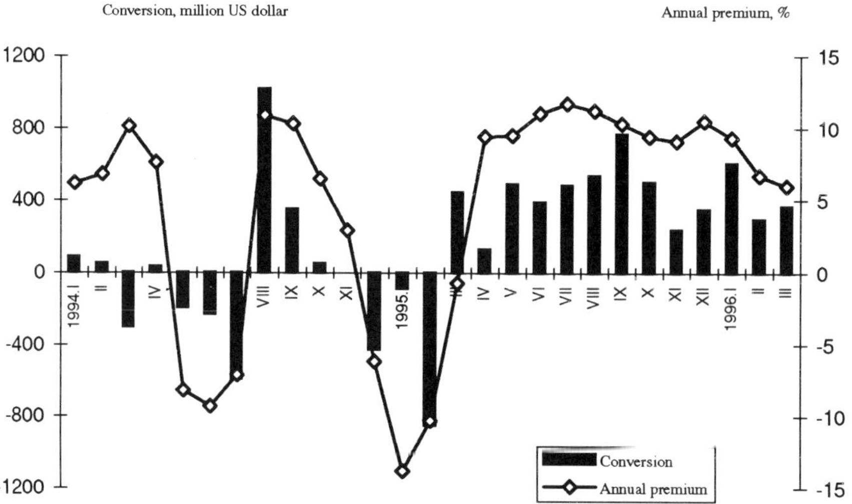

Source: Information provided by the National Bank of Hungary.

Note: Graph on conversion: negative sign represents net conversion from Hungarian currency to hard foreign currency; positive sign represents net conversion from hard foreign currency to Hungarian currency; Graph on premia: the premia are calculated on an annual basis. The premium is the excess of the Hungarian government 3 months treasury bill's return over the nominal depreciation of the Hungarian currency, and the average interest rate of hard foreign currencies. (The basket of foreign currencies is determined according to the proportions of Hungarian foreign trade.) It is a proxy to real return on government securities; For 1994 and 1995 the calculations are based on ex post actual data, the figures for the first quarter of 1996 are ex ante estimates.

response to many other factors (above all interest rates and incomes). In any case it will certainly be instructive to follow the process by comparative studies across countries.

It is of great importance to the internal and external equilibrium of the Hungarian economy that household saving rates should fluctuate as little as possible and total household savings, in real terms grow reliably. If the household saving rate should fall again, one of the harmful effects would be on aggregate demand, and ultimately on the current account. There are several ways in which savings can be helped to grow:

- It would be desirable to have as little fluctuation as possible in the real return on household savings, so that they remain lastingly positive. (Figure 5 shows the failure to achieve such stability over many years.) The trend was reversed after the first successes of ASP 95. Instead of capital flight (largely concealed), foreign capital began to flow into the country. Part of this is not intended as long-term real investment, some investors tend to buy short-term government securities and treasury bills only. These are extremely attractive investments, because the present exchange rate regime almost eliminates the exchange rate risk, and such Hungarian securities offer a sizeable, secure real return. This influx has already pushed the previously high rates of interest appreciably downwards. From the point of view of household savings, it would not be desirable for the interest level to fall too far.[31]

- Reforms must continue to narrow the range of bureaucratic public services financed from taxation (or compulsory contributions levied like taxes) and enhance the role of decentralised pension funds, health-insurance funds and housing savings banks. As these reforms make themselves felt by reducing taxes and contributions, and not only by narrowing the range of free services and transfers, they will encourage private savings. This is also needed for the expansion of the decentralised capital market where institutional investors can play a greater part.

3.5 Privatisation

A new surge of privatisation did not feature in the ASP 95 package announced in March 1995. On the contrary, the financial administration emphasized several times that the economy's grave disequilibrium must be overcome even if there are no substantial revenues imminent from privatisation. They rightly underlined that the practical implementation of privatisation must not be subordinated to short-term fiscal considerations.

Preparations for privatising several key branches had been taking place for a long time. The legislation governing these was drawn up, and the legal and organisational infrastructure for regulating the natural monopolies prepared after much delay and procrastination. Once these tasks had been done, the process speeded up suddenly. Within the space of a few months, the privatisation of the energy sector and telecommunications made a great stride forward. Several large state-owned banks and a number of sizeable manufacturing companies were also

Table 6. Annual flow of foreign direct investment into Hungary, 1990-1995 (US$ millions).

Form of investment	1990	1991	1992	1993	1994	1995
Inflow of foreign capital in cash	311	1,459	1,471	2,339	1,147	4,453
of which: Privatisation income	8	329	519	1,202	104	3,024
Inflow of foreign capital in kind	589	155	170	142	173	117
Total inflow of foreign direct nvestment	900	1,614	1,641	2,481	1,320	4,570

Source: Direct communication by the State Privatisation and Property Management (Állami Privatizációs és Vagyonkezelo Rt), except for the figure of privatisation income in 1995 which was communicated by the National Bank of Hungary.

Table 7. Labour productivity in post-socialist countries: International comparison.

		Average labour productivity (Real GDP/Employment; 1989=1)				
Country	1989	1990	1991	1992	1993	1994
Bulgaria	1.00	0.97	0.88	0.89	0.88	0.91
Czech Republic	1.00	0.97	0.88	0.89	0.88	0.91
Hungary	1.00	0.98	0.92	1.05	1.11	1.16
Poland	1.00	0.92	0.91	0.98	1.00	1.07
Romania	1.00	0.95	0.83	0.77	0.81	
Russia	1.00	0.89	0.74	0.66	0.57	
Slovak Republic	1.00	0.98	0.95	0.93	0.92	0.96

Source: Calculations of J. McHale (1996, Table 1) on the basis of the following sources: European Commission (1995), EBRD (1995) and various editions of the OECD/CCET publication: *Short-Term Economic Indicators: Transition Economies.*

privatised. The financial results of the accelerated privatisation of 1995 (as well as that of the overall privatisation process in earlier years) are shown in Table 6.

Most of the buyers were large Western firms. The contracts made with them call for strong development of these key branches. To take one example, one of the most grievous manifestations of the shortage economy for decades was the telephone shortage, with several hundred thousand families waiting for years for a phone in their homes. Since the beginning of privatisation — from 1994 to the first quarter of 1996 — 650 000 new lines have been installed. The concession contract stipulates a mandatory annual increase of 15.5 per cent in the number of telephone lines, which so far has been always outstripped by the telecommunication company.[32] In a few years the telephone service will have changed from a sellers' to a buyers' market.

It is especially worth noting that this is not just a case of new foreign owners setting about development tasks under privatisation agreements. Large international concerns that acquired property in Hungary earlier are making successive new investments, and these will contribute to modernising the Hungarian economy.

This study does not set out to analyse the experiences with privatisation in Hungary.[33] I will confine myself to the macroeconomic side-effects. Foreign direct investment in 1995, including sums paid in connection with privatisation, came to about US$4.6 billion (see Table 6). The scale of the sum can be gauged well from the fact that in 1994, the worst year of external disequilibrium, the deficit on the current account was US$3.9 billion. This fell in 1995 to US$2.5 billion, due to the factors already discussed (see Table 1).

There has been a debate about how to utilise this windfall income. There were plenty of applicants, and great pressure was applied to use the money in a "popular" way, in other words to consume it. Economic common sense prevailed at last, and it was decided to use the proceeds of privatising the key branches for reducing Hungary's state debt. Given how large the debt burden is, the saving of interest in this way seems to be the safest, and when all is said and done, the most effective investment. That is not to mention that a reduction in Hungary's indebtedness has numerous favourable external effects on the country's financial ratings and as a stimulant to investment.

4. What comes next?

To a large extent, it will be the political, rather than the economic sphere that determines subsequent development. Will the government, its each and every member and its parliamentary majority be prepared to persevere with the present economic policy? Will they not be tempted to change course, especially when they see the 1998 general elections approaching? What attitude will various groups in society take to the achievements and costs of adjustment and stabilization? What power relations will emerge between the programme's supporters and opponents? Indeed, most of the tasks entailed by it will extend beyond 1998. What will be the political composition of the next government and parliamentary majority, and what economic policy will it pursue? I have simply posed some questions here, to signify my appreciation of how vitally important the answers are to assessing the future. Even so, I leave the task of answering such questions to other studies of mine, confining myself in this work to economic and economic policy forecasts and recommendations in the narrow sense.

4.1 A prolonged process

ASP 95 was an example of "shock therapy" on a small scale, and it brought a rapid improvement in certain macroeconomic indicators. International experience, however, shows that such results are fragile, and can easily slip from economic policy-makers' grasp.

Interactions of several kinds apply between the various problems in the economy. In some cases, easing one economic difficulty may help to reduce another. Let me give two instances of such a favourable interaction, one might say a "virtuous circle". As the budget deficit lessens, the fall in the government's aggregate demand for credit has a "crowding in" effect. This makes more funds available for private lending, which is conducive to the acceleration of growth. This in turn increases budget revenue, which further reduces the budget deficit. At the same time, the reduction in the state borrowing requirement reduces the demand for foreign credit, so improving the country's external debt position. The interest premium paid on the debt is reduced. This means it is worth going substantially further in reducing Hungary's budget deficit.

The other example of a "virtuous circle" is the climate of business opinion. In the space of a few months, ASP 95 increased confidence among entrepreneurs and investors, at home and abroad. One of Hungary's business research institutes has been putting the same quarterly questions about the business situation and prospects to top company managers since 1987. According to their latest report (Kopint-Datorg, 1996), the situation in manufacturing was assessed more favourably in January 1996 than at any time in the previous decade. This is corroborated by the new surge of foreign investment, mentioned in connection with privatisation. The confidence itself becomes a growth factor, and the continuing, or in the best case accelerating, growth in turn reinforces the optimism.

However, there also exists unfavourable interactions — "vicious circles" — that must be reasonably taken into account. Let me give a few examples of these as well. Mention was made, in earlier parts of the study, of maintaining the real exchange rate, which at a given rate of inflation, requires nominal depreciation at the same pace. The depreciation becomes built into the inflationary expectations, which contributes to upholding the inertial inflation. It is extremely hard to improve the country's trading position, prevent a growth of indebtedness, and concurrently achieve disinflation. To take other examples, the forcing of growth by fiscal means may aggravate the budget deficit, and conversely, attempts to reduce the budget deficit at any price, by large tax increases, for example, may cause recession. What is a remedy for one ill turns out to exacerbate another.

Experience in Latin American countries with similar problems shows that the struggle may last even for one or two decades. First one, then another economic tension intensifies, and the therapy applied for the ill of the moment causes a further problem to arise. Some countries have relapsed time and again into one of their old problems after successful partial stabilizations. Either production falls drastically, or the balance on the current account deteriorates, or inflation speeds up, or even more than one problem arises. Chile, possibly the most successful Latin American country from the economic point of view, moved in 1978 from the rapid range of inflation to the moderate range of 20-40 per cent a year. It was another 17 years before the country finally reached single-digit inflation in 1995, but in the meantime, production continuously rose at an imposing rate of 4.8 per cent a year.[34] The chance of this happening sooner in Hungary cannot be excluded, but it cannot be relied upon either. It would be unfortunate to delude ourselves and others into thinking that a single great action like ASP 95 can suffice to let matters right themselves in two or three years.

One of the great dangers is complacency: "The situation's a bit better now, there's no need to be so strict as before." This is an enticing idea to any politician in government. There are already signs of this in Hungary. For instance, the emission of nominal wages jumped again at the beginning of the year, imports began to resume their rise, and investment activity seemed to be slowing down. We have to be constantly prepared to combat the adverse phenomena as soon as they appear.

The antecedents to ASP 95 are thought-provoking in this respect. Some researchers who studied the political economy of reforms (Drazen and Grilli, 1993) take the view that politicians are not prepared to take unpopular action until a crisis has actually occurred. The Hungarian ASP 95, as I emphasized earlier, is preventive in nature, which partly supports and partly refutes the hypothesis. It was the immediate threat, if not the crisis itself that triggered the programme. The question is how imminent the crisis has to be before politicians can summon up the courage to act. Is it too much to expect that they keep the economy "in good repair" simply by discernment of the economic situation, without a crisis looming or occurring?

I confess I am uncertain about the answer. Even consolidated, stable countries like the United States or France tend to protract and postpone long overdue fiscal reforms because the consequences of them would be unpopular.

4.2 Selecting priorities

Returning to Hungary's problems, one difficult problem is to choose the correct economic policy priorities and assign the right relative importance to the various parallel tasks. There has been much argument about this. In my view there is no universal rule, valid at all times in every country (or more narrowly, every post-socialist country). If a country has rapid inflation, or even hyperinflation, it must undoubtedly be the prime task to reduce it, at least to the annual rate of 30-0 per cent. There is enough evidence to show this is a requisite for healthy development (see Bruno and Easterly, 1995; Végh, 1992; Fischer, Sahay and Végh, 1996). What is less clear is how to choose the priorities when inflation has come down to the moderate range.

In the moderate band of inflation, disinflation becomes very costly. In most cases, it has not been achieved without a substantial rise in unemployment and a serious fall in production. So the lesser of two evils seems to be to allow the moderate inflation to continue. Care and strict control are needed to prevent it from running away. The emphasis, though, must shift to attaining the conditions for balanced, lasting growth. This includes reducing the budget deficit, cutting down state expenditure, halting the increase in external indebtedness (and where necessary, improving the debt/GDP ratio), and promoting exports and investment. All these developments will contribute to the acceleration of growth, which should also be encouraged in several other ways. As a by-product or side-effect of them, inflation may gradually slow down, so long as they are joined by the right price and income policy and monetary policy. In my view it would be unwise under such circumstances to impose an urgent and radical curb on inflation at the expense of all the other tasks.

The developments in the economies of the post-socialist countries may prove to be interesting experimental laboratories in this respect as well. The various governments have different points of departure and different economic policies. There are, and no doubt will remain, some countries where the financial administration uses real appreciation of the exchange rate to reduce the inflation rate. For my part I argue against doing this in Hungary. I continue to recommend caution, warning against real appreciation of the forint and the threat of a renewed deterioration in the balance of trade.[35]

4.3 A reassuring sign: rising productivity

Readers will gather that I feel the Hungarian economy is vulnerable in several respects. I have tried to point to the dangers, but there is one fundamentally important aspect of the Hungarian economy that fills me with confidence: the rise in labour productivity. Mention was made earlier of auspicious signs that the competitiveness of Hungarian exports is improving. This arises partly from the movement in the exchange rate, but even more important is the efficiency of the underlying real process. The trend in productivity is the key to growth (and for a small, open economy like Hungary's, export-led growth).

Table 7 compares productivity over time in several post-socialist countries.[36] Hungary shows the most favourable trend in this respect. There are several contributing factors.

Although property relations were transformed more slowly than in countries that conducted so-called "mass" privatisation (distributing fragmented property rights free of charge), Hungary's privatisation process was more inclined to generate "genuine" owners. Ownership has gone mainly to private persons or businesses already operating that can exercise real control over management and impose application of the profit motive. This has also helped to bring about a radical restructuring of many firms.

The budget constraint in Hungary has really hardened. This was promoted by legislation compatible with a market economy and conducive to financial discipline: the new acts on bankruptcy, banking and accounting. Although some stipulations in the bankruptcy act initially formulated in an extreme way caused serious problems for a time, the mistakes were quickly remedied. The ultimate result is a process of "natural selection" that allows the truly fit, efficient and profitable businesses to survive.[37]

Connected to the above changes is the elimination of the phenomenon "unemployment on the job" that evolved under the socialist system. The larger part of this painful process — accompanied by human sufferings, the tormenting feelings of losing one's job — has already taken place in Hungary, while, as it seems, many other post-socialist countries try to put it off.

One common explanation for all the changes listed so far is the very high rate of foreign direct investment. Hungary has received about half the foreign capital investment entering Eastern Europe. Apart from its benefits in macro-financial terms, this has helped to introduce new products, technologies and management methods and tighten labour discipline and organisation.

A steady rise in labour productivity is not enough by itself to produce lasting growth in the economy. There must also be a favourable development in several other circumstances, some of which have been detailed in this study. However, theory demonstrates, and the broad experience of international economic history confirms, that this is one of the most important conditions (perhaps <u>the</u> most important) for healthy, steady economic growth. This is among the factors that give cause for confidence in the future of the Hungarian economy, despite the many difficulties it faces.

Notes

[1] Work on some parts of ASP 95 had begun under the previous Finance Minister, László Békesi. The programme was then drawn up under the direction of the new Finance Minister, Lajos Bokros, and the new president of the National Bank of Hungary, György Surányi. ASP 95 was announced to the country on television by Prime Minister Gyula Horn, accompanied by the Finance Minister and the president of the central bank.

For a year, Bokros played a prominent part in devising, explaining and implementing the programme, and it came to be known colloquially as the Bokros Package. I have preferred to use a "non-personal" name here because responsibility for the programme was accepted throughout by the Prime Minister, and because the government, the majority in Parliament, and the central bank remain collectively responsible for what occurs under it — achievements and mistakes alike. Since Lajos Bokros resigned, however, the new Finance Minister and the government have committed themselves to continuing to implement the programme.

[2] Indeed it takes two or more probably three years before the effects of such a programme can be fully assessed. A study by Alesina and Perotti (1995), for instance, terms a fiscal adjustment successful if the public debt/GDP ratio shows a material improvement (of at least 5 per cent) in the third year after the firm measures were taken.

[3] Attempts at an overall assessment have been largely confined so far to articles in the Hungarian daily and weekly papers and internal reports by the government and the central bank. These I have tried to use in my study. See, for instance, National Bank of Hungary (1996a) and Ministry of Finance (1996a). Among the more detailed studies, I draw attention to Köves (1995b) and Oblath (1996).

[4] The sources of the data are: National Bank of Hungary (1995), pp. 172 and 234, and see also Tables 1, 2 and 4.

[5] Of the analyses of the Hungarian macroeconomic situation that built up in 1993-1995, I would emphasize Antal (1994); Békesi (1993, 1994, 1995); Csaba (1995); Erdos (1994); Köves (1995a, 1995b); Lányi (1994-1995); Oblath (1995); and World Bank (1995a).
For the view of those directing ASP 95, see Bokros (1995a; 1995b; 1996), and Surányi (1995a; 1995b; 1996).
For my own views see Kornai (1995a) that was written before the announcement of ASP 95, and see furthermore Kornai (1995b; 1996a) that were written during the implementation of the programme.

[6] Of the literature on the Latin American crises and protracted financial disequilibria, I relied mainly on Cooper (1992); Dornbusch and Fischer (1993); Dornbusch, Goldfajn and Valdés (1995); Dornbusch and Werner (1994); Krugman (1991); Little, Cooper, Corden and Rajapatirana (1993); Sachs (1996); Sachs, Tornell and Velasco (1995).

[7] For the sake of brevity I did not include all indicators demonstrating similarities in Tables 2 and 3.

[8] Economists watching the events in Mexico with concern, including the writer, avoided openly alarming the public and hesitant politicians with threats of catastrophe. There was a danger that such warnings would become self-fulfilling prophecies by arousing panic. It was hard to reassure the Hungarian public and the international business world, in other words to avoid arousing panic, while mobilising efforts to avert the crisis.

[9] These views are reported in the article of Kocsis (1995).

[10] The balance of the current account does not contain the balance of medium- and long-term capital flows. Therefore, a very important item, namely foreign direct investment, does not appear in the current account. However, while the large inflow of foreign direct investment, does not improve the current account, it does show up in the improvement of the country's net external debt. When calculating net foreign debt, reserves are part of the asset side, and capital inflow contributes to the reserves. Therefore, it is feasible to have a negative current account and at the same time a reduction of net external debt.

[11] The index number mentioned in the text is a quotient with the business sector's "own resources for investment purposes" as a numerator and GDP as denominator. The definition of own resources for investment purposes is depreciation plus pre-tax profit minus company taxation. The source of the data is Ministry of Finance (1996a), p. 20.
Szentgyörgyvári and Baár (1996), p.18, take another definition: profitability before tax = difference between total income and total costs, divided by total income. Taking the average for the whole business sector, this was negative in 1992, -3.2 per cent, rising to +3.3 per cent in 1994 and to +7.2 per cent in 1995.

[12] This idea was focal to my economic policy proposals, published in Hungary in the summer of 1994, before the definitive version of ASP 95 was devised (Kornai, 1995a).

[13] For the analysis of this exchange rate regime see Kopits, 1996.

[14] "Foreign inflation" means here the average inflation for a basket of currencies that reflects the actual composition of Hungary's foreign trade.

[15] The convertibility of the Hungarian forint meets the criteria of "current-account convertibility" in Article VIII of the IMF. Furthermore, it meets the OECD's convertibility requirements for certain capital transactions.

[16] National Bank of Hungary (1996a), p. 25.

[17] The study by Szentgyörgyvári and Baár (1996) provides an excellent survey of measurement of the real exchange rate and competitiveness, and the Hungarian situation and problems in this respect.

[18] Analyses showed that imports of certain products, such as passenger cars, had increased particularly. So extra consumer tax was imposed on these (alongside the import surcharge).

[19] Under the present exchange rate regime, this would amount to a formula of having a pre-announced pace of nominal depreciation much lower than the expected rate of inflation. The pre-announced exchange rate would act as a nominal anchor, pulling the rate of inflation down.

[20] See the literature already quoted in Section 2 in connection with the crises. There are also lessons for Hungary in the conclusions reached in the study by Dornbusch, Goldfajn and Valdés (1995), pp. 251-252: "A policy of bringing down inflation by slowing the rate of depreciation below the rate of inflation ... is a common way of creating overvaluation. Because the real exchange rate is sticky downward, overvaluation is not easily undone by wage-price deflation and thus, ultimately, leads to collapse and devaluation ... The temptation to use the exchange rate to obtain early results on disinflation without much unemployment is all too obvious as a shortcut, but the results are often illusory. After the collapse, inflation will be higher than it was at the outset."

[21] On the effects of unanticipated inflation, see Sachs and Larrain (1993), pp. 349-352.

[22] The best account of the debt position in Hungarian public finance can be found in Borbély and Neményi (1994; 1995).

[23] A thorough analysis of the fiscal policy of ASP 95 appears in the study by Oblath (1996) pp. 81-4 and 95-7.

[24] The index of gross debt of the general government over GDP remained practically unchanged, while the index of consolidated gross public debt over GDP has risen somewhat (see Table 4). A substantial reduction in both these indices would be desirable, so as to bring the country's macroeconomic situation closer to the norms required for EU membership.

[25] The specific expenditure-reducing changes listed above had relatively little effect on the fiscal situation in 1995. Their effect will really be felt in 1996, and still more in 1997.

[26] It was a great mistake that some of the measures in their original form conflicted with the principles of constitutionalism, and were therefore rejected by the Constitutional Court.

[27] See World Bank (1995a). Among those to comment on welfare-sector reform have been Andorka, Kontradas and Tóth (1995); Augusztinovics (1993); Augusztinovics and Martos (1995); Ferge (1995, 1996a, 1996b); and Kornai (1996b).

[28] Own calculation on the basis of data from National Bank of Hungary (1996b), p. 110.

[29] Net lending by households = gross money savings - increment in borrowing by households. (All three figures are flow variables.) The source of the figures is Ministry of Finance (1996b), Table 14.

[30] A contribution to the rise in total household savings expressed in forints was made by the fact that continuous depreciation of the forint increases the forint value of deposits held in foreign exchange.

[31] Speculative short-term inflows of capital can cause other grave problems as well. The conversion of hard currency increases the inflationary pressure, and sterilisation of this is extremely expensive. It is not possible to count on the resulting extra foreign exchange reserves, which may evaporate as easily as they arrived. It is difficult to gauge what would be the ideal interest level and return on state securities. Even if this were known, the central bank could still only exert an indirect influence, after a long lag, on the "thin" credit and capital markets, which continue to operate with a great deal of friction. On this, see Darvas (1996); Darvas and Simon (1996); Dornbusch, Goldfajn, Valdés (1995); Sachs (1996).

[32] Information provided by the telecommunication company MATÁV.

[33] On this, see Laki (1993); Major and Mihályi (1994); Mihályi (1993, 1994, 1995); and Voszka (1992, 1993, 1994).

[34] The sources of the data are IMF (1995), and for 1995: IMF (1996b), p. 65, and National Institute of Statistics (1996).

[35] Darvas and Simon (1996) take a similar position.

[36] On the comparative productivity of post-socialist countries, see McHale (1996).

[37] Regrettably, the tendencies are not unequivocal. Firms in grave financial difficulties are bailed-out far less frequently than before, but some of the business sector's financial woes tend nowadays to take the form of "non-performing bank loans", and in most cases the banks so far have been rescued from insolvency. (Even so, it must be admitted, they can rely less confidently on state assistance than they could in the past, following the liquidation of a few non-viable banks.) Nevertheless, it certainly cannot be said that Hungary has left the syndrome of a soft budget constraint behind.

References

Alesina, A. and Perotti, R., 1995, Reducing Budget Deficits, prepared for the conference "Growing Government — International Experiences", Stockholm, June 12, [mimeo].

Andorka, R., Kondratas, A., and Tóth, I.G., 1995, "A jóléti rendszer jellemzoi és reformjának lehetoségei" (The Characteristics of the Welfare System and the Ways of Reforming It), *Közgazdaosági Szemle*, 42 (1), pp. 1-29.

Antal, L., 1994, "Az örökség. A gazdaság helyzete és a feladatok" (The Legacy. The Situation of the Economy and the Tasks), *Társadalmi Szemle*, 49 (10), pp. 12-21.

Augusztinovics, M., 1993, "Egy értelmes nyugdíjrendszer" (An Intelligent Pension System), *Közgazdasági Szemle, 40* (5), pp. 415-431.

Augusztinovics, M. and Martos, B., 1995, "Számítások és következtetések nyugdíjreformra" (Calculations and Deductions for a Pension Reform), *Közgazdasági Szemle, 42* (11), pp. 993-1023.

Banco de Mexico, 1995, *Indicadores Economicos*, December.

Banco de Mexico, 1996a, *Indicadores Economicos*, February.

Banco de Mexico, 1996b, *Indicadores Economicos*, May, Internet update.

Békesi, L., 1993, "A feladat öt szöglete. Farkas Zoltán interjúja Békesi Lászlóval" (The Five Angels of the Task. An Interview with László Békesi by Zoltán Farkas), *Társadalmi Szemle*, 48 (3), pp. 3-13.

Békesi, L., 1994, "A társadalom még nincs tisztában a gazdasági helyzettel. Karsai Gábor interjúja Békesi Lászlóval" (The Society is not Aware of the Economic Situation Yet. An Interview with László Békesi by Gábor Karsai), *Figyelo*, July 14, pp. 13-15.

Békesi, L., 1995, "Mást választhatunk, de 'jobbat' aligha" (A Different Program Can Be Chosen, But a 'Better' One Hardly), *Népszabadság*, July 8, pp. 17-18.

Blanchflower, D.G. and Oswald, A.J., 1994, *The Wage Curve,* Cambridge and London: The MIT Press.

Bokros, L., 1995a, "A leendo pénzügyminiszter huszonöt pontja. Bokros Lajos szakmai cselekvési programjának alapvonalai" (The Twenty Five Points of the Future Minister of Finance. The Fundamental Ideas of Lajos Bokros' Action Program), *Népszabadság*, February 17, p. 15.

Bokros, L., 1995b, "Az államháztartásról, a stabilizációról. Dr. Bokros Lajos pénzügyminiszter tájékoztatója" (On the State Budget and Stabilization. An Exposition by Dr. Lajos Bokros, the Finance Minister), *Pénzügyi Szemle*, 40 (4), pp. 259-262.

Bokros, L., 1996, "Növekedés és/vagy egyensúly — avagy az 1995. március 12-én meghirdetett stabilizáció tanulságai" (Growth and/or Stabilization — Lessons from the Stabilization Program Announced on March 12, 1995), *Népszabadság*, March 11, p. 8.

Borbély, L.A. and Neményi, J., 1994, "Az államadósság növekedésének összetevoi 1990—1992-ben" (The Factors behind the Growth of the Public Debt, 1990—92), *Közgazdasági Szemle*, 41 (2), pp. 110-126.

Borbély, L.A. and Neményi, J., 1995, "Eladósodás, a külso és belso államadósság alakulása az átmenet gazdaságában (1990—1993)" (Indebtedness, the Development of External and Internal Public Debt in the Economy of Transition, 1990—1993) in *Rendszerváltás és stabilizáció. A piacgazdasági átmenet elso évei*, ed.: Tamás Mellár, Budapest, Magyar Trendkutató Központ, pp. 123-166.

Bruno, M., 1993, *Crisis, Stabilization, and Economic Reform: Therapy by Consensus*. New York, Oxford University Press.

Bruno, M. and Easterly, W., 1995 "Inflation Crises and Long-Run Growth", *NBER Working Paper Series*, n°. 5209, Cambridge, National Bureau of Economic Research, Harvard University, August.

Central Statistical Office (Központi Statisztikai Hivatal), 1995a, *Magyar statisztikai évkönyv 1994*, (Hungarian Statistical Yearbook 1994), Budapest.

Central Statistical Office (Központi Statisztikai Hivatal), 1995b, *A KSH jelenti*, n°. 12.

Central Statistical Office (Központi Statisztikai Hivatal), 1995c, *A nemzetgazdaság munkaerömérlege* (Labor Balances of the National Economy), January 1, Budapest.

Central Statistical Office (Központi Statisztikai Hivatal), 1995d, *Foglalkoztatottság és kereseti arányok, 1993—1995* (Employment and Relative Earnings), Budapest.

Central Statistical Office (Központi Statisztikai Hivatal), 1996a, *KSH Statisztikai Hírek*, April 2.

Central Statistical Office (Központi Statisztikai Hivatal), 1996b, *A KSH jelenti*, n°. 1.

Central Statistical Office (Központi Statisztikai Hivatal), 1996c, *Magyarország nemzeti számlái, 1991—1994*, (Hungary's National Accounts, 1991—1994), Budapest, forthcoming.

Central Statistical Office (Központi Statisztikai Hivatal), 1996d, *Fobb munkaügyi folyamatok. Negyedéves jelentés* (Major Processes of the Labor Market. Quarterly Report), Budapest.

Central Statistical Office (Központi Statisztikai Hivatal), 1996e, *Statisztikai Havi Közlemények*, n°. 4.

Cooper, R.N., 1992, *Economic Stabilization and Debt in Developing Countries*. Cambridge and London, The MIT Press.

Csaba, L., 1995, "Gazdaságstratégia helyett konjunktúra-politika" (Trade-Cycle Policy Instead of Economic Strategy), *Külgazdaság*, 39 (3), pp. 36-46.

Darvas, Z., 1996, "Exchange Rate Premia and the Credibility of the Crawling Target Zone in Hungary", *Discussion Paper Series*, n°. 1307, London: Centre for Economic Research, January.

Darvas, Z. and Simon, A., 1996, Toke beáramlás, árfolyam- és pénzpolitika (Capital Inflow, Exchange Rate and Monetary Policy), Budapest: National Bank of Hungary (Magyar Nemzeti Bank), Közgazdasági és Kutatási Foosztály, February, [mimeo].

Dornbusch, R. and Fischer, S., 1993, "Moderate Inflation", *The World Bank Economic Review*, 7 (1), pp. 1-44.

Dornbusch, R. and Werner, A., 1994, "Mexico: Stabilization, Reform and No Growth", *Brookings Papers on Economic Activity*, 1994, (1), pp. 253-315.

Dornbusch, R., Goldfajn, I. and Valdés, R.O., 1995, "Currency Crises and Collapses", *Brookings Papers on Economic Activity*, 1995, (2), pp. 219-293.

Drazen, A. and Grilli, V., 1993, "The Benefit of Crises for Economic Reforms", *American Economic Review*, June, 83 (3), pp. 598-607.

EBRD, 1995, *Transition Report*, London.

Erdos, T., 1994, "A tartós gazdasági növekedés realitásai és akadályai" (The Realities of Lasting Economic Growth and Obstacles to It), *Közgazdasági Szemle*, 41 (6), pp. 463-477.

European Commission, 1995, *Employment Observatory: Central and Eastern Europe*, n°. 7.

Feldstein, M., 1974, "Social Security, Induced Retirement, and Aggregate Capital Accumulation", *Journal of Political Economy*, September/October, 82 (5), pp. 905-926.

Ferge, Z., 1995, "A magyar segélyezési rendszer reformja, 1" (The Reform of the Hungarian System of Cash Benefits, 1), *Esély*, n°. 1.

Ferge, Z., 1996a, "A magyar segélyezési rendszer reformja, 2" (The Reform of the Hungarian System of Cash Benefits, 2), *Esély*, n°. 1.

Ferge, Z., 1996b, "A szociálpolitika esélyei" (The Prospects of Social Policy), *Vigilia*, 1996, forthcoming.

Fischer, S., Sahay, R. and Végh, C.A., 1996, *Stabilization and Growth in Transition Economies: The Early Experience*, Washington, D.C.: The International Monetary Fund, January, [mimeo].

Giavazzi, F. and Pagano, M., 1990, "Can Severe Fiscal Contractions be Expansionary? Tales of Two Small European Countries", *NBER Macroeconomics Annual*, pp. 75-116.

Giavazzi, F. and Pagano, M., 1996, "Non-Keynesian Effects of Fiscal Policy Changes: International Evidence and the Swedish Experience", *Swedish Economic Policy Review*, May, forthcoming.

Halpern, L., 1996, "Real Exchange Rates and Exchange Rate Policy in Hungary", *Discussion Paper Series*, n°. 1366, London: Centre for Economic Policy Research, March.

Horváth, P., 1996, Vizsgálatok az állami redisztribúció tanulmányozásához (Studying State Redistribution), Budapest, [mimeo].

IMF, 1994a, *International Financial Statistics Yearbook 1994,* Washington, D.C.

IMF, 1994b, *IMF Economic Review*, n°. 7.

IMF, 1994c, *IMF Economic Review*, n°. 16.

IMF, 1994d, *IMF Economic Review*, n°. 17.

IMF, 1994e, *IMF Economic Review*, n°. 18.

IMF, 1995, *International Financial Statistics Yearbook 1995*, Washington, D.C.

IMF, 1996a, *International Financial Statistics*, February.

IMF, 1996b, *International Financial Statistics*, April.

Kindleberger, C.P., 1978, *Manias, Panics, and Crashes: A History of Financial Crisis*, New York, Basic Books.

Kocsis, G., 1995, "Mégis, kinek a borére" (At Whose Expense, After All?), *Heti Világgazgaság*, October 28, p. 100.

Kopint-Datorg, 1996, *Konjunktúrateszt-eredmények a feldolgozóiparban, az építoiparban és a kiskereskedelemben, 1995. IV. negyedév* (Activity Test Results in the Manufacturing, Construction and Retail Trade, 1995, 4th Quarter), Budapest.

Kopits, G., 1996, "Hungary's Preannounced Crawling Peg", *Acta Oeconomica*, forthcoming.

Kornai, J., 1995a, "Lasting Growth as the Top Priority: Macroeconomic Tensions and Government Economic Policy in Hungary", *Acta Oeconomica*, 47 (1/2), pp. 1-38.

Kornai, J., 1995b, "The Dilemmas of Hungarian Economic Policy", in *Lawful Revolution in Hungary, 1989—94*, eds.: Béla K. Király and András Bozóki, Boulder: Social Science Monographs, Highland Lakes: Atlantic Research and Publications and New York: Columbia University Press, pp. 323-349.

Kornai, J., 1996a, "Paying the Bill for Goulash-Communism: Hungarian Development and Macro Stabilization in Political-Economy Perspective", *Social Research*, forthcoming.

Kornai, J., 1996b, "Az állampolgár és az állam: A jóléti rendszer reformja" (The Citizen and the State: Reform of the Welfare System), *Mozgó Világ*, Feb. 1996, 22 (2), pp. 33-45.

Köves, A., 1995a, "Egy alternatív gazdaságpolitika szükségessége és lehetosége" (The Necessity of an Alternative Economic Policy and the Scope for It), *Külgazdaság*, 39 (6), pp. 4-17.

Köves, A., 1995b, "Gazdaságpolitikai dilemmák és lehetoségek a Bokros-csomag után" (Economic Policy Dilemmas and Potentials after the Bokros Package), *Külgazdaság*, 39 (11), pp. 4-18.

Krugman, P., 1991, "Financial Crises in the International Economy", in *The Risk of Economic Crisis*. ed.: Martin Feldstein, Chicago and London: The University of Chicago Press, pp. 85-128.

Laki, M., 1993, "Chances for the Acceleration of Transition: The Case of Hungarian Privatization", *East European Politics and Societies*, Fall, 7 (3), pp. 440-451.

Lányi, K., 1994, 1995, "Alkalmazkodás és gazdasági visszaesés Magyarországon és más országokban. I. Tények és magyarázatok. II. Gazdaságpolitika és szelekció" (Adjustment and Economic Recession in Hungary and in Other Countries. I. Facts and Explanations. II. Economic Policy and Selection), *Társadalmi Szemle*, 49 (12), pp. 13-25. and 50 (1), pp. 3-19.

Little, I.M.D., Cooper, R.N., Corden, W.M. and Rajapatirana, S., 1993, *Boom, Crisis and Adjustment. The Macroeconomic Experience of Developing Countries*, Oxford: Oxford University Press, published for the World Bank.

Major, I. and Mihályi, P., 1994, "Privatizáció — hogyan tovább?" (Privatization — How to Go Further?), *Közgazdasági Szemle*, 41 (3), pp. 214-228.

McHale, J., 1996, *Equilibrium Employment Rates and Transformational Slumps,* Cambridge: Harvard University, March, [mimeo].

Mexican Ministry of Finance (SHCP), 1995, *Informe sobre la Situacion Economica, las Finanzas Publicas y la Deuda Publica*, Fourth Quarter.

Mihályi, P., 1993, "Plunder—Squander—Plunder. The Strange Demise of State Ownership," *The Hungarian Quarterly*, Summer, 34, pp. 62-75.

Mihályi, P., 1994, "Privatization in Hungary: An Overview" in *Privatization in the transition process. Recent experiences in Eastern Europe*, eds.: Yilmaz Akyüz, Detlef J. Kotte, András Köves and László Szamuely. Geneva and Budapest: United Nations Conference on Trade and Development and Kopint-Datorg, pp. 363-385.

Mihályi, P., 1995, *Privatisation in Hungary: Now Comes the 'Hard Core'.* presented at the V. World Congress for Central and East European Studies, Warsaw, August 6-11, [mimeo].

Ministry of Finance (Pénzügyminisztérium), 1996a, *A gazdaság helyzete 1995-96 fordulóján* (The Economic Situation at the Turn of 1995-96), Budapest, February.

Ministry of Finance (Pénzügyminisztérium), 1996b, *Tájékoztató az 1995. évi és az 1996. év eleji gazdasági folyamatokról* (Report on the Economic Processes in 1995 and at the Beginning of 1996), Budapest, March.

National Bank of Hungary (Magyar Nemzeti Bank), 1995, *Annual Report 1994*, Budapest.

National Bank of Hungary (Magyar Nemzeti Bank), 1996a, *Az 1995. évi gazdasági és pénzügyi folyamatokról,* (On the Economic and Monetary Processes in 1995), Budapest, February.

National Bank of Hungary (Magyar Nemzeti Bank), 1996b, *Havi Jelentés*, n°. 2.

National Bank of Hungary (Magyar Nemzeti Bank), 1996c, *Eloterjesztés és jelentés az 1996. évi rendes közgyulésnek a Magyar Nemzeti Bank 1995. évi üzlettervérol* (Exposition and Report to the 1996 Annual General Assembly on the Business Plan of the National Bank of Hungary), Budapest, April.

National Bank of Hungary (Magyar Nemzeti Bank), 1996d, *Éves jelentés 1995* (Annual Report 1995), Budapest, April.

National Institute of Statistics (Instituto Nacional de Estadisticas), 1996, Internet update, May.

Oblath, G., 1995, "A költségvetési deficit makrogazdasági hatásai Magyarországon" (The Macroeconomic Effects of Budget Deficit in Hungary) *Külgazdaság*, 39 (7/8), pp. 22-33.

Oblath, G., 1996, "Makrogazdasági folyamatok" (Macroeconomic Processes) in *Konjunktúrajelentés. A világgazdaság és a magyar gazdaság helyzete és kilátásai 1996 tavaszán*, Budapest, Kopint-Datorg, n°. 1, pp. 79-118.

OECD, 1995, *OECD Economic Outlook*, December.

OECD, 1996, *Economic Indicators*, March.

Sachs, J.D., 1996, *Economic Transition and the Exchange Rate Regime*, Cambridge, Harvard Institute for International Development, Harvard University, [mimeo].

Sachs, J.D. and Larrain, F.B., 1993, *Macroeconomics in the Global Economy*, New York, Harvester Wheatsheaf.

Sachs, J.D., Tornell, A. and Velasco, A., 1995, "The Collapse of the Mexican Peso: What Have We Learned?", *Discussion Paper*, n°. 1724, Cambridge, Harvard Institute of Economic Research, Harvard University, May.

Surányi, G., 1995a, "A gazdaság örökölt struktúrái gúzsba kötik az országot. Válaszol Surányi György, a Nemzeti Bank elnöke" (The Inherited Economic Structures Shackle the Country. György Surányi, the President of the National Bank Answers), Heti Világgazdaság, April 29, pp. 47-48.

Surányi, G., 1995b, "Önmagunkkal kell megállapodásra jutni. Beszélgetés árakról, bérekrol, kamatokról Surányi Györggyel, az MNB elnökével Bossányi Katalin interjúja" (It is Ourselves we Have to Come to an Agreement with. A Conversation about Prices, Wages and Interest Rates with György Surányi, President of the National Bank. An Interview by Katalin Bossányi), *Népszabadság*, December 30, pp. 1 and 10.

Surányi, G., 1996, "Jobban igen, másként nem. Szombati MH-extra Surányi Györggyel, a Magyar Nemzeti Bank elnökével. Pintér Dezso riportja" (It Can Be Done Better, but not in Other Ways. A Saturday Interview of 'Magyar Hírlap' with György Surányi, the President of the Hungarian National Bank. An Interview by Dezso Pintér), *Magyar Hírlap*, January 6, p. 9.

Szentgyörgyvári, A. and Baár, I., 1996, *A magyar nemzetgazdaság nemzetközi versenyképessége 1995-ben, kitekintés 1996-ra és 1997-re* (The International Competitiveness of the Hungarian National Economy in 1995, a Detour to 1996 and 1997), Budapest, National Bank of Hungary (Magyar Nemzeti Bank), Közgazdasági és Kutatási Foosztály, April, [mimeo].

Végh, C.A., 1992, "Stopping High Inflation", *IMF Staff Papers*, September, 39 (3), pp. 626-695.

Voszka, É., 1992, "Not Even the Contrary is True: The Transfigurations of Centralization and Decentralization," *Acta Oeconomica*, 44 (1/2), pp. 77-94.

Voszka, É., 1993, "Variations on the Theme of Self-Privatization," *Acta Oeconomica*, 45 (3/4), pp. 310-318.

Voszka, É., 1994, "Centralization, Renationalization, Redistribution: The Role of the Government in Changing the Ownership Structure in Hungary, 1989—93," *Discussion Paper Series*, n°. 916, London, Centre for Economic Policy Research, February.

World Bank, 1995a, Hungary: Structural Reforms for Sustainable Growth, Document of the World Bank, Country Operations Division, Central Europe Department, Report n°. 13577-HU, Washington, D.C, June 12.

World Bank, 1995b, *World Tables 1995,* Washington, DC.

7

The interplay between economic and political transition

Leszek Balcerowicz

1. Basic concepts and the analytical framework

Political transition in the countries of Central and Eastern Europe refers to the movement away from a one-party communist state towards political pluralism, i.e. open competition for votes as the main vehicle for achieving and maintaining power within the state. Economic transition denotes a movement from a socialist economy, a special case of a non-market economic system, towards a market economy with a growing share of private ownership. Economic transition is thus synonymous with a market-oriented reform, a special case of systemic change or institutional transformation. In addition, economic transition includes, if necessary, macroeconomic stabilization.

The essence of both political and economic transition is a change in a country's institutional system, i.e. its legal and organisational framework, which is conventionally divided into a political and economic system.

These definitions deal with transition as a process. However, it is also useful to distinguish the **transition outcomes**, i.e. the resulting political or economic systems. Among the outcomes one can further distinguish the intermediate ones (those which are likely to be changed further) and the final one (i.e. the institutional system which will remain "frozen" for a number of years).

Distinguishing the process and the outcome of transition is important for three main reasons, which I discuss with a focus on the economic transition:

1. The two sets of variables must be **conceptualised** in different ways. The process of economic transition differs in the timing of the launching of the new economic package, and in the speed and scope of its implementation.

2. Based on these criteria we can distinguish more or less radical modes of transition (see Balcerowicz and Gelb, 1994). The transition outcome, i.e. the emerging economic system, differs along such dimensions as the ownership structure, the mechanisms of corporate governance, the relative prices, the kind and the degree of competition, the tax/GDP ratio, the flexibility of the labour market, the type of the pension system, etc.

3. The process and the outcome of economic transition produce different sets of economic consequences, and these consequences additionally depend on the form of each of those variables. For example, a radical transition is capable of quickly eliminating the pervasive shortages. It also quickly improves the relative prices, increases the share of the private sector, hardens enterprises' budget constraint and introduces a large dose of competition among suppliers. As a result of these systemic changes a country achieves some **transition effects.**[1] They include a rapid increase in most measures of economic efficiency and a — partly related — rapid decline in environmental pollution (Balcerowicz, 1995).

   These transition effects are related to systemic change and will be exhausted once this change comes to an end, i.e. the economic system remains "frozen". From then on it will be this final economic system which will be the main domestic determinant of a country's long-run economic performance. For the societies of Central and Eastern Europe which have much "catching-up" to do and which need to do a lot of labour reallocation, the main criteria for judging the quality of the final economic system should be the rate of the long-run economic growth that it is capable of generating and the — partly related — capacity to create productive jobs. Economic systems, conventionally called "capitalist" or "market economies", differ considerably along the dimensions I mentioned in point 1 above.

   Furthermore, the experience and emerging institutional theory of economic growth suggest that large differences in these dimensions bring about huge differences in the long-run rate of economic growth and in the pace of job-creation. The most relevant comparisons are the US versus most of Western Europe during the last twenty years (the job creation aspect) and the Asian Tigers plus Chile versus most of the other developing countries during the last 20-30 years (the rate of both growth and job creation). One can infer that the model which would most fully meet the chosen optimality criteria is a predominantly private enterprise market economy, with free entry, outward-looking orientation, low tax/GDP ratio, flexible labour markets, macroeconomic stability, etc. (Sachs and Warner, 1996). We can call such a model an optimal final system for the post-socialist countries. The relevant question is then what determines which final system they eventually get to, and how distant or close it will be from the optimal one.

4. Based on our distinction between the process and outcome, we can further inquire whether there is a **relationship** between the mode of economic transition and the quality of its final outcome. It follows from the adopted definitions that a radical approach, **if sustained**, would produce the optimal final system. But is it not claimed sometimes that "shock therapy" in the first phase provokes social reactions which lead to the victory of political forces that opposed it and that — in this way — a radical approach is self-defeating? Are we really facing a trade-off between the speed of transition and the probability of getting close to the optimal final system?

The political and economic transition in the countries of Central and Eastern Europe has been an enormously complex historical process. To understand at least some of its general characteristics and aspects, one needs a **clear analytical model** which would incorporate the main forces at play. I believe that such a model should have the following characteristics:

1. It should be a dynamic, multi-stage model with a special role for the initial political breakthrough and the following first stage of "extraordinary" politics, which gives way to more adversarial and partisan "normal" politics (see Section 3).

2. The key analytical category in this model should be the **initial (inherited) conditions**, i.e. those which existed during the political breakthrough. The economic conditions influence — to some extent — the choice of the economic policies in the first phase and the effects of the adopted policies. The initial conditions in the socio-political sphere influence the political developments, which in turn affect the choice and effects of the economic policies. There are also random, chance factors which affect the choice and implementation of economic policy, for example, who is responsible for the policy.

3. The model must incorporate the **external influences** on political decision-making in post-socialist countries. These include:

   a) Transmission of economic reform experiences from post-socialist countries which had a "head-start" to other countries (demonstration effect);
   b) Influences and pressures from international organisations and Western governments; the power of these external factors differs across countries (Russia versus smaller post-socialist states), across time (late-comers may profit from experience which was not available to the early reformers) and across economic situations (economic crisis makes the external conditionality especially effective, and the improvement in a country's economic situation may reduce the power of external pressures to continue the reforms). These differences help to explain the variations in economic policies and, as a result, in economic transition. However, the external pressures combined with the domestic economic crisis also help to explain why overtly anti-reformist political forces sometimes engage in tough stabilization and radical reform;
   c) external economic developments which influence the economic situation during the transition and — given certain constant predispositions of the voters (see Section 2) — shape their political attitudes.

4. The political breakthrough in post-socialist Europe **empowered the voter** in the early phase of the whole transition. It is thus the voting behaviour which has acquired the decisive influence — via the selection of policy-makers and pressures on the politicians — on the pace and direction of the economic transition. The model should, therefore, include clear assumptions on **voting behaviour** in general (see Section 2). In addition, it should translate the specificity of the post-socialist situations into the special states or values of the

general variables determining voting behaviour in post-socialist countries (Section 3).

2. Political decision-making under democracy: some general observations

There are two categories of decisions in a pluralistic, representative political system with open competition:

1. Voting choices preceded by election campaigns;
2. Decisions made between elections by the elected politicians and the public administration, which may be to a differing degree "politicised", i.e. be the object of a "spoils system". Decisions made between elections shape, among others things, the economic policy. These decisions are likely to be influenced to some extent by the prospect of the next elections.[2]

The electoral campaigns and the outcome of the voting choices influence the decisions made after the elections; policies depend on who is elected (personality factors, party ideological orientation) and — to some extent — on the type of criticism of the record and proposals of the political rivals, and the kind of electoral promises that were made by the participants.[3] However, the scope for influence of the electoral outcomes on subsequent policies depends on:

1. What exactly is determined by political decision-making;
2. What are the post-electoral economic situation and the related external constraints and pressures.

In transition countries, especially in the early phase, politics (i.e. points 1 and 2 above) can make more of a difference than is typical in the West; political decisions in the first case deal with the specialised and enormous subject of institutional transformation.[4] In transition countries, politics in the first phase determines how much will depend on politics in the following phases. As for the second factor, the general observation would be that the better the post-electoral economic situation, the more room a winning opposition has. To what extent this room is actually used for change depends on the nature of the winning political forces and on the personalities of the key policy-makers. And conversely, a very acute economic crisis could dictate broadly similar economic policies, at least for the time-being, regardless of who wins (Greskovits, 1993). Such a crisis in a post-socialist country, combined with demonstration effects and external pressures, can then reduce, in the short run, the scope of operation of the first factor, i.e. the voting decisions and outcome.[5] However, even in such a situation, important differences can emerge with respect to the crucial details of the economic programme, its timing and the quality of implementation.

A simple model, aimed at explaining the political decision-making under a mass democracy, would include voters, politicians grouped in the political parties, journalists and experts who have access to mass media (Zaller, 1992). Politicians (along with their staff), journalists and experts are the main sources of political messages to the voters, i.e. messages which may influence their voting choices. Therefore, we can integrate these three groups of actors into the category of **voters' political environment**. Changes and differences in this environment are of great importance in explaining changes (differences) in voting decisions, outcomes and other aspects of political performance.[6]

Another source of political messages is the change voters perceive in conditions in their life, to the extent that they link it to the actions of political forces (see proposition 5).

Completing the list of the main determinants of the voting outcomes, one should add the **type of electoral law**. This variable can produce huge differences in the distribution of seats in Parliament, given the same distribution of votes across the party spectrum.

The mere listing of the components of the model is not sufficient to produce propositions about voting behaviour and outcomes. We also need some substantive assumptions on the main actors, especially the politicians and the voters, as the decision-making units. Without exhausting this vast subject, let me suggest the following propositions:

Proposition 1: Typical professional politicians (political parties), during "normal" times, tend to promote policies which maximise — in their view — their electoral chances, and they tend to avoid policies with a high perceived risk of electoral defeat.[7] This assumption follows from a more general assumption of a self-interested motivation of individuals and from an additional assumption that professional politicians' prospects are closely linked to their political careers.

The same assumed motivational orientation of typical politicians can however lead to different policies which they promote, as they may try to appeal to different sections of electorate. Politicians also differ in their propensity and capacity to lead the public and to shape public opinion.

Proposition 2: During **special times**, such as a grave economic and/or political crisis or a democratic political breakthrough (see Section 3), there is far more room for non-typical politicians, whom John Williamson (1994) calls "technopols" — "economic technocrats in a position of political authority". These are professional outsiders who are called on — thanks to their professional reputation — to do a special job of bringing a country out of an economic crisis and/or transforming its economy.[8] Technopols may be as self-interested as the career politicians, but their different backgrounds and different professional prospects lead them to different evaluations and choices than those typical of politicians. Technopols are likely to chose more radical economic options than the professional politicians. The reason for this difference is that his or her self-esteem would suffer if proposed policies were accepted but — being insufficiently radical — failed from an economic standpoint. Self-esteem would suffer less if reforms that could have been successful (if implemented) were politically rejected, costing him or her a job. In contrast, the self-esteem of a career politician probably suffers most if he or she loses in the political game. It is also of importance that technopols, as distinct from professional politicians, have alternative careers (in academia, international institutions, business, etc.), and their prospects depend on how they conducted economic reforms.

As special times give way to normal politics, the technopols (if they appeared at all) are driven out by the typical politicians, and former technopols who stayed in politics have to adapt to the rules of "normal" politics or give up political activity.

There are several propositions regarding **voters**:

Proposition 3: Voters differ in their political awareness, and this determines among other things the number of political messages they receive (Zaller, 1992). Political awareness rises on average with the level of education.

Proposition 4: Voters also have partly different political predispositions, i.e. relatively lasting cognitive-motivational elements which, given the received political messages, shape their political opinions and choices. The predispositions can be visualised as forming various layers depending on the ease with which they can vary with time, across countries (depending on their particular history) and within the respective societies (group-specific predispositions).

Proposition 5: The "deepest", most fundamental predispositions are constant across countries and time (at least for modern times). These constant predispositions include the tendency of voters to evaluate political options from the viewpoint of their perceived impact on the voters' life situations, including both economic and psychological dimensions. This evaluation process is not necessarily rational; it may involve a lot of emotions. Another constant predisposition consists of the tendency to judge the government by comparing the situation which prevailed during its rule with a recent past (and **not** by comparing the actual situation with the hypothetical one available under the best alternative policy option). This predisposition makes the country's inherited conditions important in determining the amount and kind of changes in political opinions, choices and outcomes (see Section 3). The combination of inherited conditions, which produce a worsening of the life situations of many voters, and the assumed predispositions generate the so-called "protest vote". Various voters in the same country experience various changes in their life situations. The assumed predisposition helps to explain, therefore, both the inter-country and the intra-country differences in voting behaviour.

Proposition 6: The predisposition of voters to judge a government by a change in their life situations during its rule stops operating (or at least works with a reduced force) in some special conditions. These conditions make voters aware that negative change is unavoidable and due to external forces. Such conditions prevailed, for example, in the Western democracies, during the second World War. Another set of conditions which could convince voters to suspend their normal judging method are those which followed the political breakthroughs and the collapse of socialism in the post-socialist countries (see Section 3). This "suspension", however, was bound to be much more limited compared to the first case and to last for a shorter time, because the factors which could explain the worsening of the economic situation were much less evident to the average voter that those during the war situation. Post-socialist voters were also suddenly exposed to adversarial political messages. These messages included political communications which denied the link between external factors (i.e. collapse of trade within the former Comecon) and the country's economic problems, while trying to put the whole blame on government policy.

Proposition 7: The variable political predispositions of voters differ across countries and time. The static differences include, for example, a different value put by various post-Soviet societies on having their own independent state (compare, for example, Belarus and the Baltic countries). The differences in this national awareness dimension,[9] due to the different history of various peoples, were probably of importance for the choice and acceptance of radical economic options. Voters in those countries, which were characterised by a high national awareness and where political power was consequently placed in the hands of pro-independence forces, could support the radical economic options proposed by these forces. This was due to the trust in them created by shared national feelings and the belief that such measures are necessary for preserving a country's independence. This is a special political predisposition operating in a special situation, which perhaps might have been able to overcome for a certain time the normal voters' tendency to judge the government by the change which happened during its rule.

The variable predispositions which change in time include the evolving party loyalties, which, once created, constitute the main basis for voting decisions for most voters. It is the evolution of these loyalties and the evolution of the party system which is at the heart of political transition in post-socialist countries.

Besides the assumptions on the characteristics of politicians and voters, there is one proposition on the nature of electoral choice:

Proposition 8: Voters cannot choose between individual positions on various issues (individual "commodities") but only have a choice between "bundles" of positions on various issues "packaged" by the parties. This has a very important implication for the political chances of radical reform. Support for such reform can be linked to some popular position on another issue, i.e. the entry into the European Union or preservation of the country independence (see proposition 7). This can be called a **positive linkage**. On other hand, the opposition to radical reform may be linked to popular position on still another issue, (for example, criticism of the loss of empire in Russian politics). We can then speak of a **negative linkage**. The possibilities of creating such positive and negative linkages differ depending on countries' particular situations, and these differences help explain the choice of economic programme made in the political sphere.

3. Specificities of the post-socialist countries and their political transition

In the previous section I sketched some general propositions on the political decision-making under democracy, noting in passing the specificities of the transition countries. In this Section I will focus on these specificities. What follows is a number of propositions, which I believe help to explain the political and economic transition in Central and Eastern Europe.

Proposition 9: As already noted, **the post-communist political transition in the respective countries had special dynamics** — it started with a political breakthrough which opened the way to a brief period of "extraordinary politics", which in turn gave way to "normal" partisan politics. The first period is characterised by two transitional factors: by the post-liberalisation euphoria and by a special state in the political sphere (political forces of the former regime are still discredited and the opposition is still united). As a result, it is early in this period that difficult economic measures were accepted in the political system and in society at large (Balcerowicz, 1995).

The timing and intensity of the political breakthrough differed across countries. Earlier breakthroughs (Poland in the first half of 1989) combined with a rapidly declining threat of Soviet intervention (the Gorbachev factor) contributed to later breakthroughs in Central and Eastern Europe, creating a sort of chain reaction. With respect to the former Soviet Union, the decisive event was the failed *putsch* in August 1991 which triggered the dissolution of the Soviet Union and the political and economic transitions in the former Soviet republics. As they started about two years after similar processes in Central and Eastern Europe, they could profit from the experience of these earlier transitions.

The post-socialist countries also differed in nature and, as a result, in psychological consequences of the political breakthrough. One can distinguish on one hand Russia and the former Soviet republics with the least developed national awareness, and the remaining countries on the other. The external liberation of the societies of the second group must have been to many Russians a loss of both prestige and a sense of history.[10] To the countries with the least developed national aspirations, the newly gained independence must have meant much less than to the countries of the Central and Eastern Europe and to the people in the Baltic States.

The differences in the depth of the political breakthrough imply that countries also differed with respect to the length and intensity of "extraordinary" politics and with regard to the related political climate for a radical economic reform existing in the first phase. But in each country the first period after the political breakthrough had some special characteristics conducive to radical economic reform. The quick launching of such a reform may therefore be regarded as the proper use of a scarce "political" capital given by history, while a delay would be a waste of these opportunities. However, the period of "extraordinary" politics was too short to complete some fundamental reforms — for example, privatisation or pension reform — without which there are no prospects for a substantial reduction in the tax/GDP ratio. Therefore, even the countries which used the first period for launching radical reforms are facing the challenge of completing them in the later stages of "normal" politics to create the optimal final economic system (see Section 1).

Proposition 10: The political and economic transition in Europe was made possible by **explicit or implicit agreements between at least some parts of the elite** of the former regime and the opposition. These agreements created a belief among those who could have resisted a radical political change that they would not be physically threatened and that they would be free to seek good positions in the emerging new system.[11] However, the same fact which constituted a necessary condition for the launching of a peaceful transition[12] also influenced its later developments in ways not favourable to the former opposition; the forces of the past could organise politically. In addition, they had certain advantages (see proposition 13). The image of members of the former elite taking advantageous positions in the new system poisoned, to some extent, the political atmosphere and might have contributed to the splits in the former opposition, thus additionally strengthening the relative position of the forces stemming from the former system.[13] Besides, this picture tended to undermine the legitimacy of the new system, and thus to weaken the popularity of those who launched it, i.e. those who ruled in the first period.

Let us now focus on the inherited conditions and their consequences for the political environment of the post-socialist voters. These conditions are the initial states of the economy, the political system, the mass media and other sources of political messages.

Proposition 11: The **inherited economic conditions** were typically rather difficult: high inflation requiring tough stabilization; a distorted economic structure with large, hidden unemployment which was to be revealed; and a dependence on the Soviet market which led to the collapse of exports and the related decline of GDP. These typical conditions made it impossible to avoid economic pain for many voters in the first phases of transition under **any** economic policy.

Proposition 12: However, there were also huge differences in the inherited economic conditions among the post-socialist economies. They differed, for example, in the rate of inherited inflation (Poland and the former Czechoslovakia were the two extremes), in the extent of structural distortions and in the related potential for open unemployment (compare the Czech Republic and Slovakia), in the amount of foreign debt (Poland, Hungary and Bulgaria versus former Czechoslovakia). Countries differed, therefore, in the amount of economic pain felt during the transition and generated by different inherited conditions. Given proposition 5, this was bound to have an impact on the reception of economic policies and the attitudes towards those who governed during the period of most intense economic pain.

A more developed analysis of the inherited conditions must consider the following categories:

a) **Conditions which allow for quick economic improvement** under the new policies without a worsening along another dimension. Such conditions include the repressed sectors which can quickly developed thanks to liberalisation and privatisation. Chinese agriculture in the late 1970s and the early 1980s was the most spectacular example (*World Development Report*, 1996). This "Chinese Syndrome" has been present in Albania which had perhaps the highest share of agriculture capable of being easily privatised among the European post-socialist economies.[14] This is an example of "hidden treasures" — a country's characteristics which were not used under a former restrictive regime but which start producing many economic benefits once economic liberalisation is carried out on a sufficient scale. Other examples of "hidden treasures" include favourable location, especially bordering with Western countries, and the possession of the attractive tourist centres. The Czech Republic achieves the highest scores on both counts.

b) **Conditions which allow for quick improvement under the right policies but with substantial economic costs.** The case in point here is inherited hyperinflation. One can also point out that the value people put on its elimination probably increases with the length of time during which they experienced it.[15] The successful macroeconomic stabilization must have been, therefore, much more appreciated by the voters in Argentina than in Poland.

c) **Conditions which do not allow for any quick improvement but produce economic pain in one form or another.** This category includes the declining sectors (for example, inefficient coal mining) or the overextended social entitlements. Poland, Romania and Ukraine seem to have been especially burdened by the first type of condition, while Hungary was by the second one. Heavy structural dependence on the former Soviet market was also a very important part of the unfavourable inherited conditions. Still another example is the foreign debt.

The post-socialist countries differed greatly in the composition of their inherited conditions. By far the best conditions, i.e. those that produced relatively more economic gain and less economic pain during the economic transition, seem to have existed in Czech Republic (large "hidden treasures", relatively good economic structure, the most stable macroeconomic situation, little foreign debt). The other extreme included the smaller countries of the former Soviet Union which inherited a very unstable macroeconomy and a heavy structural dependence on the Russian market. Bulgaria (the highest degree of dependence on the Soviet market outside the former Soviet Union and the large foreign debt), Poland (hyperinflation, large share of inefficient coal mining, large foreign debt), Romania (economy ruined by years of Ceaucescu's policies) also have inherited difficult starting conditions.

Proposition 13: There were also differences in the inherited political conditions which influenced the scope of the subsequent political liberalisation and the attitudes towards those who introduced it, i.e. ruled during the first period. Although all the socialist regimes were non-democratic, they differed quite a lot in the level of repression. The harshest regimes existed in Albania, Romania and Czechoslovakia; the most liberal, in Hungary. Gorbachev reforms brought about much political liberalisation in the former Soviet Union. Therefore, the largest improvement must have been felt in the first group of countries, the smallest, in the second.

Proposition 14: Given the typical inherited economic conditions (proposition 11), it was impossible to avoid some discontent among the voters with their economic situation during the first phases of the economic transition, regardless of economic policies (Balcerowicz, 1995). This dissatisfaction was bound to be translated, given proposition 5 (the tendency to judge the government by the perceived change in the life situation of the voters during its rule) into some votes against those who governed during the first difficult period.

However, as the inherited economic conditions differed quite a lot and the political ones to a large extent, the magnitude of positive and negative change must have sharply differed across countries too and this was bound to influence to voters' opinions and choices.

There were other factors which shaped political developments in the post-socialist countries:

Proposition 15: Political opposition was banned under socialism and could not organise into the political parties. As a result, the post-socialist political transition started with a very weak and asymmetric party system: parties stemming from the former system have, on average, more organisational and financial resources than the new parties. The former, in addition, are often allied with the post-socialist trade unions and youth organisations. The asymmetry in organisational and financial strength between the two types of parties is an important feature of the post-socialist voters' political environment and must have a certain impact on the voting decisions.[16] This impact must have been additionally deepened by the fact that the parties of the former system did not rule in the first economically difficult phase of transition.

Proposition 16: Post-socialist countries differ in the number and kind of **cleavages on non-economic issues** which can be exploited by the opposition during economic reform in the first phase (see the concept of **negative linkages** defined in proposition 8). Such negative linkages existed in Russia (the loss of empire), in Poland (opposition to what was perceived by many voters as the excessive political role of the Catholic Church) and in Romania (the Hungarian minority). On the other hand, the Czech Republic, after the separation with Slovakia, and Albania seem to have been free of such linkages.

Post-socialist countries also differed with respect to the **positive linkages**, i.e. possibilities of linking support for a radical reform to a popular position on another issue. Such a possible linkage exists especially in the Visegrad countries, where the prospect for entering the European Union is highly popular. This linkage, however, operates only weakly because the European Union has been unwilling so far to formulate strong and clear conditions on economic transformation and make a strong conditional commitment.

Proposition 17: Political liberalisation has freed the **mass media**. As a result, a change in the political and economic reality was accompanied by a radical difference in the presentation of the new and the previous reality. The controlled media under socialism did not engage in any systematic presentation and criticism of the socialist reality; being politically controlled, they rather displayed a "positive bias". In contrast the newly freed mass media focused on the negative aspects on the post-socialist reality. This shift from a "positive" to "negative" bias, largely a natural by-product of political liberalisation, constituted a radical change in the voters' political environment and must have had an important impact on their political opinions and choices. The perception of the new reality by many voters must have been worse than this reality. The scale of this revolution in the presentation of the changing reality, especially the focus on the sensationalist and negative in the post-socialist one and the amount of economic education presented by the mass media, could have differed across countries, depending among other things on the quality of journalists.

Proposition 18: In addition, the inherited statistical systems were unable to cope with a new economic reality — they under-estimated the effects and over-estimated the costs of the economic transition, especially the more radical programmes (Balcerowicz, 1995). Such inaccurate statistical messages, publicised by the mass media and by the opposition, blackened the picture of the first phases of transition in the public mind.[17]

Proposition 19: Countries could have differed in the amount and timing of various publicised scandals (fraud, corruption, misuse of public office). Such events may be compared to some extent to "random shocks" in the economy, and they may heavily influence the public opinion in any democracy, including the mature ones. In transition countries, a large amount of perceived "scandals" blamed on authorities could have outweighed to a certain degree the impact of relatively favourable starting conditions (this is perhaps the case in Albania).

4. Explaining the politico-economic dynamics

In this section I will draw on the propositions formulated in the previous one in order to explain certain facts which happened during the post-socialist transition so far.

Proposition 20: Radical approaches brought about much better economic outcomes than slow, hesitant or delayed reforms (for a comparative analysis see Balcerowicz and Gelb, 1994). It is instructive to compare the post-electoral state of the economy in Poland (the economic boom) and in Hungary (the macroeconomic crisis). The differences in the economic policies in the first period can be explained to some extent by the presence or absence of strong economic teams headed by "technopols" (see proposition 2) and this was due to a combination of the emerging political situation during and after the political breakthrough, as well as chance factors.

Proposition 21: The political position of those forces which assumed power after the political breakthrough appears to depend on the type of inherited economic conditions (see proposition 12). In the Czech Republic and Albania where this position has been relatively strong so far, the inherited economic conditions were favourable compared to other countries, i.e. they allowed a quick improvement and produced relatively little economic pain. In addition, in both countries the previous communist regimes were especially discredited and the post-communist opponents correspondingly weak.

Proposition 22: Political forces which ruled in the first difficult period of economic transition, characterised by an economic decline, sharply increased insecurity and the revolution in the relative prices, **tended to lose elections regardless of whether they engaged in more or less radical economic reform** (Lithuania and Poland in 1993, Bulgaria and Hungary in 1994, Estonia and Latvia in 1995). It is therefore a fallacy to blame "shock therapy" for electoral defeats. The winners were typically the post-communist forces which did not govern during this period. They were then simply the main, or the only, opposition.[18] Each of these electoral defeats has its own special history and some country-specific reasons;[19] they can be explained as the whole category, by the propositions formulated in Section 3. The electoral outcomes in particular may be linked to the type of inherited conditions.

Proposition 23: The winners of the second-round elections inherited economies in a different shape depending on the economic policies of their predecessors. The political forces which inherited an improving economy have had much more room for choosing different economic policy mixes than those forces which inherited an economy in crisis. In the former case (where the winners of elections had greater latitude), their views regarding further economic reform and the final economic system have had a greater scope for realisation than in the latter case. If the views of the electoral winners in the first case favour an economy with a rent-seeking and much redistribution, a slowdown of **further** reform can be expected, while in the second case its acceleration from a "lower level" is the most likely result. The joint effect of those two tendencies would be a **certain convergence of** the economic systems of post-socialist countries in the later stages of their transition. The demonstration effects and the external pressures affecting the late-comers (see Section 1) would work in the same direction.

Proposition 24: A different state of the economy inherited by the winners of the second-round elections has a certain impact on their chances in the third-round elections. Those who inherited an improving economy are clearly in a better situation than those who inherited the economy in crisis. The former can gain popularity thanks to the economic improvement (see proposition 5), and they are not forced to take the painful measures. The liberal opposition to the post-communist winners, which inherited a booming economy, is facing a special political challenge.

5. The unfinished transformation

The post-socialist countries are in different stages of their economic transition, and thus they presently have different economic systems which are the main engines for economic growth and job-creation. Even the most advanced reformers have not yet reached the optimal economic systems, as described in Section 1. This is even more true of the less advanced reformers, even though some systemic convergence can be expected (see proposition 19). The most important remaining tasks are completing privatisation, reforming the pension system and education, lowering the tax/GDP ratio, and strengthening the macroeconomic stability. Bringing the economic systems of the post-socialist countries close to this optimal model constitutes, I believe, a great historical responsibility for the politicians and societies in those countries. However, the outcome of economic transformation in Central and Eastern Europe matters for the West too, and Western governments and international institutions can influence the direction and pace of reforms in Central and Eastern Europe. The West should act more clearly and strongly in ways which are conducive to successfully finishing the economic transformation in post-socialist countries.

This includes efforts to stop giving bad examples (petty protectionism, excesses of the welfare state), efforts to give good examples (such as reforms of the common agricultural policy and the welfare state), and issuing clear warnings regarding economic mistakes in the West so these can be avoided in post-socialist countries. Finally, strengthening positive linkages is necessary to support completing reform in these countries. Such action would strengthen the political position of pro-reformist forces and correspondingly weaken that of anti-reformist ones.

Notes

[1] These transition effects are a special case of catching-up effects, available to late-comers with appropriate economic policies.

[2] This impact may generate the so-called "political-business" cycle.

[3] One should note however the phenomenon of post-electoral reversals, i.e. pursuing policies very different from the one advocated during the election campaigns (for example, Menem in Argentina in 1990/91 or Jacques Chirac in France in 1995). Research is needed on this phenomenon.

[4] True, Western governments, especially in Western Europe, have to tackle the same institutional reforms (mainly with respect to the welfare state and labour markets). But these reforms are incomparably smaller in scope than the post-socialist transformation.

[5] Similar developments took place in Sweden after 1994, where the victorious social-democrats had to continue policies similar to some extent to those started by their predecessors, the liberal-conservative coalition.

[6] A very important change in the political environment in the West after the second World War was the technological revolution in the mass media, i.e. the spread of television and the related revolutionary change in the way politics are presented and conducted. This change might have contributed to the growing dissatisfaction among the voters with modern politics (Entman, 1989; Hart, 1994).

[7] Thus, I follow, which respect to the "normal" times, the central assumption of the public choice theory of Buchanan, Tullock and others (Buchanan, 1978).

[8] A great example of a "technopol" was Moeen Qureshi, a former Senior Deputy President of the World Bank, who was a Prime Minister of Pakistan in 1993.

[9] These differences may be interpreted as variations in the psychological content of self-interest, as perceived by the citizens of various countries.

[10] This factor must contribute to the fact that most Russians, as distinct from the people of Central and Eastern European countries, have a negative view of their post-1991 regime and a positive one of the pre-perestroika system (Rose, 1995).

[11] Another reason for the lack of resistance on the part of "nomenklatura" was the fact that a change came from the very top of the one-party state. This was especially true in the case of Jaruzelski in Poland, and Gorbachev in Russia.

[12] A forceful transition was not possible because the opposition had no force. Violent transitions from dictatorships have usually led to another dictatorship (Palma, 1993).

[13] This seems especially true of Poland, where some parts of the former opposition did not take part in the 1981 "Round Table" discussions with the Communists, and later accused those who participated of making secret deals with them.

[14] I owe this observation to Iraj Hashi.

[15] These different values put on eliminating hyperinflation and on preserving price stability may be regarded as belonging to those political predispositions of the voters which can vary across countries (see proposition 7).

[16] The exceptions to the empirical regularity of the superior organisational strength of post-communist political parties include the Czech Republic and Albania. In both countries the communist parties had been especially discredited due to the particular histories of these countries.

[17] It is characteristic that, for example, in Poland, the revised figures that put the decline in GDP, 1990-91, at only 5-10 per cent as compared to the original 18-20 per cent, were not publicised at all, while the latter were given a lot of publicity.

[18] The importance of not ruling in the first difficult period for explaining the electoral outcomes is shown by the electoral defeat of the post-communist forces in Mongolia in June and by the victory of their democratic opponents.

[19] For example, the very fact of the Parliamentary elections in Poland in 1993 was due to the ill-thought initiative of the trade union "Solidarnosc" which tabled a non-confidence motion against the last Solidarity government, and this vote passed by one vote because one pro-government deputy was late for voting. The former opposition went into the elections fragmented while the post-communist forces formed a large coalition (Alliance of the Democratic Left — ADL) consisting of over 30 different organisations originating from the former regime and constituting post-socialist interest groups. As a result the ADL gained about 21 per cent of the votes (a modest result), but 33 per cent of the seats in the Parliament.

References

Balcerowicz, L., 1995, *Socialism, Capitalism Transformation*, Central European University Press, Budapest, pp. 264-268.

Balcerowicz, L. and A. Gelb, 1994, *Macropolicies in Transition to a Market Economy - A Three-Year Perspective*, Proceedings of the World Bank Annual Conference on Development Economics, Washington DC, pp. 21-56.

Buchanan, M.J., 1978, "From private preferences to public philosophy — the development of public choice", in *The Economics of Politics*, IEA, London, pp. 1-20.

Entman, M.R., 1989, *Democracy without Citizens. Media and the Decay of American Politics* Oxford University Press, New York, Oxford.

Di Palma, G., 1993, "Democratic Transition Puzzles and Surprises from West to East", *Research on Democracy and Society*, Vol. 1, pp. 27-50.

Greskovits, B., 1993, "Dominant Economy Subordinated Politics", *The Absence of Economic Populism in Transition of East-Central Europe*, Working Papers No. 1, July, The Central European University, Budapest.

Hart, R. P., 1994, *Seducing America — How Television Charms the Modern Voter,* Oxford University Press, New York Oxford.

World Bank, *World Development Report 1996 — From Plan to Market,* 1996, Washington DC.

Rose, R., 1995, "Russia as an Hour-Glass Society: A Constitution Without Citizens", *East European Constitutional Review*, Summer, pp. 34-42.

Sachs, J. and A. Warner, 1996, *Achieving Rapid Growth in Transition Economies of Central Europe*, Centre for Social and Economic Research, Studies and Analyses, No. 73, Warsaw.

Williamson, J.C., 1994, "Introduction" in: *The Political Economy of Policy Reform*, Institute for International Economics, Washington DC.

Zaller, R. J., 1992, *The Nature and Origins of Mass Opinion*, Cambridge University Press, Cambridge.

8

Political constraints and the transition experience

Gérard Roland

Introduction

Only a few years after the fall of the Berlin Wall and the introduction of comprehensive economic reform packages, political backlash is being observed nearly everywhere in Central and Eastern Europe. With a few notable exceptions such as the Czech Republic, voters are sending former communists back to power. Political backlash is particularly impressive in Russia where hardline communists and nationalists won the parliamentary votes in December 1995 and where Zyuganov led in the polls for the presidential elections for some time.

The advent of democracy and the fall of dictatorial communist regimes was acclaimed by populations in Central and Eastern Europe. Economic reforms have not met the same enthusiasm everywhere. In various countries in the last six years, there have been important political constraints to various dimensions of economic reform such as stabilization (Russia being the best example), or privatisation, as witnessed by the example of the Polish mass privatisation programme. One is also observing various forms of resistance to enterprise restructuring (Carlin *et al.*, 1994).

Despite this important backlash and the expression of dissatisfaction by populations in elections, no major policy reversal has taken place so far. Support for the continuation of reform, however, varies considerably across countries — in Russia and the former Soviet republics, support for reform policies is, to say the least, much weaker than in the Visegrad countries.

This leads us to ask what has been the role of political constraints in the adoption and implementation of reform packages in Central and Eastern European countries. After six years of experience, what general lessons can be drawn about the role of political constraints on transition strategies?

In Section 1, I summarise the most important views expressed at the beginning of the transition process on the effect of political constraints on reform strategies and discuss the political economy arguments for a "big bang" versus a gradualist approach to reforms. In Section 2, I broadly survey the role of political constraints in practice in the various countries. In Section 3, I attempt to draw general lessons from this experience to try to understand both the importance of the political backlash and the absence of major policy reversals.

One of the major lessons we draw from this experience is that the geopolitical dimension of transition has been neglected too much in the economic literature on transition (see, however, Csaba, 1995). We can argue that this geopolitical dimension allows us to shed light on some of the major stylised facts of transition such as the CMEA breakdown; the absence of major policy reversals in the Visegrad countries; the differences in the political transformation of former communists in Central Europe versus the former Soviet Union; as well as the greater difficulties in finding support for reform in CIS countries compared to Central Europe.

1. Political constraints and reform strategies

The political economy approach to reform has gained increasing attention in the last few years (see, for example, the survey in Rodrik, 1996). The success of the political economy approach to reform stems from the dissatisfaction with the pure economic approach to policy advice which tended to neglect political constraints. The political economy approach distances itself from an often naïve approach of economists that view political decisions as the result of social welfare maximisation. Even though social welfare maximisation may be a desirable goal in itself, the political decision-making process is characterised by conflicts between various interest groups. Welfare-enhancing reforms often hurt the interests of some groups who are well represented in the political decision-making process. This allows us to explain why economically efficient political decisions are often not made in important areas such as trade liberalisation (Rodrik, 1993) and public debt management (Alesina and Drazen, 1991). The political economy approach to reform is concerned not only with positive analysis (understanding why welfare enhancing reforms may be blocked or resisted) but is also interested in normative analysis, by providing tools to help reform-minded governments with agenda-setting powers to overcome the political resistance to reforms (see Roland, 1995).

It is important, when discussing political constraints, to distinguish between *ex ante* and *ex post* political constraints (Roland, 1994). *Ex ante* political constraints are feasibility or acceptability constraints; some decisions may be blocked. *Ex post* political constraints refer to the danger of backlash and reversal after decisions have been taken and outcomes observed. *Ex ante* and *ex post* political constraints must be dealt with differently. *Ex ante* constraints imply either that compromises must be made in the design of reform plans, or that decisions will be delayed until they become acceptable. *Ex post* political constraints are dealt with by trying to create irreversibility, and thus preventing important reforms from being undone.

It is important to note that political constraints play a role, irrespective of the view that one may have on the role of government in a post-transition economy. Advocates of the pure *laissez-faire* approach hope that the government will play a minimal role after transition. However, it is important to adopt decisions that remove all sorts of prohibitions on free economic activity. *Ex ante* political constraints are thus significant. But even under a *laissez-faire* approach, *ex post* political constraints are important too. Even if government prohibitions and regulations have been lifted and the size of government has been reduced, politics, like nature, abhors a void. This means that it is important to prevent anti-market coalitions from coming back to power.

The political economy argument for a "Big Bang" strategy

Even if economic arguments have been put forward mostly to justify a "big bang" approach to reform, there is also a political economy argument to defend a "big bang" strategy. Before spelling out that argument, it is useful to recall the background for the economic approach to "big bang":

- The first background is comparative economics, and its emphasis on the importance of complementarities in economic systems. One of the important themes in comparative economics is that economic systems cannot be built by taking bits and pieces from different economic systems. This is Kornai's supermarket analogy, according to which one cannot take the best elements from different economic systems. There is, for example, a strong complementarity between free markets and private ownership on the one hand, and central planning and public ownership on the other (Kornai, 1992). Complementarities between the institutions constituting an economic system means that partial reforms, which change some aspects of a system while leaving the others unchanged, may have very disruptive effects.

- The "big bang" approach has also been generated by disappointment with "reform socialism", which (in Hungary, Yugoslavia and Poland, for example) gave more autonomy to enterprise managers but always fell short of privatisation.

- Finally, the recommendation for a "big bang" comes from the literature on macroeconomic stabilization and credibility. It is now generally agreed that stabilization is best achieved through shock therapy (Sargent,1986). Radicalism in stabilization policy is an important way for genuine reformers to signal their commitment in order to become credible (Vickers, 1986; Rodrik, 1989).

Let us now come back to the political economy argument for a "big bang" approach to reform. There exists no direct political economy theory of a "big bang", but an argument can be made by using the results of the Persson-Svensson (1989) model.

The "big bang" strategy fully considers *ex ante* constraints, taking advantage of a window of opportunity (or a grace period or "a period of exceptional politics") to take as many decisions as possible early in the transition process (see, for example, Lipton and Sachs, 1990). This means that it may be necessary to advance some decisions which optimally should be delayed (for example, closing loss-making enterprises). Indeed, there is a danger that when the ideal time comes to make those decisions, the window of opportunity will have closed. A "big bang" strategy deals with *ex post* constraints by constraining a successor government, through the use of "*fait accompli*" or "scorched earth politics", to increase the cost of reversing policies adopted earlier.[1] The main instrument used to achieve this goal is the reduction in the size and wealth of government. By lifting price controls and disbanding administration, one makes it more costly to reinstate price controls. By giving away state assets to the population and to workers, one runs down government wealth and makes it more costly to renationalise assets or to expand government expenditures.

An important assumption in this line of reasoning is that there is an exogenous probability of losing power. This was probably the main perception of reformist governments in Central Europe prior to the failure of the 1991 *putsch* in the Soviet Union, and in particular in Poland in late 1989. There was indeed considerable uncertainty about a possible future Soviet intervention in this country, after the possible replacement of Gorbachev by conservative forces. Radicalism and economic reform can thus be understood as a form of "scorched earth politics". The probability of returning to power may also be partly exogenous if there is considerable uncertainty about who will be in power tomorrow, and if current policies have a low influence on re-election probability. In troubled times such as a transition period, one can argue that incumbent governments tend to be ousted, independently of their policy. It could be the case that political factors among the electorate are such that re-election is impossible, even with a minimal reform programme. The government may then prefer to go ahead with the reform in the face of a low probability of re-election, rather than be elected but implement a policy that would only slightly deviate from the *status quo*.

This rationale for a "big bang" strategy is broader than the naïve interpretation which has often been put forward in transition debates based on the experience of stabilization. This follows the premise that quick and decisive stabilization measures are necessary when the government takes office so that the government can reap the benefits before the next elections. This "naïve" view assumes that institutions are already established, a "given"; that election dates will not be changed; and that elections are the only form of future political constraints, neglecting the real dangers of political crises in uncertain institutional environments. This view also assumes that the fundamental institutional changes of transition can be achieved within the life of one legislature, as if they were the corollary of a stabilization package.

What are the limitations of the "big bang" argument? First of all, it relies on the assumption of weak *ex ante* political constraints. This is certainly true in some countries where the legitimacy of the first non-communist governments allowed them to adopt measures that were rejected under the communist regime.[2] As argued below, the precedence of political change over economic change is a good example of reform sequencing. Nevertheless, if *ex ante* political constraints are important enough, a "big bang" package may be blocked.

A second limitation of the "big bang" approach is that the cost of reversal may be smaller under certain circumstances. One of the costs of reversing transition policies is that the government may lose its credibility. If the government was not initially credible, this cost is much smaller. From that point of view, the cost to Zyuganov of reversing privatisation deals is much smaller than the cost to Vaclav Klaus. Another factor influencing the cost of reversal is the economic disruption that the reform package may have produced. If this disruption is high, the cost of reversing policies is smaller. One may argue that a greater level of disruption is associated with a higher speed of reform. When the old system is destroyed very rapidly, agents must mutually learn to adjust their behaviour to the market environment. As this process inevitably takes time, an initially high level of destruction of the old system necessarily creates disruption in production. Actual experience and observed disruption in Eastern Europe does not contradict this view. Models by Aghion and Blanchard (1994); Coricelli and Milesi-Ferreti (1993); Perotti (1994); and Castanheira and Roland (1994; 1995) show the contractionary effect of policies aiming at too quick a reduction of the public sector. Roland and Verdier (1996); show that a substantial output contraction can be generated with price and trade liberalisation because of the search externalities associated with a sudden liberalisation. When all enterprises become free to search for new business partners, the search externalities may lead to a significant outfall in output and a contraction in investment demand.

Third, a "big bang" strategy may lead to political instability if the probability of re-election is endogenous and not exogenous. Such political instability may have a negative effect on investment decisions.

Having outlined the political economy arguments for a "big bang" strategy and its limitations, it is also useful to describe the general underlying economic vision of the advocates of the "big bang" approach to transition. The inefficiency of the socialist economic system implies that transition will bring a very important Pareto improvement. This aggregate efficiency gain can be reached quickly if reforms are fast enough. The emphasis is on removing government prohibition, freeing prices to let markets work and on giving appropriate incentives through privatisation to secure the adequate supply response.

The political economy argument for gradualism

Gradualism has been identified by its opponents as a slow (possibly very slow) pace of reforms. This is not necessarily the case. Advocates of gradualism have focused on the possible advantages of an appropriate sequencing of reforms and have pointed to the costs of wrong reform sequencing.

The background for the gradualist vision of transition is twofold. First, it is derived from the success of reform sequencing of China, where earlier reforms such as de-collectivisation and the institution of special economic zones have allowed for building constituencies for further economic reforms. Sequencing is at the heart of the Chinese experience of transition, as witnessed by the dual track approach to liberalisation of prices, exchange rate, etc. According to the dual track approach, prices are liberalised as a way of creating "embryos" of free markets, while the planning system is maintained for the most important part of production in order to avoid disruptions in the state sector. The second origin of the gradualist approach is the success of glasnost in initiating transition. Analysts had never envisaged that political change in the communist regime would precede economic reform. The partial political reforms introduced by Gorbachev proved successful in undermining the power structure of communism. Without the initiation of such a sweeping process of political change, transition would not have been possible in Central Europe. Economic analysts in the early 1980's predicted unanimously that the

Soviet economic system would continue to survive and to stagnate at least until the year 2000 (Bergson and Levine, 1982).

The main source for the political economy theory for gradualism is Dewatripont and Roland (1995a, b). Even when pure economic logic would suggest a "big bang" approach, gradualism may be a way of overcoming political constraints. Gradualism may deal with *ex ante* political constraints by relaxing the feasibility constraint of a "big bang" package. The gradualist approach aims at overcoming *ex post* political constraints by using reform sequencing to build constituencies for further reforms.

Why may gradualism be more easily acceptable than a "big bang"? Why would the majority of the population reject the reform programme as a complete package at one time and still accept it as a gradual one? The answer is based on uncertainty. A gradual resolution of uncertainty gives an option for early policy reversal at a low cost if the outcome turns out to be bad. Policy reversals do not necessarily mean a return to a communist regime. Such decisions must be made, for example, by populist and nationalist coalitions. Communist regimes are only a subset of regimes where market and private property are not protected against predatory government intervention (see Weingast, 1993). The *ex ante* existence of this reversal option increases the willingness of the population to engage in the reform process.

Why may gradualism create irreversibility? The answer is that a correct sequencing may allow for the building of constituencies for further reform. Correct sequencing means starting with reforms which have a higher probability of a good outcome and with reforms bringing potential gains to a majority of the population. Such sequencing allows one to take advantage of the reform complementarities and then proceed with more difficult reforms later on. Indeed, complementarity of reforms means that it is impossible to stay in a no man's land between socialism and capitalism. Because of the uncertainty of reform outcomes, support for reform is less strong before the outcome is known. If, however, one starts with a reform which has a higher probability of a good outcome, then once a positive outcome has been realised, the majority of the population would be ***more*** willing to go ahead with further reform. Indeed, due to the complementarity of reforms, the only possibilities are either to go ahead with further reform or to go backward. The positive outcome of the initial reforms would then make the population more willing to accept further reforms.

It is useful to give a few examples of such sequencing. One example is that (observed in Eastern Europe) of political liberalisation before economic liberalisation. Populations in Central and Eastern Europe have suffered a lot from the absence of political freedom under the communist regime. Aspirations for democracy, freedom of expression and associations are very important. Even though they were not *ex ante* designed, the political liberalisations of 1989 accomplished these aspirations. It is precisely the advent of democracy that has created a window of opportunity for economic reform. From this point of view, the widespread opinion that reform sequencing in Eastern Europe was wrong and that political liberalisation should have followed, and not preceded, economic reform is misplaced. In China, economic reform could be started from within the communist party structure. In the Soviet Union under Gorbachev, it would have been impossible to decide upon even partial reform (Roland, 1993). Starting with economic reforms was simply not an option under the existing power structure.

Another example of correct sequencing is privatisation before restructuring. Enterprise restructuring is one of the most painful reforms since it entails layoffs of workers. As most social services and even income security are provided by the enterprise under socialism, and as unemployment benefits are relatively low for budgetary reasons, layoffs hurt workers much more in transition economies than in normal market economies. The above reasoning on sequencing shows that it may be advantageous to delay restructuring. If on the other hand, privatisation is made popular by giving away assets to the population and giving the latter stakes in the success of privatisation, it makes it easier to accept restructuring (Roland and Verdier, 1994). As we will see in the next section, this more or less describes the Czech sequencing of privatisation and restructuring.

What are the limitations to the gradualist approach? First, it may be useless if a sufficient window of opportunity exists. In that case, a "big bang" approach may be feasible and will also create irreversibility. Second, it necessitates a minimum of agenda-setting and government enforcement power. Indeed, contrary to a "big bang" strategy, breakdown of government can be dangerous to reform sequencing, since the latter requires maintenance of parts of the old system while new reforms are being introduced. For example, the success of the dual track approach to price liberalisation in China implied that the state be able to enforce planned deliveries between state-owned enterprises. Third, a critical mass of reforms may be necessary to signal the political feasibility of transition. If voters are ill-informed about the degree of support for reform, an overly cautious approach may indicate that there is strong opposition to reform, thereby reducing the level of support by uninformed voters. On the contrary, a bold approach to reform may signal political feasibility and create support among the less informed voters. Finally, wrong sequencing of reforms may be very damaging and lead to unnecessary early reversal. This would be the case if one first starts with a reform which hurts the majority of the population, while delaying potentially more popular reforms. In that case the reform process will be reversed without having even tried the potentially more popular reform.

It is also useful here to emphasize the general view of economic transition underlying the gradualist strategy. Contrary to the "big bang" approach, which tends to see transition as a deterministic path from an inefficient system to a more efficient system, gradualists emphasize the importance of aggregate and individual uncertainty. The end outcome of the reform process may be very successful and close to the German economic miracle. It may also prove to be a disaster, such as the Weimar Republic, or (closer to us) the Yugoslav drama. Gradualists tend to emphasize the importance of inter-temporal consumption smoothing for avoiding excessively large income and consumption shocks to the population. They also emphasize possible co-ordination failures during transition, due to the absence of pre-existing stable market institutions. Gradualists put more emphasis on the importance and the inevitable delay in the emergence of market economy institutions (Murrell, 1992; Kornai, 1990).

As one can see, both the "big bang" and the gradualist strategy address *ex ante* and *ex post* political constraints. An important issue is whether the probability of the re-election of reformers is exogenous ("big bang" strategy), or endogenous (gradualist strategy). In the former case, haste is more recommended to constrain a possible successor government. In the latter case, it may make sense to go slower to build constituencies for further reform. Both approaches also have different implications. For example, is it important to start with the most painful measures or, on the contrary, to delay them? Should one weaken the government or ensure a minimum of government power?

The discussion in this section was by necessity stylised. In reality, it is quite common to argue in favour of a mix of gradualism in some dimensions and the "big bang" strategy in others. It is now useful to look at political constraints in practice.

2. Political constraints in practice

In this section we briefly review the role of *ex ante* and *ex post* constraints in the most important areas of reform (stabilization, liberalisation, privatisation and restructuring).

Stabilization

For stabilization, *ex ante* constraints have mostly taken the form of delay. This is what one would expect from economic theory (Alesina and Drazen, 1991). *Ex ante* constraints to stabilization were the most important in Russia in the second half of 1992, as well as in the Ukraine and other CIS countries. The best example of *ex post* political constraints is the "stop and go" reform process in Russia between 1992 and 1994, where Gaidar and Fedorov managed to get stabilization measures through that were later reversed (see Litwack, 1993).

Liberalisation

Liberalisation has generally taken place in the early phases of transition. *Ex ante* constraints have taken the form of delay in the Ukraine, and one has observed gradual price liberalisation in Hungary, Slovenia and Romania. For the others, liberalisation has usually been comprehensive and has taken place at the initial stage of transition. *Ex post* constraints have also been observed in Belarus, where price controls were quickly re-established in 1992 after the liberalisation. Partial reversals took place in Bulgaria in 1993 and 1994. One also has examples of price controls being reinstated in Russia at local levels. Local authorities have however never really been able to enforce a return to price controls. Indeed, the mobility of goods implies that goods disappear from regions with price controls to those regions were prices are liberalised.

Privatisation

Privatisation, probably the most important and the most specific reform of the transition process, is also the area where political constraints have played the most important role.

There have been several manifestations of *ex ante* constraints and several ways to deal with them. First of all, one has generally observed a limitation of sales to foreign investors. In most countries, the fear was expressed that too high a level of privatisation to foreign investors would be politically dangerous. The restitution of property to former owners has also been widely used as a way to create support for privatisation. Restitution has played a role in Hungary, the former Czechoslovakia, Albania, Bulgaria and the Baltic States. Gradual sales have also been observed as a way to deal with *ex ante* constraints, particularly in Hungary and Slovenia. Probably the most imaginative way to deal with political constraints in privatisation has been the Czech mass privatisation plan. Vouchers have been used to achieve a quasi-give-away of assets to the population. This strategy resulted in a rapid transfer of state assets to private owners in the Czech Republic.

Mass privatisation plans have however not necessarily met the same political success elsewhere. The best example is the Polish mass privatisation programme. Initially designed in 1990 by two Polish economists, Lewandowski and Szomburg, the Polish programme implied that citizens would receive vouchers in investment funds which would themselves control the privatised enterprises. By contrast, the Czech programme implied that citizens would use their vouchers to acquire shares of enterprises directly. The main difference between the two plans was one of corporate governance, with the Polish programme attempting to avoid dispersed ownership and encouraging concentrated ownership. Both plans were however programmes involving "give-aways" to enterprise outsiders, e.g. the general population. The mass privatisation programme was however blocked for several years in Poland and eventually lost its momentum. A recent referendum in 1995 rejected the extension of the mass privatisation programme. In practice, it has hardly started. The Polish experience shows the difference in the degree of political constraints across countries. The Czech Republic had no experience with reforms prior to transition. Management of state-owned enterprises and worker collectives had not received increased autonomy under the communist regime but were still subject to the strict controls of central planning. The mass privatisation programme in Poland was blocked by coalitions of workers and managers who resisted "give-aways" to the population and lobbied for more "give-aways" to the workers themselves. Worker and manager lobbies were thus more powerful in Poland than in the Czech Republic. Even though the failure of the Polish mass privatisation programme is one of the most visible forms of political constraints to privatisation, one has also observed similar delays in the adoption of mass privatisation programmes in Romania and Bulgaria. The reason why the Russian mass privatisation programme did not get blocked and was eventually implemented is that it took directly into account the potential resistance of workers and managers to privatisation — it amounted to a give-away of the enterprise to its managers and workers. There is thus, in terms of political constraints, an important difference between the Czech and Russian privatisation programmes. The former is a give-away to the outside population, whereas the latter implies privatisation for insiders.

As far as *ex post* constraints are concerned, one has observed cases of reversal in various countries, but no major re-nationalisation has taken place so far. It is useful here to mention a difference between the design of the Czech and the Russian privatisation programmes. In the Czech privatisation programme, privatisation vouchers are not exchangeable against cash, which is the case in Russia. This has potential implications for re-nationalisation. When vouchers are not exchangeable against cash, voucher-holders, especially outsiders, have a stake in the success of privatisation. This dampens potential backlash against privatisation when privatised enterprises are restructured. When vouchers can be exchanged against cash however, workers who exchange their vouchers against cash can afterwards support re-nationalisation policies without suffering any economic loss. The future will tell whether this difference in the design of privatisation has any practical impact.

Restructuring

Turning now to restructuring, *ex ante* political constraints have led to gradualism everywhere in terms of the hardening of budget constraints of SOE's and of layoffs (see, for example, Carlin *et al.* 1994; Grosfeld and Roland, 1995). It is interesting to note here the relatively gentle approach in the Czech Republic with respect to restructuring, compared to the swiftness of privatisation. Indeed, the enforcement of the bankruptcy law in the Czech Republic has been delayed. On the other hand, universal banking has been encouraged. Banks are, at the same time, both creditors of enterprises and shareholders. According to economic theory, this would tend to lead to relative leniency by banks towards enterprises (Dewatripont and Tirole, 1995), compared to the behaviour of banks who are only creditors.

The only case of reversal with respect to restructuring is the softening of the bankruptcy law in Hungary. This is only partly related to *ex post* political constraints. An overly severe bankruptcy law adopted in Hungary in 1992 resulted in the number of bankruptcy filings increasing exponentially, which made it literally impossible to handle bankruptcy cases effectively in court.

3. Some lessons from the transition experience

Given our discussion in the two previous sections, it seems that the Czech government has best taken into account political constraints so far. It has taken advantage of the window of opportunity of 1989, and carefully prepared its reform programme. The mass privatisation programme takes into account *ex ante* political constraints and is designed in such a way as to prevent policy reversals. At the same time, the delay of restructuring shows a subtle understanding of reform sequencing. The Czech government is also one of the only governments which has maintained strong popular support so far. One must however add that, in the former Czechoslovakia, political constraints were more concentrated in Slovakia. The break-up of Czechoslovakia has indeed left most of the difficult restructuring cases, particularly the restructuring in the former arms industry, in Slovakia. Also, the Czech Republic had no important initial disequilibrium to start with, and state structures had not collapsed. It is important to take these initial conditions into account while evaluating the success of Czech transition. Nevertheless, political constraints have been taken into account in a skilful way.

Otherwise, one has observed an overall political backlash in the region. This would tend to reject the assumption of an exogenous re-election probability. Indeed, if this is the case, then one would observe more randomness in the behaviour of voters. Also, as we will see below, one can show that in those countries where a backlash has taken place, political constraints have not always been taken into account. Of course, not only reformist governments were ousted, and there were many other reasons for which inexperienced new governments in troubled transition circumstances were sanctioned by voters.

On the other hand, despite electoral backlash, no major policy reversal has taken place so far. Even in those countries where former communists have come back to power, this would tend to confirm the idea of "scorched earth politics". It is thus interesting to ask, what are the causes for the backlash and why have we not observed major policy reversals so far?

Explaining the backlash

Various explanations have been put forward so far for the political backlash in Central and Eastern Europe. According to Aghion and Blanchard (1994) and Przeworski (1993), the increase in unemployment following the output fall has played an important role. Sachs (1995) contests the reality of the output fall and claims that an aggregate increase in welfare has been taking place, if not in all countries of the region, at least in some of those countries where backlash has taken place, such as Poland. Sachs thinks that the return of the former communists can be explained by the fact that, as with social democratic parties in Western Europe, they back the support of pensioners and other sections of the population for welfare entitlements. Rodrik (1995) has elaborated a model where state workers initially support the transition and then gradually withdraw their support. Initially state workers support subsidy cuts financed from the private sector because the size of the private sector is too small to finance substantial subsidies and because many expect to find a job in the private sector. However, as the size of the private sector increases, state workers tend to prefer policies favouring higher subsidies to the state sector levied on the private sector, both because their likelihood of finding a job in the private sector declines and because the size of the private sector allows levying a higher subsidy.

Table 1. Growth of private consumption (%).

	1990	1991	1992	1993	1994
Czech Republic	-	-28.4	15.1	2.9	5.3
Hungary	-0.8	-5.8	-0.5	1.4	-
Poland	-11.7	7.2	3.5	5.1	1.2
Russia	-	-	-43.0	12.0	-

Sources: OECD, EBRD, Russian Economic Trends

My own tentative explanation would tend to be based on three elements: a) the increase in aggregate uncertainty related to the important economic disruptions that took place at the beginning of transition, b) the associated increases in income inequality and individual uncertainty, and c) policy mistakes in various countries.

The increase in aggregate uncertainty would tend to confirm the economic vision put forward by the gradualist camp. Indeed, aggregate uncertainty has increased a great deal with the economic disruption following the collapse of central planning, the collapse of CMEA, price and trade liberalisation, and the increase of criminality within borders and of insecurity across borders.

Despite the various controversies about the size of the output fall in various countries, there is a general consensus that this output fall has taken place and that it has been substantial (see, for example, Rosati, 1994). Table 1 shows the evolution of real private consumption in the Czech Republic, Hungary, Poland and Russia. One sees an important consumption fall the year were prices were liberalised (1990 in Poland, 1991 in the Czech Republic and 1992 in Russia). The biggest consumption fall in Hungary took place in 1991, the year of the CMEA breakdown, which can be seen as price liberalisation at the regional level. There is also a general consensus that CMEA breakdown, as well as the breakdown of the Soviet Union, have had substantial contractionary effects throughout the region (Rodrik, 1992). Only Poland seems to be approaching its 1989 output level.

The collapse of state structures has not only led to market creation, but has also led to an important increase in criminality. The "Mafia" phenomenon in Russia has reached alarming proportions. This shows the importance of having stable state structures to be able to enforce private contracts. In Russia, "Mafia" services are often used to enforce contracts. However, they also engage in massive criminal activity and extortion of the private sector. Competition and wars between competing mafias lead to an increased economic uncertainty, which is deleterious for investment in the new private sector. Similarly, the collapse of the Soviet empire and the breakdown of various countries has led to increased insecurity at the borders. Even though a break-up of Yugoslavia was expected by observers, the barbarity of the war that has raged there was clearly unexpected.

To summarise, populations in Central and Eastern Europe have been witnessing an increase in aggregate uncertainty along various dimensions. Given this increase in aggregate uncertainty, one possible explanation for the backlash is that voters have opted for coalitions less committed to reform continuation, which is consistent with the Dewatripont-Roland (1995) model of reforms under aggregate uncertainty. This can be interpreted as a way of buying insurance against possible future bad outcomes by voting into power coalitions which are more prepared to decide on policy reversals.

The effects of the output fall have been reinforced by increases in income inequality; poverty; declining basic public goods provision (for health and education, for example); a low social safety net and an increasing unemployment risk. In other words, individual uncertainty has also greatly increased. Recent research by Milanovic (1996) has shown an increase in income inequality as measured by an increase in the Gini coefficient. This increase in income inequality has been strongest in Russia and the FSU. It is also relatively strong in Bulgaria. We notice a link between the increased income inequality and the declining reform support in Russia and Bulgaria. The increase in poverty has also followed a similar pattern, with the most dramatic increases in the former Soviet Union and Bulgaria. One should also notice an increase in poverty in Poland. Figures published by UNICEF (1994) also witness the effects of the deterioration of health conditions in various countries. Data from UNICEF show a fall in life expectancy in Eastern Europe, with the exception of the Visegrad countries. Mortality for children and adults aged between 20 and 59 has also been increasing, again with the exception of the Visegrad countries. Thus, there seems to be a strong deterioration of health conditions in CIS countries. The pattern is identical for education. Secondary enrolment rates since 1989 have fallen sharply in the region, once more with the exception of the Visegrad countries. Increases in unemployment rates show an increase in unemployment risk. This represents an important increase in individual uncertainty, given the rather low safety nets existing in Central and Eastern Europe and the strong implicit employment insurance workers enjoyed under socialism. Even if the unemployed are not pivotal in elections, state workers most probably still are. It is state workers facing the prospect of restructuring who are the natural constituency of the former communist parties, hoping for a reduction in unemployment risk.

To the increases in aggregate and individual uncertainty, one should add a list of policy mistakes for which the voters have punished new reformist governments. Let us review some of the most important mistakes.

In Poland, for example, the first non-communist government has certainly under-estimated the strength of insider coalitions who were able to block mass privatisation plans. This under-estimation, together with an initially hostile attitude towards the state sector, led to a quick undermining of support and political fragmentation and instability. Przeworski (1993) documents that support for the Mazowiecki government had already fallen in May 1990. Presidential elections later in 1990 gave Mazowiecki only 12 per cent. After that, Poland underwent a period of relative political fragmentation and instability.

In Hungary, the Antal coalition probably neglected the window of opportunity offered by the change in political regime to adopt significant stabilization measures (Kornai, 1996). Ironically it is the coalition of social democrats, former communists and liberals which started implementing a tough stabilization package in 1995. The Antal coalition tended to neglect economic problems, focusing more on nationalist issues such as the fate of Hungarians in Slovakia and Romania. Former communists won their election campaign in 1994 by claiming to have more expertise than the nationalist government.

In my view, a very important sequencing mistake was made in Russia in late 1991. The failure of the August 1991 *putsch* led to the unexpected end of the communist regime in the Soviet Union. This could have been a unique opportunity to set up new elections inside Russia, write a new constitution and search for a relative consensus for new democratic institutions. Instead of that, Eltsin gave priority to economic issues. He was left with a Parliament that had been elected under the communist regime in March 1990. Not surprisingly, that Parliament started systematically blocking reform measures. Because of this, the Gaidar team obviously did not have sufficient political support for radical reforms. This important sequencing mistake shows that the opposition to reform had certainly been strongly under-estimated. Despite the success of Chubais in implementing rapid mass privatisation to insiders, the privatisation programme is now being accused of having favoured an increase of "Mafia" control over economic assets. This is probably related to the fact that reformers insisted vouchers be made exchangeable for cash. The idea of reformers was that ordinary workers and the ordinary people would exchange their vouchers for money, thereby leading to a transfer of ownership to concentrated owners. This strategy neglected the fact that "Mafia" organisations were among the only groups in society having enough wealth to acquire state assets at a low price.

Policy reversal and the geopolitical hypothesis

Why has there been no major policy reversal despite backlash by voters in elections? I would like to suggest as a hypothesis the strength of the geopolitical factor. Economists trying to understand transition have generally viewed transition as a shift towards democracy and the market. If we take some historical distance, we can see that transition also represents a very important geopolitical move, i.e. the shift of Central Europe and the Baltic States to the West. To important parts of populations in those countries, the single most important factor about transition is the change from being a satellite country of the Soviet empire to being a part of the Western block or even of the European Union. Transition represents a unique historical opportunity for several nations to become strongly anchored in Western Europe. Not only is this "anchorage" to the European Union desired by nations of Central Europe, but it also focuses expectations and gives credibility to the political and economic process of transition. Entry into the European Union implies adopting the political and economic system of the West. The potential reward of belonging to the club of Western nations makes it more worthwhile to undergo the cost of transition, and thus makes it easier to accept. Moreover, the geopolitical factor increases the perceived cost of a policy reversal, since it implies the risk of being left out of the Western club, a prospect that many in Central Europe would view as disastrous.

I would like to suggest that the geopolitical hypothesis allows us to explain a number of stylised facts of transition that overall have not received a comprehensive explanation so far. The first stylised fact is the CMEA breakdown (as well as the break-up of Soviet Union). It has been considered the single most important explanatory factor for the general fall of output in the region (see, for example, Rodrik, 1992), but it has generally been perceived as an exogenous shock. The breakdown of CMEA was however not exogenous but endogenous. It was agreed upon in early 1990 when the Czechoslovak and the Polish governments insisted on regaining their freedom of export, contrary to CMEA agreements. The Soviets at that time responded by insisting that imports for the Soviet Union would, from 1991 onwards, be paid for at low prices and in hard currency. From the economic point of view, it would have probably been better to find co-ordinated transitional arrangements between former CMEA countries to avoid the strong trade disruption that occurred in 1991. However, and this is where the geopolitical factor comes in, such co-ordination was not desired. Individual Central European countries wanted to leave the Soviet block as quickly as possible and to be the first to knock at the door of the European Union. The CMEA breakdown was thus an economic consequence of the political will prevailing in Central European countries to leave the Soviet block.

The geopolitical factor also allows us to explain the rapid expectational changes that took place among economic agents that led to a change of behaviour by managers of state-owned enterprises. It is not self-evident that the political changes of 1989 and the announcement of drastic stabilization programmes would necessarily produce important changes in expectations. Indeed, new governments with no track records and lacking credibility could have fallen prey to pressures from managers of state-owned enterprises for soft budget constraints. Previous loss of control of the centre over enterprises under socialism generally tended to increase soft budget constraints. It is thus not certain that the announcement of stabilization policies would by themselves produce hard budget constraints because if they were not credible, they would have been undone (Perotti, 1994; Coricelli and Milesi-Feretti, 1993). Evidence from enterprise behaviour in Eastern Europe since the beginning of transition strongly suggests however that stabilization policies have contributed to hardening the budget constraints of enterprises (Pinto *et al.*, 1993; Carlin *et al.*, 1994; Bouin and Grosfeld, 1995). The crucial factor leading to increased financial discipline is the credibility of a "no bailout" policy. Without such credibility, the reduction of subsidies associated with stabilization policies automatically leads to a growth in inter-enterprise arrears and the portfolio of bad loans in banks. Suppliers and banks would be prepared to extend credit to loss-making enterprises if they expect them to be bailed out. Insufficient credibility of a "no bailout" policy would not induce much change in enterprise behaviour and in private behaviour. Experience in various transition economies shows that efforts to drastically enforce hard budget constraints are often partly undone and that credibility is at best only partial. Drastic cuts in fiscal subsidies have led, in all countries, to a deterioration of the bad loan problem in the banking sector. Efforts to toughen financial discipline in enterprise-bank relationships have led to an increase in inter-enterprise arrears. Similarly, measures to get rid of inter-enterprise arrears have often resulted in higher tax arrears. Such shifts are documented in all countries. Despite these observations, the evidence produced so far on enterprise behaviour leads to the conclusion that measures to impose hard budget constraints were credible enough and therefore contributed to the reinforcement of the financial discipline of firms. Indeed, even gradual changes in expectations tend to reinforce each other. Enterprises and banks become more reluctant to accept payment arrears by their clients if they are less sure than before that bailouts will take place, even though expectations of bailouts remain high. A higher reluctance to accept payment arrears reinforces the general perception of a hardening of the budget constraint which leads to further changes and expectations resulting in further changes in behaviour, and so forth. The key question is how to explain a sufficiently strong initial credibility. It appears that the geopolitical factor seems to play an important role. The collapse of communism and the change in regime itself tended to produce changes in expectations. Interestingly, Kornai (1995) documents drastic changes in inventory behaviour taking place in Hungary at the end of 1989, indicating important changes in expectations with respect to shortages and soft budget constraints, despite the fact that no radical economic policy change was taking place at that precise time.

The geopolitical factor in Central European countries was reinforced by a "transition tournament" between the Czech, Hungarian and Polish governments where each purported to be the most advanced transition country in the hope of attracting the bulk of foreign direct investment to the region. The incentives related to the "price" of such a tournament are strong enough for countries of that size to create credibility for economic transformation. Countries which entered the transition race later, such as Bulgaria and Romania, have little hope of catching up on the more advanced countries, or even of pretending to do so, and thus less possibilities for attracting FDI.

To understand the strength of the geopolitical factor, it is useful to compare the situation of Central European countries with that of Russia, where this geopolitical factor is absent. In contrast to the former, where transition is seen as a liberation from the Soviet empire and access to the Western club of nations, transition is viewed in Russia as a traumatic experience by a major part of the population. Transition indeed represents the loss, not only of the Soviet empire, but also of territories, such as the Ukraine or the Baltic States, that belonged to Tsarist Russia. This loss does not only mean a wound to Russian nationalist pride, but it implies uncertainty for the families of those who have relatives among the millions of Russians living in the former Soviet republics and who became "immigrants" in former Soviet territories, often with the status of "second-rate" citizen. The trauma of the loss of superpower status, similar in a way to the trauma of Germany after the first World War, could, to a certain extent, be compensated for by economic gains from transition. This however has not materialised so far for the majority of Russians. Entry of Russia into the EU is not expected nor especially desired. The large area of the country implies that the impact of FDI is likely to be more diluted, thereby reducing the incentives to participate in "transition tournaments". It is thus no wonder that resistance to transition proved much harder in the former Soviet Union, as shown by the greater difficulties in hardening budget constraints of enterprises or in adopting stabilization measures. Nor is it clear that no major policy reversal will take place or is expected to take place. The uncertainty surrounding the June 1996 elections is a clear example.

The geopolitical factor also allows us to explain the difference in the evolution of former communists in the Visegrad countries and in Russia. Reform communists in Poland and Hungary strongly support the "anchorage" of their nations to the West. It is interesting to see former communist Kwasniewski insisting on early entry of his country to NATO, and there is no reason not to believe him on this, since there is broad national consensus on such a goal. In Russia, things are very different. The communist party consists mainly of hardliners who regret the demise of the former Soviet Union.

The geopolitical factor may also explain why aid from the West to Russia was not so swift in the beginning of transition. In geopolitical terms, if the entry of Central European countries into the Western block represents an important gain for the latter, observers are divided over the strategic interests of the West and of the United States vis-à-vis a weakened Russia. Advocates of help to Russia point to the dangers of a destabilized Russia headed by communist and nationalist coalitions. Others think that a weakened Russia may represent less of a threat in the years to come. Again, assessing whether the probability of national-communist coalitions coming to power in Moscow is exogenous or endogenous is key to that debate — advocates of aid viewing it as endogenous, and others seeing it as mainly exogenous.

If the hypothesis of the geopolitical factor allows us to explain the stronger resistance to reform or reduced support in Russia and former CIS countries, it also implies that, everything else equal, the cost of the reversal of transition policies is much higher in Central European policies than in Russia and in the former CIS.

Conclusion

We have tried in this paper to summarise the role of political constraints in the transition experience in Central and Eastern European countries so far. Both the "big bang" and the gradualist approaches take *ex ante* and *ex post* political constraints into account. The main difference between both is whether the probability of re-election is exogenous or endogenous. When it is exogenous, then the "big bang" approach serves to constrain a successor government, because rapid reform on all fronts makes policy reversal more costly. When it is endogenous, gradualism allows us to design reform sequencing so as to build constituencies for further reforms.

The experience of transition has shown the importance of political constraints. Stabilization plans were systematically blocked in Russia, and the Polish mass privatisation plan was blocked for several years. Privatisation is also the area of reform where political constraints have played the most prominent role. In countries where insider control was pervasive before transition, only give-away plans favouring insiders could be adopted, as is the case of Russia, in contrast to that of the Czech Republic where "give-aways" to outsiders were possible.

The Czech Republic has the best record so far in terms of dealing with political constraints. The privatisation programme took into account both *ex ante* and *ex post* political constraints. The delay in restructuring to ensure the initial success of voucher privatisation, shows a subtle understanding of reform sequencing.

Confronting theory with experience, the generalised backlash in the region (with the exception of the Czech Republic) puts into doubt the exogeneity of re-election probability. On the other hand, the absence of major policy reversals tends to confirm the idea that fast initial reforms are effective in constraining a successor government. However, we suggest that the geopolitical factor of transition has not been sufficiently taken into account so far. To citizens of Central Europe, transition essentially represents a geopolitical shift from the Soviet empire to the club of Western nations. Therefore, the benefits of transition to the market, as well as the costs of reversal, are perceived very differently in Central Europe, compared to Russia. Further research is needed to analyse the strength of the geopolitical factor in explaining transition successes in some countries and difficulties in others.

Notes

[1] This is where the Persson and Svensson (1989) model comes in. They have shown that a conservative government favouring fiscal conservatism may want to limit the policy of a democratic successor by running a budget deficit today. The cost of servicing the public debt will then constrain the policies of future governments.

[2] An obvious example is the rejection of price increases by the Polish population under the Jaruzelski regime, but the relative acceptance of comprehensive price liberalisation in January 1990 under the Mazowiecki government.

References

Aghion, P. and Blanchard, O., 1994, "On the Speed of Transition in Central Europe", *NBER Macroeconomics Annual*, pp. 283-319.

Alesina, A. and Drazen, A., 1991, "Why are Stabilizations Delayed?", *American Economic Review*, vol. 81, pp. 1170-1188.

Bergson, A. and Levine, H.S., 1982, *The Soviet Economy Towards the Year 2000*, Allen and Unwin, London.

Bouin O. and Grosfeld, I., 1995, "Credibilité des réformes et ajustement des entreprises en Pologne et en République tchèque", forthcoming in *Revue Economique.*

Carlin,W., van Reenen, J. and Wolfe, T., 1994, "Enterprise restructuring in the transition : an analytical survey of the case study evidence from central and eastern Europe", *EBRD Working Paper* , n° 14.

Castanheira, M. and Roland, G., 1994, "The Optimal Speed of Restructuring: A General Equilibrium Analysis", ECARE, Université Libre de Bruxelles, [mimeo].

Castanheira, M. and Roland, G., 1995, "Restructuring and Capital Accumulation in Transition Economies: A General Equilibrium Perspective", ECARE, Université Libre de Bruxelles, [mimeo].

Coricelli, F. and Milesi-Ferreti, G-M., 1993, "On the Credibility of "Big Bang" Programs", *European Economic Review*, vol. 37 n° 2-3, pp. 387-395.

Csaba, L., 1995, *The Capitalist Revolution in Eastern Europe*, Aldershot Edward Elgar.

Dewatripont, M. and Roland, G., 1995, "The Design of Reform Packages under Uncertainty", *American Economic Review,* vol. 85 n° 5, pp. 1207-1223.

Dewatripont, M. and Tirole, J., 1994a, *The Prudential Regulation of Banks*, Cambridge MA, MIT Press.

Grosfeld, I. and Roland, G., 1995, "Defensive and Strategic Restructuring in Central European Enterprises", *CEPR Discussion Paper*, n° 1135.

Kornai, J., 1990, *The Road to a Free Economy*, Norton, New York.

Kornai, J., 1992, *The Socialist System*, Oxford University Press, Oxford.

Kornai, J., 1995, "Eliminating the Shortage Economy", *Economics of Transition*, vol. 3 n° 1, pp. 13-37.

Kornai, J., 1996, "Paying the Bill for Goulash-Communism", *Collegium Budapest DP*, n° 23.

Lipton, D. and Sachs, J., 1990, "Creating an Market Economy in Eastern Europe: the Case of Poland", *Brookings Papers on Economic Activity*, n° 1, pp. 75-133.

Litwack, J., 1993, "The Trap of Fiscal Instability: the Case of Russian Economic Transition: 1992-Mid 1993", Stanford University, [mimeo].

Milanovic, B., 1995, "Poverty, Inequality and Social Policy in Transition Economies", World Bank, [mimeo].

Murrell, P., 1992, "Evolution in Economics and in the Economic Reform of the Centrally Planned Economies", in Clague, C. and Rausser, G., (ed.), *The Emergence of Market Economies in Eastern Europe*, Blackwell Cambridge, pp. 35-53.

Perotti, E., 1993, *Collusive Trade Arrears in the Stabilization of Transition Economies*, Boston University, [mimeo].

Persson, T. and Svensson, L., 1989, "Why a Stubborn Conservative would run a Deficit: policy with Time-inconsistent Preferences", *Quarterly Journal of Economics,* vol. 104, n° 2, pp. 325-346.

Pinto, B., Belka, M., and Krajewski, S., 1993, 'Transforming State Enterprises in Poland', *Brookings Papers on Economic Activity*, n°1, pp. 213-270.

Przeworski, A., 1993, "Economic Reforms, Public Opinion and Political Institutions", in Bresser, L.C., Pereira *et al. Economic Reforms in New Democracies,* Cambridge University Press, New York.

Rodrik, D., 1989, "Promises, Promises: Credible Reform via Signalling", *Economic Journal,* vol. 99, pp. 756-72.

Rodrik, D., 1992, "Making Sense of the Soviet Trade Shock in Eastern Europe: A Framework and Some Estimates", CEPR DP n° 705.

Rodrik, D., 1993, "The Positive Economics of Policy Reform", *American Economic Review*, vol. 83, pp. 356-61.

Rodrik, D., 1995, "The Dynamics of Political Support for Reform in Economies in Transition", *Journal of Japanese and International Economics*.

Rodrik, D., 1996, "Understanding Economic Policy Reform", *Journal of Economic Literature*, vol. 334 n° 1, pp. 9-41.

Roland, G., 1993, "The Political Economy of Transition in the Soviet Union", *European Economy*, pp. 197-216.

Roland, G., 1994, "The Role of Political Constraints in Transition Strategies", *Economics of Transition*, vol. 2 n° 1, pp. 27-41.

Roland, G., 1995, "Political Economy Issues in Ownership Transformation", in Aoki, M. and Kim, H-K. (ed.), *Corporate Governance in Transitional Economies*, World Bank, Washington, pp. 31-58.

Roland, G. and Verdier, T., 1994, "Privatization in Eastern Europe: Irreversibility and Critical Mass Effects", *Journal of Public Economics*, vol. 54, pp. 161-183.

Roland, G. and Verdier, T., 1996 "Transition and the Output Fall", ECARE and DELTA, work in progress.

Rosati, D., 1994, "Output Decline during Transition from Plan to Market: A Reconsideration", *Economics of Transition*, vol. 2 n° 4, pp. 419-442.

Sachs, J., 1995. "Postcommunist Parties and the Politics of Entitlement", *Transition newsletter*, World Bank, vol. 6 n° 3, pp. 1-4.

Sargent, T., 1986, *Rational Expectations and Inflation*, Harper and Row, New York.

UNICEF, 1994, *Regional Monitoring Report*.

Vickers, J., 1986, "Signalling in a Model of Monetary Policy with Incomplete Information", *Oxford Economic Papers*, vol. 100, pp. 1011-1039.

Weingast, B., 1993, "The Political Foundations of Democracy and the Rule of Law", Hoover Institution, Stanford University, [mimeo].

9

Comments

Vincent Koen

The contributions included in Part I offer a synopsis of many of the crucial issues related to transition strategies. Drawing mainly on the experience of Russia and Poland, I will ask three questions: i) how reliable are the data commonly used to describe what happened in the first half of the 1990s? ii) how comparable are policy outcomes over time and across countries? and iii) are the first or second-generation policy debates still relevant now that some countries are advanced enough to shrug off — rightly or not — the "transition" label?

1. (Re)-estimating the past

When it was moving through the transition from early capitalism to communism, Keynes (1925) noted that "the economic system of Russia has undergone and is undergoing such rapid changes that it is impossible to obtain a precise and accurate account of it. (...) Almost everything one can say about the country is true and false at the same time." The same holds now that Russia has embarked on the journey in the opposite direction.

Although it is often acknowledged rhetorically as important, the issue of data quality is routinely side-stepped by analysts of transition, and insufficient care is often exercised when selecting relevant statistics. I will illustrate some of the uncertainties that surround official macroeconomic estimates, in order to emphasise that first-order misunderstandings can arise from an overly casual use of the numbers. I will focus here on output, but acute problems plague price measures as well.

A prominent feature of the first stage of transition has been the collapse of output. The contraction has clearly been massive in most countries, exceeding most "Great Depressions" witnessed by them or others earlier on. But the magnitude of the actual decline in output was widely overstated by the first set of official statistics published by national accountants. In Poland, it is likely that the actual cumulative output drop did not exceed 10 per cent, as against an official estimate approaching 20 per cent. In Russia, the cumulative drop through 1994 was in the order of one third, rather than one half. Unfortunately, the re-estimations carried out down the road are often ignored by users.

One approach adopted by some of the analysts despairing of official real GDP data has been to use electricity consumption as a simple, but unfortunately simplistic, substitute. The main arguments offered in favour of such a summary statistic are that it suffers much less from under-reporting; that it is available on a timely basis; and that it has been shown to move, by and large, in tandem with the true level of activity; or that it would, if anything, understate it; given the shift in the composition of GDP towards less energy-intensive activities. Such a summary indicator also circumvents sectoral aggregation problems, which in a period of massive structural change are very important. Although highly suggestive of a strong downward bias in the official real GDP series, electricity use cannot serve as a decent proxy for actual output in the first stages of transition, and even less so in cross-country comparisons, mainly due to the instability of the parameters underlying the relationship between aggregate output and electricity input. But if watching the changes in electricity use is not necessarily very enlightening to assess the size of the cumulative output collapse, it may be helpful to identify turning points in economic activity, once the period of massive cross-sectoral output shifts has ended and the aforementioned parameters have settled down to their new levels.

If movements in real GDP are ill-measured, so is the actual size of the economy. Recent semi-official estimates for Poland show that the hidden economy represents around 15 to 18 per cent of GDP (Zienkowski, 1996). Some allowance is made in the official GUS data for the existence of an underground economy that thrived in the early stages of the transition, but only to the tune of some 6 per cent of GDP. One should not, therefore, be surprised if sometime in the foreseeable future, the official measure of nominal GDP were to be grossed up suddenly by about one-tenth — the statisticians' contribution to the catch-up process discussed below.

Clearly, given the magnitude of the discrepancies between alternative series, focusing on the wrong ones can seriously distort comparisons over time and space of the merits of different economic policies.

2. *Assessing policy successes and failures*

A second kind of bias stems from downplaying initial conditions. This can lead to spurious correlations — a poor country in a disassembling empire starting off with a war would, *ceteris paribus,* suffer a larger output decline **and** higher inflation than a relatively wealthy one enjoying its regained full independence and where peace prevails. Some of the initial conditions are also difficult to put in numbers, but it can, and has been, usefully done. As stressed by Stern, some of the countries starting with relative handicaps did better than others that inherited easier initial conditions, but that says more about the strength of the reform measures and adjustment efforts than about the irrelevance of initial conditions.

A third type of oversight in many policy assessments is the confusion between calendar and stabilization time. Too often, transition economies are compared as if both chronologies started in 1989, which translates into undue inferences such as "countries in FSU have had less virtuous policies than their Western neighbours, since output is still declining in most and inflation is still higher in most". Policies may indeed have been less bold and comprehensive in the FSU than further West, but the lag between the start of transition in the first and in the second region ought to be controlled for. The general trajectory of many of those countries — in particular the U-curve of output and the inverted U-curve for inflation — is similar once differences in timing are controlled for. Dating the beginning of transition is not certainly a trivial task, but the relevance of cross-country comparisons is much improved when some systematic effort along those lines is made.

Lastly, another temptation is to ask, as does Stern, in which countries output has by now recovered its peak pre-transition level, as a measure of success. This is misleading, however, because it glosses over the change in the composition of output, which matters as much as movements in its aggregate level and because the comparison with the past is misplaced, as Balcerowicz laments when describing voters' behaviour (proposition 5). The relevant counterfactual argument for assessing policies and policy-makers is what would have happened had other policies been pursued — the centrally planned economy was crumbling under its own weight, and policies other than radical market oriented reforms presumably could not have spared Poland, Russia and others large output declines.

3. *Inflation and growth — past and future*

As history unfolds, the controversies on reform design evolve somewhat. For example, a series of hyperinflations or near-hyperinflations, mostly in the FSU, seems to have converted a number of the critics of the "Washington consensus" to the view that under such circumstances it may be appropriate to reason along monetarist lines. But as inflation is brought down to more moderate levels, the issue resurfaces of the desirable degree of tightness of financial policies, as reflected in the contribution by Laski and Badhuri.

The debate has thus largely shifted from the merits, at the onset of transition, of "shock therapy" versus "gradualism", to the best way to cope with "moderate" inflation and to preserve and speed up growth. Laski and Badhuri paint the authorities, and their Bretton Woods allies, as obsessed quite exclusively with disinflation, and unwilling to consider the need to sustain aggregate demand. They point to the simultaneity of the recovery of aggregate demand and of disinflation in the second stage of the transition to argue that supporting demand will enhance growth. The "Washington gnomes" would reply that it was the revival on the supply side following the initial disruptions, and fostered by decisive liberalisation measures, that produced this outcome. They would argue that if Poland is now "the soaring eagle of Eastern Europe", it is largely thanks to the radical reforms launched in 1989-90, bold and comprehensive enough to be described by some as a "jump to the market". They do indeed push for further disinflation, but worry at least as much about the sustainability of the recent growth performance and the possible institutional obstacles that might stem it. In that respect as well, the emphasis is diametrically opposed to the one adopted by Laski and Badhuri. Where the latter talk about private entities as "parasites" and discrimination against state-owned enterprises, the former would see the persistence of an oversized state, high taxes, and implicit or explicit residual subsidisation of agonising mastodons. Viewed from Washington, those factors are among the threats to the continuation of disinflation and swift growth — if the investment push in infrastructure needed to underpin future growth, as highlighted by Stern as well as by Laski and Badhuri, is to materialise, further divestiture of the state is necessary.

In the longer run, as Balcerowicz stresses, the acid test for judging reforms and reformers is growth. Will the countries emerging from the transition enjoy an Asian tiger-like boom or "Euro-sclerotic" crawling along? Some of the ingredients for long-run convergence toward EU living standards are present in the region, as noted by Stern — an educated labour force, relatively open economies, a fair measure of macroeconomic stability, and large nearby export markets. But the long-run run will last decades, even under the most optimistic scenarios.

Further east, Russia remains the colossus with lead boots. No unambiguous recovery of aggregate output can yet be ascertained, at least based on the official production data, notwithstanding sporadic cries of victory during the last year or two to the effect that the turning point had been reached.

Lastly, a series of new questions arise at this stage of transition, now that former communist parties have been returned to power by voters in many countries of the region. Balcerowicz nicely discussed some of them, arguing that tough initial reforms offered post-communist parties room for complacency once they were back in charge, which will enable them to be re-elected. We have therein the skeleton of an interesting theory on why bold reformers might loose elections at least twice — in Poland at least. Another intriguing point made by Balcerowicz pertains to the economic consequences of political cycles. He contends that some "reversion to the mean" occurs, with early reforming countries slowed down by complacency and late reformers, who make a virtue out of necessity, catching up. There are reasons to wonder, however, whether countries such as Bulgaria or Ukraine will catch up soon, and to worry about the downside risks associated with procrastination and protracted stagnation.

References

Keynes, J.M., 1925, *A Short View of Russia*, published by Leonard and Virginia Woolf, London.

Zienkowski, L., 1996, "The Polish Experience in Estimates of the Hidden Economy", *Research Bulletin of RECESS*, Vol. 5, No. 1.

Stanislaw Gomulka

The contribution by Fischer, Sahay and Vegh is impressive in its coverage of countries and the wealth of statistics. Using simple regression techniques, its authors have identified a number of interesting associations between the various key variables. However, the causal links among the variables are not simple to disentangle. My concern is that the authors write as if these associations are, in fact, causal relationships. I am particularly unhappy about their claim that slow stabilization (high inflation) increases the cumulative fall in GDP and that a fixed exchange rate policy helps recovery. In fact, there are grounds to think that the cross-section positive relation between price level increases and output declines during the initial phase of transition is a case of spurious correlation (Blanchard, 1995; Gomulka, 1996). The countries which suffered greater real shocks have also experienced greater output falls. These tended to lead to larger budget deficits and therefore higher inflation. The opposite view, that the fall of output has been made worse by policies of financial restraint, is also to be rejected. Elsewhere I argued, on the basis of cross-country comparisons, that financial policies may have affected the path of recession but not the cumulative fall of output (Gomulka, 1994). This has been recently restated on the basis of evidence produced by Aslund *et al.* (1995), that "all that a responsible financial policy does is to hasten the fall in output and thus the beginning of the recovery" (Russian Economic Trends, 1996).

The policy of fixing the exchange rate has been adopted consistently for several years only by the Czech Republic. Therefore, the evidence that this policy helps recovery is virtually non-existent. In Poland, where the recovery came first and has been largest, a more flexible policy of a pre-announced crawling peg was adopted before the start of recovery and has since been credited with playing an important role in inducing export-led growth. The IMF inclination to use the fixed exchange rate policy for controlling inflation endangers rather than stimulates recovery, even though it may help long-term growth.

The contribution by Roland is a courageous attempt to offer a general theory of the role of political constraints in transition reforms. Perhaps inevitably, it exaggerates and misinterprets. Its principal thesis is that the main difference in the choice between the "big bang" and the "gradualist" approaches is whether the probability of re-election was exogenous or endogenous. This exaggerates differences between actual reform strategies. Compared to the standards of China and the pre-transition experiences of socialist countries, transition reforms have been extremely radical and fast in nearly all the countries of Central Europe and the FSU. Moreover, Roland's thesis implicitly assumes that these countries had the option of choosing a gradual approach. This assumption belittles the powerful influences of initial conditions: the double collapse of central planning and communist power; the economic crisis; and the expectations of electorates that strong policy measures and institutional reforms would, could and should be implemented. The reformers were influenced by these conditions and expectations rather than by the concern of a possible political backlash or the risk of policy reversals (Balcerowicz, 1995; Gomulka, 1995). The contribution consequently fails to note and address the continuity paradox: although voters do tend to return former communists to power, these newcomers neither reverse reform policies much nor change the direction of transition and have even accelerated reforms, as has been the case recently in Bulgaria and Hungary. Zyuganov and his hard-line supporters failed to win presidential powers in Russia possibly because of doubts that they would continue the reforms. The contribution notes correctly that to citizens of Central Europe, transition also represents a geographical shift from the Soviet empire to the club of Western nations. This point is somewhat new for economists, but it has been stressed by politicians and therefore its originality should not be claimed.

Finally, Roland singles out privatisation "as the area of reform where political constraints have played the most prominent role". If this were so, the extremely rapid progress of privatisation throughout the region should be taken as evidence of the fairly limited ability of these constraints to affect the pace of reforms, though the methods of privatisation have been affected. Roland also makes reference to the Polish mass privatisation plan, that was delayed for several years. However, this delay was in large part due to two controversial features — namely, a complicated governance structure, and a leading role given to foreign management groups. A plan of the Russian type or of the Czech type would have been probably much easier to enact and implement. Thus the concern of Polish reformers with quality rather than quantity delayed the programme.

References

Aslund, A., Boone, P. and Johnson, S., 1996, *How to Stabilize, Lessons from Post-Communist Countries*, Brookings Papers on Economic Activity, March.

Balcerowicz, L., 1995, *Socialism, Capitalism, Transformation*, OUP and Central European University.

Blanchard, O., 1995, *The First Clarendon Lecture*, Oxford, November.

Gomulka, S., 1994, "Economic and Political Constraints during Transition", *Europe-Asia Studies*, 46(1): 83-106.

LSE, 1996, *Causes of Output Decline, Sources of Recovery and Prospects for Growth in Transition Economies*, July, [mimeo].

Russian Economic Trends, 1996, 13 June, p. 4.

Silvana Malle

In assessing the relative success of various CEECs in their economic transformation, topical aspects, such as the selection of the period of reference, the grouping of the countries, and the main evaluation criteria, need to be clearly addressed, as any initial bias would impinge on the conclusions. Implicit in this assessment is a more fundamental question: what evidence do we have that transformation has been completed?

While the issue of gradualism versus shock therapy has lost much of its interest in the course of the economic transformation, its implications for policy choice remain. This is particularly true as our knowledge today goes beyond the immediate impact of the chosen transformation strategy and encompasses also the social and political backlashes and the consequent policy accommodations — a point raised by Roland. Although any model needs stylised features, excessive simplifications neither help the understanding of the crucial moments in transformation, nor give confidence that this period is over and that no reversals are possible.

If the starting point of reforms is taken to be 1989, Slovenia, for instance, did not at that time fit the description of a "planned economy", as it belonged to the typology of market socialism characterised by workers' self-management, public property and market prices. Borders were fairly open, and both visits and migrations contributed to further exposure to the West, as well as to the accumulation of savings in hard currency (which facilitated the recovery through private investment). The characterisation of Hungary as a planned economy in 1989 is also disputable, since in the 1980s planning was much diluted and the country gradually opened to foreign trade, adjusted to international prices and approved market-oriented legislation. One might also question the selection of the year when reforms began in Poland (in 1987, it started liberalising foreign trade, granting free access of domestic firms to foreign trade, and introducing hard currency schemes for exporters), or even Russia and the FSU (from the mid-1980s the Soviet Union introduced not only significant political reforms, but also the liberalisation of economic activity for individuals, and trade for co-operatives, allowing production to be based on market prices and issuing legislation on joint-ventures).

Thus, in 1989, only one effectively planned economy belonged to the group of fast reformers — the Czechoslovakian Federal Republic, if East Germany is excluded. If Czechoslovakia were taken as a model, a possible conclusion would be that, thanks to the lasting advantages of having a rigidly-planned economy, Czechoslovakia was able to maintain financial discipline and consequently to absorb the shocks of fast reforms with lesser backlashes.

If countries such as Poland, Hungary and Slovenia, which started market reforms earlier than 1989, are included among the successful group of countries, they might actually provide stronger arguments for gradualism, since the introduction of reforms before 1989 should be taken into account. One needs to be sceptical, however, about the gradualist argument, since the evidence is that pre-1989 reforms, while disrupting the planning system and relaxing financial discipline, brought about comparatively worse post-1989 stabilization and transformation problems. Hungary still suffers from high external indebtedness *per capita*, much of which was accumulated during the 1980s; Poland has benefited from a partial cancellation of external debt, but will have to bear the cost of rescheduling the residual debt for years to come. Just as the selection of the period is crucial for a meaningful assessment of the transformation process, any conclusion based on a five- or six-year period should be regarded as preliminary.

There has been — and there continues to be — much speculation about the possibility of reversals, particularly for systems such as Russia's which are more exposed to political uncertainties. Since what existed prior to a coherent package of reforms was generally financial disruption and different degrees of economic chaos, any possible reversals would indeed bring back the same situation, rather than a return to central planning. A case in point is the Hungarian crisis in 1995, which was about to develop into a textbook case of a debt-poverty trap, with real interest rates higher than real GDP growth and a rising fiscal deficit. Growth, boosted by increasing indebtedness in 1994, was severely slashed in 1995 in what Kornai calls "the March Package shock therapy". Thus, political changes matter even for fast reforming countries, contrary to Balcerowicz's hypothesis that once radical reforms have been introduced, no government change will matter and no reversal will be possible. When reversals occur and are marked by financial disruption, it is common for the business community to turn to the state for help. Thus, after chaos the real danger for fragile market economies and paternalistic democracies is corporativism, i.e. a blend of inward looking nationalist policies coupled with a good dose of state industry and banking and trade union acquiescence, a model with which Europe has already had some experience.

Should we expect Polish-type results — positive growth after three years of reforms — in any post-communist country, regardless of its political and economic geography, post-reformist government changes and initial conditions, provided that the appropriate balance of shock measures is enforced? There is little justification for this. It is hardly credible that the geoeconomic dimension does not matter (a conclusion reached in de Melo's and Gelb's model), when one considers that the five most successful transition countries all border on some of the wealthiest West European OECD countries, while the intermediate or slow reformers are more distant. As geoeconomic indicators are likely to be closely correlated with indicators of economic performance, one wonders whether they are implicit in indicators of FDI and private business growth, which appear to matter.

Another major issue is the identification of the turning point leading to positive growth. This indicator is preferable to recovery measures based on the attainment of the pre-transition output level because of sizeable changes in the output mix, quality and relative prices during the transition. But the turning point also depends on the estimated level of GDP in 1989 and on the estimated output fall after that year. It is not known what GDP was before the reforms started in countries which, by the beginning of reforms, had not yet moved to market prices. Base year prices also matter in assessing growth, since the longer the time distance from the base year, the higher the bias in estimating output fall or growth. The Czech statistics, for instance, still use 1984 base prices and this helps to boost investment growth figures. Thus, depending on the reliability of GDP estimates, output falls may have been exaggerated, positive growth may have occurred earlier, and measured positive growth rates may be overstated. With revisions of statistics underway, it is likely, as it has already emerged for Poland and Russia, that the output fall generally was exaggerated and that positive growth occurred earlier, even in fast-reforming countries.

To highlight the contribution of the real side of the economy, some models (including the one presented by de Melo and Gelb) incorporate privatisation as a determinant of the composite index of liberalisation. If privatisation is used as a proxy for restructuring, this is, indeed, a poor and potentially biased indicator since most reforming countries have either stopped at formal property rights redistribution or postponed major decisions in this field. The share of the private sector in the economy is highly dependent on the share of the expanding sectors, which are trade and services. However, much of the output of the new service sectors was previously included in the industrial output statistics. The statistical effect of separating trade and services from industry is not only to boost these sectors' output, but also to lead to an overestimation of the fall in industrial output, which in turn means an overestimation of "privatisation-restructuring effects" as a whole.

In economies characterised by the "51 per cent" private property threshold for the definition of private business, with former managers still in power, with dispersion of residual stock ownership, with opaque and illiquid capital markets and with cross shareholdings in which state banks have a major role, mass or voucher privatisation should not be interpreted as evidence of actual restructuring. It is true that private business has been growing, but this growth is by no means dramatic in the traditional production sectors. All in all, even in countries which have rapidly liberalised their economies, gradualism has prevailed in privatisation. This raises doubts, not only about the effects of shock-therapy, but also about the underlying causes and sustainability of GDP growth.

In most post-communist countries, growth has been export-led, helped by strong initial devaluations, by sales of accumulated stocks of raw materials and semi-finished products after the sudden demise of the CMEA, by lively international demand as well as by FDI. Large firms (mostly SOEs) were able to rapidly reorient their sales to the West, while still remaining dependent on Eastern inputs. These early competitive advantages are being eroded by the real appreciation of the exchange rate and by price, wage and cost adjustments, with energy costs rapidly increasing and (energy-saving) technological changes being hampered by high interest rates and inefficient banking structures.

Sustainable growth is not compatible with the worsening of domestic and external balances and needs to be built, in transition economies, on falling inflation and interest rates. If these developments do not take place, the chances of continuing success might be overestimated. Hungary, for instance, achieved 2.9 per cent growth in 1994 (after -0.6 per cent growth in 1993) at the price of a rapid worsening in the balance of payments and the general government deficit. Only the 1995 March economic package seems to have prevented a major crisis (as Kornai forcefully argues) which could have developed along the lines of the Mexican crisis. The modest 1.5 per cent growth attained in 1995 represents in itself a warning about the actual limits and precariousness of the output recovery.

A final comment on inflation. Inflation is still a problem, by and large, in all transition economies. As long as inflation and interest rates are kept higher than in more advanced economies, while capital movements are liberalised, speculative attacks remain possible with fixed or quasi fixed exchange rate policies. Capital inflows jeopardise the target of bringing down inflation, since sterilisation is difficult in weak financial markets.

Georg Winckler

The contributions presented by Kornai, Gelb, Roland and Sahay excel in offering interesting insights into the transition experiences of both CEECs and NIS. They document the great strides these countries have made toward becoming market economies, but they also demonstrate that this transition is still far from being completed. The four contributions complement each other, while remaining rather diverse with respect to the object and method of their analyses.

Although all contributions discuss interesting hypotheses and contain important conclusions, it is not easy to find a rubric under which they can be discussed together. The joint perspective around which I will organise my remarks is whether the policy recommendations of the contributions adhere to the "Washington consensus". Of course, other perspectives could be chosen as well. Yet, by using this standpoint, I hope to stimulate a debate.

The "Washington consensus", as described in Rodrik (1996), and first analysed by Williamson (1994), reflects a remarkable convergence of views that has occurred in recent years about the broad outlines of what constitutes an appropriate development and transition strategy. This "new orthodoxy", elaborated and promulgated by international institutions in Washington D.C., e.g. the IMF and the World Bank, can be described in more detail as a "decalogue" of policy "desiderata", dubbed as a kind of "ten commandments", reflecting the ten items in Williamson's list. These refer to goals of macroeconomic stability, internal and external liberalisation and structural reforms. According to this decalogue, countries should: (1) keep fiscal discipline; (2) redirect public expenditure toward health, education, and infrastructure; (3) reform the tax system by cutting marginal rates and broadening its base; (4) adopt unified and competitive exchange rates and maintain tight monetary polices; (5) secure property rights; (6) privatise; (7) deregulate; (8) liberalise trade; (9) eliminate barriers to direct foreign investment; and (10) liberalise capital flows and financial markets.

From a *theoretical* viewpoint, one may have doubts about liberalising and privatising an economy as quickly as the "Washington consensus" suggests, since, in transition economies, there are various shortcomings that may cause market failures: (1) there is a legacy of the past, for example, *bad stocks* such as bad loans; and (2) special information gaps, uncertainty or control problems may exist. In addition, as Roland points out, feedback between the implementation of markets and political decision processes has to be taken into account.

Likewise, after examining the *empirical* evidence of countries with high growth rates in the recent past, it is not obvious that compliance with the policy decalogue of the Washington consensus will bring about long-run economic growth. After studying the various policy prescriptions that East Asian Tigers did or did not follow, Rodrick (1996) remains sceptical whether, beyond maintaining macroeconomic stability (in particular the first and fourth commandments), the Tigers did much to implement the "new orthodoxy". Instead, as Rodrick (1996) points out, other policy features of the Tigers contributed to stimulating growth, e.g. the avoidance of rent-seeking activities by "hard" or "strong" states whose bureaucracies assisted, not hindered, enterprises; or good governance or just political stability as a consequence of a relatively equal distribution of income and wealth. When looking at the growth experience of Continental Europe, especially Germany, after the second World War, similar observations may emerge.

Hence, the "Washington consensus" may be still regarded, theoretically and empirically, as a controversial issue. Nevertheless, given the remarkable conversion of views about development strategies, it represents an interesting perspective under which one can evaluate transition experiences.

The contributions by Gelb *et al.* and Fischer *et al.* are much in line with the "Washington consensus". Gelb constructs various indices of external and internal liberalisation, which basically reflect compliance with commandment numbers six to nine. He aims at explaining the time profile of growth and inflation of transition countries by their stage of liberalisation. His main conclusion is that the more countries have liberalised their economies, the more they have been successful in fighting inflation and overcoming output decline. One can criticise the empirical validity of Gelb's conclusion by alluding to the fact that his set of data basically consists of two different groups of countries (see his figures 1 and 2). On the one hand, the highly liberalised central and eastern European countries that have had relatively low inflation rates and regained growth quickly; on the other hand, the less liberalised countries of the former Soviet Union struck with chaos, e.g. output decline and inflation. Combining these two groups of countries then easily yields Gelb's main result. It would have been worthwhile to find out whether this result holds true even ***within*** each of these two groups, since, otherwise, one could object that heterogeneous countries are lumped together.

If Gelb's main result holds true, there is an interesting implication with respect to the "Washington consensus"; external and internal liberalisation entails macroeconomic stability, but not necessarily (see Rodrick's analysis) the other way round. Consequently, it may be that a rapid liberalisation of the economy is one way to "cause" macroeconomic stability. Yet another way may be to start with macroeconomic stability. Yet then to liberalise, as the Czech Republic did, lagging behind Poland, Slovenia, and Hungary in the various liberalisation indices of Gelb, or as the East Asian Tigers have been doing.

Fischer *et al*'s contribution analyses the level and growth rates of output, and it indicates on the basis of econometric evidence that commandment numbers one and four, i.e. fiscal discipline and competitive exchange rates, as well as economic liberalisation (using indices of Gelb and others) are conducive to a good output performance. When estimating long-run transition growth, the second commandment, i.e. investment in education, becomes important. What points to an open issue within the "Washington consensus" is whether fixed or flexible exchange rate regimes will bring about a quicker revival of output. The authors opt for the fixed rate version, using the exchange rate as a nominal anchor to reduce inflation. However, besides initial benefits, this exchange rate policy may entail uncompetitive exchange rates due to domestic inflation. Hungary or Poland could serve as an example.

Kornai's analysis of the Hungarian programme of adjustment and stabilization of 1995 (ASP, 1995) is fully in line with the commandment of keeping fiscal discipline. Yet, whether the changes in the fiscal sphere encompass a redirection of public expenditure toward health, education and infrastructure (the second commandment) remains doubtful. For example, he reports that higher education ceased to be free.

With respect to exchange rates, there is much concern in the ASP 1995 about regaining competitiveness, by letting both the nominal exchange rate depreciation exceed the inflation rate and the latter exceed the nominal wage increase. The implementation of this recommendation is reflected by a growing gap between real exchange rate changes based on unit labour costs and those based on the consumer price index. However, there remains the question whether this strategy only produces "moderate and controlled inflation" as maintained by Kornai. Instead of attacking the overall wage dynamics directly, the policy strategy seems to take these dynamics as given and it aims at depreciating the currency over-proportionately, hoping that this may not speed up the wage dynamics. Otherwise, there may be an inflationary bias in the ASP 95.

At odds with the "Washington consensus" is the ASP 1995, to the extent that it includes measures aimed at reducing the amount of external liberalisation by introducing import surcharges.

The contribution by Roland neither explicitly accepts, nor rejects the policy decalogue of the "Washington consensus". Roland basically attacks the traditional theories of implementing reforms, be it the "big bang" or the "gradualistic" approach. He correctly points out that they neglect the political constraints of transition. However, when it comes to developing a general theory of the "Political Economy of Transition", Roland remains vague in his conclusions. Anything may be allowed. Hence, it does not come as a surprise that even keeping fiscal balance, which all the other contributions suggest as a policy desideratum, is not considered absolutely necessary.

References

Rodrick, D., 1996, "Understanding Economic Policy Reform, *The Journal of Economic Literature*, Vol. 34, pp. 9-41, March.

Williamson, J., 1994, *The Political Economy of Policy Reform*, Institute for International Economics, Washington, D.C.

Heinrich Vogel

The transformation of formerly communist countries appears to follow an almost identical pattern. The typical trajectory of GDP-growth is U-shaped, and the reasons why some countries have bottomed out in their transitional recession while others have not are usually seen in the differences in the resources, political resolve, and social engineering skills of post-communist leaders in steering the course from communist rule and a command economy towards democracy and a market economy. The lesson seems to be: the later the start, the greater the pain and the probability of turmoil, if not failure. The statistics of economic aggregates (mostly monetary), as well as the reports on political change in these countries, are confirming parallel developments — however with distinct leads and lags. The contributions (much like studies initiated by other monitoring institutions) confirm the classification of transformation countries in groups of "hopefuls" and "less hopefuls", especially when it comes to candidacy for membership in the EU or future competitiveness in the global market.

The contributions by Balcerowicz, Stern and Laski and Bhaduri are dealing with the general problems of transformation. Reading them is interesting at the very least, because the differences in country-by-country performance are being interpreted from different angles stressing different factors at work — in terms of a political-economic model (Balcerowicz), of applied neo-classical economic theory (Laski and Bhaduri), and in terms of empirical statistical analysis (Stern). Despite these different approaches, I found remarkable parallels, if not identical evaluations, in a general scepticism vis-à-vis the simplistic model of social engineering, in particular regarding the role of the state or the public sector. Clearly, efforts in monetary stabilization, privatisation strategies, and in political reform (institutional change and the ability to create a new mechanism of political consensus-building via political parties or other) make the difference in steering out from transformational recession.

A state of equilibrium, i.e. the establishment of a new social contract, is difficult as long as trust in the sincerity, or even relevance, of politics has not been consolidated. The anxiety surrounding the Russian elections of June 16 is only a faint foreboding of things to come, should the promised reform process be implemented to the point where indicators of the real economy react. Hard budget constraints are a necessary condition, but by no means a sufficient one for systemic change.

The Central European and Baltic countries, as well as Slovenia, stand out positively due to their handling of the balance between private and public sector, consistent change of the legal system, protection of property rights, institution building, and abstention from populist concessions. Russia and the other CIS-countries are lagging behind in comparative analysis, due to a specific post-Soviet way in which politics have been influencing the scope and pace of transformation. Incomplete statehood plus inherited structural or geographic handicaps may well doom some NIS to failure as independent international actors. Others may end up in a class of political and/or economic systems which differ from the standard model of transformation, with extreme difficulties of survival in a competitive global environment.

Geography matters. There can be little doubt that the combination of geographic dimensions with disastrous investment gaps is relevant for success or failure in vital sectors of the economy. This is evident in the Russian economy for several reasons. Extensive (private or collective) farming is not feasible without infinitely higher inputs of fixed investment in infrastructure, machinery, and equipment, as compared to the economies of Central Europe. Militarisation of Soviet industry and the specific patterns of geographic dispersal of "closed cities" are persistent handicaps with a distinct impact on many aspects of reform: the pace of conversion; restructuring of industries; regional employment; and voting behaviour. The structure of transportation (prevalence of rail and road) demands more capital investment, causing much greater financial strains for the public sector than in most industrialised countries, including those of Central Europe.

Employment matters more than is generally assumed. Standard statistical discussions of transformation in Russia and the CIS tend to neglect the potential of political destabilization which may spill from this ill-defined and neglected sphere. Estimates by Goskomstat as well as by the ILO (which vary by a factor of two) invite self-serving political interpretations. Besides, what makes us so sure that the reported two-digit levels of unemployment in Central Europe (produced by an infinitely more reliable statistical apparatus) are politically irrelevant, particularly when positive rates of growth in production are not reflected in additional employment? Once privatisation has become more than an act of changing property-deeds, once a new management under the pressure of open competition has started cutting large numbers of hitherto subsidised jobs, once the true indicator of market reforms (the number of bankruptcies) has begun rising, mass unemployment may well destabilize new unfinished states, particularly in the CIS.

Resources matter, even in a paradoxical way. Lack of energy has been constraining the efforts of the NIS that depend on Russian supplies to an extent which makes structural reforms almost impossible, and it is forcing them to stay together in a painful pattern of co-operation which invites geostrategic designs called reintegration, but not a free integration of viable sovereign states. At the same time, the perception of having "vast resources", expectations of sufficient revenue from energy exports to the West and a comfortable political leverage over partners in the CIS have been preserving a sense of ease in Russian mainstream political thinking, thereby reducing pressures for reform and breeding what has been called "Dutch disease", i.e. an over-valuation of the Rouble, imported inflationary pressures, and de-industrialisation. Russian economic policy seems to be trapped in complacency, ignoring time pressures and forgoing growth which could derive from feasible structural changes.

Windows of opportunity hardly open twice. There is no second take and certainly no "third way" of getting out of recession and crisis. A compressed effort in implementing the critical elements of systemic change (*à la* Balcerowicz) cannot be repeated, once it is aborted or diluted beyond political credibility. The continuation of volatility, at least in the NIS, is best described as a balancing act between true and faked stabilization of the economy and of politics, and it is more probable than not that it will persist. Here, the question whether "the glass of reforms is half full or half empty" remains open — the difference being in the eye of the beholders, i.e. governments and financial institutions of the West. I keep wondering to what extent "avoidable losses" (Laski and Bhaduri) will be avoided, regardless of possible demonstration effects from pioneering reforms in Central Europe.

László Csaba

Second thoughts about transformation strategies and outcomes

The contributions by Fischer *et al.*, Gelb *et al.*, Kornai and Roland share some methodological and theoretical commonalities. The contributions prove the relevance of standard economics for understanding the problems of transformation. This sounds trivial for some, but a growing number of people in government in CEECs do question the relevance of standard economics for their economies, because of the latters' peculiarities. Now, with some experience and hindsight, the issue seems to have reached the level of consensus that emerged for developing countries by the late 1980s — namely, good economics is valid across countries, and certain types of measures tend to produce similar outcomes in different economies. Institutional arrangements and the time component also play a relevant role in explaining the actual outcomes. The importance of the institutional factor is crucial in explaining the differences in the actual outcomes — and this is one of the most relevant findings of both "Washington contributions".

The contribution by Fischer, Sahay and Végh contains valuable quantitative evidence of past performance and underlines the importance of fundamental assumptions regarding the individual components of growth. Policy-makers in transforming countries and in international organisations are thus called on to reflect upon their mostly implicit assumptions pertaining to the relative significance of factors for development and growth. The authors rightly draw attention to the poor quality of official data. However, electricity consumption seems to be a fairly poor measures of an overall performance. In traditional industry, it may serve as a reasonable proxy. But as it is documented, the overall trend of economic change in transforming countries entails a move away from industry into services, for which the proxy is very poor. The use of this as one of the several partial indicators approximating actual change may well be a legitimate technique, but singling this out, as *the* proper indicator replacing the "proper" GDP, seems simplistic at best. One may well go as far as arguing for a limited role for all quantitative indicators in presenting an overall picture of development performance, as has been widely discussed in the literature on global sustainable development. Thus the borderline between hard facts and soft interpretations may well be on the way of withering away.

These reservations notwithstanding it is relevant to have a reasonable guess over the actual size of output drop, especially in Russia, to be able to accept or reject the claim of output drop having come to a halt by late 1995. First, according to various estimates and recalculations by the Russian Central Statistical Administration and the IBRD (Csaba, 1996a), the drop of GDP in 1991-95 was closer to one third than the official figure of one half that was previously reported. More importantly, the trajectory indicating the Russian economy's reactions to monetary signals changes fundamentally, turning it into a *demand-constrained* rather than resource-constrained economy. If the latter is true, "shock therapy" was anything but a failure in systemic terms, since it has changed the fundamentals of behaviour of that economic system, irrespective of recorded growth performance. On the latter, preliminary data released from CSA for the first five to six months of 1996 are indicative of a continued drop of 2-3 per cent in reported GDP in 1996. The latter is not too surprising, since it is more in line with the traditional thinking on the shape of the business cycle than the government forecast of 1-2 per cent growth for 1996. The latter was clearly a politically motivated figure and disregarded the typical slope and time span of evening out and later recovery in the cycle. This implies that though the overall model of recovery developed by the authors might actually prove far too optimistic for Russia, the actual situation may, among other things, be exacerbated by structural factors and excessive cuts in government spending, two further factors also discussed by the authors. In any case, if they — correctly — see the story of FSU quite differently from that of Central Europe, their model, stylising the facts of the former, could not, even in theory, be legitimately extended to the latter without further qualifications. Thus my reading of the Russian story would imply less output drop but lengthier stagnation, followed by a later and more moderate recovery, than the general model suggests.

This differentiation has, incidentally, quite important bearings on the overall theory of transformation. As the authors rightly show, the drop of output in Central Europe never reached FSU levels; it was less dramatic in time and scope. Its size is certainly not comparable to that in the Great Depression. The differentiation of performance by country group, profile, slope and length of recession cautions against the uses of regional averages in formulating sweeping generalisations on the strategies and outcomes of systemic change. A regional average is unduly biased towards the largest and least transforming economies, like Ukraine and Kazakstan, where economic policies in general, but fiscal and monetary policies in particular, have been shown to be at the largest variance not only with the IMF advice, but also with the IMF doctrine (Bofinger, *et. al*, 1995). Thus regional averages tell very little about how the IMF approach, and even less about how standard economics in general, fared in the post-socialist world. One of the empirical points this contribution convincingly proves, is precisely the usefulness of the standard stabilization cum liberalisation medicine in the medium run, whenever this medicine is actually swallowed, as opposed to cases when swallowing was only contemplated. In the Russian case, the election campaign and the rulings of the State Duma over additional monetary financing of fiscal outlays will probably translate into much higher inflation rates than the authors — following the Russian authorities — forecast. Thus, the rebound in GDP is unlikely to be robust, even within the framework of their own model.

The authors are quite right in seeing the decreasing importance of transition factors as compared to standard growth factors, the latter establishing a long-term potential for high rates of growth due to the inherent catch-up potential of lower to middle-income countries. In this respect, I can only applaud their highlighting the need to make distinctions among the various components of governmental spending, especially highlighting the need to invest more in human capital, retraining in market-based institutions and to ensure entrepreneurial and technological skills. The country report of the IBRD (1995), for instance, advises Hungary not to increase spending on education; it even considers the stabilization of these spending elements as a precondition for long term sustainable growth. Similarly, the Hungarian government's programme on public finance reform of May 1996 (Gondolatok, 1996) foresees an annual 2-3 per cent cut in real expenditure in all spheres pertaining to human infrastructure, and not only in social transfers and various income support schemes. Calls to spend more on improving the quality of government administration are equally well taken. The authors could well have made more explicit their concern over decreasing population growth by involving this factor in explaining the social security crisis — an issue well known in many other European welfare states.

Meanwhile the authors seem to have entered a bumpy path in singling out gross capital formation as the major generator of growth. As is well known, theoretical literature is less than equivocal over this issue. Some recent evidence on East Asian growth (Young, 1995) plainly questions the empirical relevance of this proposition. Others (de Long and Summers, 1993) accept the direct nexus, but underline the importance of allocative and incentive mechanisms as equally hard side-conditions for this to hold. Still others (Blomström, *et al*, 1996) reverse the causal link and single out high growth as a condition for high capital investment to become financeable. My own point is that of caution, warning against taking widely accepted assumptions as proven evidence for policy advice. In the case of the transforming countries, capital markets are less than perfect, thus there is a long way to go to improve their *allocative* efficiency. Large public sector dinosaurs also survive in several transforming countries. As long as these and incentive problems related, for example, to moderate inflation, negative rates of interest, bureaucratic over-regulation and the like remain crucial, there is always a case for seeking the way out in more efficient, better allocated, rather than simply more gross capital investment. This way of reasoning obviously undermines the use of the Levine and Renelt model and the related 200 years time horizon for catch-up. In a transition economy, it is not investment *grosso modo*, but the propensity of private agents to invest, rather than to consume or save in currency, which is the crux of the matter.

The major strength of the contribution by de Melo and Gelb is their establishing an empirical proof of the use of the stabilization cum liberalisation policies. This is all the more important as the political pendulum has moved against the forces having cultivated those policies. Turning away from IMF dogmatism, taking into account realities, focusing on real economic processes, or on the concerns of the man on the street, these are the arguments that are often heard and take theoretical forms (see most recently, Szamuely, ed., 1996). Gelb and associates, by contrast, develop a composite index of liberalisation, whose techniques are disputed by Fischer *et al.* in their contribution but which seems to have fared empirically well in indicating the interrelationships between policies and outcomes. In my own reading the only serious flaw of this index is in its use of privatisation, which is a concept open to very wide, on occasion rather unconventional, interpretation in some countries. Contrary to established terminology and procedures (Dallago, 1993; Bornstein, 1994), some countries consider any destatisation as privatisation, even if no restructuring takes place. Corporate governance, principal-agent problems, regulation and deregulation, monopoly and market power and many other issues subsumed in the established parlance on privatisation have simply been missing or seriously neglected in, and by, many transforming countries. Thus, taking official privatisation plan-fulfilment reports by and large at face value, as the EBRD seems to have done on occasion, does not seem to be a very helpful procedure.

These reservations notwithstanding, Gelb, *et. al.* proved convincingly the direct *nexus* between real GDP growth and liberalisation, as well as between disinflation and liberalisation, with a cross-country validity. These findings are all the more relevant, as they explain the nature of country-specificity, highlighted also by Fischer *et al.* Accordingly, it is the nature of policy measures and their sustaining, or the lack of the latter, that really makes the difference, not the oft-quoted cultural differences. If depth and duration of reforms also explain their outcomes, then it is not only design and sequencing which matters.

In the debates concerning the second stage of transformation, several authors employ the old-fashioned trade-off between inflation and growth. Regressions of Gelb *et. al.*, seem to have refuted these claims. This is particularly important insofar as their finding was derived from a sample of two dozen countries not functioning under free market conditions. However, the Easterly and Bruno argument does not seem to be relevant for Visegrad countries and Slovenia, where either no period of high inflation occurred, or it did only a relatively long time ago. Thus, it seems unlikely that disinflation could be expansionary also in the front-runners, whereas it is clear that no recovery can be sustained unless stabilization brings inflation gradually down to single digit levels. Meanwhile the nature of these interrelationships is such that a relaxation of strict monetary and fiscal stances — avoiding the "credit crunch" — can only bring more inflation, not more growth (Herr, Tober and Westphal, 1994).

The regressions of Gelb *et al.* are indicative of the inevitability of the sharp initial contraction of output and employment, and also prove that countries that attempted a softer landing actually fared worse, with cumulative output and income losses exceeding radical reformers'. What really is remarkable is the cross-country validity of their findings, and the normalisation of data along "Poland-equivalent reform years" is a truly useful analytical tool.

In an important novelty in their assessment, Gelb *et al.* underscore the role of large quasi-fiscal deficits in sustaining inflation. This contrasts to the initial unilateral focus on deficit cuts and rightly broadens the analyst's attention to the entire general government sector. Quick disinflation may well imply unwillingness to face the issue of quasi fiscal deficits, or simply continued reliance on flawed accounting practices, producing figures which are practically incomparable to those derived from established and internationally audited procedures.

On the interrelationships between stabilization and structural reform the authors conduct an artificial debate with Portes. My reading of both the article they quote and the discussion is that if there is a lack of structural reforms, stabilization is bound to run out of steam. This is anything but an unorthodox proposition, as recent evidence in Bulgaria, Serbia and even Russia indicates. In fact, if one compares both Washington contributions with the initial output from the Washington twins, the most conspicuous difference is their highlighting the relevance of institutional factors, time dimension, social responses, sustainability and many other elements which did not use to belong to the core elements of the Washington consensus, or conventional mainstream wisdom. In short, one may well quote Tanzi (1993) or Zecchini (1996) for detailed evidence on how one-sided emphasis on current account imbalances distorted the entire initial conceptual framework of these institutions, which had to be significantly improved and refined to come to terms with the new challenges.

Roland's contribution is important in bringing back the geopolitical dimension to a debate where strategic issues are often discussed in purely trade terms. This factor, which has played a decisive role in enlargement of the EU in each of the previous cases, or also in forming the NAFTA, may indeed explain the different social acceptance and, therefore, the statistically significant differences in outcomes of similarly conceived policies in the post-socialist country group. Coalition-building, compensation of losers, pre-committing subsequent governments have long been in the focus of interest of Roland, who has been contributing to the understanding of policy reform processes from early on. He, too, has been playing an important bridge-building function between mainstream and political economy approaches.

The present contribution is focused on the thesis of whether the probability of re-election is endogenous or exogenous for reforming governments. This is an important step in getting away from the initial simplicity of shock versus gradual approaches, as it brings in the time dimension and the political cycle with the aspiration of scientific interpretation. While appreciating the approach highly, I cannot conceal my dissatisfaction with the outcomes, especially in analytical and policy terms.

Roland seems to consider the "shock versus gradualism" issue as still a relevant question, while several authors in the literature have argued the opposite. One finds little reflection on the latter in the presentation There are at least three types of reservations which deserve reflection. First, several authors (for example, Daianu, 1994) have advanced the argument of *path dependency*. This is particularly important in Roland's framework encapsulating historical and institutional elements. In this line of reasoning not only the choice, but later moves of the pendulum seem to have, to a large extent, been predetermined by the legacy of the past. The Russian attempt at shock therapy and the Chinese strategy of evolutionary change can equally well be fitted into this view. Second, several authors (Balcerowicz, 1995, chapter 9) have highlighted that there are different maximum/optimal speeds for different types of changes. A sufficiently sophisticated radical would certainly not propose the nonsensical, as the instantaneous introduction of equity markets as a means to resolve the problem of initial asset valuation. Institution building takes time and so does the internalisation of new rules by millions of agents. Third, the evolution of economic systems is, to a large extent, inevitably spontaneous, where the role of human deliberation — both system design and policy measures — is limited at best, due to a plethora of factors (Wagener, 1992 and 1994). The above reference presents a rich literature and a variety of methodological and theoretical considerations supportive of this way of thinking. One can expect some reflection on at least these typical points by a theorist considering the shock versus gradualist dichotomy as still relevant.

China and Hungary are often invoked as prime examples of gradualist strategies. Whereas many analysts tend to reproach them for this choice, Roland seems to be supportive and reassured by the respective country evidence. Discussing these in detail would, of course, be disproportionate. However, it is legitimate to refer to the doubts surrounding this common wisdom of interpreting Chinese and Hungarian experiences. On the former, several China-watchers (Hermann-Pillath, 1994; Sachs and Woo, 1996) point to the lack of consensus, consequently a lack of strategy in Chinese reforms in the last 20 years. This, by definition, would be precisely the opposite of what Roland correctly describes as gradualism, i.e. a phased implementation of a package of preconceived measures, where analysis of their side-effects leads to spreading them over a few years. Elsewhere (Csaba, 1995, chapter 9) I tried to advance a set of arguments in the same vein, calling Hungarian gradualism a myth. What Kornai describes in his contribution aroused criticism in Hungary as another attempt to introduce shock therapy (Köves, 1995), while the parallel introduction of bankruptcy, accounting, banking laws in 1992, or opening up without either devaluation or tarification of quotas in 1988-90, is also seen by a large part of Hungarian economists as shock therapy applied to the supply side. All in all, very few observers who are familiar with the Hungarian situation would qualify Hungary as an exemplary pupil of the gradualist school.

It is also very hard to accept the argument that the CMEA shock was a major component of falling demand. First, CMEA should not be treated as an element extraneous to Hungarian, Polish or even Russian socialism; it was part of the systemic totality that came to an end by 1990. Second, early analyses of the period (Rollo and Flemming, 1992) have already raised serious doubts about this interpretation. Gravity model based analyses show that reorientation actually implied a normalisation of the trading relations among CMEA countries and also between Eastern Europe and the rest of the world. These analyses have also shown convertibility to be a timely, overdue rather than premature, step taken by these countries. Third, the same book proved that it was the nature of liberalisation and stabilization which, as in developing countries, produced adjustment recession and later recovery. Having surveyed the Washington contributions, I do not need to reiterate empirical proofs of this point.

Finally, one may want to rethink the fundamental thesis about the endogenity of re-election chances. Following the Czech elections it seems clear that in all transforming countries there is a revolt against the governments who managed the transition. This is equally true for these who opted for radical strategies and for those, like Mr. Klaus, who seems to have heeded the cautioning words of Roland against haste. This calls (or allows), for alternative interpretations, such as certain peculiarities, professional inadequacies and distributional consequences to explain the return to power of the old guard (Csaba, 1996b).

Kornai's contribution puts the Hungarian current account adjustment programme of March 1995 into an international perspective — especially the Mexican comparison is very illuminating. He makes some quite important observations that are either brand new, or were downplayed in the debates inside and outside the country. First, discussing the changes in the exchange rate regime he rightly points to the consideration of predictability and calculability. These are well known maxims in economic theory; however, these hardly played a role in the exchange rate policies of Hungary. As governments have not proved to be particularly good forecasters in terms of inflation, the real rate of exchange, as well as the timing of devaluations turned out to be rather arbitrary for most economic agents and households. Against this experience the crawling peg regime is extremely useful as a device to discipline macro-economy, especially interest rate policies, to strengthen anti-inflationary commitments and also to stabilize expectations. The crawling peg has surely been instrumental in ensuring that inflationary processes never got out of control, as was feared.

A second point is the distribution of the burden of adjustment. It is absolutely novel in Hungarian economic history that the threat of unemployment made those employed willing to agree to a 12 per cent cut in real wages in order to retain employment and improve the fiscal stance of the country. This model was normally thought to be a peculiarity of Austrian and Czech wage earners, while Hungarian and Polish workers were thought to be more combative on income distribution issues. With the further 9.5 per cent cuts in the first four months of 1996, coinciding with a drop of unemployment to 10.6 per cent, the trade-off is fairly strong. In other words, unlike in Poland, Slovenia and Slovakia, in Hungary already modest GDP-recovery generates new jobs, which does bode well for the social sustainability of stabilization and reforms.

As far as the temporary import surcharge is concerned, I tend to be less permissive than Kornai. First, I do not see the point in making an exchange rate adjustment only halfway, extinguishing the export promoting elements in this measure. Second, although the import surcharge is in theory flat and non-distortionary, its administration in practice proved to be cumbersome, delayed, and not all those entitled actually received reimbursement, or not in due time. Third, the surcharge produced a fiscal balance which looked temporarily much nicer than the actual adjustment process would have warranted. At the time of writing one can already observe the difficulty of the Ministry of Finance in coping with the task of replacing the fallout for 1997 of this revenue windfall. Last but not least, there was no justification to enhance effective protection of Hungarian producers at a time when exchange rate adjustment had already provided a cushion against imports and an incentive favouring exports. The resulting stagnation and drop of imports is hardly encouraging for the recovery of economic activity and modernisation in general. Once the government was willing to run into a major clash with its own electorate, sacrificing some of the heterodox measures described in the contribution, and replacing them with a larger but full devaluation, more efficiency gains and more sustainable adjustment performance became possible, without distorting short term indicators and without burdening the future.

I also tend to be very sceptical about other heterodox measures described in the contribution. Wage controls always distort labour markets, and are hard to dismantle. Wage bargaining in the tripartite council proved futile in real terms, as the loudest, i.e. teachers, health care workers, police and firemen, actually got the least in real terms, while silent but effective groups, like real estate business or locomotive drivers were faring well. One wonders whether heterodoxy means anything more than a cover-up operation, which more often than not distracts public opinion from focusing on the real trends in the economy.

Kornai restates his earlier warning (Kornai, 1993) against overdoing disinflation. This is perfectly right at the theoretical level. At the policy-making level, however, I do not see this danger. The June 1996 edition of the three year programme of the Hungarian government forecasts even for the year 1999, a 10 per cent inflation rate, i.e. still a two digit figure (*Világgazdaság*, 6 June, 1996). Moreover, early phases of fiscal planning for 1997 already call for a revision of the IMF stand-by agreement, which allows only a 3 per cent general government deficit for that year (*Magyar Hírlap*, 12 June, 1996). Against this background, I do not see a very grave danger of overdoing fiscal stringency, while the threat of softening up, due to the political cycle in 1997-98, looks imminent.

I also tend to see as rather worrying the June 1993 decision that softened up bankruptcy legislation. Since then only half dozen bankruptcies have occurred per month, while liquidations run by the hundred. In other words, the advantage of bankruptcy in decentralising bargaining among creditors and debtors, was replaced by either very tough closures, or government bailouts. This is not the way the market clears, and the softening of this legislation has certainly proved to be one of the most controversial innovations of the centre-right government of the day.

I see the inflation record as one of the notoriously weak points of the Hungarian economy for the years to come. The 1995 figure is close to ten times (!) the OECD average, thus the scope for improvement, preferably prior to EU accession, is significant. If there is any good news, this is the government's deliberation to eliminate all quasi fiscal deficits by 1997 by eliminating interest-free financing of the Forint equivalent of external government debt. This will make the picture clearer, and the size of future fiscal adjustments will come to the limelight very soon. One of the serious drawbacks of the year 1995 was that the year-end figures looked so good, that they gave the illusion that the adjustment problem had truly been settled. This, in turn, gave grounds, among the number-gazers and politicians alike, to think in a way that Kornai rightly condemns as complacent.

References

Balcerowicz, L., 1995, *Socialism, Capitalism, Transformation,* The Central European University Press, Budapest, London and New York.

Blomström, M., Lipsey, R., and Zejan, M., 1996, "Is fixed investment the key to economic growth?" *The Quarterly Journal of Economics*, Vol. No. 1., pp. 269-276.

Bofinger, P., Flassbeck, H., and Hoffman, L., 1995, "Ekonomika ortodoksalnoi monetartnoi stabilizatsii: primer opita Rossii, Ukraini I Kazakhstana", *Voprosi Ekonomiki*, vol. 66. No. 12., pp. 26-44.

Csaba, L., 1995, *The Capitalist Revolution in Eastern Europe,* Cheltenham and Brookfield, E. Elgar Publishing Co.

Csaba, L., 1996a, "Gazdaságpolitika és gazdasági rendszer Oroszorszgában, 1992-1996. Economic policy and economic system in Russia" in 1992-96 *Külgazdaság*, vol. 40 No. 3 pp 35-60.

Csaba, L., 1996b, "Privatisation and distribution: theory from evidence", in: Dallago, B., ed.: *Privatization and Distribution in Central and Eastern Europe*. Cheltenham and Brookfield: E., (in print).

Dewatripont, M., and Roland, G., 1996, "Transition as a process of large-scale institutional change", *Economics of Transition*, vol. 4, No. 1. pp. 1-30.

Dallago, B., 1993, "Some reflections on privatization as a means to transform the economic system: the Western experience", in Wagener, H.-J. ed., *The Political Economy of Transformation*. Physica Verlag, Heidelberg and New York, pp. 113-144.

Daianu, D., 1994, "The changing mix of disequilibria during transition: a Romanian perspective", in: Csaba, L. ed. *Privatization, Liberalization and Destruction: Recreating the Market in Central and Eastern Europe,* Aldershot and Brookfield, Dartmouth Publishing Co, pp. 189-216.

Gondolatok az államháztartási reformról (Thoughts on the reform of public finances), a document adopted by the Hungarian government, *Pénzügyi Szemle,* Vol. 40, No. 5, pp. 339-351.

Pillath, C., 1993, "China's transition to the market: a paradox of transformation and its institutionalist solution", in: Wagener, H.-J. ed., *The Political Economy,* pp. 209-241.

Herr, H., Tober, S. and Westphal, A., 1994, "Output collapse and economic recovery in Central and Eastern Europe", in: Herr, H., Tober, S., and Westphal, A. eds., *Macroeconomic Problems of Transformation,* Cheltenham and Brookfield, E. Elgar Publishing Co., pp. 1-44.

IBRD, 1995, *Hungary: Structural Adjustment for Sustainable Growth.,* Washington and Budapest, December.

Kornai, J., 1993, "Evolution of financial discipline in the post-socialist system". *Kyklos*, Vol. 46, No. 3, pp. 315-336.

Köves, A., 1995, Gazdaságpolitikai lehetõségek és dilemmák a Bokros csomag után (Possibilities and dilemmas of economic policy — after the Bokros-package), *Külgazdaság*, Vol. 39. No. 11. pp. 4-18.

de Long, B. and Summers, L., 1993, "Equipment investment and economic growth: how strong is the nexus?", *Brookings Papers on Economic Activity*, No. 2.

OECD/CCET, 1995, *The Russian Federation,* Economic Surveys series, September.

Rollo, J. and Flemming, J., eds, *Trade, Payments and Adjustment in Central and Eastern Europe,* RIIA and EBRD, London.

Sachs, J. and Woo, W., 1996, "China's transition experience re-examined", *Transition*, Vol. 7. No 3-4, pp 1-5.

Szamuely, L., ed, 1996, *Reevaluating Economic Reforms in Central and Eastern Europe since 1989.,* Tokyo and Budapest: NIRA and Kopint-Datorg Foundation for Economic Research.

Tanzi, V., 1993, "The budget deficit in transition", *IMF Staff Papers*, Vol.40., No.3. pp. 697-707.

Voszka, É., 1996, "A tulajdonváltás felemás sikeréve" (A contradictory year of success in ownership change in Hungary), *Közgazdasági Szemle*, Vol. 43. No.5. pp. 385-402.

Wagener, H-J., 1992, Wieweit ist Systemtransformation planbar? in: Albeck, H. ed, *und Geldverfassung*. Göttingen, Vandenhoek and Ruprecht, pp 99-115.

Wagener, H.-J., 1994, "Some theory of systemic change and transformation", in: Wagener, H.-J. ed, *On the Theory and Policy of Systemic Change,* Physica Verlag, Heidelberg and New York, pp. 1-20.

Young, A., 1995, "The tyranny of numbers confronting statistical realities of the East Asian growth experience", *The Quarterly Journal of Economics*, Vol. 59., No.3., pp 641-680.

Zecchini, S., 1996, "The role of international financial organisations in the transition process", in: Schönfeld, R., ed, *The Role of International Financial Institutions in Central and Eastern Europe,* Münich, Südosteuropa-Gesellschaft, pp 75-96.

Misu Negritoiu

The CEECs are now in the midst of a unique and historic transformation process. Having replaced authoritarian regimes with pluralist democracies, they have also moved from more or less centrally-planned socialist economies to largely market-based economies. As the contributions presented here emphasize, the transition process is far from over, but the speed of reforms and pace of transformation is different from country to country. I fully agree with the authors that inherited conditions and the consistency of the reform policies have played a great role in the systemic transformations in these countries in the last six years.

The situation of these countries is completely different from that of Western European countries in the aftermath of the second World War. While those countries were facing the challenge of economic recovery and partly structural adjustment, they did not, like the CEECs, also have to undertake deep systemic transformation and structural reforms.

In his contribution, Stern underscores that macroeconomic stabilization has been largely achieved in much of the region in 1993 and 1994, in many cases with the help of IMF programmes, and impressive falls in inflation took place in 1994 and 1995. This is the case of my country — Romania — too, where the last stage of price liberalisation and the elimination of subsidies was implemented in 1993, followed by interest and exchange rate liberalisation in 1994, along with tight monetary and fiscal policies. As a result, inflation has been reduced from almost 300 per cent in 1993 to less than 30 per cent in 1995. At the same time, after the early years when output declined sharply, the recovery was quick. GDP increased by 1.5 per cent in 1993, 3.5 per cent in 1994 and almost 7 per cent in 1995. According to Stern, a number of CEECs now seem to be on a path of sustained growth. From cross-country comparisons, it seems that the recovery took place sooner in countries where reform began earlier and was pursued more firmly and where macroeconomic discipline was maintained more successfully.

However, it is too early to speak about sustainable growth in CEECs. If the key transformation elements have been introduced quickly — price and trade liberalisation, macroeconomic stability, hard budget constraints, financial sector reform, small-scale privatisation and competition policy — the building of institutions, effective corporate governance, restructuring and labour reallocation will take time. Stern identifies four key areas of fundamental importance to all transition economies for the coming years: corporate governance and restructuring; financial institutions; infrastructure; and the environment. In order to make progress in these areas, these countries need politically strong and efficient governments.

Balcerowicz's contribution underlines the importance of inherited conditions as a key element of the political transition, which affected the choice of economic policies.

Inherited conditions were very different across CEECs at the time of the political breakthrough. A country such as Romania, relatively more isolated from the outside world, has been less prepared than others to face the new challenge of designing and implementing transformation policies, and it needs more time to assimilate the values of the market economy and political pluralism and to improve its human resources. At the same time, its economy has been more rigid, and consequently, the transformation more painful. But in order to make the transformation more rapid and smoother, particular attention has to be paid to improvement of the inherited legal and institutional framework, to public administration reform and to further development of human resources.

CEECs still need technical and financial assistance, trade access and private investment. If the far-ranging programme of reforms is to continue and to move onto a sustainable growth path as quickly as possible, substantial inflows of capital will be needed. At the same time, the acceleration of the reforms should increase the absorption capacity for external financing and lead to more efficient domestic resource mobilisation, which will enable them to "overcome the physical legacy" (Stern) and "get close to the optimal final system" (Balcerowicz).

The contribution by Laski and Bhaduri accuses stabilization policy of having relied on untrue assumptions, namely the stability of output (considered to be exogenously given, and not affected by credit restraint) and that of the velocity of money. In my view, output contraction was, in all cases, more severe and protracted than had initially been projected, but part of it was exogenous, being the result of adverse supply shocks, co-ordination breakdowns and market segmentation (which were due to the changes in the rules of the game against a backdrop of inferior managerial capacities), and lower adaptability on the part of enterprises. Therefore, it is probable that easier monetary policy would not have recouped these output losses anyway. The contribution also expresses doubts about the sustainability of a low rate of inflation. To some extent, in many countries this is close to the truth, given the state of flux which these economies are in. Instead, moderate inflation (20-40 per cent) should be something to be content with, given the microeconomics and the structural sources of inflation in most of these countries (as in the case of Romania). What counts more, over a relatively longer span of time, is reducing the variability of the inflation rate, while struggling to achieve lower annual rates.

Laski and Bhaduri's analysis starts with the assumption that the transition has been moulded by the economic ideas prevailing 20 years ago, and draws the conclusion that aggregate demand in the general transformation strategy has been almost completely ignored. But demand management policy presupposes fine-tuning and policy rules present in a developed market economy, but non-existent in an economy in systemic transformation with a fundamentally volatile economic environment and with heterogeneous and shifting expectations.

Laski and Bhaduri's analysis of cost push is largely accurate, but for this to continue (even in the presence of monopolies and oligopsonistic markets), demand validation is necessary; so demand restriction (surely not a first-best solution) has to continue, supported by tight wage policy and adjustment in the real sector (especially enforcement of financial discipline). Also, it is something of a *non-sequitur* to say that, if one policy does not work, its opposite would. No-one claims stabilization is not costly; the question is how costly it is, and the answer may be different from one country to another.

At least for Romania, the main factors of inflation have tended to shift over time; monetary overhang/cost push/fiscal (monetisation of deficits, as well as arrears) probably describes the right sequence. Most of this tends to show that a great deal of microeconomic transformation should constitute a foundation for stabilization anyway. Even if monetary policy is inefficient in a downturn, in an upturn, relaxing it might be highly inflationary.

Can deficit spending be used when quasi-fiscal budget deficits are overly high? Moreover, when supply response (for whatever reasons) seems inordinately low (meaning an extremely steep aggregate supply curve), most of the effect of deficit spending will be dissipated into price increases, and will therefore be inflationary. Endogenising budget deficits in the explanation of inflation in Romania leads to the conclusion that austerity is needed in fiscal policy, and not the other way around. Certainly, loss of output and increases in unemployment would arise in this case, but in the opposite case it is uncertain how the economy would fare over the longer run. The contribution seems to embrace a short-term, static view of things in CEECs.

One major assumption is that the existence of excess capacity favours quantity adjustments in lieu of price adjustments. This runs counter to our "portfolio of adjustments" view of how firms go about it. In our opinion, reserve capacities appear as semi-voluntary, while price adjustment seems to be favoured over all other options. Then, part of idle capital and unemployment can be seen as representing "natural rates of under-utilisation". Since firms will tend to favour price adjustment rather than quantity adjustment in the face of an expansionary policy, the output response can very well lag behind a substantial pick-up in inflation.

Growth is not the only ultimate goal of the transformation process. In a transforming economy, beset with the psychological legacies of a command economy, behaviour is much more heterogeneous, and, therefore, one of the most important goals of the state is to support the dissemination of market-oriented behaviour throughout the economy. The transformation is not a smooth process. Given the time constraint in which transformation has to happen, and the limited knowledge about implementing it, the construction may not be a work of architecture (building according to plans, in a "strategic" manner), but rather "*bricolage*" (or tinkering), in which the ultimate shape of the building is made up as one goes along.

All in all, an optimal approach seems hardly feasible; a second-best one is, perhaps, more appropriate. Reform must be effectively implementable. Transformation, in order to be successful, has to capitalise on what has been achieved in this respect up to now. This leads to the well known idea of a "critical mass" of reform measures to ensure a successful transformation.

10

General discussion

The debate among experts highlighted the numerous difficulties that still exist in understanding the actual evolution of the transition economies and in drawing policy lessons that can be applied generally. Some discussants (Kadar) even went so far as to question the usefulness of any policy recommendation purporting to be applicable to all transition economies because of the wide cross-country differences in economic conditions.

Five issues were at the core of the debate: a) main reasons for the successes or failures in the process of economic transformation and recovery; b) the measurement of economic performance during the transition; c) the relationship between demand stabilization and output recovery; d) the role of government in the emerging economic system; and e) the scope for policy reversal.

On the first point, some criticism was voiced with respect to the often-used distinction between "gradualism" in reform and "shock therapy". Such a distinction does not seem relevant enough to explain varying degrees of achievement among transition economies. Other factors have to be considered, particularly the impact of initial economic conditions, since they varied considerably across reforming countries. The importance of initial conditions was stressed by several discussants (Balcerowicz, Coricelli, and Gomulka).

Coricelli, in particular, provided additional evidence based on the preliminary results of his econometric analysis. When using indicators similar to those utilised by Gelb, but extended to the period before the beginning of the transition, he found "initial conditions" to be the most significant among the explanatory variables. In other words, countries that had already undertaken partial reforms before 1989 were in a better position to advance in the transition. However, Sahay sounded a note of caution regarding the robustness of projections based on these types of econometric results.

Another factor that has affected economic performance is related to the sequence of reform measures. There has been a certain degree of "path dependence" (Daianu and Rostowski) in the sense that starting with an inadequate transition strategy has compromised the chances for success in the subsequent stages of the transition.

A general consensus emerged that the assessment of CEECs' economic performance is shrouded by inadequacies in the statistical base, leading to multiple interpretations of the available data. Given the large shifts taking place in the system of relative prices and in the sectoral composition of national output, the recorded changes in aggregate variables, such as GDP and aggregate demand, are of limited value in assessing the performance of these economies. There is also much uncertainty about the pre-transition level and composition of GDP at market prices.

Better indicators would be provided by data on employment and per-capita consumption (Cooper). Others warned against taking an overly negative attitude vis-à-vis the CEECs' statistics: the poor quality of data should not lead to a suspension of analysis or evaluation. Rather, it is more appropriate to resort to a well-diversified set of variables in order to draw inferences about the overall state of the economy (Stern). Distortions in statistical measurement should be identified and taken into account when using these data. For instance, if changes in national output are not adequately captured in official statistics, other data, such as electric power consumption, could help to better estimate the direction of these changes, albeit this index is not sufficient to assess the magnitude (Gelb). Although the actual extent of the output collapse in transition economies might be overstated by the official statistics, the fall in output since the beginning of the transition appears lower in comparative terms than the 34 per cent decline in the United States during the period of the Great Depression (Sahay).

The relationship between macroeconomic stabilization and growth was the subject of ample debate and diverging views. Scepticism, if not criticism, was expressed with respect to the view that stabilization is the pre-condition for economic recovery. In Gomulka's view, correlation evidenced in some of the contributions presented here, was far from demonstrating a causal relationship between the two phenomena. Daianu pointed out that economic recovery had been proven possible even under circumstances of high inflation, suggesting that institutional governance and structural factors should be given more attention when trying to explain economic growth. A corollary debate developed on the use of fixed exchange rates as a basis for macroeconomic stabilization. Coricelli remarked that those reforming countries that had adopted such policy had a better economic performance than the others. This result is in line with evidence from market economies, but the reasons behind this may be different across the two groups. In market economies, this policy approach was usually associated with an initial growth boom, while transition economies experienced steep output declines before recovery began. Coricelli saw this as evidence of the pre-eminence of supply-side factors in explaining the latter economies' performance. In particular, fixed exchange rates might have been used as a nominal anchor for macro-stabilization in place of monetary targeting since the latter was not practical, given the underdevelopment of financial markets. Evidence to this effect builds a case for greater initiatives by international financial institutions to help transition countries establish fixed exchange rates by providing them with sufficient foreign currency reserves. Sahay agreed that the reasons were different, because problems in transition economies are predominantly on the supply side unlike market economies, where problems tend to be on the demand side. Nevertheless, she partly attributed the success of the policy based on fixed exchange rates in certain CEECs to the fact that maintenance of the exchange rate provided the public with an easily-monitored indicator of government commitment to stabilization.

The difficulties experienced by some CEECs in bringing about an economic recovery were also ascribed to shortcomings in the State's intervention in the economy. In these countries, rent-seeking behaviour among enterprises is widespread, and market competition and financial constraints are not strong enough to reduce the scope for such activity (Blommestein). Hence, governments need to rapidly build those institutions that are necessary to make a market economy function and to reduce the scope for discretionary intervention of political authorities in the economy. In Balcerowicz's view, governments should concentrate on the provision of education, defence and other public goods and should not be involved in activities in which the private sector is more efficient. Others spoke in favour of greater government intervention to smooth differences in income and wealth across segments of the population (Winckler) and, more tentatively, to provide a demand-side stimulus to the economy, for instance, through various forms of targeted investment or support for poorly performing enterprises that serve a social function (Laski and Bhaduri).

In arguing that privatisation did not achieve the goal of separating political power from economic power, Nowotny mentioned the case of enterprises owned by banks in which the state had a controlling stake. The implementation of reforms is also hampered by the fact that it has been, by and large, in the hands of a public administration that has a vested interest in retaining portions of the economic power wielded under the old regime (Zecchini). Hence, there is a need to invest heavily in upgrading and renovating human capital in the public administration in order to enable the government to play a better role in the market-based economy.

Part of the debate was devoted to the question of whether the re-election probabilities of governments in transition economies are exogenously determined, or at least independent of the economic policies they pursued. While Roland argued against this thesis, Rostowski supported it on the evidence that both fast and slow reformers have been removed from power in the CEECs. In addition, Rostowski questioned the possibility of policy reversals since this to him implied a return to central planning. Roland, instead, thought that some policy reversals are possible even without such an event. For this reason initial reformers in Poland had an incentive to reform as fast as possible in order to raise the cost of policy reversals.

11

Policy conclusions

The spectrum of analyses and views presented by the various contributors is so wide and beset with controversy that to identify a set of lessons or conclusions that have received general support is a major challenge. Perhaps, too little time has gone by to have a relatively unquestionable base for building a consensus view on how to improve the transition strategy. In the face of difficulties and caveats, an attempt is made here to extract from the different contributions a few policy-oriented conclusions that could be endorsed by a majority of contributors and are relevant when looking at policy making for the coming years.

Part of the uncertainty about the conclusions is attributable to the still limited or approximate information that is available on these economies, even after markets were established and market prices are allowed to provide meaningful gauges of economic activity. As a consequence, the first conclusion should be for governments to double their efforts to measure the new economic reality by upgrading their statistical systems. This is crucial not just to enforce tax rules at a time of unrelenting pressure from still sizable budgetary gaps, but to improve the quality of economic policy making and to be able to monitor the actual developments of the economy with the required frequency. For instance, without reliable indicators on the magnitude and evolution of the so-called informal economy, the same official GDP figures are open to widely differing interpretations.

However weak the statistics concerning the reforming economies are, they are sufficient to point to a conclusion which is generally shared, i.e. that the transition process is not yet completed even for the most advanced CEECs. The basic structure of a market-based system is already in place in several countries and macroeconomic conditions are currently better than in the initial phase of the transition. Nevertheless, not all the foundations of the new system have been built and some require extensive reinforcement. Hence, the question remains as to what direction and priorities CEECs' policies should pursue.

The political backlash against the initial leaders of the reform process has already occurred in all CEECs, but it has not given way to a throwback to older policies partly because of the high costs involved with policy reversal. For the political forces currently in power, the probability of re-election now looks more dependent (endogenous, to use Roland's terminology) on the quality of the policies that they will actually pursue, than was the case in the first political cycle following the introduction of a market-based system. At the same time, these governments should be aware that complacency with the current state of reforms and economic restructuring is not likely to bring about sustained economic growth and higher living standards over the medium term. In the view of all contributors, more action is needed and the type of policy measures and the ensuing intensity and duration of structural adjustment will make the difference, while failure to make progress in economic transformation would open up the prospect of sluggish growth, if not continuing economic decline.

It is also widely recognised that low inflation, low fiscal deficits and sustainable current-account deficits in the balance of payments are all necessary conditions to spur private fixed investment, productivity gains and economic recovery. Macroeconomic stabilization is not, however, viewed by all as being also a sufficient condition, and according to some views, the macroeconomic stability objective itself should be approached differently than in the recent past, namely by focusing more on the supply side of the economy and less on curbing domestic demand. After allowing for these differences of view, a general conclusion can be reached, namely that governments' economic programmes should aim at achieving a better balance between demand management and structural transformation measures since the two are interdependent and mutually reinforcing. In this context, the choice of the exchange rate regime and the actual exchange rate policy are of critical importance since they are faced with the risk of either feeding inflationary expectations or leading to an erosion of external competitiveness.

On the structural side of economic reform, three areas were regarded by most of the contributors as requiring urgent action by the government. First among them come the institutions underpinning the market-economy, and particularly the financial institutions. Granting independence in monetary policy conduct to the central bank and rehabilitating the banking system were considered basic conditions still to be fulfilled in most CEECs.

Second, the role of government in the economy remains a subject of great controversy. Some advocate an interventionist role, with the government taking responsibility, in particular, for an active industrial policy directed to supporting the restructuring of public firms. Others recommend limiting state involvement in production sectors and concentrating public action on ensuring a better functioning of market mechanisms. Despite these contrasting views, there is general agreement that governments should invest more in both enhancing human capital and strengthening the physical infrastructure in order to better enable firms to exploit the newly emerging market opportunities and to raise the growth potential of the economy.

The third major priority area concerns the restructuring of state-owned enterprises and the development of a competitive private-enterprise sector. To achieve this end the mere transfer of ownership of public firms into private hands does not appear adequate, as restructuring is progressing slowly. Mechanisms for effective corporate governance have yet to be developed, and this requires overcoming the many weaknesses in the legal environment, the financial system and the functioning of the equity markets.

Overall, the sense of urgency of earlier days to introduce radical reforms and adjustments has receded; countries are now well advanced in the transition and have more time and experience to complete and improve the work that they began in the early 1990s. The overwhelming evidence to date, however, suggests that rapid progress in this task is preferable to slow reform, and this conclusion is reinforced by the fact that at present, conditions in general seem ripe for pushing the transformation through.

Part II

Enterprise restructuring and private sector development

1

Comparing two Great Depressions: 1929-33 to 1989-93

Jacek Rostowski

1. Introduction: demand or supply driven depressions

If official statistics are to be believed, the fall in output in the transition economies of Central and Eastern Europe has probably been the largest anywhere in peacetime in modern history. This fall in output was certainly noticeably larger than that which occurred during the Great Depression of the 1930s (compare Tables 1 and 2-4), although it was smaller than that during the second World War in countries which served as battlegrounds (France in 1944, Germany and Japan in 1945). In spite of this, during the early transition, investment fell by far less relative to GDP than during the Great Depression, and certain categories of investment in some countries actually increased in absolute terms (e.g. in Poland gross fixed investment in machinery and equipment in industry — Table 3). This is the central paradox of the Great Transition Depression of 1989-93. Our conclusion is that the behaviour of investment shows that in a number of countries the output depression was the result of profound restructuring of the economy, following on shifts in demand resulting from price and trade liberalisation, rather than the result of a reduction in aggregate demand.

Two main explanations have been put forward for the fall in output during the transition in Central and Eastern Europe, the first posits a sharp reduction in the level of aggregate demand as the cause, the second suggests a dramatic change in the structure of demand, to which supply was unable to respond sufficiently rapidly. On the demand based view, the anti-inflationary policies pursued by reformist governments resulted in excessive tightening in monetary and fiscal policies, and via high real interest rates and/or reductions in budget deficits caused sharp falls in aggregate demand, which in turn caused output to collapse (e.g. Laski and Bhaduri, 1993 or in this volume). The supply-side approach starts from the large increase in the relative prices of energy and other inputs (and the fall in the relative prices of agricultural products), which resulted from price liberalisation. This led to many production processes becoming loss making, and having to be discontinued. Due to

I am grateful to Mario Blejer for comments, and to Milan Nikolic and Janice Bell for the collection of data.

various rigidities many resources became permanently useless, while others had to remain idle until they were redeployed or improved. Since the required micro-adjustments were large, the post-communist depressions were inevitable. If, in the transition, aggregate demand was not reduced to correspond to the level of the (much reduced) sustainable aggregate supply, then countries suffered very high inflation as well as great depression, as in Russia or Ukraine (Gomulka, 1993).

If the demand based explanations are correct, we would expect the fall in gross fixed investment during the transition to be far greater than the fall in GDP, with a resulting fall in the gross fixed investment/ GDP ratio. This follows both from theory and empirical observation. On the other hand, if the fall in output is due to a change in the structure of demand, gross fixed investment need not fall by as much

Table 1. Volume indices (1929=100).

Years	1930	1931	1932	1933
Australia				
GDP	90.59	92.12	97.61	101.26
Gross investment	71.89	55.33	56.21	80.47
Gross fixed capital formation	72.38	52.49	50.28	70.17
GI/GDP	79.36	60.06	57.59	79.47
GFCF/GDP	100.67	94.87	89.44	87.19
Germany				
GDP	93.79	84.36	76.47	84.13
Production of investment goods*	81.50	56.48	38.08	49.75
PIG/GDP	86.90	66.95	49.80	59.14
Italy				
GDP	92.96	94.37	97.89	97.89
Gross investment	72.01	63.06	72.76	66.04
GI/GDP	77.47	66.83	74.33	67.47
Canada				
GDP	95.73	83.57	74.89	69.91
Gross investment	71.61	50.35	22.47	15.55
Gross fixed capital formation	87.51	64.99	36.01	25.75
GI/GDP	74.81	60.25	30.00	22.24
GFCF/GDP	91.42	77.77	48.08	36.84
Sweden				
GDP	103.40	93.53	91.12	92.28
Gross investment	115.58	99.43	77.24	79.69
GI/GDP	111.78	106.31	84.78	86.36
UK				
GDP	99.90	94.85	95.04	96.18
Gross investment	87.20	94.08	82.48	76.80
Gross fixed capital formation	100.83	98.33	85.83	89.17
GFCF in machinery & equipment	92.90	95.85	77.19	67.24
GI/GDP	87.28	99.19	86.79	79.85
GFCF/GDP	100.93	103.68	90.31	92.71
GFCF in M&E/GDP	92.99	101.05	81.22	69.91
US				
GDP	90.59	82.88	71.76	70.25
Gross investment	70.04	43.25	16.24	16.38
Gross fixed capital formation	76.64	52.41	30.37	26.09
Gross fixed capital formation in M&E	80.00	51.43	29.61	30.13
GI/GDP	77.32	52.18	22.63	23.32
GFCF/GDP	84.60	63.24	42.33	37.14
GFCF in M&E/GDP	88.31	62.05	41.26	42.89

Sources: Liesner. 1984; *Svennilson, 1954.

as GDP. Indeed, it could remain constant, or even increase. This was the case in the United States after the second World War. Between 1944 and 1947 real GDP fell by 23 per cent, while real gross private fixed investment increased by 190 per cent (Liesner, 1989).[1] Nor was this merely a housing boom, as investment in plant and machinery increased by 108 per cent, non-residential construction increased by 133 per cent, and investment in transport equipment increased by 232 per cent. In the UK where GDP fell by 10 per cent in the same period, gross fixed investment increased by 232 per cent. And although investment in plant and machinery was flat in 1945, by 1947 it had increased by 157 per cent. Investment in transport equipment increased in the same period by 83 per cent. Out of the countries for which Liesner (1989) gives data, only Australia and Canada also took part in the war, without being battlefields. In the first, GDP fell 6.8 per cent between 1944 and 1946, while gross fixed investment increased by 183 per cent, while in the second GDP fell 4.8 per cent and gross fixed investment increased 69 per cent in the same years (disaggregated data by type of investment was unavailable for these two countries). As we shall see, the "aberrant" behaviour of investment in transition economies was nothing like as extreme as in the US, the

Table 2. Selected Central and East European countries — volume indices (1989=100).

	1990	1991	1992	1993
Gross Domestic Product				
Czech Rep.	98.8	84.8	78.8	78.4
Slovakia	97.5	86.6	80.5	76.7
Bulgaria	88.2	68.0	62.4	58.7
Hungary	96.0	86.2	81.8	80.1
Poland	88.4	82.2	83.7	87.0
Romania	91.6	79.7	67.7	68.3
Russia	98.0	85.4	68.8	59.9
Ukraine	97.4	86.5	73.5	61.8
Gross Investment				
Czech Rep.	93.5	68.4	75.0	67.1
Slovakia	105.3	89.6	109.1	106.5
Bulgaria	81.5	65.3	64.3	59.2
Hungary	90.2	79.5	74.4	74.8
Poland	75.2	60.1	52.3	59.0
Romania	61.7	45.8	45.3	44.9
Russia	100.1	83.9	46.2	39.3
Ukraine	101.9	96.5	57.9	44.6
GI/GDP				
Czech Rep.	94.6	80.7	95.2	85.6
Slovakia	108.0	103.5	135.5	138.9
Bulgaria	92.4	96.0	103.0	100.9
Hungary	93.9	92.2	91.0	93.4
Poland	85.0	73.1	62.4	67.8
Romania	67.4	57.5	66.9	65.7
Russia	102.1	98.2	67.2	65.6
Ukraine	104.6	111.6	78.8	72.2

Source: Poland: International Economic Report 1993/4, World Economy Research Institute, Warsaw School of Economics, 1994.

UK, Australia and Canada after the war. Nevertheless, it is not compatible with an aggregate demand explanation for the fall in output.

In a simple accelerator model, the optimal capital stock is proportional to the expected output level:

(1) $$K^* = \upsilon Y_2$$

If today's capital stock is optimal, investment will be undertaken to offset depreciation and to match any expected increase in output:

(2) $$I_1 = K^* - K_1 + \delta K_1 = \upsilon(Y_2 - Y_1) + \delta K_1$$

Thus, a change in national income causes a matching change in the capital stock.

Figure 1.

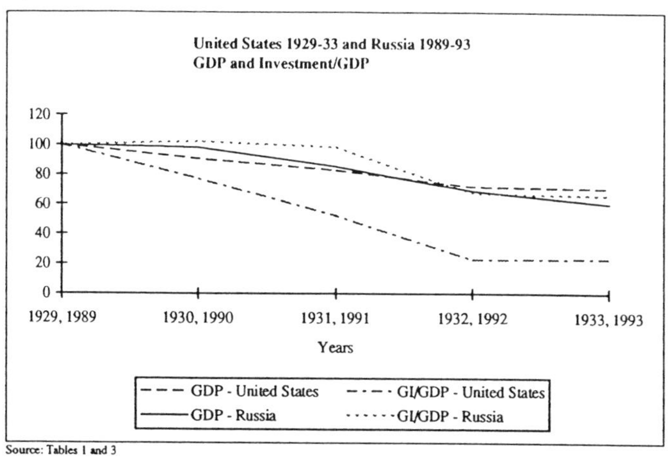

Source: Tables 1 and 3

Figure 2.

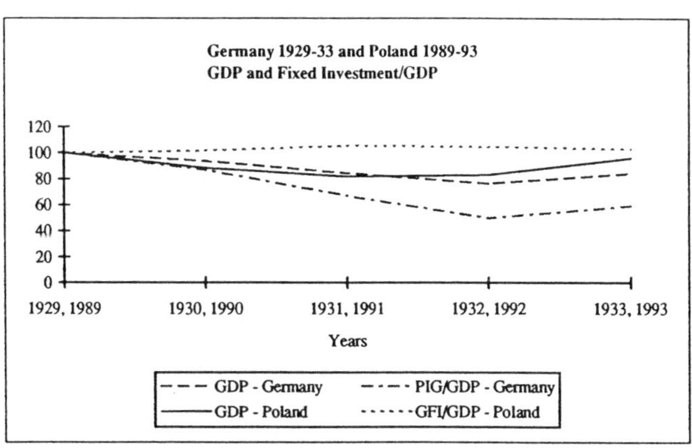

Source: Tables 1 and 2

Since the capital output ratio is typically between 2 and 3, and gross fixed investment is between 15 per cent and 30 per cent of annual GDP, a 10 per cent increase in expected (permanent) GDP would lead to a 100-200 per cent increase in gross fixed investment, if the whole of the increase in the capital stock had to take place in one period. Equally, a fall of permanent GDP by 10 per cent would lead to the complete elimination of gross fixed investment. In fact, since the adjustment of the capital stock does not need to take place in one year, and since not every increase or fall in output is believed by businesses to be a change in permanent output, there is no need for the changes in investment to be quite as violent as suggested by such a very simple model. Nevertheless, in Western market economies changes in investment are usually several times larger than the changes in output which they accompany. This is documented in Section 2 for the major capitalist countries during the Great Depression of the 1930s. In Section 3 the experience of the post-communist economies is compared with that in the West during the Great Depression. It is found that although (according to official statistics) the output collapse was in general larger during the transition crisis, investment fell by far less. In Slovakia gross investment (including changes in stocks) actually fell less than GDP. In the remaining post-communist countries, in which total gross investment falls relative to GDP, this fall is far smaller than the experience of the Western market economies during the Great Depression would lead us to expect (see Figure 1 for a comparison of Russia during 1989-93 with the United States 1929-33). It is also shown that during the Great Depression gross fixed investment, while declining slightly less than total gross investment, declined by far more relative to GDP than in those transition economies for which we have data. Moreover the case of Poland, for which we have very detailed data, shows that even when gross investment falls by more than GDP, gross fixed capital formation can increase relative to GDP. All this suggests that, in all the countries studied, reductions in aggregate demand do not provide a full explanation of the transition depression, and that supply side effects are an important part of what happened.

The behaviour of investment and of its components during the transition in Poland is examined in greater detail Section 4. It can be seen to be incompatible with both the predictions of the aggregate demand based explanation of the post-communist depression in that country, and with the experience of market economies during the Great Depression. Instead of being massive the fall in the investment/GDP ratio was quite moderate, and gross fixed investment/GDP actually increased during the transition in Poland (Figure 2).[2] What is more, this latter ratio increased very sharply in those sectors in which one would expect there to be a particular need for fixed assets to be restructured — namely, in industry and commerce. Also significant is the fact that investment in machinery and equipment rose even more than total gross fixed investment relative to output, both in the economy as whole and in industry and commerce in particular. Most striking of all is the fact that gross fixed capital formation in machinery and equipment in industry actually increased in absolute terms during the transition in Poland. On the other hand agriculture, where there was less possibility of restructuring, and which suffered a massive terms of trade shock, experienced a fall in the gross fixed investment/output ratio similar to that of the US economy during the Great Depression.

2. The behaviour of investment during the Great Depression of 1929-33

Table 1 shows the behaviour of real GDP, total real investment (gross capital formation) and (in some cases) real gross fixed capital formation GFCF, and real GFCF in machinery and equipment (GFCF-E) between 1929 and 1933 in Australia, Canada, Germany, Italy, Sweden, the United States and the United Kingdom (data was not available for other countries[3]). The countries fall into two groups. The first, consisting of the US, Canada and Germany, suffered falls in national income which are comparable to those in the transition economies (see Table 2). On the other hand, the second group (the UK, Australia, Italy and Sweden) suffered much smaller declines. In both groups, however, real investment, real GFCF and real GFCF-E fell by several times more than real national income. In the first group total real gross investment fell some 2.7 to 2.8 times as much as the fall in national income, whereas in those countries in which the depression was less severe the fall in total gross investment relative to the fall in national income was much larger (between 2.8 and 6.5 times). For those countries for which we have real GFCF (Australia, the UK and the US), it fell by slightly less than real gross investment, but still by several times more than real GDP (by 6 times, 2.8 times and 2.5 times respectively). We have real GFCF-E only for the UK and the US, and again the decline was much larger than the decline in real GDP — 4.6 times for the UK and 2.3 times for the US.

In the United States gross national product fell a cumulative 29.8 per cent in real terms, while gross investment fell 84.5 per cent. Real GFCF fell 74 per cent and real GFCF-E fell slightly less, by 69.9 per cent. Thus by 1933 investment expenditure per unit of national income had fallen to 22 per cent of its 1929 level, GFCF to 40.3 per cent of that level, and GFCF-E to 43 per cent. In Canada the results of the great depression on real GDP and real gross investment were almost identical to those in the US.[4] In Germany real GDP fell by 23.5 per cent between 1929 and 1932 (the trough of the depression in terms of national income). During that time investment expenditures fell 63.5 per cent, so that investment per unit of national income fell to 48 per cent of its 1929 level.[5]

In the UK real GDP fell 5 per cent between 1929 and 1932 (the trough year) while gross investment fell 17.6 per cent. GFCF fell 14 per cent and gross fixed capital formation of machinery and equipment fell even more: by 22.8 per cent. In Australia real GDP fell 7.9 per cent and real investment fell 51.5 per cent between 1929 and 1931, while GFCF fell 47.5 per cent. In Italy national income fell only in 1930. In that year real GDP fell 7 per cent while investment fell 28 per cent. In Sweden real GDP only fell between the years 1930 and 1932. In that time real GDP fell 11.9 per cent, while real investment fell 33.2 per cent.

There are two commonly presented interpretations of these facts. (1) The Monetarist: the unintended tightening of the monetary stance in 1929 lead to a sharp fall in national income, causing the appearance of a large amount of excess capacity, which in turn caused an even larger fall in investment and GFCF. (2) The Keynesian: an initial fall in investment demand and GFCF was the trigger. It caused a (smaller) fall in national income, which in turn caused a further fall in investment and GFCF, since firms with excess capacity had little reason to invest.

3. The behaviour of investment during the transition crisis of 1989-93

Data was obtained on gross investment and national income for eight post-communist economies. Tables 2-4 show that all the countries suffered declines in GDP which were similar in size to those experienced by the three economies in our sample which were severely affected by the great depression of the 1930s (Canada, Germany and the United States). The smallest loss of GDP (from the beginning of the transition to the trough) was suffered by Poland at 17.8 per cent, while the largest was suffered by Bulgaria at 41.3 per cent.

The largest relative fall in investment took place in Russia during 1991-3. During this period GDP fell by 29.9 per cent, slightly more than in the US and Canada in 1929-33, while gross investment fell by 53.2 per cent in Russia as against almost 85 per cent in the US and Canada (See Figure 1). This means that the fall in gross investment was only 1.8 times that of the fall in national income (compared to a factor of 2.8 times in the US and Canada). To take another comparison: during 1929-32 GDP in Germany fell 23.5 per cent and gross investment fell 63.5 per cent; during 1990-3 in the Czech Republic, GDP fell 20.6 per cent while gross investment fell only 28.2 per cent (both examples run from the peak to the trough of the depression in terms of GDP). This gives a ratio of 1.4 for the Czech Republic, only slightly more than half of the lowest figure for the sample from the Great Depression. Most important is the contrast between the behaviour of GFCF and GFCF-E during the transition and during the Great Depression for the few countries for which data is available. As discussed in Section 2, GFCF is available for Australia, the UK and the US during the Great Depression. It fell by 6, 2.8 and 2.5 times as much as GDP. Analogous data was only obtained for Poland and Hungary during the transition. GFCF increased relative to GDP in Poland, whereas it fell by only a few percentage points in Hungary (Sections 4 and 5).

Also striking is the fact that in the post-communist countries there is no inverse relationship between the size of the fall in GDP (Table 2) and the ratio of the fall in investment to the fall in GDP, as there is in our sample of countries from the Great Depression (Table 1). What we observe in the Great Depression is that when we look across countries, the greater the percentage fall in GDP the greater the percentage fall in investment, but with a declining percentage increment. The explanation of this phenomenon is probably quite straightforward. The investment aggregate used is gross investment. The greater the percentage fall in GDP and in investment, the smaller the remaining investment is relative to the economy's existing capital stock, and therefore the larger the proportion of any investment which goes to offsetting the depreciation of the existing capital stock. Since offsetting depreciation is likely to involve less risk than creating new capital, one would expect such investment to be more resistant to reduction (even as a result of falls in aggregate demand) than is investment in new capital. The absence of such a phenomenon in the transition economies suggests that investing in offsetting the depreciation of the existing capital stock is no less risky than investing in new capital. This in turn indicates the importance of relative rather than aggregate demand shifts.

4. The boom within the slump: the behaviour of components of national income and of investment during the transition to a market economy in Poland

In Poland during 1989 to 1993 we get a quite different history of the behaviour of investment and national income and their components than one would expect on the basis of Western experience (Table 3). Whereas GDP fell by 18.3 per cent between

Table 3. Poland — volume indices (1989=100).

	1987	1988	1990	1991	1992	1993
GI	87.6	95.1	75.2	60.1	52.3	59.0
GFI	97.2	102.4	89.9	86.2	86.8	88.7
- Industry	87.8	91.7	92.7	86.0	81.9	83.8
- Construction	115.6	129.0	72.8	98.0	155.3	109.0
- Agriculture	106.0	109.5	67.0	38.2	34.1	38.6
- Transport	131.8	145.6	100.5	93.1	78.4	71.3
- Commerce	82.2	85.2	97.7	111.5	151.5	185.9
GDP	95.9	99.8	88.4	81.7	82.9	86.1
- Industry	97.7	102.1	78.0	64.6	66.3	70.3
- Construction	94.6	100.3	85.5	91.3	94.7	96.6
- Agriculture	97.6	99.0	99.7	106.5	93.4	98.0
- Transport	95.4	99.0	85.2	68.2	68.9	67.3
- Commerce	89.3	95.5	100.7	108.7	108.5	121.5
GFI/GDP	101.4	102.6	101.7	105.5	104.6	103.1
- Industry	89.9	89.8	118.8	133.1	123.5	119.1
- Construction	122.2	128.7	85.2	107.4	163.9	112.9
- Agriculture	108.7	110.6	67.2	35.8	36.6	39.4
- Transport	138.1	147.1	118.0	136.5	113.8	106.0
- Commerce	92.0	89.2	97.0	102.6	139.7	153.0
GFI in mach. & equip.						
- Total	99.1	105.5	90.2	82.3	94.3	110.1
- Industry	83.3	89.5	102.8	92.2	96.4	101.5
- Construction	125.5	139.1	66.4	67.9	133.8	109.0
- Agriculture	107.6	113.2	61.2	23.4	15.7	18.4
- Transport	147.3	155.1	64.1	67.3	54.8	60.8
- Commerce	102.4	102.4	106.6	156.3	271.8	368.9
GFI in mach. & equip./**GDP**						
- Total	103.4	105.7	102.0	100.7	113.6	127.9
- Industry	85.3	87.6	131.8	142.6	145.4	144.4
- Construction	132.6	138.8	77.6	74.4	141.2	112.9
- Agriculture	110.3	114.4	61.4	21.9	16.8	18.8
- Transport	154.3	156.7	75.2	98.7	79.5	90.4
- Commerce	114.6	107.1	105.8	143.8	250.5	303.6
GFI in bldgs in industry	92.7	94.6	87.1	84.4	72.5	66.5
GFI in bldgs in ind./**GDP** in ind.	94.9	92.6	111.7	130.6	109.3	94.6

Source: Rocznik Statystyczny, Glowny Urzad Statystyczny, various issues.

1989 and 1991, gross fixed investment (GFI) fell by only 13.8 per cent, so that GFI expenditures per unit of national income actually rose by 4 per cent, rather than falling dramatically.

Even more striking are the results for the relationship between gross fixed investment and national income by main branches of output. When we look at the main sectors of output we see a divergence between those sectors in which gross fixed investment fell more than GDP produced in that sector (construction and transport) or where investment fell sharply even though GDP produced increased (agriculture), and those where it either fell far less than GDP produced (industry) or where it increased by more than GDP produced (commerce). *Thus, whereas GDP produced in industry fell 35.4 per cent between 1989 and 1991, GFI in industry fell only 14 per cent, so that GFI per unit of GDP increased by 33 per cent!*[6] (Unfortunately, we did not find data for GFI in industry during the Great Depression for any of the countries.)

How can these facts be explained? For those who hold to a Keynesian explanation according to which both national income and investment declined in Poland as a result of a decline in aggregate demand, the facts regarding GFI in industry become if anything even more difficult to explain when one notes that although GFI in construction and transport did indeed decline more than the GDP produced in those sectors, it did so by only very slightly more.[7]

On the other hand, these facts are explicable by the hypothesis that the comprehensive price and trade liberalisation and imposition of hard budget constraints, which lay at the core of the Balcerowicz Plan in Poland in 1990, constituted a massive real shock to enterprises — equivalent to a block of technical innovations — which affected the various productive sectors of the Polish economy in different ways. Such an approach makes it possible to understand why gross fixed investment in Polish industry per unit of GDP produced in that sector increased sharply instead of falling, as would have been suggested by the aggregate demand based approach. Industrial firms realised that they were not suffering from excess capacity — as would indeed have been the case if the problem had been a shortage of aggregate demand. Instead they realised that they were suffering from a shortage of the right kind of productive capacity, and that therefore they needed to invest in order to increase such capacity. The ability of the firms to invest was, however, limited by the fall in revenue which they faced due to the restrictive macroeconomic policy which was a key part of the Balcerowicz Plan, and which was necessary in order to impose hard budget constraints on the firms in the first place. Together with the fact that Poland had reneged on its international debt payments already in 1981 — so that Polish firms did not have access to international capital markets — this may explain why total GFI in industry fell in absolute terms instead of increasing in the face of the fall in capacity.

Such a "real shocks" approach to the behaviour of GDP and GFI in the Polish transition is particularly supported by the behaviour of GFI in machinery and equipment (GFI-E) in industry. This actually increased by 2.8 per cent in 1990. Since GDP produced in industry fell by 22 per cent, GFI-E/GDP in industry rose by 31.8 per cent, and this ratio continued to rise in 1991 and 1992. Even more striking, the absolute level of GFI-E in industry for the first three years of the transition was on average actually 6.8 per cent higher than in the three preceding years! This was in spite of a level of GDP produced in industry which was 30 per cent lower, and of a sharp increase in real loan rates. While incomprehensible in the light of a standard Keynesian model, this fact can be readily understood if we accept that Polish producers realised that they needed to fundamentally restructure their technical base. In such a context the data is actually compatible with a "modified" accelerator approach, with the accelerator continuing to work at a sectoral level. If price and trade liberalisation wiped out the value of a large proportion of a certain kind of the previously accumulated capital stock, excess capacity may not in fact have existed for this category, explaining the observed increase in investment in that category. In the Appendix we apply this reasoning, and attempt a very rough and ready calculation of the share of the value of machinery and equipment in industry which needed to be written down as a result of the price and trade liberalisation in Poland. We come up with a lower bound of 48 per cent of this capital being wiped out as a result of the relative price changes which accompanied the transition.

The same "real shocks" approach can explain what happened in agriculture, where GFI fell by 62 per cent even though real GDP increased by 6.5 per cent between 1989 and 1991. GFI-E in agriculture fell even more — by 76.6 per cent. Producer prices had been kept artificially high in the 1980s in agriculture, and farmers were therefore subject to a massive terms of trade shock when industrial prices were freed and utility tariffs raised (Bell and Rostowski, 1995). Farmers clearly decided that there was not going to be a great future in expanding agricultural production under the new market determined conditions. On the other hand in commerce — which had been severely repressed under communism and where liberalisation of prices and entry caused sectoral GDP to grow very fast — investment grew even faster. As a result GFI/GDP in this sector increased by 53 per cent between 1989 and 1993 and GFI-E/GDP increased by three times during the same period.

Finally, it is worth noting that the hypothesis that the depression in Poland in 1990 was due to a "credit crunch" (Calvo and Coricelli, 1992) is also hard to reconcile with the behaviour of investment in that year. Table 3 shows that for the whole economy GFI/GDP rose by 1.7 per cent, GFI/GDP in industry rose 18.8 per cent, and GFI-E/GDP in industry rose by 31.8 per cent. In industry there was an almost 30 per cent fall in gross output in that year, and yet GFI-E actually increased by 2.8 per cent in absolute real terms in this context. Since, on the credit crunch hypothesis industrial firms reduced output because they did not have the financial resources to buy inputs (particularly material inputs), and indeed were obliged in this situation to "borrow from their employees" by reducing real wages sharply, it is hard to explain why in this situation the same firms should have actually increased investment in machinery and equipment.

5. Investment and output in Hungary

Hungary is the other country for which fairly detailed investment and sectoral output statistics were obtained (Table 4). The story here has some similarity to that in Poland, but with a clear delay in the "investment recovery" as compared to Poland, so that the ratio of GFI/GDP remains several points below its 1989 level from 1990 to 1993 (between 93.5 per cent and 97.8 per cent of 1989), and only exceeds that level in 1994 (106.8 per cent). However this is in spite of an 18.3 per cent fall in GDP between 1989 and the trough of the depression in 1993, which given Western experience would have led us to expect a far larger fall in investment. When we look at GFI-E/GDP for the economy as a whole, we again have a pattern which is

Table 4. Hungary — volume indices (1989=100).

	1987	1988	1990	1991	1992	1993	1994
			GDP by sectors				
Industry	103.59	102.01	92.32	75.81	70.75	73.86	
Construction	97.67	92.35	78.10	66.39	67.64	63.28	
Agriculture	93.79	101.21	95.32	87.49	72.98	68.06	
Transport	92.35	93.57	92.67	82.08	78.51	74.49	
Commerce	116.46	101.35	111.77	102.44	85.89	81.44	
Economy	99.39	99.31	96.46	84.98	82.40	81.70	83.34
			GFI by sectors				
Industry	98.57	91.34	92.15	79.47	109.24	100.97	
Construction	79.17	81.53	103.14	122.50	109.53	113.36	
Agriculture	137.17	107.13	83.42	47.77	17.16	15.92	
Transport	105.67	104.64	91.27	96.02	133.59	158.49	
Commerce	76.69	72.02	106.69	110.44	135.21	115.02	
Economy	100.54	92.83	90.37	79.44	78.11	79.92	88.98
			GFI in mach. & equip. by sectors				
Industry		88.26	94.58	78.23	144.19		
Construction		90.49	80.70	59.09	75.88		
Agriculture		105.15	87.55	52.53	14.98		
Transport		110.46	83.04	84.45	122.41		
Commerce		85.23	138.68	131.23	174.89		
Economy	102.34	93.98	93.20	79.97	101.75	102.97	121.90
			GFI/GDP (volume indices ratios)				
Industry	95.15	89.54	99.82	104.82	154.40	136.71	
Construction	81.05	88.29	132.05	184.53	161.94	179.14	
Agriculture	146.26	105.85	87.51	54.60	23.51	23.39	
Transport	114.41	111.83	98.48	116.99	170.15	212.78	
Commerce	65.85	71.05	95.46	107.82	157.41	141.24	
Economy	101.16	93.48	93.68	93.48	94.80	97.82	106.76
			GFI in mach. & equip./GDP (volume indices ratios)				
Industry		86.52	102.45	103.19	203.79		
Construction		97.99	103.32	89.01	112.19		
Agriculture		103.89	91.85	60.04	20.53		
Transport		118.05	89.60	102.89	155.92		
Commerce		84.09	124.07	128.11	203.60		
Economy	102.96	94.64	96.62	94.11	123.49	126.04	146.27

Sources:
1. Yearbook of Economic Statistics 1989-91. KSH Budapest.
2. National Accounts Hungary 1990-93. KSH Budapest.
3. Statistical Yearbook 1987. 1988. 1989. 1990. 1991. 1992. 1993. KSH Budapest
4. National Bank of Hungary. Annual Report. 1990. 1991. 1992. 1993.

similar to that in Poland, with ratios for the economy as a whole exceeding 100 per cent by a significant amount, however, only from 1992 (before that date the ratios were slightly above 100 per cent in Poland and slightly below 100 per cent in Hungary). This is an extraordinary contrast with the behaviour of gross fixed capital formation in machinery and equipment during the Great Depression. We have data only for the UK and the US. However, in the UK where GDP fell by only some 5 per cent, GFCF-E had fallen by 33 per cent by 1933, whereas in the US, where GDP fell by 30 per cent, GFCF-E fell by 70 per cent (Table 1). Once more, this is a puzzle which a demand based explanation of the transition depression cannot explain.

As in Poland there are wide sectoral differences in the behaviour of GFI and GFI-E, and in that of the GFI/GDP and GFI-E/GDP ratios, which indicate that the high level of investment was linked to the restructuring of the economy during the transition. The "investment recovery" (relative to the 1989 level) only really starts in industry and transport in 1992, while in commerce and construction investment is higher than its 1989 level in absolute terms throughout the period (in the former case this is similar to Poland, in the latter it is not). In agriculture, as in Poland, GFI and GFI-E exhibit a continuous and very sharp downward trend, reaching 16 per cent and 15 per cent of their 1989 levels.

6. Conclusions and implications

The behaviour of investment in the post-communist economies seems to be incompatible with the view that the transition depressions were caused exclusively by a shortage of aggregate demand. In the case of Poland the behaviour of gross fixed investment suggests that little of the output fall can be attributed to insufficiency of demand. Further research needs to be done to see whether the sectoral patterns of output and of gross fixed investment observed in Poland and Hungary, and the behaviour of investment in machinery and equipment in the two countries — all of which are consistent with the view that the resilience of investment was due to restructuring of the economy — are repeated in the other countries.

It is also important to know: which are the firms which were undertaking this investment? Were they state enterprises or new private businesses? As they stand, our results cast some doubt on the hypothesis of Grosfeld and Roland (1995) that in the early transition enterprises in Central Europe engaged only in "defensive" restructuring and failed to undertake "strategic" restructuring. The resilience of investment shows that enterprises did more than merely sack workers and sell unneeded plants, which is what defensive restructuring amounts to. However, it is not impossible that all the investment was undertaken by new private firms, and that Grosfeld and Roland are right as regards the behaviour of state enterprises.

The investment facts we have described (particularly in the case of Poland) are unfriendly to a number of other hypotheses about the transition. We have already mentioned that the high level of investment in Poland in 1990 seems incompatible with the "credit crunch" hypothesis of Calvo and Coricelli. It is also incompatible with the implications of the work of Borensztein and Ostry (1992) and Borensztein, Demekas and Ostry (1993), which implies that there was very little structural adjustment in the transition economies during 1990 and 1991 at the level of the ten major sectors of industry. It has been pointed out (e.g. Rostowski 1993) that these results suffer from the level of aggregation of the data chosen, whereas the changes in output mix happened either at a higher level of aggregation (the shift from industry to commerce and other services) or at a lower level (within particular enterprises). The resilience of investment in all transition countries (as compared to what one would expect on the basis of experience in the West during the Great Depression), and the remarkable resilience of investment in machinery and equipment in Poland and Hungary in particular, shows that considerable restructuring was taking place — otherwise, why invest when output has fallen so sharply?

Appendix

A back of the envelope calculation of the amount of machinery and equipment which had to be written down in Poland after 1989 in the industrial sector can be attempted through a calibration of a very simple extension to the accelerator model presented in equation (2).

In order to calculate the value of the equilibrium value of the net capital stock in the form of machinery and equipment (M&E) in 1990 the following procedure was adopted. First it was necessary to find the historical value of the net capital stock in M&E in industry in 1989, so as to compare this to the level of GDP produced in industry in that year, and thus arrive at a guess for the equilibrium ratio of M&E net capital/Y in industry.

This was done in the following way. The real gross capital stock in industry (at 1984 prices) was obtained (Rocznik Statystyczny, 1991). The real gross capital stock in industry in the form of machinery and equipment was then estimated by applying the ratio of the value of machinery and equipment in industry to total capital in industry in 1989 at replacement cost (Rocznik Statystyczny, 1991). This ratio was 0.45. The real **net** capital stock of machinery and equipment in industry was then estimated by applying the ratio of fully depreciated capital to total capital (stopa zuzycia srodków trwalych) of machinery and equipment in industry (Rocznik Statystyczny, 1991) to the estimate of the real gross capital stock in the form of machinery and equipment in industry already obtained. This ratio was 0.28.

The figure obtained in this way was 1896 billion zloty for the net stock of machinery and equipment in industry at 1984 prices, and the level of GDP (in 1984 prices) was 3773 billion zloty for 1989. The net K/Y ratio for machinery and equipment in industry in 1989 is thus 0.5. We assume that this is the equilibrium value of υ. If we then assume, as is usual, that the depreciation rate for machinery and equipment is 10 per cent, and substitute into equation (2), to find I* (equilibrium investment), we get (in billions of 1984 zloty):

(2') $I^* = 0.5(2850 - 3773) + 0.1(1896) = -270$

as the figure for GDP produced in industry in 1990 at 1984 prices was 2850 billion zloty.

This indicates that with such parameters, investment in machinery and equipment in industry should have been zero in 1990, whereas in fact it was 327 billion zloty in 1984 prices. In fact, investment in M&E in industry in 1990 should have been zero even if we assume a depreciation rate of 0.24 (24 per cent *per annum*) which is extraordinarily high even for M&E, and the level of investment which was actually experienced in 1990 can only be obtained if one assumes a depreciation rate of 42 per cent *per annum*.

We can also use the simple accelerator approach to get a very rough idea of the amount of M&E capital which had to be written down in industry as a result of the initiation of the economic transformation in Poland. GDP generated in industry, which was 2850 billion zloty in 1990, exceeded 2800 billion zloty (in 1984 prices) only in 1994, so it seems reasonable to assume that in 1990 industrial output expected for the foreseeable future was about this amount. This gives us an equilibrium capital stock of M&E of about 1400 billion zloty. The equilibrium level of investment can also be thought of as given by:

(3) $I = \lambda(K^* - K') + \delta K'$

where λ is the proportion of the difference between K^* and K' which is eliminated each year, K' is the true value of the capital stock and K^* is the equilibrium capital stock given by

(4) $K^* = \upsilon Y^*$

where Y^* is the equilibrium (expected) level of output.

By rearranging (3) we get:

(3') $I = \lambda K^* + (\delta - \lambda)K'$

and

(3") $K' = (I - \lambda K^*)/(\delta - \lambda)$

We then get the following values for K', given the historical I (327 billion zloty) and K* estimated at 1400 billion zloty:

	$\delta = 0.1$	$\delta = 0.2$
$\lambda = 0.33$	574	1015
$\lambda = 0.25$	133	400

Given that the historical amount of capital (in M&E in industry at 1984 prices) in 1989 was 1896 billion zloty, the amount of this capital which needed to be written down in 1990 can be calculated to have been as follows:

	$\delta = 0.1$	$\delta = 0.2$
$\lambda = 0.33$	70%	48%
$\lambda = 0.25$	93%	79%

If $\lambda = 0.33$, then there is no write down of M&E capital in industry only if $\delta = 0.26$; and if $\lambda = 0.25$ then the same result occurs if $\delta = 0.24$. However, since it seems very improbable that δ should be any larger than 0.20, or even less that λ should be any larger than 0.33, we can suppose that the amount of machinery and equipment which needed to be written down in 1990 is unlikely to have been much less than about half.

Notes

[1] I am grateful to Peter Boone for pointing this out to me.

[2] In the first year this could have been because the fall in output was unexpected, but it is improbable that this could have been the case in subsequent years.

[3] Data from 1930 was available for Japan, but that country experienced no fall in national income.

[4] Data on real GFCF and GFCF-E are not available.

[5] This is based on the estimate by Svennilson (1954), Table 71, p.229. Real GFCF is unavailable for Germany.

[6] "Industry" in Poland consists of the usual manufacturing two digit sectors plus extractive industry, which accounts for less than 5 per cent of the whole.

[7] Mario Blejer has suggested that investment may have fallen somewhat more in these two sectors because they are non-tradeables, and thus did not have the opportunity (as well as the necessity) of entering new markets, which faced industrial producers. The increase in investment in commerce, also a non-tradeable, resulted from the severe repression it had been subject to before the Balcerowicz plan.

References

Bell, J. and Rostowski, J., 1995, "A Note on the Confirmation of Podkaminer's Hypothesis in Post-Liberalization Poland", *Europe-Asia Studies*, Vol. 47. No.3., pp. 527-30.

Bhaduri, A. and Laski, K., 1993, "The Relevance of Michael Kalecki Today", Vienna Institute for Comparative Economic Studies, Vienna, [mimeo].

Borensztein, E., Demekas, D. and Ostry, J., 1993, "An Empirical Analysis of the Output Declines in Three Eastern European Countries", *IMF Staff Papers*, Vol. 40., No. 1., March, Washington D.C.

Borensztein, E. and Ostry, J., 1992, "Structural and Macroeconomic Determinants of the Output Decline in Poland", *International Monetary Fund*, WP/92/86, Washington D.C.

Calvo, G. and Coricelli, F., 1992, "Stabilization in Poland", *Economic Policy*, April, pp. 175-225.

Gomulka, S., 1994, "Economic and Political Constraints During Transition", *Europe-Asia Studies*, Vol. 46, No. 1, pp. 89-105.

Grosfeld, I. and Roland, G., 1995, "Defensive and Strategic Restructuring in Central European Enterprises", [mimeo].

Kolodko, G., 1992, "From Output Collapse to Sustainable Growth in Transition Economies: the Fiscal Implications", *IMF Fiscal Affairs Dept. Working Paper*, December.

Liesner, T., 1989, "One Hundred Years of Economic Statistics", *Economist Publications*, London.

Rostowski, J., 1993, "The Implications of Rapid Private Sector Growth in Poland", Centre for Economic Performance, London School of Economics, Discussion Paper No. 159.

Svennilson, I., 1954, *Growth and Stagnation in the European Economy,* United Nations Economic Commission for Europe, Geneva, p.309.

2

Restructuring outcomes and the evolution of ownership patterns in Central and Eastern Europe

Philippe Aghion and Wendy Carlin

1. Introduction

In the early stages of the transition in Central and Eastern Europe, observers were surprised at the extent to which managers of state-owned enterprises responded to changes in the external environment. The context of a deep recession, price liberalisation, the cutting off of government subsidies and the need to sell output under competition threatened survival and produced market-oriented responses. Changes in ownership were not necessary to elicit changes in behaviour. Although in general, privatisation of enterprises seemed to have only limited explanatory power in differentiating the behaviour or performances of firms, there was one class of privatised firms that was different: former state-owned enterprises with a foreign owner. Foreign-owned privatised enterprises typically displayed a deeper form of restructuring, engaging in major investment projects and in the strategic reorganisation and reorientation of the firm. Foreign ownership meant there was an active owner for the firm with the resources to finance restructuring and to provide management expertise.

Since foreign ownership is bound to provide the route to deep restructuring for only a fraction of enterprises, a key question facing analysts of the transition is through what mechanism this second stage of restructuring — which is typically assumed to require both financial resources and managerial expertise — will come about for the majority of former state-owned firms. For some proportion of firms, incumbent managers will turn out to be competent and with the macroeconomic recovery of the economy, improved levels of capacity utilisation will allow the firm to generate the internal funds necessary to finance restructuring. In such cases, the initial post-privatisation ownership structure may still not matter very much. However, to rely on such a mechanism is to ignore a series of potentially important factors. For example, even in the case of a competent manager able to finance

The authors are grateful to participants at the OECD/CCET colloquium "Economic Transformation and Development of Central and Eastern Europe: What Lessons from the 1990s?", for their helpful comments.

restructuring, if the firm is majority owned by employees, the employees may sack the manager and thwart restructuring if it entails considerable job losses and the cost of job loss is high. Even more obvious is the failure of this mechanism to provide a solution in the case of an incompetent manager.

In general, therefore, it is necessary to consider how the immediate post-privatisation ownership and control structure impinges on the likelihood that deep restructuring will take place in the enterprise. The types of ownership which have emerged from privatisation can, at a first level, be differentiated according to whether insiders in the firm (employees or managers) have become the majority owners or whether outside owners dominate. In turn, outside ownership can be dispersed — in which case there is no dominant owner — or concentrated. Concentrated outside owners can be either financial institutions (e.g. investment funds or banks) or non-financial institutions (e.g. a company or a family or individual). The ownership form with the greatest distance from the state-owned enterprise is the case of concentrated outside ownership by a non-financial foreign company.

Firms owned by insiders will typically find it difficult to raise external finance for investment and there are obvious obstacles to the replacement of poor managers. A firm with dispersed outside ownership leaves the manager in control and hence encounters similar problems. However, there is a crucial difference: if insiders own the company, they can, in principle, prevent its sale to an owner able to instigate restructuring. In an outsider-owned firm with dispersed shareholders, the way is at least open for a new owner to build up a sufficient stake to take control of the firm. To the extent that outside participation in the firm is required for either finance or new management or both, it is important to know what determines the decision by insiders to sell their shares, and whether employees and manager owners are different in this respect.

Widespread deep restructuring has not been observed in any transition economy yet. This is not surprising when we consider that the ownership structures that have emerged from the variety of privatisation programmes have not produced concentrated ownership in the hands of outsiders able to finance growth and supply good management if needed.[1] Moreover, the severe transformational recession that has characterised each country until recently will have hampered competent managers from engaging in deep restructuring financed from internal sources.

The prevalence of insider-ownership is specific to the political conditions of the transition: the *de facto* control of enterprises by insiders meant that privatisation itself was only possible when control was legitimised through insider ownership. Russian privatisation policy epitomises the view that the opportunity to remove the state from ownership of enterprises had to be taken irrespective of the consequences for the *initial* post-privatisation structure of ownership. An explicit objective of the designers of the insider-privatisation programme in Russia was to use it as the route through which outside ownership could come about.

The exceptional case of the Czech Republic where outsider-ownership is dominant has also produced a specific form: ownership by financial institutions — the investment funds. It is immediately clear that the spectrum of initial private ownership structures for large companies emerging in the transition economies fits neither of the two broad patterns observed in the advanced economies: the Anglo-

American pattern where dispersed outside ownership is typical; and the Continental-Japanese pattern where concentrated outside ownership by non-financial institutions (Germany) or banks (Japan) is common. The rarity of insider ownership of large enterprises in capitalist economies underlies the interest in the stability of the initial ownership structures in the transition economies.

To sum up, observation of restructuring and privatisation in early transition suggests two robust findings: (i) a hard budget constraint leads insiders (managers and employees) to engage actively in survival-oriented adjustment and (ii) foreign owners of former state-owned firms do other kinds of things. By bringing both management-expertise and capital to the firm, they are able to engage in deep restructuring. Second, the observation of the initial ownership structures emerging from privatisation suggests that foreign ownership is too sparse to be relied on to drive deep restructuring in these economies. These two sets of observations provide the motivation for the core of this paper which is to explore the relationship between initial ownership and deep restructuring.

Section 2 looks first at the evidence of the impact of hard budget constraints on survival-oriented restructuring and then at differences in restructuring behaviour between insider and outsider-owned firms. In Section 3, we turn to the issue of the transfer of ownership and control in privatised enterprises. For example, in Russia, is it the case in insider-owned firms where there is an outside blockholder (holding at least a 5 per cent stake), that changes in governance are more marked than in insider-owned firms without such an outside blockholder? Similarly, in the Czech Republic, we look for signs of concentration of ownership stakes and the exercise of corporate governance by outside owners. The model of Aghion and Blanchard (1996) is used to analyse the transfer of ownership from insiders to outsiders and the potential obstacles to such share sales. Section 4 concludes by identifying implications for the design of privatisation policy of the results on deep restructuring.

2. Evidence on ownership and restructuring: a preliminary survey

2.1 Ownership structure in the Visegrad countries and Russia

The clearest available description of initial ownership structures in transition economies comes from the World Bank (1996). The diversity of privatisation methods is reflected in sharp cross-country differences in the balance between insider and outsider-owned firms (Table 1). In Poland, a majority of firms of the former state-owned sector are still in the hands of the state: apart from the state, insiders clearly dominate as owners. In Poland, three-quarters of the nearly 2 000 SOEs privatised through the most common method of so-called 'liquidation-leasing' are insider-owned (Earle and Estrin, 1996). The majority of shares in the *de novo* firms surveyed were owned by outsiders.[2] Most similar to Poland in ownership structure is Russia: privatisation has been much faster but outsiders have as little weight as owners as they do in Poland.

In both Hungary and the Czech Republic, about 40 per cent of medium and large enterprises (by value) are still in state ownership. In Hungary, privatisation by sale has resulted in outside ownership for another 40 per cent, whereas in the Czech Republic, voucher privatisation resulted in investment funds and individual voucher holders owning about half of the medium and large enterprises (by value). The negligible role of insider ownership in the Czech Republic is highlighted by the fact that only three of the nearly 1 500 Czech and Slovak firms privatised in the first wave of voucher privatisation were majority owned by insiders; insiders held, on average, less than 5 per cent of shares of firms privatised in the first wave.

Table 1. Methods of privatisation for medium-sized and large state-owned enterprises, Czech Republic, Hungary, Russia and Poland (% of total, as of end 1995).

	Sale to outside owner	Management-employee buy-out	Equal access voucher privatisation	Restitution	Other[1]	Still in state hands
Poland						
by number[2]	2	30	6	0	8	54
Russia[3]						
by number	0	55	11	0	0	34
Hungary						
by number	38	7	0	0	33	22
by value[4]	40	2	0	4	12	42
Czech Republic						
by number	32	0	22[3]	9	28	10
by value	5	0	50	2	3	40
Estonia[5]						
by value	60	12	3	10	0	15

Notes: 1) Refers to transfers to local authorities and social insurance organisations, debt-equity swaps, sales through insolvency proceedings; 2) Number of privatised firms as a share of all former state-owned enterprises, including parts of firms restructured prior to privatisation; 3) Includes assets sold for cash as part of voucher privatisation (though June 1994); 4) Value of firms privatised as a share of the value of all former state-owned enterprises. (For Poland and Russia, data by number only are available); 5) Does not include some infrastructure firms. MBOs were by competitive tender.
Source: World Bank *World Development Report* 1996, Table 3.2, p. 3.13.

Table 2. Summary of restructuring outcomes.

	Reactive restructuring	**Deep restructuring**
Czech Republic	Observed in all types of company	Highest foreign-owned firms
Hungary	Observed in all types of company with privatised firms becoming less like state owned firms over time	Higher in foreign-owned and *de novo* firms. Lower in insider and state-owned firms
Poland	Observed in all types of firms	Higher in foreign-owned and de novo firms, uneven in domestic outsider- and insider-owned firms
Russia	Employment adjustment is higher in privatised firms than in SOE; otherwise no difference across types of firms	Little deep restructuring across all types of firms

Exceptional is Estonia where a privatisation process modelled on the East German one has left the state owning only 15 per cent of enterprises and outside investors with 60 per cent (by value).

Table 2 summarises the broad patterns of reactive and deep restructuring by ownership type in the Czech Republic, Hungary, Poland and Russia. The evidence available suggests that: (i) *reactive restructuring* (that is, the labour-shedding, wage reductions, plant closures and the spinning off of social assets brought about by the hardening of firms' budget constraints) has taken place in *all* ownership types *including in state-owned and insider-controlled firms;* (ii) *deep restructuring* (involving substantial new investments and changes in technology and/or management structures) appears to be *stronger in majority foreign-owned firms.* Majority foreign-owned firms also exhibit significantly higher labour productivity growth and sales growth.

Let us first review the evidence and then attempt to explain (or 'rationalise') reactive and deep restructuring outcomes as a function of the ownership type.

2.2 Hard budget constraints, ownership type and reactive restructuring

An extensive survey of the case study evidence on enterprise restructuring, covering enterprises in Poland, the Czech Republic, Hungary and Russia between 1991 and early 1993, showed that in early transition the threat to the survival of enterprises prompted managers across a wide range of firms to initiate reactive restructuring (Carlin,Van Reenen and Wolfe, 1994). Examples of passivity were generally confined to those enterprises which through good luck had brought with them into the reform period a cushion of reserves or a position of market power. There is no equivalent survey for the period since then, but a number of more systematic country studies suggest that the findings of the Carlin-Van Reenen-Wolfe survey are quite reliable. Pinto and van Wijnbergen (1995) present a particularly rosy picture of adjustment prompted by hard budget constraints: 'a survey of [Polish] SOEs conducted over the period 1990-1993 shows adjustment patterns and management behaviour remarkably in line with what one would expect from profit oriented forward looking entrepreneurs.'

There is some evidence from both Russia and Hungary that privatisation boosts reactive restructuring. Using a sample of Russian firms (321), which is representative of industrial enterprises, Earle and Estrin (1995) provide some systematic evidence on reactive restructuring. They regress a measure of real output per employee in 1994 on the initial level of output per head (1990) and a series of ownership and product market competition variables. They find that the private ownership variable (per cent shares owned privately) has a positive impact on productivity. In conjunction with their results for the lay-off rate, this suggests that privatised firms have adjusted employment more closely to the drop in output than have state-owned companies. The inclusion of the initial level of productivity (which is always highly significant) helps to control for persistence and hence, to identify the extra contribution of private ownership to productivity.[3]

An innovative empirical study (Köllõ, 1995) provides evidence on reactive restructuring from a large panel of Hungarian firms (1 340) which operated throughout the period from 1990 to 1994. In state-owned firms, he finds evidence of a high response of employment to the decline in output in 1991, as managers sought to contain losses: there was a very marked bunching of firms around the zero profit mark. Job losers were predominantly 'marginal' workers — blue and white collar workers with low skills — and state-sector firms virtually ceased to hire. Köllõ finds that survival-oriented adjustment of employment does not differ according to whether firms remained in the state sector, were co-operatives or were privatised. However, *private* firms (as compared to *privatised* ones and SOEs) were clearly different and a comparison of employment dynamics between private firms and the rest suggests that labour-hoarding was still present in non-private firms in 1994.

When looking at the responsiveness of employment to sales over time for each ownership group separately, it becomes clear that from 1993 on, privatised firms shift from looking like co-operative or state firms to looking more like private firms: the responsiveness of employment to changes in sales increases markedly (Köllõ, 1995, Table 6). Nevertheless, as Köllõ points out, in spite of the fact that it was better-performing state firms that were privatised, they were characterised in 1993-4 by poor sales, weak investment and even higher levels of under-utilised capacity than were characteristic of the state firms (see Table 3).

Table 3. Initial conditions and restructuring indicators: Hungarian firms 1990-1994.[1]

	State-owned firm in 1990		***Private* in 1990**
	remained state-owned firm	***privatised* 92-94**	
INITIAL CONDITIONS; SIZE OF REFORM STOCK			
Profit rate 1990 (%)	3.5	5.7	12.9
Profit rate 1991 (%)	-1.8	1.2	9.0
Nominal sales 91 (1990=100)	106.5	129.9	163.1
Ave wage 91 (1990=100)	117.0	130.3	130.8
Employment 91 (1990=100)	80.9	89.7	102.9
PERFORMANCE & RESTRUCTURING INDICATORS, 1993-94			
Real sales 93 (1992=100)	98.7	101.6	105.0
Real sales 94 (1993=100)	98.0	101.7	103.2
Investment in new capacity in 92-94 (% firms)	28.2	28.3	47.3
Under-utilised capacity in 1994 (% firms)	52.3	69.4	34.5
Employment 95 (1990=100)	41.0	43.0	89.4

Note: 1) Data refers to a large panel of Hungarian firms (1 340) which operated throughout the period from 1990-1994.
Source: Köllõ (1995) Tables 1, 6, 7.

That all ownership types have engaged to various degrees in reactive restructuring is a natural consequence of the hardening of firms' budget constraints. Interesting evidence on how the hardness of the budget constraint varies by ownership type is provided by Earle, Estrin and Leschenko (1995), who explore the Russian sample further, looking explicitly at the relationship between ownership and measures of government support. A clear result is that for worker-owned firms, the probability of gaining government support through subsidies or benefits was significantly lower than for state-owned firms (controlling for the level of support in 1992 and 1993 as well as for region and sector). It seems that the budget constraint, in this sense, was harder for worker-owned than for state-owned firms (or for other types of privatised firms). The finding that the sharpest difference was between state-owned and *worker*-owned firms was true for each of the experiments using different measures of 'closeness to the state'. In some, but not all cases, *de novo* firms were also more independent of the state than were state-owned ones.

The striking result in this study is that outsider-owned firms did not emerge as clearly 'depoliticised' in the Russian sample (Earle, Estrin and Leschenko, 1995, Tables 7, 8.1, 8.2, 8.3). Of course, it is as well to keep in mind that the survey was taken in 1994, within a year of the privatisation process. Nevertheless this result serves as a warning that a key priority in Russia must be to enforce hard budget constraints and to sever dependence on the state for all ownership types. The extent to which the hardening of firms' budget constraints in turn can be affected by the attitude of the government towards banks, has been analysed in recent works (Mitchell, 1993; Aghion, Bolton and Fries, 1996[4]).

The robust finding that considerable amounts of reactive restructuring are going on under state and worker ownership raises interesting questions. In particular, are state and worker owned firms cutting back employment to a greater extent than required to reduce losses to zero? Köllõ's study of Hungarian firms seeks to answer this question. His estimates suggest that adjustment beyond the zero profit mark has characterised the median pre-transition firm:[5] a state-owned firm that had adjusted to the initial reform shock and reduced profits to zero by the end of 1991, would have showed a further cut in employment by 20 per cent to the end of 1994 if it remained state-owned and by nearly 40 per cent if privatised (assuming unchanged output) (Köllõ, 1995).

One can think of several reasons why efficient labour shedding (beyond the zero-profit mark) would be more likely to take place in foreign-owned firms (or firms with concentrated outside ownership): first, the foreign owners' commitment to profit maximisation and their ability to exert authority over the restructuring process; second, the foreign owners' ability to compensate the losers and therefore to buy out the required consensus for reactive restructuring. So, how can one account for the high amount of reactive restructuring (i.e. of net employment and/or real wage reductions) in state and insider-owned firms? Several (complementary) answers come to mind:

1. Foreign-owned firms had both the incentives and the financial ability to attract and/or keep high-quality workers, which in turn can explain the lower amount of *net* employment reduction and also the tendency towards real wage *increases* in foreign-owned firms, the opposite being true for state and insider-owned firms.

2. As argued in recent work by Aghion and Tirole (1994) on the delegation of authority in organisations, it is sometimes the case that difficult decisions affecting employees such as restructuring a company, laying off workers or imposing discipline are more easily enforced when delegated to an incumbent manager who has already invested in relationship building with the firm's employees. For example, it has been argued by practitioners in charge of the restructuring and then privatisation of British Steel that the restructuring phase (which involved a considerable downsizing of British Steel's activities and workforce) would have been more difficult (if not impossible) to implement *post*-privatisation. One reason for this may simply be that by delegating decision rights to managers with objectives *a priori* more congruent with workers' interests than those of an outside owner, one can more easily (i.e. at a lower compensation cost) secure the workers' consensus and even participation

in the restructuring effort. On the other hand, even though a rational outside investor would be aware of the above effect and therefore might find it profitable to keep the incumbent manager in charge of (reactive) restructuring *even after* outside privatisation (provided the manager shows ability and has incentives to do the job), the fear of having the outside owner exert property rights and assume full control over the restructuring process at any time would adversely affect the employees' co-operation with restructuring. This, in turn, may provide a (limited) case for insider control in the early stage of enterprise reform.

3. Descriptive statistics showing, for example, that state-owned firms have cut employment by more than domestic outsider-owned ones (see, for example, Table 4 for survey data from Poland) almost certainly reflect selection bias. Firms privatised to outsiders in Poland's 'capital privatisation' programme underwent considerable pre-privatisation restructuring. Moreover the most promising enterprises were typically privatised first. The enterprises remaining in state hands would presumably be those where surplus workers and production units are in higher number and hence where the scope for reactive restructuring is greatest.

2.3 Comprehensive restructuring and outside ownership

However, restructuring has many dimensions, not only plant closings and lay-offs. Comprehensive restructuring actually requires expertise (about the nature of markets, of marketing, of product design, and so on). It requires, to an unexpected degree (at least to a degree which was largely unexpected pre-transition), new capital: not only is capital old, but much of it cannot be used, even with low labour costs, to produce goods which are competitive on the world market.

The only clear stylised fact on ownership and restructuring that emerged from the Carlin-Van Reenen-Wolfe survey was that foreign-owned firms were different from either SOEs or SOEs privatised to other kinds of owners. Foreign owners took clear control of the firm by placing their representatives on the boards and supplementing (or, less frequently, replacing) local managers with those from the parent company. They almost always engaged in a major investment programme. This result appears to be reproduced in subsequent studies. For example in a detailed study of 27 large Hungarian enterprises, interviews were conducted with 149 top managers between October 1993 and February 1994 and clear differences were found between state-owned and privatised firms only in the case of foreign ownership (Whitley and Czaban, 1996). Even for foreign-owned firms, they found relatively modest signs of deep restructuring. Foreign-owned firms were less constrained in their access to external funds for investment, had implemented more decisive changes in organisation and management, and in each case had closed down at least one non-core activity or unit (as compared with the Hungarian-controlled firms, where such closures had occurred in only two-thirds of the cases).

As privatisation proceeded, a number of investigators have sought to identify effects of ownership on restructuring in larger samples of enterprises, focusing in particular on the distinction between insider and outsider-owned firms. The results

Table 4. Indicators of enterprise restructuring and performance in Poland, 1993.

	Dominant ownership type				
	State	Insiders	Domestic outsiders	Foreign	*De novo*
Number of employees	548	273	132[1]	423[1]	68
Profit/sales (%)	-0.7	5.5	3.5[1]	-3.2[1]	2.6
Reactive restructuring					
Real wage (% change) 1992-93	-0.5	0.6	-3.8[1]	14.6[1]	-0.8
Employment (% change) 1992-93	-5.5	-0.7	0.8[1]	-5.5[1]	13.6
Sales (% change) 1992-93	5.0	12.5	10.0[1]	19.8[1]	30.0
Labour productivity (% change) 1992-93	14.4	28.2	2.4[1]	33.4[1]	28.1
Deep restructuring					
Investment/sales (%) 1993	1.2	2.8	0.0[1]	5.8[1]	2.6
Firms introducing major new technology (%)[2]	51.6	75.0	71.4[1]	87.5[1]	73.2

Note: Figures in the table are median values, which are used instead of averages because of 'extreme' values. 1) Computed on the basis of between five and ten firms; 2) Percentage of enterprises in each dominant ownership category reporting major investment in new technology within the last two years.
Source: EBRD (1995) Table 8.8, p.134.

of these studies are inconclusive: with the exception of foreign-owned firms, there is no clear empirical evidence that distinguishes between the restructuring actions or the behaviour or performance of insider and outsider privatised firms.[6]

In the studies to date, one therefore finds at the micro level of comparisons between ownership types within an economy the same lack of clear differentiation as arises from comparisons at the macro level between the performance of the enterprise sector as a whole across the Visegrad countries, with their very different mixes of state-owned, outsider- and insider-owned firms.

In the Czech Republic, the problems of inside ownership — in terms of the entrenchment of incompetent managers and the lack of access to finance for investment — are, at least in principle, absent. Virtually all medium and large Czech firms are now outsider owned and most have outside blockholders (i.e. at least one non-state outsider owner with at least a 5 per cent stake). The Czech Republic has hurdled the phase of inside ownership and the way is open for the transfer of ownership and control to those who can make best use of the assets of the enterprises. Unfortunately there is no systematic evidence available yet on restructuring activities of outsider-owned Czech firms. In a detailed case study analysis of 10 enterprises in food processing and textiles, (Capek and Mertlik, 1996) only find signs of deep restructuring in the foreign-owned firm in their sample; the other firm acting in a clearly forward-looking manner was the management buy-out case.

In part the lack of clear differentiation of restructuring behaviour in the Czech case must be due to the fact that although outside ownership has been established, dispersed outside ownership does not necessarily lead to control of the managers, and thus to restructuring. It takes time for concentrated owners to emerge who can exert effective control over the enterprises. Enterprises often remain in a state of limbo with respect to their future orientation as they wait for the second round consolidation of shareholding to take place (see the cases described by Capek and Mertlik for examples of this).

Although domestic outside ownership in the Czech Republic has yet to produce deep restructuring, there are signs that investors in the first wave of privatisation viewed concentrated ownership favourably, i.e. as a signal that improved governance would take place. Van Wijnbergen and Marcincin focus on the Czech firms privatised in the first wave and find encouraging evidence that the presence of a dominant investor (foreign or domestic) or a high share of the stock owned by investment funds boosted share prices between the privatisation rounds and also raised share prices on the stock exchange after privatisation was complete. They are able to reject the hypothesis that the share price effect during the privatisation process could reflect insider information on the part of the dominant investors: although dominant investors bought early, they paid above the eventual market price (van Wijnbergen and Marcincin, 1995). Their interpretation of the results is therefore that the positive effect of concentrated ownership (by funds, as well as by dominant domestic or foreign investors) on share prices was a signal that market participants believed that concentrated ownership would bring improved corporate governance.[7]

The significance of investment funds as blockholders in the Czech Republic focuses attention on: (i) the ability of the funds to provide corporate governance, which in turn relates to the ability of different investment fund shareholders to act in concert or to consolidate holdings; and (ii) the emergence of core investors that purchase shares from individual share holders or from the funds. Unfortunately, there appears to be very little systematic evidence on these issues as yet. Coffee (1996) identifies three problematic features of the Czech ownership and control structure: (i) the securities market is neither transparent nor liquid (which rules out, at least in the short run, the operation of the stock exchange as a direct mechanism of corporate governance), in this respect, the Czech stock market is clearly inferior to the Polish; (ii) there is a strange system of cross-ownership between the main banks (which appears to insulate financial institutions from outside challenge), and the governance structure of the bank-related investment funds is obscure; (iii) the state still holds a 'potentially decisive' swing block of shares in the largest enterprises and banks.

Coffee's anecdotal evidence suggests that there is an important difference between the large 'independent' investment funds and those affiliated with Czech banks. Bank-affiliated funds appear to be influenced by the banks' desire to consolidate their customer base, rather than to promote active restructuring of firms in the portfolio of their funds. The major bank-related investment funds have established portfolios with much larger numbers of firms than have the large independent funds.[8] This variation in the concentration of holdings is reflected in board representation. The independent fund, Harvard Capital and Consulting (HC&C) sees itself as having a strong supervisory role in two-thirds of the companies in which it has a stake and appears to employ people to take the board positions with this objective in mind; by contrast, the investment company of the savings bank uses relatively junior employees to sit on boards and does not expect them to engage in independent monitoring of its portfolio firms. Coffee presents a summary of the views of managers and directors which points to a lack of expertise on the part of some directors (especially those from bank-related funds) about how to improve the operation of the company. Boards have apparently been willing to fire managers "but some view it more as an indication of the board's inability to take any alternative step in response to continued unprofitability".

The anecdotal evidence reported by Coffee accords with the case study results of Capek and Mertlik in suggesting that the restructuring underway in Czech firms in the initial post-privatisation period was survival-oriented adjustment that was forced on firms by the weak state of demand for output. It does not seem to have been related to the behaviour of the outside owners of the firms. Both studies confirm that comprehensive restructuring is stalled in some voucher privatised firms because of ownership uncertainty. This is expressed as a 'limbo-like' transitional stage (Coffee, 1996) and the continuation into the post-privatisation period of the 'pre-privatisation agony' (Capek and Mertlik, 1996). It is suggested that investment funds are not seen as the 'final' or 'true' owners because of their lack of access to finance for restructuring and inadequate expertise. The so-called 'third-wave' of feverish acquisition activity in 1995-96 may accomplish this.

Why might outside ownership be a necessary condition for deep restructuring? We believe that the main reason is not that the objective function of insiders is fundamentally different from those of outsiders (except for the wedges coming from imperfections in credit and labour markets discussed below). The main reason appears to be the inability of firms to raise the required amount of capital and to pay for expertise under inside ownership.

It is difficult under inside ownership to protect outside minority interests and thus to raise minority equity capital. Access to debt finance is an imperfect substitute, and is also limited.[9] Finally, expertise, which is needed for restructuring, is too expensive to buy, and for the same reason as above, experts cannot be rewarded with minority equity positions.

2.4 Political constraints and insider privatisation

A major challenge for policy-makers in Eastern Europe and the former Soviet Union is thus one of designing (mass) privatisation schemes that would:

- be politically feasible *ex ante*;
- facilitate reactive and deep restructuring *ex post.*

Whilst *deep* restructuring seems to require *concentrated outside* ownership, *ex ante political constraints*[10] make this exercise difficult.

An obvious counter-example to the latter proposition is that of the Czech Republic where voucher privatisation has led to outsider ownership. Another is that of Estonia, where direct sales to outsiders appear to have played a major role (see Table 1).[11]

But outsider privatisation appears to be more the exception than the rule. In most other countries, privatisation has in effect privileged insiders. This is true of Russia where, despite the description of privatisation as voucher privatisation, insiders are majority owners in most firms. It is also true in most of the CIS countries, and in the countries which were formerly members of Yugoslavia. In the Slovak Republic, the second wave of voucher privatisation has been halted to be replaced by privatisation plans more favourable to insiders. Enterprises are sold as management buy-outs in which the buy-out team pays in instalments over ten years and is required to meet profitability targets and investment commitments. In Poland, 'mass privatisation', a voucher privatisation programme with a limited stake for insiders, remained on the shelf until this year, and covers only 500 firms; the dominant method has been insider privatisation.

These evolutions are not hard to explain. The assumption made by many at the beginning of transition that state firms were controlled by the state, to be disposed of as the state wanted, was simply incorrect. Once central planning had disappeared and the power of ministries had been reduced, state firms were in fact controlled by insiders, who could largely block or sabotage outsider privatisation, either at the level of the firm or, more conventionally, at the political level. Except for those state firms with the worst prospects in the absence of restructuring, strict outsider privatisation, with its risk of lay-offs and unemployment, is an unattractive option for insiders.

But then, the question becomes how best to design privatisation so as to go from insider privatisation (imposed by political constraints) to outsider ownership (required for comprehensive restructuring). In other words, the way to think about alternative initial insider ownership structures is as alternative transition devices towards outsider ownership. This is the issue to which we now turn.

3. Resale to outsiders: the model of Aghion-Blanchard (1996)

3.1 Evidence on the transfer of ownership and control

One would expect transfers of ownership and control to be most visible where mass privatisation through vouchers occurred — i.e. in the Czech Republic and Russia. In Poland and Hungary with a lower pace and more deliberate style of privatisation, the initial ownership pattern seems more firmly entrenched. In Russia, the question is whether outsiders are beginning to play some part in ownership and control given the predominantly insider character of the privatisation programme.

Fortunately, the systematic analysis of the evolution of ownership and control of Russian privatised enterprises is being undertaken and provides important early insights into the consequences of the mass privatisation programme (Blasi and Shleifer, 1996). The Blasi team revisited enterprises a year after privatisation just after a Presidential Decree came into force requiring firms owned by insiders to have a majority of outsiders on their boards. A tiny handful of firms had implemented the Decree and these firms were found to have very large outsider stakes. More interestingly, in spite of the general failure of firms to implement the Decree, the majority had already some outsiders on the board or were about to appoint them. Closer inspection revealed that in about 44 per cent of firms, outsiders other than former employees or representatives from closely connected firms were to be found. This marked a clear increase in the role of outsiders from 1993 to 1994. It was found that it was firms with large average outside blockholder stakes where outsiders had been appointed to the board — i.e. concentrated holdings of at least 5 per cent, rather than simply the outside ownership share as a whole appeared decisive. It seems likely that the Decree had some indirect effect in setting as a norm outsiders on boards and therefore prompting outside blockholders to press for representation.

Signs of increased outsider representation on boards between 1993 and 1994 were matched by increased outside ownership in this initial post-privatisation period. Between the first survey in 1993 and the third one in December 1994, the average stake of outsiders in the 79 per cent of firms in which there was any non-state ownership, had risen from 21.5 per cent to 29 per cent. In nearly 60 per cent of firms there were outside blockholders and their average stake was 17 per cent. The survey results suggest that concentrated holdings of shares by outsiders are emerging in Russia and that such block-holdings matter for corporate governance — as measured by board membership. Where there are blockholders, they appear to exert pressure on managers to provide them with a seat on the board. This is a sign that they both have leverage vis-à-vis managers and wish to use it to affect the running of the enterprise.

However, the scale of share sales should not be exaggerated (nor should it be forgotten that one fifth of firms surveyed had no non-state outside ownership at all). Blasi reports that the average percentage of shares sold by employees was 4 per cent and by voucher funds, 1 per cent. Outsiders dominated insiders as buyers by three to one (Blasi and Shleifer, 1996). From the survey evidence, it appears that managers seek to retain control of the enterprise through informal mechanisms of authority in the face of the high employee ownership stakes. The absence of anonymous voting at shareholders meetings is the most obvious of the tactics in use.

3.2 A simple model of resale

Consider the following benchmark model, drawn from Aghion and Blanchard (1996).

A representative firm employs and is initially owned by n workers. The product per worker is x in the absence of comprehensive restructuring, and $y > x$ if restructuring takes place in the firm.

Comprehensive restructuring in turn requires additional capital and expertise which only an outside investor can bring, provided he/she acquires a controlling majority of the firm's equity.

In addition to funding and expertise, restructuring also requires laying off and replacing a fraction λ of incumbent workers. For notational simplicity we shall assume that $\lambda = 1$.

Let R denote the reservation wage of workers, that is the wage equivalent of their being unemployed. Let w denote the post-restructuring wage (which we also take to be equal to the wage rate in the private sector). Efficiency wage considerations will always imply that $w > R$. Let $c = w - R$ denote the workers' cost of being unemployed.

We shall now analyse resale to outside investors under three alternative assumptions, namely: (i) the firm is worker-owned and workers act non-co-operatively when selling their shares; (ii) the firm is worker-owned and workers collude when bargaining with the outside buyer; (iii) the firm is majority-owned by its incumbent manager

(i) Resale conditions when workers act non-co-operatively

An outsider will buy the firm only if he gets a majority of the shares and thus can restructure (otherwise, as a minority shareholder, he would, under our assumptions, receive no profit, and thus the price he would be willing to pay would be equal to zero). Let q^b denote the maximum price an outsider is willing to pay for one share of the firm, conditional on buying a majority of shares: q^b is equal to the net profit per share, thus to the product per worker after restructuring minus the market wage:

$$q^b = y - w.$$

Let q^s denote the minimum price at which each worker is willing to sell his share. We assume that workers do not collude. That is, they individually decide whether to sell their shares, taking the actions of other workers as given. Then q^s satisfies:

$$q^s + R(y-w) + R..$$

Under the assumption that the outsider gets a majority of the shares and thus will restructure the firm, the left hand side gives what an individual worker gets if he sells his share: the sale price, plus the reservation wage (as the sale implies, under the assumption that $\lambda = 1$, that the worker loses his job and becomes unemployed). The right hand side gives what the worker gets if he holds on to his share: profit per share plus the reservation wage (as, again, he finds himself unemployed, whether or not he sells his share).

Putting the two equations together:

$$q^s = q^b = y - w.$$

This is nothing but the well-known free-rider effect of Grossman-Hart: dispersed shareholders (in this case worker-owners) extract all the surplus from restructuring. This, in turn, implies that if the outsider were to incur *any* additional take-over cost which he cannot recover, he would not acquire the firm.

As compelling as this theoretical argument is, it does not strike us as being of much relevance in the context of transition economies. In particular, outside investors can take advantage of the liquidity problems faced by a positive fraction of shareholders, which will lead them to sell at a lower price than q^s (see Bolton and Von Thadden, 1995); this is likely to be particularly relevant in countries in transition where most workers-shareholders have no access to credit and may value current cash q more highly than future cash. There is evidence that this effect is indeed important in Russia.

Outside investors may also be able to dilute part of the incumbent worker-shareholders' claims, so that workers, if they hold on to their shares receive only a fraction of $(y-w)$, and are thus willing to accept a lower selling price. This again is likely to be especially relevant in countries in transition, in which the room for illegal dilution is higher than in the West.

Thus, in the case where workers do not co-operate, resale is unlikely to be problematic.

(ii) Collusion among workers

We have so far assumed that workers do not collude in resale, that each worker decides individually whether to sell or not. What happens if they collude? Following Holmström and Nalebuff's (1992) discussion of the Grossman-Hart result, we would expect that the presence of large shareholders reduces the free rider problem and thus makes take-overs more likely to succeed. We would thus expect collusion to make resale more likely. In fact, the effect of collusion turns out to work perversely in the case of *worker*-shareholders and make resale *less* likely.

More formally, if the workers as a group decide to sell their shares, restructuring takes place and they get $R+q^s$. But if they decide not to sell, they prevent outsider privatisation and thus keep x, the product per worker in the absence of restructuring. Hence:

$$q^s = x - R$$

whereas, as before,

$$q^b = y - w.$$

Thus, resale takes place if and only if:

(1) $$q^b \geq q^s \leftrightarrow y - x \geq w - R = c$$

If the initial shareholders were not also workers in the firm, the condition for resale to take place would become $y - x \geq 0$. This condition would automatically hold, and resale would take place even if the outsider had to spend additional funds to acquire the firm (as long as these costs were less than $(y - x)$. This is the large shareholder effect pointed out by Holmström and Nalebuff.

But the shareholders here are also workers in the firm. And under collusion, they internalise the fact that they will find themselves unemployed if the firm is sold, and therefore want to be compensated accordingly. Thus, despite the fact that restructuring is socially desirable (under our assumptions, it leaves employment constant and increases output), if the cost of being unemployed, c, is larger than the net surplus generated by restructuring, $y - x$, the sale will not take place.

Thus, when shareholders are also the workers in the firm, and when they collude in the resale process, the fear of unemployment may become a major obstacle to resale to outsiders.

More generally, when $\lambda \neq 1$, the resale condition can be shown to be:

$$y - x \geq \lambda c.$$

Therefore the bigger the probability of becoming unemployed, λ, under outsider privatisation, and/or the bigger the cost c of becoming unemployed, the less likely is resale and thus comprehensive restructuring.

In turn, the effect of aggregate unemployment on the resale condition under collusion depends on how the cost of becoming unemployed $c = w - R$ depends on aggregate unemployment. In some efficiency wage models, c is independent of labour market conditions: w and R both vary inversely with unemployment, but their difference remains constant.[12] If this is the case, then unemployment will have no effect on whether condition (1) is satisfied.

However, the idea that higher disutility from unemployment is exactly offset by the higher utility from becoming a shareholder in a firm which makes higher profits does not sound robust. And indeed, it is easy to think of realistic modifications of the original model which deliver the implication that higher unemployment will make resale less likely.

Consider for example the case where the outcome of restructuring, y, is uncertain, say equal to $x+\underline{z}$ with probability 1/2 and to $x+\overline{z}$ with probability 1/2.[13] Assume further that $x+\underline{z} - w < 0$, so that the firm closes if the outcome of restructuring is unfavourable (assume $\overline{z}$ to be large enough that restructuring is still socially optimal).

Then the expected net profit of an outsider, assuming limited liability,[14] is given by $1/2(x+\overline{z} - w)$ so that the maximum price that an outsider will pay for the firm is:

$$q^b = \frac{1}{2}\,(x+\overline{z} - w)$$

The condition for resale under collusion thus becomes:

$$\frac{1}{2}(x+\overline{z} - w) \geq x - R$$

or equivalently:

(2) $$\overline{z} - x \geq c - R$$

In contrast to (2), this latter condition depends on R and depends therefore on the unemployment rate. The reason is that the effect of unemployment on R is now stronger than the indirect effect of lower wages on expected profit.[15] Thus, under plausible assumptions, more depressed labour markets make outsider privatisation less likely.

(iii) Manager ownership

Let's now turn to resale when managers receive a large ownership share in insider privatisation.

We first need to describe what happens to managers under restructuring. Assume the state firm has one manager and the probability that he does not remain in the firm after restructuring is equal to π.[16] And, suppose that the manager holds a majority $m > n/2$ of shares as a result of the initial insider-privatisation.

Let B be the benefits of control, or more formally the difference between the manager's income when managing the firm, and his income equivalent of becoming unemployed. Following the same steps as before, resale will take place if and only if.

$$m(y - x) \geq \pi B$$

or, equivalently:

(3) $$y - x \geq \frac{\pi B}{m}$$

A comparison between (1) and (3) yields the following interesting conclusions:

1. If the private cost and/or probability of the manager losing control is not too high (so that $\frac{\pi B}{m} < \min\,(c, y - x)$) then, not only does majority ownership by the manager facilitate resale (compared to ownership by workers acting collusively), but also having the manager hold *all* the shares makes resale comparatively easier than if the manager holds $m < n$ shares. (This is a *scale*

affect: the more shares he holds, the less the manager needs to be compensated *per share*).

2. However, there are good reasons to believe that the private cost B and the probability π of managers losing control are high. In particular, being laid-off is likely to be a much more informative signal for a manager than for a worker (who may be laid-off because the plant he worked in is closed). This in turn implies that it may be much more difficult for a laid-off manager to find another job, thereby increasing B. When B and π are sufficiently large, resale will thus become less likely in the manager-ownership case.

Another consideration not captured by the above formalisation, is that the scope for collusion, which we have so far taken as given, is itself likely to increase with the importance of the shareholdings of managers. This also points towards giving shares to workers, not managers.

4. Conclusions

Three main conclusions for the design of privatisation programmes can be drawn from our review of the evidence and our discussion of the resale process:

1. **Insider privatisation should minimise the scope for collusion in resale**. In particular, the resale process should involve *anonymous* trading, and the registration of shares should not involve the firm's manager (or at least should take place *outside* the firm). Involving the firm in any way would make it easier for the manager to enforce collusive agreements among workers. By the same token, the creation of funds of workers' shares should be avoided.[17]

2. **Insider privatisation should favour workers' rather than managers' majority ownership**. This conclusion is always relevant when workers are not able to collude and remains relevant when workers do collude whenever the expected loss of private benefits to managers following outside privatisation is large compared to the expected unemployment cost for workers. This conclusion however ignores the pre-resale period, where more power to managers may well be desirable for reactive restructuring. Although whether managers need a large number of shares to be powerful within the firm is questionable. The experience of Russia suggests that managers control the firms even if, as is usually the case, they are minority shareholders.

3. **Subject to political constraints, as many shares as possible should be given or sold to outsiders at the initial privatisation stage**. Even if outside shareholders are small, as may be the case after a voucher programme, they do not have the wedge that insiders have in resale and thus will not prevent the emergence of concentrated outside ownership. Outside ownership is important for another reason, because it leads to the existence of a market for shares where insiders can sell their shares more easily, making anonymous selling easier, and thus making collusion harder.

The proposals in this paper aim to maximise the opportunities for the introduction of outside ownership and control into firms initially privatised to insiders. The key problems for which a transfer of ownership to outsiders can provide a solution are the entrenchment of poorly performing managers and inadequate access of inside-owned firms to finance for investment. This is not to deny that insider-owned firms with good managers may well evolve into dynamic companies in which comprehensive restructuring is financed by retentions. Internal funds would also enable the losers from reactive restructuring to be compensated and this, along with natural wastage, could well eliminate over-manning.

If internal funds prove inadequate, competent managers should, in principle, be able to raise equity finance through the sale of a majority stake to an outsider without losing their job. This would only be problematic where liquidity constraints on the part of worker-owners resulted in an under-valued sale. This is the danger of 'asset-stripping' in which an outsider, the 'first buyer', takes advantage of the liquidity constrained inside owners and breaks up the firm. A 'second buyer', unable to internalise the synergies realised by the first buyer, will find it too costly to reassemble the firm and will therefore offer too low a price for a second resale to take place: manager entrenchment results.

With the exception of the asset stripping case, good managers should survive an ownership transfer from insiders to outsiders. The main focus of the last two sections has been to examine how best to open up opportunities through which incompetent managers can be replaced. Where inside-ownership prevails, changes in control require changes in ownership.

In conclusion, it is important to signal that more systematic empirical research using panels of enterprises is essential if sound assessments are to be made about the pattern and speed of restructuring in the transition economies. Some of the studies referred to in this survey represent important contributions to this work. But more research is needed to identify the balance between ownership types in generating dynamism, as aggregate growth picks up across the region. This survey has noted some instances of what, from a theoretical perspective, are surprising results in terms of adjustment by insider-owned firms. These could turn out to be ephemeral or unrepresentative — or they could be indicating that insider-owned firms with good managers are of some quantitative significance in some countries. The variation in ownership types within and across countries provides rich possibilities for distinguishing between these hypotheses.

It is still too early to be sure of the structure of corporate governance that will emerge in the transition economics. In the Czech Republic's 'Third Wave', there are examples of the reconsolidation of firms which were split up prior to the voucher privatisation process into industrial holding companies. These are similar to those found in Germany and, indeed, to those in Czechoslovakia before the second World War. Yet it is in Slovakia and Poland that medium-sized firms are typically manager-owned and may come to resemble the German Mittelstand.

Poland therefore provides a particularly striking combination of Anglo-Saxon and Continental corporate governance structures. On the one hand, there is the large weight of insider-ownership and on the other, a highly liquid and transparent stock exchange onto which the investment funds will float restructured large companies. The investment funds may evolve either into industrial-financial groups on the

German model or fulfil a venture-capital role by providing access to equity finance to other companies as they sell restructured firms.

Notes

[1] The peculiar case of East Germany is an exception (Carlin and Mayer, 1995).

[2] A striking feature of the dynamic Polish *de novo* firm sector is the extent of outside ownership.

[3] Rather perplexingly, none of the variables included to try to capture the level of product market competition was ever significant in the productivity equation.

[4] These two papers focus on the effects of different recapitalisation policies on the banks' behaviour towards defaulting firms and thereby on the firms' budget constraints. A somewhat surprising result in Aghion, Bolton and Fries is that firms' budget constraints will tend to be softened, not only in the case where recapitalisation of banks by the government is full and unconditional, but also in the polar case where recapitalisation policies are too tough vis-à-vis banks, for example if recapitalisation entails the automatic replacement of banks managers. Indeed, whilst too soft recapitalisation policies may encourage bank managers to exaggerate the extent of their non-performing loans problem (e.g. by allowing firms to postpone the repayment of their debt), an excessively tough recapitalisation policy will induce banks managers to hide the magnitude of the bad loans problem, (e.g. by liquidating a smaller fraction of defaulting enterprises than would be efficient n the absence of informational asymmetries between banks and the government regarding the true proportion of non-performing loans). In either case, the firms' budget constraints will end up being too soft. This, in turn, provides some theoretical justification for 'middle-of-the-road' policies, e.g. conditional and/or partial bailouts, of the kind currently implemented in Poland.

[5] The median firm is defined by the attainment of zero profits by the end of 1991, the avoidance of bankruptcy and an inability to invest in 1992-1994.

[6] Data on Polish firms (Earle and Estrin, 1995) provide somewhat surprising results. In terms of deep restructuring, worker-owned firms rank second to *de novo* firms in the investment: income ratio and are more likely than any other class of firm to have engaged in a major investment. The data in Table 4 above come from the same survey. As would be expected, worker-owned firms are less likely than other firms to have shed social assets (Estrin and Earle 1996, Table 1.5). The result that the insider owned firms have apparently been willing and able to undertake major investments is surprising but not too much weight should be placed on it until it proves robust in larger samples and with more rigorous analysis. (The sample size in the Polish study is very small with information coming from only 13 employee-owned, 4 manager-owned, 154 outsider owned and 19 *de novo* enterprises, as well as 122 SOEs).

[7] The results from another study (by Claessens) suggest that it is the presence of a strategic investor as owner that raises share prices, not the existence of ownership concentration *per se*. Of firms privatised in the first wave, Claessens finds that: 'high absolute strategic ownership has a positive effect on prices but effective control, particularly by investments funds, does not have positive influence on price — actually a negative influence' (Claessens, 1994, p. 11, quoted Coffee, 1996, p. 142).

[8] For example, at one extreme is the investment company of the savings bank (Ceska Sporitelna) which has shares in 500 firms and at the other is Harvard Capital and Consulting with only 51 companies (Coffee, 1996, p. 151). Again, the contrast with the Polish investment funds, each with only 30 companies and with the personnel to undertake corporate restructuring, is striking.

[9] It is all the more difficult to use debt finance when insider privatisation, as in the case for example in Poland, takes the form of a discounted sale of the firm to insiders financed by long-term debt to the state, resulting in highly leveraged newly privatised firms.

[10] This includes, as we have discussed above, the need to secure a higher level of consensus for *reactive* restructuring.

[11] Whereas the Estonians moved directly from state ownership to concentrated outside ownership with a core investor, the Czech method entails a stage of ownership concentration subsequent to the initial allocation of ownership to outsiders. It is interesting that the achievement of effective corporate governance led to opposition to the Estonian government, whilst the Czech government has, uniquely, retained its popular mandate throughout the transition.

[12] In the shirking model of Shapiro and Stiglitz (1994), the difference between the value of being employed and the value of being unemployed does not depend on labour market conditions.

[13] $\bar{z}$ and $\underline{z}$ represent the additions to x associated with successful and unsuccessful restructuring, respectively.

[14] That is assuming that the actual *ex post* profit is equal to zero whenever x + z - w < 0, i.e. whenever $z = \underline{z}$.

[15] The same conclusion obtains in the initial model if workers own only a fraction α < 1 of shares in the firm. In that case, the firm will be resold to an outsider if and only if $w - R \leq y - x - \left(\frac{1-\alpha}{\alpha}\right)(x - R)$, which again depends on R and therefore on the unemployment rate in the same way as in (2).

[16] For example, the manager's ability may be known *ex ante*, but only learnt *ex post* through his restructuring performance, which is high with probability (1- π) and low with probability π.

[17] Originally conceived as an instrument whereby managers could 'group and dominate the employee vote', the funds of workers' shares (FARPs) operate in less than 5 per cent of the privatised firms surveyed by Blasi (1994). A main reason for this is that informal control by managers of their employee-shareholders has proved to be quite effective. In particular, voting at the shareholders' meetings is not confidential in 66 per cent of the firms surveyed by Blasi and therefore employees are being silenced by the fear of being laid-off if they vote against the firm's manager. Also, workers are encouraged to give proxies to middle-managers instructed by the top management. Finally, the management's control of the shareholders' meetings is not confidential in 66 per cent of the firms surveyed by Blasi and therefore employees are being silenced by the fear of being laid-off if they vote against the firm's manager. Also, workers are encouraged to give proxies to middle-managers instructed by the top management. Finally, the management's control of the shareholder register creates a managerial supervision of the employees' sales of shares to outsiders.

References

Aghion, P. and Blanchard, O., 1996, *On Privatisation Methods in Eastern Europe and their Implications*, EBRD, [mimeo].

Blanchard, O., 1996, *The Economics of Transition in Eastern Europe*, Clarendon Lectures, Oxford University Press, forthcoming.

Blasi, J. and Shleifer, A., 1996, *Corporate Governance in Russia: an Initial Look* in Frydman *et al.* (ed) (1996), Volume 2.

Bolton, P. and Von Thadden, E., 1995, *The Ownership of Firms: The Liquidity Control Trade-Off,* Ecare, Brussels, [mimeo].

Boycko, M., Shleifer, A. and Vishny. R., 1995, *Privatizing Russia*, MIT Press, Cambridge.

Capek. A. and Mertlik, P., 1996, *Organizational Change and Financial Restructuring in Czech Manufacturing Enterprises, 1990-1995*, Czech National Bank Institute of Economics [unpublished mimeo].

Carlin. W. and Mayer, C., 1995, *The Structure and Ownership of East German Enterprises',* Journal of the Japanese and International Economies, December.

Carlin, W., Van Reenen, J. and Wolfe, T., 1995, *Enterprise Restructuring in Early Transition: The Case Study Evidence* Economics of Transition, Vol. 3., No. 4 pp. 427-458 (a more detailed version was published as: *Enterprise Restructuring in the Transition: An Analytical Survey of the Case Study Evidence from Central and Eastern Europe,* EBRD, Working Paper No. 14, 1994).

Coffee, J.C., 1996, *Institutional Investors in Transitional Economies: Lessons from Czech Experience* in Frydman *et al.* (ed) (1996), Volume 1, esp. pp. 115, 153.

Earle, J.S. and Estrin, S., 1995, *Privatisation Versus Competition: Changing Enterprise Behavior in Russia*, Stanford University and London Business School, [unpublished mimeo].

Earle, J.S. and Estrin, S., 1996, *Employee Ownership in the Transition* in Frydman *et al.* (ed) (1996), Volume 2.

Earle, J.S., Estrin, S. and Leshchenko, L.L., 1995, *Ownership Structures, Patterns of Control and Enterprise Behavior in Russia.* Stanford University and London Business School, [unpublished mimeo].

Frydman, R., Gray, C.W. and Rapaczynski, A., 1996, ed., *Corporate Governance in Central Europe and Russia*, 2 volumes, Budapest: CEU Press & OUP.

Holmström, B. and Nalebuff, B., 1992, "To the Raider Goes the Surplus? A Reexamination of the Free Rider Problem", *Journal of Economics and Management Strategy* 1(1): 37-62.

Köllõ, J., 1995, *Short-Term Response of Employment to Sales in State-Owned and Private Firms in Hungary 1990-1994*, Institute of Economics, Hungarian Academy of Sciences, Budapest, [unpublished mimeo].

Pinto, B. and Van Wijnbergen, S., 1995, *Ownership and Corporate Control in Poland: Why State Firms Defied the Odds*, CEPR Discussion Paper No. 1273, esp. p. 14.

Shleifer, A. and Vasiliev D., 1996, "Management Ownership and Russian Privatisation" in Frydman *et al.* (ed) (1996), Volume 2.

Whitley, R. and Czaban, L., 1996, *Institutional Transformation and Enterprise Change in an Emergent Capitalist Economy: The Case of Hungary*, Manchester Business School, University of Manchester, [unpublished mimeo].

EBRD, 1995, *Transition Report*, London.

World Bank, 1996, *World Development Report*, Washington.

3

Corporate governance and the political effects of privatisation

Roman Frydman and Andrzej Rapaczynski

The limits of privatisation

In looking back at the experience of privatisation in the transition economies of Eastern Europe, it becomes evident that the early thinking concerning the very role of privatisation needs to be revisited. The assumption underlying much of that thinking was that firms in the state sector, presumably holding a large stock of valuable assets, would continue to play a key role in the future of post-communist economies. As a result, thorough reform of the state enterprise sector, of which privatisation was to be the core element, was a prerequisite of further economic growth.

In part, the truth of this assumption is still incontrovertible. The state sector's share of GDP was extremely high in all communist countries, including the most reformed ones, such as Hungary or Poland, and the legendary inefficiency of state enterprises, again including the "reformed" ones, had to be stopped. To what extent privatisation, in the ordinary sense of the word, had to be the primary, dominant component of such a policy, is, however, somewhat more problematic.

At the time, any doubts concerning privatisation seemed to presuppose that state enterprises could be run efficiently after all — not something many reformers were willing to entertain. But, of course, there could also be another reason against privatisation that only very few raised at the time,[1] namely that the state sector was essentially non-reformable, or its reform so costly that one had better begin elsewhere. This might very well have been the state of affairs in a number of countries which had been primarily agricultural before the communist take-over and in which industrialisation reflected most fully the dynamic of communist development.

It would take us too far afield to try to characterise this dynamic in detail. But the features of communist development we have in mind are, roughly, the following: (1) emphasis on heavy industry, often with primarily military significance; (2) location of industries according to political desiderata (agricultural areas in which transformation of a substantial portion of peasantry into new proletariat seemed desirable for political reasons, or areas in which party leaders, always eager to maximise the deployment of scarce resources in their fiefdoms, were politically powerful enough to succeed in attracting large projects); (3) no attention to natural economic advantages, such as proximity of raw materials, availability of skilled labour, etc.; (4) creation of vertically integrated, autarchic mammoth complexes with no competition for their products; (5) technological obsolescence; (6) emphasis on the quantity of output without regard to quality; (7) massive over-employment; (8) no attention to production costs; (9) political selection of managerial personnel and generally low level of competence; (10) when educational criteria were present at all, the prevalence of engineering rather than business education.

In light of these factors, it is somewhat misleading to describe the problem with East European economies as primarily one of state ownership — something that brings to mind the somewhat sluggish performance of Western utilities or state airlines, or even the patronage-ridden state-owned Italian conglomerates. What the decades of communist misallocation produced, especially in areas with little pre-existing industrial base, was a set of white elephants in the middle of nowhere, with whole cities and regions dependent on dysfunctionally huge industries with very low quality of capital stock and an organisational structure incapable of functioning in a normal economic environment.

Although this state of affairs is known *in abstracto*, it is rarely confronted in most discussions concerning privatisation. And yet, these factors, perhaps especially the low quality of capital stock, have very significant consequences.[2] The pain of transition is directly proportional to the amount of "creative destruction" that market forces are apt to inflict on the former state sector. The greater the proportion of firms without any reason for their existence under the new conditions, the less privatisation can do to soften the hard landing in a competitive environment. Under any regime, the essentially non-reformable, value-subtracting firms must be closed down if they are not to continue to drain the resources needed in other, more dynamic sectors of the economy. Whether or not to privatise such white elephants is therefore not a decision concerning their potential efficiency, but rather one concerning the relative *political costs of their closure* under the systems of private or public ownership.

Privatisation is often automatically assumed to decrease the politicisation of firm governance and to make subsidisation less likely. But this is by no means necessarily the case. The only time when the assumption clearly holds is when the assets to be privatised have potentially greater value when they are productively deployed on the market than when they are used to extract rents from the state. When, as by hypothesis here, the assets themselves have negative economic worth, there is no reason to believe that their private owners will pursue state handouts any less efficiently than state managers.

Privatisation of value subtracting firms thus makes sense only if the *political* effectiveness of new owners (who must also be expected to use their resources primarily for rent seeking) is for some reason expected to be less than that of the present management. This is likely to be true when the people now in control are already well organised and form an effective special interest constituency. Such is the case, for example, in many post-communist countries in which the old branch ministries, industrial associations, trusts etc. survived the change of the regime, and privatisation can potentially replace them with less well organised, more diffuse group of owners.

Whether such an operation is politically feasible, and how costly it is to execute, is another matter. In the absence of a promise of continuing subsidisation, it is unlikely that genuine owners can be found for the chronic losers in the state sector, except perhaps for their management and employees who have a heavy specific investment in their firms and a special stake in their survival. Since wages of the proletarian "vanguard" employed in large communist enterprises, especially in such sectors as mining, steel, armaments, or shipbuilding, were generally higher than average, these insiders can perhaps be persuaded to accept lower pay in exchange for a chance to try to preserve their jobs and positions. Employee ownership has been used in this way in advanced economies, and some have argued that it might be appropriate in transition countries as well (Earle and Estrin, 1996). But high wages in industry have already been eroded by inflation in most post-communist economies and the fundamental problem of value subtraction in many enterprises would persist even if labour costs were reduced to zero. If the proportion of such firms in the economy is not too high and the state is ready to withstand the political pressure of their bankruptcies, privatisation may perhaps be used to lessen that pressure somewhat and to assure that firms that can be turned around — something that is very difficult to predict as long as subsidies are available[3] — are in fact restructured. But in fact nearly all states in Eastern Europe have preferred to continue to keep their white elephants under state ownership and whatever shrinkage has occurred was due to a partial tightening of budget constraints. Although for some states this may have been a mistake, it is hard to say that states with a large proportion of value subtractors in their economies could have politically afforded their abrupt closure. And unless closure is seriously contemplated, privatisation is unlikely to be of much help.[4]

The goals of privatisation and the interests of the insiders

When a significant portion of the capital stock of an economy is of relatively high quality, privatisation may make sense from an *economic as well as political* point of view. But the two do not necessarily go together. The reason for this is that an effective privatisation strategy is likely to have an immediate negative impact on a number of powerful political constituencies.

Under the conditions of post-communist transition, the "victims" of well designed privatisation of most firms are the firm's employees and, most likely, the management as well. The first reason for this is well known: most communist firms were grossly overstaffed and badly mismanaged. In fact, "mismanaged" is probably not the right term; the very objectives of management under socialism were so different that it is not surprising that most managers often lacked the basic skills necessary to continue in their posts under the conditions of a market economy. But a further reason why insiders stand to lose from privatisation is that if privatisation is not viewed as a mere change of title, but as a restructuring of the incentives of firms and their employees, its primary effect is to impose a governance structure that makes the parties in control pursue the maximisation of share value as their primary objective. This in turn means that the ultimate control of firms must be transferred to parties whose primary incentives are to *defend the interests of capital.* These parties are very unlikely to be the corporate insiders who have a multitude of other interests in the firm, above all, their continued employment, which are likely to distort their behaviour.

Let us consider the case in which insiders become complete or controlling owners of the privatised enterprises.[5] That this, with rare exceptions, is not a good governance structure in the case of employee ownership is widely recognised. But the same is no less true of managerial ownership which is often supported by commentators on East European privatisation. First of all, managers are not likely (for political, if no other, reasons) to end up as 100 per cent owners. Under most insider privatisations in Eastern Europe, managers share their ownership with employees. It is often noted, sometimes with approval and sometimes with censure, that managers are usually firmly in control under this type of arrangement. But the price of this control may be very high. Unless the managers themselves can buy out the employees, they are usually interested in preserving employee ownership upon which their control depends, rather than allowing new outside owners (who can threaten the management) to come in. This means, however, that the main interest of the employees, i.e. prevention of major layoffs — the very thing that is often in the interest of the firm — is largely shared by the management.[6] Furthermore, the shared management-employee ownership, under the conditions prevailing in Eastern Europe, gives managers a strong incentive to siphon off assets to companies they or their families personally control — the very behaviour which characterised their actions, with devastating effect, in the last stages of communist reforms and the early transition period.[7] Although such managerial dishonesty may exist in all systems, the legal system in Eastern Europe is very inept at policing it and employees (like the state, although for different reasons) may be in a particularly weak position to defend their interests.

Even when the managerial share of ownership rises to higher levels, making managerial control independent from other parties, the governance situation does not necessarily improve. Again, those who extol the virtues of managerial ownership usually have in mind firms owned by their founder, whose skills are responsible for the firm's initial success, or other dynamic managers who, having proved their skill at managing, can obtain sufficient credit to "take private" the firms in which they work. But these are very different cases from those of most East European enterprises. Indeed, the situation of the proverbial second generation owner-manager, who lacks the father's skills and runs the firm to the ground, is more apt to be an appropriate parallel. For the average communist-trained manager is not very likely to change much upon becoming the owner. He has no other comparable employment opportunities and no sense of his own limitations. He is probably not very young and is rigid in his thinking. His attitude toward the new system is, on the whole, unfavourable, and he is unlikely to have the imagination, energy, or enthusiasm necessary to lead the firm in its difficult transition. But the new ownership structure simply entrenches him in control.

Finally, managerial ownership of large firms is probably generally not a good idea. The need for owners to diversify risk, as opposed to risk averseness of managers with both financial and specific human capital investment in the firm, the ease of access to capital, the need to prevent entrenchment and use the best available managerial expertise, increased specialisation, and a number of other factors have historically led to the rise of the modern corporation, with its division of ownership and management (see Fama and Jensen, 1983a; 1983b). There is no reason to believe that these factors are any less important in the case of large enterprises in Eastern Europe.[8]

A privatisation programme designed primarily to improve corporate governance of state sector firms, whether a give-away or some form of sale, will thus avoid conveying controlling equity interests to enterprise insiders. But by the same token, it will encounter serious political opposition, both because the insiders, enjoying *de facto* control at the beginning of the reforms in most countries, are likely to resist being dislodged, and because insider interests are among the best organised and most effective political constituencies. This is particularly true in those countries in which significant communist reforms had preceded the post-communist transition. One of the main features of these decentralising reforms was to confer more power on enterprise managers and workers and to allow them to develop a network of vertical and horizontal connections to other firms. Over time, these local forces formed a cohesive lobby designed to defend and expand their interests, which in time came to be treated as quasi-entitlements. Indeed, once these special constituencies had been allowed to form, any attempt to wrest from them the effective control over state enterprises has always turned out to be a task transcending the ability of East European governments. Hungary, after the failure of its centrally managed First Privatisation Programme,[9] succeeded in privatising mainly when managers were willing to go along, and that usually meant preserving their own hold over the firms. Poland, having missed the initial window of opportunity, ended up with its privatisation stalled by the opposition of a worker-manager alliance. Despite Romania's futile attempts at mass privatisation, the only privatised firms have resulted from management-employee buyouts (MEBOs). The price of rapid privatisation in Russia was the nearly complete insider control of all privatised firms. And so, in country after country, with the exception of the Czech Republic (where the communist reforms had not made headway), the story is the same.

Winners and losers in the politics of privatisation

There are two ways in which insiders can attempt to block a privatisation policy that promises to empower outsider interests. One is to create political difficulties for the reformers who attempt to introduce the new policy. The other is to impede implementation. Let us focus on politics.

The political difficulties faced by reformers seem to be a typical example of a dilemma facing a politician intent on providing a public good. Although nearly everyone is likely to benefit in the long run from the economic success of ownership reforms — since the improved efficiency of corporate governance will lead to higher growth, and most advances in life standards of the masses come from growth rather than redistribution — it is very difficult to "sell" this idea to a voting constituency. The benefits offered are to be enjoyed only in the future, and this future is, moreover, not very definite. People have difficulty thinking of these benefits as tangible and their future enjoyment in no way depends on one's having contributed to their achievement (by, for example, voting for the right party in the first place). Most importantly, except for very special circumstances, masses of people are extremely difficult and costly to mobilise. The opponents of the reform, on the other hand, are likely to be losers in the immediate future, their losses are very tangible (dismissals, loss of security, loss of control), and the class members are easily identifiable and already highly organised groups of individuals.

There are, however, two important qualifications to this picture. The first was already hinted at as the "very special circumstances" that allow masses of people to be politically mobilised. A paradigmatic case of such a situation is a regime change, when an old, despised system is rejected in favour of a new one, commonly believed to offer the hope of a better future. Even though that future may be somewhat remote, in the special historical moments we are dealing with the narrow political focus of most people is suspended and a broader, more public spirited attitude prevails.[10] This is the much spoken about "window of opportunity" for the post-communist reformers, which was used by the Poles to enact their ambitious macroeconomic reforms, but not a privatisation programme, and which the Czechs used to push through their unique mass privatisation. The same period, by contrast, was largely frittered away in Hungary in favour a more "gradualist" approach, and it was completely wasted in most post-Soviet and southern rim countries.

The other important qualification is that the goods to be delivered by structural reforms, such as privatisation, are not all "public goods". There are in fact very distinct special interests which stand to gain from the reforms — the new owners of privatised enterprises, for example, the owners of new businesses who are generally interested in the expansion of the market economy, young people whose prospects in life may be dramatically improved and who have no nostalgia for the stagnant security of the old regime, and generally those whose risk averseness does not dampen their entrepreneurial abilities. The problem is that these are largely *future* constituencies and it is very difficult to tap into them for political support at the time that the reforms are initiated. Many people simply do not know whether they will be winners or losers in the future and they may be risk averse in the early stages of the reform. Moreover, the interest groups in question grow and become organised only concurrently with the success of the reforms.

Together, these two qualifications define the choices of a reform strategy in the area of privatisation. The basic choice is one of balancing the support of the present against the future constituencies. If the initial window of opportunity is used to establish a stable reformist government and launch an imaginative privatisation strategy, reform politicians can hope to see it produce results that could bring tangible support in the future — perhaps as close as the next election.

Roughly, this seems to have been the strategy of the Czech (then still Czechoslovak) reformers. Their macroeconomic stabilization and liberalisation policies, despite strong free market rhetoric, were somewhat more cautious than the Polish ones, for example, and they produced somewhat less of a politically costly shock. (But there were also a number of other factors tending to decrease the negative public reaction to reform. Unemployment was concentrated in Slovakia and its negative political impact was eliminated after the "velvet divorce". Freedom from external debt and large foreign currency influx from tourism also helped the overall economic situation.) But where the Czechs excelled was in pushing through in record time the most extensive privatisation policy ever. Even more uniquely, the several Czech privatisation programmes did not give any special privileges to insiders. Neither managers nor employees could buy shares or assets at preferential prices, nor were managers even given a monopoly in preparing the "privatisation projects" that had to be submitted for each enterprise detailing the exact privatisation strategy (with any interested person free to submit a "competitive" project). Under these conditions, tens of thousands of stores were auctioned to the general public, creating a large class of new small business people, most often with no connection to old state institutions. A large restitution programme gave back thousands of buildings, factories, etc. to their pre-communist owners — a sure way of politically reinforcing a group that was likely to be unwavering in its support for reforms. And finally, large enterprises, including the most valuable Czech firms that could perhaps have been sold relatively easily and at high prices, were included in the mass privatisation programme which gave every participating citizen assets equal to several times his or her monthly income. The privatisation process also resulted in the creation of a large number of new financial institutions depending for their very existence on the continuation of the reform process. Together, in a Thatcher-like manoeuvre, a large portion of the population was given a vested interest in the success of a market economy firmly based on private property. And in a very tangible political way, the reform government of Premier Vaclav Klaus stands as the nearly certain winner in the next elections.

The Polish and Hungarian reform politicians, both living under Communist-dominated governments, and the Russians who soon may be, might point to many special features of the Czech situation, including the presence of very strong central government and no history of communist reforms allowing managerial and employee interests to organise. In the circumstances of their countries, it might be argued, only decisive compromises with insider interests could produce any privatisation at all.

It is difficult to know how to test the truth of such propositions and it may be better not to attempt to do so. What is somewhat more capable of an objective test is the proposition that a strategy banking on insiders produces neither a desirable corporate governance structure *nor* political support for reforms. The cases of Hungary and Russia provide the most striking examples.

Take Russia first. We have argued elsewhere that despite massive privatisation there is little evidence of any fundamental restructuring in the newly privatised Russian enterprises (Frydman, Pistor, and Rapaczynski, 1996). More recent evidence collected by Earle and Rose (1996) finds some evidence of change, but also reveals a striking picture of the political attitudes of employees of Russian firms — the group that was among two main beneficiaries of the privatisation programme (see Table 1). Looking at the likely voting pattern of the employees of state, privatised, and new private firms, Earle and Rose found that, compared to workers in new private firms and in state firms, the employees of privatised companies, who collectively are the largest shareholders of their enterprises, were the least likely to vote for reform politicians, were more sympathetic to communists, and gave higher marks to communism as a system. They are also the most negative about their firms, unwilling to work to improve things, and desirous of changing their place of employment.

This result should not be surprising. As we said already, the dominant concern of employees is their continued employment, especially in times when finding new jobs is difficult. The stake employees have in this aspect of their firms is nearly always higher than what they have as shareholders, even if the company is making money, which many Russian firms do not. Furthermore, privatised firms were not generally among the best Russian companies and the squeeze applied on them by the macroeconomic policy is likely to be, on the whole, tighter than that on the state or new private firms, because the private firms are more dynamic and the remaining state companies are likely to have been among the larger, strategic firms which may be both politically more powerful (thus more successful in keeping a portion of their subsidies intact) and, if they operate in such areas as the exploitation of Russia's rich mineral resources, more economically viable. Becoming shareholders of the privatised companies did therefore little to alleviate the hardships of transition for this group of stakeholders and, given the disappointment of expectations, may have even added to their frustration.

Earle and Rose did not interview Russian managers and we do not know whether their responses would reveal a similar disappointment. The case of Hungary, however, provides an interesting glimpse into the political effects of managerial privatisation. Hungarian managers, whose role was greatly strengthened during the years of the communist reforms, have managed to retain control of most formerly state firms. As early as the last years of the communist rule (since 1988), managers were able to change the legal form of their firms, spinning valuable assets into separate limited liability companies, or transform the whole enterprise into one or more joint-stock and limited liability companies. Following a period during which this process was commonly abused by managers, who through so-called "spontaneous privatisation" appropriated significant chunks of valuable assets for themselves, the state attempted to regain some control over the privatisation process. But the extent to which it was successful was rather limited and most ownership

Table 1. Voting behaviour of Russian employees.

Column Per cent	Budgetary organisation	State Enterprise	Privatised firm	New Private	Other	Sample
Approval of Yeltsin (n=980)	13.5	13.5	8.6	21.0	8.7	12.8
Candidate for President (n=480)						
"Leftist"	8.4	5.1	12.0	1.1	7.5	7.4
"Nationalist"	20.9	32.8	32.8	25.1	46.5	29.2
"Reformer"	51.9	43.6	32.3	49.0	45.5	43.3
"Centrist"	18.7	18.5	23.0	24.9	0.5	20.1
Party (n=423)						
"Leftists"	22.4	16.9	24.7	1.9	14.4	19.3
"Nationalists"	18.0	26.7	30.8	34.8	43.3	26.8
"Reformers"	36.6	30.2	23.2	55.5	41.8	32.4
"Centrists"	23.0	26.2	21.2	7.8	0.6	21.5
Ownership composition	24.8	31.9	28.8	12.5	2.0	100

Source: Earle and Rose (1996).

changes were *de facto* conditioned on managerial consent. Moreover, many companies were effectively excluded from privatisation, while the process of redrawing corporate boundaries continued and resulted in a chain of cross-ownerships, conglomeration, and other extremely complex corporate structures. As a result, property relations became quite confused, and managers, while often being formal owners of only a minority position, remain firmly in control of their firms.[11]

When asked about their view of the political and economic changes since 1990 and a number of other related questions, however, Hungarian managers, both absolutely and as compared to their Czech and Polish counterparts, are strikingly pessimistic, longing for state assistance to business, and supportive of more redistribution (despite the already huge transfer payments in the Hungarian budget). In Poland, where the economic situation is better and the degree of change from the old regime is more pronounced, the answers are markedly more upbeat and more pro-market, but nowhere near as much as the Czechs (see Table 2).

Table 2. Managerial attitudes in Czech Republic, Hungary, and Poland.

	Agree/Disagree (%)		
	Czech Rep.	Hungary	Poland
Changes in the economic system are generally positive	83/1	21/42	62/10
Changes in the political system are generally positive	81/1	35/16	44/20
Political and economic future of the country is promising	92/0	45/27	77/12
Prevailing political climate is favourable for business	60/23	28/69	35/57
State does not provide enough assistance to existing business	50/33	79/18	65/22
State pays insufficient attention to social justice	13/70	53/42	36/38
State overtaxes companies in my business	43/42	74/25	82/9
Sample size	151	234	149

Source: Data based on Privatisation Project/World Bank spring 1995 survey.

Table 3. Managerial attitudes across ownership types.

	Agree -Disagree (%)[1]				
	Privatised firms				
	Insiders	Individual share-holders	Foreign owners	Central govt[2]	New firms[3]
Changes in the economic system are generally positive	-8	-8	6	38	46
Changes in the political system are generally positive	32	28	56	56	40
Political and economic future of the country is promising	32	56	52	74	52
Prevailing political climate is favourable for business	-21	-28	-30	-18	-40
State does not provide enough assistance to existing business	66	68	40	60	54
State pays insufficient attention to social justice	32	6	-2	-6	-10
State overtaxes companies in my business	72	74	20	66	60
Sample size	45	15	59	21	34

Notes: 1) Percentage calculations exclude mixed or no opinion responses; 2) Only partially-privatised companies in which private parties have voting power formally sufficient to block major decisions; 3) All companies newly-founded solely by private owners only, regardless of the type of the largest owner.

Source: Data based on Privatisation Project/World Bank spring 1995 survey.

Moving to intra- rather than cross-country comparisons, the effect observed by Earle and Rose seems to hold true as well (see Table 3). When managerial views of the political and economic situation are compared across different types of firms in both Hungary and Poland,[12] we observe that the managers of privatised firms in which insiders are the largest shareholders are generally less positive about the political and economic situation and more supportive of "socialist" measures than those of the managers of new firms and firms in which the state, foreigners, or individuals are the largest owners.[13] Although these results are not statistically significant, they are consistent throughout the sample, both overall and in each country separately.[14]

Conclusion

The politics of privatisation, especially the post-privatisation effects of various policies, need to be better understood in order to evaluate the effectiveness of privatisation. The fact that privatisation cannot change the basic economic reality of many post-communist enterprises — their essential irrationality and often value-subtracting character — means that their privatisation has a primarily political significance, measured in terms of its effect on the opposition to the dismantling of the communist economic inheritance. Privatisation can make some economic difference only if the privatised assets have genuine productive potential in a competitive environment. But in order to enable this potential to be realised, the method of privatisation must ensure that enterprise insiders are not put in control of privatised firms. This usually means that the initial cost of an effective privatisation policy is an increase in the insiders' political disaffection, and that this cost must be weighed against possible political gains from creating a new pro-reform constituency through the process of privatisation itself. But as our (admittedly still limited) evidence shows, policy-makers have no realistic alternative to such a bet on the future. The reason for this is that a compromise with the insiders of privatised enterprises produces no marked increase in their political support for reform policies. On the contrary, the supposed beneficiaries of such policies turn out to be among the most hardened opponents of reform politicians and remain among the most nostalgic proponents of a more interventionist, "socialist" regime.

Notes

[1] Janos Kornai was the most notable exception. Kornai (1990).

[2] For a more extensive treatment of the significance of the capital stock in privatisation policy design, see Frydman and Rapaczynski (1994), Chapters 3 and 6.

[3] The contrasting stories of Gdansk and Szczecin shipyards in Poland are instructive in this respect. The first, formerly the bastion of the Solidarity union, is fast approaching closure after the state refused to continue its subsidies. By contrast, the Szczecin shipyard, the fate of which appeared equally hopeless not long ago, is doing rather well, having dramatically restructured (and contracted) its operations and found a rather profitable niche on the world market. See *New York Times*, 4 July 1995.

[4] In fact, good arguments could be made that post-privatisation subsidisation is a bad policy in most cases and that it might be easier to maintain the credibility of a governmental policy of

non-intervention if the subsidised firms are temporarily kept under state ownership, or at least if they are subject to a special privatisation programme, strictly walled off from the rest.

[5] Clearly, insiders may also be given a minor share of ownership and such an arrangement may or may not be good for the enterprise, depending on the size of insider stakes, the identity of other owners, etc. At this point we are merely trying to establish that insider *control* is bad for the governance of most privatised firms in Eastern Europe and that any other arrangement would be perceived as threatening the insiders' present controlling position.

[6] For a discussion and evidence of this alliance in Russia, see Frydman, Pistor, and Rapaczynski (1996).

[7] It is widely believed that this behaviour is common in Russia, where the management-employee ownership is the most widespread. For some empirical evidence, see Earle and Rose (1996).

[8] For a more extended discussion of the problems of insider ownership, see Chapter 5 of Frydman and Rapaczynski (1994).

[9] For a description of this programme, see Frydman, Rapaczynski, Earle, *et al.* (1993) and Earle, Frydman, Rapaczynski, and Turkewitz (1994).

[10] For the analysis of a distinction between normal and extraordinary politics, see Ackerman (1991).

[11] For a description of confused firm boundaries and ownership relations, see Stark (1996). For a description of the role of managers in the privatisation process, see Frydman, Rapaczynski, and Turkewitz (1996).

[12] Czech Republic was excluded from the tabulations because, given the overwhelmingly positive views of Czech managers (who gave practically no negative responses), the effect of any changes introduced by their inclusion would be due exclusively to the distribution of Czech managers across different types of firms (which differed from those in Poland and Hungary). Even so, the inclusion of the Czech Republic would not significantly change the results in the table.

[13] The only companies in which managers sometimes score lower than those in which insiders are dominant are privatised firms in which private domestic individuals are the largest shareholders (*nota bene*: new firms are excluded from this category). Given that domestic individuals who become major shareholders in official privatisation are often related to the management, these results are consistent with the general trend.

[14] Actually some results are statistically significant, but the significance comes from cross-country effects (similar to those that motivated the exclusion of Czech firms from the tabulations. The results presented here are still preliminary — further analysis might reveal statistically firmer relationships.

References

Ackerman, B.A., 1991, *We the People: Foundations*, Harvard University Press.

Earle, J.S. and Estrin, S., 1996, "Employee Ownership in Transition," in: Frydman R., Gray, C.W. and Rapaczynski, A. (eds), *Corporate Governance in Central Europe and Russia*, CEU Press, Vol. 2.

Earle, J.S. and Rose, R., 1996, "Causes and Consequences of Privatization: An Empirical Study of Economic Behavior and Political Attitudes in Russia", [mimeo].

Fama, E. and Jensen, M., 1983a, "Separation of Ownership and Control", *Journal of Law and Economics*, 26, pp. 301-25.

Fama, E. and Jensen, M., 1983b, "Agency Problems and Residual Claims", *Journal of Law and Economics*, 26, pp. 327-49.

Frydman, R., Pistor, K. and Rapaczynski, A., 1996, "Investing in Insider-Dominated Firms: A Study of Russian Voucher Privatization Funds", in Frydman, R., Gray, Ch. and Rapaczynski, A. (eds.), *Corporate Governance in Central Europe and Russia*, CEU Press.

Frydman, R., and Rapaczynski, A., 1994, *Privatization in Eastern Europe: Is the State Withering Away?,* CEU Press.

Frydman, R., Rapaczynski, A., Earle, J. *et al.*, 1993, *The Privatization Process in Central Europe,* CEU Press.

Frydman R., Rapaczynski, A. and Turkewitz, J., 1996, "Transition to a Private property regime in the Czech Republic and Hungary," in: Parker, S. and Woo, W., MIT Press, forthcoming.

Earle, J., Frydman, R., Rapaczynski, A. and Turkewitz, J., 1994, *Small Privatization; The Transformation of Retail Trade and Consumer Services in the Czech Republic, Hungary, and Poland,* CEU Press.

Kornai, J., 1990, *The Road to a Free Economy. Shifting from a Socialist System: The Example of Hungary*, Norton.

Stark, D., 1996, "Networks of Assets, Chains of Debt: Recombinant Property in Hungary", forthcoming in Frydman, R., Gray, C. and Rapaczynski, A. (eds.), *Corporate Governance in Central Europe and Russia*, CEU Press, Vol. 2.

4

Large privatisation, restructuring and foreign direct investment

Gábor Hunya

1. What matters most is restructuring

The linkages between the privatisation of state-owned enterprises, their restructuring and the participation of foreign capital in both processes are the focus of this paper. In a broad sense, restructuring includes all policy measures and economic processes which increase the efficiency of an economy or of a company (including its international competitiveness UNIDO, 1994). This may cover the whole transformation process. In a microeconomic sense, restructuring refers to the re-deployment of assets in order to increase efficiency (Ernst *et al.*, 1996). In the context of economic transformation, restructuring covers mainly the adaptation of enterprises to the new market economy framework and to shifts of demand. Economic, legal and political systems, as well as privatisation and FDI policies, are understood as the environment for restructuring companies. Macroeconomic and microeconomic evidence is combined to shed light on the restructuring processes. The results of privatisation and the consequences of foreign direct investment (FDI) will be assessed as tools of restructuring in the Central and East European countries (CEECs) — Bulgaria, the Czech Republic, Hungary, Poland, Romania, Slovakia and Slovenia. The Czech Republic, Hungary, Poland and Slovakia were selected for deeper investigation as they are the most advanced in respect of the threefold subject of this paper. Focusing on only four out of 25 post-communist countries reflects both the limited capacity of the author and the large number of countries lagging in transformation.

At the outset of transformation, the economic and policy environment of enterprises changed within a relative short period of time. The structure of demand changed, and new price and cost relations appeared due to the elimination of subsidies and the competition from imports and new private firms. The collapse of the CMEA changed foreign demand. In addition, restrictive stabilization policies led to a fall in aggregate demand and to high interest rates. All these events have confronted companies with almost insurmountable problems.

Besides the shocks, there were also economic policy measures which helped companies to adopt to the new conditions: under-valued domestic currencies, bail-out of large indebted state-owned enterprises (SOEs), and increased decision-making autonomy provided for the management. In many countries transformation steps were simply postponed or softened if the challenge they would have caused was considered too big. Consistent industrial policies were not applied, not only because 'planning' was abandoned based on the experience under communism, but also because the targets and agents of a consistent policy were both overwhelmed by the magnitude of changes. The effects of policy measures in such circumstances were unpredictable.

In a broad sense, restructuring and privatisation of the CEEC economies started immediately after the introduction of liberalisation steps. A new private sector emerged, both competing with and complementing and acting in symbiosis with the public sector. Previously underdeveloped industries, like trade and financial services, increased rapidly. The genuine private sector was too weak by itself to put the formerly centrally planned economies on a new growth trajectory, the transfer of SOEs into the private sector was necessary. Institutional changes were introduced to harden the budget constraint of state-owned enterprises and privatisation was scheduled for the immediate future.

The policies designed to speed up restructuring by mass privatisation, bankruptcy and rearranging company structures proved to be more time-consuming and more cumbersome than envisaged by creative minds. Economic transformation and restructuring was bound to be an evolutionary process (Frydman and Rapaczynski, 1994). Government policies only loosely followed some master plan of transformation; they reflected changing compromises between various economic and political powers and pressure groups. Pragmatism was not the expression of a 'lack of conceptual basis, order and design' (Csaba, 1995), but of the impossibility to apply a master plan to an evolutionary process. Models which tried to slow down the transformation process, or direct it into a 'third way', remained a fiction (Kregel *et al.*, 1992), even more than radical ones. The legal framework in the CEECs was itself in the making and allowed for economic actions not in line with the desire of governments, like 'spontaneous privatisation' and 'ambiguous restructuring' (Carlin *et al.*, 1994). Even if government revenues were lost and moral principles hurt, spontaneous processes could speed up privatisation in the absence of efficient public institutions in countries where enterprise managers were interested in getting more freedom (Hungary, Poland). In other countries, like Romania, the inertia of the former system proved to be strong, and thus privatisation and restructuring suffered delays.

Governments were usually not engaged very deeply in enterprise restructuring before privatisation, but corporatisation, splitting of large organisations, and in some countries also some financial restructuring, took place on a large scale. There is an extensive literature maintaining that the lack of an active state in the restructuring process was responsible for the mal- (or non-) adjustment of many SOEs, the liquidation of capacities and massive lay-offs (Amsden *et al.*, 1994). Industrial policy, in the sense of setting the macroeconomic framework and providing for institutions not developed by the market, was missing at the outset of transformation (Landesmann, 1994), but these activities appeared in most countries after a few years. In addition, case-by-case state involvement in the restructuring of key enterprises and banks has been practised with not very encouraging results.

In the following two parts of this paper, the speed and the results of restructuring are examined by two indicators: labour productivity in industry and changes in the commodity structure of exports. Then differences between countries concerning restructuring will be explained by peculiarities in the privatisation policy and the inflow of FDI. Subsequent sections provide evidence concerning the restructuring by foreign investment enterprises at the aggregate and industry levels. In Section 6, some results of company surveys will be cited to explain more specific features of microeconomic restructuring under specific privatisation policies.

2. Some macroeconomic evidence of restructuring

2.1 *Productivity, FDI and the share of the private sector in manufacturing*

In this section labour productivity is used as an indicator of restructuring. Table 1 gives some evidence concerning the speed of restructuring as evidenced by the growth of labour productivity, the inflow of FDI and the achieved weight of the private sector in manufacturing. Labour productivity increased in countries both with low and high private sector shares and with different intensities of foreign penetration. The link between FDI and productivity gains is closer than that between private sector share and productivity. At this stage of analysis, only the lack of a strong positive correlation between the three indicators is at issue.

At the outset of the transformation in the CEECs, privatisation was considered one of the most important tasks. No restructuring of SOEs and no recovery of production was expected to take place without the transfer of ownership into private hands. The profound setback of production in 1990-92 was a sign of real adaptation difficulties and the lack of instant restructuring. In the last few years, however, GDP and industrial output recovered in all seven CEECs, which in itself is the result of some restructuring. Production increased also in countries with predominantly public ownership. On the other hand, delaying privatisation did not save countries from depression. In the early 1990s, countries which did not privatise suffered economic setbacks similar to those in rapidly privatising countries. Although the 'horror of economic collapse because of slow privatisation' (Aslund, 1991) did not materialise, restructuring without privatisation has been slow, and longer-term growth prospects are bleak. Under state ownership, restructuring was mainly

Table 1. CEECs: labour productivity change, FDI stock per capita and private sector share in output/value added in industry/manufacturing, 1995.

Country	Labour productivity 1989=100	FDI per capita US$	Private sector share %
Czech Republic	96	257	67
Hungary	134	560	65
Poland	118	109	45
Slovak Republic	77	57	68
Slovenia	113	377	15
Romania	86	28	16
Bulgaria	99	26	21

Source: National statistics, own estimates and calculations.

passive (Grosfeld and Roland, 1995), i.e. reducing costs by shrinking output, laying off workers and spinning off subsidiaries. Strategic restructuring would have required investments, the means for which were lacking in most SOEs, and there was very little room for strategic thinking in SOEs facing the uncertainty of privatisation (pre-privatisation agony).

The adaptive strength of some SOEs came from the change in their corporate governance and, for large SOEs, also from their preserved privileged position in the relations with budgetary organs and state-owned banks. The withdrawal of the state from interfering in the matters of enterprises increased the autonomy of decision-making of managements and changed their incentives. Independence from the state was especially big under the ownership system of the post-Yugoslav self-management and the Polish workers' councils, which could effectively hinder governments from privatising such companies. In Hungary, enterprise councils also influenced the manner of privatisation without being able to block it. Another important aspect is that, with liberalisation and the termination of subsidies, most SOEs had fairly hard budget constraints and a competitive environment enforcing restructuring. The changing conditions affected medium-size firms more than giants, which have retained more direct state links.

The managers of SOEs are not generally unskilled or unable to adapt to market economy circumstances. Starting from a very depressed situation in the early 1990s, some marketing skills and minor investments facilitated the re-utilisation of some redeployed capacities, which made temporary output growth in SOEs possible. At the same time, enterprise autonomy coupled with a lack of effective control over the managers meant also that privatisation could be blocked, and asset stripping and fraud behaviour practised.

2.2 FDI, privatisation and the upgrading of export structures

Industrial restructuring in the broad sense must be reflected in growing access to high-quality foreign markets and by improvement of the export structure. The trade with the EU, which accounts for 50-70 per cent of CEEC exports, can be taken as a point of reference. In the following, the increase in the present EU-15 countries' imports from the CEECs reflects the penetration by Eastern exports of high-quality markets. Structural change in exports is demonstrated by a simple aggregate import structure of the EU-15 from five CEECs.

EU imports from the five countries investigated in Table 2 doubled between 1990 and 1994. The highest dynamics was shown by countries which had the lowest EU share in exports in 1990, the Czech Republic and Bulgaria. Here the geographic shift of exports played a more important role than in Hungary or Poland, where the re-orientation of trade had taken place already in 1987-90.

The structure of exports is a reflection of the general level and pattern of economic development. Countries with higher per-capita GDP tend to have more processed and more capital- and R&D-intensive goods in their exports, while less developed countries specialise in labour- and material-intensive industries. An upgrading of export structures means that food as well as labour- and energy-intensive products lose their weight in favour of machinery and transport equipment.

Table 2. Share of commodity groups in manufacturing exports to the EU-15, 1990 and 1994.

NACE Code		Czech Rep.*		Hungary		Poland		Romania		Bulgaria	
		1990	1994	1990	1994	1990	1994	1990	1994	1990	1994
DA	%	6	2	19	11	16	7	1	2	15	7
DB-DE	%	29	26	29	26	29	38	60	58	27	32
DF-DJ	%	44	41	32	27	39	34	28	29	41	44
DK-DN	%	21	31	20	36	16	21	11	11	17	17
Total volume											
ECU bn		2.4	7.7	2.5	4.4	4.0	7.9	1.2	2.3	0.4	1.2
Increase	%	320		173		200		200		270	

Notes: DA = Food and beverages, tobacco; DB-DE = Textiles, clothing, leather, shoes, wood, paper; DF-DJ = Chemicals, construction material, metals; DK-DN = Machinery, transport equipment; * Czechoslovakia for 1990.
Source: Eurostat, imports of EU-15 from CEECs.

As for industrial goods, the most favourable export structure and the fastest upgrading can be observed in the case of the Czech Republic and Hungary, the latter having some lead. The increase in the share of machinery in Hungarian exports to the EU-15 was 16 percentage points, leading to a 36 per cent share, in the case of the Czech Republic the improvement was 10 percentage points, and the result in 1994 was a 31 per cent share. There is no difference between the two countries concerning the change in the share of the group of labour-intensive light industry products. Due to natural conditions, energy- and material-intensive goods are over-represented in the Czech and Slovak industrial and export structures, just as food is in the Hungarian. In all CEECs, with the exception of Romania, exports of food products stagnated in volume terms, meaning a halving of their export shares.

The structure of Polish exports developed in a less favourable direction. They are dominated by a high and increasing share of labour-intensive light industry products, but there is also an increase in the importance of machinery, the share of which reached 21 per cent in 1994, the Czechoslovak and Hungarian level of 1990. Beyond industrial traditions, the low inflow of foreign capital prior to 1994 is expressed in these figures. Polish firms have been integrated with EU firms by co-operation and outward processing agreements, typical of light industry international networks, rather than by capital participation.

The two South-east European countries are characterised by an absence of structural upgrading, but they could also double their exports to the EU. Romanian exports consist mainly of light industry products, the Bulgarian ones to a large extent of energy- and material-intensive products. Both countries have low and stagnating shares of machinery exports. In these countries foreign direct investment plays a negligible role in manufacturing, privatisation has been slow and most likely the restructuring of SOEs also advanced more slowly than in the other three countries.

The above analysis provided only a sketchy picture which disregards the complexity of commodity groups. A recent research project carried out by WIIW analysed the specialisation of CEEC exports to the EU at NACE three-digit level (Landesmann, 1996). Industries were grouped as capital-, labour-, R&D-, skill- and energy-intensive, based on their characteristics in the four largest EU member states, and the representation of the products in the EU-15 imports from the CEECs was analysed.

Results show that the representation of capital- and energy-intensive products is highest in the Czechoslovak (for 1994 the Czech) and Bulgarian exports, and in Poland higher than in Hungary and Romania. Labour-intensive products are most characteristic of Romanian exports. Capital-, energy- and labour-intensive commodities had increasing shares between 1988 and 1993 in all five countries but decreasing in 1994. As for R&D-intensive products, Hungary had the highest representation and showed also a high rate of growth; the other countries had worse positions, Czechoslovakia faring better than the rest, but with no clear sign of improvement. As for skill-intensive products, the Czech Republic and Hungary are clearly ahead of the others, and only they show growing shares of these products in their exports. Unit prices of Hungarian exports in important product groups of engineering and clothing were highest and increased more rapidly than for other countries. A catching-up of Czech and Polish unit prices was observed.

The change in CEEC export structures correlates closely with the stock of FDI. The higher the degree of foreign penetration in a country, the more advanced is the structure of exports. The export structure of Hungary, and also of the Czech Republic, has shifted towards branches where foreign presence is pronounced, as shown in later sections. In both countries export shares increased most rapidly in the group of transport equipment, which was the target of foreign penetration. As will be pointed out below, in all industries foreign investment enterprises have a higher export intensity than domestic firms. Also the private sector share in manufacturing correlates with changes in the trade pattern. It must be noted, however, that time-lags are not duly considered here. After FDI inflow or a privatisation deal, years may pass before the results of restructuring appear in productivity growth or trade re-orientation.

3. Privatisation

3.1 An overview of privatisation methods

In the context of restructuring, only the assessment of the economic aspects of privatisation is important; legal, social or moral aspects will not be discussed here. It is necessary to distinguish between primary "de-etatisation" (corporatisation, voucher distribution; see also Hunya, 1992) and final privatisation. From an economic point of view, privatisation is final when non-public owners interested in the long-term value of a company assume full ownership rights over a former SOE and impose corporate governance over the management. Either strategic investors or the capital market can carry out the controlling task. In early 1996 even the advanced CEECs are still in the midst of the privatisation process of SOEs. Countries who wanted to get fast results have 'privatised on the surface' (Hunya, 1992), relying on a voucher scheme and leaving the emergence of strong owners ('deep' or 'completed' privatisation) to the capital market, which has just started to function. Restructuring was delayed until after privatisation. Also the sales strategies allowed for little restructuring before privatisation, but expected a new owner to emerge who would introduce corporate governance and restructuring with no delay.

Five basic methods of privatisation of SOEs can be identified:

- **Privatisation by vouchers** was used when primarily the denationalisation of SOEs and not their stable corporate management and rapid restructuring was the main objective. This approach was also favoured when political support for privatisation appeared to be the crucial problem. The state was deprived of its operational control over enterprises, and a broad dispersion of property rights was envisaged. The demand problem which appears in connection with sales did not apply, but supply difficulties and organisational constraints slowed down the implementation (see also OECD/CCET, 1995a).

- **Free transfer** of ownership without vouchers was practised when the target and object of ownership transfer was well defined. Restitution, the transfer of shares to pension funds or municipal administrations fall under this category. These methods appeared in most countries, but without playing a dominant role.

- **Privatisation of SOEs by sale**. The underlying assumption was that there would be a big supply of feasible SOEs and matching demand on the part of private investors, and also that some state authority was able to mediate a great number of deals. As neither of these assumptions held, except in the former GDR, the sale of SOEs has been a rather cumbersome process. Nevertheless, if applied, the expected positive results of this approach did materialise: hard budget constraints, better corporate management, restructuring of production. Financial and organisational restructuring sometimes preceded sales to make SOEs more attractive, but most of the task of restructuring was left to the new owners. After the sale of the more lucrative SOEs, partial restructuring before privatisation gained ground and sales gained again momentum in 1995 in most CEECs.

- **Sale of assets after liquidation of SOEs** to private investors without the obligation to take over financial, employment and organisational burdens. SOEs in financial difficulties sold off part of their assets; buyers were private investors. Liquidation and privatisation of whole SOEs were most frequently linked in Poland and Hungary, and sale after liquidation was just as important as sales of SOEs in corporate form (Hunya, 1995b).

- Both the **sale of companies** and of individual assets can take place **under preferential terms**, using payments by instalments, low-interest credits or leasing. Special conditions can apply to former owners, employees, managers, the population at large. Leveraged sales increase domestic demand for state-owned assets, at the same time they reduce the risk of new owners and soften their budget constraints. Similarly to voucher privatisation, this method can make a fairly large public interested in privatisation, but may decrease the effectiveness of privatisation and exclude foreign investors like in Poland and Romania, also in Hungary in 1994 and recently in Slovakia.

- **Initial public offering** of shares was tried in several countries but did nor become an often used method of privatisation. Weak stock exchanges are both reason for and the result of the rarity of this way of privatisation.

In the privatisation processes of CEECs the above methods were combined. Countries can be grouped according to the dominant approach. The voucher method was dominant in the Czech Republic and Slovakia. Sales dominated in Hungary and Poland. Next to the four countries most advanced in privatisation, there is another group that has just launched privatisation on a mass scale, applying some form of voucher privatisation: Bulgaria, Romania and Slovenia. Some country-specific remarks below point out the most important current issues and describe the role of foreigner investors in the privatisation process (for comprehensive works on CEEC privatisation, see Frydman, Rapaczynski, Earle *et al.*, 1993; Böhm, 1995; OECD/CCET, 1995b).[1]

3.1.1 Voucher-dominated privatisation

It seems that in the **Czech Republic** the less frequently used method of direct sales has brought more positive results than the voucher scheme. Five years after launching privatisation, the policy of the investment funds, which control about 70 per cent of voucher-privatised shares, and the future of the remaining public stakes remain controversial. Intermediaries helped the voucher scheme to succeed among the population and solved part of the problems feared to arise from dispersed ownership, but they may lack efficient corporate governance themselves. Majority state-owned banks and similar financial institutions were the founders of the bigger investment funds which control a considerable part of industry. In this construction privatisation meant a transfer of ownership from the state to partly state-owned financial institutions (see also Section 5, and Mertlík, 1996). Other investment funds, mainly those set up by foreign banks, are now more active in restructuring. After the two privatisation waves, the state's National Property Fund still held shares in about 1400 small and medium-sized companies and in a number of larger companies of strategic importance. In summer 1995, the government declared the willingness to privatise most of the latter also.

From the beginning of the large-scale privatisation until the end of 1994, foreign investors were involved in the privatisation process of more than 300 Czech enterprises, primarily larger industrial ones. Projects with foreign participation were subject to particular scrutiny and could be highly controversial since they affected the best enterprises in the economy. In evaluating projects with foreign investment, specific attention has been devoted by the Czech authorities to both the financial conditions of the transaction (debts versus equity, plans to increase equity, etc.), as well as employment and environmental issues. In 1994 a policy debate took place whether 'the Czech way' (domestic owners) or foreign privatisation should be preferred. The latter opinion prevailed, and foreign investors could win the privatisation tenders both in telecom and the national oil company in 1995.

Slovak enterprises participated in the first wave of the Czechoslovak voucher privatisation, but since independence, privatisation policy took different tracks. The success criteria for a nationalist government are clearly different from those of the social-liberal Czechoslovak one. In September 1995 three new laws regarding the privatisation policy were approved. The first law cancelled the second wave of the voucher privatisation while it was already in progress. The second law curbed the role of investment funds. And the third one exempted some 25 strategic companies in sectors of energy, telecommunications and arms production from privatisation. Now the government sells controlling stakes to politically reliable managers at a low price paid in instalments. Even these payments can be partly cancelled if the new owner invests in restructuring. Domestic investors are preferred even if foreign investors offer a higher price. The existing foreign sector in Slovakia either originates from the first Czechoslovak privatisation wave or represents green-field projects.

3.1.2 Sales-dominated privatisation

Privatisation and foreign investment policy in Hungary has been decisively influenced by two specific features: indebtedness and reform traditions. High foreign and domestic indebtedness made the increase of public revenues by selling state-owned assets necessary. The relatively early and rather smooth transformation made market privatisation possible and acceptable, although it also allowed for insider deals and asset stripping. Sales slowed down in 1994 for political reasons but gathered momentum in December 1995. Although institutions and concepts of privatisation have changed several times since 1990, the principal guideline — that direct sales of state-owned property should constitute the backbone of Hungarian privatisation — remained unchallenged. In 1990-94 foreign and Hungarian investors played a roughly equal role in privatisation. Hungarian investors were promoted by various preferential credit lines and leasing constructions. Management and employee buy-out deals were also supported. Compensation certificates (vouchers provided for those who had suffered in the second World War or in the communist period due to confiscation of property or political repression) were distributed to purchase shares of state-owned firms.

The privatisation of SOEs in **Poland** was carried out by three basic methods: transformation into joint-stock companies and selling of shares in them; privatisation by liquidation, i.e. contributing its assets to a new company; and liquidation proper, which takes place in the case of state-owned enterprises in financial difficulties. Privatisation advanced primarily because a great number of small companies were privatised by liquidation methods; 1 021 state-owned enterprises were transformed into joint-stock companies, of which 146 companies have been sold, 26 through public offering, the rest to strategic investors, including foreign ones. The remaining 875 joint-stock companies are 100 per cent treasury-owned, but 514 of them are included in the Mass Privatisation Programme which started in the autumn of 1995. In this respect Poland can also be put among the countries with delayed privatisation.

Foreign investors were mainly involved in buying treasury-owned joint-stock companies, but quite often privatisation started only after a foreign strategic investor had appeared. Foreign investors have also acquired shares in companies which were already private. In some cases they bought shares that the treasury had retained after privatisation.

3.1.3 Delayed privatisation

In **Bulgaria**, up to the end of 1994 only a few large enterprises were privatised. A mass privatisation programme started in January 1996. Citizens can participate in the voucher scheme either personally, or through an agent, or through a privatisation fund, but showed limited interest until the end of May. Foreigners can take part through investment funds provided they are registered as a financial institution and have been engaged in similar activities in their home country for at least five years. Privatisation funds and foreign capital may ensure better results for the Bulgarian privatisation than for the Romanian programme, which excludes financial intermediaries.

Privatisation in **Romania** still lacks a broad political base. The policy of the governments since 1990 has fluctuated between initiating and blocking privatisation. Privatisation laws have been controversial, the implementation partial or delayed. The scope of privatisation was narrowly defined because companies of 'national importance', which comprise also energy, telecom and steel companies, already privatised in some other CEECs, were excluded from privatisation.

The current mass privatisation programme offers 3 900 companies against vouchers and cash. Between 40 and 60 per cent of shares will be divested by vouchers, the rest by direct sales. Vouchers could be invested in companies until the end of March 1996, most of the persons eligible did it in the last days, some of them only under administrative pressure. There is high uncertainty concerning the future steps of privatisation. Foreign investors have been invited to bid for minority stakes in several companies.

Publicly owned enterprises in **Slovenia** had enjoyed a substantial degree of autonomy during the Yugoslav communist regime. In the self-management system, workers were considered owners of the so-called social property, having special ownership rights in their firms, but they did not have the right to buy or sell shares. Most of the companies were integrated into Western markets and featured high competitiveness and competent managements. For these reasons privatisation was not a pressing economic problem in the first phase of the transformation. After protracted debates in the Slovenian parliament, the privatisation law came into force in 1992 and was amended several times; the sluggish process of privatisation gathered momentum only in 1995. The privatisation law provides for a combination of free-distribution and commercial-privatisation methods. Vouchers were distributed to each Slovenian citizen, with the nominal value depending on the age of the respective person. They can be used by employees to acquire shares in 'their' company, or in special investment funds.

It was an obvious intention of the legislation to limit the role of foreigners in privatisation. A typical privatisation project allocates 40 per cent of the shares to the pension, restitution and development funds, 20 per cent to small investors and 40 per cent to the employees. Thus a big part of Slovenia's enterprises will be dominated by internal owners, managers and employees. This development recalls the distribution of ownership rights under the self-management system, the only difference being that employees now have *de jure* ownership rights.

3.1.4 Privatisation method chosen by political efficiency

Considering that sales resulted in more restructuring than did voucher privatisation, the question arises — why do countries where privatisation was delayed go in for mass privatisation? If sales to foreigners lead to faster restructuring, why did most countries prefer domestic owners? Without going into detail, it can be said that economic policy was mostly guided not by short-term efficiency gains, but by popularity, equality and national ideals. Lack of domestic entrepreneurial capital and the lack of interest of foreign investors for companies in riskier countries were further obstacles to sales. Mass privatisation also provides the opportunity for half-hearted privatisation which does not lead to the complete loss of state control over enterprises (e.g. Romania).

3.2 New ownership structures in manufacturing

The ownership structures emerging in the privatisation process differ widely as regards the role of foreign owners. A comparison of the Czech Republic and Hungary is presented in Table 3. It points out the results of different privatisation policies, with the Czech favouring domestic investors and the Hungarian method favouring sales to foreigners. (A similar survey for Poland is not yet possible, because many SOEs were not corporatised until recently.)

Privatisation in the Czech Republic resulted in a smaller public share than in Hungary, if shares owned by privatisation investment funds are included in the private sector. The partial reliance on free distribution in the framework of the voucher privatisation enabled the state to divest more rapidly than in Hungary by direct sales. In the voucher scheme, loss-making companies could be privatised, while in Hungary these companies were either liquidated or remained in public hands. The voucher scheme made the Czech privatisation process politically more acceptable and did not suffer deadlocks as in Hungary during 1994 and most of 1995.

Table 3. Ownership structure of nominal capital in manufacturing companies[1] in the Czech Republic and Hungary, 1994 (%).

	Czech Republic	Hungary
State-owned	26.3	33.2
Foreign	5.6	33.2
Domestic private	68.1	33.6

Note: [1] In Hungary all companies supplying tax declarations, in the Czech Republic representative sample of 247 firms.
Source: Czech Republic: Zemplínerová *et al.*, 1995; Hungary: *Ipari Szemle*, No. 6, 1995.

A more significant difference between the Czech Republic and Hungary appears in the degree of foreign ownership. Foreign investors in Hungary are as important as domestic private owners, whereas in the Czech industry, domestic owners dominate. The method of direct sales benefited foreign bidders because entrepreneurial capital was short domestically. The voucher method excluded the direct appearance of foreign owners, but their indirect presence through investment funds is more significant. The discussion of the impact of FDI will reveal that the choice between domestic or foreign dominance has a decisive role in restructuring and the future corporate strategy of firms.

4. Foreign direct investment in Central and East European countries

4.1 General features of FDI in CEECs

Several CEECs had already allowed minority foreign participation in joint ventures in the 1970s and 1980s, but this opportunity was not attractive enough to foreign investors. Except for a few showpieces, foreign investment started to flow only after the transformation to market economy had been launched. The liberalisation of prices and of foreign trade allowing the operation of fully foreign-owned firms, as well as the successful initial stabilization, were the prerequisites for investment from abroad. Those CEECs that have been unable to make major progress in transformation and stabilization have remained unattractive for investors, just like other countries in the world with unstable political and economic systems and high inflation rates.

The transformational recession, unlike recessions in market economies, was not a major obstacle to foreign investment. Markets and production lines of ailing state-owned companies were taken over by foreign firms which also supplied goods and services for which demand had been suppressed or missing earlier (e.g. household electronics, banking, management consulting). If the applied privatisation methods were friendly to foreign investors, whole companies and industries were subject to foreign take-overs.

After an initial upsurge in 1990 and 1992 and two years of stagnation, the year 1995 brought an upswing of FDI activities in the Central and East European countries. In the CEEC-7 (Visegrad countries plus Bulgaria, Romania and Slovenia) inflows doubled compared to the preceding year and reached US$10 billion, the total stock increasing to three times that amount. The former Soviet Union (FSU) received about US$3 billion, also twice as much as in the preceding year (see Table 4).

In the CEEC-7 region, only Hungary, Poland and the Czech Republic have been important FDI targets with internationally significant capital inflows — and based on *per capita* inflows, also Slovenia. These are the most advanced transforming countries with the most stable economies and political systems. Hungary participates with about 43 per cent in the total stock of CEEC-7 FDI, Poland with 23 per cent and the Czech Republic with 20 per cent (see Table 5). In 1995 all three countries realised the highest annual inflows in their history. The reason for this success was identical in all cases — sales of state-owned companies to foreign investors in the framework of privatisation and also follow-up investments in earlier established ventures. As for per capita FDI, Hungary was among the first five non-OECD target countries in the last three years, often also ahead of Southern European countries.

In another three countries of the CEEC-7, namely, Bulgaria, Romania and Slovakia, the inflow of FDI has been meagre; in 1995 it was less than in the preceding year. These countries provide a less stable environment for foreign firms, and privatisation policies give preference to domestic investors.

Table 4. Total foreign direct investment — inflow (US$ million).

	1989	1990	1991	1992	1993	1994	1995	1995
Czech Republic incl. SR	.	112	494	1004	654	869	2562	248
Hungary	300	900	1700	1700	2550	1300	4570	447
Poland[1]	.	.	247	900	1479	1342	2511	65
Slovak Republic incl. CR	.	.	.	.	135	185	181	34
Slovenia	.	.	.	.	.	395	196	99
Bulgaria	.	.	14	51	130	234	101	12
Romania	.	108	156	209	227	511	323	14
CEEC-7	300	1120	2611	3864	5175	4836	10445	107

Note: [1] Projects with more than US$ 1 million invested capital.
Source: National publications.

4.2 Targeted industries and source countries

In the three CEECs with relatively high amounts of FDI, about 60 per cent of foreign capital was invested in manufacturing by 1994. In the Czech Republic and Hungary, FDI in telecommunications (in Hungary also in the energy sector) surged in 1995 so that the share of manufacturing in the FDI stock decreased to about 50 per cent. Telecom and energy sectors have not yet been opened to foreign privatisation in Poland, so the high share of manufacturing has remained. In countries with low overall FDI, manufacturing constituted only 30-40 per cent of the invested capital, showing that investors did not initiate larger and longer-term projects, i.e. trade and services providing faster returns on capital dominated as primary investment targets.

Table 5. Total foreign direct investment — stock (US$ million).

	1989	1990	1991	1992	1993	1994	1995	1995
Czech Republic incl. SR	.	72	595	1555	2153	3191	5916	573
Hungary	550	1450	3150	4850	7400	8700	13270	1298
Poland [1]	.	353	600	1500	2979	4321	6832	177
Slovak Republic incl. CR	.	.	.	231	366	552	733	137
Slovenia	.	.	.	.	859	1254	1450	729
Bulgaria	.	.	14	65	195	429	530	63
Romania	.	108	264	533	761	1272	1595	70
CEEC-7	550	1983	4623	8734	14713	19718	30326	311

Note: [1] Projects with more than US$1 million invested capital; including smaller projects, the total 1995 stock is about US$8200 million.
Source: National publications.

The home countries of the largest multinational companies, US, Germany and the Netherlands, were the most important investing countries. Germany ranked first in the Czech Republic, Bulgaria and Hungary, and second in Romania and Poland. US-based multinationals ranked first in Poland, second in Hungary, and fourth in the Czech Republic. Austrian firms, relatively small in international comparison, used their local knowledge and geographic proximity to penetrate neighbouring countries. Austrian investment took first position in Slovakia, third in Hungary, and sixth in the Czech Republic and Poland.

There are basically three types of foreign investors present in the CEECs:

- big multinational corporations operating world-wide;
- medium-size companies from nearby countries;
- one-man ventures.

Big companies with world-wide operations like Pepsi Cola, Coca Cola, Siemens, ABB, Procter and Gamble, Philip Morris and Unilever are present with large projects in most of the countries, consciously building up their presence in the region. Their products are mainly oriented towards the local market. Car manufacturers (Fiat, Volkswagen, General Motors, Ford, Suzuki) follow two objectives simultaneously, setting up both assembly plants producing for the local market and component production integrated in their global manufacturing.

The proximity to developed European countries attracted many German, Austrian and Italian firms with little international production experience. Medium-size companies with formerly local orientation could enlarge their markets with distribution outlets and acquire cheap production facilities. Austrian construction firms, banks and transport enterprises enlarged their international activities this way to an unprecedented extent. With the opening of the borders thousands of small businessmen, traders and emigrants flooded the Eastern countries and became involved in small ventures. They came from Western Europe and the US as well as the Near East and China. They are the most numerous investors but with low capital contribution.

5. Economic impact of FDI on recipient countries

There is no direct and immediate contribution of FDI to gross capital formation. Only FDI inflow less acquisition outlays are part of gross fixed capital formation: green-field investment, restructuring investment following acquisition, capital increase. Generally less than half of FDI was of the non-acquisition type (Table 6). This calculation may actually under-estimate the amount of FDI used for new investment, because the state does not keep the whole sum of privatisation revenues; a part of it is usually recycled into the privatised company to cover restructuring investment. Table 6 is therefore a worst-case scenario; the actual foreign shares in capital formation may be somewhat higher. It is also possible to measure the investment outlays of companies with foreign involvement, called foreign investment enterprises (FIEs). These investments overlap to a great extent with the amount of non-acquisition FDI, but are calculated with different methods.

Table 6 reveals that the contribution of FDI to solving the problem of capital shortage in CEECs is generally limited. In the last few years FDI contributed to 10-15 per cent of fixed capital formation in Hungary and less than half of that in the

Czech Republic and in Poland. The contribution of foreign investment enterprises to fixed investment is more significant.

The impact of FDI beyond capital formation is perhaps even more important. Restructuring by the foreign investor in the form of modern management, organisation, marketing, access to new markets and brand names, etc., improves the efficiency of companies even with small capital investment. Domestic companies can also benefit from improved products and services supplied by foreign investment companies. Local sourcing and networking of multinational investors can induce a spreading of restructuring to domestically owned companies. But how close do foreigners come to these expectations? Research results concerning the restructuring impact of FIEs are summarised below, first at the level of industries, then at the microeconomic level.

5.1 The performance of the foreign sector

The subject of analysis below are foreign investment enterprises (FIEs) including all firms with any share of foreign ownership in the Czech Republic, Hungary, Poland and Slovakia. (A research project on FDI is currently underway at The Vienna Institute for Comparative Economic Studies, WIIW and relies on data delivered by CEEC statistical offices and assessed by local subcontractors. First results were included in Hunya, 1996a and 1996b.) Technical difficulties prevented a sorting-out of the true foreign sector, i.e. majority foreign-owned companies, but minority foreign-owned enterprises do not differ much, as the foreign investor often obtains a controlling position over the management if the majority owner is public.

Table 6. Role of non-acquisition FDI (FDI*) in gross fixed capital formation (FCF) (US$ million and %); contribution of FIEs to investment outlays (FIE %) of companies.

		1991	1992	1993	1994	1995 estimate
Czech Republic	FCF	5603	7975	8284	10812	12000
	FDI*	300	500	500	500	700
	%	5.4	6.3	6.0	4.6	5.8
	FIE %	.	.	9.8	10.5	.
Hungary	FCF	6902	7305	7186	8258	8000
	FDI	1209	798	999	1037	1200
	%	17.5	10.9	13.9	12.6	15.0
	FIE %	.	.	27.2	31.1	.
Poland	FCF	14906	14156	3639	14994	16000
	FDI*	130	600	900	800	1200
	%	0.9	4.2	6.7	5.3	7.5
	FIE %	2.5	4.7	5.7	.	.

Source: Official statistics and own calculations.

The state only retains the right to dispose of the company's capital. In FIEs the decision about restructuring usually lies with the foreign strategic investor.

Among the four countries in Table 7, only Hungary showed a high degree of foreign penetration. Already in 1993 27 per cent of the nominal capital of companies was located in foreign investment enterprises, one year later 31 per cent. The other three countries, i.e. the Czech Republic, Poland and Slovakia, were still much more closed against foreign influence, although there were industries with relatively high foreign penetration in each country.

In all four countries foreign investment enterprises had higher shares in capital than in labour and even higher shares in output, meaning that endowment with capital as well as labour productivity were higher in the foreign sector than in the domestic one. This confirms the expectation that the foreign sector uses more recent technology, but may also be related to the concentration of FDI in specific industries.

The export performance relative to output in Hungary and Poland indicates that FIEs are more export-oriented than domestic firms. Other data reveal that FIEs are more strongly represented in imports than in exports and thus have contributed considerably to foreign trade deficits. FDI targeted at penetrating the local market with the aim of selling foreign goods was wide-spread. Other factors, like high import needs at the early stage of export-oriented investment projects, may disappear later.

In the four countries on which data are available, FIEs contribute disproportionately more to fixed investment. This is a confirmation of the positive effect of FDI on economic growth and restructuring. The large amount of follow-up investment after acquisition suggests that foreign investors rapidly restructure the acquired firms. This is connected with lay-offs, so FDI does not help to solve the problem of unemployment.

Table 7. Share of foreign investment enterprises (FIEs) in the total economy[1] (%).

	Czech Republic 1994	Hungary 1994	Poland 1993	Slovak Republic 1994
Nominal capital	7.4	31.9	7.0[2]	5.0
Employed persons	6.0	22.6	5.6	3.8
Output	9.4	38.6	10.8[3]	7.7[4]
Export sales	n.a.	50.6	16.4	n.a.
Investment	16.5	38.0	11.2	11.8

Notes: [1] Czech Republic, Slovak Republic: non-financial corporations with at least 25 employees; Hungary, Poland: companies supplying tax declarations; [2] Estimated; [3] Income from sales and financial operations; [4] Value added.

Source: Based on national statistical data collected in the framework of the WIIW research project on FDI.

The very positive features concerning the activity of foreign investment enterprises may be overshadowed by the fact that foreigners picked the most healthy firms in the privatisation process so that the FIEs' performance is compared with "leftovers". While this observation is certainly valid for Hungary, in other countries the foreign sector is too small to own most of the good companies.

5.2 FIEs in Czech manufacturing

The following results are derived from a database covering all Czech manufacturing firms whose employment exceeds 24 workers and who are subject to regular statistical reporting of their balance sheets data. (This section relies on research done by Zemplínerová in the framework of the WIIW project on FDI.) In 1994 among 4 000 such companies, there were 375 FIEs, of which 104 were 100 per cent foreign-owned. The firms fully owned by foreign capital were significantly smaller in size than the average Czech manufacturing firms, and even smaller than Czech private firms. For larger investment projects, multinational enterprises preferred to involve a domestic partner in order to share the risk and reduce the amount of capital required for the venture. Larger FIEs with less than 100 per cent foreign ownership usually came into being as a result of privatisation.

FIEs active in the manufacturing sector in 1994 represented approximately 9 per cent of all firms, but 11.8 per cent of the total nominal capital and 11.2 per cent of total output. FIEs employed 7.5 per cent of the workforce in manufacturing, of which 1.3 per cent was in fully foreign-owned enterprises. The FIEs' share in manufacturing employment is slightly higher than in the economy as whole. FIE employees' salaries are on average 20 per cent higher than in domestic enterprises. These higher salaries reflect the higher labour productivity in the foreign firms. FIEs are apparently able to attract the more skilled workers and managers.

FIEs differ significantly by sub-branches of manufacturing (see Table 8). If measured by labour or output, the most intensive foreign involvement can be found in the car industry, in printing and publishing, and rubber and plastics. These industries also record the highest shares of foreign investment capital in the total. A significant part of foreign investment is recorded also in the sub-branches of electrical machinery. The preference of investors for certain activities corresponds to international trends — first of all technology- and R&D-intensive sectors are dominated by multinationals. Foreign investors find labour-intensive industries not sufficiently attractive. The assumption that cheap local labour offers a comparative

Table 8. Czech Republic: share of FIEs in labour force, investment, output and export sales of manufacturing enterprises by branches (%).

Industries	Labour 1994	Investment 1994	Exports 1994	Output 1994
Foodstuffs and tobacco	9.3	22.7	20.8	11.1
Textile	4.1	7.4	7.3	6.5
Clothing	7.0	7.3	6.2	7.1
Leather and shoes	4.7	2.4	3.0	3.6
Wooden products	3.3	2.3	10.6	5.5
Paper	6.1	3.9	9.0	9.6
Printing & publishing	20.9	39.6	13.3	31.7
Oil refining, coke	0.0	0.0	0.0	0.0
Chemicals	3.9	16.4	6.6	5.1
Rubber & plastics	21.5	43.6	52.4	28.2
Non-metal	10.9	35.2	26.3	20.5
Metals	1.7	10.3	3.2	2.2
Metal constructions	6.2	15.2	12.5	9.8
Machinery	3.6	6.3	5.2	4.0
Office machines &	3.8	2.6	7.3	5.8
Electrical machinery	12.0	33.9	26.3	13.7
Communication	3.3	7.9	5.7	4.2
Optical, medical	8.7	21.7	23.2	10.8
Cars and trailers	28.8	73.0	73.9	55.1
Other transport	1.9	2.0	3.1	1.6
Furniture	4.6	13.0	7.7	6.2
Recycling	4.2	4.1	4.9	0.0
Total manufacturing	7.5	24.8	16.4	11.2

advantage for development cannot be confirmed. With their very high capital-to-labour ratio, the labour in firms with foreign involvement has high productivity and wages.

FIEs accounted for almost one quarter of capital investment in Czech manufacturing in 1994. This is two times higher than their share in output and nominal capital. FIEs are expanding and have a more recent and probably more modern capital stock than domestic companies. Only in clothing and textiles do FIEs record lower investment shares than output shares. In these branches they may really exploit the available capacities and care little for modernisation.

In 1994, 16.4 per cent of Czech manufacturing exports came from FIEs. The export orientation of FIEs is relatively high. Exports represent 31 per cent of sales in the case of all enterprises and 41 per cent for FIEs. Firms in full foreign ownership do not have higher export ratios than the national average. The lowest export ratios are found in the production of foodstuffs and tobacco (14 per cent). An especially high export orientation (export/output more than 60 per cent) was registered for wooden products, metals, vehicles other than cars, and clothes (see Table 9). Although we lack statistics about imports, it can be assumed that the import content per unit of production in FIEs is significantly above the average national level.

Table 9. Czech Republic: share of export sales in total sales by manufacturing sub-branches and ownership, 1994.

Industries	100% FIEs	other FIEs	domestic private firms	all enterprises
Foodstuffs and tobacco	13.96	14.81	6.03	8.86
Textile	47.66	49.93	41.93	44.60
Clothing	91.92	60.56	46.60	50.56
Leather and shoes	97.96	49.62	29.08	37.78
Wooden products	5.03	77.43	41.86	42.37
Paper	12.35	44.58	18.51	33.53
Printing and publishing	3.19	5.08	9.97	8.15
Oil refining, coke	.	.	.	23.69
Chemicals	68.32	54.08	28.56	40.87
Rubber and plastics	41.50	48.53	22.19	32.45
Non-metal	12.83	45.25	36.91	38.84
Metals	51.36	65.96	32.09	45.42
Metal constructions	89.60	36.33	25.85	31.28
Machinery	58.99	37.38	35.79	35.62
Office machines and	.	47.19	59.51	58.40
Electrical machinery	36.87	59.26	14.74	26.79
Communication	86.88	41.90	42.32	44.93
Optical, medical	88.77	50.54	14.85	22.98
Cars and trailers	98.12	52.43	37.09	42.68
Other transport	.	64.53	25.12	29.21
Furniture	95.70	59.35	38.40	44.74
Recycling	.	44.35	26.14	34.85
Total manufacturing	32.48	42.91	25.92	31.36

5.3 *FIEs in Hungarian manufacturing*

The total stock of FDI in Hungary was reported to be US$7 400 million at the end of 1993, while registered foreign capital in FIEs amounted to US$6 583 million, the rest being invested in small or recently established firms not covered by statistics. Of the foreign investment capital, 30.6 per cent was placed in wholly foreign-owned companies, 50.1 per cent in majority foreign-owned companies and only 20 per cent in minority ownership. FIEs employed 20 per cent of the total workforce (in companies providing tax declarations) in 1993. FIEs are less labour-intensive than domestic firms in all branches of production, except financial services, and in all sub-branches of manufacturing. The lower labour intensity and higher capital intensity of FIEs compared with domestic companies is the result of different company strategies. FIEs are faster in restructuring and employ more labour-saving technology than do domestic firms.

The share of FIEs in business sector investment was 26 per cent in 1992, 34 per cent in 1993 and 38 per cent in 1994. In 1993 investment by domestic companies without foreign capital remained constant; the entire increase of business investment in that year was due to FIEs. FIEs invested less than average in buildings and more than average in machinery, two-thirds of which was imported. The FIEs' share in investment in machinery was 45 per cent, and in imported machinery 50 per cent. This proves that the contribution of FIEs to economic modernisation through machinery investment and imports of technology is outstanding. On the other hand, the deterioration of the foreign trade balance can partly be attributed to the investment activity of FIEs.

Half of FDI until 1993 was invested in manufacturing, where FIEs own 45 per cent of the nominal capital of companies. The highest rate of FIE presence was in construction material production (62 per cent), food industry (57 per cent) and machine-building (50 per cent). All these shares underwent increases during the last two years. The foreign penetration has been strongest in branches with relatively stable or promising domestic markets. Some sub-branches of the food industry, like edible oil production, breweries and tobacco factories, are almost

Table 10. Hungary: share of FIEs in the total economy[1] by industries, 1993 (%).

ISIC-Code	Industries	Employ-ment	FIE Capital total[2]	FIE Capital FDI[3]	Sales	Export sales	Invest-ment[4]	FDI[5]
A,B	Agriculture, hunting, forestry, fishing	0	5.2	0	0	22.4	0	1.2
C	Mining and quarrying	11.5	25.2	19.0	12.1	21.1	35.0	1.3
D	Manufacturing	30.6	45.0	31.2	40.2	51.7	61.8	49.9
E	Electricity, gas and water supply	0	0.6	0	0	0	0	0.8
F	Construction	14.6	35.9	25.8	24.7	34.5	35.5	3.9
G	Wholesale and retail trade	21.0	34.6	22.1	32.3	50.4	37.0	13.6
H	Hotels and restaurants	22.5	40.3	28.3	27.3	37.0	41.7	3.9
I	Transport, storage, communications	12.0	35.3	13.8	36.0	52.9	54.6	8.7
J	Finance	47.4	46.1	14.9	79.6	94.3	0	7.3
K	Real estate, renting	14.2	24.7	16.7	29.8	42.2	38.6	8.5
	Total	20.1	26.6	15.9	30.9	50.0	34.0	100.0

Note: 0 denotes less than 5%; [1] All companies providing tax declarations; [2] Nominal capital of foreign investment companies; [3] Foreign direct investment in nominal capital; [4] Gross capital investment; [5] Distribution of FDI among branches, %.

Source: KSH, 1995b and 1995c.

exclusively foreign-owned. Household equipment and cars can also be regarded as products with good prospects on the Hungarian market, but the size of the Hungarian market is too small to carry firms for local sales only. A relatively stable domestic market does not hinder, but rather stimulates production for exports. FIEs provided 40 per cent of sales in manufacturing, and within that about half of the sales in the sub-branches non-metallic minerals (construction materials), machine-building and food industry in 1993. Their share in total manufacturing sale increased to 55 per cent in 1994.

Table 11. Hungary: share of FIEs in manufacturing, by branches, 1993 (%).

ISIC-Code	Branches	Employment	FIE capital	FDI capital	Sales	Export sales	FDI
15-16	Food	36.0	57.5	43.0	49.2	58.8	33.7
17-19	Textiles	27.4	37.8	23.1	36.2	53.8	4.3
20-22	Paper	25.5	40.6	27.8	43.3	53.5	6.6
23-25	Chemicals	31.1	29.6	14.8	27.1	37.3	11.1
26	Non-metallic mineral products	40.0	62.1	48.2	52.5	62.8	8.4
27-28	Metallurgy	19.7	40.8	24.9	29.0	36.8	6.9
29-35	Machinery	34.7	49.5	37.7	49.4	66.3	27.6
36-37	Other	20.6	29.9	23.4	24.8	42.9	1.5
	Total	30.6	45.0	31.2	40.2	51.7	100.0

Source: KSH, 1995b and 1995c.

Export sales of FIEs made up exactly half the total exports of Hungarian companies in 1993 and 60 per cent a year later. The share was even higher in the case of the most important export branch, manufacturing (see Table 11). Two-thirds of machinery exports and almost 60 per cent of exports of the food industry came from FIEs. Manufacturing FIEs exported 30 per cent of their products, compared to the average 23.2 per cent. Machine-building FIEs exported 47 per cent of their products, those in textiles and clothing 58 per cent. In these sub-branches processing for exports must have been an important motivation for investing in Hungary. The food industry, on the other hand, was highly domestic-oriented. The relatively low export share, 16 per cent in the case of FIEs, reveals that investment in the food industry was motivated by access to the domestic market. Nevertheless, FIEs provided almost 60 per cent of the food industry export sales.

In fact, foreign investment enterprises are the most dynamic part of the Hungarian economy (and perhaps even the only one). Foreign investment enterprises have an extraordinary impact on the microeconomic development (subordinated to the global strategy of multinational enterprises) and the path of future economic development (rapidly increasing openness). They have contributed to the rapid upgrading of Hungarian exports.

6. Lessons from company surveys

The statistical evidence on the mezzo level presented in the former sections conceals the great variety of restructuring stories. From the vast literature reporting on company surveys and case studies, the latest conclusions concerning restructuring in the wake of privatisation and FDI are summarised below. However interesting the results of such surveys may be, they must be treated with caution as even the most recently published ones rely on information gathered in 1993 or 1994.

Surveys come to three general basic conclusions:

- there is great diversity of performance between individual companies, irrespective of their ownership;
- the difference in restructuring between SOEs and domestic private companies is not very large;
- restructuring in FIEs is much more significant than in domestically owned companies.

The follow-up problems of voucher privatisation in the Czech Republic are well demonstrated (Mertlík, 1996) — there is no significant difference between privatised and non-privatised companies. Similar companies with a similar history and privatisation path may have very different current positions and restructuring strategies, while companies differing in all respects may end up in identical situations. According to Mertlík, voucher-privatised firms can speed up restructuring if ownership gets concentrated; foreigners are likely to be attributed a big role in the concentration process. Another study on the Czech Republic (Zemplínerová *et al.*, 1995) measured restructuring by indicators such as change in organisation, improvement in marketing and management, quality control, and training and innovation under different ownership structures. Zemplínerová finds some restructuring taking place in most of the 242 surveyed enterprises by 1993, but the difference in the grade of restructuring varied. State-owned firms performed worse, followed by management-owned ones. Firms under dispersed owners, employees or citizens, restructured somewhat more than the former group. Firms with concentrated domestic owners and investment privatisation funds performed even better. Far ahead of all other groups, 94 per cent of the foreign-owned firms featured a higher than average grade of restructuring.

Surveys of Hungarian manufacturing firms' restructuring in 1993 (Szanyi, 1994b) found that most companies, disregarding ownership, made steps towards re-organisation, marketing and quality control. The skills of the managers (regardless of whether they were new or old in this position) in applying new methods and setting viable goals was important. These measures however could hardly compensate for the lack of investment resources to change old or inadequate machinery. One-third of the companies surveyed were able to introduce new technologies; foreign-owned ones more frequently than others, but state-owned ones were also well represented. Companies not able to invest or to overcome financial difficulties were forced to choose a foreign investor if they wanted to survive (Hunya, 1996b). A 1992 survey of Czech and Hungarian firms stated that new foreign owners found organisational changes more important than technical improvements in raising productivity, while the opinion of local company managers was just the opposite (Hitchens, 1995).

In Poland 57 large FIEs were questioned during 1994 (Jermakowicz *et al.*, 1994). The authors conclude that the largest companies made a positive contribution to

Poland's economic recovery. The automobile industry recovered due to massive investments by Fiat and GM. Another dynamic industry nation-wide was brewery, also majority foreign-controlled. The authors also point out the beneficial role of foreign investors in technology transfer and training of staff. Foreign investors targeted capital-, technology- and qualification-intensive activities, and not the traditional labour-intensive industries. The problems pointed out by this study refer mainly to the sometimes dubious performance of smaller investment projects. Many of these use existing capacities and have little new investment. They serve the local market and do not contribute to the integration of the Polish economy into international markets. Also large FIEs were established with the primary aim of penetrating the Polish market, but the foreign owners' activity increased exports as well. While 90 per cent of the foreign investors made changes in the profile and the organisational structure of the acquired Polish enterprise, only 20 per cent reduced employment.

The findings of the above study were included in a comparative survey of Czech, Hungarian, Polish and Slovenian foreign investment enterprises which investigated among other aspects the content of post-acquisition changes and restructuring acts (Rojec, 1995). The authors did not use their findings for an inter-country comparison, perhaps because of the rather small samples, but such a comparison (based on Rojec, 1995) leads to very relevant results. The most frequent restructuring activity was the introduction of new production programmes and the improvement in marketing activities, although less frequently in Hungary than in the other three countries. The training of management was much more frequent than its replacement. Foreign investors, unfamiliar with local circumstances, had to rely on the experience of the former management if the latter could be trained for the new tasks. In the Czech Republic new owners frequently reduced the staff and sold non-core businesses, less frequently in Poland and rarely in Hungary. The earlier start of restructuring in Hungary is contrasted to the Czech policy of postponing restructuring until after privatisation. On the other hand, the need for financial consolidation was much more severe in Poland and Hungary than in the Czech Republic. It seems that in Hungary and Poland technical restructuring did proceed under state ownership, but not in a financially efficient way. Unlike in the Czech Republic, SOEs' debts accumulated rapidly, and no general relief was provided by the state. The lower real interest rates in the Czech Republic also protected companies against the debt-trap, but good liquidity did not stimulate restructuring by investment because managers were unable to take the initiative ('pre-privatisation agony').

The comparative survey (Rojec, 1995) found it not very encouraging that only one third of FIEs were integrated into the investing company's network. Integration was high in Slovenia, perhaps because FIEs were more mature there than in the other countries. The larger and the more internationalised the foreign partner and the acquired company, the higher was the propensity to be integrated into the investor's network. Market-oriented investment resulted in less networking than efficiency-oriented investment.

Foreign ownership, though beneficial at the initial stage of restructuring, limits the choice of future company strategies (Csermely, 1995). Incorporation into global sourcing means narrower assortment, competition for higher-standard products inside the multinational network, and limits on R&D activity (Skoda, Elektrolux). Import dependence on other members of the multinational group may increase, without a test of alternative supplies. This increases imports and may kill the traditional domestic supplier. Market access is also restricted by the multinational owner. Little chance is left for the former SOE to retain brand-name and corporate identity. A study of the car and parts industry in Hungary (Somai, 1996) reveals great difficulties of local companies in becoming subcontractors to multinational car producers active in the country. While Suzuki from Japan is interested in increasing local sourcing to surpass 50 per cent European content, European investors (GM, Audi, Ford) operate as islands with marginal local sourcing.

7. Conclusions and outlook

- Five years after the basic framework of a market economy has been installed in the CEECs, companies are still in the process of adapting to the new circumstances. Economic recovery started both in privatised and in majority publicly controlled economies. Passive adaptation and marginal restructuring had been possible also under state ownership, but chances for strategic restructuring and sustained economic growth are better in privatised and foreign-penetrated economies.

- Restructuring in industrial enterprises is generally hindered by the slow pace of restructuring in the financial sector. This is a marked disadvantage of the domestic sector compared to the foreign one. FIEs restructure faster because they have access to investment from abroad and receive credits under the risk conditions of well-established foreign enterprises.

- Different privatisation and FDI policies have led to very different ownership structures in the CEEC economies. Fundamental differences have emerged among the countries concerning foreign control of manufacturing industries. In the Czech Republic and in Poland, a few big deals dominate the FDI scene, and the general level of foreign penetration has remained low. In Hungary, foreign penetration is relatively strong, although still weaker than in Austria or Spain.

- The manufacturing industries under foreign ownership restructured more rapidly than domestically owned companies. The gains in productivity, the intensity of investment activities and the improvement in the export performance all point in the same, positive direction.

- The future development of manufacturing enterprises under foreign ownership has become dependent on decisions in multinational corporations. The fast restructuring in Hungarian manufacturing is the result of large-scale foreign penetration, which has also made the development of whole industries foreign-dependent. In the Czech Republic and in Poland most companies try to preserve their independence even at the cost of slower restructuring, but in the hope of being able to pursue advantageous strategies.

- Rapid success in initial restructuring by foreign investment is no guarantee of future success. It is not yet obvious to what extent CEEC subsidiaries will be integrated into the global networks of multinational enterprises, whether they will succeed in advancing on the technological ladder (Radoševic, 1995), and whether their success will have a spreading effect on the CEEC economies by increasing local sourcing.

- It can be expected that major FDI in the CEECs will also in the future be confined to three countries — the Czech Republic, Hungary and Poland — for at least two reasons: (1) Established foreign investment projects will attract further investment in the form of capital increase into existing projects, competing multinational companies in the same branch or subcontractors of major multinationals. (2) No other CEEC is prepared to privatise public utilities, or speed up privatisation by sales to foreigners. The privatisation policy of other countries clearly follows ways of keeping state influence dominant in several sectors or, if they privatise, voucher methods are favoured.

- The focus of foreign firms may shift between the three leading target countries. The Czech Republic is going to privatise public utilities in 1996 and 1997, which will certainly attract large amounts of capital. The restructuring needs of companies privatised in the voucher scheme will make new foreign involvement necessary. Investment funds may be interested in inviting strategic investors. In Hungary privatisation-related FDI in manufacturing will phase out in 1996, and FDI will not be attracted by the expansion of the local market either. At the same time Hungary is emerging as a major location of export-oriented investment projects and their sub-contractors and keeps attracting investment in manufacturing. Poland, the largest market and most rapidly growing economy, will attract increasing amounts of FDI. It has also the largest non-privatised sector offering opportunities for foreign take-overs after mass privatisation has been completed. Relative to their small size, Slovenia, Slovakia and also some Baltic states will also benefit from FDI, but for other transition countries restructuring by FDI remains uncertain.

Note

[1] The information given in these sections was provided by WIIW country specialists and reflects the situation at the end of 1995.

References

ACE Quarterly, 1995, PHARE, No. 4, Winter.

Amsden, A. *et al.*, 1994, *The Market Meets its Match*, Harvard University Press, Cambridge.

Aslund, A., 1991, "Principles of privatization", in L. Csaba (ed.), *Systemic Change and Stabilization in Eastern Europe*, Dartmouth, Aldershot.

Böhm, A. (ed.), 1995, *Privatization in Central & Eastern Europe*, Central & Eastern European Privatization Network, Ljubljana.

Carlin, W. *et al.*, 1994, "Enterprise Restructuring in the Transition: an Analytical Survey of the Case Study Evidence from Central and Eastern Europe", European Bank for Reconstruction and Development, *Working Paper*, No. 14, July.

Charap, J. and Zemplínerová, A., 1994, "Foreign Direct Investment in the Privatization and Restructuring of the Czech Economy", *Development and International Cooperation*, No. 18, June.

Csaba, L., 1995, *The capitalist revolution in Eastern Europe*, Edward Edgar Publishers, Aldershot-Brookfield.

Csermely, Á., 1995, "Impediments to Exports in Small Countries in Transition, Country Study Hungary", paper read at the workshop "Impediments to Exports in Small Transition Economies", IIASA, Laxenburg, Austria, 29 June - 1 July.

EBRD, 1994, *Transition Report*, London.

EBRD, 1995, *Transition Report*, London.

Éltetö, A. *et al.*, 1995, "Foreign Direct Investment in East-Central-Europe in Comparative Analysis with Spain and Portugal", Institute for World Economics, *Working Papers*, No. 51, Budapest, May.

Ernst, M., Alexeev, M. and Marer, P., 1996, *Transforming the Core*, Westview Press, Boulder.

Frydman, R., Rapaczynski, A., Earle, J. *et al.*, 1993, *The Privatization Process in Central Europe*, Central European University Press, Budapest.

Frydman, R. and Rapaczynski, A., 1994, *Privatization in Eastern Europe: Is the State Withering Away?*, Central European University Press, Budapest.

Grabher, G. and Stark, D. (eds.), 1996, *Legacies, Linkages and Localities: The Social Embeddedness of the Economic Transformation in Central and Eastern Europe*, Oxford University Press, London, New York.

Grosfeld, I. and Roland, G., 1995, "Defensive and Strategic Restructuring in Central European Enterprises", Centre for Economic Policy Research, *Discussion Paper*, No. 1135, March.

Hitchens, D. *et al.*, 1995, "The Comparative Productivity of Manufacturing Plants in the Czech Republic and Hungary", *Economic Systems*, No. 3.

Hunya, G., 1992, "Foreign Direct Investment and Privatization in Central and Eastern Europe", *Communist Economies and Economies in Transition*, No. 4.

Hunya, G., 1995a, "A progress report on privatization in Eastern Europe", in C. Saunders (ed.), *Eastern Europe in Crisis and the Way Out*, Macmillan, London.

Hunya, G., 1995b, "An Economic Assessment of Privatization in Central and Eastern European Countries", in P. Karasz *et al.* (eds.), *Economics & Politics*, Proceedings of the Vth Bratislava Symposium and IInd East Central Europe Roundtable Conference, Slovak Committee of the European Cultural Foundation, Bratislava.

Hunya, G., 1996a, "Foreign Direct Investment and its Employment Effects in the Czech Republic, Hungary and Poland", *OECD Seminar on Migration, Free Trade and Regional Integration in Central and Eastern Europe*, Vienna, February.

Hunya, G., 1996b, "Foreign Direct Investment in Hungary: a Key Element of Economic Modernization", *WIIW Research Reports*, No. 226, February.

Jermakowicz, W. *et al.*, 1994, *Foreign Privatization in Poland*, Centre for Social and Economic Research, Warsaw, October.

Kornai, J., 1995, "Transformational Recession: the example of Hungary", in C. Saunders (ed.), *Eastern Europe in Crisis and the Way Out*, Macmillan, London.

Kregel, J. *et al.*, 1992, *The Market Shock*, Austrian Academy of Sciences/Research Unit for Socio-Economics, Vienna.

KSH (Central Statistical Office), 1995a, *National accounts, Hungary 1991-1993*, Budapest.

KSH (Central Statistical Office), 1995b, *A külföldi müködötöke Magyaroszágon 1993* (Foreign direct investment in Hungary 1993), Budapest.

Landesmann, M., 1994, "Industrial Policy and the Transition in East-Central Europe", in G. Hunya (ed.), *Economic Transformation in East-Central Europe and in the Newly Independent States*, Westview Press, Boulder.

Landesmann, M., 1996, "Emerging Patterns of European Industrial Specialization: Implications for Trade Structures, Foreign Direct Investment and Migration Flows", OECD Seminar on Migration, Free Trade and Regional Integration in Central and Eastern Europe, Vienna, February.

Mertlík, P., 1996, "Czech Privatization: from Public Ownership to Public Ownership in Five Years", paper presented at the AGENDA Group Workshop, Vienna, April.

Naujoks, P. and Schmidt, K., 1995, "Foreign Direct Investment and Trade in Transition Countries: Tracing the Link", *Kiel Working Papers*, No. 667, January.

Norman, G. and Motta, M., 1993, "Eastern European Economic Integration and Foreign Direct Investment", *Journal of Economics & Management Strategy*, No. 2, Winter.

OECD/CCET, 1993, *Methods of Privatizing Large Enterprises*, Paris.

OECD/CCET, 1994a, *Trends and Policies in Privatization*, Vol. II, No. 1, Paris.

OECD/CCET, 1994b, "Bureaucratic Barriers to Entry: Foreign Investment in Central and Eastern Europe", SIGMA, Paris.

OECD/CCET, 1995a, *Mass Privatization. An Initial Assessment*, Paris.

OECD/CCET, 1995b, *Trends and Policies in Privatization*, Vol. II, No 2, Paris.

Quaisser, W., 1995, "Ausländische Direktinvestitionen im polnischen Transformationsprozeß", Osteuropa-Institut München, *Working Papers*, No. 184, October.

Radoševic, S., 1995, "Technology Transfer and Restructuring of Technology Capability in Global Competition: the Case of Economies in Transition", paper presented at the workshop "Transfer of Technology, Trade, and Development: the Newly Industrialised Economies in the Global Competition", Venice, April.

Rojec, M., 1995, *Foreign Direct Investment and Privatization in Central and Eastern Europe*, ACE Project, Final Report, Ljubljana.

Sander, B., 1995, "Siemens — A Multinational's Strategy to Investment in the Central-East European Transformation Countries", *Kiel Working Papers*, no. 709, October.

Schmidt, K., 1994, "Foreign Direct Investment in Central and East European Countries: State of Affairs, Prospects and Policy Implications", *Kiel Working Papers*, No. 633, June.

Schmidt, K., 1995, "Motives of Large Multinationals Investing in Small Transition Countries: A Literature Review", *Kiel Working Papers,* No. 668, January.

Sereghyová, J., 1995, "Case Studies from the Czech Republic", paper read at the workshop "Impediments to Exports in Small Transition Economies", IIASA, Laxenburg, Austria, 29 June - 1 July.

Somai, M., 1996, "Autó- és autóalkatrész-gyártás Magyarországon" (Car and components manufacturing in Hungary), mimeo, Institute of World Economics, Hungarian Academy of Sciences, Budapest.

Szanyi, M., 1994a, "Experience with foreign direct investment in Hungary", Institute of World Economics, Hungarian Academy of Sciences, *Working Papers*, No. 32, April.

Szanyi, M., 1994b, "Efforts at Adaptation by Hungarian Industrial Firms During the Transformation Crisis", Institute of World Economics, Hungarian Academy of Sciences, *Working Papers*, No. 46, December.

UN ECE, 1995, 1996, *Economic Survey of Europe*, New York and Geneva.

UNIDO, 1994, *Economies in Transition: Restructuring of Large-Scale Industries*, Vienna.

Welfens, P. and Jasinski, P., 1994, *Privatization and Foreign Direct Investment in Transforming Economies*, Dartmouth, Aldershot.

Young, P. and Reynolds, P., 1994, *The Amnesia of Reform*, Adam Smith Research Trust, London.

Zemplínerová, A. and Benácek, V., 1995, "Foreign Direct Investment — East and West: The Experience of the Czech Republic", mimeo, ACE Project Workshop, Prague, 6-8 April.

Zemplínerová, A. *et al.*, 1995, "Restructuring of Czech Manufacturing Enterprises: An Empirical Study", *CERGE-EI Working Papers*, No. 74, Prague.

5

The evolution of bank credit quality in Romania since 1991

Octavian V. Cãrare and Enrico C. Perotti

Introduction

This paper examines whether the economic reforms which started in 1990 have been effective in tightening financial discipline on Romanian state-owned enterprises. Our main conclusion is that the Romanian banking systems criteria for loans show few signs of improvement since the beginning of the reform process.

At the onset of economic reform, there were strong similarities across all Central and Eastern European economies in the structure of SOEs funding. Although the government was nominally in control of enterprise governance, the influence of direct state controls over enterprises fell markedly following the onset of reform. As direct subsidies were sharply reduced during this period, bank lending became a crucial source of outside finance for the state-owned enterprise sector.

On the one hand, in a transition economy subject to large trade and price shocks, banks may have a hard time at first reducing their exposure to unprofitable enterprises. If appropriate microeconomic reform takes place over time, however, it should be possible to observe a progressive improvement in the composition of bank lending. If on the other hand banks are under political pressure due to their need for massive recapitalisation, they may direct credit to less creditworthy but politically sensitive enterprises. In addition, there may be perverse incentives even on the part of profit-maximising banks to continue direct credit to former borrowers in the presence of implicit government guarantees (Perotti, 1993). This is particularly important as the Romanian banking system faces a considerable degree of decapitalisation, as a result of inflationary pressure and a large stock of non-performing loans. It is therefore essential to assess whether banks contributed to enterprise restructuring by ceasing to finance the worst performers and redirecting resources to the more efficient producers.

Studying the disciplinary role of the banking system on enterprise restructuring requires data on the true amount of bad loans and the quality of new credit. This information is hardly available. An alternative is to assess the data related to bank borrowing and arrears from the SOE's yearly balance sheets.

The authors thank Mark Schaffer for useful comments.

In a well functioning financial market, banks' lending is driven by knowledge of historical performance and by consideration of future profitability of potential borrowers. A history of losses and failure to repay trade liabilities, and a large stock of unpaid bank loans would clearly have a negative impact on the lending decision.

Pinto and van Wijnbergen (1994) use balance sheet and survey data from Polish SOEs to determine whether the allocation of bank lending had improved since the beginning of market reforms. Their analysis shows a breakdown of the negative link between SOEs profitability and their access to new credit, and conclude that a structural break took place in the behaviour of Polish banks as a result of a broad reform of the banking system in 1992.

Regressing observed changes in bank credit on profitability to verify the sign of the correlation is not informative, as it cannot separate supply and demand effects. In principle, high profitability is positively related to credit supply (banks like to lend to good firms); but when real interest rates are high during stabilization cycles, profitability may be negatively related to credit demand (why borrow when you can finance internally at a lower cost?). In contrast, bad firms do not mind accepting high interest rates, as they do not plan to repay. Pinto and van Wijnbergen (1994) address this issue by a test based on ordered logit regressions of firms' perceived ease of obtaining bank credit on profitability. Using survey data allows some degree of identification of the supply curve. Surveys of subjective measures can be aimed at measuring some of the underlying attitudes of lenders and borrowers toward lending, borrowing and repayment. Kotzeva and Perotti (1995) developed and implemented a special survey of managers of Bulgarian SOEs, aimed at measuring subjective attitudes towards extending trade credit. They find evidence of opportunistic behaviour based on the expectation of a collective bailout.

We pursue here another approach. We examine bank lending to firms stratified by balance sheet measures of performance (profitability, growth rates), and relate it to variables such as trade receivables (a normal cause of bank lending) as well as to the stock of inter-enterprise and bank arrears. The correlation of bank loans with financial arrears over time should enable us to measure whether credit is correlated negatively with profitability because during tight policies there is less demand by "better" firms (which may in fact reduce their borrowing); or if banks passively continue to lend to uncreditworthy firms, which continue to accumulate arrears.

We apply these ideas to a detailed sample of Romanian state enterprises for the years 1991 through 1994. Our results are not encouraging. Bank credit appears to be directed increasingly towards firms that are on average larger, less profitable, and have a larger arrears position in trade and bank credit. Even lending to "better" firms seems to contain some bias towards those with the largest trade arrears. The evidence suggests that bank credit in 1993-94 has replaced state subsidies of 1990 and direct bailouts of trade arrears of 1991-92. We conclude that a large part of bank credit among SOEs in Romania is used to prop up weak firms rather than fund the enterprises with better prospects.

While macroeconomic indicators are most commonly used to assess the performance of an economy and its reform process, the importance of a timely assessment on the quality of bank lending should be self-evident. Microeconomic adjustment is the sole guarantee of long-term performance; a tight credit policy may reduce inflation, but be unsustainable because available credit is used to cover losses. If enterprises consume credit without generating an appropriate return, and decapitalise themselves by paying insiders most of their surpluses, in the medium term the banking sector will reveal its insolvent state, requiring massive recapitalisation and thus sharp monetary growth or a large budget deficit.

Section 1 briefly describes the economic context of the Romanian reform process and illustrates the structure of our working assumptions. Section 2 describes the sample and presents our empirical results. We offer some preliminary conclusions at the end.

1. A brief history of the Romanian financial transition

Until 1992 an important source of funding for SOEs consisted of direct government subsidies for the state enterprises. The agreements signed in 1991 and 1992 between the Romanian government and the International Monetary Fund required a drastic cut in such subsidies. In order to be able to receive the IMF structural adjustment loans, explicit subsidies were cut dramatically. In 1993, most SOEs reported to be zero subsidies in their balance sheets. The main responsibility for promoting further financial discipline on enterprise thus shifted to the banks.

Before 1989, the Romanian financial system served only as a channel for subsidies to enterprises. The monolithical National Bank had control over the flow of funds, and deployed them to state-owned enterprises according to a five year plan (Brainard, 1993). The only bank which had some of the prerogatives of a commercial bank was the Bank for Foreign Trade. The main source of funds was the Savings Bank (CEC), which had a monopolistic position as a retail bank paying (low) interest rates on people's savings. Real interest rates were kept very low. The financing of long-term investments was carried out through the Investment Bank. Enterprises did not have any incentive to repay loans, as future credit was independent of past repayment and no mechanisms were in place to enforce credit contracts. These features were common to all former Communist economies, although the degree of overlending did vary across countries (Perotti, 1994).

An early financial crisis developed in Romania within the state industrial sector following a first attempt at macroeconomic stabilization in 1991. The stock of inter-enterprise arrears rose rapidly 18-fold, until it amounted to a stunning 50 per cent of Romania's GDP. The implementation of the Global Compensation Scheme (GCS) in December 1991 did not bring any considerable improvement to the trade arrears problem (Clifton and Khan, 1993; Calvo and Coricelli, 1993). The CGS led to a massive shift of financial arrears to the banking sector and, ultimately, to the Romanian National Bank, which had to provide funds for clearing outstanding trade debts between enterprises. Following the GCS the money supply rose by 149 billion lei (Clifton and Khan, 1993), leading to an increase in prices of 223 per cent, some 118 per cent more than projected.

The basis for a cyclical pattern of tight monetary policy, rapid build-up in arrears and finally centralised bailout had been established. The money supply remained almost unchanged from November 1990, (Croitoru and Ciocirlan, 1994), until April 1991, increasing then by December 1991 by 71 per cent. Although interest rates were formally liberalised during 1991, certain constraints imposed severe limits on real interest rates becoming positive (Croitoru and Ciocirlan, 1994). The interest rates for credits offered by commercial banks in Romania in 1992 and 1993 varied considerably (during December 1992, for instance, interest rates for credits ranged from 15 per cent to 180 per cent, another sign that a dual market for credits was effective during at least 1992 and 1993).

In May 1992 the NBR shifted policy again, and interest rates on loans offered by the main state-owned banks, calculated on a quarterly basis, became positive in real terms for a short period during the second and third quarters of 1992; following a new credit relaxation they then plunged, only to become positive again at the beginning of 1994. The imposition of quantitative ceilings for refinancing around that date gave a clear sign that the NBR was attempting to stem the amount of credit offered by commercial banks to its borrowers. Interest rates on inter-bank credit auction rose to 184 per cent in March 1994. Commercial banks managed to shift these high levels of interest rates on overdraft corporate loans, suggesting that loan demand was quite inelastic during this period. As argued below, this may in part reflect the fact that many uncreditworthy firms maintained a high level of loan demand. The hyperinflationary environment and thus the decapitalisation of the banking system greatly diminished the commercial banks' lending capacity. Between August 1993 and February 1994 the share of inter-bank auction and overdraft funds in the commercial banks' sources increased 35-fold, from 1.4 per cent to 50 per cent, then decreased somewhat by August 1994 to some 33 per cent.

Although bank credit was restricted both by means of "official" interest rates and quantitative ceilings imposed by the NBR, there were signs that the Government facilitated for some firms an implicit subsidisation of interest rates. In the period analysed, enterprises faced two different interest rates: the "official" and the "preferential-subsidised" interest rates. This "dual" interest rate was just one of the signs of financial "softness" in the Romanian financial system, resulting in an accumulation of credit arrears on both banks' and enterprises' balance sheets.

The state sector is still the major borrower in Romania. Although the private sector accounts for an important share of GDP (estimated at 35 per cent in 1993, as reported by Business Central Europe, 1994) and for 59 per cent of the number of employees in Romania (Croitoru and Ciocirlan, 1994), the private sector still accounts for only a small part of total bank borrowing (19.5 per cent in December 1994) (NBR, 1995).

The NBR has progressively tightened its norms for commercial bank lending; as a result, all commercial banks in Romania have at least nominally developed internal procedures for loan origination and risk control. Assessing their performance is in our opinion a crucial predictor of future financial solvency and economic performance for Romania. It would not be the first time when stringent loan conditionality based on macroeconomic measures is fulfilled by transferring the burden of subsidies to the balance sheets of the banking system.

Basic question and methodology

Our analysis is based on a simple working model of enterprise demand for credit. In a hyperinflationary environment such as Romania experienced in 1990-91 there is a tendency for very negative interest rates on loans; demand for credit is then unlimited and credit needs to be rationed. As Romania started a more determined stabilization policy in 1992-93, real interest rates rose; loan rates in particular became positive and at times quite high. Enterprises which were profitable, or more generally had good future prospects, presumably became more sensitive to the high cost of credit. Although they could make the best use of more financial resources, they could not expect financial relief and thus had some incentive to protect their residual value by reducing their demand for loans. In contrast, firms with poor prospects would not be as concerned with high rates, as they were not as likely to repay them anyway; their incentives were skewed towards short-term objectives and possibly towards higher risk undertakings (Stiglitz and Weiss, 1984). In this subset of firms, demand for credit is unlimited; the volume and allocation of credit are therefore determined by the suppliers of capital, the banks. In conclusion, credit allocation for healthy firms is more determined by demand, while for weak or insolvent firms it is supply-driven.

In general it is not easy to distinguish between demand and supply effects on the allocation of credit. Simply regressing the stock of bank credit on the level of profitability of the borrower cannot allow us to assess the quality of lending performed by the banks. While better firms deserve more credit, they may demand less; so a negative coefficient on profitability may still be consistent with banks lending to the best enterprises on the demand curve they face. Pinto and van Wijnbergen address this problem by using survey responses in addition to balance sheet data; their measure of financial constraint may identify a subjective measure of "scarcity of funds", which is related to loan demand.

In our approach we make use of balance sheet information on the stock of bank and trade arrears. If banks were choosing their lending on the basis of the capacity and willingness to repay, they should be withholding loans from firms with a history of unpaid loans and overdue trade liabilities. Thus, after controlling for profitability, under the null hypothesis credit should be decreasing in the amount of financial arrears; over time, a strengthening of this negative relationship would reflect tighter financial constraints. We would also expect scaled bank credit to be independent of firm size and positively related to the stock of trade receivables (a measure of short-term assets to be funded), after controlling for its overdue component.

2. Description of sample data

We analyse balance sheet data collected from two samples drawn from the same source, the list of state owned enterprises in the "Transylvania" III Private Ownership Fund's portfolio. The first sample includes data 1991-93 data from 256 state-owned enterprises, the second includes 345 enterprises over 1992-94.

After the Privatisation Law was enacted (Law 58/1992), the institutions which had the prerogatives of interim management of SOEs, for their ownership share of 30 per cent of each SOE, were called the Private Ownership Funds (POFs). The POF 3 in Brasov is one of the five such ownership funds, each of which on a regional basis exercise control and governance over some 1 300 formerly state owned enterprises. This means that the POFs have people to represent their interests in each of the enterprises in their portfolios. Moreover, since POFs are shareholders in these SOEs, they have access to balance sheet data. The POFs play, in addition to their control and governance attributions, an important role in the mass privatisation process in Romania. The privatisation vouchers issued in 1993-1994 and the newly issued "privatisation coupons" account for the POFs ownership shares in SOEs, which are to be "traded" by voucher and coupon holders for shares of stock in SOEs.

The balance sheet data reports various financial indicators, including bank borrowing and government subsidies. Data contain information about the SOEs' profits, employment, bank arrears, inter-enterprise arrears and bank borrowing. The enterprises in the sample are randomly selected from about 1 300 enterprises in the Private Ownership Fund 3's portfolio, they are distributed geographically all around Romania and are from different branches. First sample data contains observations from 1991, 1992 and 1993. The second sample brings in observations from 1994. All the data are expressed in terms of 1991 constant Lei, the data from 1992, 1993 and 1994 being deflated with the producer price index (PPI).[1]

The first sample of 265 enterprises was selected from an initial sample consisting of 315 enterprises on the basis of completeness of data regarding employment, bank borrowing and arrears. All observations with missing variables were removed.

In addition to this first sample, we used a second sample of enterprises selected in the same way. This second sample includes a good part of the enterprises in the first sample plus an additional set of some 80 enterprises, also randomly selected from the POF 3 data base.

No systematic criterion was used for selecting the enterprises. In the POF's data base, enterprises are grouped geographically in an order corresponding with the date of their registration within the Trade Register. The sampling process was mechanical: for each county the first 5 SOEs were selected, then the next 10 were not selected, another 5 were selected, and then the next 11 not selected, and so on. The stated intent was to remove any possible identifiability of the firms in the sample. There seem to be no reasons to think of these samples as not being representative. The size of the sample covers more than 30 per cent of the enterprises in the POF's portfolio.

Hypotheses to be tested

Our null hypothesis is that, as a result of market-oriented reform, the allocation of bank credit shows an increasing sensitivity to profitability and solvency indicators, and a negative sensitivity to unpaid bank loans and overdue trade arrears. More credit would be offered to the category of enterprises that have higher profits and less financial arrears. On the other hand, such firms are less likely to demand credit, while we expect credit demand by weaker firms, those with low profitability and large arrears, to be virtually unlimited. Thus we cannot say much about the correlation between profitability and credit under the null hypothesis, but we can certainly rule out a stable relationship between credit and arrears.

Our regressions examine as possible determinants of enterprises borrowing: the size of the enterprises (we use their yearly sales as a proxy), the enterprises' scaled banking and inter-enterprise arrears (calculated as the amount of overdue trade credit for which an enterprise stays as net debtor, i.e. total payables in arrears minus total receivables in arrears) and the scaled net profit of each enterprise. We sometimes use scaled profitability in the regression, or use that information to stratify our sample and test whether the determinants for bank lending differ between better and worse performing enterprises.

The political situation in Romania suggests that enterprise size may influence the allocation of bank credit, as a proxy for the bargaining power of large enterprises. A major concern of the Romanian Government seems to be concentrated now on issues related to maintaining the "social peace". Measures taken to liquidate poor performing enterprises would generate unemployment and are likely to be resisted.

Empirical Testing

We first run a general regression over the two samples to assess the more significant variables in determining the allocation of bank credit over 1991-1994.

The basic regression we run is:

$$BB\_EMP_{it} = a + \beta_1 \cdot BAREM_{it} + \beta_2 \cdot SALES_{it} + \beta_3 \cdot IEAREM_{it} + \beta_4 \cdot PROEM_{it} + \varepsilon_{it}$$

where the dependent variable is the stock of bank borrowing divided by employment, and the independent variables are:

$BAREM_{it}$ are total bank arrears divided by employment for each year;
$SALES_{it}$ are real sales for each of the three years;
$IEAREM_{it}$ are total inter-enterprise arrears divided by employment, defined here as the difference between overdue payments and overdue receivables;
$PROEM_{it}$ are total profits over employment.

Table 1 presents the results of the regression.

The profitability of enterprises influences in a significant and positive way bank lending in 1991 and 1992, though no longer in 1993. The coefficients for the rescaled profit of enterprises decrease sharply and turn negative for 1993. This by itself is not evidence against the hypothesis of improvement in the efficiency of bank credit allocation, as it may result from a demand shift.[2]

Table 1.

Variable	1991	1992	1993
SALES	-4.17407E-05	3.313486E-04	1.112097E-04
	(-.446)	(1.644)	(4.007)
BAREM	-.008044	.333710	.726104
	(-.074)	(.578)	(4.603)
IEAREM	.243818	-.101220	.128517
	(2.955)	(-.203)	(1.573)
PROEM	.908116	.798123	-.045532
	(4.360)	(3.735)	(-1.516)
Constant	77.852736	67.838315	55.148901
	(4.320)	(5.017)	(3.466)
	R Square= .14695	R Square= .09208	R Square=.14569
	F=9.73280	F= 5.73020	F=10.95693

The coefficients on the variable SALES show an increasing correlation between the size of the enterprises and the amount of bank credit received. Until 1992 the coefficient is insignificant, but it becomes positive and highly significant in 1993. This suggests that the size of enterprises is an element of increasing bargaining power used by enterprises to gain access to bank loans.

The coefficient associated with the rescaled bank arrears shows that this is also a positive and economically significant determinant of bank credit. This is the most troublesome piece of evidence: it unambiguously suggests a worsening of the criteria.

Table 2 below reports results for the second sample, which includes data from 1994. While a comparison is difficult, we find a confirmation of several trends.

The size of enterprises contributes significantly to explain bank lending, at least until 1994: larger firms receive proportionally more credit.

Bank arrears (STBA_E) are a significant determinant of credit. In fact, the correlation appears to be becoming stronger and its economic significance to be increasing.

Inter-enterprise trade arrears (IEA_E) are also becoming more significant and having a greater economic impact. In this sample the correlation is positive and significant also in 1992.

Profitability (PRO_E) appears to have been strongly negatively correlated with bank credit in 1993, though it is not significant in 1994.

Trade receivables, a variable available only in the later sample (REC_E), has a positive sign and is significant (as it would be in a normal credit market) though only until 1993.

Overall, there are signs of some ambiguous change in loan policy in 1994. It seems therefore a natural idea to see whether over time there are different trends in credit policy for the better and the worse performing firms.

We thus split both samples in two subsamples, as in Pinto and van Wijnbergen (1994), corresponding to the upper and the lower tail of the distribution of profitability, measured as the ratio between the firm's net profit and the number of employees. The first subset of firms includes those in the upper quarter of the distribution, the second those in the lower quarter of the distribution. The

Table 2.

Variable	1992	1993	1994
SALES	8.75743E-05	8.08702E-05	3.08415E 05
	(3.227)	(3.603)	(.976)
STBA_E	-.098895	1.936130	1.627735
	(-.153)	(7.569)	(9.607)
IEA_E	.368918	.233291	.699665
	(2.910)	(3.529)	(4.552)
REC_E	.247626	.597558	.062602
	(2.147)	(9.228)	(.616)
PRO_E	.124387	-.324116	-.071711
	(.708)	(-4.342)	(-.868)
Constant	44.470075	9.525264	36.576697
	(2.904)	(1.117)	(2.953)
	R Square=.11973	R Square=.46773	R Square=.59042
	F=6.66471	F=48.85781	F=80.43584

composition of the two subsamples changes from year to year. We refer to them therefore as good and bad enterprises.

The case of good enterprises

For the best 25 per cent in 1991, 1992 and 1993, the results of the regressions are presented in Table 3.

Table 3.

Variable	1991	1992	1993
SALES	-9.87821E-04	4.298012E-04	7.520216E-05
	(-.545)	(1.220)	(1.470)
BAREM	.068570	-29.748707	-3.292976
	(.305)	(-1.401)	(-.250)
IEAREM	-.008206	-.042578	.066465
	(-.038)	(-.062)	(.509)
Constant	279.070305	149.149028	95.734386
	(4.497)	(3.656)	(2.007)
	R Square= .00815	R Square= .04585	R Square=.04717
	F= .14508	F=.83292	F=.6508

The coefficients associated with the variables in the regression over the 1991-1994 sample do not show any significant correlation with bank borrowing; moreover, the R square is extremely low. We are thus inclined to neglect this table.

Table 4 reports the regression results based on a subsample of firms with similar characteristics taken from the second sample over 1992-94. There is a marked difference between the first and second sample.

In the second sample size is positive and significant until 1994. This is a sign that for at least a significant period of time the bargaining power of large enterprises vis-à-vis banks became more important in time even for good firms.

Table 4.

Variable	1992	1993	1994
SALES	1.52218E-04	7.17119E-05	4.26191E-05
	(2.330)	(3.892)	(.933)
BAREM	-56.487727	-5.585524	-4.328547
	(-1.979)	(-1.323)	(-1.574)
PR_E	.206499	-.177421	-.272775
	(.451)	(-2.711)	(-2.356)
IEAREM	.096173	-.145738	1.165422
	(.402)	(-2.758)	(3.426)
REC_E	-.049131	.550920	.591857
	(-.226)	(13.721)	(3.609)
Constant	54.821984	-3.314487	12.867281
	(.876)	(-.301)	(.505)
	R Square= .14622	R Square=.84492	R Square=.53610
	F= 1.91811	F=70.82991	F=15.02328

Reassuringly, bank credit is negatively correlated with bank arrears, a relationship that appears marginally significant. Much more problematic is the effect of trade arrears, which have a significant negative impact in 1993 but a significant positive effect in 1994. This structural change is intriguing; it is consistent with results reported later that better performing firms received more credit in 1994 to cover trade arrears, while poor performers received more bank loans to cover bank arrears. It may also be related to the end of the large cancellation programmes of trade arrears that were completed by late 1992. In fact, it is possible that since the last "selective bailout" of 1992 those firms with low initial arrears in 1993 were actually the worst ones, which then rebuilt them rapidly.

Receivables, on which we have data only in 1992-94, are on the other hand a positive and significant determinant of bank credit for these enterprises. Finally, profitability is strongly and negatively related to credit. While this is an ambiguous sign, it is possibly the outcome of a strong reduction in the demand for credit by solvent firms reacting to sharply higher real rates of interest.

The case of bad enterprises

The results of the same regression over 1991-93 for the lower part of the distribution of firm profitability are presented in the Table 5. For the sample over 1992-94, the regression results are presented in Table 6.

Table 5.

Variable	1991	1992	1993
SALES	4.861554E-06	.004706	8.209530E-05
	(.9365)	(2.092)	(2.196)
BAR_E	.701031	-1.332031	1.256099
	(5.311)	(-1.363)	(10.875)
IEA_E	.184477	96.953953	.047524
	(2.619)	(3.392)	(.221)
Constant	33.739493	78.285355	23.098423
	(2.403)	(2.185)	(1.372)
	R Square=.48379	R Square=.23201	R Square=.64810
	F=16.55700	F=5.53851	F=44.20110

Table 6.

Variable	1992	1993	1994
SALES	-1.38240E-04	8.65766E-05	8.40262E-04
	(-1.148)	(2.195)	(3.239)
STBA_E	-1.973780	1.602583	2.496327
	(-2.017)	(4.369)	(6.100)
PR_E	.135623	-.133813	.376078
	(.293)	(-1.124)	(1.375)
IEA_E	1.663996	.140436	.502388
	(3.792)	(.525)	(.610)
REC_E	1.512149	.286559	-.202966
	(4.065)	(.909)	(-.530)
Constant	56.289789	.858126	33.042065
	(1.888)	(.077)	(.980)
	R Square=.29197	R Square=.69584	R Square=.77827
	F=4.61860	F=31.57123	F=45.62976

Some of our earlier considerations are reinforced by these results. First of all, the size of SOEs is a significant determinant for lending to these underperforming state firms.

Unlike the allocation of credit in the subsample of good enterprises, the allocation of credit to loss-making enterprises is highly correlated with the amount of accumulated bad debt. In 1992 bank arrears do not seem significant for new credit allocation, but results for later years suggest that the more bank arrears an enterprise has, the more bank credit is allocated by banks to that enterprise.

Both the coefficients associated with trade and bank arrears show a high correlation with the amount of bank borrowing received, at a high level of statistical significance.

Bank credit appeared to be positively related to the volume of trade receivables only in 1992; this may in fact simply pick up some correlation with the trade credit that became overdue in that year and was bailed out through concessionary credit. In later years, there is no significant correlation between total receivables and bank credit.

Together, these results paint a disturbing picture of an inertial, passive and possibly politically complacent banking system. While old loans may not be easily enforceable, the sheer size of the correlation indicates a strong economic significance of arrears on credit. It also points at an undermining influence of a number of large loss-making enterprises on the credibility of hard budget constraints.[3]

We now measure whether we are able to explain changes in the flow of credit, as opposed to its stock. The results of the regression are presented in Table 7.

The dependent variable represents the change in bank borrowing; independent variables are the difference in the size of each enterprise, the difference between inter-enterprise arrears and bank arrears (the variable used for rescaling is the employment in each enterprise):

$$DIFBBE_i = a + \beta_1 \cdot DIFBAE_i + \beta_2 \cdot DIFS_i + \beta_3 \cdot DIFIEE_i + \varepsilon_i$$

where:
DIFBBE is the difference from year to year in bank borrowing per employee;
DIFBAE is the difference in bank arrears scaled by employment;
DIFS is the difference in the size of enterprises;
DIFIEE is the yearly difference in the stock of real trade arrears per employee.

Table 7.

Years	Variable	Estimate	Standard error	t statistic
	DIFBAE21	-.105216	.096425	-1.091
	DIFS21	7.01095E-05	8.2554E-05	.849
1991-92	DIFIEE21	.044411	.068954	.644
	Constant	-37.947118	14.912813	-2.545
	DIFBAE32	.451379	.149060	3.028
	DIFIEE32	-.241248	.074240	-3.250
1992-93	DIFS32	3.80628E-05	2.8990E-05	1.313
	Constant	.399376	14.964356	.027

The only statistical significance available confirms a structural switch in 1993-1994; while in the previous year it was trade credit arrears which seemed to move bank lending (perhaps as a substitute for the bailout policy interrupted in 1992), in 1994 it appears that bank arrears were the driving factor behind the change in bank credit (possibly to repay the overdue loans made in 1993 to compensate for the lack of further trade arrears compensation!).

The regressions over for the second sample are in Table 8. They include the variable DIFPROE, the difference from year to year in the scaled profits of enterprises.

Table 8.

Years	Variable	Estimate	t statistic
1993-92	DIFBAE	1.078211	3.611
	DIFS	1.35081E-05	.390
	DIFIEE	.025891	.794
	DIFPROE	-.408531	-4.328
	Constant	-27.401962	-3.225
		R Square=.13743	
		F = 9.79870	
1994-93	DIFBAE	1.414809	7.988
	DIFIEE	-.172891	-2.600
	DIFS	-5.747E-05	-1.025
	DIFPROE	-9.285E-04	-.010
	Constant	22.438511	2.334
		R Square=.34195	
		F = 36.24444	

Analysing the regression results, it could be seen that changes in most variables between 1991 and 1992 are not significantly correlated with the rescaled bank credit.

The situation reverses for the period between 1992 and 1993. As bank arrears increase, the volume of bank borrowing increases too, all other things constant. In fact, the strong t statistic associated with the variable DIFBAE suggests a high level of significance of its relation: an increase in bank arrears is very likely to generate an increase in bank borrowing, *ceteris paribus*. The situation deteriorates in the period from 1992 to 1993 compared with the period before. Some other superficial signs of progress may actually hide the cause: the coefficient associated with the change in inter-enterprise arrears over 1993-94 is negative and significant. This may say that banks became more cautious when lending to those SOEs which have a significant stock of inter-enterprise arrears; however, it is then unclear why credit does not react similarly to bank loan arrears.

We conclude that overall there are few signs of a positive change in the banks' lending behaviour towards the worst performers. At the same time there are signs that better firms are reducing their borrowing from the banking system, which is thus becoming a container of poor loans. There are also indications of a further shift of soft budget constraints away from trade credit and towards bank credit. The evidence is not consistent with the initial hypothesis that, as a result of a market oriented reform of the banking system, the allocation of bank credit in Romania is improving.

Conclusions

The conclusion of our investigation on the quality of credit allocation is that Romanian banks have continued to play a passive role, funding large and unprofitable state owned enterprises. Although there are some improvements in the allocation of credit among profitable SOEs, even in that subsample there is still a strong tendency for credit to be directed at larger firms and, most recently, to those with the most trade arrears. Among firms in the subset of the more poorly performing SOEs, the evidence suggests that the quality of credit allocation is deteriorating.

An explanation for this is that Romanian banks are not sufficiently distinct from their borrowers. As in the case of the inter-enterprise arrears in Russia, both the accumulation of arrears and the distorted allocation of bank credit to state sector enterprises are a consequence of the "inconsistencies in the economic reform programme combined with underdevelopment of the financial system" (Ickes and Ryterman, 1992).

The only solution for the bad loans, as well as for the inter-enterprise arrears problem, is the imposition of harder constraints by the lenders. However, banks must then become active agents of change, something they do not seem to be doing.

While most Romanian banks may not possess much expertise to undertake enterprise restructuring, on the other hand there are hardly any other institutions who may do so or have better expertise. Privatising the banks, as Begg and Portes (1993) suggest, may help. However, changing the ownership of banks will not solve a basic problem: in many cases the expected value of a debtor's assets is less than the cost of enforcing bankruptcy. Thus, even privatised banks may find it more attractive to wait for financial relief rather than to start a liquidation process. Taking actions against debtors may signal that the bank has non-performing loans and it might cause a run on the bank. Under such ambiguous circumstances, banks would not be interested in initiating any liquidation procedures.

Foreign capital may provide the funds for privatising and recapitalising Romanian banks. However, evidence that political pressures are at work in influencing the banks' allocation of credit can only discourage foreign investors. At this stage the only alternative may be to recapitalise the banks using Government funds. Unfortunately, this would send the wrong signal to lenders, just as the repeated bailout of trade credit did in 1990-92, and presumably would result in a continuation of the poor criteria for bank lending. Only a sustained period of separation of financial and political decision-making may pave the way for a stable financial transition in Romania.

Notes

[1] The producer price index is taken by the Monthly Statistical Bulletin of the Romanian Commission for statistics (1994).

[2] A problem with this early sample is that enterprises reported their profits only when greater than zero, while those with losses reported zero profits and recorded losses on a separate entry, not available. This problem is not present in the second sample over 1991-94. However, the number of enterprises reporting no profits for 1991, 1992 and 1993 does not exceed 5 per cent of the total sample. Calvo and Coricelli (1994) also indicate a low number of Romanian enterprises reporting losses.

[3] Banks accumulating bad debt to large but politically favoured enterprises presumably receive compensation though cheap credit from the Central Bank.

References

Begg, D. and Portes, R., 1993, "Enterprise Debt and Economic Transformation: Financial Restructuring of the State Sector in Central and Eastern Europe", *CEPR Discussion Paper* No. 695.

Brainard, L., 1993, "Reform in Eastern Europe: Creating a Capital Market", in *Economic Review*, February.

Business Central Europe, 1994, November.

Calvo, G. A. and Coricelli, F., 1993, "Inter-enterprise arrears in Economies in Transition", in Holzmann, R. *et al.* (ed.) *Output Decline in Eastern Europe-Unavoidable, External Influence or Home-made?*

Croitoru, L. and Ciocirlan, L., 1994, "*Financial Deregulation and the Functioning of the Romanian Banking System Throughout 1991-1993*", Department for Economic Reform, Romanian Government.

Clifton, E. and Khan, M.S., 1993, "Interenterprise Arrears in Romania", in *IMF Staff Papers*, vol. 40, No. 3, September.

Ickes, B. W. and Ryterman, R., 1992, "*The Interenterprise Arrears Crisis in Russia*", Post-Soviet Affairs, 8: 4 October-December.

Isarescu, M., 1991, "The Prognoses for Economic Recovery in Romania", in Nelson, D. (ed.), *Romania after Tyranny.*

Kotzeva, M. and Perotti, E., 1995, *"Exogenous and Opportunistic Financial Arrears: Evidence from a Survey of Bulgarian State Managers",* [mimeo].

National Bank of Romania — Monthly Bulletin No. 12/1995.

Romanian Commission for Statistics — Monthly statistical bulletin, 1994.

Perotti, E., 1993, "Bank Lending in Transition Economies", in *Journal of Banking and Finance.*

Perotti, E., 1994, "A Taxonomy of Post-Socialist Financial Systems: Decentralised Enforcement and the Creation of Inside Money", in *Economics of Transition*, Vol. 2.

Pinto, B and van Wijnbergen. S., *Ownership and Corporate Control in Poland: Why State Firms Defied the Odds*, April 1994, International Finance Corporation.

van Wijnbergen, S., "On the role of Banks in Enterprise Restructuring", *CEPR, Working Paper* No. 898.

6

Comments

Stanislaw Gomulka

Rostowski makes a significant contribution to the still inconclusive debate about the ultimate causes of the observed large falls of output in the initial phase of transition. He provides new and quite strong support for the theory that these causes have been largely structural, i.e. the wrong composition of output at the starting point, which the change of the economic system has evidenced, rather than the stabilization policy. This theory suggests that the direction of causality has been from microeconomic supply and demand shocks to falls of output, and only then to lower investment. In contrast, during the Great Depression of the 1930s, the causality was in the opposite direction: from macroeconomic policy shocks to exceptionally large falls of investment, and then to falls of outputs. The contribution's method of analysis is based on the assumption that this difference in the direction of causality has different implications for the evolution of the investment/GDP ratios. Evidence based on these ratios can provide indirect indications of the actual direction of causality during transition.

The falls in fixed capital investment in transition economies, while smaller in relation to GDP than during the Great Depression, are still large. There are good "structural" reasons for such falls which, if developed by the author, would provide further support for his thesis. These reasons are the following:

1. Initial stocks of inventories were exceptionally large and, therefore, inventory investments should have collapsed, which they did.
2. The largest percentage fall of investment occurred in agriculture, even though the demand for food has remained high. The reason for the fall has been the near elimination of subsidies for farm equipment, a microeconomic shock.
3. Faced with radically changed market conditions, firms needed time to develop new business strategies and new investment projects.
4. The near collapse of housing investment has been caused by the sharp fall of state investment subsidies and underdevelopment of the financial sector, rather than by the overall fall of output and income.

Reforms may be looked at as a large block of innovations. They reduced the profitability of many existing capital assets, but increased the profitability of new investment projects. However, many of these new projects were "discovered" by private entrepreneurs; these initially lacked finance and were therefore keen to use the existing capital assets which they bought from (formerly) state firms at give-away prices. The implication is that the initial phase of recovery did not require large investment as initially believed (Gomulka, 1995). However, investment/GDP ratios need to recover, and indeed be high, for transition economies to take full advantage of the new economic system.

References

Gomulka, S., 1995, "The IMF-Supported Programs of Poland and Russian, 1990-1994: Principles, Errors and Results", *Journal of Comparative Economics*, Vol. 20: 316-340, July.

Jozef Brhel

I am impressed by the range of privatisation and restructuring issues raised by Aghion and Carlin, Frydman and Rapaczynski, and Hunya, as well as by the fact that all of the authors avoid the temptation of coming up with a general answer or "correct" approach. Although, rightly, they do not attempt to build an overall framework, they do cover most of the key issues in a most helpful way.

I will follow this good example by discussing these issues on the basis of the policies which we are pursuing in Slovakia, and I will add some evidence. We do not think that we have a perfect blueprint or perfect practice; we are very conscious of the fact that we are facing a complex problem of timing and availability of as many policy instruments as the number of evolving and conflicting goals we seek to pursue.

The key issues are well summed up in Hunya's contribution, in the distinction he makes between primary "de-etatisation" (or freeing from state control) and the final post-privatisation scenario, and in his characterisation of the whole process as an evolutionary one. We are just finishing the second wave of privatisation in Slovakia, and our top priority is to provide a good context for post-privatisation restructuring, which will lead to further ownership changes and which will be crucial in determining the final outcome of the whole privatisation process.

I disagree somewhat with Hunya's description of the 1990-92 production decline as the result of difficulties in structural adjustment and the lack of instant restructuring. With the benefit of hindsight, I think it is clear that whatever the form, speed or perfection of any privatisation process, recession would have been inevitable after the fall of socialism. Even a perfect capitalist system, faced with such a dislocation of markets as that experienced throughout Eastern Europe, would have experienced a downturn — as was the case in Western countries in post-war slumps or after the oil crises. The recovery from this depression in the Visegrad countries has been of similar timing and magnitude (all are now close to 1989 GDP levels), and has been based on proximity to European markets, labour force skills and organisational capacity. Differences in economic recovery that can be attributed to the various privatisation methods are difficult to detect, at least as yet, and are not sufficient to explain the huge gap in economic performance between the Visegrad countries and many other transition economies.

As regards the trade-off between instant privatisation and a more gradual process, I wish to point out some advantages which we have derived from a slower process:

1. Instant privatisation would hardly have been fair to the citizens of the former communist countries, given the small stock of savings which could be readily drawn upon, the relative lack of information and sophistication in evaluating companies, and the lack of experience in raising capital.

2. Instant privatisation would have brought a great deal of property to the market and prices could have been pushed below those attainable in a more drawn-out approach. Some delay had the advantage of increasing the sale price of assets, as well as, other things being equal, future earnings from interest and dividends if the sales were to domestic citizens. If the delays also allow domestic citizens greater access to ownership, there will be further revenue gains.

3. During our second privatisation wave consisting mainly of management buyouts, there have been many cases where simple reorganisation has brought about a rapid turnaround in corporate financial positions. If and when these companies are partially or wholly resold later, the gains from the simple, initial rationalisation will be reflected in these companies' prices. There will also be direct gains to the State budget. This has been noticeable in our second privatisation wave — the potential for simple rationalisation has been recognised and has affected the prices paid to the National Property Fund. The budgetary implications are sufficiently large to improve the country's ability to provide a sound macroeconomic framework for the future development of the private sector. The macroeconomic implications are barely mentioned in the contributions, yet they are crucial for the post-privatisation strategy.

4. The development of corporate governance structures and the financial system may affect the post-privatisation results as much as the privatisation methods themselves; yet, these are tools which take time to put into place.

5. A slower process of privatisation has helped us to 'learn by doing', thus avoiding many of the potential mistakes that can be made in any privatisation process.

6. Slower privatisation can allow a country more time to prepare itself for important foreign capital inflows for direct investment.

Frydman and Rapaczynski rightly make a distinction between potentially viable public sector companies and what they call "white elephants" with no potential future value, but perhaps sizeable political influence. In the latter case, privatisation may not be of much help, and closure is the obvious answer, subject to political constraints and costs. A few qualifications should, however, be added.

Firstly, the timing of closure of loss-making enterprises is an important issue. Immediate closure of all such enterprises would not be advisable in a situation in which there are many such firms, since adding to unemployment would not significantly improve labour market conditions for the dynamic sectors of the economy, and in which the authorities are trying to maintain sound public finances as part of a proper macroeconomic strategy. A more gradual process, which leads to the immediate closure only of those firms which are making operating losses and allows for the natural reallocation of labour towards the emerging private sector, may have its advantages.

Secondly, a gradual process may be more advantageous if these marginally productive companies have sizeable debts which are guaranteed by the State, at least until a satisfactory process of debt consolidation is in place.

Thirdly, there is a need to identify portions of such firms which are potentially viable for privatisation, even if their privatisation creates a bigger problem with the residual part of the company.

In the more usual case in which privatisation is justified by the intrinsic value of the company, Frydman and Rapaczynski are sceptical about managerial ownership. Their remarks are pertinent. Yet, in a situation of mass privatisation in Eastern Europe, was there an alternative pool of managerial expertise? Ownership is a powerful incentive to learn. Minority ownership, as is the case in Slovakia, is no lifetime (or even short-term) employment guarantee. I do not see how ownership distribution or sales can be a solution for the generalised problem of a lack of managerial skills. Again, the fundamental solution lies in developing corporate governance, management ability and management mobility in the post-privatisation period.

Of course, these conclusions would not hold if state-owned enterprises and their managements were as sluggish as some people feared in the early days of transition. The Aghion and Carlin contribution illustrates how much more complex the reality is. They point out the ability of insider owners to adjust and improve performance, notably when subject to a hard budget constraint. This is, in my view, the situation in Slovakia. They also point out that more fundamental restructuring is brought about by outside ownership, capital and expertise. Again, I agree fully.

There is no conflict between these two views. Can we go so far as to say that one reasonable line of approach is, first, to transfer control to domestic managers/owners in order to do the initial rationalisation which the state should have done, but could never do, and then to complete privatisation by bringing in a much wider range of owners? The second stage could be implemented at prices which reflect the benefits of the first round of rationalisation. The combination of these two stages would enhance the return to the State, and help to create the right macroeconomic conditions. Such an approach would, of course, need to ensure that owners at each stage have incentives to restructure. This is, approximately, our approach to privatisation in Slovakia, though it might not have been presented this way explicitly at the outset. We have taken a prudent approach with the conscious goal of deep restructuring, subject to social constraints. Our principal concern now is to provide the right environment in terms of corporate governance, regulation, bankruptcy procedures, banking facilities and macroeconomic conditions.

Before concluding, I wish to add a point of detail on Hunya's analysis. His Table 1 shows a very marked decline in Slovak labour productivity in the 1989-95 period. There was a large fall in productivity during 1990-92, associated with the closure of capital-intensive arms plants, but labour productivity has been growing since 1993 in the range of 5 to 10 per cent *per annum*. In assessing the impact of foreign investment on productivity during transition, one should take into account the effect of these closures in the base years.

Rumen Dobrinsky

The three contributions dealing with the issues of enterprise restructuring in Central and Eastern Europe nicely complement each other; while the contributions both by Frydman and Rapaczynski and by Aghion and Carlin are more focused on conceptual and theoretical problems, the contribution by Hunya provides a wealth of empirical information. This makes it possible to test some of the conceptual issues against some of the available hard facts. At the same time the three contributions are a fair reflection of the ongoing discussion of the process of enterprise restructuring and adjustment in the transition economies. As these issues are controversial, it is natural that the authors may disagree with each other on some points, or have different interpretations of some facts.

One general comment is addressed by all three contributions. The increasing number of survey-based empirical studies has revealed widely diverging patterns of enterprise restructuring and adjustment in the transition economies; this makes it next to impossible to place them into any single conceptual framework unless this encompasses a sufficiently broad range of assumptions. A narrowly defined model with a rigid set of assumptions poses the risk of leaving out a number of cases or classes of enterprise adjustment.

Another general comment is related to the theoretical aspects. The theoretical literature usually treats SOEs (especially in the framework of a centrally planned economy) as a homogeneous continuum. However, the experience of transition and some empirical studies (see, for example, Estrin and Takla, 1994) have revealed that this is not likely to have been the case. The different patterns of behaviour and performance in the transition partly reflect inherited differences among enterprises in terms of quality of physical and human capital, managerial skills, adherence to country-specific comparative advantages, etc. Thus, enterprises inherited different capacities and potentials to adjust and displayed different degrees of viability under market conditions. There were socialist "dinosaurs" (or "white elephants" as they are called by Frydman and Rapaczynski), but there were also viable enterprises capable of adjustment. It is the latter that were the first to restructure, to be privatised and/or to attract foreign investors. In analysing the typology of enterprise behaviour in the transition, it is helpful to differentiate between viable and unviable enterprises in order to highlight some of the driving forces of restructuring.

The contribution by Frydman and Rapaczynski starts with some illuminating insights on some of these issues. As argued by the authors, "the pain of transition is directly proportional to the amount of 'creative destruction' that market forces are apt to inflict on the former state sector". This alone puts certain political constraints on the speed of enterprise restructuring. It is a pity that this line of reasoning (and especially the impact of viability/unviability) is not followed later in the contribution when analysing the political effects of privatisation.

The model of transformation of ownership and control, developed by Aghion and Carlin, is applicable to the viable firms only (except for some special cases). Unviable firms are due to be closed down, sooner or later, depending on the political costs of this process.

Both of the theoretical contributions provide arguments against insider privatisation. One of the lines of reasoning is that insider privatisation can only be a second best solution: while it may not be the most efficient decision in the economic sense (in terms of corporate governance and restructuring), it may be the politically preferred solution. Aghion and Carlin further develop this argument in their model of the secondary market of privatised SOEs and come up with some conclusions and recommendations about how to design the primary market so that the secondary market is open to outsiders.

While I broadly agree with these arguments, I would like to point out, for the completeness of consideration, that there exists at least one class of to-be-privatised SOEs for which they do not necessarily hold. This is the case of firms with a large share of non-tangible assets in the form of human capital (for example, companies in which the business links are based on personal reputation, such as traders, distributors, tour-operators or companies where the value creation is based on team-work). In such firms, a large share of the value-creating assets is embodied in the current staff and is somehow their private property. If such a company is privatised to outsiders, these assets will most probably vanish, as the staff holding them will likely leave (as they have no incentives to share the return on the assets with the new owners). In such cases, insider privatisation is not only the politically acceptable solution, it is the economically rational decision as well.

On several occasions the contributions indirectly argue with each other. One of these issues is the quality of management inherited from the past. While the contribution by Frydman and Rapaczynski states that "most managers lacked the basic skills necessary to continue in their posts under the conditions of a market economy", both the Aghion and Carlin, and the Hunya contributions argue in the opposite direction. As noted earlier, enterprises in the transition economies had different starting points and this also refers to the quality of their management. Hence, it would not be fair to make a general statement on the managerial quality of enterprises in transition. Indeed, the successful restructuring of a number of firms in Central and Eastern Europe is an indication of managerial success. Actually, the Aghion and Carlin contribution provides empirical evidence that after acquiring a local company, foreign owners most often leave local managers in place and supplement them with co-managers from the parent company.

The contribution by Frydman and Rapaczynski makes reference to a very intriguing phenomenon seen in some insider-privatised companies — managers continue to siphon off assets even post-privatisation. This phenomenon has also been noted by other observers, especially in Russia (see, for example, Bim, 1996) and it seems to be one of the unique characteristics of the transition process. This perverse type of behaviour could tentatively be labelled as "insider hostile takeover". There might be different causes for this behaviour. One possible cause is that managers are aware of the fact that the company is not viable, but due to information asymmetry, the public (and even employees) may not be aware. After acquiring stakes in the firm at low or no cost, the managers may be in a hurry to extract whatever value is still available there before it goes bankrupt. Another cause may be an employee/management buy-out in which managers consider their stakes insufficiently large and seek additional rents in the absence of proper governance. Whatever the causes, "insider hostile takeovers" distort resource allocation.

References

Bim, A., 1996, "Ownership, Control over the Enterprises and Strategies of Stockholders", Paper presented at the IIASA Workshop "Russian Enterprises on the Path of Market Adaptation and Restructuring", Laxenburg, 1-3 February.

Estrin, S. and Takla, L., 1994, "Enterprise Adjustment in Transition: Does History Matter?", Paper presented at the Workshop on "Enterprise Adjustment in Eastern Europe", World Bank, Washington, DC, 22-23 September.

John M. Litwack

The contributions by Aghion and Carlin, Frydman and Rapaczynski, and Hunya all address the relationship between privatisation and restructuring during economic transition. Written in the aftermath of very ambitious privatisation programmes in several of the transition economies, they raise serious questions concerning the notion that mass privatisation can play a central role in providing the incentives and corporate governance for rapid economic restructuring. Their conclusions are rather sobering; the only strong conclusion to emerge is that, in the case of significant foreign investment, the relationship between privatisation and restructuring appears quite strong. Although we find significant "reactive" restructuring, as defined by Aghion and Carlin, in other firms, this has primarily reflected changes in financial constraints, which have affected state-owned and privatised firms very similarly.

While these three studies take a "micro", firm-level approach, it is interesting to note that, from a macroeconomic perspective, the relationship between privatisation and restructuring looks a bit more encouraging. All of the transition economies have vibrant and rapidly-growing private sectors that have been absorbing resources from the state sector. This has also been associated with a process of genuine restructuring; resources have been flowing into sectors of the economy that were neglected in the socialist past, according to a logic somewhat related to enhanced efficiency and comparative advantage. But this process has involved new private firms much more than successfully restructured privatised firms, leading to the concentration of private sector activity in areas of the economy with low capital requirements.

For firms with high capital intensity, with few exceptions, privatisation has not made much difference. Of course, one could argue that real privatisation has not yet been realised in these firms. According to Hunya, "privatisation is final when non-public owners interested in the long-term value of the company assume full ownership rights over the former SOEs and impose corporate governance over the management". From this point of view, one could interpret the contributions of Frydman and Rapaczynski, and Aghion and Carlin, as exploring the feasibility and expediency of speeding up this finalisation of privatisation before it is too late. Given the financial constraints on these firms imposed by stabilization programmes, their days of functioning without an infusion of new capital are numbered.

Frydman and Rapaczynski have stressed an important but too often forgotten point: many of these firms are simply not worth restructuring. Accordingly, the current process under which these firms are gradually disappearing, as their human and physical capital is absorbed into the private sector, may not be far from the optimal form of restructuring for the economy as a whole. In fact, some advocates of rapid mass privatisation see its value not as a means of accelerating restructuring at the micro-level, but as a means of providing the political and social prerequisites for large-scale liquidation. Whether it is accomplishing even this goal remains, however, highly questionable.

The contrary point of view portrays SOEs and former state-owned firms largely as victims of circumstance, with significant economic potential but in desperate need of an inflow of new capital and a more stable and healthy business environment. Given severe liquidity constraints, largely non-functioning capital markets, and the absence of state investment funds, the only feasible means of restructuring could become downsizing, decapitalisation and liquidation. This can be economically as well as socially costly in the presence of firm-specific capital and complementarities between factors of production.

It is the potential presence of these types of firms, hidden somewhere in the thick jungle of rusty state-owned and formerly state-owned enterprises, that motivates the concern expressed by Aghion and Carlin for facilitating the transfer of ownership to outside investors, who have both the power to discipline management and the capital for restructuring. Under dispersed employee ownership, they emphasize the interesting point that collusion among workers in the bargaining process of resale can actually decrease the likelihood of a deal, and therefore measures aimed at preserving anonymity in secondary trading could be important. One could, however, imagine situations where, due to market imperfections in the transition period, the risk and transaction costs of acquiring a firm through several individual deals would greatly exceed those associated with one large deal.

Aghion and Carlin also conclude that insider privatisation, to the degree that it is necessary, should favour worker rather than manager majority ownership, because managers are likely to reap more significant private benefits from control, and would therefore only relinquish it at a higher price. This latter proposition is complemented by the Frydman and Rapaczynski contribution, which also stresses the perceived incompetence of management inherited from the socialist period, when political considerations were often involved in the placement and promotion of managers. The skills required of a successful manager in the socialist period were also often quite different from the entrepreneurial ingenuity needed to restructure and compete in markets. Indeed, if we accept the very dismal picture of a socialist manager drawn in the Frydman and Rapaczynski contribution, we should also certainly accept the proposal by Aghion and Carlin that outsider or worker ownership is preferable to managerial ownership.

Neither of these conjectures is entirely convincing. Managers in these economies, like the firms that they manage, are a very heterogeneous group. Despite the problems exposed in the contribution of Frydman and Rapaczynski, it is also true that, in the latter technocratic years of the socialism, the primary factor considered in the promotion of managers was their ability to manage and produce impressive economic results in their respective enterprises. While, certainly, there are many managers in power without the competence to successfully restructure, there are also many who may be the most competent for this task. Unfortunately, in the design of privatisation programmes, it is usually not possible to know who belongs to which category. The chaotic situation in the transition period also limits the ability of competent management to signal their abilities directly to potential investors. Furthermore, a two-stage process by which, first, *de facto* ownership is taken away from management and widely dispersed to employees and outsiders, and then, subsequently, concentrated in the hands of a dominant investor through secondary markets, can create perverse incentives for management in the interim period. For this reason, I have always felt more comfortable with those privatisation schemes that give managers a large stake, under the hope that the need for outside funds will eventually drive them to relinquish control anyway. In this latter process, one would also expect debt-holders, in addition to equity-holders, to play a key role in developing corporate governance structures and initiating a replacement of management in the case of incompetence.

Miroslav Hrncir

After several years of a protracted "transition" depression, a remarkable recovery has recently been experienced in the countries of Central and Eastern Europe. As could be expected, this recovery appears differentiated across different parts of the region, both in its intensity and its timing. The CEFTA member countries are clearly in the lead; their recovery has turned into robust growth. Despite these developments, the need to understand the causes of the depression experienced in the initial stage of transition has not diminished. Of course, a number of hypotheses and arguments have been suggested and, with the benefit of hindsight, we can assess their validity. It must be acknowledged, however, that the extent of the fall in economic activity in individual transition economies is still an open issue. There are some apparent discrepancies between GDP figures and less aggregated data. Given the sweeping adjustments in relative prices and the institutional changes in the initial transition period, the GDP data are evidently subject to a wider margin of error. In spite of this, the depression was, without a doubt, deeper and more protracted than expected.

As for the explanation, the prevailing view rejects an interpretation based on standard business cycle theories. Rather, it is believed that transition and structural features played the dominant role. Nevertheless, we still lack persuasive and generally accepted evidence on the causes of this process. Most studies attribute the depression primarily to demand-side factors. For example, the contributions by Calvo and Coricelli highlighted the impact of the abrupt decrease of aggregate demand reflecting, in particular, excessive restrictiveness of monetary and credit policies. Unlike those demand-oriented explanations, Rostowski argues that the transformation depression resulted from the restructuring of the economy after sweeping price liberalisation.

His analysis is based on the Polish experience, and the data seem to fit his hypothesis well. It also fits the Hungarian case, to some extent. Nevertheless, to make the argument more general and conclusive, further research seems necessary. In particular, an analysis based only on macroeconomic data may be biased, due to discontinuities and distortions in the data available from the initial stages of the transition.

The experience of a number of transition economies points to the importance of institutional changes, actual as well as expected. The shift to new property structures and to new management, a sharp decrease in state subsidies, the collapse of Comecon institutions and markets, together with the restrictive stance of macroeconomic policies, evidently all contributed to the initial economic downturn. Hence, it would be appropriate to combine and compare results of macroeconomic analyses with those of institutional and microeconomic studies in order to test alternative hypotheses of the transition depression. The same approach should be applied to evaluate growth prospects of transition economies.

The key importance of well-functioning production factor markets for the ultimate success of the transition has been underlined by a number of experts. The stage of market development achieved in a given country marks the progress this country has made in the transition. This conclusion applies in particular to financial markets and to financial intermediation. Any sustainable recovery and growth in transition economies is conditional on the mobilisation of savings and their efficient allocation to prospective users. There is a fairly general consensus that banks are, and should be, the core of financial systems during transition, especially in its early stages. It is therefore relevant to ask what types of banks and what changes in their environment are required to secure satisfactory financial intermediation in transition economies.

Though the CEFTA countries can claim to have financial and banking systems that are closer to a market economy standard than others, the degree of efficiency and competition in their financial markets lags behind demand and expectations. The links and interactions between financial markets and real economy developments have been a matter of concern for both "insiders" and foreign observers. Phenomena such as the inertia of traditional ties between old, "established" banks and their state-owned clients, at the expense of the emerging new private sector, signal a continuing misallocation of credit that results in an increasing volume of "new" bad loans. This situation could make the CEECs' prospects of sustainable growth rather gloomy. Accordingly, a further radical advance is urgently needed in financial reform.

7

General discussion

A very diverse set of points were raised in the discussion and for a meaningful presentation they are organised around three major issues: a) an assessment of the enterprise restructuring that has already taken place; b) the relationship between firms' ownership structure and their performance; and c) the ownership model which should be advocated to ensure faster progress in economic restructuring.

On the first point, views on fixed capital formation during the transition were less pessimistic than was the case on the basis of official statistics. Investment was seen as having been substantial and broad-based, referring not just to foreign-owned firms but to domestic investors as well (Svejnar). This trend appeared even more remarkable in the light of prohibitively high levels of real interest rates and the inadequacy of the banking system (Rostowski and Woergoetter). Such interpretation supports the argument that the transition recession has been due to supply-side factors, rather than demand-related causes, as argued by Laski and others. Evidently, in case of revision of GDP statistics to include unrecorded output, that evaluation of investment trends might have to be modified. In Rostowski's view, however, the difference between the fall in investment, as compared to GDP, in CEECs and that experienced by the United States during the Great Depression, is so large that a very sizeable upward revision of CEECs' GDP would be needed to reverse his conclusions.

Doubts were voiced about the willingness of governments to effect privatisation in such a way as to facilitate restructuring (Laski). Any resulting, poor economic performance over the long-run might also become a political liability (Hunya).

Enterprise restructuring requires adequate funding as well as channelling of resources into the best investment opportunities. In spite of the many difficulties in complying with these two conditions, CEECs have fared reasonably well in funding investments as profitable firms drew on retained earnings rather than on the relatively inefficient banking sector (Rostowski). Perotti's analysis of what was depicted as poor and deteriorating loan quality by banks in Romania was questioned both on empirical grounds (according to Daianu, Romania has not yet experienced an explosion of arrears, and therefore true underlying corporate strength may have been under-estimated) as well as on methodological grounds, given the lack of specification of a credit allocation model incorporating the role of real interest rates (Svejnar). Nevertheless, as recently observed in many countries, the fact that a banking sector has not collapsed does not provide conclusive evidence that credit quality is adequate (Perotti). As to the methodological criticism, explicit treatment of the issue would, (according to the author), involve a straightforward extension of his currently implicit model, and would most likely show that if criteria for bank credit had been tightened, large-sized enterprises and state-owned firms would have received a still greater proportion of bank lending than was actually the case. This has negative implications for the prospects of economic restructuring as a whole.

Regarding the relationship between ownership structure and enterprise reorganisation, it was widely (Nestor and Aghion, among others) felt that foreign direct investment has generally led to improvements in performance and corporate governance, but not necessarily to lower employment (Svejnar). Should there be a necessary relationship between the two aspects, an initial macroeconomic instability might give rise to a "vicious circle", whereby lack of stability deters foreign investors, thus hindering effective restructuring and in turn undermining stabilization efforts even further (Daianu). Some questioned the premise that foreign investment is necessary for deep restructuring to take place (Rapaczynski).

The corporate governance issue of how ownership structure can influence management was also controversial. While replacement of former managers with outsiders, whether foreign or domestic, can be viewed as a sign of progress in restructuring, other more significant indicators (e.g. labour shedding and changes in wage differentiation) can be constructed to measure this development at the firm level (Rapaczynski). No blanket replacement of managers in privatised firms was advocated; rather, it was mentioned that in some CEECs, good results have been obtained by retaining and retraining past management (Hunya).

The question was raised concerning what ownership model, if any, should be recommended in order to accelerate the restructuring of these economies. Two alternative models were indicated on the basis of Western Europe experience. One model involved a wide diffusion of share ownership, with a central role played by equity markets in ensuring effective corporate governance, while the other was based on bank prominence in ownership structure, and was applied to a limited extent in Russia when financial-industrial conglomerates were created (Zecchini).

A case was also made for giving large ownership stakes to good managers (Aghion), but scepticism was expressed as to the practical implementation of this, since many privatisation schemes had already entrenched management in firms by giving them very substantial ownership stakes. Given the need in any well-functioning economic system for reallocating managers among firms, any schemes to increase managers' ownership stakes further might be inappropriate inasmuch as they reduce managers' mobility (Rapaczynski).

In his comments, Dobrinsky raised the point that a firm's intangible assets, such as benefits from teamwork, might be lost by moving to outside ownership. Aghion saw this as unlikely, since outside owners would, under normal circumstances, have incentives to internalise and maintain such assets.

Overall, the discussion highlighted several obstacles still faced by these economies on the way to achieving better enterprise performance. There was neither a clear indication of which ownership pattern might prevail in the coming years, nor a consensus on which model of corporate governance is most appropriate for these countries.

8

Policy conclusions

The empirical evidence scrutinised in Part II clearly shows that after a number of years of economic transformation, much remains to be done in order to put in place one of the main conditions for sustained growth, i.e. the restructuring of the enterprise sector. This is not to deny that fixed capital formation has continued even in a period of economic downturn and that some adjustment of a "defensive" nature has occurred even among SOEs, but these developments appear inadequate to lead to high growth over the long term.

As investment and restructuring are more likely in an expanding economy than during stagnation, the recent output recovery across the region should offer a new opportunity to accelerate structural adjustment through investment. Yet, a number of conditions have to be established by governments for this result to materialise. Attention should be paid not just to expanding the volume of capital formation but to improving its quality; this in turn, calls for a number of specific measures.

The first policy conclusion stems from the evidence that both the pace and the methods of privatisation and ownership restructuring have been, in general, hostage to political considerations, to the detriment of sound economic development. The tightness of these political constraints has to be eased.

Second, hardening of the budget constraint on enterprises has proved to be the best incentive to restructure and to improve investment quality. Hence, further hardening is needed, especially in order to induce SOEs to move from a survival-oriented reorganisation to strategic restructuring.

Third, on economic grounds, there are not sufficient reasons to give preference to enterprise insiders vis-à-vis outsiders in privatisation schemes. In contrast, insiders' weight in corporate governance should be somewhat balanced through measures that create incentives for restructuring and continuing improvements in performance. Good corporate governance also depends, to a large extent, on government action aimed at making financial and equity markets more efficient and transparent.

Fourth, no country-specific economic factors have been identified to suggest that governments should favour a model of corporate governance consolidation along the lines of financial-industrial groups, rather than a model based on the central role of stock markets. The divergent trends that are observed among CEECs are not explicable on the grounds of governments pursuing different optimisation criteria. The OECD countries' experience demonstrates that both models can lead to good governance provided that other conditions are fulfilled, such as transparency of information on enterprises' activities, well-functioning equity markets and a legal environment with effective enforcement procedures.

Fifth, enterprise restructuring, as well as investment, cannot advance if the restructuring of the banking system continues to lag behind. Improvements in the financial system, as a whole, should constitute a top priority for governmental action in order to pave the way to a more efficient enterprise sector.

Sixth, foreign direct investment has been an important instrument for carrying out extensive adjustments at the microeconomic level, but there are doubts about its ability to be the engine of long-term development. Despite these misgivings, transition economies that are lagging behind should better exploit FDI's potential contribution, particularly by removing existing barriers to foreign participation in privatisation and certain sectors dominated by public enterprises.

Overall, a general policy message stands out: governments would be well advised to monitor more closely the problems of the entire enterprise sector (not just individual public firms in distress) and to address them through measures aimed at improving the performance of markets for goods, labour and capital as well as of market-relevant public institutions, while resisting pressure to shore up specific sectors or enterprises.

Part III

Unemployment and the reform of social policies

1

Unemployment, restructuring and the pace of transition

Simon Commander and Andrei Tolstopiatenko

Introduction

The transition in Central and Eastern Europe (CEE) has left behind in its wake a flotsam of discarded technologies, trading arrangements and, perhaps most painful of all, a large mass of people without work and with, it would appear, small chances of being reintegrated into the labour force. By early 1996 around 12 per cent of the labour force was unemployed, and of those more than 40 per cent had been out of work for over one year. Wide regional disparities emerged early in the transition and these have remained. While the generosity of publicly provided unemployment benefits has been cut back and unemployment status is quite tightly correlated with poverty, those without work still retain access to significant public transfers. And despite a clear and widespread resurgence in growth since 1993/94 and the associated stimulus to job creation imparted by the private sector, unemployment has declined only very gradually.

This picture appears to be in dramatic contrast with the situation further east in the Former Soviet Union (FSU). There, unemployment has barely reared its head. Little more than 2 per cent of the labour force is now in registered unemployment, and at a maximum unemployment has yet to surpass 8 per cent of the labour force, as is currently the case in Russia. Long-term unemployment remains minimal. In further contrast to CEE, for those without work, public fall-backs have been very restrictive and of very low generosity.

These snapshots of an apparently large divergence in labour market and institutional responses to adversity can in part be attributed to the fact that they capture different stages of the transition, with the FSU merely lagging the CEE countries (CEECs). But this only explains part of the difference. For despite truly massive adverse shocks to output and trade, countries in the FSU have explicitly chosen to limit open unemployment and have severely restricted the availability of benefits. Given the obvious costs associated with unemployment, these contrasting experiences appear to offer us a fascinating natural experiment. Put baldly, what conclusions can we draw from these experiences regarding the role of unemployment in raising the aggregate efficiency of the transition? For example, can wage flexibility and employment smoothing by the employed be induced by avoiding the creation of a generous and protracted system of unemployment benefits and social assistance? As such, does the FSU approach avoid the pitfalls of high unemployment while simultaneously facilitating the desired reallocation of labour across sectors? These are obviously important questions given the widespread assumption that unemployment was necessary not only because of the initial conditions of acute labour hoarding but also for signalling reasons and the provision of appropriate incentives for restructuring and private sector growth.

To get at these issues, the paper asks several basic questions. First, to what extent has significant unemployment in Central and Eastern Europe been a necessary, if not sufficient, condition for restructuring to proceed and for private job creation? Second, how do we explain the continuing presence of low unemployment in significant parts of the FSU and what implications has this had for restructuring and the development of a private sector? Third, what are the implications of these differing unemployment paths for the overall structure of the transition and its pace? Fourth, how important will the institutional regime for benefits and its financing be in driving the pace of the transition?

Having first established some empirical regularities, the paper then pulls these various strands together in a broader two sector model of transition focusing in particular on the implications of the inter-relationship between the availability of publicly funded fall-back schemes, their financing and hence of the relative incidence of taxation across sectors, and the reallocation of labour across private and state sectors, as well as the unemployment associated with restructuring.

1. Shocks to employment

This section provides a very summary overview of the key changes in the labour market since 1990. More detailed studies are now available and the aim here is merely to provide sufficient background information for the later analysis (such as Barr, 1994; Boeri, 1996; Commander and Coricelli, 1995). Table 1 presents information on the cumulative changes in GDP, employment and unemployment since 1990. The decline in GDP has been large everywhere except Poland where three successive years of growth have largely offset an earlier and substantial fall. In general, for the CEE countries the decline in aggregate employment has matched or exceeded the fall in GDP over this period. The main exception has remained the Czech Republic where the employment decline has been small relative to output and where unemployment has remained very low at below 4 per cent. In the FSU by contrast, the declines in GDP have not only been huge but the adjustments to employment have been largely trivial. Table 2 drives this point home by giving the change in employment relative to output in the key industrial sectors of these economies. The contrast could not be more stark. In the FSU, the evidence is that firms faced with large negative product market shocks have not adjusted employment with the result that unemployment has remained low. However, what the table does not capture is that they have been forced to adjust hours, often radically and there is, in addition, evidence of wage arrears and other borrowing from workers.

Table 1. Central and Eastern Europe and the Former Soviet Union: evolution of GDP, employment and unemployment, 1990-1995.

	Cumulative Change 1995/90 (%) in		Unemployment Rate, 1995 (%)		Share of long-term unemployed
	GDP	Employment	LFS	Registrations	%
CEE					
Bulgaria	-32.5	-25.8	15.7	12.2	66.0
Czech Rep	-24.0	-8.3	3.7	3.0	31.5
Hungary	-15.2	-19.6	10.5	10.5	49.5
Poland	-1.7	-8.5	12.9	15.2	41.4
Romania	-10.7	-13.1	8.0	9.3	47.0
Slovakia	-14.0	-13.7	12.3	13.3	53.8
FSU					
Russia	-49.1	-10.2	7.9	3.1	23.1
Belarus	-45.5	-	-	2.5	-
Kazakstan	-66.0	-	-	2.4	-
Ukraine	-55.5	-32.1	-	0.4	-
Uzbekistan	-20.0	-	-	0.5	-

Source: World Bank and EBRD.

Table 2. Central and Eastern Europe and Former Soviet Union: change in employment relative to output in industry, 1990-1995.

CEE		***FSU***	
Bulgaria	-11.7	Armenia	+113.3
Czech Republic	-5.3	Azerbaijan	+69.1
Hungary	-22.0	Belarus	+66.7
Poland	-32.5	Kazakstan	+68.8
Romania	+2.4	Kyrgyz Rep.	+123.5
Slovak Republic	-0.4	Moldova	+21.1
		Russia	+55.8
		Ukraine	+72.4
		Uzbekistan	+1.4

Source: OECD/CCET, *Short-term Economic Indicators:Transition Economies*, Paris, 1996.

With these large shocks to employment do we also find significant evidence of reallocation in employment across sectors and ownership forms? Initially, the evidence suggested that aggregate rather than reallocation shocks had dominated[1] but over time, country evidence clearly indicates a sharp increase in variation in the changes of employment across branches and there has been very significant intra-branch variation.[2] Table 3 suggests that by 1994/95 there had been non-trivial shifts in the sectoral allocation of labour in the CEECs. As would be expected, manufacturing has declined across the board while services have increased, though the latter sector still remains significantly below industrial country averages.

Further disaggregating the data by ownership type, the private sector — whether by new starts or through privatisation — has grown rapidly (see Table 4). In the Czech Republic, Hungary and Poland, the private sector accounted for over 60 per cent of GDP and employment by 1996. Although it is difficult to disentangle the *de novo* firms from those that have been privatised, the former's growth has been very significant and appears to have accounted for the bulk of job creation.[3] In a number of other countries — such as Bulgaria and Romania — privatisation has been largely absent or has proceeded more gradually and the result has been a continuing large weight of the state sector in the economy.

Table 3. Central and Eastern Europe and Russia: distribution of employment in 1989 and 1995.

	Bulgaria		Czech Rep.		Hungary		Poland	
	1989	1995	1989	1995	1989	1995	1989	1995
Agriculture	19	22	12	7	17	8	27	23
Industry	46	38	46	42	41	33	38	32
of which								
Manufacturing	34	28	34	29	29	23	25	21
Services	35	40	42	51	42	59	35	45
	Romania		**Slovakia**		**Russia**		**Industrial economies**	
	1989	1995	1989	1995	1989	1995	1989	1995
Agriculture	29	40	14	9	13	15	11	5
Industry	43	30	47	38	42	38	27	29
of which								
Manufacturing	33	22	25	21	28	25		
Services	28	30	39	53	45	47	62	66

Table 4. Central and Eastern Europe and Former Soviet Union: private sector shares of GDP and employment, 1990 and 1994/95.

	GDP		Employment	
CEE	1990	1994/95	1994/95	'Pure' private
Bulgaria	9	35	35	
Czech Republic	5	70	64	
Hungary	18	60	62	
Poland	27	60	58	
Romania	16	37	52	
Slovakia	6	57	41	
FSU				
Belarus	5	12		6
Kazakstan	7	24		9
Russia	6	58		31
Ukraine	10	35		
Uzbekistan	9	29		

Source: World Bank, *World Development Report*, 1996 and EBRD, *Transition Report*, 1995.

In the FSU countries, the story has clearly been different. While Russian data show that there has been some decline in the share of industrial employment, the configuration of the services sector still remains skewed toward public services and administration. And although in Russia the greater part of total employment is in the private sector, most of this is in privatised firms. This is also the case, although to a lesser degree, in Ukraine. Firm surveys indicate some evidence of defensive restructuring, including reductions in employment and wage flexibility, but the general picture is of very limited restructuring (see Commander, Fan and Schaffer, 1996; EBRD, 1995). More generally, the growth of a private sector has clearly been less rapid than in much of CEE and much of the growth that has occurred has been through changes in ownership. Autonomous private firms continue to account for fairly small shares of output and employment. What has emerged is a significant 'unofficial' sector clustered around state firms and outside of the tax net.

These employment outcomes are obviously not independent of wage decisions. In CEECs the first flush of reforms produced large order price shocks that eroded consumption wages, often very significantly. Over time, wages have drifted back toward pre-transition levels but gradually. Table 5 presents information on the evolution of unit labour costs in CEECs and Russia. Again, there is evidence by 1995 in a number of countries — particularly Poland and Hungary — of cost side rigidities with unit labour costs back at, or in excess of, start transition levels. But it is also clear that in the Czech Republic — the most obvious case of where employment has stayed high — unit labour costs have remained low. There is little widespread evidence of predatory wage setting, with more of the evidence suggesting that insiders have commonly traded down wages for employment. And in Russia the decline in unit labour costs has been truly substantial.

Table 5. Central and Eastern Europe and Russia: change in unit labour costs, 1990-1995.

	1990	1991	1992	1993	1994	1995	Index (90=100)
CEE							
Bulgaria	—	-39	31	19	-23	-2	72
Czech Republic	-1	-24	13	-8	3	-11	72
Slovak Republic	-1	-24	13	2	3	-1	90
Hungary	7	8	1	-9	-3	-3	93
Poland	-19	30	16	-4	-13	-3	122
Romania	10	-38	5	25	-21	4	67
FSU							
Russia	—	—	-36	7	12	32	52*

Notes: * 1991=100; for 1990-92 values for Czech Republic and Slovakia are for the former Czechoslovakia.

In sum, the main difference between the FSU and the CEECs is not only the continuing importance of state firms in the former, but the limited appearance of an autonomous private sector. In the FSU, the great majority of the labour force remains employed in either state or primarily insider privatised firms.

2. Unemployment

In the CEECs, unemployment rose rapidly and has declined only gradually thereafter. Much of the decline can be accounted for by expiration of benefits and the fall in the number of registered unemployed as well as continuing shifts to non-participation.

Large regional disparities in unemployment also emerged early in the transition in CEECs and to a far lesser extent in the FSU and these have persisted. Estimates of the importance of spatial mismatch have been large, indicative of the continuing lack of labour mobility across regions.[4] Aside from inequalities in the distribution of unemployment by region, it is also clear that unemployment has tended to have a far higher incidence among new entrants to the labour force and among those with low skills. In most countries, youth unemployment has ranged between 20 and 30 per cent of the total. However, in terms of those flowing out of employment, older workers who have lost their jobs have tended to find it particularly difficult to get back into work (European Commission, 1995).

If there is widespread evidence of labour immobility, what does this imply for the play-back from unemployment to wage behaviour, a critical channel for promoting restructuring? Here, the evidence is far from clear cut. Boeri and Scarpetta (1995) find only a weak negative association between the region unemployment rate and the change in wages over the period 1990-1992 for the major CEECs. However, Kollo (1996), using individual wage observations with appropriate controls, does find clear evidence of wage curves in Hungary since 1989. Combining firm- and region-specific data, a negative effect of unemployment on wages has also been documented in Bulgaria, the Czech Republic and Poland (see Nenova and Ugaz, 1995; Estrin and Svejnar, 1996). In Russia, there seems to be some clear evidence of an inverse relationship between region unemployment and wage changes (see Commander and Yemtsov, 1995). In this latter context, changes in relative regional wages have very clearly dominated changes to relative unemployment or employment.

Turning to the flows data presented in Table 6, we find very stable inflow rates to unemployment over the course of the transition in CEECs. On the outflows side — with the obvious exception of the Czech Republic — the rate has also tended to be low and fairly stable over time. We do observe some increase in outflow rate to jobs in several countries but the apparent effect of even significant growth, as in Poland, on the outflows rate to jobs has remained quite small. In Hungary, that outflow in 1995 actually declined significantly. In short, there is little evidence that aggregate output growth has exerted a strong pull of the unemployed into work. The pool of unemployed may have become somewhat less stagnant but its low turnover has remained. Much of the action in the labour market has continued to occur through flows across employment, with job-to-job transitions dominating the flow through unemployment.[5]

The picture in Russia has remained very different. While the inflow rate has crept upwards since 1994, it has remained lower than in most CEE countries. And in strong contrast, outflows have remained above 15 per cent with outflows to jobs at over 5 per cent per month. The differences in regional unemployment has been largely driven by differences in inflows. Further, among the unemployed a persistently high share — around 40 per cent — have been people who quit their previous jobs. Those laid off have remained a stable and quite low — 25/30 per cent — share of the total unemployed.[6]

Table 6. Central and Eastern Europe and Russia: inflows to and outflows from unemployment, 1992-1995.

	Inflow rate				Outflow rate				Outflow rate to jobs			
	92	93	94	95	92	93	94	95	92	93	94	95
CEE												
Bulgaria	1.2	0.9	1.1	1.2	9.2	6.4	8.4	11.6	1.3	0.9	1.2	2.4
Czech Rep.	0.6	0.7	0..6	0.6	24.8	20.1	20.3	19.9	17.3	15.0	15.3	14.5
Slovakia	0.9	1.2	1.2	1.1	6.6	11.8	17.5	9.2	4.1	4.0	4.9	1.8
Hungary	1.7	1.5	0.9	0.9	4.3	4.8	6.1	7.8	2.3	2.3	3.1	4.0
Poland	0.6	0.7	1.0	1.1	10.1	7.8	7.4	9.1	5.2	3.2	2.0	3.0
Romania	0.6	0.3			1.3	2.4			0.9	1.6		
FSU												
Russia	0.3	0.3	0.5	0.6	18.9	15.8	14.4	16.0	7.2	6.5	5.8	7.9

Source: Boeri (1995) and OECD/CCET.

The unemployment rate has stayed thus relatively low and there has been far greater turnover in the unemployment pool. Spells of unemployment have tended to remain short; by end-1995 nearly half the unemployed in Russia were experiencing a spell of under 4 months and less than 15 per cent had been in unemployment for over a year. Unemployment benefits have remained very low at under 10 per cent of the average wage. Elsewhere in the FSU, the story appears to be very similar.

If unemployment has been contained, how have shocks been distributed in the FSU? Several rounds of the Russian Labour Force Survey give us some idea for 1992-1994 (see Table 7). First, the decline in formal sector employment has actually been large — over 15 per cent in the period — but there has been a sizeable offset from the growth in self-employment. Much of this offset has been concentrated in the 'unofficial' economy. By 1994 the latter accounted for nearly 15 per cent of those employed. There has also clearly been a large shift to non-participation, almost exclusively by women. For those in employment, real monetary compensation has drifted downwards and at end-1995 stood at roughly 20 per cent below early 1992 levels. These are likely to be over-estimates of wages given the widespread presence of wage arrears and payment lags. There has also been a sharp decline in the hours worked by those in the formal sector. Among other consequences, this would imply an even larger decline than the nearly 50 per cent drop in unit labour costs since 1991 reported in Table 5 and derived from hours unadjusted data.

In sum, the available evidence indicates that in CEE, employment declined quickly and significantly. For those who lost their jobs, a significant share passed into non-participation (particularly when pensions were relatively generous, as in employment has remained low, even when the economy has grown. In the FSU, as mainly told by Russian statistics, large product market shocks have induced some decline in formal sector employment, wage flexibility and a large fall in unit labour

Table 7. Russia: changes in employment and unemployment — labour force survey data, 1992-1994.

Category	Share of LF in 1994	Change (%) 1994.92
Employment	92.1	-8.7
Male	48.6	-6.3
Female	43.5	-11.2
Formal employment	78.9	-14.9
Male	40.1	-13.8
Female	38.8	-16.0
Self employment	13.2	+62.3
Male	8.5	+59.2
Female	4.7	+68.2
Unemployed	7.9	+51.4
Male	4.2	+61.1
Female	3.7	+41.6
Labour Force	100	-5.7
Male	52.8	+2.3
..Female	47.2	-13.4

Source: Commander and Yemtsov (1996)

costs, but little unemployment. For those experiencing an unemployment spell, this has generally been a way station to re-employment. The growth of a *de novo* private sector has been restrained. Other parts of the FSU appear to offer a similar response with, however, yet smaller declines in formal employment and smaller increases to unemployment.

3. Benefits regimes and the costs of unemployment

An obvious starting point in explaining these profound differences might be the relative generosities and coverage of the fall-back schemes on offer in these regions. And indeed the relative incentives for being unemployed have varied quite significantly across regions. In CEECs there was an initially high generosity in benefits with open-ended access. Over time this has been transformed through cuts in entitlement durations and/or in the replacement rate (see Box 1). By 1995, most CEECs permitted 12 months of benefits receipt but in both the Czech and Slovak republics this had been cut to 6 months. Replacement rates which at the start of transition ranged between 0.4 and 0.7 had fallen to around 0.4 by 1995. On expiration of benefits, the unemployed have been entitled to social assistance at yet lower replacement values. By 1995 recipients of unemployment benefits accounted for less than 50 per cent of registered unemployed in all CEECs, bar Romania.

Despite these changes, the benefits regime remains generous in CEECs relative to the FSU. In Russia, for example, unemployment benefits are close to being flat-rate benefits and fall below 10 per cent of the average wage. On expiration after one year, workers generally have no further entitlements to social assistance. Minimum wage and pension levels also remain very low. As such, in much of the FSU publicly financed fall-backs for the unemployed remain very partial and limited in duration.

Declining generosity and the increasing pass-through of claimants from unemployment insurance to social assistance has been one factor containing the direct fiscal cost of unemployment. Nevertheless, there is significant variation in expenditures per unemployed across the CEECs, as indicated in Box 1. In Poland and Hungary both passive and active labour market expenditure was in the range of 2 to 2.5 per cent of GDP. In Slovakia and Bulgaria, it was below 1 per cent and in the Czech Republic under 0.5 of GDP. These figures tend to be under-estimates, however, given the size of flows to non-participation and the importance of early retirement. In Poland, where early retirement offered a far higher replacement rate, factoring in these costs gives a truer estimate of the direct cost of unemployment of the order of 5-6 per cent of GDP (Perraudin and Pujol, 1994).

For the FSU countries, the direct fiscal burden of benefits has obviously been small. In Russia, unemployment benefits in 1995 accounted for under 0.5 per cent of GDP. However, this may not be an appropriate measure of fiscal pressure, as despite wage flexibility, a significant share of firms, whether state-owned or privatised, continue to receive subsidies and other financing supports for maintaining employment. Further, picking employment smoothing and allowing workers to participate in the unofficial economy has clear fiscal implications since much of this effort remains outside of the tax net.

Box 1. CEE and Russia: Unemployment Insurance and Labour Taxation.

	Bulgaria	*Czech Rep.*	*Hungary*	*Poland*	*Romania*	*Russia*	*Slovakia*
Expenditure on active & passive programmes as % of GDP in 1994	0.7	0.4	2.0	2.4		0.4	0.9
Unemployment Insurance System —							
Duration	12 Months	6 Months	12 Months	12 Months	9 Months	12 Months	6 Months
Eligibility:							
Min. Employ. Record	6 Months	12 Months	360 Days	180 Days	6 Months	3 Months	12 months
Quit Penalty	5 Months	Disqual.	180 Days	90 Days	...	...	Disqual.
Job Refusal Penalty	...	...	90 Days	90 Days	...	...	...
Minimum/Maximum	90%/140-155%	None/150-180%	96%/185% of min.wage	None/None	75-85%/200%	100%	None/150-180%
% of Reg Unemployed Receiving Benefits	1995=31.2	1995=45.8	1995=36.0	1995=53.3	1995=33.5	1995=77.1	1992=23.6
Unemployment Assistance System —							
Duration	Indefinite	Indefinite	Indefinite	Indefinite	Indefinite	None	Indefinite
Replacement Rate	45%	39%	27%	28%	26%		37%
Average unemployment benefit as % of the average wage:							
1990	...	...	42.0	...	73.0	26.9	...
1991	60.6	46.3	41.0	36.0	62.6	23.6	43.8
1992	38.1	24.8	39.3	36.0	59.0	11.9	31.6
1993	35.5	28.3	36.6	36.0	37.2	8.4	29.2
1994	34.3	26.6	33.0	36.0	32.5	8.0	25.3
1995	34.9	25.1	33.5	36.0	28.5	8.8	27.5
Labour and Personal Tax Rates:							
Employer Tax	42%	46%	51%	46%	41%	39%	38%
Employee Tax		13%	12%	None	1%	1%	12%
Income Tax Rate:							
-Highest	52%	47%	40%	40%	45%	30%	47%
-Lowest	20%	15%	25%	20%	6%	12%	19%
VAT (Standard Rate)	20%	23%	25%	22%	18%	20%	26%
Effective Marginal Tax Rate on Labour Income	57%	69%	73%	62%	57%	63%	68%

4. Explaining the variation in unemployment

How can these variations in the CEECs and FSU countries be explained? Aside from differences in benefits regimes, an obvious candidate is the difference in the budget constraints facing firms. In CEECs, explicit budgetary subsidies to firms have indeed declined significantly, but this is also true for those FSU countries where information is available (Table 8). For 1994, the mean subsidy-to-GDP rate in both groups of countries was around 3.5 per cent. The major outlier was Ukraine. Yet these numbers do not adequately capture the range of financing options available to firms and the changing locus of subsidy provision over time. Aside from a host of implicit subsidies, including through energy prices and local government finance, firms have continued to have access to bank borrowing on soft terms, non-payment of tax and social security payments as well as borrowing from other firms, workers and public utilities.[7] Continuing access to soft financing has been more widespread in the FSU (see Commander, Fan and Schaffer, 1996). And the subsidy story, though important, is incomplete without considering an important associated phenomenon that differentiates the FSU countries from the CEECs. This concerns the inherited structure of compensation.

One important difference in the FSU relative to the CEECs has been the Soviet inheritance of firms commonly providing a wide range of social benefits, including housing, child and health care, to their workers. This was particularly true in the larger, industrial firms and ensured that access to benefits was explicitly linked to the site of employment. Associated with this was a relatively low monetary wage.[8] Since the start of transition, changes in both the scale and scope of benefits provision have been relatively limited. Where survey evidence is available, it appears that firms in Ukraine, Russia and in Central Asia have continued to offer roughly the same menu of benefits to their workers.[9] This has implied a rise in the relative share of non-monetary compensation in total compensation. Part of this can be traced to the control structure of these firms and the insider domination that privatisation or nominal state control has conferred. Firms and governments have

Table 8. Central and Eastern Europe and Former Soviet Union; budgetary subsidies to firms, 1992 and 1994 (% of GDP).

	1992	1994
CEE		
Bulgaria	3.2	2.4
Czech Republic	4.5	3.9
Hungary	2.1	4.4
Poland	1.4	2.2
Romania	3.0	3.2
Slovakia	4.1	4.9
FSU		
Belarus	n.a	6.5
Kazakstan	2.5	5.5
Russia	31.6	4.9
Ukraine	12.8	17.0
Uzbekistan	n.a	3.1

Source: World Bank.

remained reluctant to sanction large order employment losses, preferring to adjust hours and monetary compensation. But it is also evident that many firms — particularly the larger firms — have received major compensating finance for benefits provision from various levels of government. Regional and local governments in Russia have tended to subsidise or extend *ad hoc* tax exemptions to firms that maintain large stocks of social assets.[10] These subsidies have been far from trivial and this appears to be the case in other parts of the FSU.

The implications of this two-part compensation structure are several. With benefits and benefits financing associated with state and privatised firms, there has been a strong incentive for workers to stay in those firms but to engage in part-time or moonlighting activity in the *de novo* private sector. This result is, of course, emphasized when benefits provision is a source of subsidy. It also has implications for the growth of an autonomous private sector by raising the reservation wage. This effect will be particularly pronounced if there are large start-up costs associated with benefits provision by *de novo* firms, as would arise if exclusivity in provision to incumbent workers was maintained.[11]

In sum, with non-monetary compensation an important anchor to household income and almost negligible publicly provided support available to the unemployed, the result has been strong continuing attachment of workers to firms — state or privatised — particularly to those that offer benefits (and attract subsidies). Monetary income has increasingly been secured by allocating effort to work in the informal or 'unofficial' economy which has remained almost completely outside the tax system.

5. Implications for the path of transition

To this point we have concentrated on describing the features of the respective transitions in CEE and the FSU. We have picked out the institutional differences and indicated the importance of the effective budget constraint and the structure of compensation in explaining the variation in unemployment paths across the two regions. We now go further and look more formally at the possible implications of these institutional differences for the path and pace of transition.

The structure of the model is provided in Appendix. Briefly, the economy is characterised by two sectors — state and private — and three labour market states; employment in the state sector (N_1), employment in the private sector (N_2), and unemployment (U).[12] State firms have no capital accumulation and wages are set equal to average product. It is assumed, in effect, that decision-making rests with insiders who control the firm. By contrast, the private sector sets efficiency wages and is constrained by its marginal revenue product curve. Private wages depend on the outside labour market. While flows into unemployment can come from both state and private firms, the private sector is the only source of hiring in the model.

The model also explicitly factors in the possibilities that state firms might fail and close. In that event the workers will become unemployed. Alternatively, insiders in state firms may choose to restructure. Restructuring implies that a certain proportion $(1-\gamma)$ of workers will lose their jobs and become unemployed.[13] Aside from imposing some predetermined or initial values on the probabilities of closure or restructuring, the model endogenises these probabilities by making them depend on the difference in values across various states.

With respect to unemployment, the model allows us to calibrate several critical values. The first, *b*, summarises the unemployment regime and gives us the reservation value. The second, ε, or the payroll tax ratio for state and private sectors, relates to the financing of unemployment. It is assumed that the bulk of the cost of providing unemployment benefits is financed through payroll taxes. The term, ε, gives us the relative incidence of those taxes across the two sectors. Thus, when ε=0.1 the private sector's tax incidence is negligible and the costs of benefits will have to be covered almost exclusively by taxing the state sector. A low tax incidence on the private sector, while fiscally damaging, will stimulate outflows from the state sector through the tax effect. Through the playback from unemployment to wages and by the direct effect on the private sector's viability, job creation will be stimulated. Conversely, an equivalent tax incidence (ε=1) will reduce the tax pressure on the state sector slowing the outflow and lowering unemployment. But it will also affect the hiring rate of the private sector. This set-up permits calibration and the implications of various benefits and financing regimes with endogenous restructuring are now discussed.

Figures 1 and 2 provide a first pass at characterising two systems differentiated only by the generosity of the unemployment benefits regime. In Figure 1, (*b*) is set low at 0.5 or around 12.5 per cent of the wage. This is roughly the ratio holding in Russia and other FSU countries. In Figure 2, benefits are set at 50 per cent (b=2),which approximates conditions in CEECs. The tax ratio, (ε), is set at 0.5 in both cases. The initial values for the probabilities of closure or restructuring are also equivalent. It can be seen that the main effect of an increase in benefits generosity is to double the peak level of unemployment. Further, unemployment is far longer lasting as both the rate of decline of the state sector and of growth in the private sector are held back relative to the case with low benefits.

The difference in benefits (*b*) summarises only one of the major divides between the FSU and CEECs. As we have seen, in the FSU the combination of the control regime in firms, government preferences and the low level of benefits has not only been to sponsor attachment and hence a smaller rate of decline of the state or privatised sector but also to sponsor the growth of an informal private sector outside of the tax system. By contrast, in CEECs a far higher capture of the private sector in the tax net has occurred. Figures 3 and 4 reflect this by setting the tax ratio (ε) to 0.1 and 0.8 respectively. In addition, we know from the earlier discussion that with large spatial mismatch, the hazard rate from unemployment looks very different in CEE than in FSU. To capture this feature we lower the parameter, α, which is in the hiring function (see Appendix) and can be seen as reflecting the efficiency in matching.[14] While in the CEE case only changing the tax ratio would have a rather small effect on the size and timing of unemployment peak relative to the base case, changing both the tax ratio and the matching term does have a significant effect (Figure 4). Relative to the base case, unemployment peaks at over five percentage points higher and lasts approximately double the time that can be observed in the FSU case with low benefits. Relative to the base case, the main effect of decreasing the tax inequality, for given benefits levels, is to lower slightly the rate of outflow

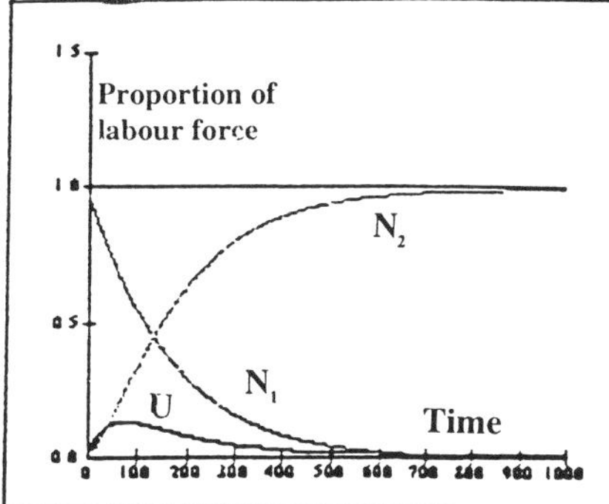

Fig 1: FSU Base Case; b=0.5; ε=0.5; α=0.1; p^0=0.15; p^0_R = 0.05

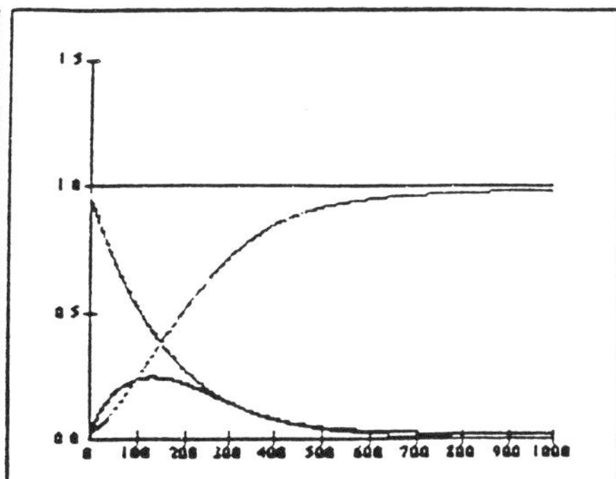

Fig 2: CEE Base Case; b=2; ε=0.5; α=0.1; p^0=0.15; p^0_R=0.05

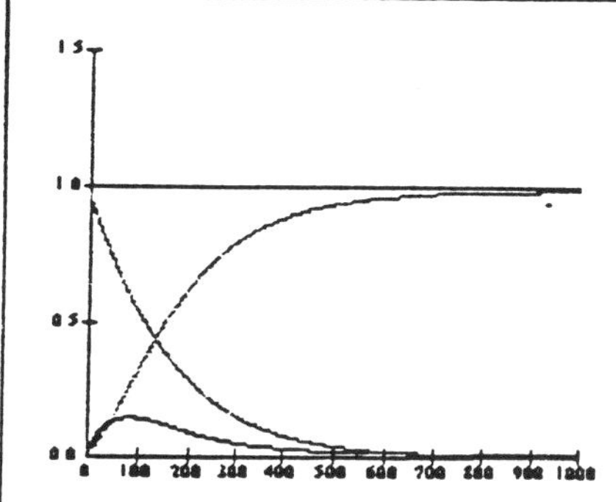

Fig 3: FSU; b=0.5; ε=0.5; α=0.1; p^0=0.15; p^0_R =0.05

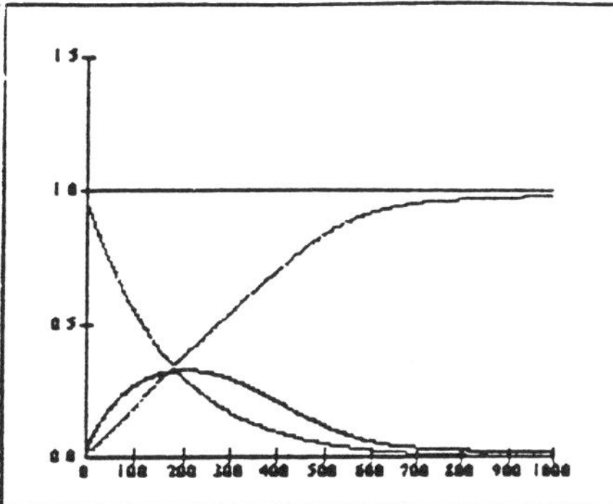

Fig 4: CEE; b=2; ε=0.8; α=0.05; p^0=0.15; p^0_R =0.05

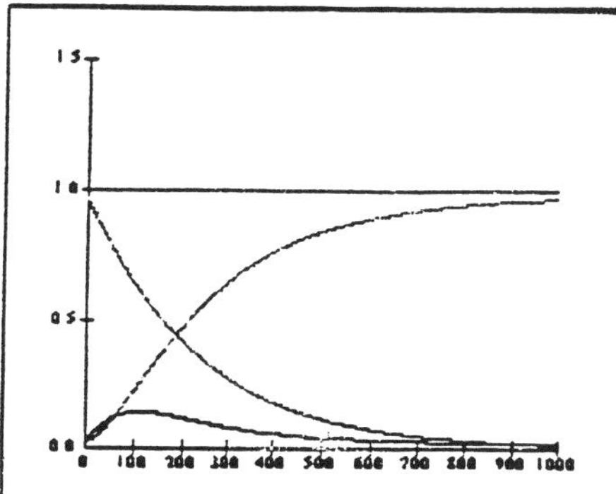

Fig 5 : FSU; b=1.5; ε=0.1; α=0.1; p^0 = 0.10; p^0_R =0.03

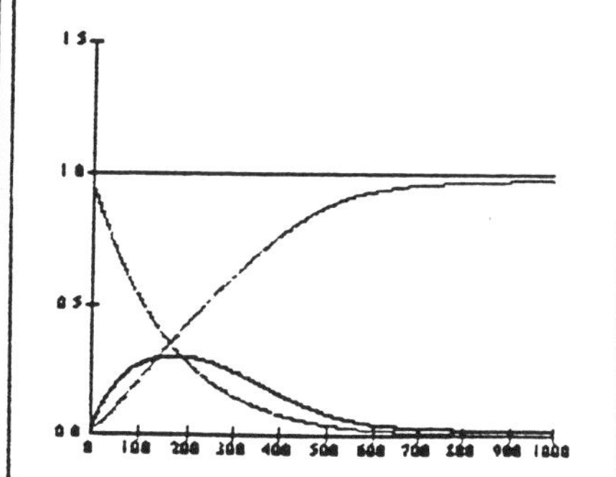

Fig 6 : CEE; b=2; ε=0.4; α=0.05; p^0=0.15; p^0_R =0.05

from the state sector. But reduction in the efficiency of matching leads to a fall in the absorption rate from unemployment by the private sector. For the FSU, by contrast, having the private sector outside of taxation actually exerts very little effect on the pace of the transition or the peak level of unemployment (Figure 3). That is because for the low level of benefits (b=0.5) and unemployment, the financing effect is small and hence the tax pressure on state firms remains limited.

The scenario outlined above (Figure 4) presents a striking picture of the effect of low benefits on the unemployment level, its persistence and the overall pace of transition. But it provides an inaccurate representation of the FSU environment in several respects. First, as already indicated, firms have still continued to receive, through a multitude of channels, significant subsidies to maintain high employment levels. While the financing incidence may not fall directly on the firm sector — except indirectly through the resulting inflation tax — we can, within the constraints of the model, think of such subsidies raising the value of staying in the state firm. Second, the probabilities of closure and restructuring have obviously been directly affected by these supports to employment. To capture this, we adjust the predetermined values for closure and restructuring so that they are significantly smaller than in CEECs or the base case. We assume the same benefits level and the low tax burden on the private sector (ε=0.1). Figure 5 shows that this shift registers little effect on the size of unemployment but the peak occurs later and there is greater persistence. The main outcome is that the speed of transition is reduced. Raising the private sector's tax effort (ε=0.5) in this scenario would actually slightly decrease the pace of transition, given the very gradual contraction of the state sector. Note also that at these lower initial probabilities of closure and restructuring it would take a very high replacement rate (b>2.5) to exert a notable effect on the size of unemployment in the transition. Further, on the assumption that current subsidies to employment are simply switched to benefits thereby raising the effective replacement rate to (b=1.5), the tax ratio is held at (ε=0.1) and the base case initial probabilities are restored, we would observe a sharp increase in the amount of unemployment generated — nearly 20 per cent at the peak — but a clear increase in the pace of the transition.

Turning back to the case of CEECs, it is already clear that high benefits have a large effect on unemployment and its longevity. Yet so far it has been assumed that this has occurred with a relatively common payroll tax burden across state and private firms. But we also know that taxation of private firms has commonly been far from complete. Tax revenues have fallen in almost all cases and in some countries — such as Hungary — the private sector has been deft in its ability to avoid payroll and other direct taxes.[15] Figure 6 shows the implications of both a high benefits regime (b=2) and weak taxation of the private sector (ε=0.4). Again, the results are not pleasant. Unemployment indeed goes high, peaking at over 30 per cent of the labour force, and is long lasting, though less so than in Figure 4. For although the additional tax pressure on state firms results in more rapid employment decline in that sector, the low effective tax ratio for private firms significantly assists its growth.

Finally, we look at the implications in the CEEC context of pursuing a more rapid programme of reform. This is handled by changing the values for closure or restructuring on the assumption that faster reform — and changes in legal and other

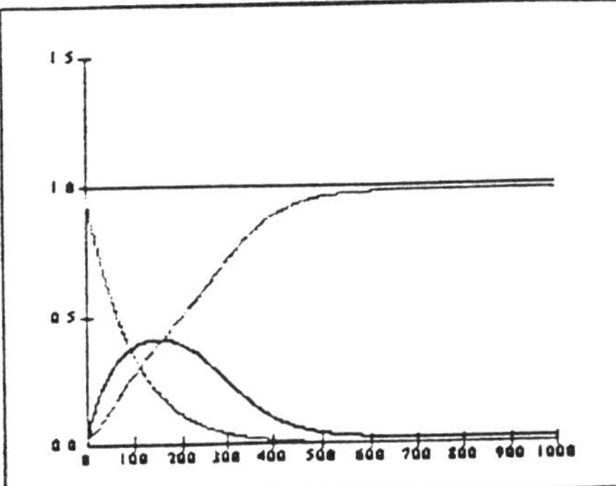

Fig 7 : CEE; b=2; ε=0.8; α=0.1;
p^0=0.25; p^0_R=0.10

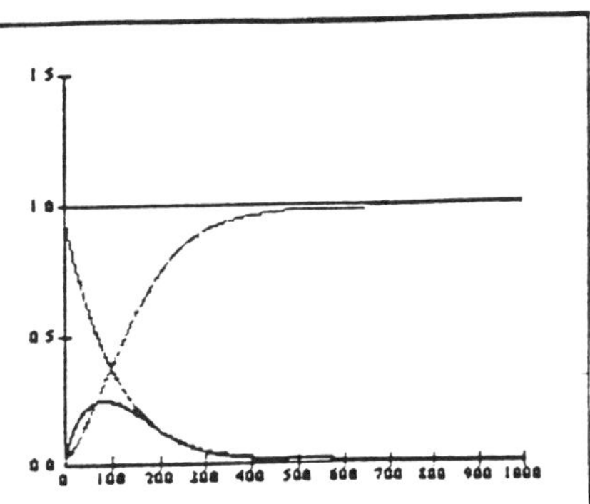

Fig 8 : CEE; b=1; ε=0.8; α=0.1;
p^0=0.25; p^0_R=0.10

institutional constraints — will tend to be associated with higher probabilities of closure and/or restructuring. Figure 7 suggests that a higher predetermined value for closure and restructuring for CEE — with its associated job losses — with a similar benefits and tax regime (*b*=2; ε=0.8) will predictably raise the unemployment peak and its rate of increase very substantially. However, unemployment will not be very long lasting and the pace of transition will be accelerated.[16] Maintaining the same closure and restructuring probabilities but reducing the benefits level (*b*=1) would lower the peak unemployment rate by around fifteen percentage points and there would be a far more rapid overall pace of transition (see Figure 8), including relative to the cases given in Figures 1 and 4.

Conclusion

This paper has attempted in the first place to outline the rather different labour market evolutions that have occurred in CEE and the FSU since the start of transition. In CEE systems of unemployment support of relative generosity have been created, giving rise to fears that these countries may in due course contract the same symptoms of labour market sclerosis prevalent in some Western European economies. By contrast, in the FSU public fall-backs have remained derisory. The incentives for workers to stay in firms have been raised and this can, in part, explain the very large wage flexibility that has been observed. In addition, the budget constraints of firms and the control regimes of firms help explain this difference. The structure of compensation as a mechanism for sustaining attachment and for promoting informalisation also appears to be important. The major fiscal implication of the adjustment path taken in most FSU countries is that most of the private sector has remained outside of the tax net. In addition, state or privatised firms have tended to extract soft financing from both government and utilities by running arrears or defaulting on taxes and other payment obligations. Not surprisingly, the revenue side of the budget has commonly come under great pressure.

The paper then attempted to calibrate these differences in a two sector, three states model of transition. These exercises indicated that benefits generosity does exert a powerful influence on both the unemployment peak that is generated, its persistence and the overall pace of the transition. The CEECs have indeed tended to drift toward systems where unemployment is likely to stay high for long.

Characterising the FSU in terms of a low benefits level and a low private sector tax coverage, the base case generates a relatively small amount of unemployment and a relatively fast transition. But it is somewhat misleading, given the size of subsidies to employment and the low relative probabilities of closure and restructuring. Assuming that such transfers are translated into benefits, shifting those subsidised workers to unemployment at that shadow benefits rate would not significantly raise unemployment but would however lead to more persistence and a much slower pace of transition.

Finally, while the paper does not deal with the issue directly, it is important to remember the consistently tight association between unemployment and poverty, whether in CEE or FSU (see Milanovic, 1995). However, in the latter, the incidence of poverty is far greater and there appears to be greater depth to the poverty that has been generated.[17] A far higher proportion of employed workers fall below the poverty line as wages have declined and, in regions with less diversified economies, income-generating opportunities have evaporated. Moreover, subsidies to employment have been one of the factors contributing to persistently high inflation and the associated inflation tax has had powerful redistributive consequences. The poverty and income distributional effects of the FSU adjustment path can already be seen to have important political economy consequences, not least a reluctance to pursue reforms and/or a clamour for the restoration of some basic elements of the controlled economy. Further, absent or negligible fall-backs may promote wage flexibility but, as this paper has tried to indicate, may also skew the development of the private sector towards informalisation while creating a larger stratum of the impoverished.

Appendix: A model of restructuring and transition

The economy consists of two sectors — state and private — and three basic labour market states — state employment, private employment and unemployment. The labour force is given by:

$$N^s + N^p + U \equiv N_1 + N_2 + U = 1 .$$

At the start of transition, virtually all employment is in the state sector; there is little private employment and no unemployment.[18]

State sector

State firms are assumed to be governed by a zero profit constraint. This is because insiders control the firm and can extract all surplus in the firm. With no capital accumulation, we can write the state firm's problem as:

$$\max_{w_1, N_1} \left\{ \frac{\overline{N}_1 - N_1}{\overline{N}_1} V_u + \frac{N_1}{\overline{N}_1} V_1 \right\}$$

subject to:

$$w_1 N_1 = p_1 Y_1$$

Wages in the state sector are set equal to average product;

$w_1 = AP_1$ or, incorporating taxes per worker;

$w_1 = AP_1 - t_1$.

In this set-up, insiders in state firms can choose to continue operating in this manner, subject to some probability of closure, or they can choose to restructure. If they take the latter route and restructure, this will result in a decline in employment, an increase in marginal product for remaining workers and a change in wage setting, with wages now set as in the private sector. Thus, with restructuring, a certain proportion of workers $(1-\gamma)$ become unemployed, the rest, (γ), remain in the restructured firm. A restructured firm is equivalent to a private sector firm.

Private sector

The private sector is assumed to be constrained by its labour demand curve and to pay efficiency wages. Further, private wages depend explicitly on outside labour market conditions so that:

$w_2 = b + c(r + \beta + H/U)$

where b= unemployment benefits; c is a constant (mark-up value), r = interest rate and H/U is the exit rate from unemployment.

Only the private sector hires and for job creation we have:

$H = \alpha(MP_2^0 - w_2(H, U) - \varepsilon t(U))$

where, w_2 = wage in the private sector; b = unemployment benefits; $t_1 \equiv t$ taxes per worker in the state sector;

$t_2 \equiv \varepsilon t$ - taxes per worker in the private sector;

α = a matching term relating the sensitivity of the hiring rate to the private sector's performance and MP_2^0 = marginal product in the private sector.

Arbitrage equations

We have three basic arbitrage equations;

$rV_1 = w_1 + p_{1U}(V_u - V_1) + p_{12}(V_2 - V_1) + \dot{V}_1$ (1) Value of being in the state sector.

$rV_2 = w_2 + \beta(V_u - V_2) + \dot{V}_2$ (2) Value of being in the private sector.

$rV_u = b + (H/U)(V_2 - V_u) + \dot{V}_u$ (3) Value of being unemployed.

where β is the probability of job loss in the private sector; H/U = the hiring rate from unemployment (probability of hiring); w_1 and w_2 are wages in state and private sectors respectively, b = unemployment benefits;

$p_{1U} = (1 - p_R)p + p_R(1 - \gamma)$ or the complete probability of moving from the state sector to unemployment; and

$p_{12} = p_R\gamma$ is the probability of moving from the state to the private sector.

The fact that state firms can stay as they are or restructure actually means that there should be four possible states. For simplicity, we do not explicitly include the value of being in a restructured firm in our basic model. We can do this because we make two assumptions. The first is that the time scale for restructuring is far longer than for the other time scales. The second is that the value of being in a restructured firm is a weighted average of the values of being in the private sector (V_2) and being unemployed (V_U). With these assumptions, our set-up is the limit case of the four states model.

From these arbitrage equations we can derive equations for the values, $(V_2 - V_U)$ or V_{2U} and $(V_1 - V_U)$ or V_{1U} as follows:

$\dot{V}_{2U} = (r + \beta + H/U)V_{2U} - (w_2 - b)$

$\dot{V}_{1U} = (r + p_{1U} + p_{12})V_{1U} + (H/U - p_{12})V_{2U} - (w_1 - b)$

Balance equations

Collecting the dynamic equations written above, we get the following expressions:

$$\frac{dN_1}{dt} = -(p_{1U} + p_{12})N_1$$

$$\frac{dU}{dt} = p_{1U}N_1 - H(U) + \beta N_2$$

$$\frac{dN_2}{dt} = H(U) + p_{12}N_1 - \beta N_2$$

Summing up the balance equations we get the consistency condition:

$$\frac{dN_1}{dt} + \frac{dN_2}{dt} + \frac{dU}{dt} = \{-(p_{1U} + p_{12})N_1\} + \left\{\frac{H}{U}U + p_{12}N_1 - \beta N_2\right\} + \left\{p_{1U}N_1 - \frac{H}{U}U + \beta N_2\right\} = 0$$

since $N_1+N_2+U=1$.

Taxation and the financing rule

Firms pay payroll taxes but the incidence across state and private firms can vary. As such, we assume different values for payroll taxes for the state (t_1) and private sector (t_2) and introduce the parameter, $\varepsilon = t_2/t_1$ where $t_1=t$ and $t_2=\varepsilon t$. We assume that virtually all of the direct costs of unemployment (viz.; unemployment benefits), $(U-U^0)$, are financed through payroll taxes. With these assumptions we have:

$$t = \frac{b(U - U^0)}{N_1 + \varepsilon N_2} = \frac{b(U - U^0)}{N_1(1-\varepsilon) + \varepsilon(1-U)}$$

Given this constraint, we can now combine with earlier expressions to find H as a function of U:

$$H(U) = \frac{\alpha U\left[MP_2 - b - c(r+\beta) - \varepsilon b(U - U^0)/(N_1(1-\varepsilon) + \varepsilon(1-U))\right]}{\alpha c + U}$$

Closure and restructuring

A feature of the model is that insiders in state firms face a probability that their firm will close, say because of the implementation of a bankruptcy law. They can also elect to restructure the firm, albeit with job losses. While the initial values are predetermined, these probabilities of closure and restructuring are subsequently endogenised by assuming that they depend on the difference between the values of various states. For example, the probability of closure of the state firm will depend negatively on the value of being in that firm as compared to the value of being unemployed. In addition we impose a constraint on each probability and consider the probability of restructuring to be equal to zero when there are no benefits to be derived from restructuring ($V_R < V_1$). The probability of closure will be equal to some exogenous value determined by institutional and other factors when ($V_1 < V_U$). With these constraints, we have;

$$p = \begin{cases} p^0 e^{-d_1 V_{1U}}, & V_1 \geq V_U \\ p^0, & V_1 < V_U \end{cases}$$

$$p_R = \begin{cases} p_R^0(1 - e^{-d_2 V_{R1}}), & V_R \geq V_1 \\ 0, & V_R < V_1 \end{cases} = \begin{cases} p_R^0(1 - e^{-d_2(\gamma V_{2U} - V_{1U})}), & \gamma V_{2U} \geq V_{1U} \\ 0, & \gamma V_{2U} < V_{1U} \end{cases}$$

where p = probability of closure of state firm and p_R = the probability of restructuring. As before, we denote $(V_1 - V_U)$ through V_{1U}, $(V_2 - V_U)$ through V_{2U} and $(V_R - V_1)$ through V_{R1} and use the following expression for the *a posteriori* probability of restructuring;

$$V_R = \gamma V_2 + (1-\gamma)V_U .$$

Notes

[1] For studies covering the period 1989-1991 in CEE, see Blejer *et al* (1993).

[2] See, *inter alia*, Estrin and Svejnar (1996); Kollo (1996); Commander and Dhar (1996).

[3] For Poland, see Konings *et al.* (1995); for Hungary, Kollo (1996).
[4] Relating the unemployed to vacancies across regions, regional mismatch was 0.25 for Poland in 1993 and 0.2 for Russia in 1994; seeCoricelli *et al.*,1995; Commander and Yemtsov, 1996.
[5] Boeri (1995); Boeri and Scarpetta (1995) and Boeri (1996) provide a set of studies of emerging unemployment dynamics in the CEECs.
[6] For a detailed analysis, see Commander and Yemtsov (1996).
[7] Schaffer (1996) puts the stock of tax arrears in the range 3-9 percent of GDP in the CEECs and 4 per cent in Russia. Real flows fall in the range of 1-2 percent of GDP. However, in CEECs arrears tend to be very highly concentrated and not a widespread source of soft financing.
[8] Survey evidence suggests that in 1993 benefits comprised roughly 30 percent of total labour costs; see Commander, Liberman and Yemtsov (1993).
[9] See Falkingham *et al* (1996) for Central Asia; Commander and Schankerman (1995) for Russia and Ukraine. The one exception appears to be child care, provision of which has declined across the board.
[10] A rough measure of the scale of support is that in Russia subsidies for housing that had been divested from firms to muncipalities exceeded 5 percent of GDP in 1995. See Le Houerou (1995).
[11] Issues discussed in more detail in Commander and Schankerman (1995).
[12] In all the results reported in this paper, the initial values — expressed as a share of the labour force — for the state sector are 0.97; for the private sector, 0.02 and for unemployment, 0.01.
[13] Throughout it will be assumed that the proportion of workers who keep their jobs with restructuring is γ=0.8.
[14] For the CEE simulation we now have α=0.05 and for the FSU at 0.1.
[15] See World Development Report, 1996, Chapter 7.
[16] Note that if α=0.05 then we have instability.
[17] In Russia over a third of the poor have incomes of less than 50 percent of the poverty line, see Klugman (1996).
[18] The full model is given in Commander and Tolstopiatenko (1996). The structure is in very much in the spirit of the two sector models developed by Aghion and Blanchard (1994) and Chadha and Coricelli (1994).

References

Aghion, P. and Blanchard, O., 1994, "On the Speed of Restructuring", MIT and EBRD, [mimeo].

Barr, N. (ed), 1994, *Labour Markets and Social Policy in Central and Eastern Europe*, New York.

Blejer, M., .Calvo, G., Coricelli, F. and Gelb A.(eds), 1993, *Eastern Europe in Transition: From Recession to Growth*, World Bank.

Boeri, T., 1995, *Labour Market Flows and the Scope of Labour Market Policies in Central and Eastern Europe*, OECD, Paris, [mimeo].

Boeri, T. and Scarpetta, S., 1995, "Emerging Regional Labour Market Dynamics in Central and Eastern Europe", in OECD, *The Regional Dimension of Unemployment in Transition Countries*, Paris.

Boeri, T., 1995, "Unemployment Dynamics and Labour Market Policies", in Commander and Coricelli.

Chadha, B. and Coricelli, F., 1994, "A Two Sector Model of Transition", *IMF Staff Papers*.

Cohen, D., 1995, *Success and Failure in Russian Reforms*, Paris, [mimeo].

Commander, S., Fan, Q. and Schaffer, M. (eds), 1996, *Enterprise Restructuring and Economic Policy in Russia*, World Bank, Washington DC.

Commander, S. and Tolstopiatenko, A., 1996, *Endogenous Restructuring*, [mimeo].

Commander, S. and Tolstopiatenko, A., 1996, *Restructuring and Taxation in Transition Economies*, [mimeo].

Commander, S. and Yemtsov, R., 1996, Characteristics of the Unemployed in Russia, in Klugman Commander, Simon and Mark Schankerman, 1995, *Enterprise Restructuring and the Efficient Provision of Benefits*, World Bank and EBRD, [mimeo].

Commander, S. and Coricelli, F. (eds), 1995, *Unemployment and Restructuring in Eastern Europe and Russia*, World Bank, Washington DC.

EBRD, 1995, *Transition Report 1995: Investment and Enterprise Restructuring*, London.

Estrin, S., and Svejnar, J., 1996, *Employment and Wage Adjustment by Enterprises in the Transition*, London Business School and University of Pittsburgh.

Estrin, S., Earle, J. and Leshchenko, L., 1996, "Privatisation and Corporate Governance in Russia", in Commander, Fan and Schaffer

European Commission, 1995, *Employment Observatory, Central and Eastern Europe*, No. 8, Brussels.

Falkingham, J., Klugman, J., Marnie, S. and Micklewright, J., 1996, *Household Welfare in Central Asia*, Macmillan, London.

Jackman, R. and Pauna, C., 1996, *How Have Labour Markets in Eastern Europe Performed?*, London School of Economics, Centre for Economic Performance.

Klugman, J. (ed), 1996, *Poverty in Russia*, World Bank, Washington DC, forthcoming.

Kollo, J., 1996, *Employment and Wage Setting in Three Stages of Hungary's Labour Market Transition*, Institute of Economics, Budapest, [mimeo].

Konings, J., Lehmann, H. and Schaffer, M., 1995, "Employment Growth, Job Creation and Job Destruction in Polish Industry, 1988-1991", CEP Working Paper 707.

Le Houerou, P., 1995, *Fiscal Management in the Russian Federation*, World Bank, Washington DC.

Milanovic, B., 1995, *Poverty and Income Distribution in Eastern Europe*, World Bank, [mimeo].

Perraudin, W. and Pujol, T., 1994, "Unemployment Benefits and Pensions in Poland", *IMF Staff Papers*.

Schaffer, M., 1996, *Tax Arrears in Transition Economies*, Heriot-Watt University, [mimeo].

World Bank, 1996), *World Development Report: From Plan to Market*, Washington DC.

2

Transformation as a demographic crisis

Michael Ellman

1. Introduction

Recently, considerable attention has been given to demographic developments in the transformation countries (UNICEF 1993, 1994 and 1995; Eberstadt, 1994; Ellman, 1994; Shapiro, 1995; Heleniak, 1995). This is entirely understandable in view of the completely unexpected and very dramatic changes which have taken place. This paper presents some relevant data and discusses their policy implications.

2. Fertility

Some data on the fall in the crude birth rate is set out in Table 1.

The crude birth rate is influenced by the age/sex structure of the population. A statistic which takes account of this is the total fertility rate, which shows the number of children an average woman would have if the age-specific birth rates remained at their current level. Some data on the total fertility rate is set out in Table 2.

Tables 1 and 2 make it clear that during the transformation there has been a significant fall in fertility. This fall has been universal, but with a wide dispersion. It was most extreme in the former GDR[1] and least evident in Hungary and Albania. Apart from the special case of the former GDR, it has been most marked in a number of countries of the former Soviet Union such as Estonia and Latvia. It has also been marked in the three eastern Slavic countries.

There are also three non-FSU countries where the decline in fertility in 1989-94 has been 20 per cent or more — Bulgaria, Romania and Slovakia. In some countries the decline in fertility has been on a scale normally associated with famine or war, in others it has been just a hiccup. Over the whole population involved (most of whom live in the three countries Russia, Ukraine and Poland) it has been substantial. It is important to note that the countries in Table 2 with the lowest fertility in 1994 were not out of line with non-transformation European countries. For example, Russia's fertility in 1994 was similar to that of the European Union (where the 1993 total fertility rate for the current 15 members was 1.46) and in excess of that of the 1993

The author is grateful to Andrea Cornia, Siv Gustaffson, Vladimir Kontorovich, Peter Rutland and Judith Shapiro for helpful comments on the draft or additional data.

Table 1. The decline in the crude birth rate 1989-94 (%).

More than 50%		*More than 10%*	
Former GDR	58	Azerbaijan	19
More than 30%		Moldova	19
Estonia	39	Slovakia	19
Armenia	37	Slovenia	16
Georgia	36	Poland	16
Russia	34[a]	Czech Republic	16
Latvia	35	*Less than 10%*	
Romania	32	Albania	6[b]
More than 20%		Hungary	3
Belarus	29	*Memorandum*	
Ukraine	26	US, 1929-33	13
Bulgaria	26	Germany, 1929-33	18
Lithuania	24		

Notes: a) This figure is derived from the revised figure for the crude birth rate in 1994 (see *Rossiya v tsifrakh 1995* (Moscow, Goskomstat, 1995) p.38. The preliminary figure used by UNICEF gives a decline of 36%; b) In 1989-1993, the decline was 22 per cent but in 1994 the crude birth rate recovered sharply.

Source: UNICEF (1995) p.110; *Wirtschaft und Statistik,* 1995, No.12 p.880 (for the former GDR); *Historical statistics of the United States, from colonial times to 1957* (US Bureau of the Census, Washington DC, 1960); *Statistisches Jahrbuch für das Deutsche Reich 1937* (Berlin 1937).

rates for Germany (1.28), Greece (1.34), Spain (1.26) and Italy (1.22).[2] One transformation country (Albania) in 1994 had a fertility rate which was very high by European standards, and others (Moldova, Poland) also had fertility rates which were quite high by West European standards. Only the former GDR has a fertility rate which is much below the west European norm. With this one exception, part of the decline in fertility can be regarded as a natural convergence of fertility in East and West Europe.

What explains this decline in fertility? This question has been discussed by Heleniak (1995); Zimmermann (1993); Maier (1993); Nauck and Joos (1995); Cornia and Panniccià (1995; 1996); Vishnevskii (1996); and Bodrova (1996). Factors which have been suggested include:

- uncertainty about economic conditions and social policies;
- unchanging relative costs of having and raising children;
- declining real wages and increased poverty. In the former GDR, however, where there was the biggest decline in fertility, average consumption rose rather than fell. Nauck and Joos (1995) sensibly note that the huge decline in fertility in the former GDR calls "into question all interpretations of the demographic consequences of the transformation of post-socialist societies that relate demographic changes directly to changes in economic welfare (or other 'objective' factors affecting living standards) on both individual and societal levels. Rather, 'subjective' factors like unstable expectations for the future and shifts in life orientation seem to play an important role in individual coping strategies for dealing with macro-social stress";

- the dismantling of pronatalist income and welfare policies (e.g. socialised child care and well-paid maternity leave):
    - in some countries, a smaller cohort of women in the most fertile age-group[3];
    - increased availability of modern contraceptives;
    - the sharp decline in the marriage rate in many transformation countries.[4]

Table 2. Total fertility rate (children per woman).

	1989	1994	% decline
former GDR	1.57	0.77[a]	51
Estonia	2.20	1.37	38
Russia	2.01	1.40	30
Latvia	2.05	1.39	32
Bulgaria	1.90	1.37	28
Romania	1.92	1.41	27
Belarus	2.03	1.51	26
Armenia	2.61	2.00	23
Lithuania	1.98	1.54	22
Ukraine	1.90	1.50	21
Slovakia	2.08	1.66	20
Moldava	2.52	2.10	17
Slovenia	1.52	1.32	13
Poland	2.05	1.80	12
Azerbaijan	2.79	2.52	10
Albania	2.96	2.70	9
Hungary	1.78	1.65	7

Note: a) 1993.
Source: UNICEF (1995) p.116; Heleniak (1995) p.4; *The demographic yearbook of Russia 1995* (Moscow 1996); Nauck and Joos (1995); and *Statistisches Jahrbuch 1995 für die Bundesrepublik Deutschland* (Wiesbaden 1995). These sources differ among themselves. Possible reasons for this include: a) the use of preliminary/revised data, b) the fact that the total fertility rate can be calculated using annual or five-yearly age-specific fertility rates which can make a slight difference to the outcome.

The table mainly uses the UNICEF data. Exceptions are Russia (where the official Russian figures have been used), the former GDR (which is not included in the UNICEF database) and those countries (Armenia and Moldova) for which UNICEF does not give 1994 data. There is no entry for the Czech republic since the UNICEF book does not give data for that country either for 1993 or for 1994. The 1994 figure in the Russian statistical handbook (1.40) is slightly larger than that given in Vishnevskii (1996), p.41 (1.39).

With special reference to the former GDR, Zimmermann (1993) suggested that economic uncertainty, the transition to the FRG child care system (in which organised child care for children under three is rare), and the expanded consumption possibilities created by reunification, are explanatory factors. Nauck and Joos drew attention to the dramatic fall in the crude marriage rate in the former GDR. Between 1989 and 1993 it fell by 61 per cent, a huge fall and very much larger than the falls in Central Europe or Russia. Since the majority of births are to married women, this was bound to reduce the birth rate.[5] The huge drops in the marriage rate and in the birth rate in a (former) country where consumption did not decline suggests that both declines were determined by some kind of social or psycho-social reaction of the population to the collapse of the GDR and of employment and the incorporation of the five new provinces in the FRG. Nauck and Joos also drew attention to the decline in organised care for pre-school children. Between 1990 and 1993 the percentage of pre-school children attending a day-care nursery fell from 25 per cent to 14 per cent and the percentage being cared for at home rose from 22 per cent to 31 per cent. The decline in organised child care partly reflects the increasing charges for it, which are a financial burden for parents (unlike the situation which used to exist in the GDR.) This privatisation of the cost of children has no doubt contributed to the reduced demand for them. Bodrova, concentrating on the situation on Russia, used public opinion surveys to analyse family formation plans. It turns out that between July 1991 and September-October 1992 the number of children thought appropriate by the Russian public for an "ideal" family fell from 2.1 to 1.53, a remarkable change in values in such a short time. The number of children couples expected to have fell in 1991-94 from 1.77 to 1.08, which probably reflected not only the change in values but also the uncertainty, chaos and poverty resulting from the collapse of the Soviet system, and the increased private costs of child care. These public opinion surveys also showed that the "ideal" number of children increased sharply in 1994 and increased further in 1995 (when it slightly exceeded the 1991 level) and the expected number of children jumped sharply in 1995 (although it was still about 11 per cent lower than in 1991). This suggests that the Russian fertility rate may recover.[6]

A debate has taken place in recent years about the development of living standards in the transformation period. Some writers (Adam, 1993; Kabaj and Kowalik, 1995) have stressed the decline in measured national income and in food consumption and argued that there was a significant drop in living standards. Other writers (Sachs, 1993 and 1995) have drawn attention to the increased consumption of fruit, the increased consumption of a number of food products by retirees, the difference between 1993 and 1994 food consumption data, the increased consumption of durables, and the decline in queues, and rejected as absurd the alleged decline in living standards. In this debate between 'pessimists' and 'optimists', the reproductive behaviour of the populations concerned, which is similar to that in the US and Germany during the great depression, is a piece of evidence, similar to that of electoral behaviour in many countries, that suggests the subjective assessment of many of the populations concerned is closer to the 'pessimistic' standpoint than to the 'optimistic' one.[7]

How should this decline in fertility be evaluated? Obviously, to the extent that the decline has resulted from a negative perception of the transformation process by the population, it is itself a negative social indicator. In Russian public discussion the decline in births is generally regarded as a negative phenomenon. An important reason for this is that a reduced number of boys being born now means less conscripts available in eighteen years.[8] This is a non-economic, but historically important, reason for evaluating the fertility decline negatively. This attitude is similar to that which prevailed in France after the first World War. It is entirely understandable in view of the two world wars in which Russia has been involved this century. Nevertheless, it seems to me anachronistic and harmful. It is anachronistic because future major wars seems likely to be less cannon fodder intensive and more technology intensive than past wars. It is harmful because it encourages the Russian armed forces to prepare for a repetition of the second World

War rather than the type of conflicts which they are actually likely to become involved in.

Another negative evaluation of the decline in fertility has been offered by UNICEF (1995). UNICEF argues that the decline in fertility is undesirable because it leads to an ageing of the population (with adverse effects on public expenditure and political decision-making) and a decline in new entrants to the labour force in 15-20 years. This ignores the fact that a decline in fertility may have positive economic effects (Cutler *et al.*, 1990). These include the reduction in the proportion of children in the population and hence of youth dependency costs, the reduction in investment requirements, and possibly an increase in the rate of productivity growth (resulting from increasing labour scarcity). Furthermore, there is also a positive environmental effect which UNICEF does not discuss. Declining births contribute to resource saving (e.g. energy and water), pollution reduction and the preservation of biodiversity. Although some economists regard ecological arguments as "unsophisticated from an economist's point of view" (Birdsall, 1988) they are relevant (Kelley, 1988) and can be translated into the language of economists (as Birdsall herself shows).

The implication both of the conventional Russian position and also of the UNICEF position, is that measures of public policy should be taken urgently to stimulate births. This has widespread support in Russia. For example a public opinion survey in Russia in 1995 showed that about half the respondents were in favour of this (Bodrova, 1996). An important factor in the Russian case is geographical. Russia has a very low population density and a constant population will affect adversely the long-term viability of some settlements, for example in some rural areas. In particular, it will adversely effect the viability of settlements in the far North and the far East. Nevertheless, I am inclined to think that attention should also be paid to the positive environmental effects. Hence in my view decisions on births should be left to parents and there is no need for any special government policies. Of course, for the children that are born, financial assistance to mothers (paid leave, family allowances), child health clinics, and nursery education are very desirable. These policies, however, should be seen as measures to enhance the welfare of the children that parents decide to bring into the world (and as a very important human capital investment) and not as means to influence the birth rate.

Part of the recent sharp decline in fertility is likely to be temporary. This is shown by such facts as the recovery in fertility in Albania in 1994 (Table 1 note b), the increase in the crude birth rate in the five new provinces of Germany in 1995 (see endnote 1) and the increase in expected numbers of children per family in Russia in 1995 (see above).[9] If a large part of the decline in births turns out to a long-term phenomenon (this is determined both by fertility and by cohort size[10]) it will also have important implications for the age of retirement, the financing of pensions and the allocation of medical care. A long-term ageing of the population would be an additional argument for an increase in the retirement age (Eatwell *et al.*, 1995) and a greater role for funding in the provision of pensions. It would also require a substantial redistribution of medical resources from the care of children to the care of the elderly.

3. Mortality

Some data on mortality are set out in Table 3.

Table 3 shows that the behaviour of the crude death rate in the transition period has been characterised by a wide dispersion. In the former GDR, the Czech republic and Slovakia it has fallen, in Poland it has remained unchanged (rising slightly in

Table 3. The increase in the crude death rate 1989-94 (%)

More than 20%		*Between 1% and 5%*	
Russia[a]	47	Hungary[d]	5
Latvia[b]	34	Slovenia	4
Moldova[c]	32	*Unchanged*	
Ukraine	26	Poland	0
Estonia	25	*Reduction*	
Belarus	25	Former GDR	-6[e]
Lithuania	21	Slovakia	-6
More than 10%		Czech Republic	-7
Azerbaijan	17		
Armenia	12	*Memorandum*	
More than 5%		US, 1933-36	8
Bulgaria	10	Germany, 1933-36	5
Georgia	9		
Romania	9		
Albania	9		

Notes: a) For Russia the latest official figure for the crude death rate in 1994 (15.7 — see for example *Statisticheskoe obozrenie* 1996 No.1, p.7) has been used rather than the preliminary figure of 15.6 used by UNICEF; b) Although the percentage increase in the crude death rate in 1989-94 was lower in Latvia than in Russia, the level of the crude death rate in Latvia in 1994 was higher than in Russia. Indeed, its level in Latvia in 1994 was the highest of any of the countries in Table 3 and remarkably high (16.4 per thousand) for a European country in the 1990s; c) With respect to the data for Moldova it should be noted that:

1. the Moldovan government is not in control of all its territory, so that it is unclear how accurate its record of deaths is and to which population figure they should be related to calculate the crude death rate.

2. the figures for the crude death rate given by UNICEF for 1990-94 differ from those given by Goskomstat (*The demographic yearbook of Russia*, Moscow 1995). For 1994 the Goskomstat figure is the one given in the official CIS publication *Demograficheskii ezhegodnik 1994* (Moscow, Statkom SNG, 1995).

3. It is not clear if the UNICEF figures for 1985 and 1989 are comparable — they show what appears to be a sharp fall in the crude death rate in 1985-89.

d) Although Hungary did not suffer from a major mortality increase in 1989-94, its initial level of mortality was high. Up to and including 1992 it had the highest crude death rate of any of the countries in Table 3 (in 1993 it was overtaken by Latvia and in 1994 by Ukraine, Estonia and Russia); e) Eberstadt (1994) writes about "a broad upsurge in death rates among most segments of the Eastern German population." Actually, in the former GDR the crude death rate rose in only one year (1990 — by 4 per cent) and since then has been steadily falling On the other hand, mortality among adult males rose significantly after 1989 and in 1993 was still about 20 per cent higher than in 1989 (communication from G.A. Cornia).

Source: UNICEF *Regional Monitoring Report* No. 3, Poverty, children and policy: responses for a brighter future (Florence, 1995); *Wirtschaft und Statistik 1995* No.12 (for the former GDR); *Historical statistics of the United States, colonial times to 1957* (US Bureau of the Census, Washington DC, 1960); *Statistisches Jahrbuch für das Deutsche Reich 1937* (Berlin 1937).

1989-91 and the falling back to its initial level)[11] and in Slovenia and Hungary it has risen slightly. On the other hand, in the European part of the former Soviet Union it has risen sharply, the most alarming increase being in the most populous of the former Soviet republics, Russia.[12] Other countries too have had significant increases, for example the three Transcaucasian countries and Bulgaria, Romania and Albania. The big increases in mortality in the European part of the FSU are quite out of line with West European experience and have substantially increased the difference between life expectancy in the countries concerned (especially for males) and life expectancy in Western Europe. Furthermore, the recent increase in mortality follows two decades in which Eastern and Western Europe were characterised by opposing trends in male mortality. During the 1970s and 1980s (Watson, 1995), "While all Western European countries showed reduced mortality rates for men, all of the Eastern European countries showed increasing mortality rates for men."

As far as the most alarming case is concerned, namely Russia, it is clear that a significant part of the increase in the crude death rate has resulted from changes in the age composition of the population. In 1990-94 the number of additional deaths in Russia (i.e. the number of deaths in excess of those that would have occurred if total deaths had stayed at the 1989 level) was 1 665 930. Of these 21 per cent were caused by the ageing of the population and 79 per cent or 1 316 297 by increases in age specific death rates (Vyshnevskii, 1996).[13] The contribution of the change in the age structure of the population was greatest in 1991 when this factor alone accounted for almost half the additional deaths. By 1994 this factor explained only 16 per cent of the additional deaths. An index which adjusts the crude death rate for changes in the age and gender composition of the population and enables death rates to be compared over time is life expectancy at birth. For Russia this fell from 70 in 1989 to 64 in 1994. This was a remarkable fall for a country not experiencing famine, war or life-threatening epidemics.[14] The fall was concentrated among men, whose life expectancy in this period fell from 64 to 58.[15] The latter is a very low figure and roughly on a par with male life expectancy in Pakistan, India or Indonesia.[16]

The increase in Russian mortality has been concentrated in men of working age. For example in 1993, when male life expectancy fell by 3 years, three quarters of the decline was accounted for by men aged 15-59 (and two-thirds by men aged 30-59).

What explains this dramatic worsening of mortality in Russia? This question has given rise to a lively debate. In political circles, the 'patriots' have blamed it on the policies of reform.[17] On the other hand, the 'democrats' have rejected this as absurd and blamed it on the Communists.[18] By 1996 the sharp decline in life expectancy had become a prominent subject of public debate.

As far as the proximate causes of the increase in mortality are concerned, they can be found in the cause of death statistics.[19] The two causes of death whose growth has had the biggest effect on the decline in life expectancy are cardiovascular/circulatory diseases (heart attacks and strokes), and accidents and violent deaths (accidents, suicides, murders, substance abuse). The increase in accidents and violent deaths was the main contribution to the decline in male life expectancy in 1987-92 but since then has declined in relative importance. For example, in 1987-91 the increase in accidents and violent deaths accounted for 93 per cent of the decline in male life expectancy (and was more than ten times as important as the increase in cardiovascular disease in reducing male life expectancy), and in 1992 accounted for 58 per cent, but in 1993 only for 42 per cent and in 1994 only 31 per cent. By 1994, the increase in cardiovascular disease was substantially more important than the increase in accidents and violent deaths in reducing male life expectancy. For women too accidents and violent deaths have been a significant cause of the decline in life expectancy, but in 1992 their increase accounted for just under half the decline in life expectancy, in 1993 for only 27 per cent and in 1994 for just 20 per cent. For women the increase in cardiovascular disease accounted for 52 per cent of the decline in life expectancy in 1993 and 64 per cent in 1994.[20]

Economists are naturally concerned with going beyond the proximate causes of death as recorded on death certificates and looking for ultimate causes of death. In Russia, accidents and violent death are frequently associated with alcohol abuse, so it is natural in a situation in which the increase in accidents and violent deaths has been such an important factor in the decline in life expectancy to look at the alcohol consumption situation in search of an explanation. In 1985-87 there was a dramatic anti-alcohol campaign in Russia (White, 1995). The number of sales outlets and their opening hours were sharply reduced, the production of spirits was sharply cut, a considerable amount of newly imported brewery equipment was not installed, and extensive vineyards were torn up. As a result, state sales of alcohol fell sharply in 1985-87. This was partly compensated for by a growth in the consumption of *samogon* (moonshine). Nevertheless, it seems likely that there was a significant decrease in alcohol consumption in 1985-87, although less than shown in statistics confined to state sales (Meslé *et al.*, 1995). This is generally considered to have been the main cause of the decline in fatal accidents and violent deaths in 1984-87 (mainly in 1986) and the significant increase in male life expectancy at birth which took place then (in 1984-87 male life expectancy rose by 3.2 years).

This interpretation of the increase of Russian male life expectancy in 1984-87 has been challenged by a medical specialist, Professor Gundarov of the Russian medical academy for post-qualification education (Gundarov, 1995). He disagrees that the sharp reduction in death rates in 1986 can be explained by the anti-alcohol campaign. He has pointed out that there were also reductions in death rates in 1986 in the East European countries, although these countries did not have anti-alcohol campaigns. Furthermore, anti-alcohol campaigns in other countries which have led to sharp reductions in alcohol consumption have not had such sharp demographic consequences. In addition, although alcohol-related deaths undoubtedly fell in Russia in 1984-87, this was partly compensated for by a rise in deaths from consumption of alcohol substitutes. Gundarov argues that the reduction in mortality in 1984-87 was a result of the upswing of hope and optimism in Soviet society as a result of the beginning of perestroika. This may have been a factor (Watson, 1995), but is difficult to know how much weight to give it.

As far as the big increase in mortality since 1987 is concerned, writers who argue that the decline in 1984-87 was caused by the decline in alcohol consumption, naturally ascribe most of the increase since 1987 to the end of the anti-alcohol campaign and a rapid growth of alcohol consumption from the low level of 1987. Official sales of alcohol have remained relatively low, and *per capita* official sales are still well below the level of 1984. When account is taken of *samogon* and illicit imports, however, it seems that by 1993 *per capita* alcohol consumption exceeded the 1984 level. Hence it seems likely that in 1987-92 the increase in alcohol consumption, via its effect on accidental and violent deaths, was the most important cause of the increase in male mortality. For 1993 and 1994 the increase in alcohol consumption seems to have been a less important factor, for two reasons. First, in those two years the increase in accidental and violent deaths accounted for less than half of the decline in male life expectancy (see above). Secondly, in 1993 the increase in alcohol consumption seems to have been much less than the increase in deaths from accidents and violence.

In view of the fact that fluctuations in alcohol consumption, although important, cannot explain all the increase in Russian mortality, it is necessary to look elsewhere for explanations of that part of the increase which cannot be explained by increases in alcohol consumption. Five such explanations have been offered: the medium-term trend, shock therapy, stress, environmental factors and medical reasons.

Russian demographers have pointed out that the 'epidemiological revolution' in the West and the USSR differed in an important respect. In both there was a long-term trend decline in infectious disease as a cause of death and a long-term growth of degenerative disease (e.g. cancer, heart attacks) as a cause of death. In the West, however, life expectancy has continued to rise despite the growth of degenerative disease. In the USSR, on the other hand, the growth of degenerative disease fully compensated the decline in infectious disease. As a result, from the mid 1960s life expectancy at birth failed to match the Western increase. It stagnated at a level which gradually lagged more and more behind that of the West. The main reason for this seems to be that "the Soviet political, medical and economic planning systems failed to respond quickly and adequately to changing health needs. Although extremely successful in dealing with the 'old' causes of death, in particular from infectious diseases and diseases of the respiratory system, they failed to respond to the rapid increase in deaths from the 'new' causes of death, i.e. circulatory, cancer and external factors. The anti-smoking, healthy-diet and more-exercise campaigns in the West were absent in the USSR." (Ellman, 1994)

Explanations of the big increase in Russian mortality in the 1990s which focus on the medium-term trend, point out that if the trend increase in male mortality which began in the 1960s is extrapolated to the 1990s, it explains most of the mortality explosion of the 1990s. For example, Avdeev, Blum and Zakharov (1996) have pointed out that the increase in mortality in the 1990s can be analysed as simply a catching up with the mortality that would have taken place in the mid 1980s had there been no anti-alcohol campaign then. In other words, the men who comprised the excess deaths of the 1990s would have died in the mid 1980s but were saved from death then by the anti-alcohol campaign. Once alcohol consumption reverted to normal they were killed by the trend increase in death rates. This idea is illustrated in Figure 1.

The policy implication of the explanation based on the medium-term trend and fluctuations in alcohol consumption are that to overcome the adverse trend it is necessary to westernise Russian society, so that the development of a dynamic civil society and higher living standards lead to the adoption of a more 'life friendly' life style (more exercise, healthier food, less smoking and drinking) and changes in the way alcohol is consumed (judged by the quantity of alcohol consumed, Russia is not strikingly more alcoholic than Finland or France).

This explanation, based on the trend since the mid 1960s and fluctuations in alcohol consumption, does not command universal agreement.[21] As pointed out above, Gundarov for one does not accept the reduction in alcohol consumption as a satisfactory explanation of the big fall in mortality in the mid 1980s. In addition, there was a decline in mortality in the early 1980s, before the beginning of Gorbachev's anti-alcohol campaign (although there were anti-alcohol abuse measures then that may have played a role). Furthermore, if one simply extrapolates the trend, it is difficult to explain the big increase in mortality in 1993 and the further increase in 1994. In both 1993 and 1994 Russian male and female mortality taken as a whole was in excess of the medium-term trend (Vishnevskii, 1996). For the particularly vulnerable group of men aged 15-59, the probability of dying in that

Figure 1. Probability of death for Russian men aged 15-59

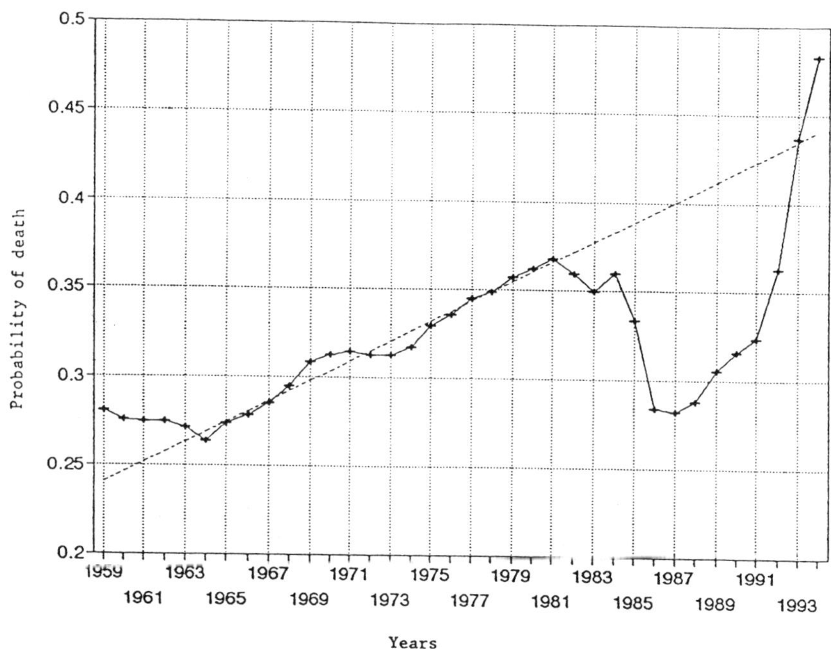

Source: E. Andreev, oral presentation at conference on "Mortality in Russia", Institute for National Economic Forecasting, Moscow April 15-17, 1996. See also Avdeev, Blum & Zakharov (1996) p.41.

age group in 1994 was considerably above trend (see Figure 1). Moreover, alcohol consumption itself is not exogenous to the socio-economic situation. A major increase in alcohol abuse is itself a social phenomenon which requires explanation in terms of the socio-economic situation (e.g. the price of vodka, or the wish to escape from an unbearable reality).

In some quarters the mortality crisis is ascribed to 'shock therapy'. This was done, for example, in the January 1994 report of the Economics Division of the Russian Academy of Sciences (*Otdelenie*, 1994). This is obviously very one-sided when one observes that the classical countries of 'shock therapy' (former GDR,

Poland, former Czechoslovakia) have not experienced a mortality crisis and that Russia which has experienced a mortality crisis has pursued a very gradual path to policy-makeration which even today after four years of attempts at liberalisation and stabilization is neither fully liberalised not fully stabilized (Ellman, 1994; EBRD 1995). However, it is not impossible that the economic situation in Russia and other CIS countries in the past few years, which includes an unsuccessful attempt at shock therapy in Russia in 1992, has contributed to the mortality crisis. The fact that US life expectancy fell in the wake of the great depression (see above) suggests that this might be the case.

Another explanation of the big increase in Russian mortality in the 1990s links it to an increase in stress (Shapiro, 1995; UNICEF, 1994; Gundarov, 1995). Shapiro suggested that "the particular causes of death and their distribution suggest a close link with stress and the crisis of transformation... it is not just pressure (the deadline to finish a conference paper, for example) which produces stress. It is the absence of strategies for coping with pressures and needs for adaptation. This may arise because individuals are ill-equipped to cope, or it may arise because the social and economic situation is so chaotic that reliable strategies are difficult to choose. I think in Russia we find both." This line of argument derives support from the upheavals which have taken place in Russia in recent years. One indicator of these upheavals is the re-emergence of the unhappy civil war phenomenon of large numbers of *besprizorniki* (street children).[22] It also derives support from the similarity between mortality patterns in contemporary Russia (predominantly circulatory and unnatural) and that in other areas where the population is subject to acute stress, such as Harlem (New York). On the other hand, this explanation has a somewhat ad hoc character.

To make the concept of 'stress' more operational, Cornia and Paniccià (1996) proxied it by an economic stress index constructed from data on real wages, employment and the rate of inflation. By combining it with data on the decline in medical expenditures, they were able to account for about half of the increase in the crude death rate in the thirteen transition countries considered. In another regression exercise, this time confined to the FSU, Brenton, Gros and Vandille (1996) also found that part of the increase in mortality could be accounted for by the economic reform process. The increase in the crude death rate was lowest in countries with low and high degrees of trade liberalisation and greatest for countries in between.

One explanation of the mortality crisis in Russia is the ecological situation in that country (Feshbach and Friendly, 1992; Feshbach, 1994, 1995). It is well known that there are many ecological problems in Russia and that pollution has often reached levels harmful to health (Revich *et al.*, 1995). This can clearly be seen from the geographical distribution of morbidity. The incidence of cancer, for example, is much higher than average in the heavily polluted mining and industrial towns. Furthermore, it is possible that environmental deterioration has contributed to the long run trend of Russian life expectancy failing to rise in line with the increase in the West. Nevertheless, it seems implausible to suppose that environmental factors can explain the mortality explosion of the 1990s (Ellman, 1994; Watson, 1995).

Another explanation of the mortality crisis in Russia is the underfunding and general inadequacy of the Russian medical system. It is clear that state funding of medical care as a proportion of GDP is low by OECD standards. Ermakov and

Kiselev (1992) sensibly argued that "The public health system in the former USSR has been thrown into economic chaos as it endeavours to shift from a heavily centralised and bureaucratised economic model towards a free market, self-sufficient and insurance-oriented system without enough financial support to achieve this." The morbidity situation is poor and in some respects alarming. In 1993-95 there was a diphtheria epidemic (with a peak in 1994 In 1992-94 there was a rapid growth of whooping cough (this fell sharply in 1995). There has been an explosion in syphilis which shows no signs of ending. (Gonorrhoea, however is declining, and statistically measured HIV and AIDS are minuscule.) The growth of tuberculosis (Ellman, 1994) is continuing. In 1994 the number of deaths per hundred thousand of the population from tuberculosis rose by 16 per cent. The only comfort for the general population is that Russian tuberculosis is disproportionately concentrated in prisons and other places of detention and that the spread of tuberculosis is an international problem which is alarming the whole world, not just Russia, the CIS or the transformation countries. Russian statistics concerning the health of pregnant women and newly born babies are also alarming (Vyshnevskii, 1996). They show a sharp increase in anaemia in pregnant women, a sharp increase in the proportion of babies born ill or who fall ill shortly after birth and a steady growth in the 1990s of the proportion of low birthweight babies.

The structure of excess mortality, however, which is concentrated among adult males, does not suggest that a sudden worsening of the medical system is the chief cause (Shapiro, 1995). Furthermore it is well known that the welfare interpretation of morbidity data is problematic (Sen, 1995). For example in Russia there was a big increase in statistical invalidity in 1990-92. This did not result, however, from a sudden deterioration in the health of the population but from a change in the pension regulations.

It is important to note that the economic situation, stress and alcohol consumption are not necessarily competitive explanations of the increase in mortality. They may be interrelated. The economic situation may generate acute stress which leads, *inter alia*, to increased alcohol consumption which in turn increases mortality (via its effects on accidents and other unnatural deaths).

In order to clarify the causes of the increase in mortality there is an urgent need for epidemiological research, possibly utilising new sources of data. At the same time it is hardly likely that an adequate and generally agreed explanation of the increase in mortality will be found before it reverts to more normal levels. (In 1995 the Russian crude death rate fell from 15.7 per thousand to 15.0 and the provisional estimate of life expectancy rose by one year to 65 — for men it was 58 and for women, 72.) Obviously, it will be easier to explain the big increase in Russian mortality in 1993 and 1994 after we have seen what follows it.[23]

4. International migration

The first half of the 1990s was a period of substantial migration from, and among, the transformation countries (UN/ECE 1995; Vyshnevskii, 1996; Zaionchkovskaya, 1994 and 1995; SOPEMI, 1995). Important features of it were:

- Mass emigration from Albania. It has been estimated that about 10 per cent of the total population (mainly young men) left that country in the early 1990s. The main destination countries seem to have been Greece and Italy. The main reasons for the emigration appear to have been political and economic. Politically, the collapse of the Communist regime led to the end of the previous stringent controls on travelling abroad. Economically, young people reacted to the enormous gulf between living standards at home and in adjacent EU countries.

- Substantial emigration from Romania. It seems that more than half a million people (out of a population of about 23 million) left Romania in the early 1990s. The main destination country was Germany. Over 180 000 subsequently left Germany, either voluntarily or repatriated on the basis of an agreement between the two governments. The reasons for the emigration were similar to those in Albania.

- Mass emigration from the former Yugoslavia. This did not result from a sudden opening of the frontiers because these had long been open. The main factor here was the armed conflicts which resulted from the break-up of the former Yugoslavia. Although there is no accurate data for total emigration from the former Yugoslavia, it seems likely that in the early 1990s roughly 1.2-1.5 million people left, the main destination country being Germany.

- Mass migration from the former GDR (to the FRG). This was a major cause of the collapse of the GDR. In 1990-91 net migration from the former GDR to the 'old' FRG was about half a million. Since the unification of Germany net migration from the former GDR has been steadily falling. It was 360 000 in 1990, 169 000 in 1991, 88 000 in 1992, 53 000 in 1993 and only 27 000 in 1994. German unification, and the policies which have been pursued by the newly united Germany have enabled the substantial migration from the former GDR to the 'old' FRG, which was one of the chief migration streams in Europe for four decades, to be ended. This has happened without the use of administrative controls. The extension of political freedom to the former GDR, and the huge transfers to this former country, have eliminated the causes of this persistent (but now ended) phenomenon.

- Substantial emigration from the former Soviet Union. About 1.1-1.2 million people emigrated from the former Soviet Union in the early 1990s. The main destination country was Germany.

- Large 'ethnic' component of this emigration. It was dominated by the emigration of Germans to Germany and Jews to Israel.

- Substantial migration within the former Soviet Union. The dissolution of the former USSR led to substantial numbers of people moving to successor states in which their ethnic group was the main one. This process began before the final collapse of the USSR (for example the war between Armenia and Azerbaijan led to substantial emigration of Armenians from Azerbaijan and Azeris from Armenia already in 1989-90). Subsequent armed conflicts (in Moldova, Georgia, Tajikistan and Chechnya) have all led to population movements. The refugees from these conflicts frequently live in poor conditions which provide good opportunities for the spread of disease. For example, the rapid spread of malaria in Azerbaijan in 1994-96 seems to be connected to the mass exodus of Azeris from territories seized by Armenian Karabakh forces. The refugees settled first in southern Azerbaijan, where malaria is endemic, but later moved round the country in search of work and spread the disease. The migration within the former USSR comprises not only people who intend to remain in their new countries (i.e. immigrants), but also temporary workers who intend eventually to return to their own country and war refugees who hope to return to their own countries/regions when stability has returned.

- Emergence of Russia as a substantial net immigration country. This was natural bearing in mind that according to the Soviet census of 1989 there were 25 million Russians living in the non-Russian republics of the former USSR and that living standards are higher in Russia than in many CIS countries. Some relevant data are set out in Table 4.

Table 4. Migration to and from Russia (thousands).[a]

	1980	1990	1991	1992	1993	1994	1995
Emigration from Russia to countries outside the former USSR	7	104	88	103	114	114	118
Immigration to Russia from countries outside the former USSR	—	—	—	—	—	45[b]	25
Apparent net emigration [c] from Russia to countries outside the former USSR	7	104	88	103	114	69	93
Emigration from Russia to countries of the former USSR	774	626	587	570	369	232	229
Immigration to Russia from countries of the former USSR	876	913	692	926	923	1 146	842
Apparent net immigration to Russia from countries of the former USSR	102	287	105	356	554	914	613
Apparent total net immigration to Russia	95	183	17	253	440	845	520

Notes: a) The data in this table, which derive from the files of the Russian Ministry of the Interior, are probably not very accurate. It does not take account of people who leave the country 'temporarily' (e.g. as 'tourists') but who never return. Nor can it take account of unregistered immigration. Furthermore, the distinction between 'temporary workers' and 'migrants' can often only be made *ex post*. Of all those who 'emigrated' to the US in 1908-1914, about 40 per cent subsequently returned home (Goldin, 1993); b) In 1994, according to the Federal Migration Service, 55 000 foreigners from beyond the former USSR were legally working in Russia. Of these, 20 000 were from China and 12 000 from Turkey. c) This figure is probably grossly misleading because of substantial non-registered immigration to Russia (sometimes of a transit nature). Russian official bodies estimated that at the beginning of 1994 roughly 300 000-500 000 people from outside the former USSR (mainly from Asia and Africa) were living in Russia.

Source: *Rossiiskii statisticheskii ezhegodnik* (Moscow 1995); *Ekonomika Rossii 1995* g Moscow 1995; *Statisticheskoe obozrenie* 1996, No.1.

From Table 4 it can be seen that in the 1990s Russia has once again become a significant net immigration country, as it was for centuries up till the late nineteenth century (Willekens and Scherbov, 1995; Bartlett, 1979). Furthermore it should be noted that the figures in the table probably substantially understate immigration into Russia from countries outside the former USSR (see Table 4 note c). In view of its low population density, substantial natural resources, large diaspora, relatively liberal political system and higher living standards than many other countries, Russia may in the future have an attraction for migrants similar to that of Australia, Canada and Argentina.

- A substantial brain drain. A number of countries or groups of countries (e.g. the US, Australia, Canada, Israel, European Union) have benefited from substantial import of human capital (Gieseck, Heilmann and Loeffelholz, 1995).
- Substantial temporary migration of workers in search of jobs. For example, there has been a significant flow of temporary workers from Ukraine and Belarus to Russia, Poland, the Czech republic, Slovakia and Hungary. Similarly, about 350 000 Poles work abroad, predominantly in Germany but also in France, the Czech Republic and Sweden (SOPEMI, 1995).
- Numerous countries have found themselves being used by transit migrants, that is people who have entered the country but actually are trying to get to a third country (SOPEMI, 1995). Some of these transit migrants succeed in reaching and staying in their destination countries, some of them stay in the transit country, often working in the informal sector, and some return to their country of origin.
- Numerous countries have been confronted by unwanted potential immigrants. This has led to problems at borders, tightening up of domestic legislation, strengthened migration control measures, repatriation/expulsion of potential immigrants etc.
- There has been no increase in emigration from Central Europe. Emigration from Poland in the 1990s appears to be lower than in the 1980s. Net emigration from the Czech republic, Slovakia and Hungary appears to be negligible. EU fears of substantial net immigration if the EU is enlarged to include Central Europe appear to be exaggerated. Central Europe has, however, become a transit area for (potential) migrants to EU countries from elsewhere.

The large number of refugees from the military conflicts in the former Yugoslavia and the former USSR constitutes one of the largest of the costs of the liberal revolution of 1989-93 (Ellman, 1995). The number involved, however, is fortunately quite small compared to the mass European population movements of 1939-43 or 1945-49.

5. Conclusions

Experience in 1989-94 corroborates the traditional view that revolutions are costly. Transformation has turned out to be a demographic crisis. Important features of this crisis are:

1. A sharp decline in fertility. This decline shows a wide dispersion. It is greatest in the former GDR and smallest in Hungary. It suggests that in the debate between 'pessimists' and 'optimists' about the short run impact of the transformation on living standards, popular perceptions in many countries (but not in Poland) were closer to those of the 'pessimists' than to those of the 'optimists'. Even in the low fertility transformation countries (with the exception of the former GDR), however, fertility is not out of line with that in Western Europe. Hence part of the fall can be considered a natural process of European convergence. The decline in fertility has important implications for the future size and age composition of the population, and hence of the labour force and armed forces. Whether or not policy measures are required to influence, or even reverse, it are a matter for national debate in the countries concerned. It has obvious implications for the age of retirement, the financing of pensions and the allocation of medical care. It seems likely that part of the decline in fertility will turn out to have been temporary.
2. A sharp increase in mortality. The change in mortality varies from a very big increase in Russia to declines in the former GDR (except among adult males), Slovakia and the Czech Republic. The increase in mortality is concentrated in the European part of the former Soviet Union and among men of working age. Its causes are uncertain. The dramatic increase in Russia (up to and including 1994 — in 1995 it declined) has given rise to an extensive debate, both academic and political, about its causes. Part of Russian excess deaths is caused by the ageing of the population (the contribution of this factor was greatest in 1991). As far as the remainder (the great bulk) is concerned, the trend (since the mid-1960s) increase in male mortality and fluctuations in alcohol consumption would seem to be important explanatory factors (in particular up to and including 1992). Other possible (partial) explanations, especially for the mortality jump in 1993-94, are increased stress (resulting from the socio-economic crisis), the environmental and medical situations. Some of the explanatory factors suggested may be interrelated. More research is needed to explain this alarming development, which is quite out of line with contemporary West European experience. It is, however, in line with (but larger and more differentiated between men and women than) US experience in the wake of the great depression and east European trends in the 1970s and 1980s. Up till 1994, in the former USSR transformation failed to end the long-run Soviet decline in male life expectancy and may have worsened it. On the other hand, as far as mortality is concerned, Poland was largely unaffected by the crisis in the FSU, and the Czech Republic and Slovakia have succeeded in leaving the Soviet empire and returning to Europe.

3. Significant flows of international migration. Albania, Romania, the former Yugoslavia and the former USSR have been significant countries/regions of emigration. Significant recipients of immigration have been Germany and Russia. This migration has been determined by economic, ethnic and military factors. An important development has been the emergence of Russia as a net immigration country. The brain drain from the former USSR has been a significant gain for the recipient countries. Some of the migration has been of temporary workers and some has had a transit character. Although substantial international migration has taken place, many destination countries have made legal immigration harder or (almost) impossible. The large number of refugees from the military conflicts in the former Yugoslavia and the former USSR was one of the largest costs of the liberal revolution of 1989-93. The absence of significant emigration from the Czech Republic, Hungary, and Slovakia, and the decline since the 1980s in emigration from Poland, are positive signs as far as the enlargement of the EU is concerned. In the first half of the 1990s, the long-standing large emigration from the former GDR to the 'old' FRG dwindled to nothing as a result of a successful policy of tackling its causes.

Notes

[1] In interpreting the extremely sharp fall in the former GDR, three special factors should be borne in mind. First, prior to the collapse of the GDR there was a downward trend in the crude birth rate. For example, in 1980-89 the crude birth rate fell by 18 per cent. Secondly, part of the fall in births resulted from changes in the age-sex structure of the population. For example about one twelfth of the decline in births in 1989-91 can be ascribed to this factor. (The main influence here was that women in the peak child bearing ages of 18-25 were more likely to move to the 'old' FRG than the population as a whole.) Thirdly, the crude birth rate in the former GDR was higher than in the FRG, probably because of the pro-natality policy of the government. For example, in 1989 the crude birth rate in the GDR was 9 per cent higher than that in the FRG. One would expect unification to lead to the removal of the policy induced additional births. Nevertheless, the crude birth rate in the former GDR in 1994 was remarkably low (5.1 per thousand inhabitants) and only 49% of that in the 'old' FRG in 1994. Furthermore, 1994 was not a freakish year. The crude birth rate in the former GDR was the same in both 1993 and 1994. It can, however, be observed that after a very sharp fall in 1989-93, the crude birth rate stabilized in 1994 and increased slightly (to 5.3 per thousand inhabitants) in 1995. This may be a precursor of a gradual convergence with that in the 'old' FRG.
Attention to the dramatic demographic developments in the former GDR was drawn by Eberstadt (1994). He drew attention to the second of these special factors, but not the first and the third.

[2] For these figures see *Demographic* (1995), pp. 104-105.

[3] This is an echo effect of World War II which was important in the USSR in the late 1980s. In the 1990s it has been much less significant, and declining in importance. For example, in Russia in 1990, of the total decline in births compared with 1989, 28 per cent was explained by the change in the age composition of the population and 72 per cent by the decline in age-specific birth rates. By 1994, of the decline in the number of births since 1989, only 12 per cent was explained by the change in the age composition of the population and 88 per cent was explained by the decline in age-specific birth rates (Vyshnevskii, 1996, p.40).

[4] This is an important demographic development, but except with respect to the special case of the former GDR, will not be discussed further in this paper. A discussion (which excludes the former GDR) can be found in Cornia and Paniccià (1995). These authors explain it by a decline in living standards and the availability of housing, and negative expectations about the future. Before the transformation, marriage rates were higher in eastern Europe than in western Europe, so that part of the decline can be thought of as a natural convergence process.

[5] The proportion of births in the (former) GDR to unmarried mothers was about 1/3 in the late 1980s and rose in the early 1990s to about 2/5.

[6] This, however, has not yet happened. The crude birth rate in Russia in 1995 was below that in 1994, and the preliminary data for births in the first quarter of 1996 suggest that the crude birth rate then was six per cent less than in the first quarter of 1995.

[7] It should be noted, however, that the debate between Adam and Kabaj and Kowalik on the one hand, and Sachs on the other, specifically concerned Poland. For that country, a statistical study of deviations in 1990-94 from the 1970-89 trend for nuptiality, fertility and mortality (Cornia and Paniccià 1996), could find no evidence for any deviation from the trend in 1990-94. Hence in the specific Polish case the demographic data appear not to support the 'pessimistic' position.

[8] See for example V.I.Kozlov, Vymiranie russkikh: istoriko-demograficheskii krizis ili katastrofa? *Vestnik rossiiskoi akademii nauk* 1995, Vol 65, No.9 pp 771-777. For a similar perspective see A.Ya.Kvasha, Demograficheskie i ekonomicheskie razvitie rossii, *Vestnik Moskovskogo Universiteta: Seriya 6, Ekonomika*, 1995, No.5.

[9] Hence analyses of the decline in fertility which explain it all by a natural convergence to the general European level (such as Vishnevskii, 1996, p.44) are one-sided. Part seems likely to be a temporary phenomenon resulting from the perceived negative impact of the initial stages of the transformation on the population.

[10] The age composition of the Russian female population, for example, is such that Russian demographers expect a births peak in 2007.

[11] According to Cornia and Pannicià (1996, p.110) when account is taken of three demographic variables (the crude marriage rate, the total fertility rate and the crude death rate) and of trends in 1970-89, "only Poland seems to have been generally unaffected by the population crisis of the transition."

[12] The increase for Russia is so large that many observers have asked whether it is a real phenomenon or a statistical artefact. The general view in the specialist literature and among all specialists consulted by the author is that it is not a statistical artefact and is — unfortunately — real. For a detailed and comprehensive description of the sources of Russian demographic data see Andreev, Scherbov and Willekens (1995).

[13] Extending the period by one year, to the end of 1995, increases the number of excess deaths not explained by changes in the age composition of the population, to roughly 1.7 million. Extending the calculation to all the CIS countries, and not just to Russia, would increase it to over two million.

[14] In the USA, in the wake of the Great Depression, there was a fall in life expectancy at birth in 1933-36 of 4.8 years. The fall was greater for men (5.1) than for women (4.5), and was greater for blacks than for whites. Black male life expectancy at birth fell by 6.5 years, and black female life expectancy at birth by 4.6. A still sharper decline in US life expectancy at birth took place in 1918, when it fell by 11.8 years. This was a result of the influenza epidemic of that year. (For these statistics see *Historical statistics of the United States, colonial times to 1957*, US Bureau of the Census, Washington DC, 1960).

[15] The current official figure for male life expectancy in 1994 is 57.8 Figures in the range 57.3-57.6 can be found in the literature, but they were (now outdated) preliminary estimates.

[16] There are large regional differences in life expectancy in Russia. In 1993 the region with the lowest life expectancy was Tuva. Male life expectancy in 1993 in Tuva (52.3 years) was approximately equal to that in Ghana in 1985-90 (52.2). There is also a large difference between male and female life expectancy in Russia. As a result Russian female life expectancy is higher than would be expected on the basis of the international relationship between income per head and life expectancy, and until 1992 it was higher than the life expectancy of black females in the USA. Similarly, the decline in Russian female life expectancy in the period 1986-87 to 1994 (3.4 years) is less than the decline in the life expectancy of US females in 1933-36 (4.5 years).

[17] See for example T.Sidorov, Esli ty zhelaesh' dobra Rossii, lyubish' i zhaleesh' ee narod, to mozhno li golosovat' za nyneshnikh demokratov posle osoznaniya etikh bespristrastnykh statisticheskikh svedenii, *Pravda* 28 November 1995; Yeltsinizm ubil 2 200 000 russkikh, *Zavtra* August-September 1995, No. 35 (91).

[18] See for example, O.Latsis, *Ryazhenye*, Izvestiya 27 March 1996.

[19] For an invaluable study of causes of death in Russia in 1965-93 see Meslé *et al.* (1995, 1996).

[20] For these figures see Vishnevskii (1996) p.72.

[21] Cornia and Paniccià (1995) pp 15-19 claim by means of a simple econometric exercise to have rejected the hypothesis that the recent increase in the Russian (and other) crude death rates can be explained by the trend. This argument is repeated in Cornia and Paniccià (1996). They, however, considered the 1970-1989 trend. As can be seen from Figure 1, in the Russian case, choice of these years is bound to give a misleading impression. The negative trend began earlier, and mortality in 1989 was still influenced by the favourable effects of the fall in the mortality rate in the mid 1980s.

[22] These are usually boys and have frequently run away from home as a result of domestic violence and neglect, which itself is usually the result of poverty and alcoholism. They usually work as thieves, normally self-employed but sometimes in co-operatives or for adults. Another negative civil war phenomenon (it is a sign of urban impoverishment) which revived in the early '90s, is urban-rural migration. In 1991-95 the urban population fell by 1.5 million and the rural population rose by 1.3 million. (A significant number of the new rural inhabitants were not migrants from Russian towns but immigrants from the near abroad.)

[23] Preliminary data for the first quarter of 1996 suggest that the crude death rate for that period was slightly above that for the first quarter of 1995. Whether this is a short-term fluctuation, a statistical artefact, or a resumption of the adverse trend, will not be clear till definitive data for all of 1996 are available.

References

Adam, J., 1993, Letter to the editor, *Economics of Planning*, Vol. 26, No. 2.

Andreev, E., Scherbov, S. and Willekens, F., 1995, *Sources of information on the population of Russia,* Demographic report 19, University of Groningen, Netherlands.

Avdeev, A., Blum, A., and Zakharov, S., 1996, "La mortalité en Russie a-t-elle vraiment augmenté brutalement entre 1991 en 1995", INED, Paris, Dossiers et Recherches No. 51, March, [mimeo].

Bartlett, R.P., 1979, *Human capital. The settlement of foreigners in Russia, 1762-1804*, CUP, Cambridge.

Birdsall, N., 1988, "Economic approaches to population growth", in H. Chenery and T.N. Srinivasan (ed), *Handbook of development economics*, Vol. 1, North Holland, Amsterdam. p. 497.

Bodrova, V., 1996, Osobennosti reproduktivnogo povedeniya naseleniya rossii v perekhodnyi period, *Voprosy statistiki*, No. 2.

Brenton, P., Gros, D., and Vandille, G., 1996, "Output decline and recovery in the transition economies: causes and social consequences", CEPS, Working Document No. 100, Brussels, pp. 13-14.

Cornia, G.A. and Paniccià, R., 1995, "The demographic impact of sudden impoverishment: Eastern Europe during the 1989-94 transition", UNICEF, Florence, Innocenti Occasional Papers EPS 49; 1996, "The transition's population crisis: An econometric investigation of nuptiality, fertility and mortality in severely distressed economies", *Most*, No.1.

Cutler, D.M. *et al.*, 1990, D.M. Cutler, J.M. Poterba, L.M. Sheiner and L.H. Summers, "An aging society: Opportunity or challenge?", *Brookings Papers on Economic Activity* 1.

Demographic, 1995, *Demographic statistics 1995*, Eurostat, Luxembourg, p. 456.

Eatwell, J. *et al.*, 1995, *Transformation and integration: Shaping the future of central and eastern Europe*, IPPR, London, Chapter 4.

Eberstadt, N., 1994, "Demographic shocks in eastern Germany", *Europe-Asia Studies*, Vol. 46, No. 3. There is a summary of this paper in, "When the Berlin wall fell, so did birth rates", *Transition* (World Bank), Vol. 5, No. 2-3, February-March 1994.

EBRD, 1995, Social indicators and transition, *Transition Report 1995*, London, pp. 21-25.

Ellman, M., 1994, "The increase in death and disease under 'katastroika'", *Cambridge Journal of Economics*, Vol. 18, No. 4, August, pp. 336-349 and 927-928.

Ellman, M., 1995, "The state under state socialism and post-socialism", in H.-J. Chang and R. Rowthorn (eds), *The role of the state in economic change*, Clarendon Press, Oxford.

Ermakov, S.P. and Kiselev, A.A., 1992, "Economic aspects of health", *World Health Statistics Quarterly*, Vol. 45, No. 1.

Feshbach, M., and Friendly, A. Jr., 1992, *Ecocide in the USSR: Health and nature under siege* , Aurum, London.

Feshbach, M., 1994, *Environment and health atlas of Russia*, ed M.Feshbach (Center for Post-Soviet Studies, Md.); 1995, *Ecological disaster: Cleaning up the hidden legacy of the Soviet regime*, The Twentieth Century Fund Press, New York.

Gieseck, A., Heilemann, U. and von Loeffelholz, H.D., 1995, "Economic implications of migration into the Federal Republic of Germany, 1988-1992", *International Migration Review,* Vol. 29, No. 3, fall.

Goldin, C., 1993, "The political economy of immigration restriction in the United States, 1890 to 1921", NBER Working Paper, No. 4345, p. 8.

Gundarov, I.A., 1995, "Pochemu umirayut v rossii, kak nam vyzhit'?", Moscow, Media Sfera, pp. 20-21, 39.

Heleniak, T., 1995, "Dramatic population trends in countries of the FSU", *Transition,* Vol. 6, No. 9-10, September-October, p.2.

Kabaj, M. and Kowalik, T., 1995, "Who is responsible for postcommunist successes in eastern Europe?", *Transition* Vol. 6, No. 7-8, July-August.

Kelley, A.C., 1988, "Economic consequences of population change in the third world", *Journal of Economic Literature*, Vol. XXVI, December, p. 1719.

Maier, F., 1993, "The labour market for women and employment perspectives in the aftermath of German unification", *Cambridge Journal of Economics,* Vol. 17, No.3.

Meslé *et al.,* 1995, F. Meslé, V. Shkolnikov, V. Hertrich and J. Vallin, *Tendances récentes de la mortalité par cause en Russie, 1965-1993*, Paris, INED, 1995, Dossiers et Recherches, No. 50, [mimeo].

Meslé *et al.,* 1996, F. Meslé, V. Shkolnikov, V. Hertrich and J. Vallin, *Tendances récentes de la mortalite par cause en Russie, 1965-1993*, Vol 2, Annexes, Dossiers et Recherches, No. 50, INED, Paris, [mimeo], pp. 53-54.

Nauck, B. and Joos, M., 1995, "East joins West: child welfare and market reforms in the "special case" of the former GDR", Innocenti Occasional Papers, EPS 48, UNICEF, Florence, pp. 47.

Otdelenie, 1994, Otdelenie ekonomiki, Rossiiskaya akademiya nauk and Mezhdunarodnyi fond 'reforma', Sotsial'no-Ekonomicheskie Preobrazovaniya v Rossii: Sovremennaya Situatsiya i novye podkhody, Moscow, [mimeo].

Revich, B. *et al.*, 1995, B. Revich, E. Gurvich, Yu. Prokopenko, B. Prokhorov, *Regional'nye i lokal'nye problemy khimicheskogo zagryazneniya okruzhayushchei sredy i zdorov'ya naseleniya* (pervyi vypusk), Evraziya, Moscow.

Sachs, J., 1993, "Reply to Jan Adam", *Economics of Planning,* Vol. 26, No. 2.

Sachs, J., 1995, "Old myths about Poland's reforms die hard", *Transition*, Vol. 6, No. 11-12, November-December.

Sen, A.K., 1995, *Mortality as an indicator of economic success and failure*, UNICEF, Florence, pp. 25-28.

Shapiro, J., 1995, "The Russian mortality crisis and its causes", in A. Aslund (ed), *Russian economic reform at risk*, Pinter, London and New York.

SOPEMI, 1995, *Trends in international migration. Annual report* 1994, OECD, Paris, pp. 58-60.

UN/ECE, 1995, "International migration in Central and Eastern Europe and the Commonwealth of Independent States", Chapter 5 of *Economic Survey of Europe in 1994-1995*, UN, New York and Geneva.

UNICEF, 1993, "Public policy and social conditions", *Regional Monitoring Report*, No.1, Florence.

UNICEF, 1994, "Crisis in mortality, health and nutrition", *Regional Monitoring Report*, No.2, Florence, pp. 68-69.

UNICEF, 1995, "Poverty, children and policy: Responses for a brighter future", *Regional Monitoring Report*, No. 3, Florence, pp. 42-44, 110.

Vishnevskii, A.G., 1996, A.G. Vyshnevskii (ed), *Naselenie Rossii 1995*, Moscow, pp. 63-68, 77-91.

Watson, P., 1995, "Explaining rising mortality among men in eastern Europe", *Social Science and medicine*, Vol. 41, No. 7, pp. 925, 930.

White, S., 1995, *Russia goes dry*, Cambridge, CUP.

Willekens, F. and Scherbov, S., 1995, "Demographic trends in Russia", in H. v.d. Brekel and F. Deven (ed), *Population and family in the Low Countries*, 1994, Kluwer, Dordrecht, p. 218.

Zaionchkovskaya, Zh.A., 1994, Migratsiya naseleniya i rynok truda v rossii (Moscow, Institute for national economic forecasting); 1995, Razvitie vneshnykh migratsionnykh svyazei Rossii, *Sotsiologicheskii zhurnal*, No.1.

Zimmermann, K.F., 1993, "Labour responses to taxes and benefits in Germany", in A.B. Atkinson and G.V. Mogensen (eds), *Welfare and work incentives,* Clarendon Press, Oxford, pp.237-238.

3

Labour market policy and the reallocation of labour across sectors

Richard Jackman and Catalin Pauna

1. Introduction

This chapter is concerned with the process of reallocation of labour across broad industrial sectors. There are two main reasons for being particularly interested in this issue. First, one of the most conspicuous features of the pre-reform labour market of the formerly socialist economies as compared to that of market economies is the very different structure of employment across broad industrial sectors. The large-scale movement of labour from agriculture and manufacturing industry into the service sector is evidently one of the major tasks of economic restructuring.

Second, the reallocation of labour is a task that must fall upon the "external" labour market. It can be achieved only by the physical mobility of workers who leave one enterprise and find work in another. It is thus the dimension of restructuring where any deficiencies in the workings of the labour market, such as impediments to labour mobility or poorly developed employment exchanges, are likely to have the most severe effect. By contrast, at least part, and possibly a large part, of the adjustment to new technology or commercial business practices involves restructuring within the enterprise, in the sense of introducing new working practices or organisational structures within firms and it is in this context that issues of corporate governance, privatisation, capital markets and the like are critical.

To what extent have the economies of Central and Eastern Europe (CEE) succeeded in reallocating labour towards sectors where it is more productive? Can one assess the efficiency of their labour markets in achieving such reallocation? What explains differences between countries, and what policies can now help in this process? Do high rates of unemployment assist or hinder labour market reallocation? Has the Czech Republic maintained low unemployment by delaying economic restructuring, or has it been able to combine full employment and labour market reallocation, and if so how? In this paper we attempt answers to these questions.

Our main conclusions are first that the labour market of most of the transition economies have been dominated by economy-wide shocks entailing employment decline in almost all sectors rather than by reallocation across sectors. Even so, as the recovery gathers strength, reallocation is taking place and in the lead economies in this regard (the Czech Republic and Poland) up to half of the reallocation that may be required has been achieved within the first five years of the transition. This speed of reallocation compares well with that of less developed market economies such as Greece or Portugal which are adjusting to the European Single Market. Second, the effectiveness of labour market reallocation appears to proceed as rapidly in interventionist countries like the Czech Republic as in free market countries like Poland. The Czech full employment "miracle" has not been bought at the cost of a slower pace of restructuring.

This chapter is in four sections. The first attempts a measure of the change in the structure of employment required and the amount so far achieved. The second section identifies measures both of the speed and the efficiency of restructuring, and the effectiveness of new job creation. We argue that new job creation is the most important aspect of restructuring and we show that this measure bears little relationship to aggregate measures of economic performance, such as GDP growth or unemployment. The third offers some thoughts on decision-making within state-owned enterprises (SOEs), where it is argued that the key to understanding the disparate performance of the economies of Central and Eastern Europe lies in the worker orientated management of the SOEs. The final section looks at policy.

2. The reallocation of labour across sectors

Despite the pivotal importance of the concept of restructuring in the economics of transition, there seem to have been few attempts to measure it. We attempt to quantify various measures of restructuring, in the sense of labour reallocation, in order to answer the following types of question:

- How much restructuring is required in each economy?
- How much restructuring has taken place since the reforms?
- How far has the restructuring been successful in reducing the initial structural imbalance (i.e. has it been in the right direction, or "convergent")?
- Is the pace of restructuring fast or slow by comparison with the current pace of employment reallocation in market economies?
- Is high unemployment correlated with faster, or better directed, restructuring?

Some models of labour market reallocation have been formulated in terms of ownership. Perhaps most influential have been models developed by Blanchard (1991) and Aghion and Blanchard (1994). Their basic paradigm envisaged three stages in the transition. The initial stage would be characterised by a sharp fall in state sector employment and a sharp rise in unemployment. In the second stage the growth of private sector firms would draw workers from the pool of unemployment. Unemployment would decline until it reached an equilibrium level, after which, in the third stage, further growth in the private sector would depend on private firms being able to bid away workers from the residual state sector. Some economists went as far as to argue that unemployment could be regarded as an "indicator of the extent to which the restructuring process has got under way" (McAuley, 1991).

We would argue that it is misleading to identify labour market reallocation with the development of private ownership. Employment in the private sector can grow simply because enterprises are privatised with no change in any worker's place of employment. Such privatisation may raise efficiency but in general will not remove the need to shed labour from the formerly state-owned manufacturing enterprises. In the context of the labour market, restructuring is more fundamentally an issue of industrial composition. A shift out of agriculture, for example, is needed in most transitional economies whether or not agriculture was initially in state or private ownership. Likewise one can expect a substantial expansion of employment in activities such as airports or telecommunications, whether or not state owned. Of course the change in industrial composition will in general be associated with a decline in the state sector (manufacturing) and growth in the private sector (services), but it is the sectoral rather than the ownership shift which necessitates labour reallocation.

This is not to rule out the need for labour mobility between enterprises within the same sector. Differences in management qualities, market access or product mix may allow some enterprises to flourish while others in the same sector decline, and, even within narrowly defined sectors, state firms may be losing out to *de novo* private activity. None the less, in this paper we will focus on labour mobility across broadly defined (1-digit) industrial sectors, because this is.where problems of structural adjustment can be expected to be most severe. In industrialised market economies, there is considerable labour mobility within sectors, but very much larger problems associated with de-industrialisation and the absorption of manufacturing workers into other sectors. Similarly, prior to the reforms, inter-enterprise labour mobility was quite high in Eastern Europe and of the same order of magnitude as in many Western European countries (Jackman and Rutkowski, 1994, Table 7.1). But in the past the bulk of this mobility took the form of people moving between basically similar jobs in similar types of enterprise, and even if job mobility of this form were to remain high, as appears to be the case in Russia and elsewhere in the FSU (see e.g. Commander *et al.,* 1995), it would make no contribution to bringing about the enormous changes in the broad structure of employment that are required.

A second reason for looking at broad industrial sectors concerns the need to distinguish restructuring — which implies change from a less to a more efficient allocation of resources — from simple turbulence, or change in no particular direction. We need to ask whether labour reallocation is moving people to where they are likely to be more productive, and this requires a view of what structure is the ultimate objective. How might one determine a "warranted" or "terminal" employment structure for each country, that is to say the structure that could be expected to develop in the long term given current policies, the "long term" being perhaps a period of time over which the workforce and the built environment are taken as given but the labour allocation and investment adjust fully to the new regime.

Estimates of the comparative advantage of individual countries in particular sectors (e.g. Hare and Hughes, 1992) typically build in features of the economy, such as the inherited capital stock, which will themselves change during the process of transition. Additionally, they are more feasible for traded goods sectors than for (private or public) services, though the bulk of employment in an efficient allocation is likely to be in the service sector.

Tables 1-2. Structure of employment (in %).

Sector	Bulgaria	Czech R.	Hungary	Poland	Romania	Slovakia	South OECD	North OECD
1989								
Agriculture	19.0	11.7	16.6	26.8	27.9	13.8	10.7	4.1
Mining	2.6	3.6	2.0	3.4	2.3	1.0	0.4	1.0
Manufacturing	34.9	34.0	28.6	24.5	33.0	32.1	22.0	26.3
Electricity, gas, water	0.8	1.4	2.6	1.1	1.2	1.6	0.9	1.1
Construction	7.8	7.3	7.0	7.8	7.0	11.6	8.1	6.4
Trade	9.2	11.5	11.3	8.9	5.9	11.1	19.3	17.4
Transportation	6.8	6.5	7.7	7.2	6.9	6.4	6.0	6.0
Finance	0.6	0.5	0.8	1.0	0.3	0.4	6.1	8.6
Community services	18.4	23.5	23.4	19.3	15.3	22.0	26.5	28.7
RI-South	24.2	17.2	16.5	23.0	31.3	18.4	-	10.0
RI-North	27.3	19.6	19.6	27.7	33.4	21.6	10.00	-
1994								
Agriculture	23.2	7.0	8.7	26.7	35.6	10.2	8.3	-
Mining	3.1	2.0	1.0	2.7	2.6	1.6	0.4	-
Manufacturing	29.4	29.7	23.7	20.3	24.5	26.8	20.5	-
Electricity, gas, water	1.1	2.0	2.9	1.9	1.7	2.3	0.8	-
Construction	5.9	9.3	5.4	5.7	5.6	8.9	8.3	-
Trade	10.9	15.0	15.4	14.6	6.7	12.3	19.5	-
Transportation	7.2	7.6	8.4	5.7	5.6	7.8	6.0	-
Finance	1.4	1.6	1.9	1.6	0.6	1.2	7.2	-
Community services	17.7	25.9	32.5	20.8	17.2	29.0	28.5	-
RI-South	28.2	14.6	12.7	21.8	34.4	13.6	-	-

Notes: 1) South OECD countries are France, Greece, Italy and Spain, North OECD countries are Denmark, West Germany, Great Britain and the Netherlands; 2) RI is the coefficient of restructuring, defined as the overall excess employment in sectors where the proportion employed in the Eastern European country exceeds employment in the comparator countries, respectively North, OECD).
Source: OECD-Labour Force Statistics (1993) and authors' computations.

Table 3. Restructuring indices, 1989-1994.

	Speed		Efficiency		New Job Creation (%)
Bulgaria	40.5	(48.2)	70.0	(66.8)	3.9
Czech R.	44.2	(39.6)	90.7	(87.2)	28.0
Hungary	60.3	(54.5)	84.1	(76.0)	12.8
Poland	35.3	(44.4)	70.6	(64.8)	23.3
Romania	21.1	(30.5)	64.8	(84.2)	3.4
Slovakia	48.7	(48.8)	92.5	(90.3)	19.1
Greece*	26.3		57.0		41.9
Portugal*	70.1		85.9		89.9

* 1989-1993.
Note: Indices in brackets exclude agriculture.
Source: Authors' computations.

Instead, we start from the idea that, to a first approximation, the structure of employment in the Central and Eastern European countries (CEECs) should in the long run become more or less the same as in neighbouring market economies. The differences in the inherited employment structure of the CEE economies as compared to a neighbouring market economy can be attributed to the distortions of the planned economy, reflecting the material bias of production, obsolete technology and inappropriate relative factor prices. As these features are removed, the employment structure of CEECs should come to resemble that of Western European market economies.

One advantage of a direct comparison with a market economy unadjusted for the specific features of the transition economies is that it avoids the need for reliable data on output or the capital stock. Time inconsistent and error-infested statistical measures of output or capital stock are a major impediment to any empirical investigation of the economic reform in Eastern Europe, particularly when attempting inter temporal and cross-country comparisons. Labour market data in the former socialist countries for historical reasons tend to be more reliable than other types of quantitative information.

In Table 1, using OECD data which permit direct comparison by broad industrial sector, we document the employment structure of the CEECs in 1989 with that of Western European comparator economies. For purposes of comparison, we divided Western European countries into a Northern group (Denmark, (West) Germany, Netherlands, UK) and a Southern group (France, Greece, Italy and Spain), to allow for the considerable differences in employment in agriculture.

The table indicates the scale of the problem. In comparison with either group of market economies, there is obviously excessive employment in agriculture, mining and manufacturing industry everywhere. Services, particularly trade and finance (which cover business and professional services in addition to banking, insurance etc.) are underdeveloped in all countries. It is noticeable also that "community services" (which include health and education as well as public administration) employ fewer people than in the market economies. On the other hand, employment in construction and transport is much the same.

It is evident from Table 1 that the extent (as against the nature) of structural imbalance differs considerably between countries. In the final rows of the Table, we calculate an "index of restructuring" which measures the proportion of the workforce in each country which would need to change sector to enable the country to attain the same structure of employment as that of a comparable Western European economy, as characterised by either the Northern or the Southern group, in 1989.

As compared with the structure of employment in the Southern European countries, the extent of restructuring required in Romania, at 31.3 per cent of the workforce, was at the outset, nearly double that required in Hungary (16.5 per cent). While Romania is something of an outlier, the extent of restructuring required was also significantly greater in Bulgaria and (because of its abnormally large agricultural sector) in Poland than in the Czech or Slovak Republics, which are quite similar to Hungary. To attain the same structure as the Northern countries requires a further reallocation of about 3 per cent in each of the countries.

Turning now to the second question, the amount of restructuring achieved, an obvious measure is simply to replicate Table 1 for a recent year, say 1994, and compare the structural imbalances "now" with those that existed at the outset. The data for such a comparison are shown in Table 2. For various reasons, including German reunification, it is not possible to obtain data on a comparable basis for the Northern group of countries after 1989, so this comparison is undertaken with regard to the Southern group only. This makes very little difference since the direction of labour reallocation is the same on either basis in almost all sectors in every country. The remarkable feature of Table 2 is that the imbalances appear as great now as they were in 1989. While the proportion employed in manufacturing has fallen everywhere, and the proportions employed in trade and finance risen, the proportion employed in agriculture has risen in some of the countries, and, most remarkably, the restructuring index shows very little improvement and has actually slipped back in some countries.

The apparent lack of progress in restructuring despite substantial job losses reflects several phenomena. First, there is a problem of "moving goalposts" — the market economies are themselves in the process of relatively rapid structural change, and the transition economies need quite a rapid pace of employment reallocation simply to avoid falling further behind. (In all cases employment changes in market economies are moving them further away from the employment structure of the transition economies.) If one calculates the gap in employment structure between the transition economies in 1994 and the comparator economies in 1989, all the transition economies show some improvement, most notably the Czech and Slovak republics. Even on this measure, however, progress in Poland and Bulgaria has been very limited and in Romania it has been almost non-existent.

The second reason concerns the peculiar role of the agricultural sector as an "employer of last resort". In some countries, particularly those where employment in agriculture was initially high, the collapse of regular employment has led to a reversion to small-scale farming. There is thus a perverse tendency for those countries which had the greatest surplus of employment in agriculture in 1989 to experience the slowest declines, or even in the case of Romania a sharp increase, in agricultural employment between 1989 and 1992. We return to the special character of agricultural employment in the next section.

Third, and most important, a significant part of the change in the employment structure that has been observed has not been attributable to the reallocation of labour across sectors, but simply reflects the uneven incidence of macroeconomic recession. A sector with excess employment at the outset may be shedding labour, but if its rate of employment decline is slower than average its share of employment will be increasing. In Bulgaria, for example, the shares of employment in mining, in electricity and water and in transport have all risen even though the initial shares in these sectors were already too high, presumably because they are less vulnerable to recession.

Some further evidence for this last point is found from evaluating gross changes of employment by sector between 1989 and 1992, and 1992 and 1994 respectively. Between 1989 and 1992 the rate of job destruction ranged from 25.0 per cent in Bulgaria to 10.2 per cent in the Czech Republic, while job creation ranged from 6.7 per cent in Romania to only 0.2 per cent in Bulgaria. There is clear inverse relationship between job destruction and job creation measured at the sectoral level, consistent with the dominant role of aggregate shocks relative to sectoral reallocation. It is notable that in most cases even where the share of employment in a particular sector was rising, the absolute level of employment in that sector was falling. Such changes in the structure of employment that took place between 1989 and 1992 were thus achieved almost entirely by differential rates of job loss with no need for labour mobility across sectors.

The later period, from 1992 to 1994, showed a reduced rate of job destruction in all countries and a more rapid rate of job creation, and no longer an inverse correlation between the two. By this stage, there was evidence of significant job creation, notably in Poland and the Czech Republic, which had achieved relatively rapid rates of growth in the business service sectors, that is trade and finance.

3. Labour reallocation and aggregate unemployment

To assess the extent of effective labour reallocation across sectors, it is clearly necessary to look not at employment shares but at the actual numbers employed in different sectors. With employment falling by 15-20 per cent in some countries, the immediate issue is how to treat the emergence of unemployment. In large part this depends on whether unemployment is regarded as temporary or permanent. To the extent that the CEECs are adopting policies and institutions similar to those of Western European countries, they must presumably expect rather similar unemployment rates in the long term. We therefore adopt the principle of the comparator market economies as indicators of likely long term unemployment rates.

It turns out, however, that average unemployment rates in CEECs are now much the same as in Western Europe. Thus we can regard current CEE unemployment rates as perhaps close to their likely long run equilibrium levels at least in relation to Western Europe as it was at the end of the 1980s. We may then take the allocation of the labour force in the comparator country, including the unemployment rate, as the standard against which labour reallocation can be measured. Thus for each CEEC we calculate, given the size of its 1994 labour force, how many people would be employed in each sector and how many would be unemployed if it were to have the same structure of employment and the same unemployment rate as the comparator Western European economy (as of 1989).

For this purpose we return to the Northern and Southern groups of comparator market economies set out in Table 1. The differences between these groups can be attributed in part to permanent features of the economic landscape such as climate or population density. It is conspicuous that in comparison with Northern Europe the CEE imbalance is concentrated almost exclusively in agriculture, where the CEE average of around 24 per cent contrasts with only 4 per cent in the Northern European countries. It would seem appropriate to allow for persistent differences along these lines in CEECs also, and in the comparisons that follow we use the Northern countries as the comparator group for the Czech and Slovak republics and for Hungary and the Southern countries as a comparator group for the others (Poland, Bulgaria and Romania).

This provides a basis for comparing the actual changes in employment, measured in terms of overall sectoral declines or increases, with those which would be required for the structure of employment to adjust to that of the comparator market economy. The data and calculations for each of the CEECs are presented in

Table A in the Appendix. The first three columns set out the data — actual employment and unemployment in 1989 and 1994 and the employment structure based on the comparator market economy. The next two columns contrast the changes in employment which have occurred with those which would have been required to replicate the employment structure of the comparator economy.

On this basis we may construct a measure which takes account not only of the totality of sectoral employment changes but also of the direction of such changes. The "warranted" or "convergent" change in employment (column 5) can then be compared with the actual change in employment between 1989 and 1994 (column 4). Where the two figures have the same sign, either positive or negative, we can measure the amount of restructuring achieved by the smaller of the two. Where the actual and convergent changes have opposite signs, no restructuring is deemed to have taken place. Hence for each economy we can compute the total extent of labour reallocation in the convergent direction, that is restructuring achieved (column 6), as compared with labour reallocation going in the "wrong" direction or overshooting the adjustment required (column 7).

These calculations permit a number of measures of the success of labour reallocation. First we can ask what proportion of the labour reallocation "required" has taken place in the first five years, which we may measure as the absolute sum of the numbers in column 6 divided by the absolute sum of those in column 5. This gives a measure of the speed of restructuring. The results of these calculations are presented in Table 3, which suggests that on average about 40 per cent of the employment changes to achieve convergence had already taken place by 1994, with the highest figure being for Hungary (60 per cent), and the lowest for Romania.

It is also possible to derive a measure of the "efficiency" of labour market reallocation, that is to say the proportion of the total employment change that has been convergent towards the warranted structure. This is measured by the absolute sum of the numbers in column 6 as a proportion of the absolute sum of those in column 4. If labour reallocation is costly, it is important to avoid unnecessary structural change, and one may wish to balance these costs against the costs of slower adjustment. In all countries over 60 per cent of employment changes have been convergent, with the Czech Republic achieving the highest efficiency, over 90 per cent, on this criterion.

By way of comparison, we have made similar calculations for two relatively non-industrialised market economies in southern Europe, Greece and Portugal, which have recently become members of the EU and are now to some extent subject to the rigours of the European Single Market. In terms of the speed of restructuring, Portugal has achieved a more rapid change than any of the CEECs while Greece is at the lower end of the range. Similarly, Portugal does well on the efficiency index while Greece is worse than any of the CEECs. The differences between these two countries, and the differences amongst the CEECs, are evidently larger than the differences between the two groups.

The measure of restructuring we have adopted comprises two qualitatively rather different activities: job losses in sectors with excess employment and job creation in sectors with deficient employment. But clearly, destroying redundant jobs, for all the social costs involved, remains an economically easier task than creating new jobs. The amount of new job creation required for convergence varies from over

24 per cent of the labour force in Romania to about 16.5 per cent in Poland and Slovakia to 12.5 per cent in Bulgaria, Hungary and the Czech Republic, the low figure for Bulgaria being largely because of the sharp drop in its labour force which permits a larger part of the restructuring process to be achieved through differential job loss.

In the final column of Table 3, we have calculated a new job creation index, which is the number of new jobs created in the sectors with deficient employment as a proportion of the total new job creation required for convergence. On this measure, the Czech Republic is the most successful of the transition economies, with 28 per cent of new job creation already achieved, followed by Poland, Slovakia and Hungary. Bulgaria and Romania have made virtually no progress at all on this definition. It is also noteworthy that, on the basis of the new job creation index, both Greece and to an even greater extent Portugal are far ahead of any of the CEECs.

The final question concerns the relationship between restructuring and unemployment. Does unemployment assist the process of restructuring? Clearly, the answer depends on the measure chosen. We would argue that the objective of restructuring from a labour market perspective is to create jobs in the growth potential (deficient employment) sectors. It is a hypothesis that this process may be assisted by a rapid rate of job destruction and transitional unemployment, but job destruction and unemployment should not be seen as policy objectives, but only as a means to an end, the objective being new job creation.

On this measure, as we have already noted, the Czech Republic is the most successful of the CEE economies and this experience appears to suggest that employment growth in private services may be assisted by a more gradual pace of job loss in the state sector. The next most successful economy on this criteria, however, is Poland which, by contrast, is an economy of high unemployment (in particular in relation to its output growth). The relationship between unemployment and the pace of job creation in the growing sectors is shown in Figure 1, which suggests that there is no clear-cut relationship, with the Czech Republic a clear outlier.

The explanation of the absence of any correlation between restructuring and unemployment appears a relatively simple one, namely that unemployment is not the route by which workers move between sectors. The Hungarian Household Panel Survey (Kollo, 1993) found that most workers in private firms were recruited directly from state firms, whilst a majority of the unemployed who found jobs returned to state sector employers, and in fact more people entered unemployment from the private sector than unemployed people found work in the private sector. Similar results were found in the former Czechoslovakia (Vecernik, 1992), in Poland (Boeri, 1993) and a survey of recruitment by private sector firms in Bulgaria (Beleva *et al.*, 1995) found that virtually none hired unemployed people.

The evidence that growing firms recruit from those in work rather than from the unemployed does not mean that there is no link between unemployment and restructuring. If growing firms are recruiting from the state sector the wage they will have to pay will obviously depend on the wages paid in state firms which in turn may be sensitive to the unemployment rate. However, in economies where flows out of unemployment are low (Boeri, 1994), wage setting in firms would in principle be much more sensitive to the income available to the unemployed, in particular the level and duration of unemployment benefit, than to the impact of changes in the unemployment rate on their prospects of finding another job.

Figure 1

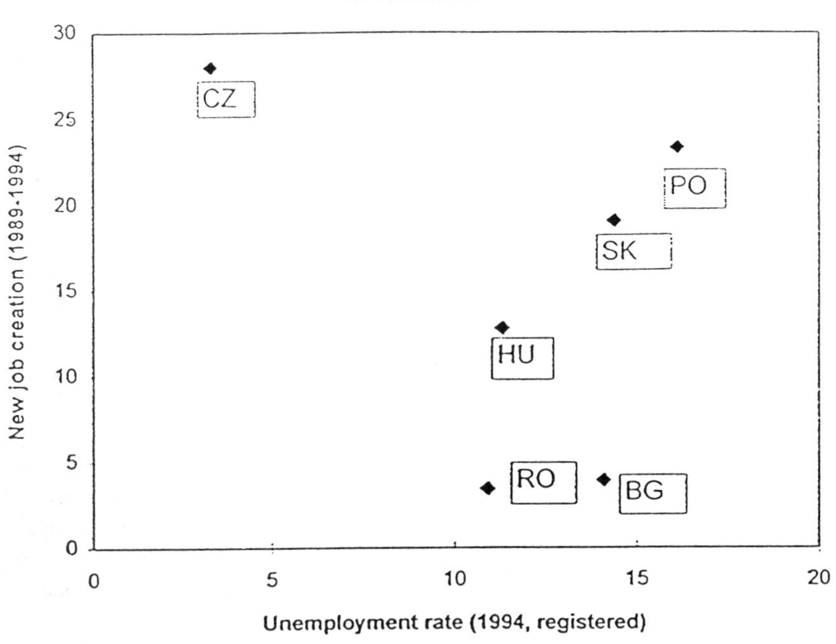

Source: Table 4 and 5.

The finding that unemployment is unnecessary for successful restructuring, as measured in terms of labour mobility, raises two further questions. First, if the Czech full employment achievement is not accounted for by slow restructuring, how is it to be explained, and indeed what are the main causes of the very different evolution of unemployment (both absolutely and relative to output) across countries? Second, what policy actions can countries now take to enable them to reduce unemployment without prejudicing the progress of economic transition?

4. Employment decisions of state firms

Given the dominant role of the collapse of output in the immediate aftermath of the recession, it would be natural to presume that the unemployment rate of an economy would be determined primarily by the magnitude of the aggregate decline in output. But, as shown in Table 4, there are in fact large and significant differences between output and employment changes and between employment and unemployment changes in the first years of transition. In some countries the fall in output has been associated with much larger falls in employment than in others. Given the initial concentration of output and employment in state firms, it is in their behaviour that some understanding of the differences in behaviour may be sought.

Table 4. Output, employment and unemployment in Central and Eastern Europe (in %).

	1989-1992		1992	1989-1995		1994
	ΔGDP	ΔE	U	ΔGDP	ΔE	U
Bulgaria	-26	-25	16	-25	-25	13
Czech R.	-19	-9	3	-15	-9	3
Hungary	-18	-21	12	-14	-26	10
Poland	-17	-13	14	-3	-16	16
Romania	-26	-4	8	-19	-11	11
Slovakia	-21	-15	11	-16	-13	15

Source: GDP, EBRD *Transition Report 1995*, pp. 185-207.

How might one model the wage and employment decisions of worker- or manager-controlled enterprises subject to the disruptive consequences of economic transition? We do not attempt a systematic review of this issue, but instead focus on the critical question of when an enterprise facing an adverse demand shock resorts to laying off workers. We follow the standard presumption that, in the interval between the collapse of central planning and the institution of private ownership, the prime objective of the state-owned enterprise has been the welfare of its workforce. In attaining this objective, it is important to recognise that the SOE can separate output and employment decisions, and that the production function is not necessarily a binding constraint. Price and output decisions are made to maximise revenue in the product market subject to the constraint of demand. Wage and employment decisions are then made in the interests of workers' welfare, subject to the financial constraint. (For a model developing this idea, see Jackman *et al.*, 1992).

Some evidence in support of this interpretation is given in Table 5. Over the period 1990-93, the correlation between changes in output and changes in employment across narrow (2-digit) sectors in manufacturing in Poland is only 0.30. Notably, the correlation between product price and output is negative, though again weak, while the correlation between product price and the number of employees is positive. Most strikingly, there is a much stronger correlation between revenue and employment. All this appears consistent with the idea that employment is determined by the number of workers firms can afford to pay rather than by their production requirements.

Enterprises facing an adverse shock can then choose to reduce production but maintain employment. In such an enterprise, worker effort must necessarily fall in line with the fall in productivity, and if there is no change in the relative product price the real consumption wage must also fall in the same proportion. In Romania, for example, survey evidence suggests that average hours worked have fallen from around 2 100 a year in 1989 to only 1 500 a year in 1992.

To explain differences in behaviour across countries, it is helpful to envisage three stages of enterprise response to adverse shocks. First, it may be able to protect both wages and employment in the face of falling revenues by reducing other costs, by not replacing workers who leave and taking advantage of any remaining softness

Table 5. Poland — Correlation between changes.

1989-90		Employees	Product price	Industrial prod.	
	Employees	1.00			
	Product price	0.54	1.00		
	Industrial prod	0.50	0.49	1.00	
1990-91		Employees	Product price	Industrial prod.	Revenue
	Employees	1.00			
	Product price	0.31	1.00		
	Industrial prod	0.49	0.42	1.00	
	Revenue	0.47	0.92	0.69	1.00
1991-92		Employees	Product price	Industrial prod.	Revenue
	Employees	1.00			
	Product price	0.67	1.00		
	Industrial prod	-0.09	-0.11	1.00	
	Revenue	0.20	0.00	0.70	1.00
1992-93		Employees	Product price	Industrial prod.	Revenue
	Employees	1.00			
	Product price	-0.04	1.00		
	Industrial prod	0.27	-0.66	1.00	
	Revenue	0.09	0.91	-0.29	1.00
1990-93		Employees	Product price	Industrial prod.	Revenue
	Employees	1.00			
	Product price	0.40	1.00		
	Industrial prod	0.30	-0.37	1.00	
	Revenue	0.71	0.78	0.20	1.00

Source: Central Statistical Office.

in the budget constraint. Second, it can maintain employment with lower work effort and lower real wages. It will want to cut wages for so long as the wage income it can pay exceeds the income its workers can get outside the firm, i.e. primarily unemployment benefit. Only when other sources of savings have been exhausted, and wages have been cut to the outside opportunity, will it be forced into laying off workers.

There is evidence that labour shedding in the first phase took the form mainly of voluntary separations. This process takes various forms: retirements and early retirements; in some countries emigration or others wanting to leave the labour force; but above all workers leaving to take (what they hope will be) better jobs in the growing sectors of the economy dominated by *de novo* private firms. A number of studies have documented a rate of separation from state sector firms in the first few years of the transition no higher than their normal levels prior to the reforms (see, for example Beleva *et al.*, 1995, for Bulgaria, or Earle and Oprescu, 1995, for Romania).

One of the most important differences between countries has been the extent to which various forms of deficit finance have been allowed to continue. Poland and Hungary have perhaps been least tolerant, as was Bulgaria in the initial stages of the transition. The ending of the soft budget constraint in these countries has forced a greater degree of adjustment of wages and employment. In Romania, by contrast, much of state owned industry, particularly heavy industry and mining, continued to receive financial support. In the Czech Republic, selective subsidy and other forms of directed support have permitted many state enterprises to maintain employment despite being subject to major demand shocks.

Where SOEs are obliged to cut into their wage bills, and therefore to reduce either wages or employment or both, the key issue is the expected income of workers laid off from the enterprise. It has been clear from an early stage that the labour market prospects of unemployed workers were very weak. The alternative sources of income for most workers consist largely of unemployment benefits, casual informal work or the support of their families. Differences in unemployment benefit regimes constitute a further element in understanding the different experiences of the different countries.

Unemployment benefit regimes in CEECs appear at first sight rather generous, with replacement rates as high as 75 per cent in Hungary and around 60 per cent elsewhere. In fact, these ratios give a misleading picture: benefits are often capped and their real value in some countries is quickly eroded by inflation. Even more importantly, the duration of benefit entitlement is limited, to only six months in the Czech Republic and typically about a year elsewhere (Boeri, 1994; Scarpetta and Reutersward, 1994). In some of the countries, in particular Poland, the benefit regime was initially more lenient in terms of eligibility and duration, and this allowed some unemployment and particularly long-term unemployment to build up. One consequence has been that it has become difficult for benefit officers to monitor the activities of the unemployed so that it is for example common for unemployed people to work in the informal sector.

It is perhaps the combination of hard budget constraints at the level of the enterprise and a relatively generous stance on benefits in Hungary and Poland which accounts for the willingness of enterprises in these countries to lay off workers rather than cut wages. From the perspective of a worker managed firm, unemployment benefits reintroduce, at the level of the household, the soft budget constraint in the sense of providing public financial support for the enterprise conditional on making its workers unemployed. In the Czech Republic, and to some extent also in Romania, a different policy stance, more supportive of firms but tougher on unemployed people, has encouraged enterprises to retain their workers.

5. Policy

From the outset, labour market policy in the transition economies has been based on the recognition of the need for substantial reallocation of labour across sectors. It was thought that employment restructuring might lead to high albeit temporary unemployment, because the speed of job loss in declining sectors could be expected to be very much more rapid than the rate of new job creation in the growing sectors. Further, the sectoral reallocation of labour could be impeded by various obstacles to labour mobility, such as poorly developed employment exchanges or the absence of an effective housing market. In this framework, the key elements of labour market policy were seen to be (a) subjecting firms to hard budget constraints to force rapid restructuring, (b) encouraging labour mobility and wage flexibility and (c) provision of benefits, or some form of "social safety net", for those temporarily stranded between the collapse of jobs in the state sector and the growth of the private sector.

We have argued that such a perspective may have been mistaken. It is not in our view correct to think that unemployment in the transition was an inevitable component of reallocation. The Czech Republic, which has achieved the most rapid rate of new job creation in the growth sectors (trade and finance), has the lowest unemployment rate in Europe. Overall, our empirical work suggests that there is no correlation between the rate of new job creation and the rate of decline of employment in the sectors with excessive employment. The belief that unemployment is needed in the particular circumstances of the transition, because it would facilitate the movement of workers into growth sectors, seems to us mistaken — private firms appear to recruit almost exclusively from those with jobs in the state sector or new entrants to the labour force rather than from the unemployed.

Thus we would question the rationale of policies directed at speeding up the shake-out of labour from the excess employment sectors. By creating open unemployment, such policies burden the public finances and additionally may create problems of deterioration of morale and work habits amongst those made unemployed. It remains an option for state firms to maintain employment, and the extent to which they exercise that option can be influenced by policy. What principles ought then to guide policy?

Clearly the main objective must be to encourage the growth of the new private sector. While high rates of unemployment do not of themselves contribute to this objective, policy initiatives to reduce unemployment could well be harmful to private sector employment. For example, a policy of indefinite and indiscriminate support for maintaining employment in declining firms financed by taxes on private firms would have a severe adverse effect on the private sector. Rather what is needed are policies to equate the private and social costs of layoffs, as against the present situation where the state subsidises layoffs but not employment.

One extreme would be simply to abolish unemployment benefits, as is approximately the case in Russia. The main effect of this policy has been to bring about very sharp cuts in real wages in conjunction with the maintenance of high levels of employment in state (or formerly state) firms. Registered unemployment in Russia remains very low, and, even on Labour Force Survey measures, the 1995 rate is below 8 per cent. Given a decline of output in Russia of close on 50 per cent this is a remarkably low number. But the consequence has been an enormous increase in hardship, poverty and inequality in Russia to an extent which would be unacceptable in most of Eastern Europe.

An alternative approach, for which the Czech experience offers some support, is one based on restricting the availability of unemployment benefits on some "workfare" principle. In such programmes, the state provides income support in conjunction with requiring unemployed people to undertake some publicly useful work. Workfare not only diminishes the possible attractions of unemployment, particularly to those with informal sector opportunities or to the idle, but also tends to encourage the unemployed to search more actively for regular work. Hence it leads to lower wages being set in firms than if unemployment benefits were set at the same level but with no work obligation.

The balance of policies in the Czech Republic has involved a relatively short duration of "unconditional" unemployment benefits, followed after six months by a work guarantee programme on workfare lines. By accompanying this policy with selective support of state firms, the Czech Republic has achieved a better balance in terms of both encouraging the growth of jobs in the private sector and restraining the decline in employment in the state sector. (For more detailed evaluation of the Czech experience, see Boeri and Burda, forthcoming; Ham *et al.,* 1995.) This policy mix may offer a more attractive model for other CEECs.

Looking further into the nature of unemployment in the transition economies, it is notable that both the eligibility and the duration of unemployment benefits are limited, yet many people seem able to support themselves for long periods of unemployment. For example, in Bulgaria, only 24 per cent of those reported as unemployed in the June 1994 Labour Force Survey were receiving unemployment benefits, leaving 550 000 people (over 15 per cent of the labour force) reporting themselves as unemployed without benefits and in most cases without other forms of state income support.

Clearly, it is possible that many of those registered as, or reporting themselves, unemployed may also have some form of casual or informal work, given in particular that many of the East European countries have sizeable agricultural sectors, and some also have thriving informal sectors. There has been widespread concern, not least in the countries themselves, about abuse of the benefit system, though there is little hard evidence. However, in Poland one survey found that 46 per cent of unemployed people had some form of work, albeit often only casual or part-time (World Bank, 1995), while a second survey found that around 35 per cent of employers were hiring informally people registered as unemployed (Mroczkowski, 1996). Unemployment is thus becoming linked to the growth of the (non-taxpaying) shadow economy.

The transition economies typically have both high benefits, albeit with restricted coverage, and high employment taxes, which together create strong incentives for evasion. This suggests a possible new role for active labour market policies: by linking payment of benefit to some temporary job, the employer is of necessity brought into the formal sector. Traditionally, evaluations of active labour market policies in CEECs, as in OECD economies, have tended to be unfavourable, reflecting the fact that active policies are designed to overcome impediments to mobility when the problem in most CEECs has been an overall shortage of jobs (OECD/CCET, forthcoming; Puhani and Steiner, 1996). But these evaluations have been primarily concerned with the future job prospects of participants rather than with the growth of the shadow economy. A gradual introduction of workfare style active labour policies, say in terms of providing a temporary job or training after six months unemployment for those under 25, as a condition for continued receipt of benefit could have an important role in retaining people in the official labour market, and discouraging the growth of the shadow economy.

The main conclusion of this paper is that unemployment in the transition economies has been neither necessary nor efficient from the perspective of labour market restructuring. It has rather been the consequence of misguided policies which have subsidised socially inefficient job destruction. The outcome has been high and persistent unemployment. Labour market policy is thus still required to restrain the growth of wages, either through reducing unemployment benefits or by combining benefits with workfare-based active labour market policies.

DATA APPENDIX

Sources:

i) OECD employment by sector. The data is from *OECD-Labour Force Statistics (1993)*. The southern group of OECD countries consists of France, Greece, Italy and Spain, the northern group consists of Denmark, Germany (West), the Netherlands and the United Kingdom. The figures for each group are weighted averages.

ii) Eastern European countries. The main data source is *Employment Observatory - Central and Eastern Europe, 1996*, (European Commission (DG V), Brussels), except for Romania, where we use the *Statistical Yearbook (1995)* published by the Romanian Commission for Statistics. These data derive primarily from administrative sources, typically enterprise based Censuses, supplemented by various *ad hoc* estimates of the private sector and, since 1992 or 1993 by labour force surveys. Data is end year. Further details for individual countries are as follows:

Bulgaria

The primary sources of data for the whole period are the National Statistical Institute and the Ministry of Labour and Social Welfare. The labour force and employment figures are administrative data derived from establishment Censuses together with official estimates of employment in the private sector.

Czech Republic and Slovakia

Up to and including 1992, the data are based on establishment surveys. The figures are total number of jobs (i.e. multiple job holders are counted more than once) and exclude apprentices and women on maternity leave. After 1993, the data come from the Labour Force Survey, which however adopts a broadly similar industrial classification.

Hungary

Up to 1991, the data are derived from the labour accounts of the Central Statistical Office. From 1992, they come from the Labour Force Survey, with broadly similar industrial classification. The unemployment rate is the official one and includes women on maternity leave.

Poland

Data are from administrative records throughout plus sample surveys of small enterprises conducted by the Central Statistical Office and also, in the case of agriculture, from Census figures and the Labour Force Survey.

Romania

Data come from administrative sources of the National Commission for Statistics. Figures include official estimates of employment in the private sector.

Table A.

	Labour Force			Change in employment 1989-94	Employment differential 1989	Convergent	Non-Convergent
	Actual 1989	Actual 1994	Comparator country	(2)-(1)	(3)-(1)		
	(1)	(2)	(3)	(4)	(5)	(6)	(7)
Bulgaria							
Agriculture	814	732	317	-82	-497	-82	—
Mining	114	98	15	-16	-99	-16	—
Manufacturing	1496	927	698	-569	-798	-569	—
Electricity	36	35	26	-1	-10	-1	—
Construction	333	186	258	-147	-75	-75	-72
Trade	395	344	613	-51	218	—	-51
Transportation	290	227	192	-63	-98	-63	—
Finance	26	44	203	18	177	18	—
Community services	788	558	853	-230	65	—	-230
Unemployment	—	537	517	537	—	—	—
Total	4292	3688	3688	-604	|2037|	|824|	|353|
Czech Republic							
Agriculture	631	340	151	-291	-480	-291	—
Mining	197	99	30	-98	-167	-98	—
Manufacturing	1839	1444	1165	-395	-674	-395	—
Electricity	78	96	45	18	-33	—	18
Construction	392	454	292	62	-100	—	62
Trade	620	729	802	109	+182	109	—
Transportation	351	370	267	19	-84	—	19
Finance	25	78	418	53	393	53	—
Community services	1243	1261	1310	18	67	18	—
Unemployment	—	172	549	172	—	—	—
Total	5376	5043	5043	-333	|2180|	|964|	|99|
Hungary							
Agriculture	820	328	130	-492	-690	-492	—
Mining	100	39	26	-61	-74	-61	—
Manufacturing	1408	889	998	-519	-410	-410	-109
Electricity	130	108	39	-22	-91	-22	—
Construction	345	201	251	-144	-94	-94	-50
Trade	555	578	687	23	132	23	—
Transportation	380	315	229	-65	-151	-65	—
Finance	38	73	359	35	321	35	—
Community services	1152	1221	1123	69	-29	—	69
Unemployment	24	568	471	544	—	—	—
Total	4952	4320	4320	-632	|1992|	|1202|	|228|

<table>
<tr><th></th><th>Labour</th><th>Force</th><th></th><th>Change in employment</th><th>Employment differential</th><th>Convergent</th><th>Non-Convergent</th></tr>
<tr><th></th><th>Actual 1989</th><th>Actual 1994</th><th>Comparator country</th><th>1989-94 (2)-(1)</th><th>1989 (3)-(1)</th><th></th><th></th></tr>
<tr><th></th><th>(1)</th><th>(2)</th><th>(3)</th><th>(4)</th><th>(5)</th><th>(6)</th><th>(7)</th></tr>
<tr><td>Poland</td><td></td><td></td><td></td><td></td><td></td><td></td><td></td></tr>
<tr><td>Agriculture</td><td>4557</td><td>3920</td><td>1510</td><td>-637</td><td>-3047</td><td>-637</td><td>—</td></tr>
<tr><td>Mining</td><td>578</td><td>394</td><td>70</td><td>-184</td><td>-508</td><td>-184</td><td>—</td></tr>
<tr><td>Manufacturing</td><td>4173</td><td>2970</td><td>3320</td><td>-1203</td><td>-853</td><td>-853</td><td>-350</td></tr>
<tr><td>Electricity</td><td>182</td><td>276</td><td>123</td><td>94</td><td>-59</td><td>—</td><td>94</td></tr>
<tr><td>Construction</td><td>1321</td><td>839</td><td>1230</td><td>-482</td><td>-91</td><td>-91</td><td>-391</td></tr>
<tr><td>Trade</td><td>1515</td><td>2137</td><td>2916</td><td>622</td><td>1401</td><td>622</td><td>—</td></tr>
<tr><td>Transportation</td><td>1222</td><td>835</td><td>914</td><td>-387</td><td>-308</td><td>-308</td><td>-79</td></tr>
<tr><td>Finance</td><td>172</td><td>241</td><td>966</td><td>69</td><td>794</td><td>69</td><td>—</td></tr>
<tr><td>Community services</td><td>3282</td><td>3096</td><td>4058</td><td>-236</td><td>776</td><td>—</td><td>-236</td></tr>
<tr><td>Unemployment</td><td>—</td><td>2910</td><td>2459</td><td>2910</td><td>—</td><td>—</td><td>—</td></tr>
<tr><td>Total</td><td>17002</td><td>17618</td><td>17618</td><td>616</td><td>|7837|</td><td>|2764|</td><td>|1150|</td></tr>
<tr><td>Romania</td><td></td><td></td><td></td><td></td><td></td><td></td><td></td></tr>
<tr><td>Agriculture</td><td>3056</td><td>3564</td><td>966</td><td>508</td><td>-2090</td><td>—</td><td>508</td></tr>
<tr><td>Mining</td><td>259</td><td>260</td><td>45</td><td>1</td><td>-214</td><td>—</td><td>1</td></tr>
<tr><td>Manufacturing</td><td>3613</td><td>2453</td><td>2123</td><td>-1160</td><td>-1490</td><td>-1160</td><td>—</td></tr>
<tr><td>Electricity</td><td>133</td><td>170</td><td>79</td><td>37</td><td>-54</td><td>—</td><td>37</td></tr>
<tr><td>Construction</td><td>767</td><td>561</td><td>786</td><td>-206</td><td>19</td><td>—</td><td>-206</td></tr>
<tr><td>Trade</td><td>649</td><td>671</td><td>1865</td><td>22</td><td>1216</td><td>22</td><td>—</td></tr>
<tr><td>Transportation</td><td>757</td><td>561</td><td>584</td><td>-196</td><td>-173</td><td>-173</td><td>-23</td></tr>
<tr><td>Finance</td><td>35</td><td>60</td><td>618</td><td>25</td><td>583</td><td>25</td><td>—</td></tr>
<tr><td>Community services</td><td>1677</td><td>1722</td><td>2595</td><td>45</td><td>918</td><td>45</td><td>—</td></tr>
<tr><td>Unemployment</td><td>—</td><td>1224</td><td>1573</td><td>1224</td><td>—</td><td>—</td><td>—</td></tr>
<tr><td>Total</td><td>10946</td><td>11246</td><td>11246</td><td>300</td><td>|6757|</td><td>|1425|</td><td>|775|</td></tr>
<tr><td>Slovakia</td><td></td><td></td><td></td><td></td><td></td><td></td><td></td></tr>
<tr><td>Agriculture</td><td>345</td><td>214</td><td>74</td><td>-131</td><td>-271</td><td>-131</td><td>—</td></tr>
<tr><td>Mining</td><td>25</td><td>34</td><td>15</td><td>9</td><td>-10</td><td>—</td><td>9</td></tr>
<tr><td>Manufacturing</td><td>801</td><td>564</td><td>570</td><td>-237</td><td>-231</td><td>-231</td><td>-6</td></tr>
<tr><td>Electricity</td><td>41</td><td>48</td><td>22</td><td>7</td><td>-19</td><td>—</td><td>7</td></tr>
<tr><td>Construction</td><td>289</td><td>187</td><td>143</td><td>-102</td><td>-146</td><td>-102</td><td>—</td></tr>
<tr><td>Trade</td><td>278</td><td>258</td><td>393</td><td>-20</td><td>115</td><td>—</td><td>-20</td></tr>
<tr><td>Transportation</td><td>161</td><td>163</td><td>131</td><td>2</td><td>-30</td><td>—</td><td>2</td></tr>
<tr><td>Finance</td><td>9</td><td>25</td><td>205</td><td>16</td><td>196</td><td>16</td><td>—</td></tr>
<tr><td>Community services</td><td>549</td><td>610</td><td>642</td><td>61</td><td>93</td><td>61</td><td>—</td></tr>
<tr><td>Unemployment</td><td>—</td><td>366</td><td>269</td><td>366</td><td>—</td><td>—</td><td>—</td></tr>
<tr><td>Total</td><td>2498</td><td>2469</td><td>2469</td><td>-29</td><td>|1111|</td><td>|541|</td><td>|44|</td></tr>
</table>

<table>
<tr><td></td><td>Labour
Actual
1989</td><td>Force
Actual
1994</td><td>Comparator
country</td><td>Change in employment 1989-94
(2)-(1)</td><td>Employment differential 1989
(3)-(1)</td><td>Convergent</td><td>Non-Convergent</td></tr>
<tr><td></td><td>(1)</td><td>(2)</td><td>(3)</td><td>(4)</td><td>(5)</td><td>(6)</td><td>(7)</td></tr>
<tr><td>Greece</td><td></td><td></td><td></td><td></td><td></td><td></td><td></td></tr>
<tr><td>Agriculture</td><td>930</td><td>794</td><td>354</td><td>-136</td><td>-576</td><td>-136</td><td>—</td></tr>
<tr><td>Mining</td><td>21</td><td>19</td><td>16</td><td>-2</td><td>-5</td><td>-2</td><td>—</td></tr>
<tr><td>Manufacturing</td><td>715</td><td>580</td><td>779</td><td>-135</td><td>64</td><td>—</td><td>-135</td></tr>
<tr><td>Electricity</td><td>36</td><td>40</td><td>29</td><td>4</td><td>-7</td><td>—</td><td>4</td></tr>
<tr><td>Construction</td><td>239</td><td>261</td><td>288</td><td>22</td><td>49</td><td>22</td><td>—</td></tr>
<tr><td>Trade</td><td>624</td><td>792</td><td>684</td><td>168</td><td>60</td><td>60</td><td>108</td></tr>
<tr><td>Transportation</td><td>241</td><td>249</td><td>214</td><td>8</td><td>-27</td><td>—</td><td>8</td></tr>
<tr><td>Finance</td><td>169</td><td>221</td><td>227</td><td>52</td><td>58</td><td>52</td><td>3</td></tr>
<tr><td>Community services</td><td>695</td><td>765</td><td>951</td><td>70</td><td>256</td><td>70</td><td>—</td></tr>
<tr><td>Unemployment</td><td>290</td><td>398</td><td>577</td><td>108</td><td>—</td><td>—</td><td>—</td></tr>
<tr><td>Total</td><td>3961</td><td>4118</td><td>4118</td><td>157</td><td>|1302|</td><td>|341|</td><td>|258|</td></tr>
<tr><td>Portugal</td><td></td><td></td><td></td><td></td><td></td><td></td><td></td></tr>
<tr><td>Agriculture</td><td>829</td><td>505</td><td>410</td><td>-324</td><td>-419</td><td>-324</td><td>—</td></tr>
<tr><td>Mining</td><td>20</td><td>21</td><td>19</td><td>1</td><td>-1</td><td>—</td><td>1</td></tr>
<tr><td>Manufacturing</td><td>1107</td><td>1062</td><td>902</td><td>-45</td><td>-205</td><td>-45</td><td>—</td></tr>
<tr><td>Electricity</td><td>38</td><td>31</td><td>33</td><td>-7</td><td>-5</td><td>-5</td><td>-2</td></tr>
<tr><td>Construction</td><td>384</td><td>362</td><td>334</td><td>-22</td><td>-50</td><td>-22</td><td>—</td></tr>
<tr><td>Trade</td><td>655</td><td>867</td><td>792</td><td>212</td><td>137</td><td>137</td><td>75</td></tr>
<tr><td>Transportation</td><td>180</td><td>210</td><td>248</td><td>30</td><td>68</td><td>30</td><td>—</td></tr>
<tr><td>Finance</td><td>154</td><td>310</td><td>263</td><td>156</td><td>109</td><td>109</td><td>47</td></tr>
<tr><td>Community services</td><td>1009</td><td>1099</td><td>1102</td><td>90</td><td>93</td><td>90</td><td>—</td></tr>
<tr><td>Unemployment</td><td>300</td><td>304</td><td>668</td><td>4</td><td>—</td><td>—</td><td>—</td></tr>
<tr><td>Total</td><td>4677</td><td>4772</td><td>4772</td><td>95</td><td>|1087|</td><td>|762|</td><td>|125|</td></tr>
</table>

Source: OECD-Labour Force Statistics (1993) and authors' computations.

References

Aghion, P. and Blanchard, O., 1994, *On the Speed of Transition in Central Europe*, NBER Macroeconomics Annual

Beleva, I., Jackman, R. and Nenova, M., 1993 *The Labour Market in Bulgaria*, in Commander and Coricelli (eds.) op. cit..

Blanchard, O., 1991, *Notes on the Speed of Transition, Unemployment and Growth in Poland* [mimeo].

Boeri, T., 1993, *Labour Market Flows and the Persistence of Unemployment in Central and Eastern Europe,* paper presented at OECD Workshop on *The Persistence of Unemployment in Central and Eastern European Countries* Paris.

Boeri, T., 1994, *Transitional Unemployment, Economics of Transition*, vol. no., pp.-25.

Boeri, T. and Burda, M., forthcoming, *Active Labour Market Policies, Job Matching and the Czech Miracle,* European Economic Review

Commander, S. and Coricelli, F., editors, 1995, *Unemployment, Restructuring and the Labour Market in East Europe and Russia*, The World Bank, Washington, D.C.

Commander, S., McHale J. and Yemtsov, R., 1995, *Russia,* in Commander, S. and Coricelli, F. (eds.) op. cit.

Earle, J.S. and Oprescu, G., 1994, *Employment and Wage Determination, Unemployment and Labour Policies in Romania*, in Commander, S. and Coricelli, F. (eds.) op. cit.

Ham, J., Svejnar, J. and Terrell, K., 1993, *The Czech and Slovak Labour Markets during the Transition,* in Commander, S. and Coricelli, F. (eds.) op. cit..

Hare, P. and Hughes, G., 1992, *Industrial Policy and Restructuring in Eastern Europe,* Oxford Review of Economic Policy, vol. 8, no. 1.

Jackman, R., Layard, R. and Scott, A., 1992, *Unemployment in Eastern Europe*, paper presented to NBER Conference, Cambridge, MA, February, 1992.

Jackman, R. and Rutkowski, M., 1994, *Labour Markets: Wages and Employment* in N. Barr (ed.) *Labour Markets and Social Policy in Central and Eastern Europe: The Transition and Beyond*, Oxford University Press for the World Bank, September.

Kollo, J., 1993, *Unemployment and Unemployment Related Expenditures*, Blue Ribbon Commission, Budapest.

McAuley, A., 1991, *The Economic Transition in Eastern Europe: Employment, Income Distribution and the Social Safety Net*, Oxford Review of Economic Policy, vol.(4) 93-105.

Mroczkowski, T., 1996, *Informal Employment in the Transition Economy of Poland*, Department of International Business, Washington, D.C.

OECD/CCET, forthcoming, Proceedings of *technical workshop, *What can we learn from the experience of transition countries with labour market policies*? Vienna, Nov. 30-Dec., 1995.

Puhani, P and Steiner, V., 1996, *Public Works for Poland? Active Labour Market Policies during the Transition,* ZEW Labour Economics, Human Resources and Social Policy series, Discussion Paper no. 96-01, Mannheim, Germany.

Scarpetta, S. and Reutersward, A., 1994, *Unemployment Benefit Systems and Active Labour Market Policies in Central and Eastern Europe: An Overview* in T. Boeri (ed.) *Unemployment in Transition Countries: Transient or Persistent*?, OECD, Paris.

Vercenik, J., 1993, *Czechoslovakia and the Czech Republic in 1990-93*, Institute of Sociology, Academy of Sciences, Prague.

World Bank, 1995, *Workers in an Integrating World*, World Development Report 1995.

4

Central and Eastern European labour markets in transition

Marek Góra

1. Introduction

The transition in the Visegrad countries (Czech Republic, Hungary, Poland and Slovak Republic) has been a long lasting process. Monitoring the process has been very interesting because it is both similar and dissimilar to "normal" performance of OECD economies. At the beginning of the transition, due to lack of information we could only make educated guesses about what was really happening. This was particularly true in the case of labour market developments. The data necessary for analysis were either non-existent, incomplete or not fully reliable. Now, after a few years of the transition we know quite a bit about Visegrad economies, including the performance of their labour markets. Moreover, we also have a general view of how Visegrad labour markets differ from those in developed countries and how they differ from each other.

There are a large number of excellent papers and reports on labour markets in the Visegrad economies. Some of them focus on specific issues, others on specific economies. Because of the extremely low Czech unemployment rate, most of them focus on the Czech labour market (see, for instance, Boeri and Burda, 1995). There are also studies comparing the Czech and Slovak republics, which are especially interesting because of the split of former Czechoslovakia into two separate states (Burda and Lubyova, 1995; Svejnar *et al.*, 1995), and comparative studies on such important issues as active labour market policies (Boeri, 1995; Lehmann, 1995; Rutkowski, 1996; and the papers quoted above). OECD/CCET reports provide very detailed information on the economies analysed in this paper.

However, statistics available for Visegrad countries are confusing to some extent since some pieces of information are not fully consistent with others. The most striking is the relationship between the aggregate activity level and unemployment.

The author would like to thank Hartmut Lehmann for his valuable comments on an earlier version of this text; Agnieszka Chlon for her assistance; Richard Woodward for his help in editing this text; and Mária Ladó, Martina Lubyova and Vit Šorm for their help in obtaining selected data from national sources. The author highly appreciated the easy access to all necessary data offered by the Polish Central Statistical Office.

Among the four countries referred to in this paper, the country with the shortest and shallowest recession following the switch of economic regimes has experienced the highest unemployment in the region. The relationship between output and unemployment is often not strong, but in the case of the Visegrad countries it looks as if it does not exist at all or is even reversed. A set of factors besides output fluctuations must have existed that played the major role in differentiating unemployment rates across these countries. In my opinion, the institutional framework of labour markets play the most important role.

The paper provides a very general view on the transition in the Visegrad economies.[1] It ends with the following conclusions. First, differences among Visegrad economies are not restricted to the difference between the Czech labour market and all the others. I try to show that each of the four countries has gone its own way of adjustment to transition shock. Each experienced some success but also paid a kind of price for that success. However, the paper points out that it is not labour demand that differentiates the labour markets. Second, the Visegrad labour markets, while different from each other, are not necessarily so different from what those in what we usually refer to as Western economies.

The following sections of the paper refer to selected labour market issues analysed for all the countries or for selected ones. More specific results refer mostly to the Polish labour market. In particular, in the last part of this paper I present a set of arguments for the thesis that non-labour market problems have a particularly strong effect on unemployment in Poland.

2. Aggregated labour market performance

In this section I present a comparison of behaviour of selected aggregated variables that are related to the labour market performance of the economies analysed. The variables are: unemployment rate, GDP growth, employment, size of labour force and labour productivity. Table 1 provides a synopsis view of the changes in the variables.

Table 1. Changes of selected variables during the transition.

	Unemployment rate	GDP (depth and length of recession)	Employment	Labour Force	Labour Productivity (GDP/E)
Czech Republic	↑(*)	↓↓↓	↓	↓↓↓	↓↓
Hungary	↑↑	↓↓	↓↓↓↓	↓↓↓↓(*)	↑↑↑
Poland	↑↑↑↑	↓ (*)	↓↓	– (*)	↑↑
Slovak Republic	↑↑↑	↓↓↓↓	↓↓↓	↓↓	↓

Note: Number of arrows ranks the countries: one arrow denotes the smallest change; four arrows the largest. Stars (*) denote cases of outliers, in which magnitude of changes was very different from that in the other countries; (–) denotes a change close to zero. E=number of employed workers.

Arrows that I use in the table are easier than indices for a quick comparison. The synopsis picture provided in Table 1 is illustrated by five figures presented in Annex A. Each figure illustrates one column of the table.

Table 1 provides a relative ranking of developments of selected variables in the economies analysed. A look at the table and the figures reveals that each of the four countries exhibits a different pattern of adjustment in the period of the transition.

Czech Republic

The relatively strong recession did not lead to much labour shedding. Although some labour shedding occurred, its impact on the labour market was reduced by relatively large outflows from the labour force. The gain is a very low unemployment rate; the cost is a strong decrease in labour productivity.

Hungary

GDP decline was smaller than that of the Czech Republic, but it was associated with large-scale labour shedding (the largest among the countries analysed). However, extremely large outflows from labour force caused the unemployment rate to remain low. The gain is the increase in labour productivity; the cost is the huge occupational deactivation of population.

Poland

The length and depth of recession were the least dramatic among the countries of the region. There was some labour shedding (moderate) and — which is the important feature of the Polish economy — there was virtually no decrease in the labour force. The gain is that productivity went up significantly; the cost is that the unemployment rate increased to the highest level in the region.

Slovak Republic

The Slovak economy behaved in the most "natural" way. The large output contraction caused relatively large labour shedding associated with some occupational deactivation. Productivity did not decrease much; unemployment increased more or less proportionally to depth of recession.

The overall picture of the labour market performance of Visegrad economies raises many questions which require a deeper investigation of behaviour of these economies. This paper focuses on a few selected problems.

3. Labour demand

Let us start with an attempt to find out whether it is labour demand that differentiates the economies of the region.

3.1 Absorption of unemployed workers into employment

The solution to the problem of unemployment lies in an increase in outflows from unemployment; the best solution lies in an increase in the outflow to jobs. From that point of view Visegrad economies are generally divided into a group with high outflows (Czech Republic) and a group with low outflows (the remaining group of economies). It is commonly stressed that high levels of unemployment in Visegrad economies (with the exception of the Czech Republic) have been built up because of extremely low outflows while inflows were at a moderate level by international standards (see e.g. OECD/CCET, 1993; OECD/CCET, 1995). Boeri (1995) provides recent annual outflow rates to jobs for the economies analysed (in 1994: 0.153 for Czech Republic; 0.049 for Hungary; 0.031 for Poland and 0.020 for Slovak Republic). These results show that the difference in performance between the two groups of economies remained large until recently.

While these outflow rates are very informative and useful for various types of analysis, they may be misleading in the case of labour markets in transition. Outflow rate relates outflows to the number of unemployed. This means that if unemployment is overstated (for any reason) the outflow rate (UE/U)[2] under-estimates the real dynamics of labour markets. Later in this paper, I will discuss the issue of overestimation of unemployment. Here, I will just present an alternative method of assessing the effect of labour demand on unemployment. Instead of the outflow rate I calculate the "absorption" rate (or hiring rate from unemployment), calculated as a ratio of outflow from unemployment into jobs to employment (UE/E). This measure says to what extent unemployed workers are absorbed by employment. Therefore possible over- or under-estimation of unemployment does not cause a perception bias of the scale of labour demand. Table 2 provides results of this calculation.[3]

Table 2. "Absorption" rates of unemployed into employment (administrative data).

	Czech Republic	Hungary	Poland	Slovak Republic
1992	0.0073	0.0035	0.0032	0.0073
1993	0.0040	0.0061	0.0038	0.0038
1994	0.0057	0.0075	0.0061	0.0035

Source: Statistical Yearbooks (Czech Republic, Hungary, Poland and Slovak Republic) and Boeri (1995).

Note: The rates provided in the table have been calculated as UE/E, where UE is outflow from unemployment to jobs and E is employment.

For 1994, — surprisingly — differences across the economies analysed are rather small. Moreover, the Czech rate is not the highest one. In 1992, it was two times larger than the Hungarian and Polish rates, but more recently the situation has changed.[4] The Visegrad economies absorb unemployment at similar paces. For 1994, Hungarian and Polish rates are even above the Czech one. What matters for the labour market situation is the stock of unemployment that has already been built up, not the current level of labour demand.

If the stocks have been built up mostly due to employment adjustments and therefore reflect economic performance, then even high absorption rates will not cause a miracle. However, if the build-up of mass unemployment also reflects an impact of labour market institutions then the absorption rate says more about the labour market performance than the outflow rate. The issue of the need of a reform of the institutional framework of the labour market in Poland is discussed in Section 4 (see also Góra, 1996).

3.2 Privatisation

Privatisation has played an important role in the labour reallocation in Visegrad economies. However, studies on privatisation are usually focused on non-labour reallocation issues so it is difficult to compare the impact of privatisation on labour markets in various countries of the region.

Labour force survey (LFS) results provide an opportunity to compare the role of the ownership change (both growth of the private sector and privatisation of formerly public firms). Below I present results of a comparison based on the Polish and Hungarian LFS.[5] Hungarian results come from Tóth (1996) and have been calculated for the period from April 1992 to March 1993. Polish results cover three yearly periods starting in 1992 (May to May panels).

In the period from Spring 1992 to Spring 1993, despite the large reduction of workers in the public sector, the quick growth of the private sector provided jobs for a number of workers comparable with the number of workers laid off in the period analysed.[6] The increase of jobs in the private sector during its quick growth halted the initial decline in employment in the whole economy.[7] In the same period employment was still being reduced (see Table 3).

Table 3. Change of employment stocks in Hungary and Poland (as percentage of the initial stock; LFS panels Spring 1992-Spring 1993).

	Hungary (%)	Poland (%)
Change of employment stock	- 8.0	0.0
of which:		
public sector	- 10.1	- 5.2
private sector	- 4.1	+ 5.2

Source: Tóth (1996), Polish LFS individual data and own calculations.

However, the private sector dismissed much fewer workers than the public sector. The positive impact of employment growth in the private sector is constantly present in the Polish economy (see Table 4).

Table 4. Change of stocks of employment by ownership sector in Poland (as percentage of the initial stock; LFS panels).

Yearly panels	Public sector	Private sector
May 1992 – May 1993	- 5.2	+ 5.2
May 1993 – May 1994	- 6.3	+ 7.9
May 1994 – May 1995	- 3.1	+5.7

Source: LFS individual data; own calculations.

In the panel May 93-May 94, three-quarters of all employment shifts from the public sector to the private one occurred due to privatisation of public firms (or their parts); in the panel May 94-May 95, that share was around two-thirds. These are rather rough approximations. Nevertheless, we can say that privatisation must play a major role in labour market transitions in Poland.

Before 1993, the Polish LFS does not enable us to calculate the privatisation component of employment shifts from the public sector to the private sector (these shifts themselves cannot be calculated). So, it is impossible to compare the results for the Polish economy with the corresponding results for the Hungarian economy as presented in Tóth (1996). In the Hungarian panel April 1992 — March 1993, the privatisation component of the total number of job to job transitions equals 80 per cent. However, even if the figures obtained for both economies (1992-1993 for Hungary versus 1993-1995 for Poland) are not directly comparable, they show roughly the same scale of the role of privatisation in job to job transitions.

Ways of privatisation in Hungary and Poland differ from each other much more strongly if we analyse not only job to job transitions but also transitions that pass through unemployment. The exit from unemployment to employment in the private sector is more than twice as high in Poland as in Hungary. It is also remarkable that the private sector in Poland plays an important role in the absorption of people previously not employed. They constituted 17 per cent of total private sector employment in 1993 according to LFS data. This effect is particularly strong in the case of young workers, whose main employment opportunities are in the private sector.

The flow rates provided in Table 5 show that private sector employment decisions contribute not only to easier exits from unemployment but also to more frequent inflows into unemployment. However, altogether the balance of private sector hiring and separations is strongly positive for employment. Especially if a person is unemployed, opportunities to be hired come from the private sector. In Hungary (see Tóth, 1996), private employment opportunities are of the same order as for public employment.

Table 5. Annual inflow and outflow rates into/from unemployment by ownership sector (Poland; LFS panels).

	Public sector		Private sector	
Yearly panels	inflow rate	outflow rate	inflow rate	outflow rate
May 1992 – May 1993	0.039	0.123	0.047	0.247
May 1993 – May 1994	0.035	0.111	0.045	0.247
May 1994 – May 1995	0.027	0.102	0.041	0.277

Source: LFS individual data; own calculations.

Note: Inflow rates have been calculated as $E_{pu}U/E_{pu}$ and $E_{pr}U/E_{pr}$; outflow rates: UE_{pu}/U and UE_{pr}/U.

4. The evolution of labour supply (Poland and Hungary)

As shown in Section 2, Visegrad economies strongly differ from each other with respect to the evolution of labour supply. Hungary and Poland are the two extremes.[8] Between the end of 1989 and 1994, Hungary lost 16.9 per cent of its labour force. In the same period, the Polish labour force grew by 2.1 per cent.[9] Population growth, and thus growth of labour force, is higher in Poland and lower in Hungary. That must have influenced the labour market situation in both countries. However, the difference in population growth cannot be the only factor determining labour supply developments.

Tables 6 and 7 illustrate a simple method of analysis of the labour supply developments. The method controls for the scale of cohorts entering working age each year. The analysis is focused on inflows and outflows into and from labour force. In the tables two periods are covered, namely the initial period of the transition (1990-1991) and the whole period of the transition for which we have data (1990-1994).

In both countries large groups of people entered pension systems. A substantial fraction of these flows out of labour force occurred due to early retirement schemes.[10] This type of policy to cut labour supply played an important role in Hungary as well as in Poland. However, Hungary and Poland differ from each other if we take into account also the "additional" net flow (inflow or outflow). The additional flow is defined as the residual number of people necessary to balance the stocks. This flow consists of people who leave the labour market for other than retirement reasons or enter the labour market for reasons other than simply coming of working age. If the net number of people flowing in or out is unnaturally large, we can suspect the presence of factors encouraging or discouraging participation in the labour market. I do not discuss such factors in this paper. Instead, I focus only on results of their presence.

Table 6. Labour force developments in Hungary (1990-1994).

	1990-1991	1990-1994
Change of stock of labour force (LF)	-294	-931
of which:		
change of stock of employment	-676	-1427
change of stock of unemployment	382	496
Inflow into LF (cohorts entering working-age)	348	870
Outflow from LF (people entering pension system)	402	954
Additional net inflow/**outflow** (ADD)	-240	-847

Source: Central Statistical Office (Hungary), Tóth (1996) and own calculations.
Notes: 1) Stock data are end of year data, so change of a stock in the period 1990-1991 means the change in the period from 31/12/1989 to 31/12/1991; 2) If ADD > 0 then ADD is net inflow into LF; If ADD < 0 then ADD is net outflow from LF (details are provided in Annex B).

Table 7. Labour force developments in Poland (1989-1994).

	1990-1991	1990-1994
Change of stock of labour force (LF)	209	372
of which:		
change of stock of employment	-1947	-2466
change of stock of unemployment	2156	2838
Inflow into LF (cohorts entering working-age)	1136	2986
Outflow from LF (people entering pension system)	2286	4048
Additional net **inflow**/outflow (ADD)	1359	1434

Source: Central Statistical Office (Poland); own calculations.
Notes: 1) Stock data are end of year data, so change of a stock in the period 1990-1991 means the change in the period from 31/12/1989 to 31/12/1991; 2) If ADD > 0 then ADD is net inflow into LF; If ADD < 0 then ADD is net outflow from LF (details are provided in Annex B).

Hungary

The increase in unemployment is much smaller than the decrease in employment. The increase in unemployment was equal to 57 per cent of the loss of employment in the first two years of the transition and only 35 per cent if we calculate that percentage for the whole period (see also Tóth, 1996). However, it was not only the outflow to the pension system that absorbed the remaining 65 per cent of the decrease in unemployment. Parallel to that outflow we have an additional outflow of roughly the same scale.

Poland

The increase in unemployment is larger than the decrease in employment. The effects of the policy to cut down labour supply (early retirement and very loose disability regulations) were overridden by the flow of people entering the labour market (see also Góra and Sztanderska, 1995). The additional inflow into labour force equalled more than one-half of the increase in unemployment (63 per cent in the first two years of the transition; 51 per cent if we take into account the whole period). So given demographic developments and policies to cut down labour supply, unemployment would have been much lower than the actual level registered at labour offices if the additional inflow had not appeared.

5. Worker flows (Poland)

5.1 Job to job transitions

Beginning from 1993 we can estimate the scale of job to job transitions in the Polish economy. In the panel May 93-May 94, job to job transition rate equals 0.060; in the panel May 94-May 95, that rate equals 0.055. In both panels, job to job transitions are mostly driven by the job to job transitions within the private sector (see Table 8).

Table 8. Job to job transitions by ownership sector in Poland (1993 – 1995).

	May 93 – May 94		May 94 – May 95	
	E_{pu}	E_{pr}	E_{pu}	E_{pr}
E_{pu}	0.020	0.020	0.014	0.022
E_{pr}	0.013	0.064	0.014	0.058

Source: LFS individual data; own calculations.

5.2 Selected indicators of labour market performance

The Polish labour market is commonly described as one characterised by high unemployment, moderate inflows, and very low outflows (see OECD/CCET, 1993).[11] Table 9 provides selected measures of labour market performance of the Polish economy. They have been calculated in exactly the same way as the ones provided in Alogoskoufis *et al.* (1995). The figures provided in Table 9 say more if they are compared with appropriate figures for OECD countries (see Table 9a).

The comparison of the Polish results and the results for selected other economies enables us to conclude that the Polish labour market does not differ very strongly from the labour markets of France, Germany, Spain or the UK.[12] In particular, the opinion on the moderate inflows and extremely low outflow rates in Poland proves to be only partially correct after 1992.

The bottom part of Table 9 provides information on unemployment spells duration. The share of long-term unemployed is not particularly high (it is similar to the average in Western European economies). At the same time, the average duration of unemployment spells is high. Both pieces of information suggest that there are two groups of workers among the unemployed, namely a group flowing out from unemployment relatively quickly and another group of people who are unemployed for a very long time. The latter group makes the average duration so long.

Table 9. Annual gross worker flows (percentage of source population)*.

	1992/1993	1993/1994	1994/1995
Unemployment inflow	7.8	7.4	6.0
Unemployment outflow	53.9	51.7	53.5
Employment inflow (H/E)	..	17.9	16.3
Employment outflow (S/E)	..	16.2	14.6
Gross worker turnover (WT=(H+S)/E)	..	34.5	30.9
Duration of unemployment (months)**	13	14	15
Proportion of LTU (%)***	36.5	38.1	40.4

Source: LFS, Central Statistical Office, own calculations
Notes: *Calculation based on May to May panels; ** Average duration of uncompleted spells among the current stock of unemployed; *** In May 1993, 1994, 1995 (respectively); (..) – data not available; H – hiring (UE + NE + EE); S – separations (EU + EN + EE); EE – job to job transitions.

Table 9a. Annual gross worker flows in selected OECD countries, 1987 (percentage of source population).

	France	Germany	Spain	UK
Unemployment inflow	3.88	3.01	1.61	7.8
Unemployment outflow	69.62	93.33	16.80	120.40
Employment inflow (H/E)	28.86	22.33	19.80	6.55
Employment outflow (S/E)	30.69	21.47	20.92	6.61
Gross worker turnover (WT=(H+S)/E)	59.55	43.80	40.72	13.16
Duration of unemployment (months)	8.02	8.04	6.12	10.67
Proportion of LTU (%)	39.52	36.98	51.48	42.16

Source: Alogoskoufis (1995).

5.3 *Quarterly outflows from unemployment*

Quarterly outflows from unemployment have a strongly seasonal pattern in Poland. The highest rates are observed in Spring and the lowest in Winter (see Figure 6). Average outflow from unemployment is around 0.25; average outflow to jobs is around 0.17. Both averages are not particularly low by European standards. However, Figure 6 illustrates two interesting facts. The first is that seasonal fluctuation of outflow rates is virtually identical each year (variations of the rates became smaller in 1995). This is strange since the period covered includes not only the period of the transition but also the period of the switch from recession to quick recovery. Outflows from unemployment did not react to that switch. The second remarkable feature of the Polish labour market is the behaviour of quarterly outflows from unemployment to non-participation. These outflows have exactly the same seasonal pattern as outflows to jobs. The more unemployed start jobs, the more unemployed flow out of the labour market. That is a strange relationship. A possible explanation of such behaviour of outflows can stem from the impact of the shadow economy. In fact some people who start shadow economy jobs answer the LFS questionnaire as if they were inactive. If this explanation is correct the real outflows from unemployment to employment are larger.

5.4 Steady-state unemployment

The panels used for calculation of the labour market performance indicators enable us also to calculate the steady-state (target) unemployment rate for Poland. For calculation of that rate (û) the following formula has been used:

$$\hat{u} = \frac{s+z}{s+h+n}$$

where: s = (EU+EN)/E; h = UE/E; z = (NU-UN-EN)/L; L = U+E; n = growth rate of L.

It is striking that starting from a similar level the target unemployment rate deviates more and more downwards from the actual unemployment rate (see Table 10). Although the difference between the two became pretty large, the period covered by observation is rather short, which makes it premature to draw strong conclusions.

Table 10. Actual vs. steady-state unemployment rate*.

	1992/1993	1993/1994	1994/1995
Unemployment rate (%)	12.3	13.5	12.6
Steady-state unemployment rate (%)	12.6	12.2	9.2

Source: LFS, Central Statistical Office, own calculations
Note: * Calculation based on May to May panels

6. The incidence of unemployment (Poland)

In Section 3, I presented results of estimation of the additional inflow into the Polish labour market. In this section I focus on unemployment incidence despite its source. However, even this section provides additional arguments to support the view that in the case of Poland the unemployment rate is over-estimated.

6.1 Unemployment incidence by category of unemployed

There are strong differences in unemployment incidence among various groups. In Table 11 one can see the following general regularities:

- unemployment rate for women is higher than that for men;
- unemployment rate for youth is extremely high;
- unemployment rate in big cities is significantly below the average unemployment rate; however, unemployment rate in rural areas is the lowest;
- the higher the educational attainment, the lower the unemployment rate.

Information on unemployment provided in Table 11 requires some more explanation.

Table 11. Unemployment incidence (1995 average, LFS).

Group description	Incidence (%)
Population at large	13.3
Youth	31.1
Women	14.7
Household heads	7.2
Big cities	12.1
Urban areas	16.4
towns under 10 000 inhabitants	17.3
Rural areas	11.9
University education	3.2
Secondary education	12.3
Primary education	15.7
primary vocational	16.7
Share of long-term unemployed	40.0

Source: LFS, Central Statistical Office

6.1.1 Female unemployment

The issue of gender differences in the labour market is very complex and goes beyond the scope of this study. I constrain the presentation to the most general information. The inflow rate to unemployment for women is very similar to that for men. What really makes unemployment rates for both genders different is the outflow rate. The rate for women is around 2/3 of the one for men (see Góra *et al.*, 1995). However, it is difficult to judge to what extent this is due to discrimination against women in the market or their own behaviour in the market; job search intensity is much lower for women than for men (see Góra, 1995).

6.1.2 Youth unemployment

In the case of unemployed youth, search intensity is much below the average level. However, unlike women, young unemployed have a very high exit rate to employment. This should help, so why is the scale of youth unemployment so large? Analysis of labour market flows provides the answer, namely, the inflow rate for youth is extremely high (more than twice as high as the average inflow rate for the whole population, see Góra *et al.*, 1995).

Although the scale of inflow explains why the stock of youth unemployment is so large, the question arises why the scale of inflow is so large. It is really large — around two-thirds of the total output of the education system[13] in Poland registers at labour offices. However, it seems strange that so many school-leavers register at labour offices after four years of pretty quick economic recovery. In fact the Polish labour market is harsh for older people, not for the young. So why?

I propose the following answer: School-leavers are strongly motivated to be unemployed by the existing structure of institutions. To make a long story short, instead of helping the school-leavers to avoid unemployment, the existing regulations require them to be unemployed before the help is provided. In the case of school-leavers the help means benefits and free tuition for various courses. The latter is probably even more important since the educational system, while ensuring a good general level of education, has not been able to adjust to new requirements of the labour market. So young people do not need much – just some computer skills, languages, etc. – and that is for free IF they stay unemployed for some time or at least register at labour offices (LOs). So school-leavers, which means the majority of the youth entering the labour market, use the opportunity. Unemployment jumps every June – September.

According to LFS (Aug 94 – Aug 95 panel),[14] the share of school-leavers successfully entering employment equals 0.33; flowing into unemployment 0.52; and remaining non-participating 0.15. These results are consistent with the information coming from administrative sources; based on the same panel estimation, the exit rate to jobs for unemployed school-leavers equals 0.49. It is much above the rate for the remaining group of unemployed (0.36).

Evaluation of active labour market policies is usually based on the impact of various active measures on outflows from unemployment. Policies targeted at school-leavers not only help them to find jobs but also strongly encourage them to become unemployed.[15] The net effect of that is ambiguous. Hence, evaluation of policies focused only on outflows can be misleading.

6.1.3 The impact of education

Incidence of unemployment is strongly dependent on education. Education pays an important role in Poland nowadays. Both employment opportunities and wages are strongly positively related to education (see Rutkowski, J., 1996). On the other hand, that situation sheds light on the central problem of the labour market, namely unskilled workers. More precisely, the group having the largest problems in the labour market are unskilled (especially young) women living outside big cities (see Góra *et al.*, 1995).

This fact strongly suggests that both the problem of female unemployment and the problem of youth unemployment are in fact dependent on the underlying major problem of lack of skills among the unemployed. Of those who are unemployed and do not have skills, women and youth workers are the weakest. It is easier to find a job for an unskilled man than for a woman. On the other hand, unskilled unemployed are weakly motivated to seek a job since they know that their wage will be low anyway. Most young uneducated women are usually married or live with their parents, so they are not bread-winners (unemployment incidence for household heads is substantially below the average rate driven upward by the remaining groups of unemployed).

The marginal effect of education on the probability of exit to jobs (multinominal logic regression, see Góra, 1995) is much stronger for women in comparison to men. This does not mean better employment opportunities for better educated women but worse employment opportunities for women with less education.

6.2 Registration and unemployment benefits

Data on unemployment registration and benefit claimants can be taken not only from administrative data sources. Some information can also be obtain from the LFS, namely, we can match labour market status of people with their declaration of their status at LOs. Table 12 provides the most interesting information.

Table 12. LFS vs. registration at LOs.

	U_{reg}/U	U_{reg}/Reg	U_{ben}/U_{reg}	U_{ben}/Ben
1992	0.69	0.94	0.73	0.95
1995	0.78	0.65	0.51	0.71

Source: LFS individual data; own calculations.
Notes: 1) U_{reg} – LFS unemployed registered at LOs; U_{ben} – LFS unemployed receiving registered and receiving benefits; Reg – total number of people declaring registration at LOs (not necessarily LFS unemployed); Ben – total number of people declaring they receive unemployment benefits (not necessarily LFS unemployed); 2) Reg and Ben cover only those people who are LFS unemployed or non-participating. People who are employed (LFS) do not answer appropriate questions. It is likely that some of them are also benefit claimants.

First, the share of people who claim they are registered and are LFS unemployed in the total number of LFS unemployed, although increasing, is rather low. There is also a large group of people who are not unemployed according to the LFS definition but claim they are registered. The percentage of such people among all declaring registration is even higher than in Spain (25 per cent among unemployment benefit claimants and 30 per cent among non-benefit claimants (see Blanchard *et al.*, 1995), where because of extremely high unemployment such an effect might be expected on a large scale.

If we took into account that a large group of unemployed do not really seek any job (even though they declare that they do) the share of LFS unemployed (really seeking jobs) in the total number of people registered at LOs would go down to less than 50 per cent.

6.3 *Low search intensity*

In the period from May 1992, the starting date of LFS in Poland, to November 1995 around one-quarter of the LFS unemployed did not perform any search activity.[16] They were just registered. Low search intensity of the unemployed is also observed in other countries. For instance in Spain the same category accounts for 40 per cent of total unemployment (see Blanchard *et al.*, 1995). However, in Poland being registered at an LO hardly means seeking a job. Out of those people who were registered as unemployed at labour offices in any sub-period of 1990-1994 and started jobs afterwards only 5-6 per cent found a job at a labour office (see Góra *et al.*, 1995). This percentage is not just a calculation result; it is fully in line with anecdotal evidence and knowledge of people registered at LOs. That fact is even more striking if we realise that the ratio of unemployed to LO staff members equals around 1 300:1.[17] Finding a job at an LO is rather rare. Most of those people who successfully find jobs do it on their own. Here we have another analogy with Spain where LOs intermediate about 9-10 per cent of all matching (see Blanchard *et al.*, 1995).

The question arises: How does low search intensity affect chances of finding a job? One might argue that the very limited number of vacancies causes the unemployed not to seek jobs intensively. The multinominal logic analysis of transitions from unemployment to employment suggests the opposite (see Góra, 1996). Those unemployed who seek jobs not only at LOs but also on their own have a significantly higher probability of finding a job than unemployed who are just registered at LOs (0.170 and 0.127 respectively (quarterly), hence they also have shorter average unemployment spells. This effect is even stronger for those unemployed who seek jobs very intensively. Their exit to job probability equals 0.188 which means that the average unemployment spell is around one-third shorter than the average spell of those who are only registered and do not perform any active job search. Shorter unemployment spells mean not only a decrease in unemployment but also less severe social consequences of unemployment.

The low search intensity of the unemployed in Poland is not a result of the discouraged workers effect. The percentage of LFS long-term unemployed who register but do not engage in any search activity is slightly below the corresponding percentage of all unemployed.

In Poland, a large group of those people who declare no other search activities than registration at an LO most likely do not seek any job in fact.

6.4 Over-estimated unemployment rate in Poland

Institutional incentives cause registration at LOs to be attractive for a group of people who are not necessarily unemployed. According to unpublished estimations of the Polish central statistical office around 14 per cent of people claiming unemployment benefits were involved in unregistered employment in the first eight months of 1995. Góra *et al.* (1995) show that the problem of unregistered work of registered unemployed is not the most important one. Much more important is that a large number of registered unemployed either do not seek any job or are unable to start a job if they were offered one. Among non-benefit claimants the percentage was probably much higher. LOs do not have real motivation to monitor non-benefit claimants since they do not pay these people. For the registered unemployed people the situation looks different. They are motivated to register even if they do not claim benefits (see Góra, 1996).

Is LFS data on unemployment sensitive to institutional regulations? Perhaps. In a country in which registration covers a large number of people who do not really seek jobs we can observe the following effect: People are registered and when asked whether they seek a job they say "yes" because they are registered. Consequently, they are considered as LFS unemployed. If those people were properly investigated at LOs, they would be deregistered and in the questionnaire they would say "no" answering the question on job search. So, improper work of LOs can have an effect on the overstating of the scale of LFS unemployment.

However, even if we do not go so far and do not blame over-registration at LOs as being the reason for the overestimation of unemployment, then LFS still over-estimates unemployment in Poland. Answers to the LFS question on the job search method show that around 3-3.5 per cent of people classified as LFS unemployed explicitly declare they do not seek any job — despite their positive answer to the direct question on whether they seek a job. Without any additional assumptions, this means that the average LFS unemployment rate in 1995 was not above but slightly below 13 per cent.

Conclusions

Labour markets in the Visegrad countries have experienced a similar transition from the excess labour demand typical for centrally planned economies (i.e. zero unemployment) to regular market adjustment. However, transitions have significantly differed from each other in Visegrad economies. The chapter highlights the differences and points out the main gains and losses in each case.

In this chapter I tried to present a critical view on labour market developments in Visegrad countries (Czech Republic, Hungary, Poland and Slovak Republic) during the transition. Given the limited availability of adequate data, I focused my presentation on specific problems and on the four countries.

The paths of transition and consequently the rates of unemployment strongly differ in Visegrad economies. The first and most intuitive explanation of such differentiation is the difference in labour demand developments in each of the economies. However, the relation between GDP developments and unemployment does not show a reasonable pattern. The highest unemployment rate is observed in Poland, the country with the shortest and the shallowest recession in the region. Even more surprisingly, hiring rates from unemployment do not differ substantially among the economies analysed. Hence, low unemployment absorption into employment cannot exclusively be blamed for higher unemployment in some countries than in others.

An important factor in explaining different labour market performance in Visegrad economies is the evolution of labour supply in these economies. This is the factor that strongly differs in the region. The two extremes, namely Hungary (large contraction of labour force) and Poland (virtually no change of labour force in comparison to the pre-transition period) are analysed in detail in the chapter. In both countries, policies have been used extensively to cut labour supply. In Hungary, the retirement policy and general deactivation of the population have been parallel, while in Poland results of the retirement policy have been offset by an inflow into the labour force which is not related to population growth.

The main conclusion of the paper is that Visegrad countries have chosen different paths of adjustment during transition, and therefore particular details of the outcome of transition in the region are difficult to compare. Moreover, some indicators — such as the rate of unemployment — probably must be read differently in each case. If labour market policies are a substitute for the social safety net, then the rate of unemployment reflects the scale of a whole set of social problems rather than exclusively labour market problems (Poland can serve as an example here). In the period of transition, the institutional framework implemented in each country can heavily affect labour market performance.

The chapter shows that institutional differences are really important and drive labour market performance in these economies. In the case of Poland, analysis suggests that unemployment was only partially caused by the recession of 1990-1991. Hence, the solution to unemployment in Poland probably lies not only in economic growth. In 1995, the economy reached the pre-transition level of output with employment around 13-15 per cent below the pre-transition level. Growth helps, but even growth as strong as that observed in Poland cannot absorb unemployment caused, to a large extent, by non-economic factors, such as unemployment policies which provide a kind of substitute for the social safety net. Consequently, the Polish rate of unemployment reflects the scale of a whole set of various social problems rather than only the scale of labour market problems. This could be the case — in varying degrees — in other Visegrad countries.

Even though institutional frameworks of some Visegrad labour markets are imperfect, labour market performance in these economies is not necessarily much worse than in Western European OECD countries. Limitations in the availability of appropriate data allow the author to estimate main labour market indicators (based on workers flows: annual inflows, outflows, hiring, separations, workers turnover, average duration of unemployment spells and steady-state unemployment) only for Poland. The encouraging conclusion with respect to Poland is that the indicators do not differ substantially from the results available for European OECD countries. The chapter also provides selected information on the impact of privatisation on labour market developments in Visegrad countries.

Notes

[1] The text left aside some important issues, such as the level of labour hoarding carried over from the command economy (see Góra, 1993), disinflation, and so on.

[2] The following notation will be used throughout the paper: U=number of unemployed workers, E=number of employed workers, N=number of inactive workers; UE, NE, EE refer to numbers of workers shifting to employed status from unemployment, inactivity or employment, respectively; EU, EN refer to shifts from employment to unemployment and inactivity, respectively; UN=movement from unemployment to inactivity; etc.

[3] In order to avoid the problem of low availability of information on yearly outflows, the rates provided in the table have been calculated indirectly using the following formula:

$$\frac{A_t}{E_{t-1}} = \frac{A_t}{U_{t-1}} * \frac{U_{t-1}}{LF_{t-1}} * \frac{LF_{t-1}}{E_{t-1}}$$

where: LF is labour force stock (E+U); E is employment stock (end of year); U is unemployment stock (end of year); A is outflow from unemployment to jobs; A_t/U_{t-1} is outflow to jobs rate; U/LF is unemployment rate.

[4] The absorption rate provides an important piece of information on labour market performance. However, it can also be misleading if applied for time comparisons of labour demand in one country since high values of UE can cause an increase in E, and thus a decrease of the ratio. So the use of the rate should be limited to static comparisons of labour markets, which is the aim of the author in this part of the text.

[5] Unfortunately I have not been successful in getting the same type of data for the other two economies analysed.

[6] In 1992, both sectors employed roughly the same number of workers. This is why the rates are exactly the same.

[7] The period before 1992 is covered only by administrative data.

[8] The Czech Republic and Slovak Republics lie in between Hungary and Poland. Nevertheless, it would also be interesting to make the same type of calculation for CR and SR. However, I have not been able to obtain appropriate data on yearly inflows into pension systems in those countries.

[9] Indices provided in Figure 4 (Annex A) illustrate changes of average labour force (each year), so the indices slightly differ from the ones in the text and Tables 5 and 6.

[10] For a detailed analysis of outflows from labour force in Hungary see Tóth (1996)

[11] This opinion is also formulated with respect to most other transition economies (for instance, Hungary; see OECD/CCET, 1995).

[12] Unfortunately, I do not have data appropriate for calculation of the same indicators for other Visegrad countries.

[13] The share of school-leavers (higher than primary educational attainment) registering at LOs was 57 per cent in 1995. However, if we take into account in fact that university graduates do not really

experience unemployment we can narrow the analysis to those with below university educational attainment. That leads to a share of around 2/3.

[14] August was chosen as the best moment to analyse behaviour of school-leavers.

[15] A new regulation on school-leavers has been introduced at the very beginning of 1996. Unemployment benefits – now called "stipends" – are paid only those school-leavers who are "active" which means they take part in programmes (with the special focus on training courses). This regulation clearly suggest that school-leavers should postpone seeking jobs. This will probably result in even better effectiveness of training. The transition from school to work is a difficult problem, so providing some help is probably a good idea. Given the huge inflow of school-leavers into unemployment it would be better for all parties if all the measures for school-leavers are available for all of them, not requiring registration.

[16] 24 per cent of all LFS unemployed – although they claim they seek jobs – cannot name any job search method they used. That share reaches as much as 31 per cent in the case of registered LFS unemployed (32 per cent among unemployment benefit claimants).

[17] The proportion concerns only those LO staff members who directly deal with the unemployed and try to help them to find a job.

References

Alogoskoufis, G., Bean, C., Bertola, G., Cohen, D., Dolado, J. and Saint-Paul, G., 1995, *Unemployment: Choices for Europe*, CEPR, London.

Blanchard, O., Jimeno, J.F., Andrés, J., Bean, C., Malinvaud, E., Revenga, A., Saint-Paul, G., Snower, D.J., Solow, R., Taguas, D., and Toharia, L., 1995, *Spanish Unemployment: Is There a Solution?,* CEPR, London.

Boeri, T., 1995, "Labour Market Flows and the Scope of Labour Market Policies in Central and Eastern Europe", OECD/CCET Technical Workshop, *What can we learn from the experience of transition countries with labour market policies?,* OECD/CCET.

Boeri, T. and Burda, M., 1995, "Active Labour Market Policies, Job Matching and the Czech Miracle", *European Economic Review* (forthcoming).

Burda, M. and Lubyova, M., 1995, "The Impact of Active Labour Market Policies: A Closer Look at the Czech and Slovak Republics", in Newbery, D, (ed.) *Tax and Benefit Reform in Central and Eastern Europe*, CEPR.

Dyba, K. and Svejnar, J., 1995, "A Comparative View of Economic Developments in the Czech Republic", in Svejnar, J. (ed.), *The Czech Republic and Economic Transition in Eastern Europe*, Academic Press.

Employment Observatory No. 8, European Commission.

Góra, M., 1993, "Labour Hoarding and Its Estimates in Central and Eastern European Economies in Transition", in *Employment and Unemployment in Economies in Transition: Conceptual and Measurement Issues*, OECD/CCET and Eurostat.

Góra, M., 1995, "Outflow from Unemployment to Employment in Poland", *Seventh Annual Conference of the European Association of Labour Economists*, Vol. VI, Lyon, September.

Góra, M., 1996, "Institutional Sources of the Increase in Unemployment in Poland", in Mickiewicz, T. and Smith, A. (eds), *Economic Transition in Poland: Constraints and Progress*, School of Slavonic and East European Studies (forthcoming).

Góra, M. and Sztanderska, U., 1995, "Labour Market Dynamics in Poland: 1990-1994", Programme "Social Policy Reforms", Institute of Public Affairs, Warsaw [mimeo].

Góra, M., Socha, M.W. and Sztanderska, U, *1995, Analiza polskiego rynku pracy w latach 1990-1994*, Central Statistical Office/Ministry of Labour and Social Policy [in Polish].

Lehmann, H., 1995, "Active Labour Market Policies in the OECD and in Selected Transition Countries", Policy Research Working Paper No. 1502, The World Bank, Washington.

OECD/CCET, 1993, *The Labour Market in Poland*, OECD/CCET, Paris.

OECD/CCET, 1995, *Social and Labour Market Policies in Hungary*, OECD/CCET, Paris.

Rutkowski, J., 1996, "High Skills Pay Off: The Changing Wage Structure during Economic Transition", *The Economics of Transition* (forthcoming).

Rutkowski, M., 1996, "Labour Market Policies in Transition Economies", *MOCT-MOST* 6, pp. 19-38.

Statistical Yearbook, Central Statistical Office, Warsaw.

Svejnar, J., Terrell, K. and Münich, D., 1995, Unemployment in the Czech and Slovak Republics, in Svejnar, J. (ed.), *The Czech Republic and Economic Transition in Eastern Europe*, Academic Press.

Tóth, I., 1996, *Employment and Unemployment in Hungary*, Budapest [mimeo].

Annex A

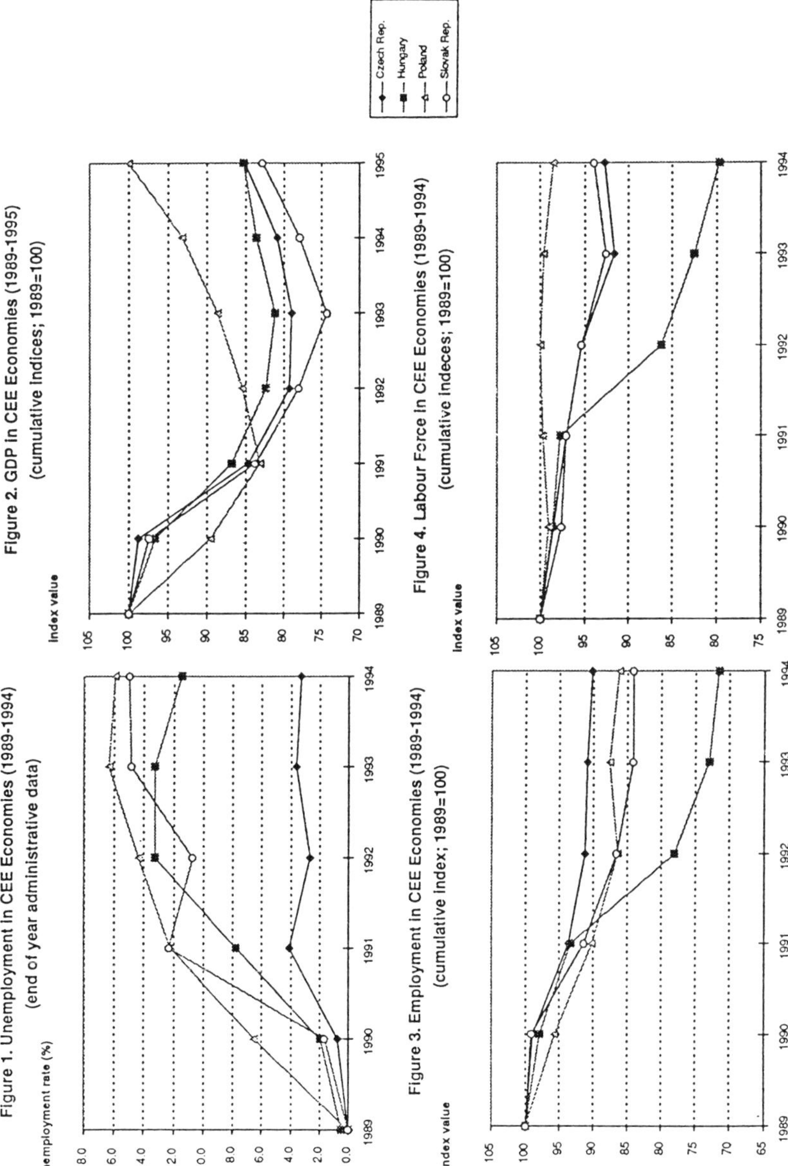

Figure 1. Unemployment in CEE Economies (1989-1994) (end of year administrative data)

Figure 2. GDP in CEE Economies (1989-1995) (cumulative Indices; 1989=100)

Figure 3. Employment in CEE Economies (1989-1994) (cumulative Index; 1989=100)

Figure 4. Labour Force in CEE Economies (1989-1994) (cumulative indeces; 1989=100)

Figure 5. Labour productivity in CEE Economies (1989-1995)
(cumulative index; 1989=100)

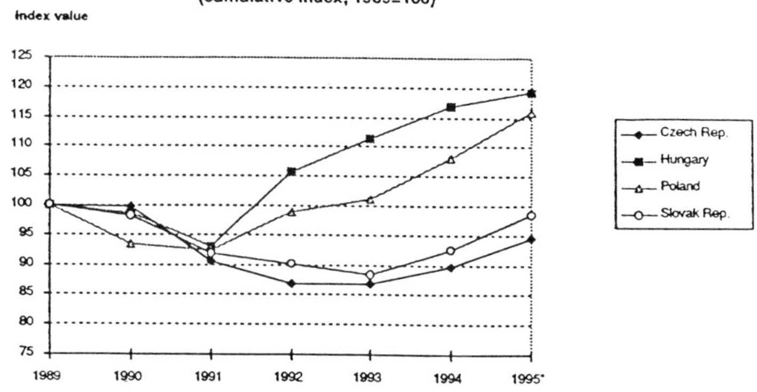

Figure 6. Outflows from Unemployment
(Poland; LFS quarterly panels)

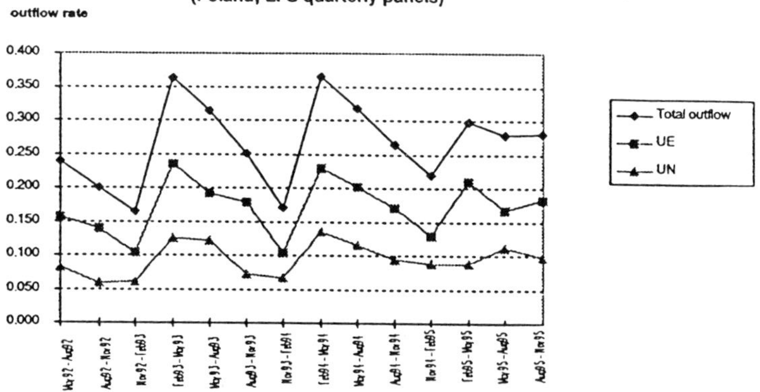

Annex B

Additional inflow/outflow has been calculated in the following way:

1. $\Delta E_t = E_t - E_{t-1}$
2. $\Delta U_t = U_t - U_{t-1}$
3. $\Delta LF_t = \Delta E_t + \Delta U_t$
4. We assume: Inflow into LF = the number of people reaching working age in year **t**
5. We assume: Outflow from LF = the numbers of new pensioners in year **t**
6. If (4) and (5) are close to reality, the following should hold:
   $\Delta LF_t = I_t - A_t$
7. If (6) does not hold, it means that an additional factor (ADD) has to be introduced into that equation in order to balance the stocks. Now,
   $\Delta LF_t = I_t - A_t + ADD$
8. If ADD>0 then we observe an additional net inflow into the labour force
9. If ADD<0 then we observe an additional net outflow from the labour force

In the equations above:
E - employment (end of year data); U - unemployment (end of year data); LF - labour force; I – inflow into labour force; A – outflow from labour force.

5

Reforming tax and benefit systems in Central Europe: lessons from Hungary

David M. Newbery

1. Introduction

Hungary was the first transition economy to make serious and sustained efforts to transform its economy, first from central planning to a form of market-guided socialism of the New Economic Mechanism of 1968, then, in response to sluggish growth in the 1980s, increasingly towards the West European model. A key objective of the reform strategy was the replacement of annually renegotiated bilateral bargaining relationships between ministries and their client enterprises by a stable, legal, and uniform set of taxes and market institutions for allocating resources, to provide better incentives for longer term investments in efficiency and productivity. Hungary therefore embarked on major reforms of indirect taxes in 1987 and direct taxes in 1988, before the fall of the Berlin Wall signalled a wider and more irresistible commitment to transition in Central and Eastern Europe (CEE). Whereas Hungary has continued its gradual, government-directed reform programme, which stretches back to the decentralisation reforms of 1968, Poland and Czechoslovakia chose a more radical approach to transition with a 'Big Bang' of price and trade liberalisation, current account convertibility, economic stabilization, and, as rapidly as feasible, the attendant institutional and fiscal reforms to create the institutions of a market economy.

It is convenient to consider these Visegrad countries together, as they are at a comparable state of institutional maturity, and share the plausible aspiration of joining the European Union, while lying at the centre of Europe with its shared historical experience[1]. Fiscal reform is central to the process of transforming a Soviet-type economy to a market economy, for with the emergence of a significant

Support from the British Economic and Social Research Council under the project R00023 3787 Tax and Social Security in Hungary, from the Commission of the European Communities under Contract ACE-92-0432-R is gratefully acknowledged. The paper draws on work commissioned by the Commission of the European Communities under PHARE Contract Taxation and Tax reform in Central and Eastern Europe, reported in Newbery (1995b), and on collaborative work with Tamas Révész reported in Newbery and Révész (1995a,b). I have benefited extensively from close collaboration with Sarah Jarvis, Paul Kattuman, Steve Pudney, Gerry Redmond and Holly Sutherland, as well as colleagues in Hungary at the Statistical Office.

private sector, the boundaries between the public and private sectors needs to be more sharply drawn. The old system in which the bulk of taxes came directly or indirectly from state-owned enterprises, and were just one part of the system of allocation of resources, has to be replaced by a legally-based, incentive-oriented and preferably stable system of raising the revenue needed for continuing public activities. Many of the old revenue-raising purposes, for providing subsidies to enterprises and financing capital formation, are no longer appropriate to a market economy and should disappear with the restructuring of the state sector. Other activities, some of which may have been financed directly by enterprises, such as many social services, education and housing facilities, must now either be transferred to the private sector (in the case of housing, resort hotels, etc.) or to the state (Rein and Wörgötter, 1995). In addition, the state inherits new responsibilities with the emergence of open unemployment requiring unemployment insurance payments, while lagging infrastructural investment is unlikely to be entirely privately financed. Although telecommunications is a natural industry to privatise and attract direct foreign investment and expertise, transport infrastructure will continue to require state finance, assisted by the growth in revenue from vehicle taxation. Finally, the whole system of social security (pensions, health) now requires explicit sources of revenue from workers and firms to replace the often implicit transfers within the state sector.

It might appear that the detailed design of an entirely new tax system would be a challenging task, but in practice the choice was fairly tightly circumscribed by the desire of these countries to join the European Union eventually. This meant that enterprise taxes were to be replaced by a standard corporation tax, based on Western accounting concepts of profit net of depreciation and interest, a personal income tax, social security taxes financed by employer and employee contributions, withholding through Pay-As-You-Earn, value added taxes (VAT) to replace turnover taxes, excise taxes on fuel, alcohol and tobacco, and *ad valorem* customs duties. There are no commonly agreed models for local taxation, property taxation, and even personal capital income taxation, and perhaps for that reason the design of these important elements of the tax system in most transitional countries is still in flux.

If the broad design features of the new tax system were reasonably clear, governments still needed to make difficult decisions about the balance between taxes, the tax rates, the level of revenue as a share of GDP with implications for the amount of redistribution to be achieved through the tax system, the mechanisms to be employed, and the general level of expenditure. Such decisions were always going to be difficult, but were made far more difficult by the unprecedented collapse in output in the transition countries. Figures 1 and 2 show the evolution of real GDP and industrial output in the Visegrad countries from 1989 to 1995 (estimated). The trajectories are shown on logarithmic scales, so that equal proportional changes are shown by equal vertical changes, with equal slopes having equal proportional rates of change. The Czech and Slovak republics separated in 1992, and their previous evolution is that of the combined CSFR. The figures also show the evolution of the US economy from 1929 to 1935 (exactly 60 years earlier) through the Great Depression.

Fig. 1 Real GDP in Depression
Central Europe 1989-95 US 1929-35

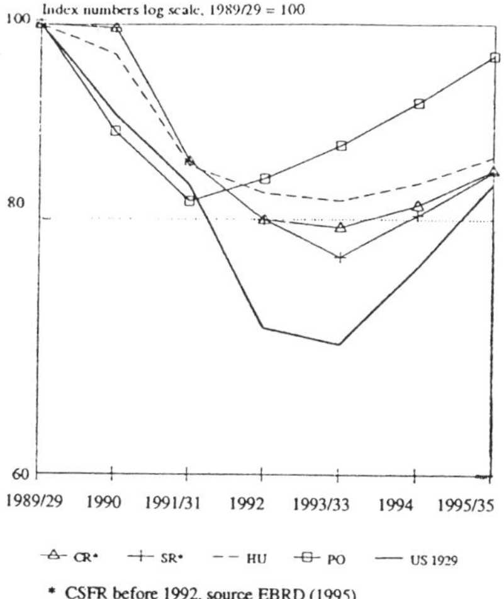

* CSFR before 1992, source EBRD (1995)

Fig. 2 Real Industrial Output
Central Europe 1989-95, US 1929-34

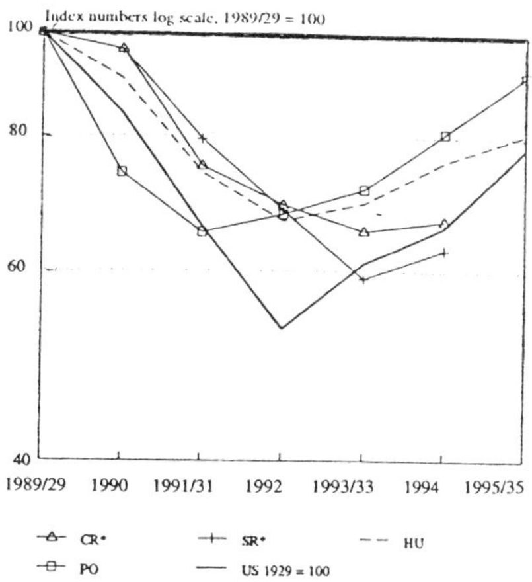

* CSFR before 1992
EBRD (1995), US Dept. of Commerce

Fig. 3 General Government Revenue
Pre- and Post-Reform

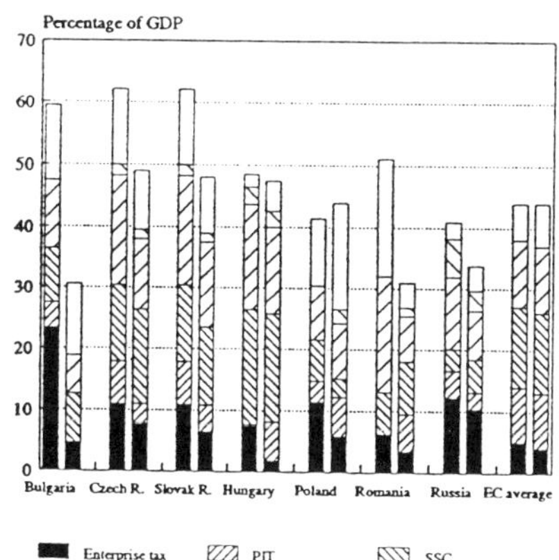

EBRD Transition Report Oct 1994 T6.5
Left column is pre-reform
EC dom. ind. and trade taxes combined

Fig. 4 Dependency Ratios
1985 and 1992

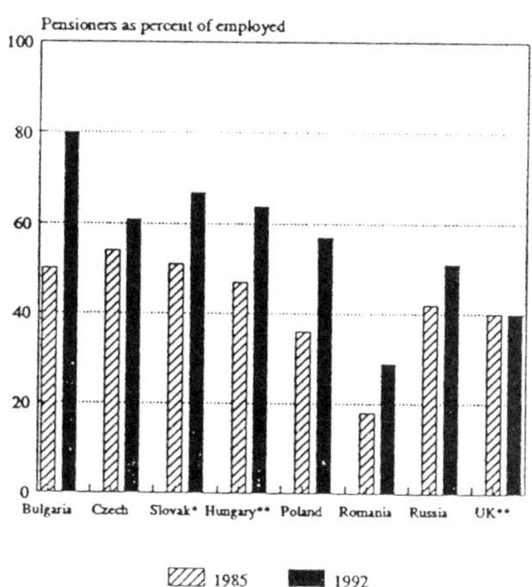

IMF World Economic Oct 1994 T18
* for 1990 not 1985
** old ager or National Insurance only

Figure 1 shows the US experiencing a deeper trough in GDP than the Visegrad countries (though many other transitional countries have fared worse), but, with the exception of Poland, none of the countries has achieved the same rapid rebound from the trough. In contrast, Figure 2 suggests that with the possible exception of the Czech and Slovak republics (for which 1995 data were not available), real industrial output now appears to be growing at US recovery rates.[2] Compared to the Visegrad countries, most of the countries of the former Soviet Union have experienced substantially larger falls in output (IMF, 1994).

Even without a fall in output, fiscal reform in the context of a movement to a market economy was bound to create tensions. Soviet-type economies secured most of their revenue through a relatively small number of over-large state-owned enterprises, whose financial flows (if not their economic activity) were transparent to the ministry of finance and closely monitored. Essentially all profits were available for reallocation through the state financial system, and wages (effectively after-tax) could be centrally determined. The typical Western market economy collects a very small share of revenue from profits taxation, relies more heavily on personal income tax, but collects a smaller fraction of GDP in tax revenue. Figure 3 compares the Visegrad countries together with Bulgaria, Romania and Russia pre- and post-reform (taken in most cases as 1989 and 1993) with the average for the EU. The figure shows clearly the relatively larger share of GDP taken in taxes and other revenues compared to the EU, and the substantially larger share of enterprise taxes pre-reform.

The reforming countries were thus posed with a difficult choice. Should they replace the fall in enterprise taxes by increases in other taxes or by cuts in public expenditure and a lowering of the overall share of taxation in GDP? The case for reducing public expenditure was strong on theoretical and practical grounds. Under the old system, although the state extracted most of the profits from the enterprises, it also directly or indirectly financed much of their investment. In a market economy, responsibility for enterprise investment falls upon the company and the capital markets, and is no longer a charge to the state. Similarly, many of the subsidies were part of a complex web of interventions in prices between enterprises and external markets that would disappear with liberalisation. The more difficult question concerned the burden of taxation on individuals, where arguments for increasing taxes or cutting expenditure seemed more finely balanced.

Here again, the Visegrad countries differ from Western market economies in the very high share of dependents (mostly voters) to active workers. This will be one of the sterner tests of a successful transition to a market economy. Figure 4 shows the very high dependency ratios (the ratio of pensioners to workers) for various CEECs compared to the UK, and the dramatic increase since 1985. Given that pensioners vote and are the prime recipients of transfers, the political dynamics of fiscal reform are likely to be extremely difficult. One of the key questions to explore, therefore, is the relative position of pensioners and workers, how they have fared during the transition, and what role financing pension payments plays in the structure of taxation.

Fig. 5 General Government Expenditure Pre- and Post-Reform

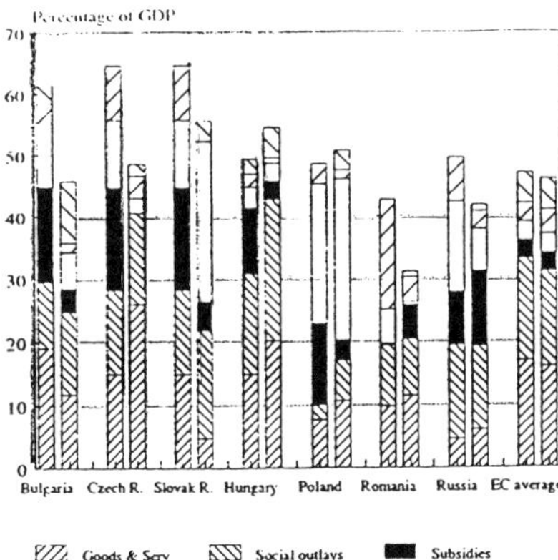

EBRD Transition Report Oct 1994 T6.6
For EC soc outlays=transfers to indivs
EC subsidies are to enterprises

Fig. 6 Real Government Revenue and Expenditure Czech and Slovak Republics* 1989-93

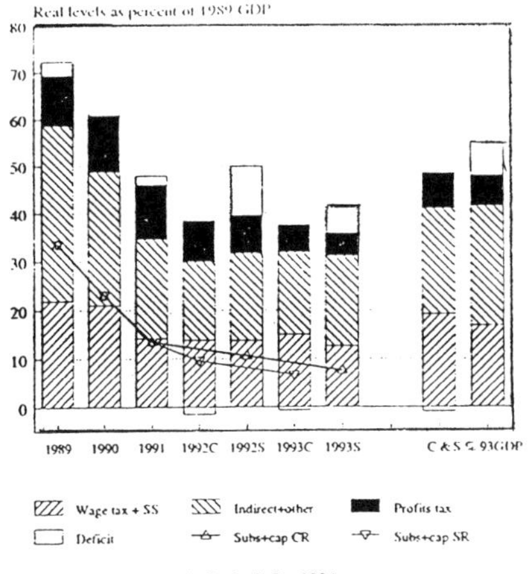

IMF World Economic Outlook Oct 1994
* CSFR 1989-91, after shown as C or S

Fig. 7
Real Government Revenue and Expenditure
Hungary 1987-94

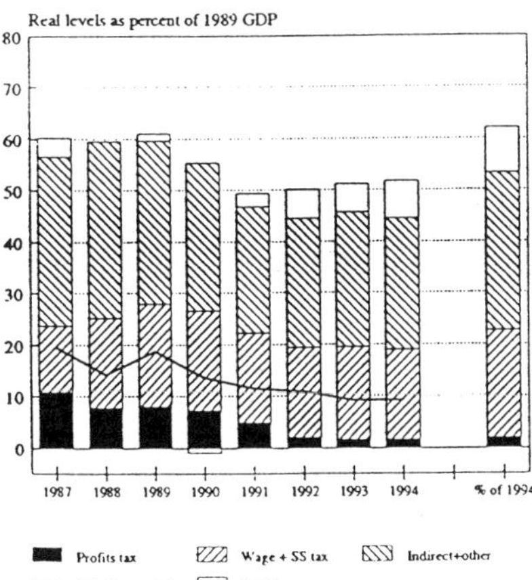

IMF World Economic Outlook May 1996
* Surplus shown negative

Fig. 8
Real Government Revenue and Expenditure
Poland 1989-94

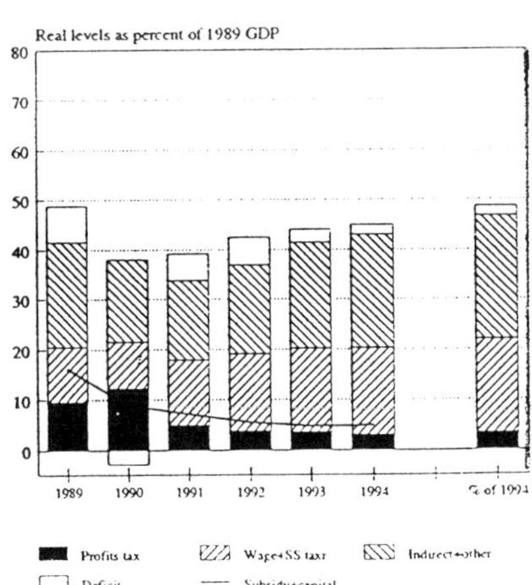

IMF World Economic Outlook May 1996
* Surplus shown negative

2. Government revenues and expenditure

Compared to richer EU countries, and certainly compared to countries of comparable purchasing power, the East European countries have a higher share of government expenditure in GDP than predicted for market economies. Figure 5 shows that while Bulgaria, the Czech and Slovak republics, Romania and Russia have succeeded in cutting expenditures, Hungary and Poland have not, perhaps because of the considerable increase in social outlays in both cases. Figure 5 also reveals the sharp decrease in subsidies (except for Russia) and expenditure on capital formation, in both cases moving towards the EU average. Social outlays have increased as a share of GDP and interest payments have risen, though high inflation in some countries may exaggerate the real cost of such interest rates, as the real value of the national debt is inflated away.

Figures 6-8 show the evolution of real government revenue and expenditure in the Visegrad countries between 1989 and 1993 (1987 and 1993 in the case of Hungary, where the tax reforms came earlier). Expenditure is given by the total height of the column, except when the budget is in surplus, in which case the surplus is shown below the line and should be subtracted. Revenues and expenditures are expressed as a percentage of 1989 GDP, while the right hand column re-expresses the 1993 levels as a per cent of 1993 GDP to show the evolution of tax shares. As real GDP fell in all four countries over this period, even maintaining a constant revenue and expenditure share in GDP would have necessitated cuts in revenue and expenditure.

In the Czech and Slovak republics, shown in Figure 6, the fall in both revenue and expenditure has been quite dramatic, with revenues falling by nearly 50 per cent in real terms. (After the divorce of 1992, the columns are labelled for the country e.g. 1992C = the Czech Republic in 1992.) Indirect tax revenue has fallen most sharply, and profits taxation has fallen less than in most other transition countries, perhaps reflecting the delayed restructuring of the large enterprise sector. On the expenditure side, subsidies and capital expenditures have fallen by over two-thirds (shown by the continuous line) but while the initial small deficit in Czechoslovakia has been replaced by a very small surplus in the Czech Republic, the Slovak Republic is still running large deficits.

Neither Hungary (Figure 7) nor Poland (Figure 8) has succeeded in cutting expenditure as a share of GDP, implying that expenditures have fallen in line with GDP (though Poland has increased its tax share in GDP). On the revenue side, profits taxes have collapsed in Hungary and have halved in Poland as would be expected with the lowering of the profits tax rate, recessionary circumstances, and an increased share of the small firm sector. Hungary introduced a personal income tax in 1988, essentially payable by enterprises, as wages were grossed up to leave the same after-tax wage, and enterprises with-held through PAYE. Consequently wage (or personal income) taxes and social security (SS) taxes increased between 1987 and 1989 in real terms as profits taxes fell, and total taxes increased in real terms until GDP started to fall in 1990. Indirect taxes have decreased modestly in real terms and as a share of GDP.

In Poland, the share of direct personal taxes has moved up to a similar level to that in Hungary and the Czech Republic. Neither Hungary nor Poland have

Fig. 9

Real Income & Expenditure per eq. adult
5-year moving averages disjoint samples

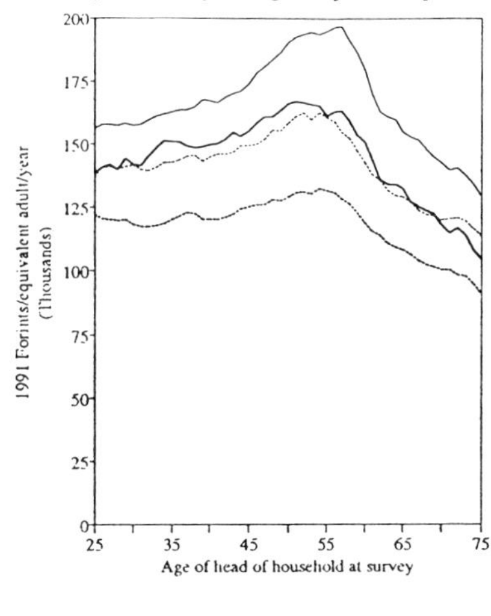

— 1987 Exp ---- 1991 Exp — 1987 Inco ---- 1991 Inco

Fig. 10

Real Changes 1987-91 per eq. adult
income, expenditure - double MA (panel)

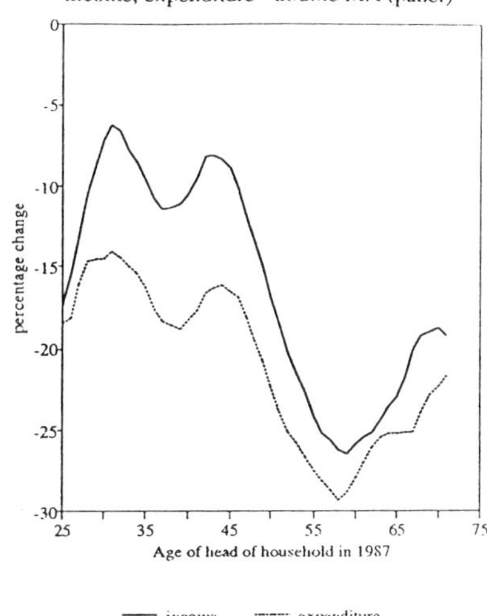

— income ---- expenditure

Fig. 11

Real Changes 1987-91 per eq. adult
double MA (disjoint samples)

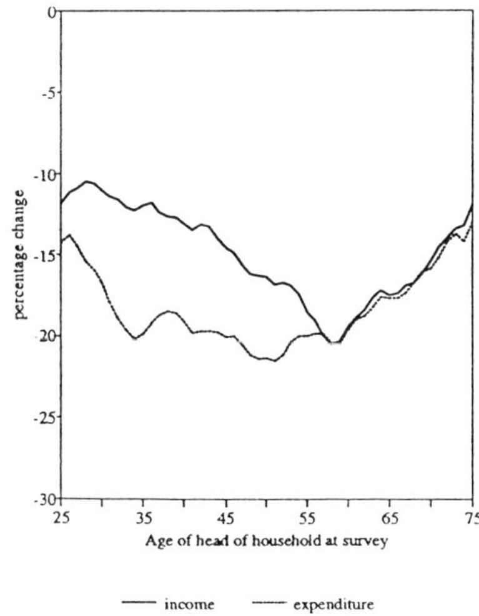

Fig. 12

Net indirect taxes
Hungary 1987-91 Active households only

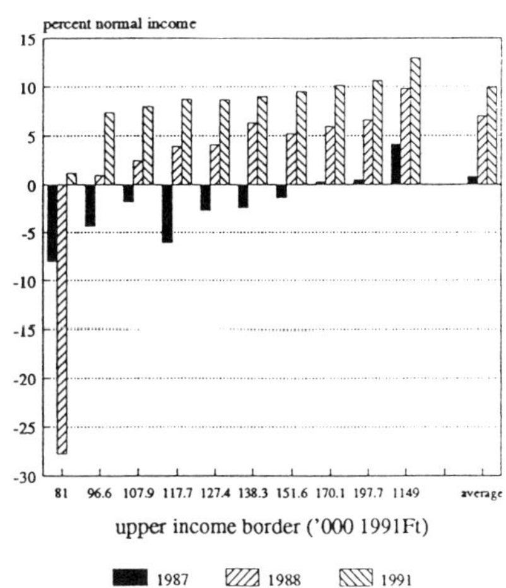

TaxSys

succeeded in addressing persistent government deficits. Hungary has reduced subsidies and capital investment by less than half as much as Poland.

3. The impact of transition on Hungarian households

In Hungary, the transition started in 1987 with the first tax reforms and the gradual liberalisation of the economy. The shift in taxes from enterprises to individuals was in principle compensated by grossing up incomes so that after-tax incomes did not fall on that account. At the same time social insurance payments by both firms and individuals were separately identified and became part of the formal tax and benefit system. Looking at the impact of these changes on individuals is complicated by the rapidly deteriorating external circumstances, and we have already seen in Figure 1 that GDP fell sharply during the transition in all transitional countries after 1989. The combined effect of systemic change, tax reform, and external trade shocks resulted in a significant decrease in real income and expenditure. How was this impact distributed across the population?

At the household level this question can be addressed using the biennial household budget surveys (HBS) conducted by the Hungarian Central Statistical Office (HCSO). These surveys replace one-third of the households in each round, thus creating a panel in which households are resurveyed three times, in this case in 1987 (before the tax reforms), 1989, and 1991.[3] Tamas Revesz has constructed a panel of 2 800 households over this period and has computed income and expenditure per equivalent adult (using the OECD equivalent scales) for each household of the panel. (Details of the surveys, the panel, and their representativity are given in Revesz, 1994). Figure 9 shows income and expenditure per equivalent adult in 1987 and in 1991 by age of head of household at the time of the survey (1987 or 1991), computed as a five-year moving average centred on the age reported (so that the observation for a household aged 30 is the average of households aged 29-32). This smoothing is particularly necessary for younger and older households, who are relatively few in number as heads of households, and the graph has been truncated to the range of ages from 25-75.[4] The figure also shows the characteristic hump shape in which income and expenditure peak at age 50-55, and decrease rapidly thereafter. It shows the considerable decline in both real income and expenditure over this transitional period.

Figures 10 and 11 show the percentage decline in two different ways. Figure 10 shows the decline in income and expenditure using the panel sample of households who were observed in 1987 and again in 1991. The households are grouped by age of head of household in 1987 and the percentage decline in income and expenditure from 1987 to 1991 are computed from the five-year moving average figures for each year, and this percentage decline is further smoothed by taking a five year moving average (hence double MA of the figure title). The changes compound two effects — of the change in age and hence position in the income or expenditure curve of Figure 9, and the impact of the transition on all households. The first effect is removed in Figure 11, which uses the same samples as Figure 9 (the whole HBS sample for 1991, and the available rather smaller sample for 1987), which have only one-third of the households in common. Figure 11 compares the change in income and expenditure of households whose head was, e.g. 45 in 1987 and the obviously different households whose head was the same age, (e.g. 45) in 1991.

The differences between Figures 10 and 11, which are drawn to exactly the same scale for easy comparison, are quite striking, and show the importance of allowing for the ageing effect of panels. Both Figures 10 and 11 show that expenditure fell more than income. Figure 11 shows that income fell more for 60 year-olds (at the point of retirement for men, many of whom experienced lower participation rates in the years leading up to 60 as a result of the transition). The average fall in income was 15 per cent and of consumption 19 per cent. At the aggregate level, GDP remained constant in real terms from 1987-89, and then fell 19 per cent between 1989 and 1991. Household consumption fell 2 per cent between 1987 and 1989, and then fell a further 9 per cent between 1989 and 1991, or an overall 11 per cent.[5] Thus the household level data tell a rather different story — less of a decline in personal income than in GDP, but more of a fall in consumption than suggested by the aggregate statistics.

Notice also in Figure 11 that consumption actually fell more in proportional terms for working age households than for the retired, though Figure 9 reminds us that the retired had both lower income and expenditure, suggesting a reduction in inequality between age groups. (The overall inequality of the population revealed by Lorenz curves and Gini coefficients did not change perceptibly in the samples over this period — see Newbery, 1995a.)

Figure 10 shows us the experience of unchanging groups of different ages during this period. Note that the experience of these groups is more extreme as they experience either the benefits or penalties of ageing on top of the transitional impact. The income and expenditure of those originally aged 60 and now moving into retirement are clearly larger than (differing) groups who remain 60, for obvious reasons. Those in their mid-30s had a rougher time than those of 30 or 45 (whose incomes begin to rise more rapidly with age then). Those who were below 50 cut their consumption by considerably less than those over 50, with those newly retired in 1987 having the highest cuts in expenditure of those whose status did not change. What this suggests is that older households bore the costs of the transition proportionately more heavily than younger households, though the poorest, oldest pensioners needed to cut their expenditure proportionately less than most other households, suggesting the existence of some safety-net protection.

Pudney (1995) has undertaken a more systematic analysis of the change in household welfare during this period making more intensive use of the panel nature of the data. With the same families observed at three different moments (1987, 1989, and 1991) it is possible to see whether large changes in family circumstances are reversed in the subsequent period and exhibit regression towards the mean, or whether some households experience cumulatively larger changes in their relative position. Pudney uses simulation techniques to look at the possible long run consequences of income mobility (changes and relative positions of households) implied by the transitions between different income levels in the data. He finds strong evidence of regression to the mean (that is, households that experienced a larger than average decline in the first period experienced an offsetting movement in the second period and conversely for those that did relatively well) but these relative movements are consistent with a remarkably stable distribution of consumption. In short, despite the great turbulence of the transition, there is very little distributional mobility, so that the relative position of different household types (described by their demographic structure) remain remarkably stable. Thus taking a household of two adults as a benchmark of equivalised consumption taken as 100, families with two or more earners have current consumption of 113, but predicting their relative position 16 years ahead they would still enjoy consumption of 110, i.e. 10 per cent higher than the reference two-person household at that date. Families with no earners currently enjoying consumption of 86 would in 16 years' time receive consumption of 82. Families with two children currently enjoy 108 and would in 16 years' time enjoy 113 (all assuming the same patterns of mobility and tax and benefit systems remain unchanged into the future).

There are several possible explanations of this remarkable stability in welfare distributional outcomes. One is that the households themselves have been able to maintain their positions by adjusting their savings to absorb fluctuations in income, in which case they must have reasonable confidence in the future stability of their relative earnings position. The other alternative is that the tax and benefit system has been quite remarkably successful in preserving the existing distribution of welfare between different categories of household, in which case the tax system is surely overcompensating for changes in relative position. The final possibility is that the income changes have been completely random, and have affected different kinds of households approximately equally, and the tax and benefit system is equally powerful in protecting families in any category. The evidence is thus consistent with, but does not definitely establish, the proposition that the tax and benefit system has provided a very high degree of insurance against shocks to relative well-being, and that this level of insurance was excessive given the costs. The next section looks at the costs of providing this level of insurance against redistribution.

4. The structure and evolution of the personal tax burden in Hungary[6]

How can one best measure the costs of sustaining the apparently very successful degree of relative welfare insurance (as measured by the stability in the relative distribution of expenditure per equivalent adult)? Revenue needs to be raised to pay for redistributive transfers, and the costs of raising this revenue take two related forms measured by the average and marginal tax burden on individuals. The revenue raising potential of the tax system can be measured by the average tax rates on individuals, making some assumptions about tax incidence, while the disincentive effects are best measured by marginal tax rates, which measure the fraction of additional income generated that is transferred to the budget and not returned to the same individual. Under strong assumptions, the optimal tax system will have constant marginal tax rates, and uniform lump-sum transfers (which may depend on demographic status), except perhaps for income taxes. The advantages of non-constant marginal income tax rates should not be exaggerated (Atkinson and Stiglitz, 1980; Newbery, 1994), and the most effective mechanism for redistribution is through transfers rather than taxes. We shall show that the Hungarian tax system has evolved towards one with an effectively constant marginal tax rate, and this can then be used to characterise the tax system, and ask whether it is too high or not.

This suggests that a tax system is best understood by looking at average and marginal tax rates across the income distribution, to identify burdens, disincentive effects, and departures from the simple optimal tax system described. To that end it is useful to think of the simplest equivalent tax system to the complex reality, in which the only tax is an income tax paid by the employee, who then can purchase untaxed goods. In practice, employers pay employment taxes (social security and unemployment insurance) as a proportion of the gross wage, and with-hold employees' social security contributions and income tax, paying a net wage which is spent on taxed goods. It should not make any difference who pays the employment taxes, as employers are concerned with the gross labour cost and employees are concerned with the purchasing power of their net income, so it is the total size of the tax wedge between the two that is important. In what follows we shall therefore express taxes as a percentage of gross labour cost, and this will be exactly equivalent to the simple tax system described.

4.1 The evolution of the Hungarian tax system

The main structural change in the Hungarian tax system came on January 1, 1988 with the introduction of the personal income tax (PIT) and value added taxes (VAT), the latter replacing the old system of turnover taxes. Wages paid by enterprises were grossed up and PIT was withheld at source, leaving the same after-tax wage as before, though incomes earned elsewhere were now subject to the marginal PIT rate. In 1989 the enterprise profits tax (EPT) was reformed and since then the tax rates and tax brackets for PIT, VAT, and to a lesser extent EPT have been revised almost every year.

Table 1 gives the tax rates payable on a single person's taxable income (gross income less allowances) at nominal prices — married couples are taxed as single persons, with the child allowance taken by the higher marginal tax payer.

Table 2 corrects for the (substantial) changes in the price level to give the tax brackets for each year on taxable income measured at 1991 prices. The left hand column of Table 2 gives the taxable income at 1991 prices, the second column gives the cumulative percentage of taxpayers recorded by the Ministry of Finance for the 1991 tax year, and the far right hand column gives the percentages of main earners in the 1991 Household Budget Survey facing this marginal tax rate. It will be seen that only 12 per cent (= 9.2 per cent + 2.7 per cent) of main earners faced the two highest tax rates of 40 per cent and 50 per cent in 1991, (and the percentage of all earners would have been less). The number at the bottom of each cell in the main part of the table gives the relevant marginal tax rate applying to the range of incomes covered by the cell. Thus in 1991 44.4 per cent of taxpayers faced a marginal tax rate of 30 per cent or less, and only 4 per cent faced the highest rate of 50 per cent (though the Household Budget Survey, discussed below, only records 2.7 per cent of main earners facing this rate, looking at the right hand column).

Between 1988 and 1991 employees had a tax allowance of 1 000 forints per month, which was replaced by a tax credit of 250 forints/month in 1991, zero in 1992, 200 forints/month in 1993, and abolished in 1994. This gradual erosion of the tax allowance has steadily increased taxes on the lower income earners. The gross annual wage of the 20th percentile male main earner in the 1991 household budget survey was 121 000 ft., (= £917 at the 1991 average exchange rate of 132 ft./£,

Table 1. Rates of personal income tax 1988-94.

Taxable income (Ft./year 000s)	1988	1989	1990	1991	1992	1993	1994
0-48	0	0	0	0	0	0	0
48-55	20						
55-70		17	15	12			
70-90	25	23					
90-100	35	29	30	18			
100-110					25	25	
110-120							20
120-150	39			30			
150-180	44	35		32			25
180-200							
200-220					35	35	
220-240							35
240-300	48	42					
300-360			40	40			
360-380	52	49					
380-500							40
500-550			50	50	40	40	
550-600							44
600-800	56	56					
800+	60						
Price level (1988=100)	100.0	115.5	135.1	174.3	214.4	262.6	-

while the median was 190 000 ft. = £1,440) and this group has certainly been affected by the lowering of tax thresholds as will be shown later in Table 3.

To make further progress in examining the distributional consequences of the tax system and changes to the tax rates and brackets, we use the HBS data which for each household, gives details of their income, tax payments, benefits, and expenditure (needed to compute indirect taxes).

4.2 Evolution of indirect taxes and subsidies

VAT was introduced in 1988, replacing a variety of indirect turnover taxes, though excise taxes on goods such as alcohol, tobacco, and motor fuel were kept, while the subsidies on district heating, household fuels, public transport, medicine, and some foodstuffs, were kept but some categories were gradually eliminated. Newbery and Revesz (1995b) give the tax and subsidy rates for the years 1987, 1988, 1991, and 1994 by commodity and as a percentage of total expenditure. These show that indirect taxes were sharply raised in 1988, and then fell slightly in 1991. Indirect taxes were slightly progressive in each year (especially if the lower groups are ignored), but only if motor fuel is included. Since a large part can reasonably be considered as a road user charge rather than a tax, it should arguably be ignored. In

Table 2. Rates of personal income tax 1988-91 at 1991 prices.

Tax inc '000 Ft '91	cum % 91 no.s	Tax rates in each bracket for years, percentages: 1988	1989	1990	1991	1992	1993	1994	'91 % HBS earners
55	7.4				0				6.0
62	8.5							0	
66	10.1						0		
71	11.7			0					
82	15.2	0	0			0		20	
90	18.0				12				15.7
106	24.7		17						
116	29.2			15					
122	31.9	20			18			25	21.9
135	37.8		23				25		
150	44.4				30				12.4
157	47.3	25							
163	49.8					25			
209	65.6	35							
214	67.0							35	
226	70.1		29						
261	77.2	39							
300	83.2				32				32.1
309	84.2							40	
332	86.6						35		
362	88.9		35						
387	89.7			30					
406	91.7					35			
418	92.0	44							
500	95.2				40				9.2
543	96.0		42						
627	97.3	48							
645	97.5			40					
905	99.0		49						
1046	99.2	52							
1394	99.6	56							
top		60	56	50	50	40	40	44	2.7

Horizontal lines give highest taxable income in 1991 prices attracting this rate.
Right hand column gives percentage of main earners in households in this 1991 tax bracket.

that case the indirect tax system then looks less progressive in 1987 and 1988, and also decreases more between 1988 and 1991.

The argument for comparing indirect taxes to expenditure, rather than income, relates to the question of how to treat savings, bearing in mind that savings produce a

Fig. 13
Average Tax Rates, All Households
Hungary 1991, Income deciles (yr end)

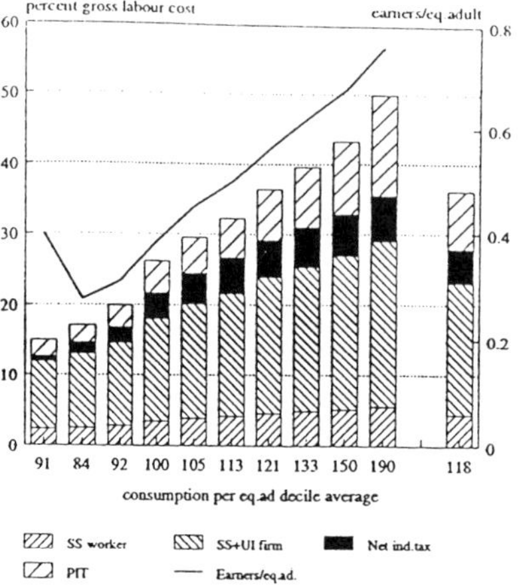

Fig. 14
Average tax rates, all households
UK 1991, Income deciles

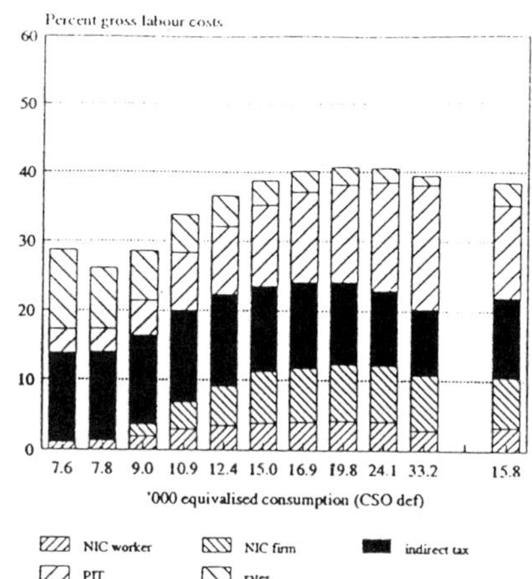

TaxdecUK

Fig. 15
Average tax rates, all households
Hungary 1991, Consumption deciles

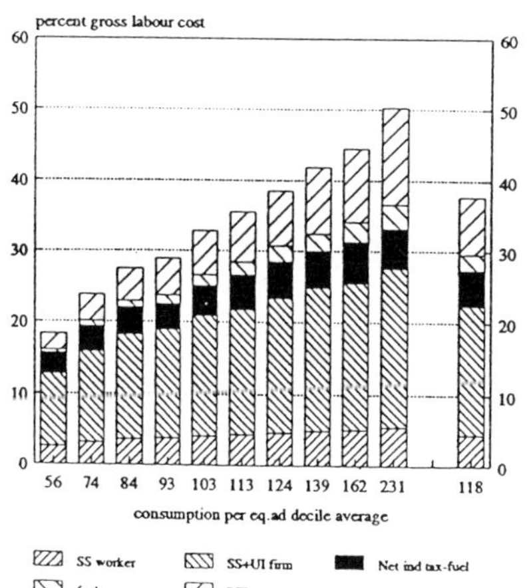

TaxdecC1

Fig. 16
Average Tax Rates, Active earners
Hungary 1991, Income deciles (yr end)

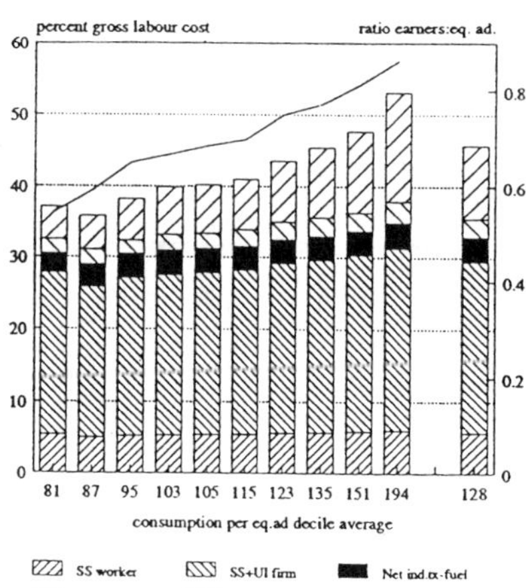

future flow of taxed income, which will be spent on taxed commodities. The assumption made here is that future indirect tax rates will be at least as high as at present, and that in equilibrium the consumer is indifferent between current and future consumption given the after-tax rate of interest on savings. This implies that the present value of future taxes is at least as high as the value of taxes on the money were it to be spent now. Thus it is appropriate to measure the incidence of taxes relative to expenditure rather than income.

This argument does not apply so obviously to subsidies, which are being phased out. It therefore seems better to measure subsidies as a share of current income, on the assumption that savings will not enjoy subsidies when spent in the future. Figure 12 shows the share of net indirect taxes, which is a hybrid of indirect taxes as a share of consumption and subsidies as a share of income, and is described as a share of normal (or life-time) income. Ignoring the somewhat non-monotonic (or random) behaviour over the third and fourth groups in 1987, the indirect and subsidy tax system remains progressive but shifts from one of net subsidy to net taxation, with somewhat more than half of the movement taking place with the reform of 1988, and the remainder with the phasing out of many subsidies by 1991.

4.3 The combined effect of direct and indirect taxes

In addition to income taxes and indirect taxes and subsidies, workers are also subject to social security (SS) payments made directly, and social security and unemployment insurance (UI) paid by firms on the workers employed. Figure 13 shows the average tax rates for all Hungarian households. The taxes distinguished are social security (SS) payments by workers, social security and unemployment insurance (UI) by firms on the workers employed, the net indirect taxes (i.e. indirect taxes less subsidies) less motor fuel taxes, and motor fuel taxes (a considerable part of which might reasonably be considered a road user charge rather than a tax), and PIT.[7] The taxes are shown as a percentage of the total cost of employment, defined as the gross wage plus firm contributions to SS and UI. The HBS sample was divided into deciles on the basis of net (after PIT and SS) income per equivalent adult (OECD equivalent scales).[8] Thus the bars in Figure 13 represent 10 per cent of the sample, and the deciles are marked by the consumption per equivalent adult (in '000 forints), as a measure of permanent or lifetime income, and in all figures the extreme right-hand column gives the average for the sub-population. The ratio of active earners to numbers of equivalent adults is shown by the continuous line, showing a sharp drop between the first and second decile for all households in Figure 13.

Figure 13 can be compared with its counterpart for a market economy, in this case the UK. Figure 14 gives the average tax rates as a share of gross labour costs for all UK households in 1991, directly comparable to Figure 13 (and with the same vertical scale), and taken from CSO (1993). Indirect taxes are computed as a share of expenditure, then grossed up by the ratio of income to expenditure, as in Figure 13. Note that the range of equivalised income is far larger in the UK than in Hungary[9], that national insurance contributions (NIC, the equivalent of the Hungarian SS + UI) are progressive in the UK, that local property taxes are important and very regressive, and that PIT appears more progressive in the UK than Hungary) but that the range of income is far wider, exaggerating the appearance of greater progressivity. Note also that the overall burden is considerably lower in the UK, largely because of the far smaller levels of SS, and that indirect taxes are relatively and absolutely heavier in the UK.

It will be seen in Figure 13 that the lowest decile selected on income has a higher consumption per equivalent adult than the second decile, and the proportion of active earners per equivalent adult is higher. This may be because the lowest decile contains many temporarily low income earners with high lifetime consumption expectations, and negative savings. Figure 15. uses the same sample as Figure 13, but ranks the households into deciles by consumption per equivalent adult, thus removing the reversal of consumption ranking. Figure 15 covers a wider range of average consumption levels but a slightly narrower range of average tax rates, as subsidies are less concentrated in the first decile.[10]

Figures 13-15 describe taxes averaged over the whole population, but the disincentive effects will be concentrated on those earning. Figure 16 shows the average tax rates for those households with active earners (defined as households with no pensioners), also for 1991. The boundaries between the subgroups represented by each bar in Figure 16 are the same as in Figure 13, but the bars for active earners represent different percentages of the sample population.

Figure 16 reveals that the proportion of active earners to equivalent adults rises monotonically across the deciles of active earner households, as does consumption per equivalent adult, though again the bottom decile is somewhat atypical in paying a higher share of taxes than the next decile. This reflects the larger share of earnings to total income in this decile.[11] Note that the average tax rate is higher on active earners primarily because of higher direct tax payments.

Three important assumptions have been made in plotting these average tax rates. The first is to treat all the SS contributions as a tax, rather than allocating some part as a contribution to future pensions. The correct solution would be subtract an estimate of the present value to the worker of benefits derived from additional contributions made by the worker or on his behalf. This will depend on the relationship between retirement pensions and contributions, the time between the contribution and the pension, and the subjective discount rate modified by any uncertainty on the part of the contributor as to the credibility of future pension payment commitments. In Hungary, the only determinants of future pension are the number of years' contribution, not the amount contributed, and the final wage (or best three years' wages over the previous five years). Extra income more than five years before retirement is thus completely taxed through (marginal) SS contributions, while the present value of additional gross income paid shortly before retirement, if it occurs at a period of peak wages, will generate greater benefits than extra tax liabilities. This last effect has been ignored.

The second assumption has already been mentioned, and relates to the treatment of savings. Net indirect taxes are a hybrid of indirect taxes as a share of consumption (reflecting the future taxation of returns to savings) and subsidies as a share of income, which are assumed to be phased out. Finally, no account is taken of taxes on intermediate goods, in contrast to the position taken by the UK CSO in their presentation of tax incidence published annually in *Economic Trends.* VAT on intermediate goods used to produce goods subject to VAT would be rebated in any

Table 3 Evolution of tax structure in Hungary (%).

		1988	1989	1990	1991	1992	1993	1994
marginal tax rates on gross wage								
PIT bot. M. qu. 3 ch.		0	0	0	12	25	25	
PIT med. M. wage + 2 ch.		35	29	30	32	25	35	35
PIT top M. qu.		39	35	30	32	35	35	35
SSC+UI		10	10	10	10.5	11	12	11.5
SSC+UI firm		43	43	43	44.5	49	51	49
Total direct bot qu.		53	53	53	67	85	88	
Total direct med. wage*		88	82	83	87	85	98	96
Total direct top qu.		92	88	83	87	95	98	96
Gross labour cost		143	143	143	145	149	151	149
marginal tax wedges on gross labour cost								
PIT bot. M. qu. 3 ch.		0	0	0	8	17	17	
PIT med. M. wage + 2 ch.		24	20	21	22	17	23	23
PIT top M. qu.		27	24	21	22	23	23	23
SSC+UI		7	7	7	7	7	8	8
SSC+UI firm		30	30	30	31	33	34	33
Total direct bot qu.		37	37	37	46	57	58	
Total direct med. wage*		62	57	58	60	57	65	64
Total direct top qu.		64	62	58	60	64	65	64
		1988	1989	1990	1991	1992	1993	1994
Indirect tax rate (as % of consumption taken as after tax income)								
	bot. qu.+2 ch.	9.9	11.3	11.6	12	12	12	12
	med. wage*	11.2	11.9	12.6	13.2	13.2	13.2	13.2
	top quint.	11.6	12.3	13	13.6	13.6	13.6	13.6
as % of gross wage GW or GLC:								
GW	bot. qu.+2 ch.	8.9	10.2	10.4	9.3	7.7	7.6	10.6
	med. wage*	6.2	7.3	7.6	7.6	8.4	7	7.1
	top quint.	5.9	6.8	7.8	7.8	7.3	7.2	7.3
GLC	bot. qu.+2 ch.	6.2	7.1	7.3	6.4	5.2	5	
	med. wage*	4.3	5.1	5.3	5.3	5.7	4.6	4.7
	top quint.	4.1	4.7	5.5	5.4	4.9	4.8	4.9
Total marginal tax (direct and indirect)								
as % of gross wage								
	bot. qu.+2 ch.	62	63	63	76	93	96	
	med. wage*	94	89	91	95	93	105	103
	top quint.	98	95	91	95	102	105	103
as % of gross labour cost								
	bot. qu.+2 ch.	43	44	44	53	62	63	
	med. wage*	66	62	63	65	63	70	69
	top quint.	68	66	63	66	69	70	69

Note: Gross wages are for male main earners, bottom quintile is boundary wage, similarly for top quintile.

* on median male wage plus 2 children.

Indirect tax rates for 1989-90 interpolated.

case, and for other goods the assumption is that producer prices are set on international markets, so intermediate taxes fall on factors not final prices.

The average rates vary considerably over the income distribution of all households, as inactive households are concentrated in lower deciles and pay lower

Fig. 17
Average transfer rates, All Households
Hungary 1991, Income deciles (yr end)

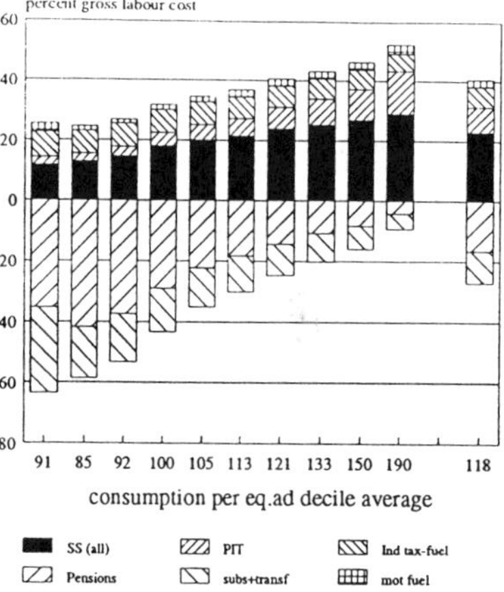

TaxDecYE

Fig. 18
Average transfer rates, Active Earners
Hungary 1991, Income deciles (yr end)

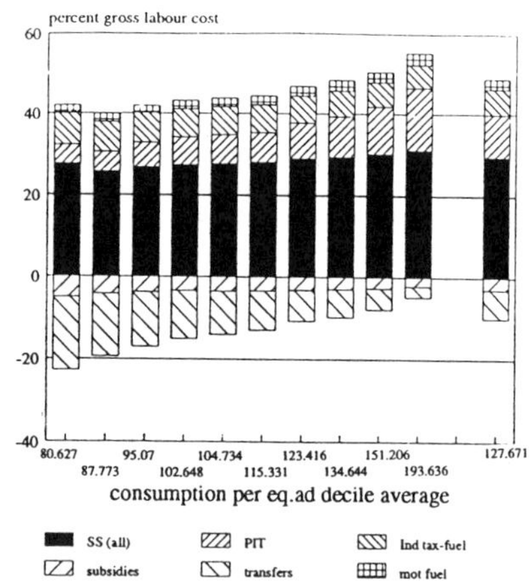

TaxDecAY

Fig. 19
Marginal tax rates, Active earners
Hungary 1991, Income deciles* (yr end)

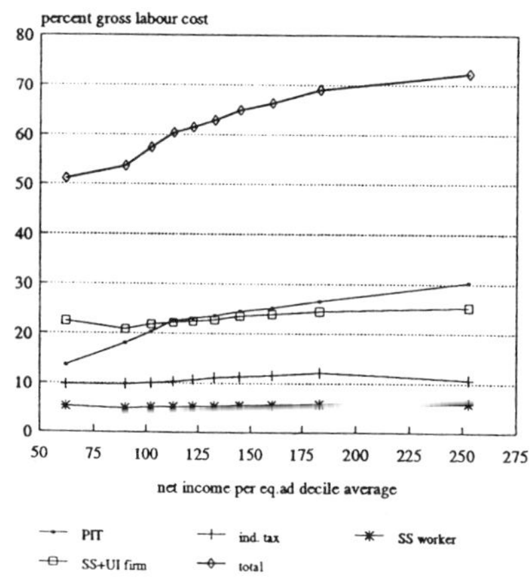

TaxdecAY
* Points indicate decline mean value

Fig. 20
Evolution of Marginal Tax Rates
Hungary 1988-94

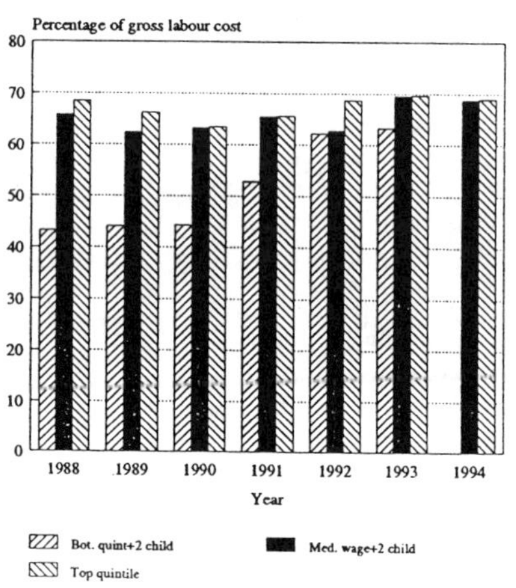

Taxsys

average tax rates. In contrast, the variation in average tax rates for active households (Figure 16) varies much less. Figures 17 and 18 distinguish between taxes (above the axis) and transfers (below the axis) given through the tax system, (mainly for children in the case of active households and pensions for inactive households, but excluding transfers in kind for e.g. health and education), shown below the line. Subsidies on goods are also shown below the axis (so the net indirect tax is the sum of indirect taxes and subsidies). Figures 17 and 18 reproduce the samples of Figures 13 and 16. Pension payments can be compared with contributions (all social security contributions, which also include unemployment insurance and some contributions to the health system). As expected, richer families are more likely to be working and making net contributions to the pension fund.

The burden of indirect taxes as a proportion of consumption per equivalent adult is slightly progressive for all households, ranging from a low of 10.7 per cent for the second decile up to 15.9 for the top decile. If taxes on petrol are excluded, the degree of progressivity decreases considerably, reflecting the concentration of car ownership and use in the higher deciles. Some part of motor fuel taxation should be considered a payment for the use of the road system, and not properly a tax, and this fraction might amount to between one half and the full amount, depending on the degree of congestion of the road network and hence the efficient level of road charges.

Subsidies as a percentage of consumption per equivalent adult are also progressive across deciles (see Figure 18, which distinguishes subsidies from other transfers — there are no pension payments by sample definition), and the net indirect tax (taxes less subsidies) then appear very progressive across all households (see Figure 16).

4.4 Calculating the total average and marginal tax burden on individuals

Table 3 gives the legally specified tax rates from 1988-1994 on marginal income earned in a firm paying social security contributions. The top segment of the table gives the rates as conventionally defined on the gross wage. The marginal income tax payable by the first owner in the household can be computed from his net income. All other direct taxes and contributions are proportional and thus have constant marginal rates. The marginal PIT is computed for three types of earner: a male main earner at the 20th percentile (of male main earners in that year) with three children (in some years there was no allowance for the first two children, so this is the most generous treatment of a family on low earnings), a male main earner on the median wage with two children, and a male main earner at the 80th percentile with no children (though the presence of up to two children would have made no difference to the marginal rates). Starting from the relevant gross wage, the taxable earnings can be computed from the allowances, (which are the same for single and married persons, and only vary with the number of children).

In addition to PIT, the employee pays social security contributions and unemployment insurance (SS, UI), as does the firm, on the gross wage at the uniform rates shown. The gross labour cost to the firm is the sum of the gross wage and the SS + UI contributions paid by the firm, and is shown in the table. The marginal tax wedge as a percent of the gross labour cost can then be computed once the relevant taxes have been identified.

The marginal indirect tax rate is defined as the extra indirect tax (net of subsidies) paid on additional goods purchased when income (or expenditure) increases by one unit.[12] It may be estimated in different ways as described more fully in Newbery and Revesz (1995b). The marginal indirect tax rates for earners at different positions in the income distribution are shown as a percentage of expenditure (which is taken as the relevant tax rate on net income), using the figures presented in the appendix tables, and also as a percentage of gross labour costs.

In countries like the UK, many transfers and subsidies are means-tested, so that increased income leads to withdrawals of benefits, and the implied marginal tax rate can be high. In Hungary, all benefits paid by the central government are conditioned on status (numbers of children etc.) and not income, so there is no marginal cost in reduced benefits from earning extra income. Most subsidies are paid on non-discretionary items such as medicines and district heating, and can be argued to be independent of income, and therefore to have a zero marginal effective rate. The *marginal* direct and indirect tax rates shown in the table for the median earner do not therefore need to be adjusted for loss of benefits, nor do those for earners in other categories (in contrast to the average rates shown in Figures 13-18).

The resulting marginal tax rates as a percentage of gross labour cost can be computed for each household, as well as for the three representative households shown in Table 3. Figure 19 shows the result of aggregating across active households by the same income groups as in Figures 16 and 18. The only progressive tax (with an increasing marginal rate) is the PIT. The total measures the total marginal tax wedge between the cost of employment and the purchasing power of the employee.

The last three lines of Table 3 show the total marginal tax as a percentage of gross labour cost as it evolved over time for the three selected household types. The marginal tax rates facing the median wage earner and those in the top quintile have hardly changed since 1988, and are remarkably close to each other. The results are also presented graphically in Figure 20. The main change has been for those in the bottom quintile with two children, where the marginal rate has increased from 43 per cent between 1988 and 1990 to 63 per cent by 1993. This process has happened despite the fall in real income of the whole population, and with it that of the bottom quintile. Almost half of the marginal tax rate is borne by firms in social security and unemployment insurance, which exceed all direct taxes and contributions made by workers even in the top quintile, and which are proportional, not progressive like PIT. Indirect taxes are a relatively small component of the total marginal tax burden.

The most striking feature of the tax reforms, brought out most clearly in Figure 18, is the gradual convergence of all marginal tax rates on active earners across the income distribution to a common and very high rate of 70 per cent of gross labour cost.

5. The desirability of reducing redistributive taxes and transfers

The tax reforms introduced in Hungary in 1988 and subsequently reformed periodically since then have had the effect of moving an exceptionally progressive tax system with increasing marginal tax rates to one in which marginal tax rates are fairly uniform over the income distribution, with most of the redistribution taking place through transfers and the provision of such services as education, health and the like. As such, the reforms have moved the structure of taxation towards that found in many market economies, though the marginal tax wedge of 70 per cent of the gross labour cost is very high by international standards. Does it follow that taxes are too high? What does economic theory, and, more to the point, welfare economics, have to say about setting personal tax rates?

The most coherent normative theory of public economics, as set out for example in Atkinson and Stiglitz (1980), is utilitarian, in that it concerns itself with the consequences of social choices for individuals. This ethical framework has considerable appeal, the more so if tempered by concepts of rights. The theory is most directly applicable to the revenue raising side of the budget, as a theory of optimal taxation. The theory addresses the following problem: how should taxes be set to raise revenue for redistribution and other public expenditures at least social cost. The expenditure side of the budget is complementary, in that the larger part of redistribution typically occurs on the expenditure rather than tax side. In a simple world with no market failures, government activity would be purely redistributive (and to that extent directly addressed by the theory of optimal taxation). In practice, market failures are pervasive and provide an important rationale for government intervention, both on the tax side (corrective taxes such as those on road users), but again more importantly on the expenditure side.

Optimal tax theory, as set out in Atkinson and Stiglitz (1980) and summarised in Stern (1987), takes a Bergson-Samuelson social welfare function as embodying utilitarian normative precepts, and a rather simple description of the economy (competitive, with no market failures) to obtain quite striking results for the choice of commodity taxation. Given some further defensible assumptions about consumer preferences it is possible to draw rather sharper conclusions for the design of a set of taxes.[13] Under these assumptions, the optimal tax involves a proportional income tax (or, equivalently, uniform commodity taxes) and an optimal lump-sum demo-grant (i.e. a grant that depends on demographic circumstances, such as family size, age, and possibly sex). It is also plausible that the income tax system should be progressive.

Ideally, taxes should fall on final consumption, not on intermediate goods, so that distortions are confined to consumption and not needlessly visited upon production. A VAT achieves this, though arguably at considerable additional complication, which may not be justified if tax administration is weak.[14] The main implication of this principle is that trade taxes are hard to justify (except on tax administration grounds, or possibly as part of the transition process).

The main argument for taxing corporate income (as distinct from personal income) rests on the possibility of taxing foreign incomes (Gersovitz, 1987) or rents. Natural resources like oil are typically subject to specific taxes designed to capture as much of the rent as possible in a non-distortionary way. Corporate income taxes (CIT) may provide a way of taxing some personal incomes and so the personal income tax and CIT need to be integrated and considered together. The main practical reason for keeping CIT is to avoid giving windfall gains to owners. A related practical reason in transitional economies is that when privatising enterprises subject to CIT, foreigners can take advantage of foreign tax credits, while domestic entrepreneurs need pay less, so the CIT is rather like non-voting state equity in the enterprise, reducing the difficulty of raising the required finance.

These general principles are useful for defining the broad structure of the tax system, but are not sufficient. The main area in which they are incomplete has to do with the tax treatment of intertemporal transactions, such as lending and borrowing. They also need to be extended to deal with such issues as the taxation of tobacco and alcohol (which interact with the provision of medical care) and the taxation of road vehicles and road fuel (which can be thought of as user charges rather than taxes).

The previous section demonstrated that the Hungarian tax system conforms quite well in its structure to the general precepts of optimal tax theory, with the possible exception of intertemporal taxation, and particularly pension finance. If the structure of taxation is a defensible approximation to the prescriptions of modern public economics, what of the level, measured by the size of the transfer and the (marginal) tax rates? If we bear in mind that a substantial (but declining) share of the enterprise sector is still state-owned, then its profits taxes and dividends are alike in being available to finance investment. The state enterprise sector may then either make a contribution to the general budget (equal to profits less investment) or, if profits fall short of investment, may constitute a claim on expenditures. Private enterprises pay profits tax, and so make a net (but small) contribution to the budget, and can be lumped together with the net flows from the state enterprise sector, leaving us to concentrate attention on the taxation of personal income.

We can approximate the personal tax system by a proportional income tax (converting commodity taxes into their income tax equivalent), a uniform demo-grant, and a fixed revenue requirement to provide for exhaustive (and non-redistributive) government expenditure (e.g. for General Public Services and defence, unsatisfied investment demands, and to service the foreign debt). This simplification enables us to describe the tax system by two parameters: the tax rate, and the fixed revenue requirement. What determines the optimal tax rate, noting that the higher the tax rate, the larger will be the redistributive benefits (given the fixed revenue requirement)?

Four factors influence the optimal choice of this tax rate (Stern, 1976). The first is the degree of inequality in skills (which is hard to observe, but is related to the degree of pre-tax earnings inequality when workers are paid their marginal product). The higher the degree of inequality, the higher the tax rate is likely to be, other things being equal. The degree of skills inequality appears to be lower in socialist economies, possibly because education is more uniformly allocated than in market economies. One might argue that there are no strong reasons for expecting large differences in the underlying skill distribution between countries at European levels of education, and differences in wage inequality may reflect the operation of implicit tax systems in the more egalitarian CEECs, rather than differences in the distribution of marginal products. Atkinson and Micklewright (1992) provide extensive statistical comparisons of wage dispersions in CEECs compared to Britain. They find that in the 1970s, the USSR and Poland had a higher ratio of the top to bottom decile of earnings than Britain (at about 3.0), though Hungary and Czechoslovakia were systematically lower, at about 2.5.[15] In the 1980s, Poland's ratio fluctuated widely, but eventually fell to that of Hungary and Czechoslovakia (Hungary actually increased somewhat), while Britain's inequality rose steadily over the 1980s along with the USSR to 3.3.

The second factor is the level of required government expenditure to be financed by taxes on workers and consumers — the higher the fraction of GDP required, the higher the tax rate. Hungary and Poland have high foreign debts that need servicing, while the Czech and Slovak republics are better placed in this regard. The main problem facing transitional economies is that enterprise revenue has fallen or is likely to fall sharply, while infrastructural investment demands (especially in transport) have increased, both increasing the uncovered component of required revenue. The other difference with market economies is in the level of foreign interest payments, where Hungary's ratio of foreign debt to GDP puts it among the most heavily indebted developing countries. Given Hungary's intention to retain its international credit standing, debt repayment places a heavy initial claim on the budget. Poland also has a high foreign debt but has been more successful in obtaining debt relief, while the Czech and Slovak republics had little official foreign debt by 1994.

The third factor is the elasticity of substitution between taxed and non-taxed activities (work and leisure in the benchmark case of a comprehensive tax system in which all goods and services can be taxed). The higher this elasticity, the lower the optimal tax rate, provided taxes are adequate to cover the fixed expenditure requirement. Soviet-type economies have remarkably extensive control over incomes (via state enterprises) and over access to consumption and work, greatly reducing the opportunities for substituting untaxed for taxed activities. The transition threatens this in various ways (Kornai, 1992). The move to a market economy with numerous smaller firms leads to a loss of information about tax liabilities, while the reform of the tax system disrupts existing procedures. Reduced tax efficiency reduces the fraction of income falling within the tax net, raising the marginal cost of tax collection and reducing the optimal tax rate.

Finally, the more egalitarian the government, the higher the tax rate. Most CEECs appear exceptionally egalitarian by Western standards, comparable only to very rich and homogenous countries like Sweden. The transition in Eastern Europe is eroding political commitment to the previous degree of equality, and with it, the desired marginal tax rate.

These theoretical considerations pull in different directions. The first two arguments suggest that an increase in taxes might be justified. Marginal products of labour (and hence the correct measure of wages) may become more dispersed with a move to a more internationally exposed market economy, arguing for more redistribution. Pudney (1994) finds a significant growth in earnings inequality in Hungary after 1988, to levels comparable with Western Europe, as does Barr (1994). The component of required public expenditure on infrastructure, debt service, and unemployment support not covered by falling enterprise taxes may have to rise as the CEECs reach the limit of prudent international borrowing and attempt to restructure their economies, again requiring tax increases. The last two arguments suggest that optimal tax rates might well fall as a result of transformation, as the ability of the tax system to collect revenue efficiently falters, and public support for equality erodes.

The theoretical arguments appear balanced, and therefore unhelpful. We need to quantify the arguments and see what factors have a large influence on the outcome. Newbery (1994) has done this for a simplified model of CEECs, roughly calibrated to Hungary, and finds that the decrease of tax coverage and/or collection efficiency has a dramatic effect on the optimal tax *rates*. Depending on the exact parameter values, the effect of reducing the tax coverage from 100 per cent to 75 per cent of expenditure would roughly halve the amount of redistributive transfers and the rate of VAT.[16] As reduced tax coverage would lead to a fall in the share of taxes in GDP anyway, a decrease in the optimal rates implies an even greater fall in the desirable share of taxes in GDP, so that a failure to maintain pre-existing tax shares as the tax base erodes is not a reason for increasing the tax rate on the diminished base. This effect appears substantially more important than the increase in inequality, whose effect could be offset by relatively minor decreases in aversion to inequality. Finally, falls in enterprise tax revenue, or increases in required public expenditure, would seem to be primarily (up to three-quarters for most plausible sets of parameter values) at the expense of redistributive transfers, and again provide little justification for sharp increases in personal taxation.

Of course, it would be premature to draw such sharp policy conclusions from what is a highly simplified model of these economies, ignoring important political realities, and with the standard, if often unrealistic assumptions of full employment and rational well-informed consumers. Nevertheless, these findings are consistent with the claims that the redistributive share of the state is too large in these economies, and should, in the medium term, be reduced, even at the expense of greater inequality, to provide greater incentives for productive growth. Instead, in Hungary, we find that the marginal tax rates have been increased as the economy moves further through the transition. The most obvious tax that needs to be reduced is the heavy SS tax on firms and individuals, which could most usefully be replaced, at least partly, by a defined contribution pension scheme. If workers were convinced that pension contributions made at any date would directly increase the real value of their future pension, they might view the contribution as (forced) savings rather than tax, and they might then have less incentive to reduce their assessable wage base.[17]

6. Detailed tax design questions

Once the broad outline of the tax system has been settled, to be compatible with future EU membership, and the level of taxation as a share of GDP decided, perhaps as a long-run target, there remain a variety of detailed questions of fiscal design. These include the balance between direct and indirect taxation, the degree of progressivity of the direct tax system, the degree of coverage and differentiation of the value added tax and excise taxes, and the form of financing of social security.

The balance between direct and indirect taxes has a degree of arbitrariness, for there is little apparent difference between a uniform VAT on all goods, and a proportional income tax on all incomes. That suggests that progressivity in the overall tax system is best achieved through the direct tax component, while the revenue to be raised from indirect taxes can be set to reduce the number of income tax payers who are required to file an individual tax return, as well as reducing the overall degree of tax evasion. Income taxes are typically evaded by under-reporting or not registering, and become more important as an increasing fraction of income comes from self-employment or is not withheld by the employer. Such income can be taxed when spent through indirect taxes, but some goods and services may be hard to subject to VAT.

The relative merits of the two systems of taxation can be put thus: indirect taxes tax all consumers on some goods and services, while income taxes tax the entire potential consumption of some fraction of income earners or income. Direct and indirect taxes are therefore complementary, and together reduce problems of evasion and incomplete coverage. Not surprisingly, we find a considerable similarity in the balance between direct and indirect taxes across countries as shown in Figure 3, which suggests that between one-half and two-thirds of personal income and expenditure taxes together are collected from income taxes, the balance from indirect taxes, mainly domestic.

The next important question to settle is whether VAT should be levied on all goods and services at a uniform rate (the most broad-based simple system) or whether different goods and services should be taxed at different rates, and whether some goods should be either zero rated or exempt (the distinction being that zero rated goods can claim back taxes on inputs, but exempt goods cannot). Does differentiating tax rates on goods and services provide an additional leverage over income redistribution that cannot be more effectively achieved through the income tax and transfer system, or is it preferable to treat indirect taxes as the proportional component of the overall tax-raising side of the budget, with most redistribution achieved through targeted transfers and some progressivity in the income tax system?

Newbery and Révész (1995b) find that the indirect tax system in Hungary, which has VAT rates of 0, 15 and 25 per cent, together with various excise tax rates and subsidies for some goods, does have some redistributive effect, but this is almost entirely confined to the taxation of motor transport fuel, and subsidies, mainly to medicine. The trend of reform in Hungary has been towards unification of the rate, and Hungary now has a smaller zero rate range of goods than most EU countries. Heady and Smith (1995) have looked at the desirability of a uniform tax rate in the Czech and Slovak republics. They find that making VAT uniform would have adverse distributional effects which could be eliminated by adjusting other taxes and benefits, but only at the cost of increasing the overall marginal tax rate. Similarly, improved targeting of social benefits can reduce poverty and government expenditure, but again at the cost of increasing marginal tax rates. Their simulations not only identify the almost inevitable trade-off between and equity and efficiency, but allow one to quantify the cost in terms of increased marginal tax rates of improvements in equity.

Of course, it does not follow that a move from the present system of taxes to a uniform VAT, even with compensating adjustments elsewhere would have no distributional effect — Heady and Smith show that such changes can lead to a large number of households gaining or losing, even if the pattern of gains and losses is random across the income distribution. This suggests that, while it may be desirable for tax simplicity and administrative convenience to move to a uniform VAT, it may be appropriate to move slowly so that the changes are lost in the noise of normal relative price movements. For countries at an earlier stage of transition, it might be worth considering making the move to uniform taxes as quickly as possible, given that the first step will necessarily have a dramatic impact. In this context, the Czechoslovak device of compensating families with a lump sum that insured a majority would not suffer from the initial price shock, subsequently to be phased out, has considerable political logic.

Jarvis and Pudney (1995) look at the scope for redistributional government policies in Hungary, the impact of recent changes in the tax-benefit system, and the potential for improving the income distribution by different targeting techniques. The authors point out that the succession of fiscal reforms in Hungary has been undertaken without a clear strategy, and particularly without a foundation of research to establish that the areas chosen for policy reform are indeed the areas that really matter in terms of the ultimate objective.' They apply an innovative technique for identifying desirable directions for tax and benefit reform using the 1991 HBS. They ask how one could best reduce a particular measure of poverty by making lump-sum transfers to households classified by some characteristics (such as number of children and other demographic attributes, location, employment status, industry of employment). The authors are careful to point out that their findings cannot be immediately translated into policies, and are best seen as a diagnostic technique for identifying better and worse correlates of poverty. These may in turn cast some doubts on the poverty-reducing efficacy of industrial and regional policies, and public rental subsidies.

The other major finding of their approach is that poverty would be reduced by making transfers from employed families with children to pensioners and unemployed, starting from the 1991 system of benefits. It is, however, worth noting that the design of tax and benefit policies is likely to be guided by a more comprehensive view of distributional justice than those captured by poverty lines, and will have to take account of disincentive effects and risk reduction (or social insurance), as well as political realities and contractual obligations (to pensioners).

The two most obvious reforms that await most countries (including the developed market economies) are the proper taxation of capital income and a better system of pension finance (and they are related). It is hard to understand why transitional (and other) economies do not introduce indexed government securities (as in the UK) to provide more incentive for savings in periods of high inflation, better public financing of the deficit, and a more sensible system of mortgage finance for property (which would avoid the front-end loading of high nominal interest rates, and would have avoided the fiasco of the large transfers made by for example the Hungarian government to mortgage holders. Indexed debt is almost essential for private pension provision, the more so if the equity market is underdeveloped. Indexed debt makes taxing nominal gains in periods of high inflation obviously foolish (which is not to say that it will not be done, as in the UK), but at least allows savers the option of being taxed on their real interest. Imputing real interest at for example 3 per cent on the money value of other savings and taxing on the imputed interest might be better than the normal practice of taxing the nominal interest.[18]

The conventional wisdom on pension reform, advanced in particular by the World Bank (1994), is a three-pillar approach, and it is interesting that the Hungarian Parliament endorsed essentially this approach in 1991 (OECD/CCET, 1995). The three pillars are i) a universal flat-rate tier, financed by general revenues; ii) an earnings-related tier with benefits closely linked to contributions; and iii) voluntary supplementary pensions. Augusztinovics (1995) makes a further distinction that current earners and pensioners have some claim on state assets (in proportion to years of service), and so two schemes are needed — one to manage these existing implicitly funded claims, the other to set up a fund to pay for claims arising from contributions made from now on. Newbery (1991) argued that shares in privatised companies could usefully be placed into the pension fund to cover the first of these sets of obligations, but although there was the intention to provide the social security fund with assets, these have not yet been transferred.

Whatever is done about existing claims arising from past contributions, the case for closely linking the second tier to current and future contributions is compelling on efficiency grounds, and, given the argument here that there is excessive redistribution, defensible against such criticisms. The opposing argument advanced by Jarvis and Pudney (1995) and again by Hancock and Pudney (1996) is that pensioners are the group that account for the largest share of total poverty, refuting the general claim in World Bank (1994) that 'in most countries poverty rates are higher among the young than the old'. It remains to be seen whether policy-makers in Hungary can devise a method of better targeting benefits that enables the burden of taxation on younger generations (who could contribute to an earnings-related funded pension plan) to be reduced while commanding adequate political support.

7. Lessons

What lessons can be drawn from the growing number of detailed studies of tax and benefit reform in transitional economies of the kind set out in Newbery (1995b)? One of the salutary lessons of careful case studies is that matters are invariably more complex when studied in detail, and lessons learned from one country should be tested out, preferably using simulation techniques like those used by Heady and Smith (1995), before their adoption elsewhere. Nevertheless, it is useful to stand back and ask what lessons emerge from such studies.

The first lesson is that profits tax revenue is almost bound to fall, both in absolute terms and as a share of GDP, but this does not necessarily mean that the share of total tax revenue in GDP will fall — Hungary provides a good counterexample — though whether maintaining the original high tax share is desirable must be doubtful. The second observation is that cutting subsidies to the traded, manufactured sector appears reasonably simple, though consumer subsidies may be more difficult to cut (for example in Hungary). Falling tax revenues combined with falling output do not necessarily imply increased public deficits (which were avoided in the Czech

Republic), just as an apparently successful rebound as in Poland does not guarantee that deficits will disappear. Raising direct and indirect taxes on individuals is clearly possible, and the adverse distributional impact of moving to uniform indirect taxes may be offset by adjustments in the tax system, possibly at some cost of increased marginal tax rates (the Czech Republic).

Overall, the benefits of simplifying the tax system and minimising the administrative burden have a relatively low cost in distributional terms, compared to the revenue gains. Creating a system to handle unemployment insurance appears to have been done more successfully than the admittedly far harder problem of reforming the system of pension payments, which affects a far larger fraction of the population. It is evident that issues of local taxation, property taxation, and capital income taxation have frequently been neglected, but there are few clear models to follow, and most involve politically unattractive choices.

Although the Visegrad countries, being committed to accession to the EU, have chosen to replace turnover taxes by VAT, it may be that other countries would be wise to delay this change, concentrating meanwhile on moving to a more uniform system of purchase taxes, *ad valorem* and excise taxes on the conventional excise goods (fuel, alcohol and tobacco). Although less efficient in principle than a VAT, as they fail to exempt production, the opportunity cost of using scarce administrative resources to introduce a VAT might be too high in some economies. Later, when more of the economy is in private ownership, VAT may become attractive if it increases company compliance for profits tax, as VAT returns give a useful presumptive estimate of turnover and hence profits.

The expenditure side of the budget is the best place to concentrate redistributive policies, which this paper argues are currently too expensive — both because they are generous and often poorly targeted. Jarvis and Pudney (1995) point out that too little strategic thinking is being directed at improving the targeting of transfers to achieve the desired redistribution at minimum total cost. Perhaps because the theory and practice of taxation is reasonably well codified and readily comparable across countries, most tax systems (at least at the central government level) seem moderately sensible, at least in broad outline. It is far harder to judge whether the system of expenditures and transfers is cost effective, and that requires detailed, painstaking, statistical analysis using household surveys. Perhaps the greatest weakness in the current state of economic knowledge is the extent to which incentives matter in the design of pension schemes, and how much a shift to defined contribution systems would reduce the disincentive effects of high marginal taxes on labour income, and how far it would displace private savings and exacerbate the problems of budget deficits. At the very least a satisfactory system of indexing interest income against both inflation and taxation is needed to guard against any such fall in private savings if pensions are to be reformed (and would be desirable in inflationary deficit-prone economies in any case).

It is perhaps unfortunate that while the OECD and EU countries offer a reasonable example for the design of the taxes on current incomes and expenditures, their own record on deficits, pensions, and the taxation of capital, property, and interest in many cases provide such poor examples for the transition countries to follow. Perhaps, like the Czech Republic, they can use the opportunity of radical reform to avoid some of the mistakes of Western market economies.

Notes

[1] The EBRD adds Slovenia to its group 1 countries, the most advanced in the transition process, (EBRD, 1995, pp. 23-24), while the World Bank also includes the war torn countries of Croatia and FYR Macedonia in its first group of countries with the highest average degree of liberalisation over the period 1989-95.

[2] Comparing levels of output pre- and post-reform is peculiarly difficult, both because of the change in definitions as the countries adopt the SNA system of national accounting, and also because of the difficulty of measuring the true size of the private sector. Figures reported in EBRD (1994, p. 165, fn 2) suggest that Poland may have reached its previous peak output by 1994, suggesting that figures 1 and 2 may overstate the collapse, though the discussion on pp. 186-7 suggests that official output-based GDP measures may overstate 1993 growth.

[3] The HBS for 1993 starts with a completely different panel to that of 1991, and so the panel element is severed at that point. The research reported here was undertaken before the 1993 HBS became available, but is still able to capture the combination of tax and benefit reforms during the transition.

[4] Further information and additional graphs are presented in Newbery and Revesz (1995a). As a rough guide, the density of the sample is roughly triangular, rising rapidly from nearly zero at age (of head of household) of 20 to a peak at age 35, and then falling roughly linearly with age to zero at age 85.

[5] *National Accounts Hungary 1991-93*, p. 25.

[6] This section is an abbreviated version of Newbery and Revesz (1995b), which gives more details on the computations.

[7] Except in Figure 13, where net indirect taxes are shown, as these less fuel would be negative for the bottom decile.

[8] The HBS gives two different measures of earnings, one based on the year-end interview, the other derived from the two-month diary keeping. The HCSO then takes the maximum of the year-end and grossed-up (but undeflated) diary records as its measure of earnings (and has similar procedures for taxes and social security contributions). The data presented here are based on year-end interview data, which are systematically lower than the CSO derived measures.

[9] The definition of an equivalent adult used by the CSO is quite different from the OECD measure used in producing the Hungarian estimates but is highly correlated with the OECD measure at this level of aggregation, so the ratio of the top to the bottom will not be affected.

[10] Figure 13 uses the year-end measure of income, while Figure 15 uses the recorded measure, which is slightly different, accounting for small differences in the denominator of gross labour cost.

[11] The SS by both employees and employers are computed from the year-end main earnings and bonuses, on the untestable assumption that all other earnings are not subject to such contributions. A higher ratio of earnings to income thus increases the ratio of SS to the estimated value of gross labour cost, taken as the total income plus employer's SS.

[12] As argued, it is more logical to express indirect tax rates on their tax base of consumption, and to adjust by the share of consumption in income when relating indirect taxes to income.

[13] If consumers are essentially identical (except for observable and unalterable characteristics, such as age) and preferences are separable, then commodity taxes should be uniform (provided all goods can be taxed). See Atkinson and Stiglitz (1980, Ch 14), and, for extensions, Deaton and Stern (1986). Part of the case for the defence is that detecting departures from separability is empirically difficult (Deaton, 1987).

[14] Koltay (1993) argues persuasively that Hungary would have been better advised to adapt its turnover tax towards a purchase tax, and leave the move to a VAT until a later date, once the tax authorities had acquired sufficient experience. The other argument for a VAT is that it provides information to enforce tax collection, particularly from corporate taxation (Gil Díaz, 1987), though this presupposes the willingness and ability of the authorities to match up tax returns.

[15] That is, the ratio of the 90th percentile point to the 10th percentile point.

[16] Note that the direct tax equivalent to an indirect tax rate of t on the producer price is $t/(1+t)$, so having the indirect tax rate with unchanged coverage would reduce tax revenue by less than half.

[17] Semjén (1995) notes the strong incentive to pay minimum wages to record years of employment history, and pay the balance in forms of income that do not attract SS contributions. This incentive to avoid or evade contributions would be reduced if pensions were based on the amount of contributions.

[18] Hungary had to successively reduce the tax rate on interest income to 10 per cent and to extend coverage to previously exempt foreign currency savings, in periods when inflation was over 30 per cent

per annum. If interest rates are 23 per cent (the bank deposit rate in December 1994) and inflation is 21 per cent (same month), the real interest rate before tax is 2 per cent, and after tax is –0.3 per cent, even at this low tax rate. A tax of 1 per cent of the asset value would only have reduced the real after tax rate to 1 per cent.

References

Atkinson, A.B., 1970, "On the measurement of inequality", *Journal of Economic Theory,* 2, pp. 244-63.

Atkinson, A.B., and Micklewright, J., 1992, *Economic Transformation in Eastern Europe and the Distribution of Income*, Cambridge University Press, p. 94.

Atkinson, A. B. and Stiglitz, J.E., 1980, *Lectures on Public Economics,* McGraw-Hill.

Augusztinovics, M., 1995, "Combined gestation and retirement financing: macroeconomic viability and transition", Budapest: Institute of Economics.

Barr, N. (ed.), 1994, *Labour Markets and Social Policy in Central and Eastern Europe: The Transition and Beyond*, New York and Oxford: Oxford University Press.

CSO, 1993, "The effects of taxes and benefits on household income, 1991", *Economic Trends*, London: CSO.

Deaton, A.S., 1987, "Econometric Issues for tax Design in Developing Countries", Ch 4 in Newbery and Stern, 1987.

Deaton, A.S. and Stern, N.H., 1986, "Optimally Uniform Commodity Taxes, Taste Differences, and Lump-sum Grants", *Journal of Public Economics* 20(3), pp. 333-46.

EBRD, 1994, *Transition Report 1994*, London: European Bank for Reconstruction and Development, London.

EBRD, 1995, *Transition Report 1995*, London: European Bank for Reconstruction and Development, London.

Feldstein, M.S., 1972, "Distributional equity and the optimal structure of public prices", *American Economic Review.* 62(1), pp. 32-6.

Gersovitz, M, 1987, "The Effects of Domestic taxes on Foreign Private Investment" Ch 23, pp. 615-36 of Newbery and Stern, 1987.

Gil Díaz, F., 1987, "Some Lessons from Mexico's Tax Reform" Ch 12 of Newbery and Stern, 1987.

Hancock, R and Pudney, S., 1996, "State pension and the welfare of pensioners during economic transition: an analysis of Hungarian Survey Data", University of Leicester: CEES DP 96/1.

Heady, C. and Smith, S., 1995, "Tax and benefit reform in the Czech and Slovak Republics", Ch 1 in Newbery, 1995b.

IMF, 1994, *World Economic Outlook*, October, International Monetary Fund, Washington DC, chart 2, p. 75..

Jarvis, S. and Pudney, S., 1995, "Redistributive Policy in a Transition Economy: The Case of Hungary", in Newbery, 1995b.

Koltay, J., 1993, "Tax reform in Hungary", Ch 14 in *Hungary: an Economy in Transition*, edited by Székely, I. P., and Newbery, D.M.

Kornai, J., 1992, "The PostSocialist Transition and the State: Reflections in the Light of Hungarian Fiscal Problems", *American Economic Review,* Papers and Proceedings, 82(2), May, pp. 1-21.

Newbery, D.M., 1991, "Reform in Hungary: Sequencing and Privatisation", *European Economic Review,* 35, May, pp. 571-80.

Newbery, D. M., 1994, "Optimal Tax Rates and Tax Design during Systemic Reform", Working Paper IPR67, Institute for Policy Reform, Washington DC, January (forthcoming in *Journal of Public Economics*).

Newbery, D.M., 1995a, "The distributional impact of price changes in Hungary and the UK", *Economic Journal,* July 1995, pp. 847-63.

Newbery, D.M., 1995b (ed)., *Tax and Benefit Reform in Central and Eastern Europe*, London: Centre for Economic Policy Research, ISBN 1 898128 197.

Newbery, D.M. and Revesz, T., 1995a, "The Impact of the Transition on Hungarian Households: A Note", Cambridge: Department of Applied Economics, January.

Newbery, D.M. and Revesz, T., 1995b, "The Burden of the Hungarian Personal Tax System", Cambridge: Department of Applied Economics, March, Appendix Table 6 and Figures 1-3).

Newbery, D.M. and Stern, N.H. (eds), 1987, *The Theory of Taxation for Developing Countries*, Oxford, Clarendon Press.

OECD/CCET, 1995, *Social and Labour Market Policies in Hungary*, Paris: OECD, p. 127.

Pudney, S., 1994, "Earnings Inequality in Hungary: A Comparative Analysis of Household and Enterprise Data", *Economics of Planning*, 27, pp. 251-76.

Pudney, S., 1995, "Household welfare change during economic transition in Hungary: an application of semiparametric estimation", University of Leicester, mimeo ACE report

Rein, M. and Wörgötter, A., 1995, *Social Protection and the Enterprise in Transitional Economies*, CEPR, London.

Semjén, A., 1995, "Tax policies in transforming economies with a special focus on Hungary", Budapest: Institute of Economics.

Stern, N.H., 1976, "On the Specification of Models of Optimal Income Taxation", *Journal of Public Economics,* 6(1,2), pp. 123-62.

Stern, N.H., 1987, "The Theory of Optimal Commodity and Income Taxation: An Introduction", Ch 2 of Newbery and Stern, 1987.

Revesz, T., 1994, "An Analysis of the Representativeness of the Hungarian Household Budget Survey Samples", DPET 9403, Department of Applied Economics, Cambridge

World Bank, 1994, *Averting the Old Age Crisis: Policies to Protect the Old and Promote Growth*, Oxford: Oxford University Press.

6

Comments

Tito Boeri

The authors of these contributions have succeeded in providing a comprehensive overview of labour market adjustment in various transition economies, and in placing this issue against the backdrop of OECD economies. As a matter of fact, the authors did such a good job that they inevitably exposed themselves to the ongoing controversies surrounding labour market adjustment and unemployment persistence in OECD countries.

Why is the experience of transition economies so relevant for OECD countries? The main lessons which can be drawn from these countries relate to the nature and extent of the labour reallocation process. The transition to a market economy involves large shifts of jobs and workers across industries, firms and occupations, and the three contributions nicely complement each other in addressing these dimensions of the reallocation process. They are much less convincing when the authors assess the desirability of the pace and direction of labour market adjustment in the various countries.

The performance indicators proposed by Jackman, which measure the speed of convergence of these countries to the structure of employment of OECD countries, are quite debatable, not only because of measurement problems (for transition economies, the author largely relies on administrative sources, which typically under-report the small business sector, hence employment in services), but also because it is problematic to identify *a priori* an employment structure to which these countries should converge. Why, rather than taking the OECD countries as reference, should one not target the employment structures of market economies at comparable levels of GDP *per capita* (at PPP)? It may also be desirable for the CEECs to have, during the transition, a large hidden unemployment in agriculture as this could contribute to alleviate poverty. One should not necessarily take as a model countries that experienced a drastic reduction of the employment share in primary sectors.

It is also difficult to take the speed at which the employment (or value added) share of the private sector has been growing as an indicator of performance. A rapid privatisation process often leads to either insider ownership or a very dispersed outsider ownership structure, not capable of exerting effective governance over the firm. The evidence presented in Part II suggests that the direct sales route to privatisation may be conducive to better economic performance, but it is well-known that this route is time-consuming.

As it is so difficult to identify criteria against which evidence on the labour reallocation process in these countries can be evaluated, I would propose a criterion on which a wider consensus could be reached. This criterion can be stated as follows — given that adjustment necessarily requires a certain amount of external reallocation (that is, it cannot be achieved entirely by reallocating labour within each firm), it is desirable that this reallocation does not marginalise a large number of people of working age. In other terms, the reallocation process should involve outsiders as much as possible. This criterion has the advantage of putting the experience of transition economies into a perspective that can be particularly valuable for OECD countries, all of which are struggling to prevent further declines in labour supply. In this respect, recent comparative analyses of gross job flows in the OECD area seem to indicate that better labour market outcomes are not so much associated with rising mobility of workers across jobs, but rather with a greater participation of the unemployed and those temporarily out-of-labour force in this reallocation. From this angle, the reallocation process in transition economies is far from satisfactory. Analyses conducted at OECD have shown that the unemployment pool in these countries is stagnant, and data from recent labour force surveys seem to indicate that flows from outside the labour force to employment are relatively modest.

As regards policy implications, the authors seem all to agree on blaming the unemployment benefit systems. This overstretches the role played by unemployment benefits in the adjustment process. It is difficult to believe that unemployment benefits are too generous when they last between less than 6 to 12 months, i.e. far less than in most OECD countries, in which re-employment prospects of the unemployed are particularly gloomy and average benefits are roughly at the level of the statutory minimum wage (which is often significantly below actual wage minima established by collective agreements).

Furthermore, fiscal pressures on the private sector and the negative effects of unemployment benefits funding on gross job creation should not be overemphasized. Fiscal pressures are mainly related to the pension systems or categories of social spending (e.g. health expenditure) other than unemployment benefits as well as to the shrinking of the tax base, due to widespread tax avoidance and evasion in the emerging private sector.

Evidence on unemployment outflows does not lend support to the view that unemployment benefits have strong disincentive effects on job search. The claims of the authors are based on comparisons of unemployment rates and benefit levels in countries like, on the one hand, Russia and the Czech Republic, and, on the other, Poland and Hungary, but there are other comparisons which can shed more light on the impact of unemployment benefit systems. For instance, why not base one's inferences on the effects of the tightening of unemployment benefit systems introduced in most of these countries at the beginning of 1992? We have also tried to draw lessons on the impact of "active" vs. "passive" employment policies by comparing the experiences of the Czech and Slovak republics (two countries that have much more in common than the Czech Republic and Russia). Our general findings — which will need to be supported by further evidence — are that a lack of job vacancies, rather than the disincentive effects associated with the unemployment benefit systems, has been a major factor behind low unemployment outflows in these countries.

In the interest of brevity, I will briefly list four areas where analysis is likely to yield important results for the design of strategies to prevent the build-up of large pools of outsiders in economies undergoing rapid structural change.

The first area concerns the availability of financing for the restructuring of firms. In certain countries, such as Hungary, there is evidence that, due to credit constraints, some firms went too far in reducing their employment levels in order to restore their viability. It would be interesting to see whether this "excessive labour shedding" has taken place also in other countries.

The second area concerns the effectiveness of job placement services in increasing the marketability of the outsider vis-à-vis the insiders. Preliminary work we have done on the staffing of employment services seems to indicate that a decentralised and service-oriented public employment service can play an important role in boosting outflows to jobs, but more evidence on this is needed to formulate firm policy recommendations.

Third, an area that quite surprisingly has received limited and decreasing attention in the literature on transition economies is that of wage bargaining institutions. The institution-building process in this area could leave room for experiments aimed at bringing the outsiders into the game, e.g. an involvement of the unemployed in wage setting negotiations.

Finally, work disincentives and "poverty traps" may possibly arise in the passage from the unemployment benefit regime to social assistance, which, unlike unemployment benefits, is means-tested. A closer look at how this transition is handled could yield important policy implications. It should be recalled that in some transition economies there are at present more unemployed people receiving social assistance than unemployment benefits. Thus, options related to adopting a more "activist" approach to the delivery of social assistance should be considered. This could involve a closer link between the public employment service and social welfare centres for the purpose of providing benefits and enforcing work-tests for the long-term unemployed.

Randall Filer

The discussants have a far easier task than the authors of the contributions. No matter what conclusion is drawn and how carefully it is supported, all the discussant has to do is to say: "but we can't believe this because the data is bad." In reading the authors' contributions. I am consistently left with a disturbing feeling: there are numbers, but do they mean anything? How can I identify what to believe?

My reluctance to go on the record with conclusions regarding the transition started when I first went to the Czech Republic in 1993, and I realised that, according to official statistics, Czech real wages fell by 28.1 per cent between 1989 and 1991. This obviously had to be an accurate and meaningful number — it even contained a decimal point! As a result of this massive, if perhaps temporary, fall in wages, I expected, in line with economic theory, a series of effects on household consumption and saving. To my surprise, the economic reality that I witnessed in

Prague did not confirm these expectations. This suggests that perhaps the transition calls for an adaptation in our traditional research strategies. Most of us are taught that the "proper" way to do economic research is to develop a theory and then to test it on the basis of data. In the context of the transition, this process may need to be reversed. If the data is inconsistent with well-accepted theory, we may need to question the data before revising the theory. We should subject all purported data from CEECs to serious consistency checks. Only when an entire pattern of findings is consistent with our basic understanding of economic behaviour can we accept that the data is reasonably accurate. This informed scepticism is what is missing in almost all contributions here.

A question should also be raised regarding the choice of comparison groups. There seems to be an implicit assumption that "geography is destiny." Thus there is a search, as Jackman says, "for a comparable European Union economy." Yet the fundamental fact remains that there is no comparable European Union economy. No matter how bad the statistics are, everyone would agree that real incomes are orders of magnitude higher in Western Europe than in Central and Eastern Europe. Given current growth rate differentials between the two areas, the transition economies cannot expect to catch up with the EU for several decades. Since services are typically luxury goods, no expert should be surprised that the structure of the labour force in the Czech Republic or Bulgaria is vastly different from what it is in Germany, with a much lower fraction employed in services. This is not an indication of an underdeveloped service sector, as much as it is an accurate indicator of the level of real income.

Rather than being concerned about labour market reallocation, one should worry about economic growth since the labour market will adjust itself. A more interesting question is: how does the structure of the labour force in Central and Eastern Europe compare with that in Malaysia or Thailand? What underlies the assumption that transition economies should look like Germany? Is the reason that they share a border with Germany, while in fact they share many more economic conditions with other undercapitalised, post-colonial economies?

My final comment regards the role of unemployment benefits. The authors look at benefit levels; other analyses, however, suggest that the critical policy parameter is not the level but rather the duration of benefits. For both Hungary and Slovenia, for example, the hazard of leaving unemployment for a job is very low except in the weeks before benefit expiration, when the hazard increases to ten or more times its rate in the previous weeks. This suggests that, if unemployment benefits have to be reformed, the appropriate policy is to make them as short as possible, while relying on general assistance to protect the truly needy, and inducing others to accept employment as quickly as possible. Shortening benefit durations early in the transition may have contributed to the low unemployment level in the Czech Republic and also may represent an approach valid for the rest of the region.

Fabrizio Coricelli

As the transition progresses, it is becoming increasingly apparent that fiscal issues are central to the overall economic transformation — tax and benefit reforms are a key factor to sustain reforms and growth. These reforms involve decisions on the size and role of the public sector in the new market economy, as well as on the extent of income re-distribution in the face of the growing income inequality associated with market reforms.

As well documented in the contributions by Newbery and Ellman, transition has the peculiar feature of implying a highly non-linear path for macroeconomic variables. Reforms leading to long-term gains are likely to imply sharp costs in the short run. As a result, there are issues of inter-generational equity, since older generations will live in the period of costly adjustment, without benefiting enough from the long-term gains stemming from the increased productivity of the economy. Of course, the solution of most distributional issues crucially depends on the efficiency of financial markets; countries undertaking successful reforms should be able to borrow initially to smooth their consumption. However, most transition economies face severe constraints on their borrowing capabilities. Moreover, the underdevelopment of financial markets implies that budget deficits are initially financed by money creation, with a direct impact on inflation.

Probably policy-makers and their advisors in CEECs have given too much attention to the budget deficit rather than to the issues of size of the public sector and the composition of taxes and expenditures. As emphasized by Tanzi (1993), budget deficits are a misleading indicator in economies in transition. Indeed, successful restructuring of the economy requires a budget deficit. I have shown in a simple model of restructuring that imposing excessively tight year-by-year constraints on budget deficits will encourage governments in CEECs to slow down restructuring. This point is rightly stressed by Newbery, who points out that restructuring implies higher taxation — of course, when borrowing is not a feasible option.

If one assumes that unemployment may be an indicator of the magnitude of restructuring and reallocation of resources across sectors, there is evidence that budget deficits in the initial stages of transition mainly reflected the dynamics of restructuring rather than the behaviour of output. In an econometric test based on panel data concerning six Central and Eastern European countries, in the period 1989-93, I found that the behaviour of budget deficits (as a share of GDP) is affected by the behaviour of unemployment, while the GDP variable is not statistically significant.[1]

The fiscal effect of restructuring works out through both tax revenue and expenditure. The reallocation of production factors from the public sector to private firms reduces the tax base in the short run, as taxation of private sector is difficult. On the expenditure side, restructuring implies transition unemployment, thereby increasing public expenditure. The fact that direct expenditure on unemployment benefits has not been very large should not be interpreted as an indication of a low fiscal impact of unemployment. Indeed, a large component of social expenditures, including pensions, is due to labour market adjustment.

The experience of the most advanced reforming countries (Czech and Slovak republics, Hungary and Poland) shows that pressure on the budget has come mainly from the rise in expenditure, rather than from the collapse of tax revenue. *Ex post*, one could conclude that successful reforms were supported by social expenditures. However, the form taken by these expenditures has been inefficient and dangerous from a long-term perspective. In fact, most of the increase in social expenditures concerns the pension system that has been used as a social stabilizer. Given the unfavourable demographic trends, the result has been to rapidly bring the pension system to bankruptcy. Although the temporary increase in social expenditures was justified from the point of view of inter-generational equity and to boost support for reforms, the way in which it was effected was myopic and very inefficient. Transition economies should have been better advised to design temporary schemes of income support (even relatively generous ones), while at the same time reforming the pension system in the direction of a capitalisation scheme. The initial fiscal costs could have been financed either through borrowing or through an increase in labour taxation. In fact, taxation increased anyway, without contributing to the establishment of a sustainable pension system.

Note

[1] The regression results are:
B/GDP = 0.43 (0.39) - 0.06 (-0.56)* GDPgrowth + 0.42 (3.60)* Unemployment rate.
See Coricelli (1996).

References

Coricelli, F., 1996, "Fiscal constraints, reform strategies, and the speed of transition: The case of Central-Eastern Europe", *CEPR Discussion paper series*, No. 1339.

Tanzi, V., 1993, "Fiscal policy and the economic restructuring of economies in transition", *International Monetary Fund Working Paper series*, WP 93/22, March.

Jan Svejnar

The contribution by Ellman identifies very important issues, such as the decline in fertility and the increase in the death rate in the former Soviet Union, and it shows that the diverse explanations still leave many questions unanswered. Fertility rates seem to be converging towards the rates that are seen in Western Europe but this is just a hypothesis. Ellman also provides some counter-evidence in the sense that the decline in fertility may be temporary, and in some of the reforming countries the fertility rate may rebound. Furthermore, in the region of the former GDR, the decline in fertility has been much deeper; what are the reasons for this outlier case? In analysing this issue, it would be worth considering the huge positive wage effects, as well as the reduction of risk within this society as compared with the CEECs. As regards the rise in mortality rates, there are a number of reasons for this but its concentration in time remains to be explained.

The contribution by Newbery is an exemplary policy-oriented study, since it presents new evidence, it surveys evidence from other studies, discusses relevant theory and draws policy conclusions. In my view, however, a number of issues still remain open. Why do these countries have such a high ratio of government expenditure to GDP, and why have some of them, namely the Czech Republic, Slovakia, Bulgaria, Romania and Russia, succeeded in cutting this ratio, while Poland and Hungary have not? Profit tax revenue has declined dramatically in

Hungary and Poland but not so much in the Czech Republic or Slovakia. The reason suggested by Newbery is basically that there may be delays in industrial restructuring in the Czech and Slovak republics. However, the two republics have very open economies, with the lowest tariffs in Central and Eastern Europe, and in Europe in general; industrial concentration has been reduced; and profits have shown resiliency. As a result the profit tax revenue remains significant.

As far as Hungary's reforms are concerned, an interesting result of Newbery's calculations is that there has been no perceptible change in income distribution, as measured by the Gini coefficient. This is consistent with the findings of some studies concerning the Czech and Slovak republics, but it runs against some other findings. Further research is needed to assess the impact of reforms on income inequality.

On the question of what the optimal tax rate should be, Newbery focuses on the degree of skill inequality. It is interesting to note that skill inequality is treated as an exogeneous variable, whereas in labour economics the level of human capital is totally endogenous, a result of choices by the individuals. Furthermore, it is argued that CEECs have lower skill inequality than other European countries. This assertion might be based on the observed smaller inequality in income and wage distributions, but such evidence does not seem conclusive.

Stefano Scarpetta

There are several areas which one can debate with the authors. Among them, I would like to focus on: (1) the comparisons between CEECs and the NIS on policy stance and labour market performance; and (2) the regional dimension of unemployment in transition countries and the implications of wide regional disparities for the setting of labour market, social policies and, more generally, structural policies.

Labour market performance and policy setting in CEECs and the NIS

Several considerations presented by the authors refer to the debate on the optimal pace of reform, in particular to the labour market implications of different reform choices (for more details on this issue see, among others, Blanchard, 1995). In my view, deciding on a reform approach cannot be just a matter of theoretical considerations, but should also be a matter of empirical analysis. As stressed by Commander and Tolstopiatenko, the experience of five to six years of transition in CEECs and in the FSU offers a unique occasion to compare the results of different transition strategies. In rather broad terms, FSU countries seem to have followed a gradualist approach to the transformation of their economy with quite restrictive income support schemes, high State subsidies and relatively soft budget constraints for SOEs. Leaving aside measurement problems, labour market data for FSU countries suggest relatively less labour shedding, with in some cases even increased employment relative to output, low unemployment rates, low persistence of unemployment, large flows in and out of the unemployment pool, at levels which are comparable with those in the United States. At the same time, however, FSU economies have been characterised by a high incidence of poverty, even among those at work.

The broad picture in CEECs, which have generally followed a faster reform approach, indicates high (with the notable exception of the Czech Republic) and persistent unemployment rates (albeit slowly declining in the recent past); low flows in and out of the unemployment pool and, in particular, low flows from unemployment to jobs and large flows of discouraged workers out of the labour force.

If the slower pace of economic reform in FSU economies could be considered, at least partially, responsible for the relatively less advanced stage of economic transformation, then it may be interesting to assess the labour market effects of further progress in the reform process. In particular, what would be the effects of phasing out implicit and explicit state subsidies to SOEs, of imposing a hard budget constraint to these firms and of improving the collection of taxes and social security contributions? Most likely, these firms would be forced to cut social benefits to their workers and to restructure themselves, which would inevitably lead to significant labour shedding. Would then the very restrictive unemployment benefits be sustainable or would social pressure lead to an increase in the levels (and possibly the duration) of these benefits in order to avoid widespread poverty? This is an issue which has not been sufficiently explored by the authors but which deserves further attention in order to promote a better understanding of the role of different reform strategies on the speed and, possibly, the success of the transition process.

The regional dimension of unemployment in transition countries

An issue which has only marginally been discussed by the authors is the regional dimension of unemployment in transition economies and its policy implications. As documented in a recent publication of the CCET (OECD, 1995), the transition has made visible new inter-regional disparities that are mainly due to the different reactions of regions to market signals in the new economic framework (Scarpetta, 1995). Under the previous system, disparities in regional economic performance were reduced by a continuous redistribution of resources and, consequently, they were not fully translated into different living standards. Since the launch of the transition process, disparities in regional or sectoral performance have no longer been mitigated, thereby giving rise to different labour market pressures and wider inequalities in living standards. For example, if we rank regions in each CEEC by unemployment level and then group the regions into quartiles, we observe that in 1994 there were two to three times more unemployed persons in the most disadvantaged regions than in the most developed regions. Moreover, a simple index of regional mismatch suggests that about one third of the unemployed should, in theory, be re-located in order to attain the same unemployment-to-vacancy ratio across regions. These figures are large by OECD standards, being close to (or even higher than) those observed in countries like Italy or Spain, with historically severe regional disparities. A further widening of these disparities has been prevented by slowing down enterprise restructuring and through large flows from unemployment to non-participation in the labour force in high unemployment regions. In fact, high levels of regional unemployment have led to high social pressure to slow down the pace of restructuring (Boeri and Scarpetta, 1996).

The existence of wide regional disparities sheds more light on certain features of aggregate labour market performance which were underscored by the authors. Gora, for example, suggests that there are two groups of workers in Poland: one group includes the short-term unemployed and workers with a low risk of becoming unemployed; the other includes workers with a high risk of unemployment which is generally of long duration and which may lead to discouragement and withdrawal from the labour market. I would argue that most of those in the second group live in backward regions, where there are few job openings and scant signs of a developing private sector. For example, in the least developed regions of Poland, the long-term unemployed accounted for 50-60 per cent of total unemployment in 1993, while they accounted for no more than 20 per cent in other, more developed, areas.

The existence of wide disparities in regional economic conditions should also be considered when assessing the speed and success of restructuring by the pace of sectoral labour reallocation, as proposed by Jackman and Pauna. This is particularly the case given the lack of geographical labour mobility and the high sectoral specialisation of many regions. In this context, it would be interesting to assess whether the relatively less advanced stage of restructuring in Poland (Table 3 in Jackman and Pauna) can also be explained by relatively higher regional disparities and greater difficulties in re-locating workers across sectors/regions.

Regional disparities also raise the issue of the appropriateness of different policy measures, particularly labour market policies. Active labour market programmes are set, in most cases, at the local level and are funded by the government according to regional labour market conditions. By contrast, income support schemes are not geared to cope with wide regional disparities. This is particularly true for those schemes which are based on a flat-rate formula or on country-wide standards. For example, the Polish unemployment benefit system is generally considered to be quite restrictive, being based on a flat rate equal to 36 per cent of the average wage. However, these benefits may be considered as relatively generous in certain backward areas where wages are likely to be close to the minimum wage (38 per cent of the average wage in 1992/93).[1] In these cases, unfortunately, the risk of creating disincentives to job acceptance is high.

Note

[1] Regional wage data suggest that unemployment benefits were close to 60 per cent of the average wage in the trade sector of the most backward regions of Poland, and the latter is likely to be much higher than the wages attached to the few vacancies available in these regions.

References

Blanchard, O., 1995, *Clarendon Lecture on the Economics of Transition*, November, [mimeo].

Boeri, T. and Scarpetta, S., 1996, "Regional Mismatch and the Transition to a Market Economy", *Labour Economics*, forthcoming.

OECD/CCET, 1995, *The Regional Dimension of Unemployment in Transition Countries: A Challenge for Labour Market and Social Policies*, Paris.

Scarpetta, S., 1995, "Spatial Variations in Unemployment in Central and Eastern Europe: Underlying Reasons and Labour Market Policy Options", in OECD/CCET, 1995, *The Regional Dimension of Unemployment in Transition Countries: A Challenge for Labour Market and Social Policies*, Paris.

Krzysztof J. Ners

The first stage of transition was marked by impressive gains in macroeconomic stabilization and economic recovery in most CEECs. This, however, does not mean that the transition is over. Macroeconomic reforms have not been accompanied by the social equivalent of the Balcerowicz-type economic reform package. Together with "transition recession", this situation has led to a crisis in public finances, with the State still being unable to cope with the social stress. Any attempt to finance the budget deficit through such means as increasing taxation, higher employers' contributions to social funds, or floating public bonds would have a suffocating effect on the emerging private sector that is the major hope for economic recovery and job creation.

The priority assigned to economic adjustment and liberalisation has not been complemented by equivalent action on the social side, whether through budgetary measures or through direct social assistance. There is a danger that the CEECs' economies will stagnate at different stages of their transition, retaining many structural features of the communist past, including the old social policies.

The reform of the tax system is a crucial step for reforming and modernising the social sector. Only the scarcity of available budgetary resources could reinforce politically difficult decisions in two key areas: pension and health care.

The reduction of the very heavy social security tax on individuals and companies would probably be the key element of a tax and public finance reform. Furthermore, it would contribute to reducing unit labour costs and to bringing to light the informal economy. This tax reduction could be achieved by changing the current pension system into a defined-contribution, multi-pillar pension scheme.

Concerning Russia's demographic crisis, it should be noted that countries that applied the so-called "shock therapy", such as Poland, Czechoslovakia and Hungary, have not experienced mortality rates as high as those observed in Russia. To explain the critical situation in this country, it is necessary to consider other factors in addition to the transition itself, namely the serious degradation of the environment as well as the inadequacy of the health care system.

7

General discussion

The discussion among experts was centered on three substantive issues: 1) the problem of high unemployment; 2) the reform of the tax and social benefit systems; and 3) the determinants of high mortality rates.

On the question of unemployment, contrasting views were expressed about the magnitude of the problem, its causes and possible measures to deal with it. Wörgötter noted that there may not actually be a trade-off between industrial restructuring and unemployment since some countries have progressed on the former front without generating high unemployment rates. Negritoiu, instead, argued that economic reform and macroeconomic stabilization can hardly create jobs in the short-term. Hence, the problem remains as to how to cope with the short-term costs of economic restructuring in terms of unemployment, while advancing in this process.

The measurement of unemployment itself raises daunting problems (Balcerowicz) as the official statistics do not adequately capture developments in the informal economy or in hidden unemployment. It was also noted (Zecchini) that in measuring and analysing unemployment, an attempt should be made to distinguish its structural component from the transitory one that can be attributed to the change in economic system and to on-going structural adjustments. The two components of unemployment require different policy responses. In this connection, broad similarities exist in the unemployment issues of transition economies and of OECD countries, with a supposedly large structural component and unsustainable levels of public expenditure to deal with its consequences. It is, however, an open question as to whether in the light of such a similarity, recent OECD policy recommendations for OECD member countries are suitable for transition economies as well.

Much attention was devoted to the generosity and coverage of the social welfare system, as well as to the choice of policy measures to tackle this problem, their effectiveness and the financial costs involved. Public interventions directed to keep unemployment low could at best affect its composition, i.e. its division into an open part and hidden one (Balcerowicz), but they would ultimately prove financially unsustainable. Sustained reform policies, such as liberalisation and privatisation, are the best measures to increase true employment and decrease true unemployment.

Among alternative policy measures, granting unemployment benefits is not a simple choice, since it raises a host of difficult issues for governments. These benefits represent for many transition economies a new addition to a system of social protection that has retained many important parts of the old system. According to Wörgötter, one of the consequences has been to create an environment characterised by high taxes, pressures to increase transfers and declining incomes.

While the transfers might be seen as a way to encourage social consensus, it cannot be assumed that these systems can be sustained, particularly at the relatively low income levels prevailing in these countries.

Reducing unemployment benefits is not, however, an easy solution either since it involves several drawbacks. Svejnar pointed out that evidence from the Czech and Slovak economies does not indicate that important work disincentives are associated with unemployment benefit provisions. Reducing unemployment benefits would, therefore, not necessarily lead to significant declines in unemployment, while it would certainly reduce political support for reforms. In contrast, Wörgötter questioned the extent to which a package of high tax rates, high transfers and a high level of social benefits is necessary in order to maintain political support for reform. By another token, according to Boeri, the evidence from other transition economies suggests that in fact reductions in expenditure for unemployment benefits lead to increases in outlays for social assistance and early retirements.

Sustainability of current labour market and social policies has become a critical factor for the ultimate success of the reform strategy. Nevertheless, this problem does not appear intractable. Gelb stressed that in the last five years, cuts in public spending by Central European countries have been made and are of a size with no comparable historic precedent. This was corroborated by Kornai, who highlighted the public expenditure reductions achieved by Hungary in the period 1994-1996. The assumption of a "fiscal barrier to reform", namely of progress in structural reforms being hampered by the need to maintain fiscal balance, has been proven unrealistic, since the most advanced reforming countries have also been the most successful in retaining fiscal revenue (Gelb). The slowest reformers tend to be in a difficult position since they not only have the least capable tax administrations but have also suffered the greatest declines in their revenue base. In this respect, Filer noted that Chile may offer a better benchmark than Western Europe when assessing the appropriateness of the tax and expenditure reforms of CEECs.

On the expenditure side, Vogel highlighted the interconnections between, on the one hand, enterprise restructuring, and on the other hand, reform of public expenditure. Public authorities have to prepare themselves to take over the responsibility for social services that have been provided by enterprises as a burdensome legacy of the old economic system.

In the social sphere, governments are also called to deal with people's deteriorating living conditions, as health and life expectancy conditions have worsened. Possible explanations for the dramatic increase in mortality rates in the former Soviet Union were evaluated by Ellman and Gros without a consensus opinion emerging. There is no clear evidence that the recent worsening in infant mortality is correlated to the different stages of reforms in the reform process; rather, it reflects mostly country specific factors (Gelb). Among the countries of the former Soviet Union, there is instead some evidence pointing to a linkage between the slow pace of reforms and the rise in mortality rates (Gros). Limited reforms disrupt the old economic system without delivering rapid improvements in economic conditions, whereas major reforms ultimately lead to relatively lower social hardship. In the former Soviet Union increased mortality rates may also be attributed to regional factors related to environmental degradation. More studies are, therefore, needed on this problem. Balcerowicz stressed, instead, that in CEECs the most important factor in explaining mortality rates is lifestyle, with curative medicine playing a secondary role. A reduction in mortality rates could be expected from: a) the changes in relative prices, to the extent that they favour healthier food consumption than under the previous system; and b) psychological factors, such as the decreasing stress and increasing hope due to progress in the reforms.

8

Policy conclusions

After rising for several years in connection with the economic transformation process, unemployment rates have eventually peaked almost everywhere in Central and Eastern Europe, but are at present receding slowly and still remain disturbingly high. Of course, these summary figures do not provide a full picture of the evolution of the unemployment problem. To identify the determinants of unemployment and its linkages with the pace and depth of economic restructuring, a detailed analysis across countries and sectors, also allowing for different policy approaches, has been presented. It depicts a rather complex situation calling for multipronged policy action which cannot be reduced to the simplistic axiom that higher growth will ultimately produce lower unemployment.

Evidently, job shortages are a primary cause of the problem. Given that the private sector has become the main source of job creation, the first conclusion to be drawn is that policies aimed at promoting the multiplication and development of private enterprises should also be considered as a top priority for the purpose of reducing unemployment.

Joblessness is, in addition, a reflection of high rates of job destruction in non-viable enterprises, while, in the light of available evidence, it appears to be scantily related to the process of labour reallocation towards expanding firms. Reallocation has progressed to a considerable extent in several economies, notably the Visegrad countries; however, recruitment has been drawn more from other enterprises than from the unemployed. The rates of absorption of the unemployed into jobs have been relatively low and quite similar across these economies. Against this backdrop, it seems disputable to recommend policies directed at delaying the shedding of excess labour in enterprises since, aside from some benefits, there are costs for the firms to be restructured and for the public budget. It seems that the authorities should, instead, focus on the factors that hamper the return to employment, especially those related to the characteristics of the unemployed and the functioning of labour markets.

Among these factors, the generosity of unemployment benefits (probably, in terms of their duration more than their level) has been singled out as contributing to the persistence of high unemployment. Whether a pre-eminent unemployment factor or not, this benefit system should be amended in the direction of linking benefits to some incentives to work. In the same perspective, it does not seem appropriate that unemployment insurance is used as a tool for income support in the context of social assistance programmes. Furthermore, social policies need to be better co-ordinated with labour market policies in order to minimise both disincentives to work and costs for the public budget.

As regards labour market efficiency, several improvements could be introduced, for instance, in job placement services, in fostering regional mobility, with a view to reducing unemployment concentration, and in labour retraining. These are all components of an "active" labour market policy which is strongly advocated for all these economies, in particular, to replace sterile subsidisation of employment in non-viable firms.

Cost effectiveness is another criterion that should guide the authorities in adjusting labour market and social policies in order to make them affordable for their economies. These policies have already had perverse effects on the volume and composition of budgetary expenditure as well as on fiscal revenue. As a result of generous retirement treatments, that were partly dictated by the need to ease unemployment and to facilitate economic restructuring, pension payments have become a heavy burden for the budget in most CEECs. Pension schemes, therefore, require changes in the direction of more closely reflecting the level of accumulated social security contributions, even though this approach may raise concerns, or even outright opposition, on redistributive grounds. A given income redistribution effect can, however, be attained by acting on a wider range of expenditures and taxes.

Funding of employment-related and social expenditure has already led to an excessive wedge between labour cost and take-home pay. The containment of such expenses should give the authorities an opportunity to narrow this wedge, with a view to stimulating labour demand and, at the same time, discouraging the development of the informal economy. It might be useful to raise Wörgötter's point, questioning the necessity of an extensive tax and spend package in order to keep support for reforms. There are great dangers of low-income countries pursuing very ambitious social spending programmes. This might be true but in fact every time a government has reduced social spending, it has unleashed serious social tensions.

Overall, the unemployment problem in CEECs tends to acquire characteristics similar to those that have made joblessness high and persistent in the advanced economies of the rest of Europe. These experiences do not generally offer promising policy models for the transition economies, but rather provide an incentive to learn how not to repeat the same mistakes.

Part IV

External policies

1

Currency convertibility in transforming economies: was it a mistake?

Richard N. Cooper

1. Introduction

A striking feature of the economic transformations since 1990 is the rapidity with which former communist countries adopted *de facto* currency convertibility, at least for current account transactions, and even formally accepted the obligations of Article VIII of the International Monetary Fund. This stands in marked contrast to the long delay by most OECD countries to make their currencies convertible after the end of the second World War, and the even longer delay by most developing countries in moving toward currency convertibility. By spring 1996 all seven former CMEA countries in Central Europe had currencies that were in practice convertible for current account transactions (with the arguable exception of Romania), and four of those (along with Slovenia, Croatia, and Mongolia) had formally accepted Article VIII. Twelve of the former 15 republics of the USSR had currencies convertible in practice, and five of those had accepted Article VIII within less than five years of the disintegration of the USSR. In contrast, Western European countries took nearly 16 years from the end of the war to accept Article VIII (in February 1961), although in practice their currencies had been convertible since 1959; Japan took three years longer, for a total of nearly 19 years. And in spring 1996, well over 30 years after independence and IMF membership, as many as 54 developing countries (41 in Africa) still maintained exchange controls under the "transitional" Article XIV — a practice that demonstrated remarkable tolerance, one might even say laxity, by the management of the IMF with respect to the pre-eminent basic rule of this important financial club.

What explains this huge discrepancy in behaviour? Were the former communist countries wise in moving so rapidly (by comparison with others) to current account convertibility? Or in retrospect were the OECD countries and developing countries mistaken to have taken so long? Or were the circumstances so different that countries were generally correct in taking the different courses they did? Finally, we must at least allow for the logical possibility that the circumstances were different, but that the OECD countries were mistaken in having delayed so long, and the former communist countries were mistaken in moving so quickly.

2. Pros and cons of convertibility

Full currency convertibility is technically easy to achieve: simply permit everyone, residents and non-residents alike, to buy and sell home currency for other currencies freely and without restriction. Convertibility for current account transactions (foreign trade in goods and services, including the remittance of earnings), such as is required by the Articles of Agreement of the International Monetary Fund, is more complicated, since the allowable market is limited to a certain class of transactions — or, put another way, it is designed to exclude certain transactions, especially the purchase by residents of foreign financial assets. It therefore requires some detailed rules and close monitoring, to prevent transactions supposedly made for current purposes from concealing what in fact are capital transactions.[1] When people speak of the difficulty or even the impossibility of a country achieving convertibility, therefore, they must have in mind, not convertibility *per se*, but the economic or political consequences of convertibility.

While convertibility strictly refers to the freedom to purchase foreign exchange for domestic currency, convertibility would not be economically meaningful if licensing were required for the activities that require foreign exchange, for example importing goods or services. In what follows, therefore, I will use convertibility in the economically meaningful sense, rather than in the narrowly legal sense, of the term. That is, convertibility cannot be considered independently of the accompanying regime for foreign trade. In particular, a currency is *de facto* convertible if would-be importers for a wide range of goods or services are free to buy foreign exchange and to import with minimal requirements, possibly subject to import duties that are not prohibitively high.

I will try in the next few paragraphs to sketch the concerns of many policy-makers in the early 1950s, and indeed by some in developing countries today, without trying to give historically accurate weights to these concerns. After that, I will sketch some of the advantages alleged for currency convertibility for former communist countries in the period 1989-91, when their move to market economies was first launched in earnest.

The typical objection to a move to convertibility is that it would lead to an unsustainable loss of foreign exchange reserves and a balance of payments crisis. This objection obviously presupposes that the government has pegged the exchange rate, or at least has taken a view on how rapid a change is permissible. If the exchange rate is pegged (including a crawling peg), then an unsustainable outflow of funds, for example through a current account deficit, must be met by some contractionary monetary policy, which in many countries will often imply the need for a smaller government budget deficit. In either case it may lead to a decline in output and income in the short run — something that is never politically popular — and if it persists, it was widely believed, to slower growth in the long run.

The alternative is to alter the rate of exchange between home and foreign currency by enough to stop the outflow — either by allowing it to float, or by depreciating by so much that market participants believe it will depreciate no further, that imported goods become so expensive in home currency that demand for them will fall significantly, and that exports become so profitable that their supply will increase significantly (or, depending on the significance of our country in the world product market, that the price of exports will fall sufficiently in foreign currency that foreign demand will be greatly stimulated). For a period in the 1950s some "elasticity pessimists" doubted that any exchange rate could clear the foreign exchange market, by which they really meant that the required depreciation might be very large. That in turn could have other undesirable consequences, to wit: a sharp increase in the domestic price level, driven by the rise in the prices of tradable goods, which might trigger higher inflationary expectations, either because the public cannot distinguish a once-for-all rise in the price level from an acceleration of inflation, or because the price increase would in fact trigger an inflationary process whereby wage-earners and others attempted to restore their real incomes by insisting on higher nominal wages (and other incomes).

If wage earners are restrained, the currency depreciation might nonetheless result in a marked deterioration of the distribution of income, especially if the staple food and other key consumption goods are tradable goods, such that their relative prices will rise with currency depreciation. That in turn might lead to serious social and political unrest, even political instability.

These are the kinds of concerns that opponents or sceptics of currency convertibility held in the 1950s, and hold even today in some quarters. In addition, several other inhibitions should be mentioned. First, it might be argued that the practical distinction between current and capital transactions is difficult or impossible to sustain, and that to prevent outflows of resident capital requires controls over current transactions as well, with a view to ensuring domestic savings are invested domestically — i.e. as an adjunct of a policy to stimulate economic growth. Second, some governments felt they had a clearer idea than private investors could of what activities were required to generate and sustain economic growth, or they took a view of where sectoral growth was especially meritorious. Short of undertaking the desired sectoral investments themselves (as many governments in developing countries did, through state-owned-enterprises), they needed some instrument for steering investment in the desired direction. Allocation of credit was the principal chosen instrument, for example in France, Japan, and South Korea, but allocation of foreign exchange played an important adjunct role, and in the early 1950s was perhaps even more important. Even when allocation of foreign exchange was not undertaken aggressively in pursuit of particular objectives, its possible withdrawal was a potent source of discipline over firm managers who were not otherwise inclined to follow the guidance of the planning ministries.

Finally, once exchange controls are in place, there is another, usually unstated, justification for keeping them in place: foreign exchange allocation is a useful channel for political favouritism and/or personal enrichment, by political leaders and by administering officials alike. Especially in poor countries, where control of the government is viewed as one of the few, and perhaps the only sure, route to riches, allocation of foreign exchange under an over-valued currency is one of the ways government authority can be used to enhance tribal, regional, or personal wealth. Despite this array of concerns with moving to convertibility from a system of tightly rationed foreign exchange, many reform-minded economists accepted the need for a convertible currency as a key component of a market-oriented economy. The question was one of timing. Early reformers in the Soviet Union argued that while convertibility was desirable, it should come, as in post-war Western Europe, late in the process. Thus Abel Aganbegyan, head of the economics section of the Soviet Academy of Science and adviser to Gorbachev on economic reform, argued that convertibility should be a "long-term objective", to be approached gradually, but he was hardly troubled by the numerous exchange rates applicable to different Soviet industries in the late 1980s and he showed no sense of urgency in establishing convertibility. Even the famous 500-day plan of September 1990, urged by Academician Shatalin and his reform-minded team and noted for its boldness (which led Gorbachev to back away from it), foresaw convertibility coming late in the reforms, possibly years after the 500-day initial push. And reformer (and former finance minister) Boris Fedorov wrote in late 1990 of current account convertibility as "a medium-term target" (Fedorov in Williamson, 1991).

Others thought that currency convertibility should be an integral part of a programme of economic transformation from a centrally-planned to a market economy, to be introduced early in the programme, with price liberalisation. One illustration is to quote the argument put in an IIASA report transmitted in mid-1990 to Soviet Deputy Prime Minister (for economic policy) Abalkin and to the Shatalin team (Cooper in Peck, Aven, and Richardson, 1991; see also McKinnon, 1991, Sachs, 1993; and Balcerowicz, 1995).

There are several reasons for preferring that the opening of the economy occur early rather than late. First, the key to a modern, flexible and innovative economy is competitive markets, wherein information on new patterns of demand or new technological developments is transmitted to the entire economy through price signals, to which both households and enterprises can respond by adapting their behaviour. The Soviet Union has intentionally concentrated production of most manufactured goods in one or relatively few enterprises. Monopolies do not respond to market signals in the same way as other enterprises, and their responses are not socially optimal. Some method must be found for introducing competitive pressures on Soviet enterprises at an early stage of restructuring so that enterprises feel these pressures in making their decisions. One way to do this, and for some sectors the only effective way, is to introduce foreign competition, so that Soviet enterprises have a price and a quality standard that they must match in order to sell at home or abroad. A second reason for introducing currency convertibility early is to encourage from the beginning an alignment of Soviet prices with world prices of traded goods and services, subject to such deviations as the economic authorities wish explicitly and consciously to make. If, as we assume, this alignment with world prices is the final objective, then starting the process early would be more advantageous than going through a domestic price liberalisation and then having a second major price realignment when the economy is opened. The alternative of administrative price adjustment to approximate world prices is inadvisable, both because it perpetuates the principle of administrative control of prices (as opposed to market determined prices) and because such control cannot be fully effective in a world with millions of products of diverse qualities. A third reason for favouring early convertibility of the rouble is to provide goods to Soviet workers whose incentive to work is now adversely affected by extensive shortages. Opening the economy would offer a wide array of new goods, albeit for purchase at high prices. It would not only provide effective wage goods, but would also help reduce the rouble overhang, since firms and households would be more willing to hold financial assets, which are not high by Western standards. It would also provide the Government with revenue from taxes levied on imports, as we propose below. Finally, convertibility would provide a strong stimulus to develop export markets. At the exchange rate required to make the rouble convertible, exports would be extremely profitable for newly independent enterprises. Autonomous enterprises would have a strong financial incentive to develop export markets, and that would push them from the beginning to take into account not only the price but also the quality of products that are sold in the world market.

While the argument was made for the then-USSR, it has more general applicability to the shift of any command economy to a market-oriented one. And in fact currency convertibility was introduced in the early reform packages of many of them, or soon thereafter. We will explore below the extent to which the concerns expressed by those anxious about currency convertibility came to pass, followed by a discussion of some of the considerations inhibiting a move toward convertibility in Europe in the late 1940s and early 1950s.

3. Trade and payments liberalisation in Eastern Europe

By 1994 all the former communist countries of Eastern Europe (as well as the three Baltic states) were rated by the European Bank for Reconstruction and Development to have earned the highest mark under the heading of price and trade liberalisation, on a scale of one to four. But both the timing and the speed of liberalisation varied substantially from country to country. Hungary and Poland began price liberalisation in the 1980s (Slovenia, then part of Yugoslavia, began even earlier). But Poland experienced the "big bang," encompassing full price and payments liberalisation as well as a major stabilization programme in January 1990. Hungary took important steps during 1990, but continued to liberalise more gradually, particularly the allocation of foreign exchange. Czechoslovakia introduced its own

Table 1. Trade and exchange rate practices.

	Initial major liberalisation	Exchange rate regime, 1995	Accepted Article VIII	Import tariff, 1994 average	Import tariff, range in 1994
Bulgaria	3/91,7/91....	Float	n.a.	17[a]	5 - 55
Czech Rep.	1/91	Fixed	10/95	5	0 - 80
Hungary	12/90....	Managed	1/96	15	5 - 83
Poland	1/90	Managed	6/95	13[a]	0 - 43
Romania	1/91, 1/92, 5/92....	Float	n.a.	12[a]	0 - 60
Slovak Rep.	1/91	Fixed	10/95	2	0 - 25
Slovenia	2/92	Managed	9/95	11[a]	0 - 25
Estonia	6/92	Fixed	8/94	<10	0 - 16
Latvia	5/92	Managed	6/94	<15	0 - 55
Lithuania	6/92...	Fixed	5/94	~ 10	0 - 30

Note: a) 1992

Sources: IMF, *Annual Report on Exchange Arrangements and Exchange Restrictions*, various years. *International Financial Statistics*, April 1996.

version of the big bang in January 1991, but that did not need to be so radical as Poland in terms of stabilizing actions, and it was modestly less radical in freeing the allocation of foreign exchange (see Table 1).

Albania, Bulgaria, and Romania took a series of liberalising steps during 1991 and 1992, which in the latter two cases carried them less far than Poland and Czechoslovakia, but left them all with currencies that were in practice convertible for most current transactions. Slovenia separated from Yugoslavia in 1992 and introduced its own currency; the Baltic states separated their currencies and economic systems from Russia in May and June of the same year, all three introducing radical and abrupt liberalisation, although the details differed (for example Estonia fixed its new currency with respect to the German mark, whereas the new currencies of Latvia and Lithuania were allowed to float until 1994). Poland, Hungary, Czechoslovakia, and Estonia began with fixed (albeit depreciated) exchange rates.

Albania, Bulgaria, Romania, Slovenia, Latvia, and Lithuania initially adopted flexible exchange rates, although in 1994 the last two switched to fixed rates (Lithuania formally, Latvia in practice) as they managed to bring inflation under control. Hungary continued to depreciate the forint from time to time, adopting a formal crawling peg in 1995, and Poland also adopted a managed float/crawling peg once the stabilization had taken hold. By 1995 Slovenia had also adopted a managed float, i.e. the authorities intervened regularly in the foreign exchange market to influence movement of the exchange rate.

Countries also simplified and generally lowered their tariffs and eliminated import quotas and requirements for import licensing at around the same time they introduced convertible currencies (the Baltics introduced new tariff systems at generally low rates). In most cases these early tariff systems were refined and raised somewhat (particularly the maximum rates) as time went on, but remained low (i.e. averaging 5 to 17 per cent) by the standards of most developing countries. Estonia and Lithuania began at virtually free trade, but then imposed revenue tariffs.

As noted at the outset, these changes were much more abrupt than the liberalisation of trade and payments introduced by Western European countries in the 1950s and by most developing countries over the 1980s and 1990s. How are we to assess their relative success? We look at five measures: economic growth, consumption, export performance, inflation, and capital flows.

Economic Growth — One standard is to look at what happened to total economic output (GDP, or an approximation thereof). Output declined in all Eastern European countries relative to 1989, by amounts that ranged from 17 or 18 per cent (Slovenia and Poland) to 52 and 61 per cent (Latvia and Lithuania) — see Table 2. By 1994 output was growing in all of these countries, although it continued to fall in some other republics from the former Soviet Union (Fischer, Sahay, and Vegh, 1996, Table 2). Even though reforms began in 1990 or 1991 for most of our countries (except the Baltics), output reached its bottom in 1993 for all except Poland (1991), Romania (1992), and Slovenia (1992). Recovery resumed more quickly, in other words, in Poland and the Baltics, countries that liberalised relatively quickly, than in gradualist Bulgaria and Hungary. However, quick liberaliser Czechoslovakia also experienced economic decline for three years.

Total output, however, is suspect as a measure of success in these reforming economies. First, total output is poorly measured, particularly in the early years of reform; new economic activity permitted or encouraged by the liberalisation is greatly under-counted, due to inadequacies in statistical collection. Second and more important, much of the output in the former communist countries was socially without value (although it used resources), so substantial reductions in output by the existing enterprises was warranted and indeed (although rarely acknowledged by officials) was actually desirable.

Real Consumption — A more appropriate measure of the impact of liberalisation involves looking at real consumption.[2] Column 2 of Table 2 shows an estimate of the cumulative decline in real consumption between the year preceding major liberalisation (1989 for Hungary and Poland, 1990 or 1991 for others) and 1995. The change ranges from an increase of 8 per cent in Poland to a decline of 25 per cent in Slovakia (and, for comparison, of 34 per cent in Russia; consumption data for the three Baltics are not available). This measure does not permit a clear award between rapid and gradual liberalisation, since Slovakia was originally in the rapid category; but the favourable experience of Poland relative to Hungary and the Czech Republic against Bulgaria and Romania suggests that rapid liberalisation is not necessarily more costly. Consumption can be sustained and even increased if a country runs a growing current account deficit. Among our countries there is little marked trend in current account positions during the 1990s; if anything, there is a modest tendency toward declining deficits or larger surpluses. The notable exception is Hungary, which ran substantial deficits in 1993 and 1994, although the deficit declined after the adoption of an austerity programme and small devaluation in the spring of 1995.

Table 2. Performance Indices, 1995 (1990 = 100).

	Output	Real Household Consumption	Exports (US$)	Consumer Prices	Real Monthly Wages
Bulgaria	74	87	82	4267	45
Czech Republic	81	95	228	253	98
Hungary	83	93 [a]	103	381 [a]	88 [a]
Poland	93	108 [a]	133	3922 [a]	71 [a]
Romania	77	79	109	6578	97
Slovak Republic	78	75	248	272	84
Slovenia	89	n.a.	190	1172	107
Estonia	67	n.a.	404[b]	361[b]	n.a.
Latvia	49	39[c]	143[b]	355[b]	119[b]
Lithuania	40	n.a.	1075[b]	1225[b]	75[b]

Notes: a) 1989=100, b) 1992=100, c) 1993.

Sources: Col. 1, Fischer et al. (1996) Col. 2, OECD (4/1995) Cols. 3-5, *International Financial Statistics*, WEFA (1996), and WIIW (1995).

Export Performance — A third possible standard of success would be export performance. Much work following Little, Scitovsky, and Scott (1970) and Balassa (1971) has suggested that one of the most insidious — and growth-inhibiting — consequences of heavy restrictions on imports is their discouragement of exports, through several channels but especially the exchange rate. To the extent this argument is correct, liberalisation of imports should encourage exports, and in general the faster the faster.

Column 3 of Table 2 shows the annualised percentage increase in dollar value of exports from the year before the major year of reform (the year of the reform in the case of the Baltics) to 1995. There it can be seen that the relative gradualists among our countries — Bulgaria, Hungary, and Romania — also experienced the slowest growth in exports; indeed exports from Bulgaria actually declined.

Several comments should be made about the export environment. First, countries varied in their trade dependence with other members of the Council for Mutual Economic Assistance (CMEA), ranging from 3 per cent of GDP for Romania to 16 per cent for Poland in 1990. And of course the Baltics traded heavily within the former Soviet Union (ranging from 27 to 34 per cent of 1990 GDP) and Slovenia within the former Yugoslavia.[3] Their rapid growth of exports may be explained in part by the diversion of products from formerly internal trade to new export markets. Second, the overall economic performance of the major export market for all these countries, the European Union, was mediocre in 1991 and 1992, after rapid growth in 1989-1990; and final demand of the EU actually declined by nearly 2 per cent in 1993, followed by modest recovery in 1994 and 1995. Third, export growth is dependent on competitiveness, and especially for manufactured goods that depends in some measure on labour costs, measured in foreign currency, as well as on quality, packaging, and a host of other factors. A move to currency convertibility accompanied by currency depreciation to ration limited supplies of foreign exchange will lower wages measured in foreign currency, unless labour successfully bargains for a proportionate increase in wages. The extent of the liberalisation in general will influence the extent of the required depreciation, and that in turn will influence wage costs measured in foreign currency. Table 3 sets out monthly wages in manufacturing in our countries, converted into dollars at the prevailing exchange rate. An inspection of the rows shows that wages in dollars generally dropped in years of major liberalisation, the notable exception being Hungary, where liberalisation was stretched over several years. Wages dropped by 30 per cent in Poland in 1990, and by a similar amount in the Czech Republic in 1991. They dropped by over 50 per cent in Bulgaria in 1991, and by a similar amount in Romania over the two years 1991-92. From these low points wages in dollars grew, often rapidly, as domestic wage increases exceeded the rate of currency depreciation. This is a pattern that one would expect, indeed welcome, as new export markets are established and developed.

A comparison down columns of Table 3 offers a direct comparison of manufacturing wages across the different countries. The sometimes striking differences reflect differences in productivity, as well as the different extent and timing of trade liberalisation and currency depreciation. It is noteworthy that monthly manufacturing wages in the former Soviet Union, other than the Baltics, were all under US$25 in 1992, and remained under US$100 (except for Kazakstan) in 1995, reflecting the strong depreciation of the rouble and its successor currencies in the other republics.

Inflation — To the extent convertibility requires substantial depreciation, the authorities may be concerned with triggering or aggravating inflationary expectations. One manifestation of that might be greater capital outflows, discussed

Table 3. Monthly manufacturing wages (in US$).

	1989	1990	1991	1992	1993	1994	1995 [a]
Bulgaria [b]		137	64	97	120	113	122
Czech Republic		190	133	162	196	231	303
Hungary	154	170	185	224	237	249	249
Poland	149	105	158	168	175	191 [a]	290 [c]
Romania	168	123	100	61	74	80	101
Slovak Republic				161	175	196	239
Slovenia				628	666	735	968
Estonia				44	78	137	219
Latvia				32	79	142	198
Lithuania					47	84	136
USA		1496	1534	1576	1619	1674	1694

Notes: a) Second quarter, b) public sector, c) gross wage.
Source: calculated from OECD (4/1995) *International Financial Statistics* Bosworth and Gur (1995), p. 131.

immediately below. Actual inflation did indeed rise substantially in all the East European countries, relative to the suppressed inflation prior to liberalisation. Column 4 of Table 2 shows the consumer price level in 1995 relative to pre-reform levels. The figures show that Hungary, a gradualist, performed much better on this measure than did Poland, which moved rapidly. But the Czech Republic and Slovakia also moved quickly, and they performed rather better than Hungary. And Bulgaria and Romania, both gradualists among these countries, experienced markedly higher rates of inflation than the other countries. Among the Baltics, Estonia, which moved rapidly, ultimately experienced less increase in prices than did Lithuania, which liberalised more slowly. Of course, movements in prices of these magnitudes reflect largely the degree of control over closely related fiscal and monetary policies, the lower inflation countries having maintained much more effective monetary control. Thus the observed inflation can be attributed only in small part to the liberalisation. But the *ex post* data offer little comfort to those who favour gradualism.

Capital Outflows — Another indirect measure of the acceptability of the liberalisation of foreign exchange transactions, necessarily with extensive depreciation, and of higher uncompensated inflationary expectations, is the extent to which capital left the country, despite widespread formal controls on international capital outflows. While private capital left various countries from time to time, the balance of payments statistics (including errors and omissions) reveal no major recorded or unrecorded outflows of private capital from East European countries, in sharp contrast to both China and Russia, for instance, where for quite different reasons substantial outflows have occurred. Of course, there still may have been substantial outflows concealed by roughly equivalent inflows that also were not recorded, for example under-reporting of exports offset by increased investment abroad, including in foreign currency. Both Poland and Czechoslovakia ran substantial but transitory current account surpluses in the year of their major reforms, due in part to the sharp price-induced decline in real incomes in those years.

It is difficult on these measures to distinguish sharply between those countries which liberalised quickly and those which did so more gradually, although as noted those which liberalised quickly seemed to have, on balance, slightly better performance on the indicators discussed. Extending the sample to include other formerly communist countries, especially the republics of the former Soviet Union, offers one possibility for sorting out the influence of liberalisation, since the extent of liberalisation is much more varied if those countries are included.

Such an exercise has been carried out by Anders Åslund and his colleagues (1996, Table 3). They regress cumulative output decline through 1995 against a "liberalisation index" for each of 24 former communist countries in 1994, taken from the World Bank. (Unfortunately for our purposes, the liberalisation index goes beyond price, foreign exchange, and foreign trade liberalisation to include private sector entry and other factors). The regression suggests that cumulative liberalisation mitigated the decline in output significantly, countries that liberalised less having experienced, on average, a sharper decline in output. However, closer inspection of the data suggests that the steepest declines in output occurred in former republics of the Soviet Union; if dummies are inserted for membership in the rouble zone or for being riven by war (Armenia, Azerbaijan, Croatia, Georgia, Macedonia, Tajikistan), the significance of the liberalisation variable disappears. A similar result obtains for unemployment (de Melo, Denizer and Gelb, 1995, Table 8). While the demise of CMEA in 1991 was no doubt a serious short-term economic disturbance to Eastern European countries, the disintegration of the Soviet Union was an even greater disturbance to its constituent members, whose economies were closely linked through decades of Moscow-directed central planning, with its emphasis on economies of scale and monopoly production, especially in manufacturing.

Further afield, output fell between 1989 and 1994 by about a third in both Cuba and North Korea, two completely unreformed communist systems heavily dependent on the former Soviet Union for trade and aid. Too many things were happening at the same time to sort out persuasively the impact of trade and payments liberalisation.

It is noteworthy, however, that cumulative liberalisation does help to explain economic growth in 1995, and the explanatory power is only slightly diminished by including dummies for membership in the rouble area and being worn-torn (Åslund and others, 1996, Table 5), suggesting that early and more extensive liberalisation yields earlier and stronger returns in terms of output. Moreover, the effect is even stronger than revealed if, as is likely, unrecorded output growth in new economic activity is higher in the countries that have liberalised more extensively.

Income Distribution — One of the concerns about currency convertibility in post-war Western Europe involved the distribution of income. A move to convertibility, accompanied either by reductions in output or by currency depreciation, was thought to fall especially heavily on the low-wage worker, since Europe at that time was still heavily dependent on food imports, whose domestic price could be expected to rise with currency devaluation. Table 3 measures Eastern European wages in dollars in the early 1990s. But the figures there also offer some indication of what has happened to real wages in the transforming economies, and indirectly something about the distribution of income. We have already seen that consumption fell substantially less than income; much pre-reform production was destined for the military services and investment in the defence-supporting industries. Cutting such production would not directly affect the distribution of income, except insofar as workers employed in those industries found themselves moving from high- to low-wage activity, or from employment to uncompensated unemployment. This change would arise from changes in the structure or level of output. The distinctive contribution to changes in the distribution of income arising from trade and payments liberalisation would arise from changes in relative consumer-good prices that arise, directly or indirectly, from such liberalisation. The most obvious example would be a liberalisation-induced rise in the prices of staple foods, especially grain.

On the other hand, the relative price of housing, still under price control in most reforming countries, and in any case experiencing extensive inertia, should fall in the face of liberalisation-induced increases in commodity prices, and the share of housing in household budgets may be expected to fall as money wages increase in even partial response to the rise in commodity prices. Column 5 of Table 2 shows the real monthly wage in manufacturing in 1995 relative to 1990 (1989 for Poland and Hungary, 1992 for the Baltics), where the real wage has been calculated using the consumer price index. The change ranges from increases of 19 per cent in Latvia and 7 per cent in Slovenia to declines of 55 per cent in Bulgaria and 29 per cent in Poland (all of the Polish decline occurred in 1990, wages having kept up with prices thereafter). There is no obvious pattern according to the pace of liberalisation. Hungary preserved the real wage much better than Poland (although the positions would be reversed if 1990 were used as the year of comparison), a fast liberaliser, but not significantly better than the Czech Republic, also a fast liberaliser, which preserved real wages much better than Romania and especially Bulgaria, gradualists. Wage data are in any case incomplete, particularly in view of a sharp increase in activity in the service sectors, much of it informal. For example, a comparison of household consumption (column 2) with real wages (column 5) for Hungary and Poland raises serious questions about one or both sets of data — or points to an exceptional increase in non-wage income in Poland.

A careful study of income distribution in the Baltic states in 1994 compared with 1990, based on household survey data, suggests a considerable increase in dispersion of income in all three countries, with the Gini coefficient rising from 0.24 by 0.10 in Estonia, 0.11 in Lithuania, and 0.17 in Latvia, with some caveats for lack of complete comparability between the 1990 and the 1994 data (Cornelius and Weder, 1996, Tables 1 and 2). More comprehensibly, the ratio of income in the top decile of the surveyed population to that in the bottom decile, a common rough measure of income inequality, rose from around 3.2 in 1990 in all three Baltics to 5.0 in Estonia, 6.6 in Lithuania, and 8.9 in Latvia in 1994. Most of these increases came about because of increased wage dispersion, wages accounting for half to two-thirds of household income, and most of that in turn came mainly from relative reductions in wages at the low end of the wage scale rather than increases at the high end, at least in terms of reported income.

These figures, however interesting, do not establish the relevance of trade and payments liberalisation on income distribution, since the analysis concerns money income, without regard to the pattern of household expenditure and changes in the pattern of relative prices. At the times of liberalisation, most Hungarian domestic prices were already free from control, as were Polish food prices. Bulgaria and

Czechoslovakia, however, maintained a full set of price controls (Bosworth and Ofer, 1995).

A detailed study is required of the post-liberalisation rise or fall in relative prices plausibly attributable to liberalisation of international trade and payments, and a comparison of these relative price effects with expenditure patterns by household income class, before and after liberalisation. (For example, the relative prices of household appliances presumably declined with liberalisation, and product quality greatly improved).

4. European convertibility in the late 1940s

Early acceptance of IMF Article VIII was inhibited by several factors in the late 1940s. Britain, while diminished, was still the key industrial economy of Europe, especially as a trading nation at the economic and financial centre of the Sterling Area, which comprised most of what is now the British Commonwealth plus several other countries. The key to Europe was thus Britain. But Britain was reluctant to move to convertibility for a variety of mutually re-inforcing reasons. First, sterling balances around the world, especially in Africa and India, were still large, and (external) convertibility would have permitted the holders of sterling to import from anywhere, straining Britain's reserves. Second, the short-lived July 1947 experiment in convertibility, a condition of the 1946 Anglo-American loan, had led to an intolerable loss of reserves. Third, Britain's re-construction (and new housing construction) needs were still being met, so Britain had little productive capacity for additional exports (an argument that was applied elsewhere in Europe). Fourth, there was a "dollar shortage," i.e. a tendency for the United States to export more than it imported; correcting this with currency devaluation was thought by some to be of dubious value, because US demand was allegedly price-inelastic and in any case European exports were supply constrained, as in the third point. Fifth, convertibility on current account was incompatible with the price controls that still prevailed in Britain and elsewhere (except Germany after mid-1948), and these in turn were an essential component of the Labour Party's programme (Britain's Chancellor of Exchequer Sir Stafford Cripps denounced advice to devalue the pound on the (correct) grounds that it favoured a "free economy" — quoted in James, 1995).

These arguments were generally accepted, in whole or in part, by many contemporaries. Diebold's (1952) classic study in European trade and payments focuses largely on the struggle to overcome bilateralism, and does not even discuss the possibility of a general move to currency convertibility. Kindleberger (1950) expounded on the existence and permanence of a dollar shortage. Triffin (1957 and 1966, collecting his memos and papers of the late 1940s and early 1950s) focuses on the need for monetary stability and accepts the need for fixed exchange rates in that context. Only Friedman (1953, memo written in late 1950) argues the case for flexible exchange rates and convertible currencies, a view which was considered idiosyncratic and even quixotic at the time.[4] The practical problem was seen to be the restraints on growth implied by the bilateral trade restrictions prevalent in the late 1940s. The solution was to create the European Payments Union (EPU) in

1950, which provided for a limited but gradually increasing current account convertibility among the Western European currencies (and the Sterling Area, encompassing Australia, India, Pakistan, New Zealand and Britain's still extensive colonial empire).

After the large 1949 devaluations and the 1951 election which returned the Tories to power in Britain and brought price liberalisation, some British officials were much more sympathetic to convertibility, if necessary even floating the pound to achieve it (James, 1996; Kaplan and Schleiminger, 1989). Canada had floated its dollar during the Korean War commodity boom in 1950. But Britain was still concerned about the sterling balance and a dollar shortage and wanted to continue to discriminate against dollar goods, for example through invocation of IMF Article VII. Eichengreen (1993) examines the possibility that European currencies could have been made current account convertible in 1950, in lieu of establishing EPU. He examines four of Kornai's five criteria for convertibility: a realistic exchange rate consistent with payments equilibrium, sufficient foreign exchange reserves, absence of a monetary overhang, and adequate wage discipline (Kornai's fifth criterion, that firms face hard budget constraints, was judged not relevant to Western Europe in 1950). Using a series of relatively simple quantitative tests, Eichengreen concludes that modest devaluation after the 1949 devaluations would have met the first criterion; the second was attained by 1950 (at least compared to the late 1920s); the third did not apply after 1950 except [significantly] to Britain and Ireland, due in part to sterling balances; and wage restraint was maintained adequately during the 1950s. However, Eichengreen argues that wage restraint might not have obtained in the absence of the EPU, and therefore cannot be taken for granted under the counter-factual alternative of currency convertibility.

The basic argument is as follows: Europe after the first World War had cut itself up economically and politically over the distribution of income. Political leaders wished to avoid this after the second World War. The "post-war settlement" involved an exchange of wage restraint by labour for a commitment by business (or government, through corporate taxes) to re-invest business earnings rather than distribute them to owners of capital, with a view to raising productivity and economic growth, and hence ultimately also real wages (but not the wage share). Many devices were introduced to this end. The Marshall Plan helped facilitate this implicit bargain by permitting some investment that was not financed out of household income or retained earnings. The EPU permitted a more favourable terms of trade for Europe, by discriminating against dollar goods, than would have been possible under currency convertibility, amounting to 1 - 2 per cent of GDP (Eichengreen, 1993). This amount, by permitting larger-than-otherwise consumption and/or investment, may have been enough to ensure wage restraint.

There was also a co-ordination problem. While Eichengreen shows that currency convertibility could have worked overall, any individual country might have found itself with a dollar deficit matched by an (inconvertible) surplus against other countries. Thus a co-ordinated move to convertibility was required. The EPU ultimately permitted this, although other mechanisms no doubt could have been found. This argument is ingenious and appealing (Eichengreen also ties it to the need to revive the German economy). But the weakness is the United Kingdom. If, as Eichengreen concedes, Britain had an unacceptably large monetary overhang until 1955, and if, as suggested above, Britain was the key to European equilibrium, then convertibility would not have been possible until after 1955 without funding the sterling balances (as many contemporaries urged) or tolerating a further once-for-all rise in British prices, followed by another devaluation. But convertibility was well advanced by the mid-1950s and might have been achieved in 1956 had it not been for the financial set-back created by the Suez Crisis.

I will not explore for Western Europe in the 1950s the performance criteria discussed above for Eastern Europe in the 1990s. Suffice it to say that economic growth during the 1950s was generally above 3 per cent a year (2.8 for Britain, lowest among the major countries); inflation was generally 2 - 3 per cent a year, except in France, where average annual inflation of 5.6 per cent reduced the value of money by 42 per cent over the decade; and the volume of export growth, both permitting and encouraged by liberalisation of trade and payments, was 7-15 per cent a year, except for Britain's paltry 1.7 per cent.

5. 1950s vs. 1990s: what explains the difference?

It is useful to recall the climate of opinion that prevailed in Western Europe of the late 1940s, and to contrast it with Eastern Europe in the late 1980s, for substantial differences therein go some way toward explaining the divergent approaches to convertibility. The world had just emerged in the late 1940s from the Great Depression of the 1930s and a devastating war that had its origins in part in the social hardship of that Depression. One legacy of that experience was high sensitivity to unemployment. Moreover, the Great Depression at a minimum had raised questions about the stability and long-run viability of a capitalist, free market economic system, and had persuaded many that government must play a much greater role in economic management — not only in sustaining aggregate demand, the main lesson of the Keynesian revolution in economic thinking, but also in directing investment and more generally in "planning" the evolution of the structure of output and even patterns of consumption.

A second legacy was a strong distaste for floating exchange rates, associated with the turbulent and disorderly periods immediately following the first World War and again in the early 1930s, as documented and interpreted by Nurkse (1944).

A third legacy from the interwar period was the presence in most Western European countries of sharp ideological cleavages reflected in political parties, at least along Marxist/anti-Marxist lines, but often also accompanied by cross-cutting cleavages along religious or monarchist/republican lines. Britain, France, and Italy, in particular, were all plagued by bitter ideological differences among leading members of the political community.

Eastern European countries by the late 1980s, in contrast, had experienced 40 years of full employment and enforced ideological uniformity in the body politic which was all-but-universally rejected as having been imposed from outside. There was wide public consensus in most countries on the desirability of breaking sharply with the recent past and moving toward greater economic (as well as political) freedom. This was understood to mean shedding the system of central planning in favour of a market-oriented allocation of resources, and this in turn implied a radical change in the composition of output. Controls over the allocation of foreign exchange were associated with the general system of centralised controls under communist rule, as well as with corruption by officials, and as such were to be rejected as heinous. Moreover, the previous unavailability of many foreign goods, especially processed foods and household durables, meant that availability even if at high prices represented an improvement, and a decline in measured real wages would not be indicative of a parallel decline in the sense of material well-being.

In addition, the major foreign currencies had been floating against one another for nearly 20 years, since 1973, with attendant inconvenience but without obvious disaster or strong negative associations.

These differences do not represent arguments why currency convertibility would have been more successful in one period than in another. Rather, they suggest why a rapid move to currency convertibility was more acceptable politically in Eastern Europe in the 1990s than it would have been in Western Europe in the 1950s. Insofar as temporarily higher unemployment can be associated with a rapid move to currency convertibility (which is not in fact established by the recent record of Eastern Europe, but cannot be ruled out either), the different approaches reflect different antecedent conditions and different social values based on those antecedent conditions. West Europeans (especially the British) inherited economic controls established during a major war they had just won, and they were intrigued with the possibility that peacetime controls might reduce or eliminate the manifest instability of a capitalist economy; East Europeans inherited economic controls from a largely externally-imposed political regime which they wished to shed as quickly and as completely as possible.

4. Conclusions

Few hard conclusions can be drawn from this examination, and those that can are largely negative. First, a rapid move to currency convertibility (on current account) by the transforming countries of Eastern Europe does not seem to have hurt those countries that undertook it compared with those that moved more gradually, on the usual criteria for economic improvement; indeed, on balance they seem to have performed rather better, but the evidence is not conclusive and in particular the number of observations is too few (even when augmented by the former republics of the Soviet Union) to make strong conclusions after allowance is made for other differentiating features among countries. Second, Western European countries almost surely could have moved to currency convertibility more rapidly than they did in the 1950s, especially if arrangements had been made for partial funding of the sterling balances held by Commonwealth countries, but the intellectual climate and political consensus were not present for making the move, and for absorbing such short-run turbulence as may have followed a move to convertibility.

Third, the experience of the Eastern European countries in the early 1990s, although admittedly embedded in special circumstances, at least raises strong doubts about the justification for preserving exchange controls in many developing countries — a much heavier burden of proof should be levied on those countries by the international community and in particular by the International Monetary Fund, whose Articles of Agreement call for currency account convertibility as a basic condition for membership in the Fund.

Notes

[1] For example, it may be expedient to limit the amount of foreign currency a resident can buy for the purpose of foreign travel — a current transaction — to prevent the export of capital for purchase of assets abroad. Travel arranged and pre-paid through a monitored travel agency would be unrestricted.

[2] In most of these countries total real consumption tracks per capita consumption closely since, remarkably, population in all is growing very slowly or, in a few cases, declining slowly.

[3] Data are from Fischer, Sahay, and Vegh (1996), Table 1.

[4] Triffin (1966, pp. 180-194, internal IMF memos written in 1949) argues that in the interests of trade liberalisation the IMF should encourage member countries to adopt flexible exchange rates, under IMF surveillance, as a strictly transitory measure.

References

Åslund, A., 1995, *How Russia Became a Market Economy*, Brookings Institution, Washington.

Åslund, A., Boone, P. and Johnson, S., 1996, *How to Stabilize: Lessons from Post-Communist Countries*, "Brookings Papers on Economic Activity", No. 1.

Balassa, B., 1971, *The Structure of Protection in Developing Countries*, Baltimore: Johns Hopkins University Press for International Bank for Reconstruction and Development.

Balcerowicz, L., 1995, *Socialism, Capitalism, Transformation*, Budapest: Central European University Press.

Bosworth, B. P. and Ofer, G., 1995, *Reforming Planned Economies in an Integrating World Economy*, Washington, Brookings Institution, esp. p. 120.

Cornelius, P. K., and Weder, B. S., 1996, "Economic Transformation and Income Distribution: Some Evidence from the Baltic Countries," *IMF Working Paper*, WP/96/14, February.

Cooper, R. N., 1990, "Currency Convertibility in Eastern Europe," in *Central Banking Issues in Emerging Market Economies*, Federal Bank of Kansas City.

Cooper, R. N., 1991, "Opening the Soviet Economy," in M.J. Peck, Petr Aven, and Thomas Richardson, eds., *What is to be Done? Proposals for the Soviet Transition to Market*, New Haven: Yale University Press.

Diebold, W., 1952, *Trade and Payments in Western Europe: A Study in Economic Cooperation, 1947-51*, New York: Harper & Row.

Economist Intelligence Unit, 1996, *Country Report* for various countries, London: EIU.

Eichengreen, B., 1993, *Reconstructing Europe's Trade and Payments: the European Payments Union*, Manchester: Manchester University Press.

Federal Reserve Bank of Kansas City, 1990, *Central Banking Issues in Emerging Market Economies*, Kansas City: Federal Reserve Bank.

Fischer, S., Sahay R., and Vegh C. A., 1996, "Stabilization and Growth in Transition Economies: The Early Experience," *IMF Working Paper*, March.

Friedman, M., 1953, "The Case for Flexible Exchange Rates," in *Essays in Positive Economics*, Chicago: University of Chicago Press.

Gros, D. and Steinherr, A., 1995, *Winds of Change: Economic Transition in Central and Eastern Europe*, London: Longman.

International Monetary Fund, "Exchange Arrangements and Exchange Restrictions", *Annual Report*, Washington: IMF, various years.

Economic Reviews for Estonia (4), Latvia (6), and Lithuania (7), 1993, Washington: IMF.

James, H., 1996, *International Monetary Cooperation since Bretton Woods*, New York: Oxford University Press, esp. pp. 95 and 99-101.

Kaplan, J. and Schleiminger, G., 1989, *The European Payments Union: Financial Diplomacy in the 1950s*, Oxford: Clarendon Press, esp. pp. 160-166.

Kindleberger, C. P., 1950, *The Dollar Shortage*, Cambridge, MA: The MIT Press.

Kornai, J., 1990, *The Road to a Free Economy*, New York: Norton.

Little, I.M.D., Scitovsky, T. and Scott, M. F., 1970, *Industry and Trade in Some Developing Countries: A Comparative Study*, London: Oxford University Press.

McKinnon, R. I., 1991, *The Order of Economic Liberalization: Financial Control in the Transition to a Market Economy*, Baltimore: Johns Hopkins University Press.

Mussa, M., 1986, "The Adjustment Process and the Timing of Trade Liberalization," in Armeane M. Choksi and Demetris Papageorgiou, eds., *Economic Liberalization in Developing Countries*, Oxford: Basil Blackwell.

Mussa, M., 1982, "Government Policy and the Adjustment Process," in Jagdish N. Bhagwati, ed., *Import Competition and Response*, Chicago: University of Chicago Press.

Nurkse, R., 1944, *International Currency Experience*, League of Nations, Geneva.

OECD, 1993, *Exchange Control Policy,* Paris.

OECD, 1994, *Integrating Emerging Market Economies into the International Trading System*, Paris.

OECD, *Short-Term Economic Indicators: Transition Economies*, quarterly, Paris.

Peck, M. J., Aven, P. and Richardson, T., eds., 1991, *What Is To Be Done? Proposals for the Soviet Transition to Market*, New Haven: Yale University Press, esp. pp. 117-118.

Russian Federation, *Russian Economic Trends 1995,* Vol. 4, No. 2,: Whurr Publishers, London.

Sachs, J., 1993, *Poland's Jump to the Market Economy*, Cambridge, MA: the MIT Press.

Triffin, R., 1957, *Europe and the Money Muddle: from Bilaterlism to Near-Convertibility, 1947-1956*, New Haven: Yale University Press.

Triffin, R., 1966, *The World Money Maze*, New Haven: Yale University Press.

WEFA Group, 1996, *Eurasia Economic Outlook*, Eddystone, PA.

Wiener Institut für Internationale Wirtschaftsvergleiche (WIIW), 1996, *Countries in Transition, 1995*, Vienna.

Williamson, J., ed., 1991, *Currency Convertibility in Eastern Europe*, Washington: Institute for International Economics, esp. p. 90

Zloch-Christy, I., ed., 1996, *Bulgaria in a Time of Change: Economic and Political Dimensions*, Aldershot: Avebury.

2

Exchange rate policies in post-communist economies

Dariusz Rosati

1. Introduction

The process of opening up to international markets has been a common feature of economic transformation in post-communist economies. This has been achieved through liberalisation and active foreign exchange rate policies. But individual experience of transition economies has differed widely, reflecting different starting conditions and modalities of adopted reform programmes. The purpose of this paper is to summarise these various experiences in order to draw some conclusions on the optimal path of exchange rate policies during transition. The key finding of the paper is that fundamental changes in the economic conditions underlying this process call for greater flexibility in foreign exchange policies.

In Section 2, the main policy dilemmas faced by East European countries at the outset of transition are discussed, including such crucial issues as the scope of convertibility, the choice of the exchange rate regime, and the extent of initial devaluation. The paper argues that a fixed exchange rate regime combined with broad currency convertibility is a preferred policy package at the initial stage of reforms. In Section 3, an attempt is made to show that, after the initial depreciation, the equilibrium exchange rates in East European countries tend to appreciate in real terms as a result of reversing expectations, productivity changes and increasing capital inflows. In the first, "stabilization-cum-liberalisation" phase, there is a tendency for the equilibrium rate to fall, while in the second, "growth" phase there is a tendency for it to rise. The swings in the equilibrium rate call for shifts in the nominal exchange rates, but the actual pattern should depend on the initial position of the exchange rate. The policy implications are discussed briefly in the last section. Although the paper is basically concerned with six Central European

Ministry of Foreign Affairs, Republic of Poland. The paper was prepared when the author was with the United Nations Economic Commission for Europe, Geneva. *The views expressed in this paper are those of the author and do not necessarily reflect the views of UN/ECE. The author would like to acknowledge helpful comments received on earlier drafts of the paper from Richard Portes, Daniel Gros, Eduard Hochreiter and Michael Landesmann.*

transition countries, the conclusions seem to be of more general significance and can also be applied to other transition countries.

2. The early decisions: devaluation, foreign exchange regime, convertibility

When launching their market reform programmes, the transition countries were confronted with a number of important policy questions for which no easy answers were readily available. Typically, the initial decisions included a radical opening of the national economy through liberalisation of current account transactions, which was accompanied by substantial devaluation of domestic currencies. In most cases these programmes, including foreign exchange policies, proved quite successful in dampening inflation and establishing some measure of external balance; but with the benefit of hindsight it is also possible to identify some policy errors, arising from some unrealistic assumptions and — quite obviously — imperfect knowledge about the peculiarities of market-oriented transformation, including the lack of necessary information.

2.1 Initial devaluation

Domestic currencies were believed to be strongly overvalued under central planning, and substantial devaluation was considered a necessary precondition for removing restrictions on trade and restoring a fundamental balance between the supply of, and demand for, convertible currencies. The dollar-shortage syndrome (including the existence of widespread foreign exchange controls under central planning and the notorious lack of hard currencies) and the anticipated effects of the intended price liberalisation, all called for a devaluation by a substantial margin. Indications to the contrary, such as the inflationary effect of excessive devaluation and its possible recessionary impact on production costs, did not receive much attention.

In fact, the dollar-shortage syndrome proved to be the key factor in deciding on the scope of initial devaluation. Confronted with the risk of missing stabilization targets and of wasting precious hard currency reserves, the policy-makers preferred to err on the side of undervaluation rather than of overvaluation (Halpern and Wyplosz, 1995). In practice, the devaluations were clearly excessive. This was one of the major policy mistakes made in Poland; in fact, the zloty was devalued to the level which was even lower than the actual black market rate. As a result, while shifting the trade balance from a deficit into a strong surplus, the devaluation produced a strong inflationary shock and contributed to deep recession. Similar effects were observed in Czechoslovakia, even though the extent of initial "overshooting" was substantially smaller than in Poland.

But what should be the extent of initial devaluation? In principle, the key factors determining the initial exchange rate adjustment are the flexibility of wages and prices and the intensity of macroeconomic imbalances. The more flexible domestic wages and prices are, the smaller the necessary devaluation needs to be, as the necessary adjustment can be assured through a reduction of real wages. Similarly, the higher the monetary imbalance is, the larger the necessary devaluation needs to be.[1] Thus, the scope can be approximated by the difference between the official rate and the equilibrium rate.

But to arrive at a reasonable estimate of the equilibrium rate is a very tricky task under conditions of a transforming command economy which had remained in disequilibrium for decades.[2] One problem is that it is never directly observable. Another is that the equilibrium rate tends to change in reaction to policy decisions taken in the early stage of transition. In the absence of better indicators, a black market rate can be used as a starting point, although caution is needed in interpreting the black market premium as a measure of the official rate overvaluation (Montiel and Ostry, 1994). With limited information, the most logical approach would be to assume that the equilibrium rate is located somewhere in the range between the official rate and the black market rate. One possible solution could be to start with the geometric average of the two rates, weighted with the shares of transactions conducted at each rate in the total volume of foreign exchange market (Rosati, 1989).

But even in that case some "overshooting" seems to be inevitable, because of the ratchet-type impact of devaluation on the demand for foreign currency and on the composition of asset portfolios of residents. Assume that in a high-inflation country there is a shortage of dollars on the official market at the official rate of E(o), and that the black market rate, reflecting the dollar marginal price under speculative demand arising from currency substitution, including a risk premium, is E(b).[3] Note that the speculative demand is there because the domestic currency is expected to depreciate further. Clearly, the (medium-term) equilibrium exchange rate, E(e), would be located somewhere between E(o) and E(b), but rather closer to E(o), because normally one would expect a higher proportion of monetary transactions involving foreign exchange to be conducted at the official rate, i.e. a larger part of total demand for foreign exchange is satisfied on the official market (e.g. demand for regular import payments).

However, a devaluation to E(e) may not be large enough to restore credibility in the new exchange rate as it is still below the black market rate which is perceived by the general public as a benchmark. In such a case, the devaluation is not sufficient to reduce the speculative demand for dollars and to induce a shift in the asset portfolios of residents in favour of domestic currency denominated assets. Thus, the initial devaluation would have to be larger than necessary to attain medium-term equilibrium at the level E(e); the required "threshold" level would probably be not very far from the black market rate, E(b). Now, if this "threshold" rate is reached, the expectations are reversed, the demand for dollars falls, and there will be a subsequent tendency for the domestic currency to appreciate. But if the devaluation falls short of the threshold level, there is no change in residents' behaviour and the equilibrium will be more difficult and more costly to achieve through stronger demand-reducing policy measures (for a more formal exposition, see: Rosati, 1993a). This is clearly a time-inconsistency problem; the locus of the demand curve shifts downwards in response to the change in expectations which, however, can be instigated only through an excessive devaluation. The level of the "threshold" and the extent of necessary overshooting will mostly depend on how credible the stabilization programme is: with full credibility, the "threshold" would be equal to E(e), while with zero credibility, it would be equal to E(b). In this context, the role of the IMF in "lending" credibility to the government stabilization programme, including some form of a currency stabilization fund, is indeed essential.

It can be shown, that under some simplifying assumptions, the extent of the initial devaluation depends only on the black market premium, which reflects the expected corrective inflation, and the proportion of total demand for foreign exchange satisfied at the black market rate (see Appendix). Assume, that the (unknown) equilibrium rate, E(e), is a weighted average of the official rate, E(o), and the black market rate, E(b):

$$(1)\ E(e) = (1-k)\ E(o) + k\ E(b),\ 0 < k < 1$$

where k denotes the share of black market transactions in total foreign exchange transactions. The real absorption in the economy is y, but nominal demand is higher by the amount of inflationary overhang OH. The excess demand, which cannot be met by additional supply on the goods market because of shortages, translates into higher demand for foreign currencies on the black market. In the short term, both the supply of foreign currencies and the level of real absorption is constant; under these conditions, the black market premium, μ, would be a function of the proportion of overhang h, to domestic absorption y. Assuming linearity,

$$(2)\ \mu = [E(b)-E(o)]/E(o) = a\ (h/y)$$

If price liberalisation can be expected to raise the domestic price level by ¶ = h/y, (2) can be written as:

$$(3)\ \mu = a¶$$

Substituting (3) into (1), dividing by E(o) gives, after some manipulations:

$$E(e)/E(o) - E(o)/E(o) = -k + (k\ a¶ + 1)$$

Defining the rate of required nominal devaluation as d = [E(e) - E(o)]/E(o), one obtains:

$$(4)\ d = ka¶ = k\mu$$

As can be seen, the extent of necessary devaluation depends positively on the black market premium, which itself depends on the expected rate of corrective inflation, and the parameter k, which represents the proportion of demand for foreign exchange satisfied on the black market.

It is worth noting, that the postulate of targeting the "threshold" level located somewhere between E(e) and E(b) implies that there is no need for taking *a priori* into account the corrective inflation in setting the new level of exchange rate. This is because the level of the black market rate, relative to the level of the official rate, already reflects the extent of market imbalances, and thus it allows an anticipation of the inflation burst after price liberalisation. Consider formula (4): a real devaluation means that d > ¶, or, d/¶ > 1, which would imply that k a >l. Because k is smaller than one, while the value of the coefficient a may be greater than one, it is impossible to establish *a priori* a fixed relationship between ¶ and d. Moreover, it is not necessary to decide *a priori* whether devaluation should be real (as postulated by Oblath, 1994), or only nominal (Berg and Sachs, 1992), although in most cases reaching the "threshold" level would probably mean some degree of real depreciation *ex post*. It follows that there are values of corrective inflation for which a real devaluation is necessary, although much more likely are the situations when k a < 1, i.e. only a nominal devaluation would be sufficient.

2.2 *Fixed vs. floating exchange rate regime*

Another early decision to be taken was to choose between the fixed and the floating exchange rate systems. High levels of domestic inflation called for a fixed rate regime, on the grounds that it provided a 'nominal anchor' for domestic price stabilization (Poland, Czechoslovakia, Hungary).[4] Some other countries, which decided to go for a floating rate regime (Bulgaria, Romania), did so not because they believed the float to be generally superior in restoring macroeconomic equilibrium, but rather because they felt that the alternative option was hardly feasible due to the insufficient international reserves and, consequently, low credibility of their stabilization programmes.

The nominal anchor approach offered important advantages in the early stage of transition: it helped to break up the inflationary inertia, both inherited from the communist past and linked to the initial liberalisation of domestic prices and, through dampening the volatility of the changes in nominal variables, it reduced overall uncertainty of business activities. Moreover, the fixed rate could have worked as a disciplining device for domestic producers (Hrncir, 1994; Gaspar, 1995). For countries with high levels of external debt (Hungary, Poland), it also helped to stabilize the budgetary cost of debt servicing. According to the modern theory of optimum currency areas, an irrevocably fixed exchange rate regime in a small open economy would generally be a preferred solution because the gain from "predictability" of the exchange rate would more than offset the risk of importing instability from abroad through currency pegging. In fact, if the currency of the peg is a traditionally low-inflation currency, the fixed rate regime would allow a transition country to "import" policy credibility and stability from a low-inflation country (Willett and Al-Marhubi, 1994).

The main problem with the fixed rate regime is that under conditions of high inflation it involves a risk of substantial real appreciation of domestic currency. To reduce the risk, a deep initial devaluation is required, which itself is destabilizing and pro-inflationary. Second, unless the devaluation is very substantial, a relatively high level of foreign reserves is needed to make the foreign exchange rate anchor a credible and working instrument. What is perhaps most important, is that the credibility cannot be assured by the peg itself: the fixed rate does not offer any credibility unless it is buttressed by sound financial policies and is seen by the market players as defendable and sustainable.

These problems were realised early and addressed in a variety of ways. Given the uncertainties surrounding the initial stage of reform programmes, most transition countries preferred to secure some room for flexibility. Except for Estonia and (later) Lithuania, none of the countries which opted for a fixed exchange rate did it in the form of a very rigid commitment through establishing a currency board. In Poland, the exchange rate was fixed initially for between three to six months, but it eventually remained unchanged for 16 months. In Czechoslovakia, no official commitment whatsoever was made as to a possible time horizon of the fixed rate, and yet it has been maintained since then. Hungary adopted an adjustable peg, with varying frequency of small devaluations. In other countries, where a floating rate regime was implemented, the operation of the system involved frequent and sometimes very substantial interventions by the central banks (Romania, Bulgaria, Latvia, Slovenia).

As it turned out, only the Czech Republic maintained the initial level of the exchange rate unchanged. Slovakia adjusted the exchange rate once in 1993 after the split of the Czechoslovak federation in an attempt to realign its currency with the stronger currency of its newly established neighbour. Hungary has been applying a policy of occasional micro-devaluations, with their frequency accelerated after 1993, while Poland abandoned the fixed rate in late 1991 and switched to an (exogenous) crawling peg regime, combined with occasional "step" devaluations. Notwithstanding the differences in the flexibility of foreign exchange regimes, the countries concerned succeeded in strengthening their external balance and managed to bring inflation down to the levels which are among the lowest in the region.[5]

Domestic price stabilization was generally more difficult to attain in the countries which adopted a floating rate regime (with a notable exception of Slovenia). Among East European countries, Bulgaria and Romania recorded the highest inflation rates during 1991-1994, and their balance of payments remained continuously under pressure. The inflationary experience of most former Soviet republics corroborates further this observation, even though part of the difficulties should perhaps be linked to other factors, such as the generally hesitant progress of structural reforms and various trade shocks (arising from the break-up of the former Soviet Union and former Yugoslavia).

The lesson which can be drawn from this early experience is that a credible fixed rate regime is probably a preferred option in the early stage of post-communist stabilization, in particular in countries with high inflation (Corden, 1993; Williamson, 1993; Obstfeld, 1995). The nominal anchor it provides is more effective in containing inflation, and if the government commitment to defend the rate is perceived credible, the fixed rate can help in reducing speculative demand for foreign currencies and overall uncertainty.[6]

Another lesson is that the virtues of the fixed exchange rate regime are likely to disappear in the medium-term. If inflation is not put under firm control because of lax fiscal and/or monetary policies, the resulting real appreciation of domestic currency will undermine exports and encourage imports, leading to a depletion of international reserves and eventually to a collapse of the foreign exchange market. This scenario, tested already in several Latin American countries, demonstrates *inter alia* that there is a need for a change in foreign exchange arrangements once the initial inflation is reduced to manageable levels. It is worth recalling, that in a longer term perspective, the main objective of the exchange rate policy should be to avoid major misalignments in the real exchange rate rather than to defend domestic price stability. The latter should in turn be the primary objective of domestic monetary (and fiscal) policies. This means that an irrevocably fixed rate may impose too much rigidity on domestic policies in a highly uncertain environment of the early stage of transition (Hrncir, 1994). After the initial disinflation, when inflationary expectations have been reversed, the country should aim at maintaining the nominal exchange rate at the level consistent with the sustainable current account deficit which would be financed by autonomous, "normal" capital inflows (Williamson, 1993). This implies a shift to a "flexible" exchange rate arrangement, preferably a crawling peg at a predetermined rate, in order to better target the equilibrium real exchange rate (Fry and Nuti, 1992; Wettstein, 1994). By contrast, the problem of domestic inflation should be addressed by domestic financial policies; unless domestic fiscal and monetary policies are sufficiently and credibly restrictive, no exchange rate anchoring can secure lasting stabilization (Corden, 1993).

In principle, the same recommendation applies to a floating rate regime. The major difference concerns the expectation forming mechanism: when the "fundamentals" are correct and domestic policies follow a non-inflationary course, the pegging does reduce the uncertainty, has a stronger psychological effect on the expectations than the float, and thus is more effective.

Moreover, as shown by Obstfeld (1995), the float is bound to produce more volatile changes in the real exchange rate because of the sluggishness of money output prices; this makes it a less desired option in the early stage of stabilization.

2.3 Convertibility

Because currency convertibility was considered under central planning as a next to impossible task, the idea of early convertibility was initially received with reservations by many experts.[7] It was argued that early convertibility would not be credible unless accompanied by deep devaluations; that would be both economically costly and politically dangerous. But most East European policy-makers seem to have been more receptive to the arguments to the contrary: early convertibility was supposed to allow for "imports" of correct relative prices from international markets, to impose a measure of competition on domestic producers through imports of foreign substitutes, and to boost credibility of the reform programmes (Nuti and Portes, 1993; Rosati, 1993b; Dedek, 1995). Theoretically, the transition countries could contemplate various degrees of convertibility, starting with a narrowly defined convertibility restricted to trade transactions only, next including also other current account transactions, and finally going for an unrestricted convertibility including capital account transactions. However, low levels of international reserves, the dollar shortage syndrome, and the overall uncertainty about the outcome of reforms reduced the choice to a narrow concept of convertibility, essentially restricted to transaction on the current account. In practice, nearly all East European countries (except Romania) adopted the so-called "internal" convertibility, which combined free access to foreign exchange for residents for commercial (trade and services) transactions with some restrictions on transfers and on transactions effected by non-residents, and with extensive controls on capital account transactions. The "internal" convertibility was formally applied under the IMF's Article XIV which allowed for some temporary exchange controls, provided that countries concerned intended to eliminate them once external balance improved sufficiently.

The shift from Article XIV convertibility to full current account convertibility under Article VIII has been, however, slower than initially expected. The three Baltic states officially declared Article VIII convertibility in 1994, while Poland, the Czech Republic and Slovakia followed in 1995.[8] Other countries still prefer to maintain some currency controls, partly because they are not confident of the sustainability of the recent strengthening of their external balance position. But the main reason might be that the key benefits of convertibility, such as the realignment of relative prices and import of competition, could have been achieved without necessarily going for full liberalisation of current account transactions.

An interesting regularity is that none of the countries decided to introduce capital account convertibility in the first phase of transition. True, there are serious arguments in favour of capital convertibility: short-term capital flows provide crucial financing for trade, while capital movements play a pivotal role in economic development (IMF, 1995). But counter-arguments are no less important. Under increased uncertainty, imperfect or non-existent markets, and low reserves, domestic currencies are particularly vulnerable to speculative attacks and to a risk of capital flight. In addition, the absence of capital controls in a small country virtually disarms monetary policy, leaving the government with fiscal policies as the only instrument of macroeconomic control.

It should be noted, however, that even though formal capital account liberalisation has been postponed, in some important areas of capital transactions a *de facto* capital mobility is already rather substantial. For instance, there are practically no restrictions on the inflow side for both direct and portfolio investment. Also, many of the existing restrictions on capital outflows are difficult to enforce in practice (for a discussion of the Czech case, see Dedek, 1995).

The experience of transition countries in restoring external balance in the post-planning period suggests that the sequence of convertibility steps they adopted was basically correct. The sequence goes from the "internal convertibility" which should preferably be implemented in one go and right from the start of reforms, through Article VIII convertibility introduced at a later stage, and then to full convertibility in a more distant future, when the fundamental market institutions are already firmly in place and working.

3. Changes in the equilibrium exchange rate

3.1 Changes in productivity

With the initial dilemmas solved in one way or another, new problems have been emerging in the course of transition. Perhaps the most important one is the challenge posed by the underlying changes in the equilibrium exchange rate, arising from large shifts in productivity and from increasing capital mobility. It can be shown that these changes follow a pattern which is broadly common to all transition countries.

A large nominal devaluation at the beginning of transition was considered necessary to secure a degree of real depreciation sufficient to stimulate exports and curb imports, in order to achieve an external balance position consistent with the medium-term stabilization targets. The preoccupation with preserving export competitiveness through exchange rate policies has remained strong among policy-makers, and in view of rapidly rising prices the currencies in most countries were allowed to further depreciate in nominal terms (Table 1). However, the changes in real rates followed a different pattern; in fact, all transition countries witnessed varying degrees of real appreciation of their currencies in the period following the initial price stabilization (Table 2).

Table 1. Eastern Europe: changes in nominal exchange rates, 1992-95 (in national currency units per $US, IV quarter 1991 = 100).

	Bulgaria	Czech Rep	Hungary	Poland	Romania	Slovakia
Q4/91	100.00	100.00	100.00	100.00	100.00	100.00
Q1/92	116.65	99.91	102.22	109.51	150.77	99.91
Q2/92	113.38	99.07	103.66	123.07	174.43	99.07
Q3/92	110.73	93.82	100.89	122.86	288.13	93.82
Q4/92	119.44	98.87	106.59	135.08	329.94	98.87
Q1/93	128.90	100.35	111.88	146.55	399.85	100.66
Q2/93	130.16	99.40	115.86	152.12	488.44	100.03
Q3/93	135.35	101.88	123.55	168.52	624.81	111.15
Q4/93	152.93	101.87	129.75	185.64	815.01	114.11
Q1/94	227.01	103.56	134.29	196.54	1141.27	114.23
Q2/94	271.05	101.18	134.58	202.47	1274.89	111.30
Q3/94	281.16	97.20	138.10	205.62	1301.84	108.85
Q4/94	320.91	96.46	143.15	213.34	1348.47	107.53
Q1/95	324.97	92.52	148.02	218.12	1380.17	103.57
Q2/95	323.00	89.45	161.24	213.92	1462.94	101.10
Q3/95	330.28	90.97	170.37	217.96	1567.14	102.72
Q4/95	337.87	90.65	178.23	222.73	1817.05	102.32
Q 1196	368.05	92.71	188.58	228.94	2105.86	104.08

Note: Calculated from national statistics.

These developments tend to be viewed with some concern by many observers (Havlik, 1994; Hrncir, 1994; UN/ECE, 1994). It is frequently argued that the real appreciation erodes competitiveness of the tradable sector, and may eventually lead to a major balance of payments crisis. This view implies that the initial level of exchange rate corresponds to the equilibrium level and that the equilibrium exchange rate does not change over time; therefore, if inflation at home is higher than abroad, the nominal rate should depreciate to maintain the real rate broadly constant. In other words, it is assumed that the Purchasing Power Parity theory holds in the course of transition, and that the nominal rate should change broadly in proportion to the changes in relative prices.

The fears about eroding competitiveness of transition economies may not always be justified, at least for some transition countries. First of all, it is very doubtful whether the transition countries did set their initial exchange rates at the equilibrium levels and, therefore, whether their currencies are now undervalued or overvalued (Oblath, 1994). In fact, as discussed above, the deep initial devaluation most probably led to a substantial undervaluation of East European currencies. Moreover, the PPP theory clearly cannot be expected to hold in the presence of large real disturbances and asymmetric shocks, which affect real output. In the first phase of transition, output tends to fall because of restrictive demand policies and the sluggishness of supply-side response to the relative price changes, and, under persistent labour hoarding in post-socialist firms, labour productivity tends to fall. This tendency, clearly evident from statistics on "transitional recession", is accommodated by a combination of initial nominal devaluation and nominal wage

Table 2. Eastern Europe: changes in real exchange rates 1992-95 (IVQ1991=100).

Deflated by CPI

	Bulgaria	Czech Rep.	Hungary	Poland	Romania	Slovakia
Q4/91	100.00	100.00	100.00	100.00	100.00	100.00
Q1/92	100.91	97.37	95.35	97.00	100.31	97.00
Q2/92	82.63	94.94	92.36	99.82	91.60	95.80
Q3/92	71.61	87.63	87.69	92.61	130.10	89.82
Q4/92	66.75	87.87	87.49	92.65	110.76	90.24
Q1/93	60.95	80.42	83.71	91.72	98.19	82.17
Q2/93	53.66	78.25	84.74	89.31	81.88	79.36
Q3/93	51.33	78.55	87.65	94.14	74.18	85.07
Q4/93	51.56	76.33	87.49	94.96	67.05	82.98
Q1/94	67.07	75.48	85.76	92.75	76.71	80.81
Q2/94	58.16	72.88	83.03	89.54	72.19	77.57
Q3/94	52.91	68.11	81.85	85.47	68.51	73.65
Q4/94	49.30	65.36	80.11	81.73	64.22	69.96
Q1/95	44.06	61.16	76.00	77.30	62.25	65.75
Q2/95	41.28	57.91	76.37	71.66	63.50	63.42
Q3/95	40.39	58.20	77.97	71.86	64.72	63.23
Q4/95	38.01	56.97	77.46	69.67	68.72	61.75
Q1/96	38.73	56.34	75.81	67.25	74.43	62.00

Deflated by PPI

	Bulgaria	Czech Rep.	Hungary	Poland	Romania	Slovakia
Q4/91	100.00	100.00	100.00	100.00	100.00	100.00
Q1/92	104.53	97.09	99.24	103.02	100.31	97.57
Q2/92	94.15	94.29	96.59	106.80	91.60	95.79
Q3/92	84.37	87.98	91.35	100.59	130.10	90.53
Q4/92	89.04	90.54	91.14	103.65	110.76	93.63
Q1/93	90.99	85.56	91.90	104.31	98.19	85.18
Q2/93	87.26	82.77	94.04	102.73	93.57	83.90
Q3/93	88.96	83.66	98.89	102.80	83.64	91.51
Q4/93	97.21	82.91	100.24	105.25	82.03	90.74
Q1/94	132.63	83.12	100.53	104.33	89.74	89.41
Q2/94	117.47	80.17	98.20	102.75	79.88	86.34
Q3/94	108.98	76.11	97.36	97.90	75.81	77.68
Q4/94	110.37	74.70	96.76	93.44	73.59	78.38
Q1/95	101.15	69.16	90.55	88.95	72.01	72.66
Q2/95	94.58	65.74	90.99	84.04	70.67	69.55
Q3/95	92.46	65.80	92.09	82.65	69.77	69.82
Q4/95	87.82	65.05	91.75	81.13	75.54	69.06
Q1/96		65.55	94.07	80.89	80.61	69.76

Note: An increase in the index represent a depreciation of the real forex rate.
Source: Calculated from national statistics.

controls, resulting in a fall in real wages. The equilibrium real exchange rate may therefore depreciate further, which would call for a depreciation of the nominal rate, if the initial position was that of the equilibrium or of overvaluation.

The situation changes in the second phase of transition, when capital and labour have been reallocated from less to more efficient sectors, and workers and managers, responding to a new incentive structure, become more productive through acquisition of new skills, greater work effort and better discipline. These two mechanisms — the reallocation of resources to new uses and a more efficient use of resources in the existing plants — allow for an increase in efficiency and produce an exogenous increase of productivity. Since this productivity improvement is stronger relative to the productivity gains taking place in other (market) economies, the equilibrium real exchange rate tends to appreciate.[9]

It is important to keep in mind the difference between the real appreciation resulting from faster increases of domestic prices relative to foreign prices under the fixed nominal rate, which leads to an overvaluation of domestic currency, and the appreciation of the equilibrium real exchange rate. Under the Purchasing Power Parity theory, only the first type of real appreciation can take place, because the theory assumes the constancy of the equilibrium rate. But it is clear that real disturbances, such as the terms-of-trade shocks or efficiency improvements resulting from institutional reforms or structural change, can cause the equilibrium rate to move in either direction. The idea that the shift from central planning to a market system should bring about substantial efficiency gains has been suggested by many authors (see, e.g. Oblath, 1994; Portes, 1994; Rosati, 1994; Hrncir, 1994; Halpern and Wyplosz, 1995). According to one recent study, with the same capital and land per worker, the transition countries would achieve an output per worker 42-52 per cent higher than under central planning (Bergson, 1994). The reasons are simple: market reforms and deregulation result in a change in the incentive structure of workers and managers and in the removal of distortions in relative prices, which in turn allow for a more efficient use of the existing capacities and for expansion of activities with higher returns. Note that the improved discipline and work effort under market rules can bring about immediate efficiency gains (they can be called X-efficiency gains — see Leibenstein, 1975), but the effects of resource reallocation can materialise only after the necessary adjustment takes place in production.

It should be obvious that the productivity growth during transition is faster than in a "normal" market economy which, by definition, operates at, or close to the optimal point on the "full-capacity" production possibilities frontier. It can therefore be assumed that this differential in productivity growth rates will result in a real appreciation of the equilibrium exchange rate of transition countries' currencies, relative to market economies' currencies.

There are several types of real exchange rate adjustment mechanisms discussed in development economics literature. For instance, the familiar Balassa-Samuelson concept of real exchange rate appreciation driven by productivity growth differentials between tradable and non-tradable sectors (Balassa, 1964; Samuelson, 1964) rests on two assumptions: that productivity tends to increase faster in tradable than in non-tradable sectors, and that the labour force in low-income countries is less productive in tradable goods. Under these conditions, and if prices of tradables are determined on international markets, faster productivity increases in the tradable sector lead to higher wages in all sectors, thereby raising the overall price levels and causing an appreciation of the real exchange rates.[10]

Another theory, associated with the works of Bhagwati (1984), and Kravis and Lipsey (1983), links the real exchange rate appreciation with differences in endowments of capital and labour. Because rich countries have higher capital-labour ratios, the marginal productivity of labour in those countries is greater than in poor countries, and therefore the wage levels in the latter will be lower. As a result, the non-tradables, which are labour-intensive, will be cheaper in poorer countries. Higher factor productivity in tradables induces, however, capital and labour to reallocate from non-tradables to tradables, thus raising the relative price of non-tradables. For a small open economy, this will also result in a rise of the domestic-to-foreign price ratio, and the domestic currency will tend to appreciate.

Neither of these theories fits well to the realities of post-communist transformation. In the transition countries, productivity gains are likely to be both larger and of more across-the-board nature (including non-tradables sectors, such as services), as they arise from the one-time move from the "constrained" to the "full-capacity" production possibilities frontier and from the shift along the frontier towards the optimum.

The conventional way to test hypotheses on real exchange changes would be to look into statistics on price and nominal exchange rate changes in Eastern Europe. But the picture thus obtained may be misleading: the changes in nominal values can only indicate deviations from the base year level of the real exchange rate, rather than the changes in the equilibrium real exchange rate itself. Moreover, the price changes may not fully reflect changes in unit labour costs. Take the standard formula for the "statistical" real exchange rate change (Devarajan, Lewis and Robinson, 1993; Obstfeld, 1995):

$$(5)\ RER = (E_t/E_o)/[(P_t/P_o)/(P^*_t/P^*_o)]$$

where E stands for the nominal price of foreign currency in domestic currency units, and P and P* are domestic and foreign price levels, respectively. In accordance with the Purchasing Power Parity theory, the formula assumes constancy of the equilibrium real exchange rates. But, as argued earlier, this assumption is untenable given the massive structural and institutional changes occurring in the transition countries (Halpern and Wyplosz, 1995). Wide fluctuations in the statistically measured real exchange rates, reported in Table 2, seem to confirm the view that the PPP theory does not hold in the transition period. Another message from Table 2 is the tendency for the real rates to appreciate. After a fall in 1990-1991, these rates appreciated strongly between the end of 1991 and the end of 1995 in all central European countries. When deflated by the CPI, the real exchange rates increased by between 29 per cent in Hungary and more than 250 per cent in Bulgaria. The extent of real appreciation is considerably smaller when the nominal rate index is deflated by the PPI, but the general tendency remains broadly the same. During 1994-1995, the real appreciation (PPI-deflated) exceeded 20 per cent in the Czech Republic, Poland and Slovakia, and only in Romania did the real rate remain broadly unchanged. The acceleration of this tendency in 1995 is mostly a reflection of the fall of the dollar rate against other convertible currencies (the US dollar depreciated by some 15 per cent against the German mark between the first halves of 1994 and 1995) and an opposite trend can be expected to prevail in 1996.

Nevertheless, the tendency to real appreciation is likely to continue. The differential between CPI-deflated and PPI-deflated real rates suggests that the main reason behind this tendency is a faster increase of non-tradable prices, mainly services. It is also worth noting that the observed differences between CPI- and PPI-deflated exchange rates seem to confirm the Balassa-Samuelson proposition that productivity gains in tradable sectors are faster in the tradable sectors.

3.2 *Real exchange rate changes and export performance*

Under the hypothesis of the constant equilibrium rate, the reported changes in the real exchange rates would not be consistent with the overall improvement in export performance of all East European countries between 1992 and 1994 (Table 3). The statistics suggest that the appreciation of the real exchange rate (the nominal exchange rate deflated by price indices) do not have any significant impact on export performance of transition countries in the post-stabilization period: it is evident that in most cases higher export growth was accompanied by real appreciation of the exchange rates (a declining trend represents an appreciation). This suggests that other factors may have been at work.

One possible explanation, which has been discussed in the previous Section, relates to productivity changes. Their impact on export performance can be tested with the following cross-section log regression model:

$$(6)\ \log(X_{94}/X_{92}) = a + b_1 \log(E_{94}/E_{92}) + b_2 \log(P_{94}/P_{92}) + b_3 \log(L_{94}/L_{92})$$

where X, E, and P stand for the dollar value of exports, nominal exchange rate and domestic PPI, respectively,[11] while L represents labour productivity level, implied by the ratio of GDP to employment. As productivity gains can only take place in a growing economy (assuming that the employment levels are less flexible than the output levels), the equation (6) has been estimated for the period 1992-1994 when symptoms of economic recovery in Eastern Europe could already be observed. The

Table 3. Foreign trade of East European countries, 1990-95 (growth rate of dollar values, in %).

	Exports					
	1990	1991	1992	1993	1994	1995[a]
Bulgaria	-21.30	-34.20	13.90	-8.70	11.80	-2.90
Czech Rep.	-10.50	5.60	3.00	15.50	15.40	18.40
Hungary	0.60	5.10	4.40	-16.50	20.00	14.20
Poland	24.70	-18.50	-11.60	7.80	20.50	38.70
Romania	-43.40	-7.10	5.20	13.90	22.60	26.20
Slovakia	-10.50	5.60	6.50	-18.70	35.30	34.60
Slovenia	20.80	-6.30	8.00	-0.90	11.90	31.40
	Imports					
	1990	1991	1992	1993	1994	1995[a]
Bulgaria	-23.70	-51.50	64.90	-3.40	-4.80	4.90
Czech Rep.	0.30	-7.20	14.40	0.50	19.10	47.30
Hungary	-0.70	30.20	-2.90	13.70	15.50	17.10
Poland	-2.50	24.30	3.90	16.30	13.50	37.60
Romania	18.10	-17.60	8.20	10.50	-3.50	37.00
Slovakia	0.30	-7.20	-1.10	5.70	14.90	37.20
Slovenia	47.00	-12.50	0.10	17.70	11.50	40.10

Note: a) January-June.
Source: UN/ECE Database

following results have been obtained for seven transition countries[12] (the values of t-statistics in parentheses):

$$\log(X_{94}/X_{92}) = \underset{(1.135)}{0.027} - \underset{(-2.242)}{0.062} \log(E_{94}/E_{92}) + \underset{(2.109)}{0.572} \log(P_{94}/P_{92}) + \underset{(1.756)}{1.583} \log(L_{94}/L_{92}), \quad R^2 = 0.7871,\ \text{Adj.}R^2 = 0.5741$$

The equation shows a clear, though not very strong, relationship between the export performance on the one hand, and the changes in nominal exchange rates, prices and implied productivity, on the other hand. All structural parameters (except for the intercept) are statistically significant at 10 per cent confidence level, but because of the small size of the sample the results should be interpreted with caution. The interesting result here is the negative correlation between the nominal depreciation of domestic currencies and export performance, and the positive correlation between PPI and export performance; this means that exports accelerated despite the appreciation of the PPI-deflated real exchange rate. The strong cyclical upturn of Western demand in 1994 played certainly an important role in eastern export expansion; however, this does not exclude the possibility that the loss of competitiveness due to the appreciation of the real rate was alleviated by the simultaneous appreciation of the equilibrium exchange rate, driven by productivity gains.

The impact of productivity changes on export competitiveness can better be examined by looking into the changes in the real exchange rates deflated by unit labour costs (ULC).[13] As can be seen from Table 4, the extent of real appreciation is even smaller than in the case of PPI-deflated exchange rates. Productivity gains between 1991 and 1994 were particularly substantial in Poland and Romania, where real unit labour costs in industry diminished by between 25 and 35 per cent. As a result, the ULC-deflated real exchange rates depreciated considerably in the two countries and also in Bulgaria, where the depreciation of the nominal rate in 1994 was deepest. Moreover, since the exchange rates in East European countries were undervalued in the initial stage of transition, the margin of competitiveness may still be substantial. The resulting gap between the nominal exchange rate and the equilibrium rate, even though it has diminished in some countries since 1991, was sufficiently large to secure a solid expansion of exports, after a lag necessary for some basic restructuring.

Table 4. Eastern Europe: Unit labour costs and real exchange rates 1992-95 (IVQ 1991=100).

Changes in real unit labour costs (ULC)						
	Bulgaria	Czech Rep	Hungary	Poland	Romania	Slovakia
Q4/91	100.00	100.00	100.00	100.00	100.00	100.00
Q1/92	83.04	93.59	99.11	88.99	75.75	100.20
Q2/92	102.20	97.94	107.10	88.20	84.76	104.64
Q3/92	106.84	108.17	109.92	86.14	98.87	110.56
Q4/92	107.53	106.43	99.48	87.06	88.80	107.03
Q1/93	110.04	103.27	100.46	85.26	67.06	111.87
Q2/93	125.56	109.76	108.01	84.43	75.14	130.28
Q3/93	141.84	116.91	102.35	81.33	79.56	140.40
Q4/93	136.73	111.88	106.35	77.89	73.27	145.96
Q1/94	120.99	105.67	98.31	77.93	66.28	130.03
Q2/94	108.52	110.65	109.10	79.94	57.12	142.14
Q3/94	100.73	118.57	107.76	73.27	60.22	136.14
Q4/94	99.78	118.47	104.02	74.97	64.08	142.48
Q1/95	97.86	96.77	86.16	71.71	60.95	132.73
Q2/95	108.84	103.49	89.71	75.40	72.63	135.68

Changes in real exchange rates deflated by ULC						
	Bulgaria	Czech Rep	Hungary	Poland	Romania	Slovakia
Q4/91	100.00	100.00	100.00	100.00	100.00	100.00
Q1/92	125.88	103.75	100.14	115.77	132.42	97.37
Q2/92	92.13	96.28	90.18	121.09	108.06	91.53
Q3/92	78.96	81.33	83.11	116.76	131.59	81.88
Q4/92	82.80	85.07	91.61	119.05	124.73	87.47
Q1/93	82.69	82.85	91.47	122.35	146.43	76.15
Q2/93	69.50	75.41	87.07	121.68	124.52	64.40
Q3/93	62.75	71.56	96.62	126.40	105.13	65.18
Q4/93	71.10	74.11	94.26	135.12	111.96	62.17
Q1/94	109.62	78.66	102.26	133.87	135.40	68.76
Q2/94	108.25	72.46	90.01	128.53	139.84	60.74
Q3/94	108.20	64.19	90.35	133.61	125.87	57.06
Q4/94	110.62	63.06	93.02	124.64	114.84	55.01
Q1/95	103.36	71.46	105.10	124.05	118.14	54.75
Q2/95	86.90	63.53	101.42	111.47	97.31	51.26

Note: An increase in the index represents a depreciation of the real forex value.
Source: Calculated from national statistics.

But the medium-term prospects, except in Poland, may be less optimistic. The margin of initial undervaluation may have been largely eroded in those countries where the ULC-deflated real exchange rates appreciated strongly — chiefly the Czech Republic and Slovakia. In fact, real export growth slowed down very substantially in the former country in 1995, and a part of the explanation is to be looked for in the combination of the fixed exchange rate regime and very weak productivity advances. Slovakia's export growth has been stronger, but it may have reflected the one-time effect of establishing new trade contacts by the country which acquired independence only a few years ago and did not have strong traditions of foreign trade before. By contrast, Hungary's competitive position appears to have improved recently due to aggressive devaluation policies and real wage restraint imposed during 1995.

3.3 *Capital inflows*

Another factor which has contributed to the appreciation of the equilibrium exchange rate in the more advanced East European countries is the increasing capital inflow to the region. The phenomenon, which emerged on a larger scale only in 1994, has assumed very substantial proportions during 1995 and 1996. It has been reflected by the rapid increase in the level of international reserves in most East European countries (except Romania). The figures reported in Table 5 show that during the eighteen-month period between December 1993 and June 1995 the level of official foreign reserves nearly tripled in the Czech Republic, Poland and Slovakia, and more than doubled in Bulgaria. This should be seen as a remarkable and even surprising performance, given the precarious external balance position of the transition countries at the beginning of the 1990s.

The causes of capital inflows are not uniform across the region; also, their relative significance have been changing overtime. The first impulse came in 1993, when Western investors, lured by the extremely low equity prices in Eastern Europe, decided to invest in the emerging stock markets, mainly in former Czechoslovakia,

Hungary and Poland. As a result, significant investments were channelled into the region, through direct participation in privatisation of state enterprises, "green-field" investment projects, and portfolio investments on the stock markets. These early inflows, dominated by FDI, were mainly concentrated in Hungary, the Czech Republic and Poland. The second wave followed up on the rapid development of domestic money markets in the transition countries. The emergence of public debt

Table 5. Official international reserves[a] in US$ billions, end-of-period.

	Bulgaria	Czech Rep	Hungary	Poland	Romania	Slovakia
Dec.92	0.90	0.80	4.30	4.30	0.80	
Jun.93		2.30	4.80	3.50	0.70	
Dec.93	0.70	3.90	6.70	4.30	1.00	0.40
Jun.94	1.10	5.20	6.00	5.20	1.30	0.70
Dec.94	1.00	6.20	6.80	6.00	2.00	1.70
Jun.95	1.50	11.20	8.00	10.70	1.80	2.40
Dec.95		13.40	10.90	14.00		

Note: a) Excluding gold.
Source: National statistics.

instruments and further expansion of capital markets, under generally high domestic interest rates, opened up very attractive opportunities for financial investments during 1994 and 1995. A combination of high government borrowing, high interest rates and expectations of real appreciation of domestic currencies led to relatively high yields on treasury bills in Poland, Hungary or Bulgaria.[14] Such high yield differentials were also observed in the past, but they did not attract significant foreign investment simply because the risks involved in investing in treasury bills in Eastern Europe were also high. During 1994-95, these risks substantially diminished due to a number of reasons. First, Bulgaria and Poland succeeded in obtaining a significant reduction of their external debt to commercial banks; second, the Czech Republic, Hungary and Poland were given relatively favourable investment rating standards by international investment agencies (Moody's and Standard & Poors); third, strong economic recovery in the region also helped to strengthen foreign investors' confidence in the region.

Can these large capital inflows be considered as "normal" and sustainable in the medium-term perspective? The answer is difficult because statistics on the structure and origin of the flows are still rather uncertain. Moreover, there is no uniform pattern of capital flows across countries; for instance, the sources of inflows to the Czech Republic and Poland, the two countries with the largest increases of international reserves, seem to be quite different. The most important single source of capital inflows in the Czech Republic (also in Slovakia) has been direct borrowing by domestic companies from foreign banks, mostly motivated by high interest rates at home. Given the fixed and credible exchange rate, the difference of 4-6 percentage points between interest rates charged on bank credits in the Czech Republic and in Western countries was a powerful incentive to borrow abroad. The other important contribution to the stock of official international reserves has been the inflow of foreign direct investment.

By contrast in Poland, the most significant source of capital inflows has been revenue from unofficial "cross-border" export transactions, mostly sales of goods and services to German tourists.[15] These proceeds are incorrectly classified as short-term capital flows because they are typical current account transactions; if they were included in the current account, Poland's huge trade deficit would most probably turn into a healthy surplus. On the other hand, the share of foreign direct and financial investment has been much smaller, probably below 30 per cent of total reported capital inflows. These preliminary observations suggest that the registered increases in international reserves in the transition countries may be in the dominant proportion caused by relatively stable financial flows, such as commercial borrowing, "unofficial" export revenues and foreign direct investment, and that the share of short-term, speculative inflows in total capital inflows is still relatively low. While this pattern can change in the future, there should be no immediate concern about the possibility of a sudden reversal of these flows. On the other hand, large capital inflows clearly pose a serious problem for monetary policies: characterised by relatively low money-to-GDP ratios, the level of money stock in the transition economies is strongly affected by the changes in foreign reserves. Indeed, the rapid growth of international reserves after 1993 caused domestic money supply to overshoot predetermined limits, and may have been partly responsible for persistent inflation.

4. Conclusions and policy implications

The upward shift in the equilibrium exchange rate of more advanced transition countries poses a new challenge to their exchange rate policies. Both exports and imports tend to grow fast as a result of the productivity advances and strong output and demand expansion both in Western and in transition countries (Table 3). Moreover, the existing asymmetry in regulations on capital mobility and improving investment opportunities in Eastern Europe have created potential for large and sometimes destabilizing capital inflows. The key policy issue is to accommodate the underlying changes in the equilibrium exchange rates in such a way as to minimise the negative impact of capital inflows on the domestic monetary situation and maintain the necessary competitive margin in exports.

Under a fixed, or otherwise controlled exchange rate, and rapidly changing structural conditions, there is always a risk of a misalignment in the exchange rates. The policy of nominal changes should therefore broadly follow the path of the equilibrium exchange rate. Drawing on the experience of East European transition countries, the optimum pattern of exchange rate policies during transition could be, in a stylised form, presented as the following sequence:

1. Initial devaluation-cum-convertibility;
2. A period of a fixed exchange rate regime;
3. A period of a crawling peg regime (exogenously determined), with occasional adjustments;
4. A flexible rate within a pre-determined band.

The sequence reflects changing policy objectives. In the first stage, a shift from non-convertibility and foreign exchange rationing requires deep devaluation; next, a fixed exchange rate regime is necessary to dampen inflation and reduce uncertainty. But once price stability has been broadly established, the policy focus shifts to another objective; in order to avoid excessive overvaluation of domestic currency and better target the equilibrium rate, the fixed rate regime should be replaced by an adjustable rate regime. Initially, a crawling peg is preferable for it offers the advantage of predictability. Finally, a flexible rate system should be installed in order to better accommodate changes in the demand for and supply of foreign exchange, arising from gradual liberalisation of capital flows. The flexibility should be limited to a predetermined band, however, to prevent excessive volatility of exchange rates.

How to cope with large capital inflows is a different policy issue. Massive inflows of foreign capital may pose serious risks to the financial stability of the receiving country. First, they put an upward pressure on domestic currency and if the currency is allowed to appreciate in real terms, this may hurt export sectors. The result could be a sort of a "Dutch disease", which may eventually lead to a major foreign exchange crisis (actually, some symptoms of exports losing competitiveness have been observed in 1995 in the Czech Republic). Second, an increase in net foreign assets is a source of additional money supply which may go out of control if capital inflows are large relative to domestic money stock. This may lead to accelerated inflation, especially in the case of a small, open economy. Third, if the incoming capital is of a speculative nature and is primarily invested in highly liquid, short-term financial instruments (treasury bills, deposits with domestic banks), the risk of sudden capital flight is substantial. How should the transition countries react to these risks?

Central banks have a number of possible policy options to deal with excessive capital inflows. The most obvious policy response is to allow the domestic currency to appreciate. But this may lead to a loss of competitiveness by export sectors and widened current account deficit, which may eventually reverse the capital flight, leading to a balance of payments crisis. Another possibility is to "sterilise" the inflows of foreign exchange through "open market operations": the central bank sells securities to commercial banks, thus reducing the stock of reserve money and their capacity to extend credit. The sterilised intervention may, however, be ineffective, As it tends to push up interest rates (as the central bank bids for resources of commercial banks), this will attract even more foreign capital into the country and the resulting inflow may overwhelm the efforts by the central bank to reduce domestic money supply. In addition, sterilisation is costly, as it involves paying higher interest rates to commercial banks, as compared with revenues obtained on foreign exchange assets.[16] Yet another possibility is to impose a tax on capital inflows, e.g. in the form of a widened spread between the "sell" and "buy" exchange rates. This solution, however, is bound to hamper trade through increasing transaction costs. Finally, the central bank can increase mandatory reserve requirements of commercial banks, in order to curb their credit capacities and thus limit the impetus of money growth.

All these measures are of a short-term nature and have typically adverse side effects. Moreover, they do not address the real causes of excessive capital inflows. If the cause is the high interest rate differential, to restore interest rate parity would require an adjustment on the fiscal side, in order to reduce the government demand for domestic savings. If the cause is the exchange rate misalignment, a real appreciation will most probably be inevitable, either through a nominal revaluation of the domestic currency or through accelerated inflation.

These observations point towards suggested policy solutions. Under the fixed exchange rate and inward capital mobility, the freedom to pursue an independent monetary policy becomes severely restricted: the central bank cannot simultaneously target monetary aggregates, interest rates and the exchange rate. If domestic interest rates are high relative to foreign interest rates, the country risks to be overwhelmed by speculative capital inflows. Given the small size of capital and money markets in the transition economies, relatively small amounts of capital can easily destabilize the monetary situation, causing the domestic money supply to go out of control. Under such conditions, sterilisation of foreign capital inflows is largely ineffective, because it inevitably tends to raise domestic interest rates and encourage more capital inflows. Moreover, it is costly, as it forces the central bank to pay high rates of return on domestic bonds. The solution would be to set interest rates and future depreciation of domestic currency at levels which are consistent with the interest rate parities.

The two main dangers associated with this strategy are the inflationary impact of lower interest rates and the adverse impact of currency appreciation on export competitiveness. But the inflationary tendencies would be counter-balanced by the nominal appreciation (or a slow-down in the rate of crawl) of the domestic currency and by a likely deceleration in the growth of domestic money supply resulting from the outflow of speculative capital. On the other hand, exports should not suffer if the equilibrium exchange rate is indeed falling due to improved productivity, provided there is restraint on growth of wages.

Notes

[1] According to Oblath (1994), the extent of initial devaluation should be larger in the case low degree of "openness" of the economy. However, stronger autarchy does not have to be necessarily associated with a more distorted exchange rate (compare Bulgaria and the Czech Republic). There is no clear correlation between the extent of overvaluation of currency and the degree of openness; even in a closed economy the official rate may be set close to the equilibrium rate (though a tendency to an overvalued rate would probably prevail).

[2] As Oblath (1994, p.34) observed with a dose of pessimism, "there are no solid grounds for assessing what constitutes an equilibrium exchange rate for an economy in transition".

[3] The risk premium might be substantial because foreign currency transactions on the black market were illegal under central planning.

[4] In Hungary, the exchange rate worked *de facto* as a nominal anchor, though it was never declared as such by the Hungarian authorities (Szentgyorgyvari, 1994).

[5] Hungary may be an exception; only after a set of drastic policy measures, including a substantial devaluation of the forint, was introduced in March 1995, the country has shown some symptoms of regaining external balance.

[6] Willett and Al-Marhubi (1994) are sceptical about the stabilizing effect of an "explicitly temporary peg". But under high inflation, even a temporary fixed exchange rate can considerably reduce inflationary expectations if it forms a part of a credible stabilization programme, including liberalisation of foreign exchange market.

[7] As Williamson (1991) observed, "...Until late 1989, it was taken as axiomatic that any transition would be a long-drawn-out affair, with the changes spaced over many years. Convertibility was regarded as an aim for the next century, which would match the time it took for Western Europe to re-establish convertibility after the second World War...". And he concludes: "... To summarise, the convertibility should not be attempted in advance of the fundamental transformation to a

market economy..." (p.27-28). For a similarly sceptical view, see Kregel, Matzner and Grabher (1992).

[8] In May 1995, Poland officially notified the IMF of its intention to observe Article VIII convertibility as from 1 June 1995. The Czech Republic and Slovakia declared the Article VIII convertibility as of 1 October 1995.

[9] The idea can also be illustrated with a simple numerical example. Assume that initially the time necessary to produce a basket of similar typical goods and services is 10 hours in the US and 30 hours in Poland, and that the wage rates per hour are US$6 and 5 zlotys, respectively. The initial equilibrium exchange rate (assuming zero capital flows) would thus be: RER_0=30*5/10*6=150zl/60US$=>2.5zl/US$. If the nominal rate is also set at this level, the zloty is neither undervalued nor overvalued. Now assume there is a reform-induced, across-the-board, increase in productivity in Poland, say, by 30 per cent; that is, the time necessary to produce the same basket of goods and services is now reduced to 21 hours. The new real equilibrium exchange rate of the zloty will now be RER_1-21*5/10*6=105zl/60US$=> 1.75 zl/US$, which means that the purchasing power of the zloty in terms of dollar goods increased by 30 per cent. If the nominal rate remains unchanged, also the degree of undervaluation of the zloty would be 30 per cent [(1.75-2.5)/2.5].

[10] In a recent paper, Halpern and Wyplosz (1995) have used the Balassa-Samuelson model to show the trend to real appreciation of the equilibrium rate in East European countries and to estimate the extent of misalignment between the nominal rates and the equilibrium rates. They find that, except for the Czech Republic, East European currencies do not seem to be undervalued. If their findings are correct, they would confirm the view that the initial exchange rate position of transition countries was that of undervaluation.

[11] Given the relatively high inflation rates in Eastern Europe, changes in foreign prices have been ignored for simplicity.

[12] Bulgaria, the Czech Republic, Hungary, Poland, Romania, Slovakia and Slovenia.

[13] The index of unit labour costs (ULC) was calculated as the ratio of the index of real product wages (wage index/PPI) and the index of productivity changes (output index/employment index).

[14] For instance, in Poland in the first half of 1995 the rates of return on Polish Treasury bills exceeded the yields obtained on short-term bills in western countries by 8-10 points.

[15] According to a study by Central Statistical Office (GUS), the value of cross-border, unregistered exports in 1994 was US$2.1 billion (Rzeczpospolita, 7.09.1995). Some recent estimates put the corresponding figure for 1995 at US$6-7 billion.

[16] For instance, the Czech National Bank spent CZK 110 billion (nearly US$4 billion) on sterilisation operations during the first half of 1995 only.

References

Balassa, B., 1964, "The Purchasing Power Doctrine: A Reappraisal", *Journal of Political Economy*, Vol. 72, December 1994, pp. 584-596.

Berg, A. and Sachs, J., 1992, "Structural adjustment and international trade in Eastern Europe: The case of Poland", *Economic Policy,* No. 14, April, pp. 117-174.

Bergson, A., 1994, "The Communist Efficiency Gap: Alternative Measures", *Comparative Economic Studies,* Vol. 36, No. 1, Spring, pp. 1-12.

Bhagwati, J., 1984, "Why Are Services Cheaper in the Poor Countries?", *The Economic Journal,* Vol. 94, June, pp. 279-286.

Corden, M., 1993, "Exchange Rate Policies for Developing Countries", *The Economic Journal,* Vol. 103, January, pp. 198-207.

Dedek, 0., 1995, *Currency convertibility and exchange rate policies in the Czech Republic*, Ceska Narodni Banka, Institut Ekonomie, VP. 38, Praha.

Devarajan, S., Lewis, J.D. and Robinson, S., 1993, "External Shocks, Purchasing Power Parity, and the Equilibrium Real Exchange Rate", *The World Bank Economic Review,* Vol. 7, No. 1, pp. 45-63.

Dornbusch, R. and Werner, A., 1994, "Mexico: Stabilization, Reform and No Growth", *Brookings Papers on Economic Activity,* Vol. 24, No. 1, pp. 253-316.

Fry, M.J., and Nuti, D.M., 1992, "Monetary and exchange rate policies during Eastern Europe's transition", *Oxford Review of Economic Policy,* Vol. 8, No. 1.

Gaspar, P., 1995, "Exchange Rate Policies in Economies in Transition", Institute for World Economics, Hungarian Academy of Science, Working Paper No. 56, Budapest, August.

Halpern, L. and Wyplosz, C., 1995, "Equilibrium Real Exchange Rates in Transition", *CEPR Discussion Paper Series,* No. 1145, London, April.

Havlik, P., 1994, "Exchange rates, wages and competitiveness of Central and Eastern Europe", *The Vienna Institute of Comparative Economic Studies,* Vienna, November, [mimeo].

Hrncir, M., 1994, "Exchange Rate Regime in the Transition Period, in Barta V., and Schneider, Ch.M., eds., *"Stabilization Policies at Crossroads? An Interim Report from Central and Eastern Europe"*, IIASA, Laxenburg, June, pp. 133-168.

IMF, 1995, *IMF Survey,* February 6.

Kravis, I. and Lipsey, R., 1983, "Toward an Explanation of National Price Levels", *Princeton Studies in International Finance,* No. 52, Princeton University, November 1993.

Kregel, J., Matzner, E. and Grabher, G., 1992, *The market shock,* Agenda Group, Austrian Academy of Science, Vienna.

Montiel, P.J., Ostry, J.D., 1994, "The Parallel Market Premium: Is It a Reliable Indicator of Real Exchange Rate Misalignment in Developing Countries?", *IMF Staff Papers,* Vol. 41, No. 1, pp. 55-76.

Mundell, R., 1962, "The Appropriate Use of Monetary and Fiscal Policy under Fixed Exchange Rates", *IMF Staff Papers,* Vol. 9, March.

Nuti, M. and Portes, R., 1993, "Central Europe: the way forward", in Portes, R., ed., *Economic Transformation in Central Europe. A Progress Report,* CEPR-EUROP, Luxembourg, pp. 1-20.

Oblath, G., 1994, "Exchange Rate Policy and Real Exchange Rate Changes in Economic Transition", in: Gacs, J. and Winckler, G., eds., *International Trade and Restructuring in Eastern Europe,* IIASA, Physica-Verlag, Heidelberg, pp. 15-46.

Obstfeld, M., 1995, "International Currency Experience: New Lessons and Lessons Relearned", *Brookings Papers on Economic Activity,* Vol. 25, No. 1, pp. 119-220.

Portes, R., 1994, "Transformation traps", *The Economic Journal,* Vol. 104, September, pp. 1178-189.

Rosati, D.K., 1989, "Exchange rate policy and macroeconomic stabilization" (in Polish), Foreign Trade Research Institute, Warsaw, November, [mimeo].

Rosati, D.K., 1993a, "A glass half-empty", in Portes, R., ed., *Economic Transformation in Central Europe. A Progress Report,* CEPR-EUROP, Luxembourg, pp. 211-273.

Rosati, D.K., 1993b, "How to Make Inconvertible Currencies Convertible?", in *The Economics of New Currencies,* CEPR, London, November, pp. 222-226.

Rosati, D.K., 1994, "Output decline during transition from plan to market: a reconsideration", *The Economics of Transition,* Vol. 2, No. 4, pp. 419-442.

Samuelson, P.A., 1964, "Theoretical Notes on Trade Problems", *Review of Economics and Statistics,* Vol. 46, May, pp. 145-154.

Szentgyorgyvari, A., 1994, "Possibility for Using the Exchange Rate as Nominal Anchor for the Domestic Price Level: Some Evidence from the Hungarian Case", in Barta, V., and Schneider, Ch. M., eds., *Stabilization Policies at Crossroads? An Interim Report from Central and Eastern Europe,* IIASA, Laxenburg, June, pp. 107-118.

UN/ECE, 1994, *Economic Survey of Europe in 1993-1994,* New York.

Wettstein, P. , 1994, *Die Rolle der Wechselkurspolitik beim Ubergang von Plan- zu Marktwirtschaften,* Ruegger, Chur/Zurich.

Willett, T.D. and Al-Marhubi, F., 1994, "Currency Policies for Inflation Control in the Formerly Centrally Planned Economies", *The World Economy,* Vol. 17, No. 6, November, pp. 795-816.

Williamson, J., 1991, "The Economic Opening of Eastern Europe", Institute for International Economics, Washington, D.C.
Williamson, J., 1993, "Exchange Rate Management", *The Economic Joumal*, Vol. 103, January, pp. 189-197.

3

Access to Western markets, and Eastern effort levels

Edward E. Leamer

1. Introduction

A natural time and place to look for historical analogues to the dramatic liberalisation of Eastern Europe is post-war Europe. It is possible that Eastern Europe will now begin the process that Western Europe experienced after the second World War. As shown in Figure 1, the 1950s witnessed high growth rates of *per capita* GDPs in most of Western Europe, and the convergence effect seemed quite strong, with rapid growth of per capita incomes especially in the war-ravaged countries of Germany, Austria, Italy and Spain.

These data support a very optimistic view of the future of Eastern Europe, and suggests that growth in real *per capita* incomes is likely to be at the very healthy rate of 3 per cent per year, and there is a good chance that it could be 4 per cent or even 5 per cent per year. But, of course, we need to ask ourselves the question: What is different now? In this paper I will develop ideas regarding two of the myriad forces that will determine the courses taken by different Eastern and Central European countries:

- Human effort levels;
- Natural and man-made restrictions on access to Western marketplaces.

There are many anecdotes that suggest that the Communist method of production involved very low-pace operations. These operations probably acculturated the workers to low-pace (and low effort level) operations; an important driver of the future of Eastern Europe is thus willingness of the workforce to accept the high-wage, high-pace contracts that are now being offered. An analogous situation exists in many developing countries in which multinational firms pay a high premium relative to local jobs, but also expect hard work in return. The attractiveness of low

Partially supported by NSF Grant SBR-940911. Assistance of Andrey Pavlov is gratefully acknowledged.

Figure 1.

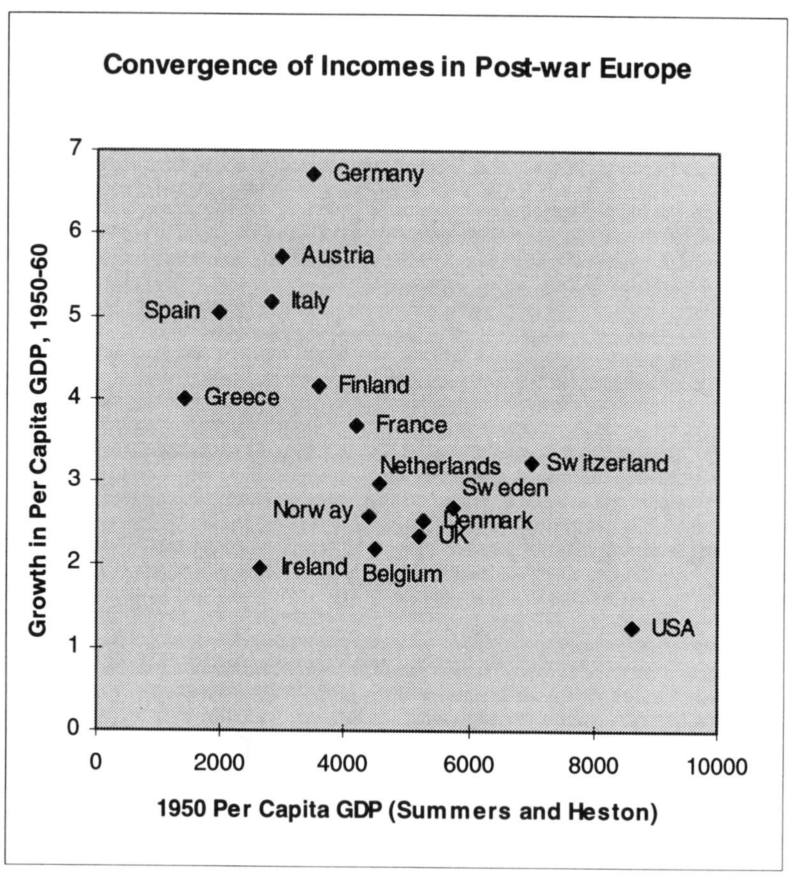

wages to multinational investment depends very much on the willingness of the workforce to achieve reasonably high levels of productivity. It is not wages that matter, it is unit labour costs.

A role that human effort might play in the development process is discussed theoretically in the context of a three-sector static general equilibrium model with variable pace of operations. A story that may or may not be true can introduce the idea. In Los Angeles, after getting on an elevator, the doors wait ten seconds before they close. In Hong Kong the doors wait only three seconds. In other words, equipment can be operated at different speeds. Workers who are willing and able to perform efficiently at high speeds save capital costs and, in a competitive setting, those savings are passed fully on to workers in the form of higher wages.

If the pace of operations is variable within an industry or across industries and if workers prefer low pace, a competitive labour market can be expected to offer a set of contracts, some high-pace, high-wage contracts and some low-pace, low-wage contracts. In a two-sector model, the savings are greatest in the capital-intensive sector and the economy may bifurcate, with the high-wage, high-pace operations in the capital intensive sector and the low-wage, low-pace operations in the labour-intensive sector. This bifurcation changes substantially the way the economy responds to external or internal shocks. For example, increased competition in Western Europe from low-wage Eastern European countries may have its initial and primary effect on the low-wage, low-pace contracts but leave the high-wage, high-pace contracts intact.

The second driver considered here is access to Western European marketplaces. In contrast to the section on pace of operations, the discussion of market access is entirely empirical. Measures of distance to marketplaces are constructed and shown to be closely correlated with *per capita* GDPs and their rates of growth. Countries that are "close to the action" are shown to have large locational advantages, enjoying high *per capita* GDP, high growth, and comparative advantage in manufactures, especially capital intensive manufactures. Geographically, Central and Eastern Europe are extremely well positioned, and if the Western market is kept open, history suggests that, after an initial adjustment, growth will be quite substantial. Protectionism in the West may increase the effective distance between East and West, and may be a major deterrent to growth.

Section 2 presents the theoretical model developed to explicitly take into consideration the pace at which workers are willing to work, and evaluates how well its conclusions fit available data. Section 3 examines the economic importance of distance to major markets. Section 4 summarises the results and draws conclusions that are relevant for Eastern Europe.

2. Compensation for pace in a two-sector model with exogenously determined product prices

This section presents a three-sector two-factor model with variable pace of operations. It is assumed that increasing the pace of operations affects the production function in the same way as factor-neutral technological change. With s standing for the speed of operations, the production function is written as:

$$Q = sF(K, L)$$

where Q is the output, K is the capital input, L is the labour input and F(.) is a production function exhibiting constant-returns-to-scale. The variable s is not literally "speed" as measured by a clock-watch, but instead stands for a kind of human effort that increases equally the productivity of capital and labour time. For example, s might be attentiveness, which makes breakdowns of the equipment less likely. If s is speed, it is assumed that the equipment does not break down more rapidly at high speed. (Workers are assumed to have preference for low speed, but capital does not care at all.) Finally, it should be mentioned that s is here assumed to be continuously and completely variable. A sewing machine can make 10 stitches a minute or a million stitches. It would not be difficult to alter the theory below to restrict the values of s in some sectors. My preference would be to assume that the pace of operations in labour-intensive sectors is greatly variable but the pace in capital-intensive sectors is technologically limited.

A competitive labour market will award the marginal increase in output all to the workers willing to work at the higher pace. The wage rate w(s) applicable to speed s is a solution to a zero profit inequality:

$$spF(K,L) \geq rK + w(s)L$$

where p is the price of the product, r is the interest rate per hour, w(s) is the wage per hour for workers operating at speed s. This can be inverted to solve for the wage rate:

$$w(s) \leq \left(\frac{pFs}{L} - \frac{rK}{L}\right) = (pfs - rk)$$

where pf is labour productivity for s = 1 workers and k is the capital/labour ratio. To facilitate the graphs and the algebra, the capital intensities are now assumed to be technologically fixed.

Suppose also that the economy has two sectors, a labour-intensive sector (Apparel) and a capital-intensive sector (Machinery). Suppose that only apparel is consumed and that these sectors make real wage offers in terms of the apparel good:

$$\frac{w(s)}{p_A} \leq \left(f_A s - \frac{r}{p_A} k_A\right)$$

$$\frac{w(s)}{p_A} \leq \left(\frac{p_M}{p_A} f_M s - \frac{r}{p_A} k_M\right)$$

These two inequalities are depicted by two lines in Figure 2. These lines start below zero since at very low speeds the value of output is not enough to cover the capital rental costs and these losses must be covered by charging workers to work. The capital rental costs are higher in the capital-intensive sector and the offered wages at low speeds are more negative in the capital-intensive sector than the labour-intensive sector. As the pace increases, workers can be awarded higher wages in both sectors because they save capital rental costs. The capital savings from speed are greatest in the capital-intensive sector which therefore offers the highest wages for high-speed work. Workers can be expected to maximise their wages at every level of speed, and labour contracts will lie along the upper envelope of these wage offers, which is the heavy piece-wise linear curve depicted in Figure 2. The low-speed contracts between s_1 and s_2 are offered in the labour-intensive sector. Speeds above s_2 are offered in the capital-intensive sector.

A representative worker and a third sector (textiles) are added to the model in Figure 3. An indifference curve of a representative worker is shown tangent to the zero profit lines of the three sectors. Each point of tangency, depicted as a dark dot, selects a labour contract, a wage-speed combination. These three contracts are ordered from lower left to upper right in the figure. In words, the pace of operations increases with the capital-intensity of the sector and the wage rate increases by just enough to make the representative worker indifferent among the three contracts.

The equilibrium depicted in Figure 3 is not unique. The tangencies between the three lines and an indifference curve can be altered by movements in the intercepts of the lines combined with an appropriate change in the slope. The movement of the three intercepts must be in unison since they are proportional to the interest rate times the price of the capital equipment, and inversely proportional to the price of

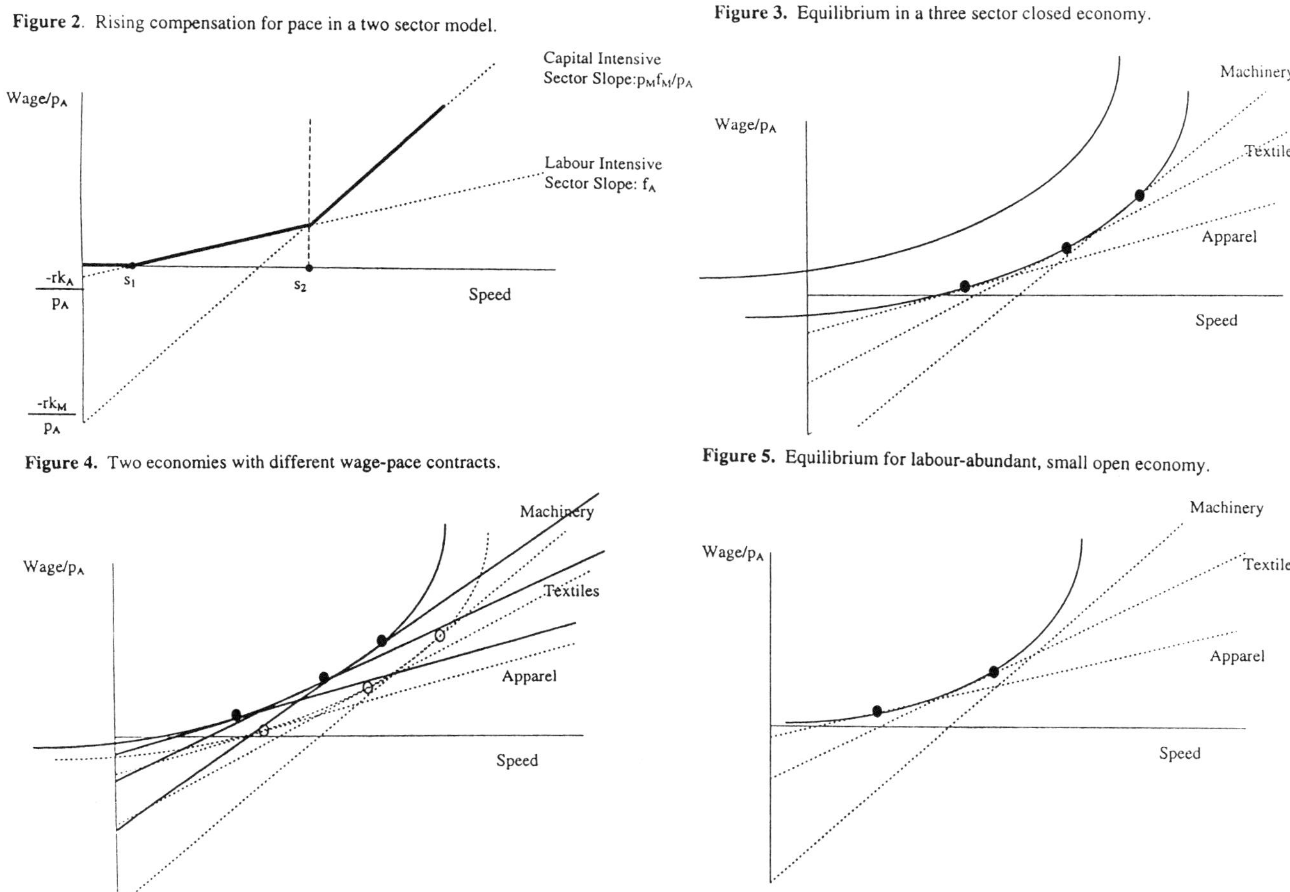

Figure 2. Rising compensation for pace in a two sector model.

Figure 3. Equilibrium in a three sector closed economy.

Figure 4. Two economies with different wage-pace contracts.

Figure 5. Equilibrium for labour-abundant, small open economy.

apparel. The slope of the apparel zero profit line is technologically fixed, but the slope of the machinery and textile lines varies with their product prices. With this much freedom to move the lines and choose a different worker indifference curve, there seem to be many alternative equilibria for a closed economy. In fact, once the cost of capital (in terms of the apparel numeraire) is selected, everything else follows. This cost of capital selects the intercepts of the three zero-profit lines. This fully determines the apparel zero-profit line since its slope is fixed. Next is selected the worker indifference curve that is tangent to this apparel zero-profit line. Then the slopes of the other two lines are adjusted to make them tangent to this worker indifference curve. This "algorithm" has been used to determine another possible equilibrium depicted in Figure 4 where the light dots represent the original contracts and the heavy dots the contracts applicable with a lower cost of capital. This lower cost of capital selects an apparel zero profit line that has the same slope but an intercept closer to zero. Then the worker indifference curve is selected that is tangent to this apparel zero profit line. The other two tangencies are selected by adjusting the intercepts proportional to the assumed change in the cost of capital, and then rotating the lines to make them tangent to the selected worker indifference curve. With the lower cost of capital applicable to the new equilibrium in Figure 4 both slopes of the textile and the machinery lines have to be reduced in order to create the indicated tangencies. In words, with cheaper capital, the wage-pace trade-off is more favourable to workers in the sense that at every rate of speed the wage rate is higher. The price of both the capital-intensive goods, textiles and machinery, relative to apparel is less, which means that the marginal compensation for speed is less. Workers in these sectors experience an "income" effect which they may spend on both higher wages and lower speeds but also a substitution effect which shifts their choices toward lower speed and lower wages. In other words, since speed saves capital costs, relatively little speed is purchased when capital is cheap.

A small open economy has a much more limited set of possible equilibria because the prices of tradables are set in external marketplaces. This fixes the slopes of the zero-profit lines and allows only the intercepts to vary proportionately with capital costs. Given these fixed slopes, most countries will find themselves in specialised equilibria such as the one depicted in Figure 5. In order to ensure that the available capital and labour are fully employed, the pair of products selected by the tangency conditions must have capital/labour ratios that capture the capital/labour supply ratio. Thus Figure 5 is labelled as an equilibrium for a labour-abundant country since it excludes the capital-intensive good.

Industriousness and the compensation for labour and capital with capital flows

Next we consider the effect of economic "culture", the willingness to work hard. "Is this the difference between Asia and Latin America?", I ask rhetorically. Are there countries in Eastern Europe with relatively large shares of their labour forces willing to work at high pace? Are there other countries with most workers accustomed to the comfortable low-pace Communist method of production? What difference will this make? The answer is that willingness to work at high pace saves capital costs, encourages capital inflows and creates comparative advantage in capital-intensive manufactures.

Contrast two communities that have identical supplies of capital and labour, one with workers willing to do high speed operations and another with workers who prefer to take it easy. If Figure 5 represents the equilibrium for a slothful community, then the industrious community can be modelled by a shift in the indifference curve in favour of higher rates of speed. This shift of preferences would leave the low-speed low-wage contracts in Figure 5 completely unfilled and these released workers seeking the high-speed jobs in the capital-intensive sector would increase the rental rate of capital, which shifts the zero profit lines downward, producing the new equilibrium in Figure 6. In the equilibrium applicable to the industrious community, workers opt for higher speeds in both sectors. Wages in the industrious community may either exceed or fall short of wages in the equivalent sector in the slothful community. The increased cost of capital is a force for wage reduction, but the preference for pace is a force for wage increases. In summary, the slothful community, other things equal, has a lower return to capital and a wage-pace offer curve that provides lower pace relative to wages. If the preference for sloth is great enough, the slothful community can have lower wages and lower pace in both sectors compared with the industrious community.

Capital mobility

Differences in industriousness among countries can create an equilibrium in which capital has an incentive to flow from the slothful to the industrious countries and for labour possibly to flow in the opposite direction. This labour flow toward the low-pace countries is not especially compatible with the facts. Workers do not generally migrate from the US into Mexico. If preferences are more extreme than the ones depicted in Figure 6, then it is possible that the labour contracts offered in the slothful community are too low-pace and too low-wage to be attractive to the industrious workers, in which case industrious workers who prefer the wage-pace *trade-off* in the slothful community cannot find actual job opportunities to their liking, and they choose to stay at home.[1]

Regardless, capital certainly has an incentive to migrate toward the industrious community until rates of return are equalised and the wage-offer curve conforms in all countries. With capital mobility, the global equilibrium is thus entirely determined by the community preferences toward pace. The tangency of a worker indifference curve to the common wage-pace offer curve selects an industry of specialisation, which selection is supported by an appropriate capital inflow or outflow to equate the country's capital/labour ratio to the capital intensity in the selected industry. Then the global equilibrium has highly industrious communities that produce only the capital-intensive good using high-speed, high-wage operations. There may also be mixed communities which have both a high-speed, high-wage operation in the capital-intensive sector and a low-speed, low-wage operation in the labour-intensive sector. And there will be slothful communities that have low-speed, low-wage operations in the labour-intensive sector. With mobile capital, sloth creates comparative advantage in labour-intensive goods; industriousness creates comparative advantage in capital-intensive goods.

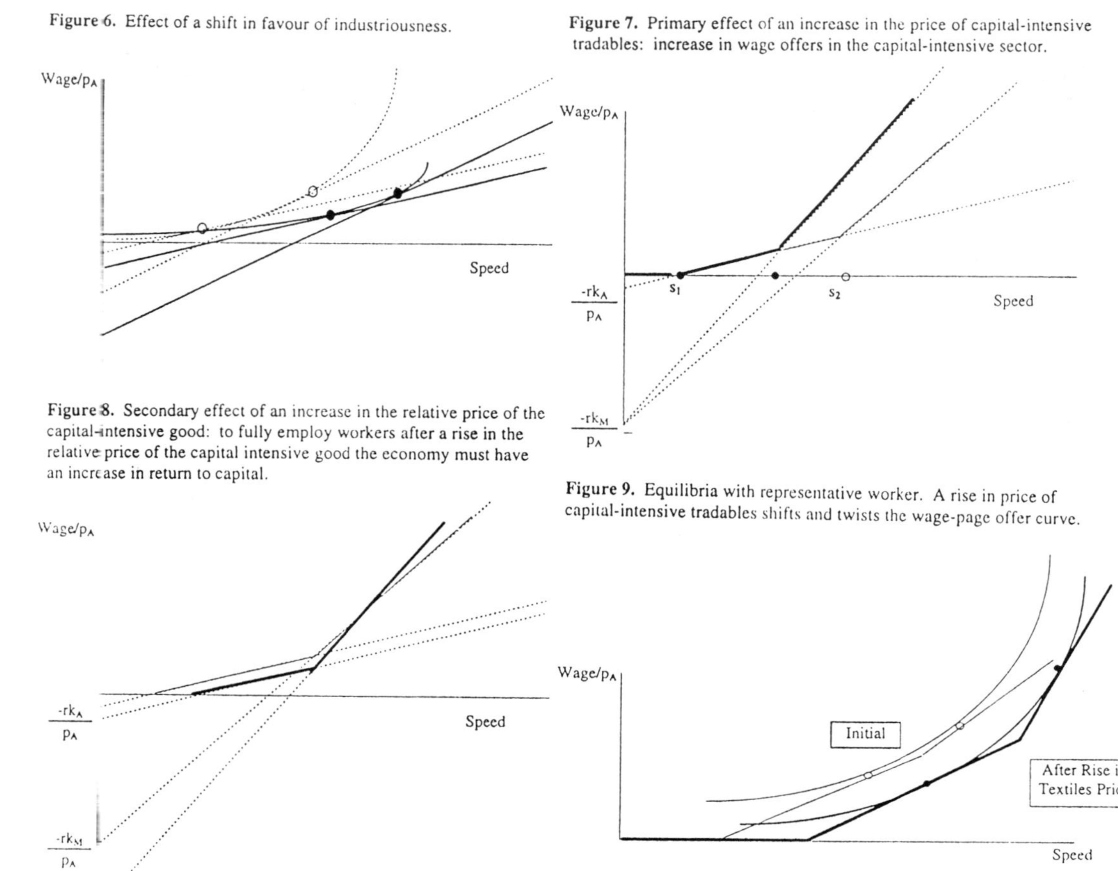

Figure 6. Effect of a shift in favour of industriousness.

Figure 7. Primary effect of an increase in the price of capital-intensive tradables: increase in wage offers in the capital-intensive sector.

Figure 8. Secondary effect of an increase in the relative price of the capital-intensive good: to fully employ workers after a rise in the relative price of the capital intensive good the economy must have an increase in return to capital.

Figure 9. Equilibria with representative worker. A rise in price of capital-intensive tradables shifts and twists the wage-page offer curve.

Effect of a rise in the relative price of the capital-intensive good

In the Heckscher-Ohlin model and in this model as well, a change in the external product markets is signalled to local labour markets by changes in relative price of tradables. The traditional Stolper-Samuelson Theorem applicable to a country producing apparel and textiles indicates that a rise in the price of the capital-intensive good, textiles, reduces the nominal wage and thus also reduces the real wage in terms of the numeraire good apparel. If a country makes all three products, as depicted in Figure 3, then a rise in the relative price of textiles and machinery rotates upward these two zero-profit lines and eliminates the low-pace, low-wage jobs in the apparel sector. A new set of tangencies may be found with these rotated zero-profit lines, in which case the apparel sector is put out of business and workers move to move demanding jobs in more capital-intensive sectors. The higher pace is more than compensated with higher wages, and workers are better off in the sense of being on a higher indifference curve. If a country is not fully diversified, or does not have the capital to support a shift in product away from apparel, then a modified Stolper-Samuelson result depicted in Figures 7, 8, and 9 applies. Initially, as in Figure 7, the rise in the price of textiles makes the wage offer curve applicable to the textile sector steeper because each increment in speed which generates the same increase in physical output produces relatively less more revenue at the higher textile price. This has the effect of raising the compensation only for high speed work. Although the initial impact is confined to the high-wage, high-pace jobs, the effect spills over to the apparel sector if workers attempt to move to the higher paying jobs. The potential shift of workers from apparel to machinery could only be accomplished if the supply of capital were to increase since the capital released by a worker leaving the apparel sector is less than the capital needed in machinery. With capital fixed, something else has to give. The higher demand for capital that comes from the attempt to transfer workers to the capital-intensive sector increases the capital return. This shifts the compensation curves proportionately downward as depicted in Figure 8. The new wage-pace offer curve is twisted, providing lower wages in the low-wage, low-pace jobs but higher wages for the jobs with the highest pace.

To express this differently, Asian competition that raises the relative price of capital-intensive tradables is harmful to low-pace, low-wage US workers but can make the high-pace workers better off.

The original Stolper-Samuelson theorem is: "A rise in the price of the capital-intensive good causes a reduction in the nominal wage rate and an increase in the return on capital." Through a two-step process with a representative worker, depicted in Figures 7, 8 and 9, we are now close to this result. The increase in the relative price of the capital-intensive good causes a rise in the return on capital rises and a reduction in wages at low pace, but can cause an increase in wages at high pace. A representative worker would not actually select one of these very high-wage, high-pace contracts since there are lower pace contracts that are preferred. One equilibrium with a representative worker is depicted in Figure 9. The low-wage contract has increased speed with little reduction in wages. The high-wage contract has both higher wages and higher pace. Thus as a result of Asian competition, the slothful work harder for about the same pay, but the industrious work harder for more pay.

Implications for Eastern Europe

This theory of pace of operations suggests that willingness to work at high pace will be an important determinant of economic success in Eastern Europe. According to this theory, industriousness contributes to economic growth by increasing the productivity of workers and capital, and by attracting foreign capital. Communities of industrious workers will pay high wages and produce a capital-intensive mix of tradables. These communities will be insulated naturally from the increasingly intense competition in the markets for labour-intensive goods. The world's slothful workers in the labour-intensive sectors will find themselves working harder and harder just to maintain the same wages.

Empirical evidence

This theory of pace of operations helps to explain four sets of empirical facts: wage differences across industries, productivity differences across countries, the absence of capital flow to the low-wage developing countries, and the increasing income inequality in the liberalised low-wage developing countries. Table 1 shows the close relationship between wages and capital-intensity in the United States, exactly what the theory of pace suggests — the high-wage high-pace jobs occur in the capital-intensive sectors where they speed saves the most capital costs. But this relationship between wages and physical capital intensity might also be interpreted as suggesting complementarity between human capital and physical capital. However, after controlling for educational differences and working conditions there remain very large differences in wages across firms and industries. This fact has given rise to a literature on "efficiency wages," e.g. Katz and Summers (1989) and Dickens *et al.* (1989). The theory of efficiency wages alludes to the difficulties in monitoring worker performance and the need to overpay workers who are infrequently monitored in order to assure the highest level of effort. The theory of the pace of operations is very close in spirit to efficiency wages. In both cases, high wages are compensation for effort. In the case of efficiency wages it is monitoring problems that give rise to high wages. Here it is capital costs. Table 2 shows that the sectoral distribution of wages in Germany and Japan is almost identical with the US. It seems likely that if monitoring were the concern, different cultures would produce different efficiency wages. Thus the similarity in wages across countries reported in Table 2 is evidence in favour of pace compared with monitoring.

Another set of empirical facts that is explained by Figure 5 is the total factor productivity differences among countries that tend to apply across all sectors. For example, Dollar and Wolff (1993) report that Korean labour productivity in 1986 relative to the US varied from a low of 21 per cent in food products to a high of 67 per cent in petroleum and 58 per cent in iron and steel.[2] Incidentally, if the proportional reduction in the speed of operations is the same in all sectors, then industriousness is not a source of comparative advantage, since the relative outputs are unaffected. But industriousness can in principle be a source of comparative advantage in either sector. Dollar (1991) found that productivity in Korea achieved two-thirds of the German level by 1978. Two thirds of the convergence over the1966-78 period came from capital deepening, one-third from convergence of total factor productivity (increases in speed?). Capital deepening was dominant in

Table 1. US wages and investment per worker, 1990, by 3-digit SIC sector.

Sector		Investment per worker	Earnings per worker
322	WEARING APPAREL,EXCEPT FOOTWEAR(322)	582	13,408
324	FOOTWEAR,EXCEPT RUBBER OR PLASTIC(324)	746	14,776
323	LEATHER PRODUCTS(323)	1,458	17,917
321	TEXTILES(321)	3,269	18,251
332	FURNITURE,EXCEPT METAL(332)	1,416	18,630
331	WOOD PRODUCTS,EXCEPT FURNITURE(331)	2,717	19,862
390	OTHER MANUFACTURED PRODUCTS(390)	1,951	19,919
361	POTTERY,CHINA,EARTHENWARE(361)	2,895	21,842
311	FOOD PRODUCTS(311)	5,769	21,928
356	PLASTIC PRODUCTS(356)	5,090	22,269
381	FABRICATED METAL PRODUCTS(381)	2,914	24,580
342	PRINTING AND PUBLISHING(342)	3,778	25,234
369	OTHER NON-METALLIC MINERAL PROD.(369)	4,945	25,687
355	RUBBER PRODUCTS(355)	5,122	26,146
362	GLASS AND PRODUCTS(362)	6,525	27,092
383	MACHINERY ELECTRIC(383)	6,061	28,397
372	NON-FERROUS METALS(372)	7,814	29,919
382	MACHINERY,EXCEPT ELECTRICAL(382)	4,322	29,976
341	PAPER AND PRODUCTS(341)	17,966	30,644
313	BEVERAGES(313)	8,540	30,949
354	MISC. PETROLEUM AND COAL PRODUCTS(354)	8,500	32,000
352	OTHER CHEMICALS(352)	9,299	32,371
385	PROFESSIONAL & SCIENTIFIC EQUIPM.(385)	4,468	33,204
371	IRON AND STEEL(371)	8,571	33,680
384	TRANSPORT EQUIPMENT(384)	6,003	35,084
314	TOBACCO(314)	6,829	37,073
351	INDUSTRIAL CHEMICALS(351)	27,388	38,010
353	PETROLEUM REFINERIES(353)	53,056	44,444
300	TOTAL MANUFACTURING(300)	5,804	26,911

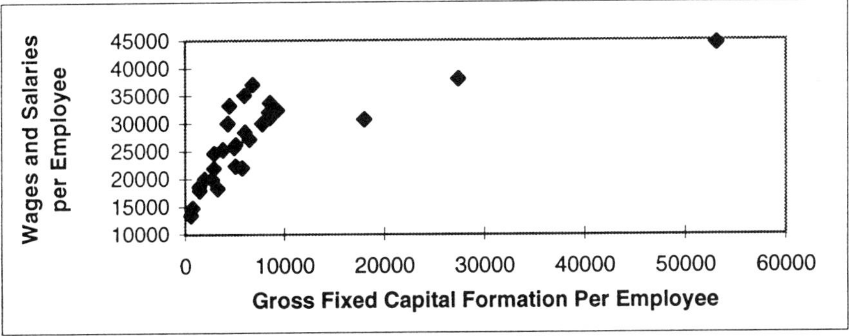

Source: 1990 US Data from INDSTAT3, Unido Database 1996.

Table 2. US, Japanese and German earnings per employee, 1990.

Sector	USA Earnings per worker	Japan Earnings per Worker	West German Earnings per Worker	Japan: US	Germany: US	Japan: Germany
322	13,408	12,921	18,683	0.96	1.39	0.69
324	14,776	19,704	21,928	1.33	1.48	0.90
323	17,917	18,208	20,239	1.02	1.13	0.90
321	18,251	18,639	23,849	1.02	1.31	0.78
332	18,630	21,583	27,542	1.16	1.48	0.78
331	19,862	20,287	25,332	1.02	1.28	0.80
390	19,919	22,697	23,508	1.14	1.18	0.97
361	21,842	21,721	22,733	0.99	1.04	0.96
311	21,928	18,790	24,102	0.86	1.10	0.78
356	22,269	23,522	27,038	1.06	1.21	0.87
381	24,580	26,632	29,000	1.08	1.18	0.92
342	25,234	31,775	32,268	1.26	1.28	0.98
369	25,687	26,249	30,533	1.02	1.19	0.86
355	26,146	27,990	30,592	1.07	1.17	0.91
362	27,092	30,586	28,948	1.13	1.07	1.06
383	28,397	25,457	31,603	0.90	1.11	0.81
372	29,919	32,118	31,565	1.07	1.06	1.02
382	29,976	31,124	33,550	1.04	1.12	0.93
341	30,644	27,169	29,200	0.89	0.95	0.93
313	30,949	25,106	31,583	0.81	1.02	0.79
354	32,000	31,655		0.99		
352	32,371	34,968	35,836	1.08	1.11	0.98
385	33,204	26,795	28,901	0.81	0.87	0.93
371	33,680	38,579	31,436	1.15	0.93	1.23
384	35,084	33,722	35,359	0.96	1.01	0.95
314	37,073	60,800	34,976	1.64	0.94	1.74
351	38,010	38,931	41,470	1.02	1.09	0.94
353	44,444	47,359	47,333	1.07	1.06	1.00
300	26,911	26,367	31,236	0.98	1.16	0.84

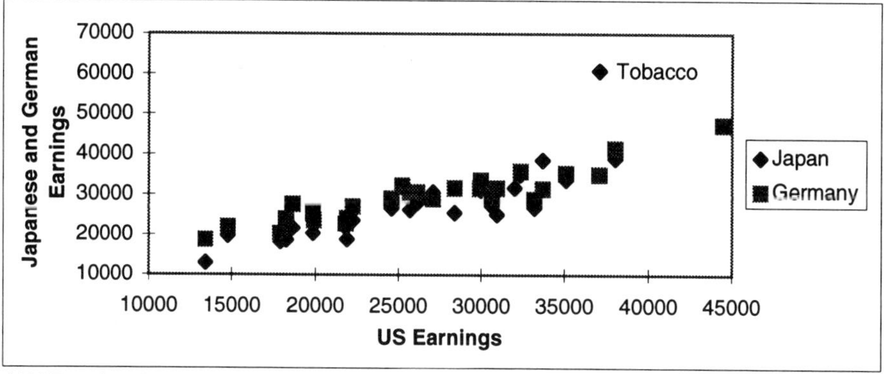

1990 Data from INDSTAT3, Unido Database 1996.

the heavy industries and TFP convergence in the light industries. An interpretation of these findings is that the pace of operations is largely fixed in capital intensive sectors but more subject to variability in the labour-intensive sectors.

Another empirical puzzle answered by Figure 6 is: "Why doesn't capital flow to the low-wage countries?" Lucas (1988) has stimulated a cottage industry producing models with increasing returns to scale to answer his question: the theory of pace described here offers one simple answer. The low-wage countries have workers who prefer low-pace contracts and the rates of return to capital are accordingly low. If there is a flow, capital seeks communities with workers who are willing to work hard. These communities can have high productivity and high wages.

Finally, there is the increasing income inequality that has been shown to exist in the liberalising developing countries. A simple Heckscher-Ohlin-Samuelson model with two factors suggests that economic integration of the developed and developing countries will drive down wages of the unskilled labour in the high-wage countries but drive up wages in the low-wage countries; in other words, income inequality will worsen in the high-wage countries but improve in the low-wage countries. But Robbins (1995) cites a number of studies of liberalisation in Chile, Argentina, Colombia and Costa Rica that suggest that increasing trade is associated with increasing wage dispersion. Likewise, anecdotal evidence from Eastern Europe suggests that some workers are doing extremely well, but others have been much hurt by the collapse of Communism. The theory of pace that is discussed here has an interesting explanation for these facts. Prior to liberalisation, the labour markets could not compensate much for pace, and the wage levels and pace of work didn't differ much across workers. After liberalisation, the wage-pace profile steepens, and those workers with ambition and industriousness can receive substantial increases in compensation.

3. Access to Western markets

Access to Western marketplaces must be important for the future of Eastern Europe, but how important? How much do barriers to markets deter growth? This is not an easy question to answer since economic openness is notoriously difficult to measure and since the effects of openness have eluded persuasive quantification. Here I will take an entirely different tack and treat artificial barriers to commerce as economically equivalent to natural barriers. In other words, because of the behaviour of governments, I will act as if Eastern Europe has been economically very far from the West for three decades. Suddenly it is very close. What effect might this have? An answer to this question is here provided by estimating the impact that economic distance has on *per capita* incomes and on product composition of international trade. Distance to markets is shown to have a very large effect on *per capita* GDP, few "far-away" countries have decent living standards. Distance also has a profound effect on international comparative advantage. After controlling for resource supplies including physical and human capital, the far-away countries export crops and import manufactures.

The distance measure in this paper is suggested by the traditional "gravity" model which explains trade between pairs of countries as a function of their distance and other variables. The subject in this section is not trade between pairs of countries, but rather the impact of distance on *per capita* GDP and product composition.

Table 3. Distance to self.

USA	488	Sri Lanka	41	Pakistan	30
Brazil	468	Ireland	39	Central African Republic	30
Australia	443	Liberia	38	Gabon	30
China	369	Costa Rica	37	Djibouti	30
Canada	350	Denmark	34	Bhutan	30
India	273	Taiwan	33	Ethiopia	30
Argentina	273	Switzerland	32	Congo	30
Mexico	239	Dominican Rep.	31	Zaire	30
Indonesia	220	Haiti	30	Bangladesh	30
Peru	182	Tunisia	30	Uganda	30
Colombia	177	Algeria	30	Rwanda	30
Turkey	154	Morocco	30	Burundi	30
Venezuela	147	Guatemala	30	Bolivia	30
France	121	Barbados	30	Tanzania	30
Spain	121	Trinidad	30	Solomon Is	30
Poland	113	Syria	30	Zambia	30
Thailand	109	Jordan	30	Malawi	30
Paraguay	106	South Korea	30	Seychelles	30
Chile	105	Mauritania	30	Comoro Isl.	30
Japan	100	Niger	30	Fiji	30
Czechoslovakia	98	Dominica	30	Zimbabwe	30
Sweden	98	St.Vincent	30	South Africa	30
Italy	92	St. Lucia	30	Madagascar	30
Finland	89	Belize	30	Botswana	30
Yugoslavia	87	Grenada	30	Swaziland	30
Ecuador	87	Senegal	30	Lesotho	30
Philippines	84	Gambia	30	Netherlands	29
UK	83	Iran	30	Belgium-Luxembourg	28
Germany (FRG)	82	Burkina Faso	30	Iceland	28
New Zealand	82	Kuwait	30	Sudan	28
Hungary	80	Sierra-Leone	30	El Salvador	22
Malaysia	75	Guyana	30	Israel	20
Ghana	74	Saudi Arabia	30	Jamaica	18
Uruguay	72	Cape Verde Is.	30	Cyprus	15
Nepal	71	Surinam	30	Mauritius	7
Greece	60	Bahrain	30	Papua-New Guinea	3
Honduras	56	Benin	30	Malta	2
Nicaragua	54	Togo	30	Singapore	2
Kenya	53	Nigeria	30	**Bulgaria**	
Portugal	51	Qatar	30	**Romania**	
Norway	50	Ivory Coast	30	Tonga	
Austria	48	Cameroon	30		
Panama	42	Oman	30		

Distance within countries

As a first step in measuring distance to markets we need to decide how close a country is to itself. A value of zero will not work in the formulae discussed below, and, more importantly, a value of zero fails to distinguish a geographically large country like the United States from a geographically small country like Singapore, the former having large internal impediments to trade while the latter having hardly any. To decide on a measure of within-country distance we can imagine that countries are circular and ask what is the expected distance between randomly selected points within a circle of radius r. The answer is approximately the radius r, which is the measure of internal distance that will be used.

Data on country areas A are transformed into radii on the assumption that countries are circular, and the internal distance formula thus becomes:

$$D_{ii} = \left(\frac{A_i}{\pi}\right)^{\frac{1}{2}}$$

These distance numbers are reported in Table 3. The areas exclude mountain regions which are presumed not to involve economic commerce. Note that the United States at 488 miles is the country that is the farthest from itself. Other self-distant countries are Brazil (468), Australia (443), and China (369). In the distance measures now to be discussed, countries are weighted by economic size and these self-distances do not matter much except for the United States. There are a lot of missing area figures. Some have been filled in arbitrarily but unimportantly with the figure of 30 squared. The missing figures at the bottom are also inconsequential because the GDP figures are also missing, but these GDP numbers are effectively zero for the calculations below.

Distance formula suggested by gravity model

According to the traditional gravity model[3,] trade between a pair of countries is proportional to the product of their GDPs divided by the distance between them raised to a power that is usually estimated to be around 0.6.

$$T_{ij} = \alpha(GDP_i \times GDP_j) / D_{ij}^{0.6}$$

If world trade is homogenous of degree one in GDPs, then the scale factor α must be inversely proportional to world GDP. Summing this over all importers produces the formula:

$$\frac{T_{i.}}{GDP_i} = \alpha \sum_j \frac{GDP_j}{D_{ij}^{0.6}} = \frac{\alpha\left(\sum GDP_j\right)}{D_i^{0.6}} = \frac{\beta}{D_i^{0.6}}$$

where D_i is a measure of the distance of country i to the world's markets[4]:

$$D_i = \left(\sum_j w_j D_{ij}^{-0.6}\right)^{-\frac{1}{0.6}}, \text{ where } w_j = \frac{GDP_j}{\sum GDP_j}.$$

Table 4. Distance to GDP.

	1960	1990	Change %		1960	1990	Change %		1960	1990	Change %
Canada	536	629	17.2	Syria	3147	3145	-0.1	Ethiopia	4857	4875	0.4
Belgium-Lux.	670	766	14.4	Israel	3194	3205	0.3	India	5151	4912	-4.6
Germany (FRG)	727	831	14.3	Jordan	3228	3235	0.2	Nepal	5286	4924	-6.8
Netherlands	731	833	14.0	South Korea	4212	3267	-22.5	Philip-pines	5792	5036	-13.1
UK	717	857	19.5	Panama	3016	3308	9.7	Congo	5041	5163	2.4
France	788	885	12.3	Mauritania	3255	3415	4.9	Zaire	5046	5169	2.4
Switzerland	986	1084	10.0	Niger	3302	3464	4.9	Bangladesh	5603	5206	-7.1
USA	1001	1115	11.4	Dominica	3311	3576	8.0	Uganda	5205	5251	0.9
Japan	2257	1175	-47.9	St.Vincent	3325	3578	7.6	Rwanda	5246	5297	1.0
Italy	1180	1214	2.8	St. Lucia	3323	3592	8.1	Burundi	5325	5387	1.2
Czecho-slovakia	1165	1279	9.8	Belize	3345	3603	7.7	Kenya	5435	5459	0.4
Austria	1274	1377	8.1	Grenada	3358	3631	8.1	Brazil	5216	5520	5.8
Ireland	1236	1381	11.8	Venezuela	3361	3642	8.3	Thailand	6097	5573	-8.6
Denmark	1238	1384	11.8	Senegal	3486	3679	5.5	Bolivia	5374	5673	5.6
Spain	1522	1548	1.8	Gambia	3558	3751	5.4	Tanzania	5853	5861	0.1
Bulgaria	1578	1550	-1.7	Colombia	3454	3755	8.7	Paraguay	5603	5927	5.8
Jamaica	1355	1568	15.7	Iran	3788	3766	-0.6	Solomon Is	6374	5959	-6.5
Hungary	1517	1617	6.5	Burkina Faso	3707	3861	4.2	Sri Lanka	6375	6044	-5.2
Norway	1523	1658	8.9	Kuwait	3966	3948	-0.4	Papua-N.G.	6598	6071	-8.0
Romania	1682	1755	4.3	China	4645	3953	-14.9	Zambia	6038	6096	1.0
Poland	1640	1761	7.4	Ecuador	3704	4015	8.4	Singapore	6669	6134	-8.0
Sweden	1614	1767	9.5	Sierra-Leone	3874	4069	5.0	Malawi	6112	6149	0.6
Yugoslavia	1695	1777	4.9	Guyana	3828	4106	7.3	Seychelles	6269	6183	-1.4
Haiti	1552	1780	14.7	Saudi Arabia	4182	4167	-0.4	Comoro Isl.	6258	6242	-0.3
Portugal	1801	1836	1.9	Cape Verde Is	4039	4216	4.4	Chile	5962	6281	5.4
Tunisia	1829	1899	3.8	Liberia	4024	4217	4.8	Fiji	6483	6289	-3.0
Algeria	1838	1913	4.1	Surinam	3948	4224	7.0	Zimbabwe	6255	6301	0.7
Mexico	1695	1933	14.0	Bahrain	4259	4227	-0.7	Malaysia	6909	6309	-8.7
Dominican Rep.	1721	1959	13.8	Sudan	4215	4260	1.1	Indonesia	6957	6428	-7.6
Finland	1914	2042	6.7	Benin	4143	4296	3.7	Argentina	6124	6447	5.3
Malta	2013	2078	3.3	Togo	4147	4305	3.8	Uruguay	6160	6484	5.2
Greece	2161	2172	0.5	Nigeria	4154	4306	3.6	Australia	6955	6643	-4.5
Morocco	2159	2246	4.0	Qatar	4351	4314	-0.8	Taiwan	8087	6658	-17.7
Iceland	2098	2261	7.7	Ivory Coast	4144	4320	4.2	South Africa	6629	6686	0.9
Turkey	2510	2465	-1.8	Ghana	4168	4332	3.9	Tonga	6886	6695	-2.8
Guatemala	2205	2473	12.2	Cameroon	4455	4584	2.9	Madagascar	6775	6717	-0.9
El Salvador	2330	2603	11.7	Oman	4729	4648	-1.7	Botswana	6741	6788	0.7
Honduras	2343	2613	11.5	Pakistan	4861	4668	-4.0	Swaziland	6837	6863	0.4
Nicaragua	2549	2830	11.0	C.A.R.	4628	4727	2.1	Lesotho	6933	6971	0.6
Cyprus	2873	2863	-0.4	Gabon	4642	4783	3.0	New Zealand	6960	6996	0.5
Barbados	2652	2929	10.5	Djibouti	4856	4854	-0.1	Mauritius	7145	7010	-1.9
Trinidad	2695	2979	10.6	Peru	4549	4872	7.1				
Costa Rica	2793	3082	10.4	Bhutan	5241	4872	-7.0	**Average**	**1683**	**1785**	**7.4**

Table 4 reports distance numbers in 1960 and 1990 based on this formula. Countries are ordered by their closeness to markets in 1990. Canada in both years is the country that is measured to be closest to markets. How can this be right? How can Canada be "closer" than the United States? This comes from the fact that we have dealt with country size for computing internal distances but not country size for determining country-to-country distances. The Canadian-US distance between their economic centres does not allow for the great distance between Vancouver and Miami, for example. Thus you should probably move Canada down the list roughly to the US number. Then Belgium is the "closest" country.

The distance measures reported in Table 4 can be summarised simply: closeness to markets means residing in Europe and North America. Northern Africa is not too bad either. Notice that Eastern Europe is particularly and literally well positioned, especially the Czech Republic.

Another general implication of the data in Table 4 is that economic growth in Asia is bringing Asian economies closer to the action. The average distance of Japan to markets fell by 48 per cent from 2 257 miles to 1 175 miles. Likewise, Korea, Taiwan, China, the Philippines,.... On the other hand, the locational advantages of Europe and North America are diminishing. The UK is farther from markets by 20 per cent; Canada by 17 per cent. Having made that observation, a comment on what is being measured is now appropriate. A feature of the formula is that if economic growth occurs on Mars, then the average distance to markets of all Earthly countries increases. But growth on Mars is unlikely to have much affect on Earth. Why should it enter the formula at all? The answer is that the measurement is only useful for comparisons, not absolute statements. The relative locational advantages of Europe versus Asia diminish over time. This occurs mostly because of increased advantages in Asia, not diminished advantages in Europe.[5]

Access to markets and per capita GDP

The dramatic effect that market access has on *per capita* GDP is revealed by Figure 10 and Figure 11. In 1960 only Australia and New Zealand were able to escape the curse of being far away. By 1990, two other countries had escaped, namely Singapore and Taiwan. Except for these, there is a very clear relationship between *per capita* GDP and distance to markets.

The Eastern European countries are very well located and should be expecting to benefit from that location. These countries are in the range of 1 200-1 800 miles to markets, for which the zoomed view in Figure 12 is relevant. If the Czech Republic conformed with this pattern, its distance to markets of 1 279 miles would afford it a GDP *per capita* like Italy or Austria. Clearly this figure makes one very optimistic about the future of Eastern Europe, but it also illustrates how dark is the cloud of protectionism hanging over the East.

Table 5 gives a numerical evaluation of the darkness of the cloud by reporting distance-to-markets numbers for Eastern Europe on the assumption that Western Europe is moved away as the rest of the world stays put. Western European trade barriers that act like a 500-mile increase in distance between East and West increase the Eastern European distance to markets by slightly more than 500 miles.[6] Another way to say this is that are as far as trade is concerned, Western Europe is pretty much the only prospect for Eastern Europe because most of the rest of the world's GDP is located naturally too far away.

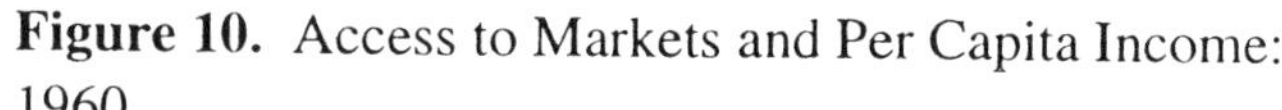

Figure 10. Access to Markets and Per Capita Income: 1960

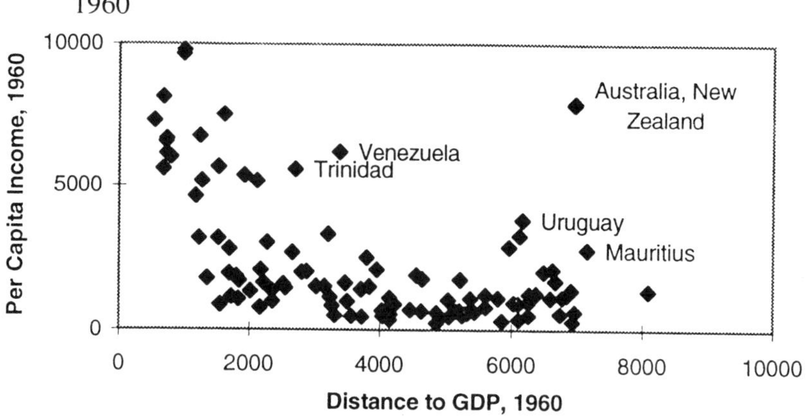

Figure 11. Access to Markets and Per Capita Income: 1990

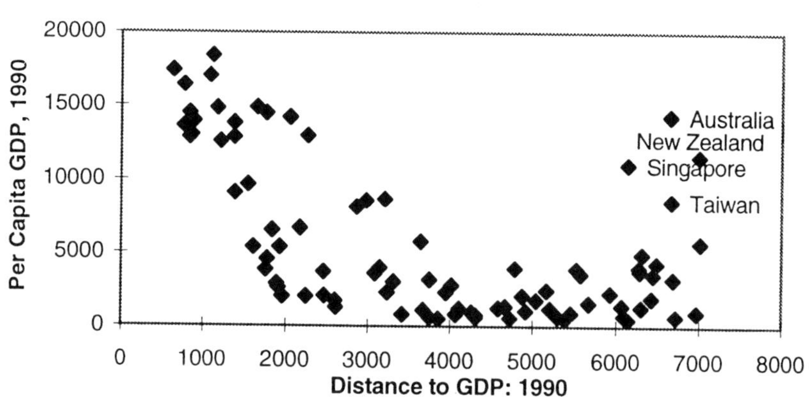

Figure 12. Access to Markets and Per Capita Income: 1990

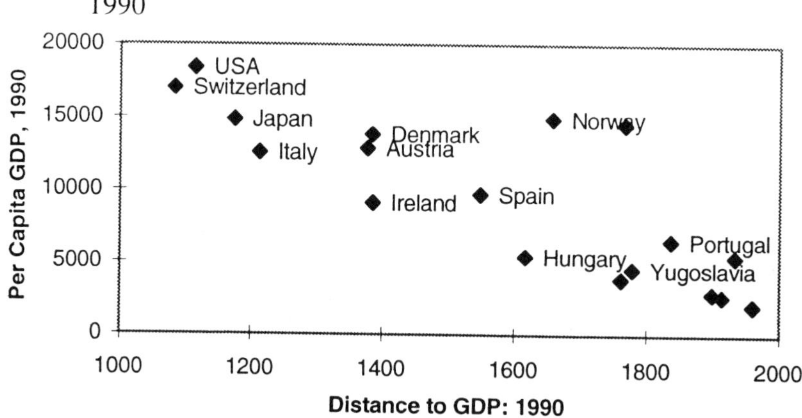

Table 5. Distance of Eastern European countries to World GDP, 1990.

Effect of hypothetical increase in distance from Eastern European countries to Western European countries

Distance to GDP

Increment	0	500	1000	2000	3000
Czechoslovakia	1279	2131	2705	3516	4093
Bulgaria	1550	2442	2979	3753	4316
Hungary	1617	2378	2919	3709	4284
Romania	1755	2454	2976	3745	4309
Poland	1761	2446	2955	3705	4252
Yugoslavia	1777	2501	3034	3821	4398

Increase in Distance to GDP

Difference	0	500	1000	2000	3000
Czechoslovakia	0	852	1426	2237	2814
Bulgaria	0	891	1428	2203	2766
Hungary	0	761	1303	2093	2667
Romania	0	699	1221	1991	2554
Poland	0	685	1194	1943	2491
Yugoslavia	0	723	1256	2043	2620

Product mix and access to markets

What about product mix? What can we expect in terms of trade patterns of Eastern Europe and how does this depend on access to markets? An attempt to determine the impact of market access on product mix is summarised in the regressions reported in Tables 7 and 9. Both are estimated from data on 56 countries in 1965 and refer to the 10 commodity aggregates used in Leamer (1984). These commodity categories are reported in Table 6 and include two raw materials, four crops and four manufactures.

Table 7 reports regressions of the logarithm of absolute trade dependence ratios on the log of distance and the log of GNP. Both distance to markets and economic size suppress trade in all categories. Forest products are most affected by economic distance. Cereals are least affected. Generally the elasticities with respect to distance are approximately -1.0 and the elasticities with respect to economic size are about -0.2. These two numbers are used to define an adjustment factor that inflates the amount of trade of far-away large countries to be used in the comparative regressions in Table 9. These conform with regressions reported in Leamer (1984) except that they include the square of the capital/labour ratio and also the distance in thousands of dollars. The factor supply variables are defined in Table 8.

The estimated nonlinearities suggest that moderately capital-abundant countries have comparative advantage in labour-intensive manufactures but as capital accumulates the comparative advantage shifts up the ladder of development in favour of capital-intensive manufactures first and then machinery and chemicals. Generally the results parallel ones reported in Leamer (1984); the literate non-professional workforce was a source of comparative advantage in manufactures in 1965. Land affords comparative advantage in the crops. However, the reason for

Table 6. Commodity aggregates.

PETRO	Crude and refined petroleum
MAT	Raw Materials
FOR	Forest products including wood manufactures
TROP	Tropical agricultural products
ANL	Animal products
CER	Cereals and related agricultural products
LAB	Labour-intensive manufactures
CAP	Capital-intensive manufactures
MACH	Machinery including transportation equipment
CHEM	Chemicals

Source: Leamer (1984).

Table 7. Impact of distance and market size on trade dependence by commodity, 1965.

Dependent Variable is LOG(ABS(NetExport(i)/LABOR_65))
Included observations: 56

	PETRO	MAT	FOR	TROP	ANL	CER	LAB	CAP	MACH	CHEM
Estimates										
C	11.9	12.6	17.8	13.9	15.4	11.3	14.8	15.1	13.4	12.1
LOG(DIST60)	-0.9	-1.1	-1.6	-0.8	-1.2	-0.7	-1.1	-1.1	-0.8	-0.8
LOG(GNP65)	-0.2	-0.2	-0.3	-0.5	-0.4	-0.2	-0.4	-0.4	-0.3	-0.3
t-Statistics										
C	4.6	3.6	6.3	5.6	4.5	4.8	5.9	6.0	6.0	6.4
LOG(DIST60)	-3.3	-3.1	-5.5	-3.3	-3.4	-3.1	-4.5	-4.2	-3.7	-4.0
LOG(GNP65)	-2.2	-1.1	-2.9	-4.6	-3.0	-2.4	-3.6	-3.6	-3.2	-4.5
Summaries										
R-squared	0.18	0.16	0.36	0.31	0.22	0.18	0.31	0.30	0.25	0.33
Adjusted R-squared	0.15	0.13	0.34	0.28	0.19	0.15	0.29	0.27	0.22	0.31
S.E. of regression	1.38	1.85	1.50	1.32	1.79	1.24	1.33	1.33	1.18	1.00
Mean dependent var	2.93	2.40	2.45	3.32	2.62	3.44	2.55	3.34	4.16	2.95
S.D. dependent var	1.49	1.98	1.85	1.55	1.99	1.34	1.57	1.56	1.34	1.20

doing this exercise is the distance coefficients. The remarkable distance estimates in Table 9 conforms exactly to the theory outlined in the previous section. Distance creates comparative disadvantage in manufactures overall, but especially so for the more capital-intensive products. Distance countries have comparative advantage in the crops. This table offers a very clear message for Eastern Europe – future industrialisation is heavily dependent on access to Western markets.

Table 8. Factor supply variables.

CAPITAL	Discounted and accumulated investment flows
LAB1	Professional workers
LAB2	Non-professional, literate workers
LAB3	Illiterate workers
LABOR	LAB1+LAB2+LAB3
LAND1	Arable land
LAND2	Land under permanent crops
LAND3	Permanent meadows and pastures
LAND4	Forests and woodland
COAL	Coal production
MINERALS	Values of minerals production
OIL	Crude oil production

Table 9. Determinants of comparative advantage, 1965.

Dependent Variable is Net Exports(i)*ADJUST/LABOR_65
ADJUST = DIST60*(GNP^0.2) , normalized to mean 1.0

Variable	PETRO	MAT	FOR	TROP	ANL	CER	LAB	CAP	MACH	CHEM
CAPITAL65/LABOR_65	-2.5	-5.1	2.5	-0.1	25.6	6.7	0.9	-9.8	-20.5	-4.2
(CAPITAL/LABOR)^2	0.0	0.1	0.0	0.0	-0.6	-0.1	-0.1	0.2	0.5	0.1
LAB1_65/LABOR_65	-349.4	-182.5	355.0	197.0	-56.1	-269.5	-245.4	-422.0	-589.6	-261.9
LAB2_65/LABOR_65	40.6	13.2	-43.7	-51.6	-159.0	-101.7	29.4	116.5	173.5	38.5
LAB3_65/LABOR_65	41.7	-33.0	-23.5	6.0	-136.9	-97.7	7.0	61.1	83.6	24.5
LAND1_65/LABOR_65	-14.8	-5.5	3.4	-0.3	-22.2	20.1	-1.0	2.8	7.7	0.6
LAND2_65/LABOR_65	-8.7	18.5	-14.7	84.3	-69.6	40.0	-2.5	14.7	79.2	16.6
LAND3_65/LABOR_65	0.1	1.0	-2.0	-0.8	4.2	6.4	-1.1	-1.9	-5.9	-1.1
LAND4_65/LABOR_65	-0.5	-0.8	1.6	0.1	0.8	-0.9	0.2	0.4	0.9	0.3
COAL_65/LABOR_65	0.0	0.8	-1.4	0.5	-3.4	0.7	0.1	2.1	4.6	1.1
MINERALS_65/ LABOR_65	-0.1	0.8	0.0	0.0	-0.2	-0.1	-0.1	0.0	-0.1	0.0
OIL_65/LABOR_65	2.4	0.1	-0.2	-0.1	-0.4	-0.2	0.0	0.0	-0.2	0.0
DIST60/1000	-3.2	4.2	2.9	12.8	26.8	12.1	-3.9	-19.9	-30.5	-8.0
CAPITAL65/LABOR_65	-1.2	-1.2	0.6	0.0	1.8	0.9	0.4	-1.6	**-2.3**	**-2.2**
(CAPITAL/LABOR)^2	0.8	1.2	-0.4	-0.1	-1.7	-0.8	-1.1	1.5	**2.4**	**2.8**
LAB1_65/LABOR_65	-1.8	-0.5	0.9	0.4	0.0	-0.4	-1.3	-0.7	-0.7	-1.4
LAB2_65/LABOR_65	**2.4**	0.4	-1.2	-1.0	-1.3	-1.7	1.8	**2.3**	**2.3**	**2.4**
LAB3_65/LABOR_65	**2.4**	-0.9	-0.7	0.1	-1.2	-1.6	0.4	1.2	1.1	1.6
LAND1_65/LABOR_65	**-3.3**	-0.6	0.4	0.0	-0.7	1.3	-0.2	0.2	0.4	0.1
LAND2_65/LABOR_65	-0.6	0.6	-0.4	1.9	-0.6	0.7	-0.2	0.3	1.2	1.1
LAND3_65/LABOR_65	0.2	1.2	**-2.5**	-0.7	1.6	**4.7**	**-3.1**	-1.7	**-3.6**	**-3.1**
LAND4_65/LABOR_65	-1.1	-0.8	1.6	0.1	0.2	-0.5	0.4	0.3	0.4	0.7
COAL_65/LABOR_65	0.0	0.8	-1.5	0.4	-1.1	0.4	0.2	1.6	**2.3**	**2.5**
MINERALS_65/ LABOR_65	-1.2	8.8	0.2	-0.3	-0.8	-0.6	-1.3	0.1	-0.7	-0.4
OIL_65/LABOR_65	**44.0**	1.0	-1.4	-0.5	-1.0	-1.2	-0.6	-0.1	-0.8	-0.4
DIST60/1000	-1.6	1.0	0.7	2.2	1.9	1.7	**-2.0**	**-3.3**	**-3.4**	**-4.2**
R-squared	0.98	0.70	0.33	0.35	0.34	0.72	0.57	0.46	0.64	0.65
Adjusted R-squared	0.98	0.61	0.14	0.17	0.15	0.64	0.44	0.31	0.53	0.55
S.E. of regression	23.21	47.46	48.46	66.42	160.35	82.30	22.23	67.38	99.90	21.49
Mean dependent var	2.28	14.71	3.00	25.53	38.12	19.27	-13.75	-38.53	-80.79	-20.69
S.D. dependent var	166.43	76.31	52.26	72.78	174.02	136.54	29.81	80.93	146.39	32.18

4. Summary and conclusions

The first part of this paper develops a theory of pace of operations. A competitive labour market can be expected to offer high-pace, high-wage contracts in capital intensive sectors and low-wage, low-pace contracts in labour-intensive sectors. This bifurcation affects the way economies respond to external and internal shocks. For example, given existing economic structures, increased competition in Western Europe from low-wage Eastern European countries may have its initial and primary effect on the low-wage, low-pace contracts but leave the high-wage, high-pace contracts intact.

The developed theory of pace of operations helps to explain four sets of empirical facts that have puzzled economists: wage differences across industries, productivity differences across countries, the absence of capital flow to the low-wage developing countries, and the increasing income inequality in the liberalised low-wage developing countries.

United States data is presented which show the close relationship between wages and capital-intensity, exactly what the theory of pace suggests — the high-wage, high-pace jobs occur in the capital-intensive sectors where speed saves capital costs the most. While this relationship between wages and physical capital intensity might also be interpreted as suggesting complementarity between human capital and physical capital, after controlling for educational differences and working conditions there remain very large differences in wages across firms and industries. The theory of the pace of operations explains high wages as compensation for effort, similarly to the theory of efficiency wages. However, in the case of efficiency wages it is monitoring problems that give rise to high wages; here it is capital costs. Evidence presented shows that the sectoral distribution of wages in Germany and Japan is almost identical with the US; it seems likely that if monitoring were the concern, different cultures would produce different efficiency wages. Thus the similarity in wages across Japan, Germany and the United States is evidence in favour of pace compared with monitoring.

An empirical puzzle answered by the theory of pace is: "Why does capital not flow to the low-wage countries?" A simple explanation is that the low-wage countries have workers who prefer low-pace contracts and accordingly the rates of return to capital are low. Capital seeks communities with workers who are willing to work hard; these communities can have high productivity and high wages.

Increasing income inequality has been shown to exist in liberalising developing countries. A simple Heckscher-Ohlin-Samuelson model suggests that economic integration of the developed and developing countries will drive down wages of unskilled labour in high-wage countries but drive up wages in low-wage countries; in other words, income inequality will worsen in high-wage countries but improve in low-wage countries. However, evidence from Latin America suggests that trade has increased wage dispersion in liberalising low-wage countries. Likewise, anecdotal evidence from Eastern Europe suggests that some workers are doing extremely well, but others have been hurt by the collapse of central planning. The theory of pace explains these observations nicely. Prior to liberalisation, the labour markets could not compensate much for pace, and the wage levels and pace of work did not differ much across workers. After liberalisation, the wage-pace profile steepens, and those workers with ambition and industriousness can receive substantial increases in compensation.

In Eastern Europe, willingness to work at a high pace will be an important determinant of economic success, as industriousness contributes to economic growth by increasing the productivity of workers and capital and by attracting foreign capital.

The second part of this paper discusses the importance to trade of distance to major markets, and implications for the CEECs. Geographically, Central and Eastern Europe are extremely well positioned, and provided that the Western market is kept open, history suggests that, after an initial adjustment, growth will be substantial. Protectionism in the West may increase the effective distance between East and West and may be a major deterrent to growth. Because of the behaviour of governments, Eastern Europe has effectively been very distant from the West for three decades. Suddenly it is very close. This effective change in economic distance can be expected to have a significant impact on *per capita* incomes and on product composition of trade, and an attempt is made to estimate this impact.

Distance measures presented in the paper for 127 countries can be summarised simply — closeness to markets means residing in Europe and North America, and to some extent Northern Africa; the data further reveal the dramatic effect that market access has on *per capita* GDP. The evidence suggests that the short distance to markets of the Czech Republic would afford it a *per capita* GDP comparable to those of Italy or Austria. While this is grounds for optimism about the future of Eastern Europe, it also illustrates how dark is the cloud of protectionism hanging over the East. As far as trade is concerned, Western Europe is pretty much the only prospect for Eastern Europe because most of the rest of the world's GDP is located naturally too far away.

As far as industrial structure is concerned, distance creates comparative disadvantage in manufactures overall, but especially so for the more capital-intensive products. Distance countries have comparative advantage in the crops. The data thus offer another clear message for Eastern Europe — future industrialisation is heavily dependent on access to Western markets.

Notes

[1] Furthermore, for discussing labour migration issues, it seems appropriate to abandon the representative worker assumption, in which case labour may sort itself into industrious communities and slothful communities.

[2] These numbers admittedly are not total factor productivity figures and do not account for differences in capital per worker.

[3] The gravity model has been used, for example, by Gros and Steinherr (1993) to project the future trade of the former Soviet Union.

[4] Incidentally, an apparent feature of the distance measure if that a tiny country with $D_{ii} = 0$ is perfectly close to the market since $D_i = 0$ also. But a country that is geographically small must also be small in a GDP or population sense, both of which decrease with the square of the radius while D_{ii} decreases with the radius. Thus the decline in the weight applicable to a small country fully corrects for the apparent problem with the formula.

[5] A different formula could be developed to allow comparisons over time.

[6] It is something of a surprise that an increase in one of the distances can lead to an even greater increase in the overall measure of distance to markets. The derivative of the overall distance with respect to one of the distances is the product of the share of the selected country in the overall index times the ratio of the overall distance to the selected distance. Thus the anomaly of greater-than-one sensitivity occurs when a close country with a large GDP is moved farther away.

$$\frac{\partial (D_i)}{\partial (D_{ik})} = \frac{\partial \left(\sum_j w_j D_{ij}^{-0.6} + w_k D_{ik}^{-0.6} \right)^{-\frac{1}{0.6}}}{\partial (D_{ik})} =$$

$$\left(-\frac{1}{0.6} \right) \left(\sum_j w_j D_{ij}^{-0.6} + w_k D_{ik}^{-0.6} \right)^{-1-\frac{1}{0.6}} (-0.6\, w_k) D_{ik}^{-1-0.6}$$

$$= \left(\frac{w_k D_{ik}^{-0.6}}{\sum_j w_j D_{ij}^{-0.6} + w_k D_{ik}^{-0.6}} \right) \left(\frac{D_i}{D_{ik}} \right)$$

References

Dickens, W. T.; Katz, L. F.; Lang, K.; Summers, L H, 1989, "Employee Crime and the Monitoring Puzzle", *Journal of Labour Economics,* vol. 7, no. 3, July.

Dollar, D., 1991, *Convergence of South Korean productivity on West German levels, 1966-78,* World Development, vol. 19, n2-3, Feb.-March.

Dollar, D. and Wolff, E. N., 1993, *Competitiveness,Convergence and International Specialization*, Cambridge, Mass., The MIT Press.

Gros, D. and Steinherr, A., 1993, *Redesigning Economic Geography after the Fall of the Soviet Empire*, Centre for European Policy Studies, Working Document No. 75, March.

Katz, L.,; Summers F., Lawrence H., 1989, "Industry Rents: Evidence and Implications" *Brookings Papers on Economic Activity.*

Leamer, E. E., 1984, *Sources of International Comparative Advantage: Theory and Evidence*, Cambridge, Mass., The MIT Press.

Leamer, E. E., 1995, "In Search of Stolper-Samuelson Effects on US Wages", *Brookings Conference Volume.*

Leamer, E. E., 1995, "The Heckscher-Ohlin Model in Theory and Practice", *Princeton Studies in International Finance*, February No. 77.

Lucas, R. E., Jr., 1988, "On the Mechanics of Economic Development", *Journal of Monetary Economics*, Vol. 22, No. 1, July.

Robbins, D. J., 1995, *Trade Liberalisation and Earning Dispersion — Evidence from Chile*, May.

4

Interrelations between subregional co-operation and EU enlargement

András Inotai

1. Introduction

Since the end of December 1991, ten Central and Eastern European countries[1] (CEECs) have signed and begun to implement the contents of Association Agreements with the European Union. Between 1994 and 1996, all of them officially applied for membership as well. Slovenia's similar agreement with Brussels has been ratified most recently. It is expected to be followed quickly by an application for membership.

Before political and economic transformation started, all of these countries, except Slovenia, formed part of the military, political and economic bloc dominated by the ex-Soviet Union. The three Baltic countries were republics of the USSR, with extremely limited manoeuvring room, while the other CEECs were integrated into the Warsaw Pact and the CMEA. At the same time, Slovenia was part of the former Yugoslavia. As a result of dramatic changes between 1989 and 1991, all countries left either their earlier alliance system or their previous state. The post-Berlin disintegration process[2] of the region was accompanied by an anxiously desired reintegration into the world economy, in general, and the established (Western) European economic system, in particular. There were some, mainly Western, views stressing the necessity of containing the disintegration process and of re-establishing some kind of regional co-operation (or even integration) framework including the transforming countries. However, for both political and economic reasons, this was clearly rejected by all CEECs, and economic disintegration, as indicated by the separation of Czechoslovakia, continued.

Despite the apparently similar pattern of the transformation from a one-party system to a multiparty democracy and from a planned economy towards a market economy, differences among the transforming countries, rooted both in their historical heritage and their experience in the last decades, became increasingly obvious. Certainly, it was first of all their Western-oriented strategy fuelled by the seizing of the "window of historical opportunity" which acted against a more comprehensive regional co-operation. However, different economic realities, such as their level of economic development, their initial progress in macro- and microeconomic transformation, as well as different patterns of their trade with the European Union[3] resulted in a low level of attention being paid to regional activities.

Following the eu(ro)phoria of the first years, considerations about the economic strategy started slowly to be modified. Evidently, the main priority of Western (and EU) orientation did not change, which is clearly proved by the Association Agreements concluded by all transforming countries. However, some opportunities for regional co-operation were rediscovered, even if not on the all-regional level. Three different subregional groupings were created, with the participation of 10 countries. The CEFTA includes the Central European emerging market economies (Czech Republic, Hungary, Poland, Slovakia, and, as of January 1996, Slovenia). Also, the three Baltic countries have formed a free trade area and want to create a customs union by 1998. Finally, Romania and Bulgaria became part of the Black Sea Co-operation. It has to be noted that these subregional co-operation patterns reveal substantial differences. First, CEFTA and the Baltics only include associated countries, while the Black Sea Co-operation covers a much larger and more heterogeneous geographic area. The planned level of subregional co-operation is the highest in the Baltics where a customs union has been envisaged. CEFTA is implementing a free trade area, which is only a long-term goal of the Black Sea Co-operation. The respective groups have rather different institutional backgrounds. There is a relatively strong institutional network in the Baltics, a loose framework in the Black Sea Co-operation, and practically no government-level institution in CEFTA. Moreover, the levels of intraregional trade and economic co-operation differ substantially.

This paper concentrates on the interrelations between the EU and CEFTA, the member countries of which are considered to be the most serious applicants for membership during the first wave of Eastern enlargement of the European Union. Although a comprehensive and detailed analysis of interrelations should not miss the non-economic factors (security, political and socio-cultural ones), we have a much more limited objective here. Taking into account the nature of the conference and the limited size of this paper, the analysis will focus on economic issues.

Section 2 presents the theoretical and economic policy framework of regional co-operation, seen both from the EU and by Central and Eastern Europe. Section 3 provides a brief analysis of intra- and interregional trade and FDI patterns. The impact of the EU on subregional co-operation, as well as the relatively modest influence of subregional co-operation on the EU, are dealt with in the following two sections.[4] The last section draws some conclusions and offers a few thoughts for the future.

2. Theoretical and economic policy approaches

Especially in the early nineties, the importance of subregional co-operation was rather differently assessed by Western European experts and those coming from the transforming countries. The former have usually overestimated, while the latter under-estimated the relevance of this factor regarding their preparation for and future membership in the EU.

The Western approach was based on two theoretical pillars. First, following the gravity theory, they argued that geographic proximity, accompanied by common economic, structural and cultural heritage has to support regional co-operation. Second, the training ground theory has been revitalised, with strong reference made to the history of European integration processes. According to this view, regional co-operation or even integration should be considered as a stepping stone towards larger integrations and global competitiveness. Countries should, first of all, learn the rules of the game in the regional framework in order to become "global players". Frequent allusions to the imitation of the European Payments Union (EPU) by the transforming countries are a good example for this approach. According to this concept, the sequencing should be from national to subregional, from subregional to regional, and finally, if necessary, from regional to global division of labour.

Practical reasons for this basic attitude towards regional co-operation seem to be more important. It is obvious that the collapse of the Eastern European integration framework in general, and that of the Soviet market in particular, have led to substantial declines in GDP. They have also resulted in the abolition of various industries previously oriented towards this large and low-quality market, in rapidly increasing unemployment, in growing regional differences and in some other adverse economic developments. The slowing down or the stopping of decline and the "managing" of the process of "creative destruction" were justified goals that were expected to be achieved through the revitalisation of regional economic links. Even more importantly, regional co-operation should have provided a framework in which both the speed and pattern of the transformation process and the risks and threats to Western security generated by the economic collapse of the region could have been kept under control.

In addition, viable (sub)regional co-operation was generally considered as basic proof of "EU-maturity" of the associated countries. Predictable political relations among neighbouring countries and rapidly growing intraregional economic contacts became preconditions of EU membership, since Brussels (and the member states) have repeatedly emphasized that no Eastern enlargement can take place if it were to integrate transforming countries with unclear regional ties and, consequently, internalise regional risks and uncertainties.

Although never really pointed out, there might have been additional practical reasons for more (sub)regional co-operation. On the one hand, a larger and more open regional market could have provided better prospects for Western firms looking at the vast and unsaturated Central and Eastern European markets.[5] On the other hand, the regional framework could have produced a certain "trade diversion" (or, in a better term, "rediversion") towards Central and Eastern Europe and, as a result, ease the competitive pressure on EU companies and markets, originating from the emerging market economies. The positive impact on exports of the GSP treatment and the Association Agreement, as well as the partially "forced" reorientation towards Western markets, due to the collapse of the CMEA and the USSR, and to the decline of domestic demand became manifest in the first half of the nineties. Although the market shares of Central and Eastern Europe in the extraregional imports of the EU remained on a moderate to low level, or was in some cases even insignificant, already this slight and initial change was felt by some Western firms as a threat. More importantly, growing Central (and partly Eastern)

European competition did not remain restricted to "sensitive" sectors but was felt in several other sectors as well.[6]

The Western European approach produced heated discussions mainly in Central Europe, which was eager to be integrated with Western Europe within the shortest possible time. The Western approach was debated both on the theoretical and the practical level. The theoretical arguments stressed that the gravity model cannot be applied to the transforming economies.

Even more fundamental criticism was attached to the "sequencing theory". The emerging market economies have always emphatically stressed that (sub)regional co-operation must not be considered either as a substitute for integration into the EU or as a precondition for membership. The theoretical underpinnings of this position can be found in the positive and negative experiences with insertion into the global economic division of labour, as shown by many national economies. Decade-long attempts at regional integration, as a training ground to a higher level of extraregional competitiveness, have repeatedly failed in Latin America. In turn, export-oriented policies of most Asian (Far Eastern) countries proved successful on the global scale. As a result and consequence of this global competitiveness, intraregional economic relations also started to develop quickly. One of the most important explanatory factors behind this development was rapid domestic growth, leading to higher aggregate demand which was partially met by intraregional imports. Another main factor was an efficient and competitive production structure, which, in many cases shaped with the substantial participation of foreign direct capital and multinational companies, created the preconditions of meaningful inter- and intra-industry specialisation within the given region (Inotai, 1991). In sum, historical experience shows that, with the exception of the core countries of the EU itself,[7] more fundamental (sub)regional co-operation was the result of and not a precondition for efficient integration into the global (or "anchor") economy.

No less relevant were (and partially still are) the practical barriers to a quick and fundamental improvement of the conditions for (sub)regional co-operation. Distorted production structures, unilaterally oriented towards the ex-Soviet market or established on a non-market basis, resulted in lack of competitiveness in global markets and limited potential for enhancing regional trade.[8] As a consequence of market-oriented transformation and the collapse of CMEA, old state-owned foreign trade organisations that carried out the bulk of intraregional trade were eliminated, broken into pieces or substantially transformed. In addition, the decline of output and domestic demand, as well as the generally high economic and social costs of transformation, strengthened “short-termism” among policy-makers. The extremely rapid reorientation towards the West, a kind of "flight from the East" forced by political, economic and emotional reasons, has also contributed to the temporary neglect of regional co-operation.

Some Western attitudes also proved counterproductive to regional economic relations. First, Western emphasis on more regional co-operation was perceived as protection of Western markets for Westerners, and the redirection of Central and Eastern European exports into the regional framework imposed by the splitting of Europe after the second World War.

Second, Western plans and suggestions to improve regional co-operation have strengthened Central and Eastern European fears of being treated as a bloc, which, in many respects, they had never been historically, and which they firmly expected to have rid themselves of after 1989.

Third, no proposal on more extensive regional co-operation could be immune to the suspicion that the old CMEA times may be re-established in a new edition, with all the negative impacts on the economic development of more quickly transforming countries (bandwagon theory).

Fourth, any new and institutionalised regional co-operation framework which included countries with different political and economic features of the region was considered not only as an attempt at new "bloc-building" but, even more, as a substantial delay in the integration process and an argument to postpone the time of accession.

Finally, and in contrast to Western Europe after the second World War, the transformation of Central and Eastern Europe was not embedded into a new European "grand design" which could have provided a clear vision for the emerging market economies, in order to minimise emergency measures, reduce the justified concerns about security and economic modernisation, and combine the possibilities of (sub)regional co-operation with the priority of integration into the EU and other Western structures.

Under these circumstances, the countries of Central and Eastern Europe remained mainly competitors, suspicious of each other and less ready for genuine (active) regional co-operation (except in cases of external pressure or threat). As a consequence, they could not make use even of their limited regional bargaining power. Similarly, it proved extremely difficult to shape a joint position in selected issues vis-à-vis the EU and even less to co-ordinate their pre-accession strategies. However, most recently, there have been some encouraging signs of more substantial economic co-operation within CEFTA to be pointed out in the next section.

3. Intra- and interregional trade and investment flows

Trade among CEFTA countries has never been very important, either in volume or as a share of total trade. Still in the CMEA framework, intraregional exports amounted to about US$3 billion. However, this figure has to be taken with some reservations, due to the serious price and exchange rate distortions, as well as to the rather artificial pattern of specialisation. As a result of economic and political changes, intraregional exports fell to about US$2 billion by 1991-92. Although this was a significant decline, it was still much less than the fall experienced in trade with the ex-USSR or with the ex-GDR. The relatively highest intraregional trade was carried out by ex-Czechoslovakia, whose share in total trade amounted to 12 or 13 per cent in the mid-eighties. In turn, Poland's and Hungary's intraregional trade did not reach the 10 per cent mark even in the "best years" of CMEA co-operation.

Regarding the trends in intraregional trade, three main periods can be defined. A declining trend had already started in the second half of the eighties. In this first period, the share of intraregional exports and imports fell by 1 to 3 points for all three countries. The second period covers the years 1989 to 1992, and is characterised by a further and steeper decline of intraregional exchange of goods. In

Table 1. Intraregional trade of CEFTA countries (US$ million).

		Exports to				
		Poland	Czechoslov[a]	Slovakia	Hungary	total
Poland	1991	*	688	—	111	799
	1992	*	498	—	171	669
	1993	*	343	167	174	684
	1994	*	425	204	194	823
	1995	*	639	339	249	1227
Czechosl.	1991	521	*	—	477	998
	1992	503	*	—	478	981
	1993[a]	350	*	2579	271	3200
	1994[a]	550	*	2341	347	3238
	1995[a]	921	*	2762	364	4045
Slovakia	1993	161	2271	*	250	2682
	1994	146	2131	*	356	2633
	1995	350	2740	*	370	3460
Hungary	1991	140	221	—	*	361
	1992	145	288	—	*	433
	1993	167	173	139	*	479
	1994	222	197	144	*	563
	1995	337	207	213	*	757
		Imports from				
Poland	1991	*	521	—	140	661
	1992	*	503	—	145	648
	1993	*	350	161	167	678
	1994	*	550	146	222	918
	1995	*	921	350	337	1608
Czechosl.	1991	688	*	—	221	909
	1992	498	*	—	238	786
	1993[a]	343	*	2271	173	2787
	1994[a]	425	*	2131	197	2753
	1995[a]	639	*	2740	207	3646
Slovakia	1993	167	2579	*	139	2885
	1994	204	2341	*	144	2689
	1995	339	2762	*	213	3314
Hungary	1991	111	477	—	*	588
	1992	171	478	—	*	649
	1993	174	271	250	*	695
	1994	194	347	356	*	897
	1995	249	364	370	*	983

Note: a) as of 1993, Czech Republic only; Mainly based on Czech and Hungarian statistics; mirror statistics may indicate small differences in some bilateral trade flows.
Source: National statistical yearbooks and foreign trade statistics.

Poland's total exports CEFTA's importance sank from 7 to 5 (in imports to 4) per cent. Czechoslovakia experienced a decline from 11 to 8 per cent in exports and to 5 per cent in imports. For Hungary, the previous CEFTA share of 8 per cent went down to 4 per cent in exports and to 6 per cent in imports.

The third stage of CEFTA trade started in or around 1993 and can be attributed to two factors. First, and most importantly, the volume of CEFTA trade increased dramatically as a result of the split of Czechoslovakia. At present, the "externalisation" of Czech-Slovak trade represents the lion's share of the intraregional flow of commodities. The volume of intra-exports jumped to US$7 billion in 1993, and reached US$9.5 billion in 1995, of which US$4.9 and

Table 2. Share of the European Union and the CEFTA in the foreign trade of the CEFTA countries (total exports and imports of each of the CEFTA countries = 100).

	1985	1989	1990	1991	1992	1993	1994	1995
Exports by:								
Poland								
to EU	23.2	32.1	47.2	55.6	58.0	63.2	62.6	68.9
to CEFTA	9.4	7.1	5.1	5.3	5.1	4.8	4.8	5.3
Czechoslovakia[a]								
to EU	9.1	26.3	31.4	43.3	52.9	42.3	45.7	55.1
to CEFTA	12.4	11.4	9.7	10.4	7.9	26.4	22.9	23.7
to CEFTA-SLO[b]						5.1	6.3	7.5
Slovakia								
to EU						22.5	28.9	
to CEFTA						49.5	38.7	
Hungary								
to EU	15.8	24.8	32.3	45.7	49.8	46.5	51.0	63.5
to CEFTA	9.1	8.2	5.8	4.3	4.1	5.2	5.3	5.9
Imports by:								
Poland								
from EU	20.4	33.8	45.6	49.9	53.2	57.2	57.5	66.2
from CEFTA	9.0	7.3	4.5	4.2	4.1	3.7	4.3	5.6
Czechoslovakia[a]								
from EU	8.6	26.4	31.9	39.8	47.8	42.7	45.1	56.4
from CEFTA	13.8	11.0	10.6	6.7	4.6	21.4	18.2	17.5
from CEFTA-SLO[b]						4.0	4.1	4.1
Slovakia								
from EU						25.2	34.5	
from CEFTA						45.9	40.7	
Hungary								
from EU	21.2	29.0	31.0	41.1	42.7	40.1	45.4	61.4
from CEFTA	8.9	8.4	7.0	5.8	5.9	5.2	6.2	6.5

Notes: a) as of 1993, Czech Republic only; b) CEFTA without exports to and imports from Slovakia; calculations based mainly on Czech and Hungarian statistics.
Source: National statistical yearbooks and foreign trade statistics, IMF Direction of Trade Statistics, Yearbook 1995.

$5.5 billion, respectively, is represented by trade between the Czech and the Slovak republics. The second and more promising development is, however, the "rediscovery" of the (sub)regional market in all CEFTA countries. Excluding the Czech-Slovak trade, intraregional exports almost doubled in three years, from US$2.1 billion in 1993 to US$4 billion in 1995 (for details see Table 1).

Moreover, intraregional trade started to grow more dynamically than overall trade, resulting in slightly increasing shares. In the last two or three years, intraregional exports of Hungary grew from 4.1 to 5.9, and imports from 5.2 to 6.5 per cent of total exports and imports. The corresponding figures for Poland are 4.8 and 5.3 per cent in exports and 3.7 and 5.6 per cent in imports. Also Czech exports to Poland and Hungary registered a dynamic growth from 5.1 to 7.5 per cent (much less in imports). However, they were not able to compensate for the rapid loss of Slovak share, as a natural consequence of trade developments in the first years after separation (Table 2).

Due to the short period surveyed and to the likely impact of various factors, it would be premature to explain the relative vitality of intraregional trade by just one factor. To be sure, the CEFTA agreement **did** have a positive impact. However, the regained growth path, structural changes, to some extent the inflow of FDI, and, certainly, the "calming down" of the dramatic geographic reorientation of trade relations should not be ignored as regional trade-creating factors.

Despite these similarities, CEFTA trade reveals two special features. First, it is much more important for the Czech Republic and Slovakia, and not only because of their mutual trade. Also, without considering their bilateral trade relations, these two countries are more linked to CEFTA than either Poland or Hungary.[9] Second, the Czech and Slovak republics have substantial trade surpluses, while Poland and Hungary are importing more than what they are exporting to the region. It would be mistaken, however, to draw the conclusion that the trade surplus countries are necessarily more developed or competitive. A detailed analysis could prove that bilateral trade balances are influenced by different export and import patterns, still valid barriers to the free flow of commodities and to distortions in domestic prices. What is, in fact, a much more important dilemma, is the discrepancy between the relatively higher reliance of the Czech Republic on subregional trade, accompanied by a substantial and structure-based surplus in subregional trade and the country's apparent "flight" from East-Central Europe on the political and "economic philosophy" levels.

A comparison of trade relations of the individual countries between CEFTA and the EU makes clear the substantial differences between the two groups. For Poland and Hungary, trade with the EU is about 10 times more important than trade with CEFTA. For the Czech Republic, this difference is much smaller, with the EU's share being two or three times higher than that of CEFTA. Finally, at least until 1994, Slovakia traded more with the CEFTA than with the EU (see Table 2).

Over the past decade, the share of the EU has been constantly growing in total exports from and imports to the Central European countries. Between 1985 and 1992 (for Poland until 1993) this trend was accompanied by a continuously decreasing share of subregional trade. Although the CEFTA countries have important trade relations with other countries also, it is very likely that this contrasting development was partially based on a "crowding out" of subregional exports and imports by commodity flows generated in trade with the EU.[10] It is interesting that after 1992-93, both the EU and CEFTA started to register higher shares in exports and imports, leading to a relative market share loss of third countries.[11] Obviously, the Czech-Slovak issue has to be dealt with separately. After the "jump" of 1993, contrasting trends, manifested in growing EU and decreasing CEFTA shares, can be observed until most recently.

No less interesting than the shifts in geographic patterns are the changes in the commodity patterns of total, EU and CEFTA trade of the individual countries. Unfortunately, no comprehensive and comparable data sets are available to carry out all-embracing research. In addition, the separation of Czechoslovakia makes any comparisons over time very difficult. Nevertheless, some basic trends, mainly revealed by Czech and Hungarian data, can be pointed out. Two key questions can be raised. First, what is the specialisation (despecialisation) pattern of the CEFTA countries in their trade with the EU and CEFTA? Are these two patterns similar or different? Second, what kinds of changes have occurred in the specialisation (despecialisation) pattern over time, concentrating on the last years? In other words, is the pattern of trade with the EU increasingly similar to or different from the

Table 3. Commodity pattern of foreign trade of CEFTA countries (total exports and imports of individual countries = 100).

SITC		0+1+4	2	3	5	6	7	8
Exports by								
Poland	1985	8.2	7.4	15.7	6.1	23.2a	39.4	23.2[a]
	1989	11.3	6.0	9.7	7.7	19.0	33.6	6.7
	1993	11.1	5.6	9.7	6.8	26.5	21.0	19.4
	1994	11.6	4.7	9.1	6.7	27.5	19.8	20.5
	1995	10.1	4.5	8.2	7.7	27.6	21.1	20.9
Czecho-	1985	3.1	3.3	4.3	6.0	16.7	53.6	11.3
slovakia[a])	1989	5	3.3	6.3	6.5	20.5	40.1	13.8
	1993	8.0	6.1	6.2	9.5	29.9	27.6	12.7
	1995	6.9	6.0	5.3	10.4	32.4	26.3	12.6
Slovakia	1993	6.5	5.1	4.6	12.0	38.8	19.4	13.4
	1995[b]	5.7	5.0	4.2	13.2	40.5	18.8	12.2
Hungary	1985	20.5	4.1	5.1	11.5	12.3	33.5	11.3
	1990	22.4	4.7	3.1	12.4	18.5	25.6	10.7
	1993	20.1	5.7	4.1	12.1	16.1	24.1	17.8
	1994	19.4	5.2	4.0	11.2	16.6	25.6	17.9
	1995	21.0	4.8	3.2	11.8	17.4	25.6	16.2
Imports by								
Poland	1985	9.2	10.2	22.2	8.9	19.0[a]	30.5	19.0[a]
	1989	11.7	8.4	12.7	10.9	14.9	33.4	8.0
	1993	11.2	4.6	12.5	13.3	18.5	29.6	10.2
	1994	10.3	5.2	10.5	14.7	20.2	28.8	9.9
	1995	9.4	5.4	9.1	15.0	21.6	29.9	9.3
Czecho-	1985	7.1	8.3	30.7	6.8	8.9	31.1	4.8
slovakia[a]	1989	8.0	7.0	21.9	7.9	10.0	27.8	12.3
	1993	7.7	5.0	11.1	12.1	15.9	36.1	11.7
	1995	7.8	5.0	9.4	13.2	17.9	35.6	11.1
Slovakia	1993	9.0	5.2	20.9	11.3	15.1	29.3	9.0
	1995[b]	7.5	5.8	17.9	13.5	17.6	29.0	8.0
Hungary	1985	6.8	6.9	22.0	13.4	16.5	27.4	6.1
	1990	7.2	5.3	14.2	14.9	15.5	34.6	7.8
	1993	5.8	3.1	13.3	11.9	18.2	36.6	11.1
	1994	6.6	3.7	11.8	12.7	19.8	34.1	11.3
	1995	5.6	4.1	11.6	14.3	23.0	30.7	10.6

Notes: a) as of 1993, Czech Republic; b) preliminary figures
Source: national foreign trade statistics and own calculations.

pattern of trade with CEFTA countries? (Tables 3, 4 and 5 provide the available data set.)

In total exports of Poland and the Czech Republic, energy- and raw material-intensive manufactured goods (SITC 6) represent the leading one-digit commodity group, while for Hungary, machinery (SITC 7) is the leading sector. The same pattern holds for the Czech, Polish and Hungarian exports to the EU.[12] In addition, Polish and Hungarian labour-intensive consumer goods (SITC 8) have strong representation. In exports to the CEFTA, this pattern undergoes substantial changes. The Czech export pattern is complemented by machinery and chemicals,[13] while the Hungarian pattern is largely different. In the latter case, agricultural products (SITC 0+1+4) and chemicals (SITC 5) dominate the export pattern to CEFTA. In total imports, machinery is the main one-digit commodity group for all CEFTA countries. The same holds for the structure of imports from the EU. However, imports from the CEFTA countries show a shift towards chemicals and

Table 4. Commodity pattern of foreign trade of CEFTA countries with the European Union (total exports to and imports from the EU of individual countries = 100).

SITC		0+1+4	2	3	5	6	7	8
Exports by								
Poland	1988	17.6	11.1	11.5	5.7	22.4	13.5	15.3
	1990	19.1	9.3	9.8	8.6	22.9	11.2	16.7
	1993	10.1	6.2	7.3	5.0	23.9	18.3	26.7
	1994[a]	9.3	5.1	8.9	5.0	28.5	18.2	24.9
	1995	7.6	4.7	6.7	5.7	29.2	21.6	24.5
Czecho-	1985							
slovakia[b]	1989	6.8	4.9	5.0	10.3	26.7	10.1	8.3
	1993	6.4	8.1	4.6	9.8	32.2	23.6	15.3
	1995	5.1	8.5	4.9	9.0	34.5	3.9	13.9
Slovakia	1993							
	1995							
Hungary	1985							
	1990	24.1	6.5	2.4	11.6	22.3	16.3	12.5
	1993	18.1	6.4	1.7	9.4	17.6	20.0	26.7
	1994	15.4	6.4	1.2	8.7	19.0	24.9	24.3
	1995	13.3[c]	5.9[d]	3.3	9.2	40.6[e]	27.6	40.6[e]
Imports by								
Poland	1988	11.2	3.1	0.4	21.5	18.7	31.5	7.0
	1990	13.3	2.2	3.0	11.2	18.7	37.2	10.3
	1993	10.1	2.0	4.4	13.7	21.2	35.0	10.7
	1994[a]	8.1	2.7	3.8	15.9	25.2	33.4	10.5
	1995	6.9	2.8	3.0	16.0	26.5	34.9	9.7
Czecho-	1985							
slovakia[b]	1989	5.9	5.2	0.1	14.4	7.7	30.6	4.6
	1993	7.8	2.7	1.2	14.1	13.4	46.9	14.0
	1995	7.5	2.7	1.5	14.9	16.8	44.2	12.2
Slovakia	1993							
	1995							
Hungary	1985							
	1990	4.2	3.2	0.6	23.4	16.9	42.2	9.5
	1993	5.9	2.4	0.5	15.4	23.3	37.7	14.8
	1994	6.2	2.4	0.6	14.8	22.4	39.8	13.9
	1995	3.7[c]	2.9[d]	1.7	15.6	39.2[e]	36.8	39.2[e]

Notes: a) based on trade with EU-15; b) as of 1993, Czech Republic; c) SITC 0+1; d) SITC 2+4; e) SITC 6+8.
Source: national foreign trade statistics and own calculations.

energy — and raw material-intensive manufactured products in the Czech Republic and towards energy and the SITC 6 group in the case of Hungary.

Based on this rather rough analysis, the general conclusion can be drawn that the export and import pattern of trade with the EU is much more "developed" than that of CEFTA. While trade relations with the EU concentrate on manufactured goods, including machinery products, subregional trade is more based on raw materials, energy and agricultural products. As a result, trade with the EU fits much more into the category of intra-industry trade, while the pattern of CEFTA trade reveals clear signs of a Heckscher-Ohlin-type, inter-industry specialisation. This overall finding is supported by more detailed statistical surveys as well. The share of intra-industry trade in machinery products (SITC 7) is always lower for the subregional trade than for the CEFTA countries' trade with the EU.[14] In the last years, a double commodity pattern of trade, with concentration on less dynamic inter-industry components in the

Table 5. Commodity pattern of foreign trade of CEFTA Countries with CEFTA (total exports to and imports from CEFTA of individual countries = 100).

SITC		0+1+4	2	3	5	6	7	8
Exports by								
Poland	1985							
	1989							
	1994	6.0	7.3	23.2	13.8	26.1	15.3	8.1
	1995	5.5	5.8	20.5	13.4	30.4	15.9	8.5
Czechoslovakia[a]	1985							
	1989[b]	6.2	6.4	4.0	8.1	11.2	16.7	10.4
	1993	9.7	2.7	11.0	12.6	25.5	5.2	11.2
	1995	9.2	3.5	9.2	16.1	29.0	24.9	8.2
Slovakia	1993							
	1995							
Hungary	1985							
	1990	15.2	5.2	0.5	13.1	8.7	43.3	12.6
	1993	22.4	7.0	1.5	22.0	13.4	13.1	6.5
	1994	24.4	6.4	8.6	24.5	16.7	11.6	7.7
Imports by								
Poland	1985							
	1989							
	1994	8.7	5.1	5.0	29.2	28.2	16.4	7.3
	1995	14.0	4.0	7.0	25.0	28.3	16.1	5.7
Czechoslovakia[a]	1985							
	1989[b]	10.2	2.4	1.8	8.6	17.0	17.3	15.4
	1993	7.3	5.2	10.7	14.3	31.5	21.7	9.3
	1995	7.6	4.8	8.7	16.6	34.9	18.2	9.1
Slovakia	1993							
	1995							
Hungary	1985							
	1990	10.0	3.5	7.5	8.6	18.4	40.7	7.4
	1993	5.5	8.6	24.1	11.6	33.7	13.0	3.5
	1994	4.3	11.4	27.8	12.4	27.9	13.0	3.2

Notes: a) as of 1993, Czech Republic; b) large part of exports and imports were classified under SITC 9.
Source: national foreign trade statistics and own calculations.

subregional turnover, has been evolving. If it were sustained for a longer period, prospects for subregional trade would remain rather limited. This is, however, fortunately not very likely, due to the strong impact of the EU on CEFTA countries, the structure-transforming role of FDI and, most importantly, of prospective full membership in the EU.

Some further characterisation of the trade pattern can be provided by examining the changes in the commodity pattern of individual countries in the last years. In total exports, the sharp decline of machinery (except for Hungary after 1990!) can be attributed to the collapse of the CMEA and the artificial production and trade structure created and maintained by Eastern integration. Overall, there is a significant growth of exports of consumer goods. While for Hungary and Poland commodity restructuring took place among manufactured goods, there was a clear shift from manufactured products to raw materials in Czechoslovakia already before 1993. This trend was substantially strengthened after 1993, as many food items and industrial inputs became part of the bilateral **foreign** trade. In exports to the EU, the share of manufacturing, mainly based on machinery (Czech Republic and Hungary)

Table 6. Specialised and despecialised one-digit commodity groups in EU and CEFTA trade of CEFTA member countries (based on the commodity structure in the last available year).

		Czech Rep. (1995)	Hungary (1994)	Poland (1995)
Exports to EU	special.	SITC 2	SITC 2	SITC 6
		SITC 6	SITC 6	SITC 8
		SITC 8	SITC 8	
	despec.	SITC 0+1+4	SITC 0+1+4	SITC0+1+4
		SITC 5	SITC 3	SITC 3
		SITC 7	SITC 5	SITC 5
Exports to CEFTA	special.	SITC 0+1+4	SITC 0+1+4	SITC 2
		SITC 3	SITC 3	SITC 3
		SITC 5	SITC 5	SITC 5
				SITC 6
	despec.	SITC 2	SITC 7	SITC 0+1+4
		SITC 6	SITC 8	SITC 7
		SITC 7		SITC 8
		SITC 8		
Imports from EU	special.	SITC 5	SITC 5	SITC 6
		SITC 7	SITC 6	SITC 7
		SITC 8	SITC 7	
			SITC 8	
	despec.	SITC 2	SITC 2	SITC0+1+4
		SITC 3	SITC 3	SITC 2
		SITC 6		SITC 3
Imports from CEFTA	special.	SITC 5	SITC 2	SITC 0+1+4
		SITC 6	SITC 3	SITC 5
			SITC 6	SITC 6
	despec.	SITC 7	SITC 0+1+4	SITC 7
		SITC 8	SITC 7	SITC 8
			SITC 8	

Note: Only most important specialisation and despecialisation cases listed.
Source: see Tables 3, 4 and 5.

and industrial consumer goods (mainly Poland and Hungary) was rising dramatically. In turn, agriculture became despecialised for all CEFTA countries. In exports to the CEFTA countries, the Hungarian figures provide more relevant information than the Czech ones which suffer from the distortion of the recently created Slovak trade. There is a strong "naturalisation" trend between 1990 and 1994. The decline of the machinery share from 43 to 12 per cent in four years is the consequence of the collapse of the CMEA, the changing (or eliminated) network of trade organisations, the substantial drop in investment activities, and also Western competition. The latter seems to be primarily "responsible" for the decline in the share of industrial consumer goods. At the same time, the share of agricultural products, raw materials, energy, chemicals and even energy- and raw material-intensive industrial goods reveal substantially higher shares[15] (additional information is provided in Tables 6 and 7).

The dominant position of the EU is manifested also in calculations of export and import market shares for main commodity groups. Comparing the volume of Hungarian exports to the EU and to CEFTA, a difference of 30 to 1 characterises

Table 7. Trends in specialised and despecialised one-digit commodity groups in EU and CEFTA trade of CEFTA member countries (based on the comparison of the commodity structure in selected years).

			Czech Republic (1993-1995)	Hungary (1990-1994)
Exports	parallel changes			
		growing	SITC 6	
		declining	SITC 8	
	opposite changes			
		EU up, CEFTA down		SITC 7
				SITC 8
		EU down, CEFTA up	SITC 0+1+4	SITC 0+1+4
			SITC 5	SITC 3
				SITC 5
				SITC 6
Imports	parallel changes			
		growing	SITC 5	SITC 6
			SITC 6	
		declining	SITC 7	SITC 7
			SITC 8	
	opposite changes			
		EU up, CEFTA down		SITC 0+1+4
				SITC 8
		EU down, CEFTA up		SITC 2
				SITC 3
				SITC 5

Note: Only most important specialisation and despecialisation cases listed, including sharp changes in one direction, with unchanged share in the other direction.
Source: see Tables 3, 4 and 5.

industrial consumer goods, 20 to 1 machinery, and about 10 to 1 the SITC 6 group and raw materials. With the exception of raw materials and energy, where the CEFTA share is substantial, indicating the "natural" pattern of division of labour, similar trends prevail in imports. All this is the unavoidable consequence of the dramatic trade reorientation of the CEFTA countries.

Regarding the future, relative shifts of the position (weight) of the EU and the CEFTA in selected commodity markets have to be followed carefully. Do they show changes in one direction (growing or declining shares), or is this development contrasting (higher shares for the one and lower shares for the other group)? Between 1993 and 1995, in the case of the Czech Republic, the EU share was growing in all commodity groups, while the share of CEFTA declined overall (except for raw materials). It is likely that EU markets have started to increasingly replace the traditional Slovak market. This trend can be observed without any exception in the Czech imports from EU and CEFTA — a clear sign of replacing CEFTA (in practice, Slovak) products by EU goods. The Hungarian development between 1990 and 1994 is less clear. Although the EU's share grew in exports (except for energy), the CEFTA share also grew in many commodity groups (agriculture, energy, chemicals, SITC 6). Contrasting trends were only observable in machinery and consumer goods (although, there is a slight improvement in the latter, between 1993 and 1994). With the exception of agriculture, the same trends characterise imports from the EU and CEFTA (detailed statistics can be found in Tables 8, 9 and 10).

Table 8. Share of EU and CEFTA in total exports of the CEFTA countries, by main commodities (exports in each commodity group = 100).

SITC		0+1+4	2	3	5	6	7	8
Exports by								
Poland								
1988	EU	50.1	50.5	31.8	20.5	33.1	11.5	54.2
	CEFTA							
1993	EU	57.1	70.2	47.1	45.6	56.6	54.7	86.4
	CEFTA							
1994[a]	EU	55.6	75.8	67.6	51.2	71.7	63.7	83.9
	CEFTA	2.5	7.5	12.2	9.8	4.5	3.7	1.9
1995	EU	53.0	72.5	57.5	51.5	74.2	71.7	82.1
	CEFTA	3.0	7.1	13.7	9.4	6.0	4.1	2.2
Czechoslovakia[b]								
1989	EU	33.3	33.2	24.2	34.1	29.8	5.7	21.4
	CEFTA	6.2	6.4	4.0	8.1	11.2	16.7	10.4
1993	EU	34.0	56.4	31.5	43.6	45.5	36.2	50.9
	CEFTA	32.2	11.8	46.8	38.0	22.6	25.0	23.4
1995	EU	40.	78.2	51.7	47.9	58.7	50.1	60.6
	CEFTA	31.4	13.7	41.4	36.6	21.2	22.5	15.5
Hungary								
1990	EU	34.7	43.9	25.2	30.0	38.9	20.5	37.7
	CEFTA	3.9	6.3	0.9	6.1	2.7	9.8	6.8
1993	EU	42.0	52.1	19.8	36.1	50.6	38.6	69.8
	CEFTA	5.8	6.3	2.0	9.4	4.3	2.8	1.9
1994	EU	40.4	62.1	15.8	39.3	58.5	49.6	69.1
	CEFTA	6.6	6.4	11.4	11.5	5.3	2.4	2.3

Notes: a) based on trade with EU-15; b) as of 1993, Czech Republic only.
Source: national foreign trade statistics and own calculations.

Table 9. Share of EU and CEFTA in total imports of the CEFTA countries, by main commodities (imports in each commodity group = 100)

SITC		0+1+4	2	3	5	6	7	8
Imports by								
Poland								
1988	EU	22.6	9.4	0.7	49.9	36.5	25.8	29.1
	CEFTA							
1993	EU	55.8	26.9	21.5	63.1	70.4	72.6	65.0
	CEFTA							
1994[a]	EU	51.3	34.2	23.9	70.6	81.3	75.8	69.5
	CEFTA	3.6	4.2	2.0	8.5	6.0	2.4	3.2
1995	EU	47.2	33.1	21.6	69.3	79.3	75.3	67.6
	CEFTA	8.3	4.1	4.3	9.3	7.3	3.0	3.4
Czechoslovakia[b]								
1989	EU	18.8	15.2	0.2	39.6	19.1	21.4	19.2
	CEFTA	10.2	2.4	1.8	8.6	17.0	17.3	15.4
1993	EU	53.5	23.1	4.8	49.7	36.0	55.4	51.1
	CEFTA	20.4	22.0	20.6	25.2	42.3	12.8	17.0
1995	EU	54.3	30.7	9.2	63.6	53.0	70.0	62.3
	CEFTA	17.0	16.9	16.1	21.9	34.2	9.0	14.4
Hungary								
1990	EU	18.1	18.7	1.4	48.5	33.8	37.8	37.9
	CEFTA	9.7	4.7	3.7	4.1	8.4	8.3	6.7
1993	EU	40.7	30.9	1.4	52.0	51.3	41.3	53.6
	CEFTA	4.9	14.5	9.4	5.1	9.6	1.8	1.6
1994	EU	42.5	29.1	2.3	53.0	51.2	52.9	55.7
	CEFTA	4.1	19.0	14.5	5.4	8.6	2.3	1.8

Notes: a) based on trade with EU-15; b) as of 1993, Czech Republic only.
Source: national foreign trade statistics and own calculations.

Table 10. Changes in the market shares of EU and CEFTA by main commodity groups.

	Czech Republic 1993 and1995	Hungary 1990 and 1994
Exports: similar trends		
increasing	SITC 2	SITC 0+1+4
		SITC 2
		SITC 5
		SITC 6
decreasing		
opposite trends		
EU up, CEFTA down	SITC 0+1+4	SITC 7
	SITC 3	SITC 8
	SITC 5	
	SITC 6	
	SITC 7	
	SITC 8	
EU down, CEFTA up		SITC 3
Imports: similar trends		
increasing		SITC 2
		SITC 3
		SITC 5
		SITC 6
decreasing		
opposite trends		
EU up, CEFTA down	SITC 0+1+4	SITC 0+1+4
	SITC 2	SITC 7
	SITC 3	SITC 8
	SITC 5	
	SITC 6	
	SITC 7	
	SITC 8	

Note: Sharp changes in one direction, with unchanged share in the other direction are included.
Source: see Tables 8 and 9.

In sum, the following main conclusions can be drawn:

1. there is a substantial difference in the size of trade with the EU and with CEFTA;
2. at least until 1993, this difference was rapidly growing as a result of dramatic trade reorientation;
3. the overall picture holds for most one-digit commodity groups as well;
4. while trade with the EU is concentrated on manufactured exports and imports, and increasingly points to intra-industry patterns, trade patterns with CEFTA countries changed in favour of raw materials and raw material-intensive manufactured goods, relegating subregional trade in machinery and consumer goods to a negligible position;
5. in order to provide meaningful impetus to intra-CEFTA trade, substantial growth of intra-industry trade is indispensable, which, however, in the longer term, remains much more influenced by extraregional factors (EU membership, FDI) than by intraregional elements (free trade, GDP growth).

For all CEFTA countries, the role of foreign direct investment is crucial for economic modernisation and integration into the world and the European economy. In this field, the difference between the volume of foreign and regional capital flows is even larger than in the trade volumes. For all countries are poor in capital and all of them need substantial amounts of net capital inflows, regional co-operation in direct capital flows is and will remain extremely limited for the foreseeable future.[16]

However, FDI can play an important role: in preparation for EU membership; in lobbying in Brussels for membership; and also in fostering regional co-operation. Multinational companies follow different strategies, with different impacts on subregional trade creation. Those firms which are located in one member country would like to export their products from this production (and distribution) base to the whole region. Therefore, they are extremely interested in complete free trade in CEFTA. Those who have set up production in all CEFTA countries may specialise in producing different commodities, and exchange them in subregional trade. This has already led to significant trade creation. Finally, there are also foreign companies which have bought different national markets and now maintain them closed for competition coming both from the EU and from CEFTA.

In the medium term, indirect impacts originated by FDI may be favourable for subregional trade. First, FDI interested in sourcing and involving local companies into its international production and distribution networks, is creating specialisation patterns which may offer good opportunities for intra-industrial subregional co-operation. This is particularly the case, if companies in the different CEFTA countries are specialising in the production of different goods. In this way, exports to the EU may create, in the second round, a higher subregional trade potential (very much similar to the sequencing process in East Asia). Second, higher growth and income is also expected to create additional demand for subregional products. Third, FDI in border areas can have substantial spillover effects for neighbouring countries and contribute to the creation of cross-border development poles with strong trade-creating capabilities.

We should not forget about the trade-diverting (or at least not trade-creating) factors either. Each of the CEFTA countries is fiercely fighting to get more FDI and convince potential investors of its benefits within the region. Different economic policies, still-existing trade-policy constraints, under-financed domestic entrepreneurs, under-capitalised small and medium-sized companies, the non-availability of a regional network of suppliers and the already developed pattern of subcontracting with extraregional partners have to be added. Finally, as already mentioned, the behaviour of the foreign investor can substantially influence subregional co-operation by asking for more national protectionism or by helping dismantle the still existing barriers and convert the CEFTA countries into a more homogeneous and harmonised market of significant size and growth potential.

4. Impact of the European Union on subregional co-operation

The relations between the EU and the CEFTA countries can best be described as a classic policy-maker/policy-taker pattern. Considering that the CEFTA's GDP is only 4 to 7 per cent of the aggregate GDP of the EU (based on exchange rate or on

PPP), and the latter accounts for about 60 per cent of the CEFTA's total external trade volume, a particularly strong impact of the EU can be predicted. It has to be noted, however, that this impact is only partially felt as a direct influence on subregional co-operation. A large part of it manifests itself in indirect ways, by affecting the member countries of CEFTA, and through this, the impacts will be transferred to the pattern of subregional co-operation. Also, some of the adjustment requirements of the transforming economies have to be met anyhow, irrespectively of adjustment to EU rules. However, sometimes the implementation of these tasks is attributed to the direct impact of the EU. Finally, the influence of the EU is not necessarily always positive. In a number of cases Brussels has been supporting and improving the framework conditions of subregional co-operation. In other cases, however, the EU's impact cannot be assessed in an unambiguously positive way.

4.1 Positive impacts

Four main areas of strengthening subregional co-operation can be identified: trade, adjustment, the PHARE programme and longer-term economic policy objectives.

1. By far the most important impacts derive from trade. The CEFTA countries were the first transforming economies which concluded Association Agreements with Brussels. The trade section of these agreements came into force in March 1992,[17] well before the CEFTA countries would have designed the subregional trade framework. Just the opposite, intraregional trade started to suffer from the disintegrative impacts produced by the collapse of the CMEA and the challenge of economic and political transformation. As a result, the Association Agreements created a more favourable trade environment for the Central European countries than conditions for intraregional trade. Strengthened by the general "flight to the West" attitude and by the financial supremacy of Western European firms, the agreements have substantially enhanced trade diversion from the subregion towards the EU.

In order to stop this trend, similar agreements became a must on the subregional level. In December 1992, CEFTA was created with the aim of achieving free trade in industrial products by 2001, at the same time as stipulated by the Association Agreements. Although CEFTA did not apply temporary asymmetrical dismantling of tariff and non-tariff barriers, since member countries were on a more or less similar general level of development, most CEFTA measures became closely harmonised with the timetable set in the agreements with Brussels.

There are several signs of this attitude. First, when the Copenhagen summit of the EU shortened the process of abolishing still existing barriers to the exports of transforming countries to the EU, CEFTA followed suit and started to accelerate the liberalisation timetable as well. Second, most recently, and parallel with the ever stronger preparation for membership, CEFTA agreed on further liberalisation steps resulting in free trade in most industrial products by 1998, and in a more advanced liberalisation scheme in agricultural trade than that stipulated by the Association Agreements with the EU. Third, Hungary, which established a system of global quota for the imports of sensitive products, determines EU and CEFTA quotas on a yearly basis.

Another trade policy instrument are the rules of origin, according to which those products, which have at least a 60 per cent (in some cases 50 per cent) local content, enjoy free or preferential access to the EU market. Local content includes domestic inputs as well as inputs originating in the EU and the CEFTA countries. It has to be admitted, that this measure has been most important in order to create a unified trade environment between the EU and the CEFTA countries. In the last years, its subregional trade creating impact remained very modest (if any) which is due to the low volume of intra-industry trade among CEFTA countries.

It is difficult to quantify the impact of the EU on subregional trade creation. On the one hand, trade policy measures could only partially correct the substantial trade diversion in the first years of the transformation. Among other factors, this can be attributed to the different pattern of trade with the EU and the subregion, the financial power of EU firms, different levels of management and marketing, and psychological barriers to buying subregional commodities. On the other hand, and in a more positive way, deeper integration with the EU has already shown its influence on the development of subregional trade. Considering the relatively high share of exports in GDP and the dominating weight of the EU in foreign trade of the CEFTA countries, commodity flows between the CEFTA countries and the EU represent a substantial factor of economic growth in the subregion. Higher growth results in higher domestic demand, part of which can be met by subregional imports. Also, the large EU market allows the building up of production capacities which enjoy economies of scale advantages and, thus, create an export potential also towards the neighbouring countries. Moreover, the rapid increase of trade with the EU has already started to shape (partially new) production and export patterns and to increase the propensity for intra-industry trade. In the medium-term, this impact will certainly be revealed in subregional exchange of goods as well. Finally, the strong impact of the EU on a more balanced and harmonised growth in the member countries of CEFTA may lead to similar business cycles, which create favourable general conditions for subregional co-operation.

In sum, CEFTA demonstrated a defensive and follower-type pattern in the area of trade and trade-related issues. Until most recently, trade liberalisation steps were adjusted to earlier implemented liberalisation in trade with the EU or were understood as a sign of "good behaviour" or "EU maturity" of the associated countries. On one occasion only, CEFTA countries took the initiative to forge a common position towards Brussels. As the EU introduced various protectionist measures shortly after the entering into force of the trade section of the Association Agreements (in 1992 and 1993, affecting steel, agriculture), there was a strong and harmonised protest by the CEFTA countries. However, this was a temporary and damage-limiting alliance which was abandoned after the normalisation of trade relations with the EU.

2. The defensive pattern is even more obvious in the overwhelmingly one-way adjustment to EU rules, standards and laws. In order to become full members of the EU, the associated countries are obliged to adopt and implement (enforce) the rules of the game developed in the EU during decades of the integration process. Already the tasks of transformation have created a parallel (but not necessarily simultaneous) process of establishing a market economy environment and institutional framework.

Even stronger are the adjustment requirements concerning the *acquis communautaire*, a part of which is contained in the Association Agreements, and are carefully summarised in the White Book presented at the Cannes summit of June 1995. Each of the candidate countries started its legal, technical and environmental harmonisation, introduced EU conforming quality controls and has implemented or is about to implement its national competition law based very much on the corresponding EU legislation. In consequence, "unconscious" subregional legal and institutional harmonisation also has been taking place, because uniform external standards imposed on the whole region, as a precondition for future membership, have to be met by all countries of the region. Through this process, the EU as the key external agent (or modernisation anchor) is creating a legal, institutional and economic framework which is also likely to boost subregional trade and economic relations.

3. Much less influence on subregional co-operation could be registered in the framework of the PHARE programme, although international financial support, if adequately designed, can easily become a major subregional contact-creating factor.[18] However, neither the structure nor the size of the PHARE programme could meet this objective. Since the allocation of PHARE resources occurs fundamentally on the national level, and little room has been left for financing investments with direct impacts on subregional co-operation (first of all in transborder infrastructure), PHARE substantially remained a programme supporting the transformation process **within** each of the associated countries. An exception to this rule is represented by the Multiphare framework, which, however, mainly aims at financing projects more with the participation of EU countries and less between and among neighbouring transforming countries exclusively.[19] The transforming countries can perhaps also be blamed for the lack of subregional co-operation, because everybody was interested in short-sighted national "priorities" instead of thinking in forward-looking regional patterns.

4. Finally, and in a prospective context, the impact of the planned European Monetary Union on the economic policy harmonisation of the CEFTA countries has to be mentioned. Obviously, meeting the Maastricht criteria is not a precondition for membership in the EU. However, strong divergence from one or more of the Maastricht indicators (e.g. inflation) in the candidate countries may not be tolerated once accession is on the agenda. Therefore, today all CEFTA countries are already undertaking serious economic policy steps in order to reduce the difference between their economic performance and the EU pattern. Of course, and for very different reasons, there is no room for joint economic policy-making or a substantial regional harmonisation of economic policies. However, economic policy harmonisation with the EU will inevitably lead to less diverging national economic policies on the subregional level as well.

4.2 *Adverse or ambiguous impacts*[20]

Beside the unambiguously favourable direct and indirect impacts of the EU on subregional co-operation, also the not so transparent and sometimes detrimental effects have to be summarised. They can be divided into four groups: trade, economic adjustment, infrastructure and regional development.

1. The most important impacts which can at least partially be quantified, stem from the development of trade. Despite the EU Association Agreements, several EU barriers to market access have not been eliminated in the first years, or will remain in force even after 2001 (i.e. in agriculture). The limited trade liberalisation has various negative consequences on subregional trade. First, it reduces the import potential of the CEFTA countries, because of both slower growth of aggregate demand and shortage of convertible currencies.[21] Second, it transmits a negative psychological message to economic policy-makers of the region who, at least in the last few years, have tried to imitate the EU both in liberalisation and in protectionism. Third, it may aggravate subregional trade conflicts, if CEFTA farmers try to find alternative outlets for their produce in other countries within the region. Taking into account the sizeable difference between the absorption capacity of the EU markets and that of the CEFTA, it is easily understandable why the subregional market cannot become a viable alternative to selling in Western Europe.

Another bottleneck exists in the sequencing of trade liberalisation. Since the CEFTA countries first signed a generous free trade agreement with the EU (except for agriculture), they have opened up their domestic markets to a much more powerful partner, both concerning the volume of trade with and the economic weight of the EU. Subregional liberalisation was a consequence of liberalisation vis-à-vis the EU, and, to some extent, a damage limitation effort to stop further diversion of trade flows. However, just at the time of catching up with standards applied in the agreements with Brussels, the first negative consequences of an early and too hasty opening up started to become manifest. Domestic lobbies in all Central European countries became aware of the not always positive impact of international competition, and wanted to protect at least the remaining part of their "traditional" markets. The timing of the subregional trade liberalisation overlapped with the first wave of perceiving the loss of markets by influential domestic lobbies. As a result, their attack was directed towards freer subregional trade, even if the latter amounted to but a fraction (about one-tenth) of trade with the EU. Two factors have underlined this behaviour. On the one hand, domestic players have recognised that it was easier to exert efficient pressure on trade policies towards subregional neighbours possessing a similarly modest bargaining and retaliating power, than against a trade giant, on which the lion's share of foreign trade, and also prospects for growth and restructuring, crucially depend. On the other hand, subregional trade liberalisation affected similar production and export patterns, with a high degree of competitive features and a low level of complementary features. During the critical years of economic transformation, this structurally determined competition was considered particularly harmful to the countries of the subregion.[22]

Paradoxically, while the rapid expansion of trade relations with the EU has offered survival and even development chances to a number of economic activities in the CEFTA countries, the rapidly growing market share of the EU has contributed to the decline of subregional trade.

First, more powerful and financially better prepared EU exporters were able to crowd traditional subregional suppliers out of the market.[23]

Second, the conquering by Western firms of important sectors of the national production and consumption markets has destroyed a substantial part of production and export capacities established for the subregional market. In more than one case, national economic policies have supported or at least silently allowed this process.

Third, new trade links with the EU, favoured by the Association Agreement, have not only diverted part of the potential subregional trade but have eliminated the structural linkages as well. The story of subcontracting in the textile-clothing sector is the most obvious case in point.[24]

Fourth, due to the economic recession in the EU in 1993, EU firms strove to increase their market share in CEECs. Financially weak enterprises of the transforming countries were, in their majority, not able to resist the competition of Western firms, and lost market shares in domestic markets as well as in other markets of the subregion.

Fifth, and in some market sections most importantly, the aggressive subsidisation of EU agricultural exports to Central and Eastern Europe has deprived the transforming countries of their traditional markets, with long-lasting economic, social and even political consequences for the respective national economies.

Hopefully, a growing deficit with the EU will not become a barrier to the development of subregional trade. In historical perspective, the growth of subregional trade used to be interrelated with the general trade balance position of the given country. Extraregional deficits were tolerated as long as adequate subregional surpluses could be generated. In turn, substantial subregional deficits were accepted as long as they could be financed by extraregional trade surpluses. The twin deficit, however, quickly led to trade balance constraints, the first "victim" of which used to be the less important, weak and underdeveloped subregional partner. At present, the high level of foreign exchange reserves in all CEFTA countries as well as the declared convertibility of the national currencies provide a guarantee against such an adverse development. However, it cannot be excluded that the continuing trend of substantial deficits in trade (and current account) with the EU may seriously impair the prospects of subregional commodity flows.

Finally, as a result of heavy trade reliance (dependence) on the EU, countries forming a subregion cannot get rid of "disintegrative" impacts deriving from various steps of the policy-maker EU. One factor may consist in the different economic orientation of the member countries of a subregional group in case of EU enlargement. Obviously, this does not apply to the CEFTA, for all countries are primarily linked to Germany. However, this is not an irrelevant factor of "disintegration" in the Baltics, where Estonia is much more oriented towards Finland and Sweden than the other two Baltic states. Consequently, the EU's latest enlargement has produced rather different impacts on co-operation within the Baltic subregion (Kala-Rajasalu, 1996).

Also, and maybe surprisingly, association agreements may not only strengthen but also undermine subregional co-operation. There are two patterns of such developments. One is initiated by one country of the subregion, and used to be driven by specific economic interests. Estonia's symmetrical free trade agreement with the EU strongly differs from the temporarily asymmetrical pattern applied for the two other Baltic countries (or to the CEFTA countries). The other is generated by the EU, since association agreements with practically the same content were signed by all transforming countries, which have rather different levels of economic development. As countries of the same region are expected to comply with similar trade policy requirements and according to the same timetable, their different "adjustment capacities" may deepen subregional differences. The ambiguous role of the Association Agreements consists exactly in their nature of strengthening and disrupting subregional trade at the same time.

2. This ambiguous impact is particularly manifest in the general economic policy adjustment of the associated countries. Uncritical propagation and implementation of pure principles of market economy (textbook economics) have already destroyed part of the production and export structures that would have been capable of intensive regional co-operation. Moreover, a too speedy adjustment to EU rules (*acquis communautaire*), and an unhealthy competition among the CEFTA countries to fulfil the adjustment criteria, without taking account of the economic realities of the individual countries, has already given way to short-sighted national efforts, with a detrimental impact on subregional co-operation.[25] Certainly, each Central European country has to be interested in a rapid and efficient adjustment to the EU rules. At the same time, however, the regional implications of this adjustment also have to be considered, because the disruption of the regional framework may produce a level of instability which can hardly be compensated by better short-term adjustment only.

3. Unfortunately, until now subregional co-operation has not been supported by large European infrastructure projects. The former West-East infrastructure pattern, linking the agricultural and manufacturing production potential of the Central European countries with the energy and raw material production potential of the ex-Soviet Union was replaced by East-West corridors between the EU and the transforming countries. As the Soviet-dominated CMEA did not create meaningful economic co-operation among the Central European countries (except for intra-industry trade satisfying the demand of the Soviet market), the present pattern also blocks the establishment of a genuine infrastructural background for more subregional trade. The latter would require the rapid development of North-South railway, highway and telecommunication links. Unfortunately, the countries involved are unable to finance such projects (even if they recognised the importance of such links, which is far from certain for each of them). The PHARE programme has not been scheduled for such purposes, and the Trans European Network programme of the EU practically forgets about the region.

4. Until most recently, transborder programmes were financed within INTERREG, a very important policy instrument applicable, however, to the border regions of an EU and a non-EU country exclusively. The historical economic development gap within Europe has a clear West-East pattern, with Western regions more developed than Eastern regions in the Central European transforming

countries. In addition, INTERREG programmes include the Western regions of the transforming countries, as direct neighbours on the Eastern external border of the EU. Consequently, this kind of programme, in the absence of compensating projects, may even further exacerbate the differences within the subregion. In most cases, substantial differences in development levels are more hindering than supporting subregional co-operation.[26]

5. Impact on the European Union of subregional co-operation[27]

In comparison with the influence of the European Union on different aspects of (sub)regional co-operation, the latter's impact is essentially weaker. Most importantly, this results from the overwhelmingly policy-taker status of the transforming countries. The CEFTA's impact on the EU cannot even be compared with some smaller and less influential members of the EU, because the Central European emerging market economies are still outside the integration framework, and cannot efficiently influence developments in various areas which are crucial for their longer-term perspectives (starting with the institutional reforms to be discussed during the IGC, through the CAP and the future of the financial transfers). In addition, their development level and the special problems of transformation offer them a rather weak bargaining position. Also, one should not ignore the low level of regional co-operation which also contributes to the insufficient implementation of joint regional interests.

Despite these barriers, CEFTA has been continuously influencing the decision-making process within the EU. Most of this impact cannot be measured in “headline” changes in the EU's general attitude and policies. Nevertheless, they have already been contributing to shifts in emphasis and priorities. This process will certainly be strengthened in the coming years.

In a direct way, during 1992, Central European countries could efficiently press Brussels to formulate clear criteria for membership, after the signing of the Association Agreements, without any clear commitment by the EU to future accession. This endeavour led to the formulation of the Copenhagen criteria and acknowledgement by Brussels that Eastern enlargement **could** take place, once specific criteria are fulfilled. For the future, the bold trade policy agreements concerning the rapid dismantling of still valid tariffs and quotas on intraregional trade in agricultural products have to be mentioned. Although the virtual level of protection and competitiveness of the CEFTA countries cannot be compared with those of the EU members, the former have initiated a free trade in agricultural commodities as well, a step which is not foreseen in the Association Agreements. It is hoped that the earlier implementation of free trade within Central Europe, in general, and the liberalisation of agricultural trade, in particular, will be able to affect the future of the Common Agricultural Policy and lead to free access by the transforming countries to the agricultural markets of the EU.

Additional direct impacts can be expected from more co-ordinated national pre-accession strategies and constantly harmonised negotiations on accession after the starting of official talks on membership conditions. The enforcement of regional interests within the EU has been a thorny and sometimes costly learning process during past enlargements as well. It is a justified expectation that, in crucial stages of negotiations, the CEFTA countries will be able to co-ordinate their priorities and not permit any undermining of their already weak bargaining position. In a more positive way, they have to draw lessons from the latest enlargement and the innovative ideas of the Nordic countries and Austria on how to protect special interests, outside the earlier pattern of the *acquis communautaire*. (In this context, the acceptance by Brussels of the support to be provided to Arctic agriculture can be stressed.)

Much more diversified are the indirect impacts. While most of them can already be felt, their real intensity will only be perceived after the first wave of Eastern enlargement.

First, Eastern enlargement, not for the first time, will shift the pattern of European unification towards a "developmental integration". Following most of the previous enlargements (with the exception of the last one by three EFTA countries, and the partial exception of the first enlargement), the accession of the CEFTA countries requires several specific methods and a new distribution of resources which could truly emphasize the "developmental" (modernisation) tasks of the EU.

Second, as any previous enlargement, the inclusion of the CEFTA countries will necessarily change the internal balance of power of the Union. This has always been the case during different accessions. However, the Eastern enlargement is expected to take place in a changed European framework and at a time when the old (Western) European ***status quo*** has been seriously questioned, with or without further enlargement.

Third, irrespective of the resolutions to be taken by the IGC, the CEFTA countries will exert a significant impact on the institutional, decision-making and voting procedures of the EU. The unequivocal strengthening of an alliance of small countries would, however, be an overhasty and superficial judgement, for neither are all potential members small (Poland), nor can it be predicted that each of the small newcomers will necessarily take the same position in all major issues for decision.

Fourth, the forthcoming Eastern enlargement will substantially enrich the EU with elements of an extended external network towards the East and the South East of Europe.

Fifth, the impact of the CEFTA countries on the global competitiveness of Western Europe has to be underlined. On the micro-level, this impact has already been fully recognised. Changed or changing attitudes of multinational and small- and medium-sized companies, increasing foreign direct investments in the region and rapid shifts in the commodity pattern of exports (and imports) reveal the recognition of cost advantages of Central and Eastern European production locations.

Sixth, it is less known that the Central European region, the most promising candidate for the first wave of EU enlargement, can easily become (and partially it **is** already) the new growth centre of an enlarged EU. This centre could cover a new subregional integration area, spreading from Slovenia over Central Europe up to the Baltics, and could provide the continent with substantial growth impulses.

Seventh, CEFTA countries will not only contribute to the geographic, historical, ethnic and linguistic diversity of a unified Europe. More importantly, they will bring into the integration substantial socio-political flexibility, keener competition and a well-developed and innovative human resources, a key element of the 21st century's global competition.

Finally, regional co-operation leading to integration into EU is likely to break the "bloc mentality" that is still observable from time to time in some circles in Western Europe. Breaking such a mentality is a precondition for the longer term economic and political unification of the continent.

6. Concluding remarks and some thoughts on the future

Experience of the last few years shows that subregional co-operation and integration into EU structures are increasingly interrelated. However, this interrelation is not a balanced one. Although more intensive subregional co-operation can exert some influence on the EU, the latter's impact on the subregion is much stronger. This imbalance originates both from the policy-maker status of the EU, its historically shaped higher level of socio-economic development and the medium-term disintegrative effects of the transformation process in the policy-taker countries.

Therefore, the prospects for subregional co-operation are essentially influenced by the opportunity of accession to the economic growth pole and modernisation anchor of the Central European countries, which is the EU. Very much in conformity with international experience, it is the Eastern enlargement of the EU which would create the adequate framework for a spectacular intensification of subregional economic contacts. The positive impact of membership on growth, structural development, legal, economic and political security and international direct investment is expected to make subregional trade grow much more dynamically than trade with the present EU member countries. Joint infrastructural projects, transborder developments, further harmonisation of economic policies and not least, the perception of joint interests within a large integration are likely to support this trend during a prolonged period of time. As a result, the share of intraregional trade may reach 10 to 15 per cent of the total trade of the respective countries (with a further relative decrease of the Czech-Slovak trade, fully compensated for by a strong increase in most other bilateral relations). Even more importantly, the structure of subregional trade will undergo substantial changes and develop an intra-industry pattern, characteristic of the trade between and among developed EU member countries.

Prior to membership, however, subregional co-operation is likely to maintain its mostly defensive nature. All countries of the subregion will remain primarily interested in satisfying EU requirements, making the necessary adjustment to EU rules and achieving EU membership as soon as possible. Subregional co-operation will remain subordinated to the clear priority of accession to the EU. A more active attitude can only be expected if serious economic and/or political interests of the region were at stake. Even in such a situation, joint positions would be likely to be shaped on a temporary basis and aim at damage limitation.

Despite this fundamental character of subregional relations, a lot can be done during the pre-accession period to achieve more intensive co-operation. Regular consultations between decision-makers is already the general practice. Although each of the candidate countries will negotiate the terms of its accession to the EU separately, there is plenty of room for shaping common positions and for organising joint activities transmitting a regional image. In addition, developments within the EU, both during the IGC and regarding the EMU and other issues, have to be followed carefully and analysed jointly. Certainly, the possibility to influence EU developments from the outside remains rather limited. However, in some vital areas, where current EU decisions may seriously threaten the position of future members, joint attitudes should be considered with more emphasis than to date. Finally, the planning of a modern regional infrastructure based on regional (and not on narrow-minded national) priorities has to be started and organically connected to other major trans-European projects.

Strategic planning must not forget about those candidate countries which may not become members of the EU during the first Eastern enlargement. Taking into account the extreme political sensitivity of this issue, but also the already given intraregional economic links, the Eastern enlargement strategy of the EU has to follow a very clear timetable which has to be announced before the first wave of Eastern enlargement takes place. Such a prospective design would not only foster the reliability of Brussels and its commitment to completing the unification of Europe. Maybe even more importantly, it will further develop subregional co-operation and let the newcomers benefit from their geographically and economically transit position and not to convert them into the Eastern-most fortresses of a closed Europe. Appropriate financial transfers, direct investments and harmonisation programmes have to support the implementation of this "grand design".

Notes

[1] Bulgaria, the Czech Republic, Estonia, Hungary, Latvia, Lithuania, Poland, Romania, Slovakia and Slovenia.

[2] The term post-Berlin is used here to indicate the new security, political and economic realities on the European continent after the fall of the Berlin wall.

[3] In 1989, the EU's share accounted for about one-third of Polish and about one-fourth of Hungarian and Czechoslovak total trade. In Romania's trade turnover the EU reached about 15 per cent and it remained below 10 per cent in the case of Bulgaria. In 1994, the EU represented 60 per cent of Poland's external trade, a slightly lower share for Slovenia, nearly 50 per cent for Hungary and the Czech Republic, a bit less for Romania and about 30 to 33 per cent for Slovakia and Bulgaria. (See: WIIW Database and national statistics.) Even more important are the differences in the commodity structure of exports to the EU. In 1994, one-third of Slovenia's exports to the EU consisted of machinery and transport equipment (SITC), followed by Hungary (29 per cent) and the Czech Republic (26 per cent). In contrast, this commodity group represented less than 17 per cent of Polish exports to the EU, and remained about or below 10 per cent in the case of the transforming countries of the Balkans. (See: Eurostat, External Trade Monthly Bulletin, no. 7. 1995).

[4] Here, and in formulating some concluding remarks, the author has substantially relied on the main preliminary findings of an international project financed by ACE and entitled "Correlations Between Subregional Cooperation and European Integration" (ACE 94-0642-R). This project, directed by the author, compares correlations in four different subregions (Benelux, Iberian peninsula, CEFTA and Baltics) and has been supported by valuable contributions from Belgian, Estonian and Portuguese experts. The final report is expected to be finished by the end of June 1996.

[5] This feature became particularly clear during the Western European recession of 1993, where some Central and Eastern European markets helped to reduce the volume of macroeconomic decline and saved a number of microeconomic actors in various EU countries from serious problems.

[6] Between 1989 and 1994, CEFTA's share in total EU extraregional imports grew from 2.1 to 4.5 per cent. The corresponding figures were 0.9 and 2.7 per cent in machinery (SITC 7) and 2.8 and 6.0 per

cent in other manufactured articles (SITC 6+8). The changes are even more relevant in the main export markets of the transforming countries, Germany and Austria. For a detailed analysis see Inotai (1995).

[7] The development of economic relations between Spain and Portugal supports our argument from global ("anchor") to (sub)regional integration. Prior to these countries' accession to the European Community, they had a "back-to-back" pattern of bilateral relations. The situation dramatically changed after membership, so that today Spain is the main trading partner of Portugal and the second most important foreign investor in this country. (For more details see Lorca and Graca Moura, 1996.)

[8] The adverse psychological impact of CMEA times is still present in most countries. Often, products coming from the region can hardly get rid of bad "labels", even if they are, as it is increasingly the case, competitive with similar Western goods (either in quality or in price, or in both). In turn, particularly in the first years of transformation, there was a highly uncritical attitude towards Western goods and services (everything coming from the West was considered more developed, higher-quality and generally better than domestic regional products and services). Interestingly, this behaviour did not characterise the higher-income consumers only, but was at times even more characteristic of the lower-income consumers insisting on keeping pace with others (strong status symbol and demonstration effects).

[9] In 1995, the Czech Republic accounted for 42.6 per cent of intraregional exports, followed by the Slovak Republic (36.5 per cent). In turn, Poland's (12.9 per cent) and Hungary's (8 per cent) combined share was just over 20 per cent. A similar pattern prevails in imports (38.2 per cent for the Czech Republic, 34.7 per cent for Slovakia, 16.8 per cent for Poland and 10.3 per cent for Hungary).

[10] A much more detailed analysis based on selected commodities (or commodity groups) would be needed to evaluate the exact nature and impact of this "crowding out" process.

[11] Here, also the impact of the enlargement of the EU by three EFTA countries has to be considered.

[12] This structural correspondence can partly be explained by the fact that the EU is the most important export market for all countries.

[13] Mainly due to the "externalisation" of Czech-Slovak commodity flows.

[14] In 1994, intra-industry trade in machinery products between Hungary and Poland amounted to 32 per cent, while this index reached slightly more than 50 per cent both in Hungary's and Poland's trade with the EU. Similar, although less pronounced, deviations characterise the pattern of Czech trade in machinery products. Slovak figures only indicate a higher intra-industry trade of the machinery sector on the subregional level than in the country's trade with the EU (Plucinski, 1996).

[15] It has to be taken into account that higher shares do not necessarily mean higher volume, because there was a substantial decline in trade volumes in the early 1990s.

[16] There is some Czech investment in Slovakia and *vice versa*, still as a consequence of the split of Czechoslovakia. Also, a low volume of Hungarian investments can be registered in Slovakia.

[17] The split of Czechoslovakia led to the renegotiation of the Association Agreement but did not virtually change the trade policy framework stipulated in the agreement still signed with Czechoslovakia.

[18] For an enlightening experience see the impact of OEEC and the Marshall Plan on Benelux co-operation before the Treaty of Rome (Van den Bempt, 1996). Also, regional infrastructural projects financed mainly by EU transfers have substantially improved trade and economic relations between Spain and Portugal, but, only after accession.

[19] The most recent financing of the modernisation of border stations between Hungary and Romania, or the rebuilding of the Danube bridge between Hungary and Slovakia are encouraging new developments, but still more an exception than the rule.

[20] It is not part of this paper to deal with the historically adverse effects on East-West trade of the European Communities trade policy in general and the common agricultural policy in particular. Nevertheless, it has to be noted, that from the first half of the seventies, this policy had been substantially fostering the reliance of small Central (and Eastern) European countries on the Soviet market, instead of supporting stronger or weaker efforts to diversify previously one-sided economic relations.

[21] Recently, the latter problem has been solved by the virtual implementation of convertibility in the member countries.

[22] This is nothing new. Even a moderate recession in the EU, consisting of economically much more developed countries, produces the same trade policy answers. In the case of less developed countries plagued with a much more substantial decline and burdened with the uniquely high costs of transformation, short-term economic policy considerations and measures, strongly influenced by politics, do not follow the reasoning of "pure economics".

[23] Here, we do not refer to those Western exports which have replaced non-competitive and low-quality products mutually delivered according to government-level ex-CMEA-agreements. Reference is made to that part of subregional trade which, in comparable conditions, could have easily resisted the export pressure coming from the EU.

[24] While all associated countries were able to substantially increase their clothing exports to the EU, because subcontracting was excluded from the group of "sensitive items", all of them became large net importers of textiles. As a result, the textile industry has practically disappeared, leaving the clothing industry a "reversed footloose" sector.

[25] Obviously, also the very different impacts on the domestic economy and society, a topic outside the area of this paper, have to be analysed.

[26] An exception to this rule is the situation if border regions represent virtual or potential regional growth poles (e.g. the Vienna-Bratislava-Gyor triangle involving Eastern Austria, Western Slovakia and North-western Hungary).

[27] Of course, the European Union can be influenced not only by regional groupings, but also by selected countries of a given region, or by a region as such, without meaningful co-operation.

References

Inotai, A., 1991, *Regional Integration among Developing Countries, Revisited,* The World Bank, Washington, April (WPS 643).

Inotai, A., 1995, "From Association Agreements To Full Membership? The Dynamics of Relations Between the Central and Eastern European Countries and the European Union", Institute for World Economics, *Working Paper No. 52,* Budapest.

Kala, A. and Teet R., 1996, "Correlations Between European Integration and Subregional Cooperation in Baltic States". Background Report from Estonia to the *ACE Project No. 94-0642-R.* Tallinn, February (manuscript).

Lorca, A. and Diego Graca., M., 1996, "Economic Relations Between Spain and Portugal: The Consequences of EEC Membership". Unpublished manuscript prepared within the ACE project no. 94-0642-R on "Correlations Between European Integration and Subregional Cooperation".

Plucinski, E., 1996, "Zur Entwicklung des inter- und intraindustriellen Handels der Visegrad-Staaten." World Economy Research Institute, *Working Papers 151,* Warsaw, May.

Van den Bempt, P., 1996, *Subregional Cooperation in Europe. The Benelux Experience.* Report prepared within the ACE project no. 94-0642-R on "Correlations Between European Integration and Subregional Cooperation" (manuscript).

5

Foreign direct investment in Eastern Europe and the former Soviet Union: results from a survey of investors

Hans-Peter Lankes and A.J. Venables

Synopsis of the survey and some conjectures

Introduction

Since the onset of economic transition there have been widespread expectations that foreign direct investment (FDI) would contribute significantly to this process. Transition involves institutional change and a learning process and, at its best, FDI can support these by transferring technologies, managerial and labour skills, marketing channels and a market-based business culture. In addition, it was often felt that substantial amounts of FDI were needed to supplement domestic savings in a quest to "catch up" with living standards in the West.[1] Given the region's closeness to major centres of economic gravity, cost advantages in production, market size and potential growth, the conditions appeared to be there for investment supply to respond to this challenge.

A few years into the transition, it is fair to say that FDI has not lived up to these expectations. However, this judgement needs to be qualified. First, 1995 may have been a turning point, with cumulative flows increasing by more than one-third from US$18 billion to US$29 billion. And second, while FDI may have under-performed in the aggregate, a handful of transition economies in Central Europe and the Baltic states did manage to attract inflows that are remarkable both in relation to their size and in international comparison.[2]

Assuming that FDI could, indeed, contribute as expected to the process of transition it is important to understand what drives the investment decisions. The explanation and prediction of investment in general, and FDI in particular, is not one of the strengths of the economics profession. Nevertheless, the accumulated evidence, especially from developing countries, has led to some understanding of the elements in the economic environment that are propitious to FDI and those that

This project is part of the research programme of the EBRD. Most of the interviews for the survey were conducted by IFO Institut für Wirtschaftsforschung, Munich. Thanks go to Donata Hoesch and Mark Schankerman for comments on the survey document.

deter it. But, are there features specific to the transition process that deserve attention and that could help explain the time pattern of investments, their form and their geographical distribution?

Beyond aggregate data, there is little reliable statistical information that could be used to address these questions. There have been a variety of survey-based studies of foreign direct investment in the transition economies.[3] However, most studies have been concerned with individual countries or a subset of the countries of the region and have been too small to allow generalisation or have had a narrowly circumscribed focus. Issues of risk and finance, particularly important where financial markets themselves are in transition, are rarely addressed. Most importantly, perhaps, in view of the questions formulated above, there appear to be no studies that relate results directly to indicators of economic transition.

The study that is presented here in synopsis attempts to fill some of these gaps while also providing an updated profile of foreign investments and investor motives and perceptions. Actual and potential FDI destinations in the survey covered all transition economies of Central and Eastern Europe and the former Soviet Union (CEE/FSU), sharpening the role of the level of transition as a discriminating variable. To better assess the geographical and time pattern of investment, the survey instrument supplemented questions referring to general locational characteristics with others focused on investor strategies. Of particular importance in this regard were the position of projects within the multinational investors' production networks, conditions for external trade, linkages between foreign investments (e.g. herding phenomena) and issues of control. Finally, detailed questions related to country and commercial risk perceptions of investors, and the willingness and ability to take on such risks and mitigate them through the structure of investment finance.

After a brief description of the survey, key results are summarised. The synopsis concludes with some conjectures on the future pattern of FDI in the transition economies which are compatible with these results.

Description of the survey

A total of 11 000 firms world-wide were contacted in January 1995. Of these 1 435 responded, of which 628 indicated they were willing to be interviewed at senior executive level. Executives from 117 of these firms with 145 investments in Eastern Europe and the former Soviet Union were interviewed between June and November 1995. To qualify for the survey, the company needed to have an operational, planned, postponed or abandoned project in the mining or manufacturing sectors of an EBRD country of operations; in addition, its headquarters had to be in Western Europe.

The 145 surveyed investments cover 16 EBRD countries of operations, employ 39 000 workers and have a total foreign equity contribution of US$2.8 billion. Table 1 provides further information on the sample.

Table 1. Summary description of investment projects in the survey.

Status		Function		Control mode	
Planned	38	Distribution and services	24	License/ sub-contract	16
Operating	91	Supply of regional or local markets	72	Joint venture	72
Postponed/ abandoned	16	Exports from the region	44	Wholly owned by foreign parent	53
Total	**145**		**140**		**141**

Industry		Country (Group)	
Primary	39	Czech Rep. and Hungary (Group I)	44
Heavy manu-facturing	34	Poland and other eastern Europe (Group II)	57
Engineering and related industries	50	Russia and other CIS (Group III)	44
Light manufacturing	22		
Total	**145**		**145**

Key results

1. *Project function* is fundamental to an assessment of investor decisions.

- The decision to invest in CEE/FSU involved the relocation of production from or investment foregone in the West in 7 per cent of cases for distribution investments, 20 per cent of cases for market investments, and in 71 per cent of cases for export investments.[4]
- Controlling for transition level, chances of an export project being abandoned are three times higher than for a market-oriented investment.
- Export investors stress the importance of production cost reduction in general and availability of cheap skilled labour in particular — this is the single most important motivating factor in their investment decision.
- Salaries of skilled workers in export investments[5] are at 16 per cent of their Western (parent company) level, while productivity is reported to be, on average, 72 per cent of the Western level. Since other, unspecified cost factors are less advantageous, overall unit costs of exporters represent 67 per cent of those in Western Europe.
- Compared with cost factors and market access, the opportunities offered specifically by the process of economic transition in Eastern Europe ("one-off

opportunities") are judged to be of only moderate importance by distributors and market investors, and negligible by export investors.[6]

- However, judged on its own, first-mover advantage (FMA) is classified as an important investment motive by distributors and market investors.[7] Responses have a bimodal distribution, with FMA viewed as either very important or not important at all. Two-thirds of market investors considered FMA to be "very important", one-third not important at all; for export investors the pattern is almost exactly the opposite.

- The low-cost acquisition of assets is not generally a significant motivation for investors, even controlling for countries' privatisation strategy. Those who did find it important were in their vast majority aiming to supply the local and regional markets.

- "Proximity" considerations, particularly the "ease of contact with customers", score highest by far in explaining why investment rather than export was chosen to supply a market in CEE or FSU. As was to be expected, for heavy industry projects transport costs are also relevant.

2. A project's *position within the production chain* of its multinational parent corporation differs by project function.

- Export investments are somewhat more "upstream" within the multinationals' production chain and sell almost half of their product within the corporation (i.e. to the parent company or other subsidiaries), while for market investors the share is only 3 per cent.

- In both cases input supply is roughly one-third from within the corporation (imports).

- There is no clear tendency for the vertical position of the projects relative to the corporations' other activities to change over the medium-term future.

3. *Locational choice* is driven by a combination of motivating and deterring factors. Significant explanatory power for the nature, number, size and success of projects is vested with measures of a country's progress in market-oriented transition.

- Using information from the large initial sample of 1 435 firms and controlling for population size, the number of investment projects in a country is highly sensitive to its transition indicator.[8]

- In the interview sample, controlling for various other host country characteristics including income and size, a one point increase in the transition indicator raises the probability that investments are of the export type relative to the market type by 224 per cent.

- A country's level of transition relates not only to the incidence of projects by function, but also to the likelihood of success. One point "up" in the transition indicator of a country is associated with an 80 per cent fall in the chance of a project being eventually abandoned/postponed.

Table 2. Investor motivation by country group (1 unimportant, 5 very important)

Country Group (see Table 1); number of respondents in brackets	I (26)	II (39)	III (23)
Natural resources	1.69	1.56	**2.69**
Unskilled labour costs	2.50	2.13	2.13
Skilled labour costs	3.23	2.53	**2.50**
Energy costs	2.00	1.56	1.77
Infrastructure:— telecoms	2.15	1.59	1.35
Infrastructure:— transport	2.42	2.15	2.09
Local market size	2.73	**4.05**	**3.75**
Access to other CEE/FSU markets	2.57	**2.59**	**2.63**
Access to EU/EFTA markets	1.77	1.79	1.18
Presence of other foreign owned/ controlled firms	2.04	2.08	1.43
Opportunities from privatisation programme	2.46	2.20	1.87
Political stability	**4.00**	**2.95**	1.83
Stability of macroeconomic policy	**3.77**	**2.74**	1.48
Regulatory environment	**3.39**	2.36	1.65
Cultural closeness	2.54	2.10	1.56
Geographical closeness	**3.33**	**2.59**	2.12
Tax/investment incentives	2.00	1.79	1.65
Effectiveness of local financial sector	1.42	1.59	1.22

- Table 2 presents "straightforward" scores for a list of motivating factors by group of countries. To gain a sense of the significance of different factors in determining the choice of location a multinomial logit model was estimated, yielding the effect of projects' scores on each factor on the relative probabilities of locating in II versus I, III versus I and III versus II. Among the statistically significant results:
    - Investors for whom political, macroeconomic or regulatory stability is of great concern tend to locate in Group I (Czech Rep., Hungary) and Group II (Poland and other Central and Eastern European) rather than Group III countries (CIS).
    - Projects which attach importance to skilled labour are relatively concentrated in Group I countries.
    - Projects which attach importance to unskilled labour and natural resources are relatively concentrated in Group III countries.
    - Local market-oriented investors are relatively attracted to Group II and Group III countries.[9]

- Among other factors that have been suggested, geographical closeness is associated with the decision to invest in Group I and Group II countries, while cultural affinity, fiscal issues, the local financial system, and local infrastructure appear to be of minor importance to locational choice for investors in any of the groups.[10]

- Unit cost savings are highest in country Group II (35 per cent), then Group I (26 per cent), and least in Group III countries (22 per cent). The differences are primarily due to differences in labour productivity.

4. The choice of *control mode* appears to be strongly influenced by considerations of country risk.

- 60 per cent of the manufacturing firms in the sample had considered a control mode other than that chosen. Joint ventures were more likely to be chosen by firms which value access to local knowledge, markets and officials and less likely to be chosen by firms concerned with maintaining control over sales strategies, production quality and intellectual property rights.
- The proportion of joint ventures (rather than full ownership) rises from 35 per cent (Group I countries) to 55 per cent (Group II) to 62 per cent (Group III).
- A one point rise in the transition indicator raises the probability of "wholly-owned" versus "joint venture" by 486 per cent, i.e. almost five-fold, holding other factors constant. This relationship is also statistically very powerful.
- Perhaps explaining this, respondents viewed "joint venture" as an effective risk-mitigation device, and ranked it highest on the "availability" scale (compared to, e.g. political risk insurance and IFI co-investment).
- But forming a joint venture is also the "least preferred" of six risk mitigation options.
- Wholly-owned projects sell one-third of output within the foreign parent corporation, while the share is only 8 per cent for joint ventures. For inputs, shares are more similar (41 per cent and 30 per cent).

5. There is some evidence of *"herding"*:

- The presence of other foreign investors in the same country was a factor in encouraging country choice among a significant number of respondents. Where there were similar investments by competitors in the same country, 20 out of 38 respondents indicated that this encouraged their investment decision.
- The increased confidence in an investment location that derives from the presence of other foreign investors (not only competitors) appears to be relatively higher for market investors and for investors in the CIS.

6. The *tax regime and tax incentives* are of little importance to the investment decision.

- The stability of the tax regime is regarded as at least as important as overall tax rates — both, however, score quite low for investors in all country groups.
- FDI incentives available to all investors, although scoring very low on average, are moderately important to a subset of investors. The same is true for special tax and incentive arrangements negotiated specifically for a project.

7. Barriers erected by *trade policy* are a significant impediment for foreign investors in country Groups II and III.

- Very few investors in the Czech Republic and Hungary report barriers of significance to the procurement of imported inputs; in countries of Group II (particularly in Poland) and Group III, almost half of respondents report a problem.
- In Group II countries, tariffs on imports from the EU are viewed as the most important barrier (38 per cent of respondents), while in Group III countries, tariffs are less of an obstacle but foreign exchange controls are viewed as significant (30 per cent of respondents).
- Barriers affecting exports are a negligible problem for Group I investors, but are a significant impediment for one-quarter of Group II and one-third of Group III investors.
- For projects in Group II the only export barriers reported with any frequency are import tariffs imposed by other transition economies, while for projects in Group III there are considerable intra-FSU trade frictions (taking the form both of import barriers and other controls in the FSU country of sale, and export barriers and foreign exchange controls in the host country).
- 12 per cent of export investors in Group III countries perceive non-tariff barriers to be a significant obstacle on EU/EEA markets.

Figure 1. Rankings of the EBRD transition indicators (1995) and perceived country risk.

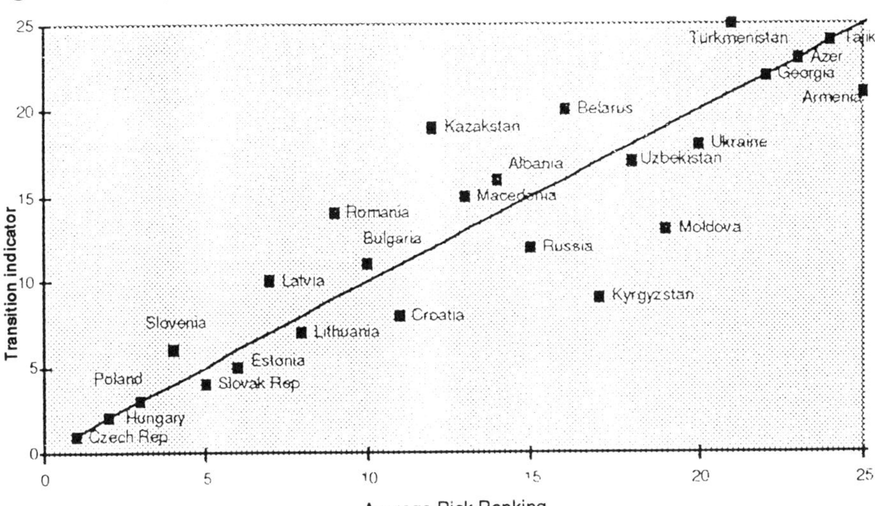

Source: EBRD.

8. *Country risk perceptions* among investors are sophisticated and closely correlated with countries' transition level. Country risk has created a backlog of potential investments.

- Countries fall into distinct groups characterised by significant step increases in country risk perception:[11] (1) Czech Republic and Hungary; (2) Poland, Slovenia and Slovakia; (3) the three Baltic states; (4) the countries of South-Eastern Europe; (5) the CIS countries except for countries at or under threat of war; (6) Georgia, Azerbaijan, Tajikistan, Armenia.

- The correlation between EBRD's average transition indicators in 1995 and perceived country risk is -0.85. The following figure plots country risk against transition indicator rankings.

- Respondents that already had an investment in a country rated its risk (substantially) better than those that did not. This is true for all countries except Bulgaria, which was rated riskier by actual investors than potential ones.

- Among different elements of country risk,[12] regulatory risk and macroeconomic risk stand out as most significant for investors in all risk groups, followed by transfer risk.

- Perceptions of commercial risk (market, production, procurement) are sensitive to increasing country risk, but deteriorate less than proportionally. "Market risk" perceptions are most sensitive.

- Three-quarters of respondents suggest they would invest anytime in the low-risk countries of the survey (depending on opportunities). This proportion falls rapidly with perceived risk rising, while the share of those who wait for risks to recede or to become easier to assess before they invest, rises from one-third in the countries perceived to be of medium risk to over half in the two top risk categories.

9. *Financing modes* are highly responsive to perceived country risk.

- Finance is generally viewed as a greater problem than the availability of good projects in all (four) country risk groups, but in particular at the low and the high risk end of the spectrum. At the same time, the share of those who can see neither good investment opportunities nor possibilities of financing them rises drastically, from none in the lowest to more than half in the highest risk group.

- The share of parent companies willing to provide full recourse to creditors only slightly exceeds one-third for investments in the lowest risk countries, and falls rapidly in the medium and higher risk categories. Still, in the medium-to-high risk category, which for most investors encompasses South-Eastern Europe and parts of the CIS, limited recourse would reportedly be offered by one in five potential investors.

- The share of investors unwilling to offer any recourse to the parent company rises from none in the low risk countries, to almost two-thirds in those of high perceived risk.
- Two-thirds of investors report that they apply a rate-of-return criterion to their investment decision; for three-quarters of these, the benchmark return varies with the level of perceived risk.
- The risk premium on the benchmark rate of return represents 5 per cent or less in countries of the lowest risk group for three-quarters of investors. For the same approximate share of respondents, in medium-risk countries the cut-off rate is 10 per cent or less, in medium-to-high risk countries 25 per cent or less and in high risk countries 45 per cent or less. For comparison, the same share of respondents apply a risk premium of 10 per cent or less to investments in Latin America, and 7.5 per cent or less to investments in South-East Asia.

Some conjectures

What drives the locational pattern of investments over time? Can we say anything about how the profile of investments has changed and will change in the future?

Ideally, we should have panel data to answer these questions. Also, sample size and composition do not allow for broad generalisations about the amount of investment that particular countries or the region as a whole should expect. Nevertheless, some conjectures appear to be supported by the evidence.

- *What drives locational choice (abstracting from characteristics of individual investments)?*

***Conjecture 1**: As transition progresses, investment flows into a country and into the region as a whole increase only mildly but flows accelerate substantially once there is a critical mass of investments.*

Locational choice is determined by (relative and absolute) opportunities and risk perceptions. Both are functions of progress in transition; the perception of good investment opportunities and the willingness to take on financial exposure fall drastically with rising risk; opportunities are constrained and risk is raised by insufficient depth of reforms.

Risk perceptions and investment opportunities are both not only functions of the transition level, but also of the presence of other investors. The evidence for this is in the asymmetry of risk perceptions between current investors and others and in the survey's results on herding. Thus FDI can be a positive function of itself, which explains sudden cumulative effects.

A note regarding FDI-supporting policies — risk mitigation alone, e.g. through insurance, may not be sufficient to trigger the investment decision. Given the relationship between "transition" (as opposed to "general level of development") and "opportunities", this is a problem specific to the transition economies.

- What drives the composition of investment over time, in a particular location, by function, control mode and industrial sector?

Conjecture 2: *The share of cost-motivated, export-oriented investments into any particular transition economy will increase over time, while that of market-oriented and natural resource investments will recede (this does not necessarily apply to aggregate FDI across all transition economies).*

The initial FDI flows into a transition economy, once risk recedes sufficiently, are dominated by investors whose opportunity cost of waiting is particularly high because one-off opportunities offered by the transition process are particularly relevant for them. This includes market-oriented investors for whom the first-mover advantage may be significant, as well as natural resource investors attracted by the opportunity to acquire strategic assets at a low cost.

Only when the transition process proceeds further do investors move in for whom cost competitiveness is a particular concern and thus timing is less crucial. Lower opportunity costs for these are demonstrated by the high incidence of relocations/foregoing of investments in other sites — i.e. these investments are not "married" to a location.

Note that one implication of this may be that the net trade balance effect of FDI for the host country will improve over time, since import ratios are similar for market and export investments but export ratios obviously differ (see the evidence on procurement/sales). It is at a more advanced stage of transition that the host economies will become more integrated into world-wide production networks.

Conjecture 3: *The share of fully-owned subsidiaries will rise relative to that of joint ventures as the transition proceeds.*

This derives directly from the evidence that shows JVs to be primarily a risk-mitigation device while at the same time they are, in fact, quite unpopular. Once risk recedes, particularly regulatory risk, new investments will therefore tend to be more of the fully-owned type and existing JV partners tend to be bought out.

Notes

[1] For an overview of such calculations of investment "needs", see EBRD Annual Economic Outlook 1993, section 4.3.

[2] See Table 3 in the Annex for FDI data; for comparison, note that the total FDI flow into the non-OECD area is estimated at US$90 billion in 1995, a third of which was accounted for by China (World Debt Tables, World Bank, 1996).

[3] The EBRD's *Transition Report 1994* provides an overview of these in chapter 9.

[4] "Distribution investment": investment in a sales base to promote exports from outside the region; "market investment": manufacturing investment with sales directed primarily at the local and regional (CEE or FSU) market; "export investment": manufacturing investment with sales directed primarily at the Western European or world market.

[5] Only for investments that are operational or at an advanced stage of planning; the data refer to averages of project-by-project information.

[6] These opportunities included low cost acquisitions in privatisation programmes, acquisition of brands, sites and other assets, and first-mover advantage over competitors.

[7] This may establish a systematic difference between FDI in transition economies and that in, say, developing countries.

[8] "Transition indicators", on a scale of 1 to 4, are taken from the EBRD's *Transition Report 1995* and represent averages of nine indicators of a country's progress in market-oriented reform.

[9] These are results from the estimation of a multinomial logit model, i.e. these results control for the influence of all other motivating/deterring factors (19 in total).

[10] ibid

[11] These results refer to the average perception of risk by country on a scale of 1-4 (based on comparator country groups outside the region) among all respondents who felt confident in making that assessment.

[12] The survey distinguished among the following types of country risk: transfer risk, expropriation risk, regulatory risk, risk of labour unrest, macroeconomic risk.

6

Comments

Peter Havlik

There are certainly sound economic reasons for early convertibility and rapid trade liberalisation and Cooper mentions some of them.

How can these theoretical arguments be supported by the empirical evidence? The fact that most transition countries have chosen this option does not in itself prove its validity, just as the different approach followed by Western Europe 50 years ago does not prove the opposite. Unfortunately, none of Cooper's 'performance' criteria provides us with any conclusive evidence for recommending either a slow or a rapid liberalisation. Apart from the problem of how to distinguish between quick and slow liberalisers (Cooper does not provide us with such a classification), Cooper cannot (and probably nobody can) find convincing evidence to recommend one approach or the other. Besides, even the slow reforming CEECs are much faster liberalisers than the Western European countries were after the second World War.

Judging on the basis of performance criteria, such as economic growth, length of recession, inflation, export performance, external competitiveness, capital flows, it seems that, neither the speed nor the extent of trade liberalisation really mattered. One should therefore consider other aspects of the recent performance of the transition economies. One of them is mentioned by Rosati, namely the 'price' (or costs) of adopted policies as measured by the impact of initial currency undervaluation. This aspect is also mentioned by Cooper as one of the reasons why Western Europe was reluctant to proceed faster towards trade liberalisation in the 1950s. Another aspect is related to the appropriateness of the exchange rate policies during the transition, an issue that was extensively discussed by Rosati.

The choice of the initial level of exchange rate, i.e. the degree of undervaluation at the beginning of the transition, affected inflation, exports, competitiveness, etc. Measured in terms of the Exchange Rate Deviation Index (ERDI — the ratio of the nominal exchange rate to the purchasing power parity, expressing both in terms of national currencies per US dollar), the initial undervaluation with respect to the US dollar is estimated in the following Table.[1]

Undervaluation and dollar wages in selected transition countries.

Country (liberalisation year)	Liberali-sation year ERDI	Liberali-sation year avg. annual wage (US$)	1995 ERDI	1995 avg. annual wage (US$)	US$ wage growth (%) from liberal. year to 1995
Russia(1992)	8.0	398	1.5	1,313	230
Ukraine (1992)	7.6	381	3.7	542	42
Bulgaria (1991)	4.5	728	3.2	1,272	75
Romania (1992)	4.2	991	2.9	1,680	70
Czech Republic (1991)	3.5	1,544	2.2	3,668	138
Slovak Republic (1991)	3.1	1,535	2.3	2,882	88
Poland (1990)	2.7	1,301	1.8	3,540	172
Hungary (1989)	2.2	2,146	1.5	3,871	80
Slovenia (1991)	1.4	7,326	1.2	11,340	55

Source: Own estimates based on European Comparison Programme (ECP), 1993; WIIW database.

Even if PPP cannot serve as a proper yardstick for determining the equilibrium exchange rate, it is still interesting to see how it compares with the initial exchange rate chosen by the transition economies. Several points in this respect are striking:

- Except for Slovenia, the initial ERDIs were much higher than in the less developed OECD economies (e.g. Turkey, Greece, Portugal) and, with a few notable exceptions (Slovenia, Hungary and Russia), they remain so even now;

- The initial ERDIs are directly correlated with the degree of "need for liberalisation": the higher the initial ERDI, the less liberalised was the economy at the outset of reforms; the lower the ERDI, the more competitive/liberalised was the economy initially and the higher the dollar wage could be;

- Despite large real appreciations afterwards, the current ERDI levels still indicate considerable undervaluation; this is required to maintain currency convertibility and a sustainable current account position in the b.o.p.;

- The excessive initial devaluations had a negative impact not only on prices (higher inflation) but, in the medium term, on trade and industrial restructuring as well. Extremely undervalued currencies lessened the pressure to improve export competitiveness, thereby slowing the necessary structural adjustments. Besides, these policies often gave rise to complaints about "Eastern wage dumping".

Thus, the questions to be asked should deal less with the speed of convertibility and trade liberalisation and more with their extent, the appropriateness of exchange rate policies and the costs of these policies, given the specific conditions of each transition economy. That many transition economies were perhaps too enthusiastic about trade and foreign exchange liberalisation has been confirmed by later policy corrections (e.g. tariff increases). Likewise, that the initial undervaluations were too large has been confirmed by huge real currency appreciations afterwards (see e.g. the Czech Republic and Russia).

As regards the comparison of the Western European experience of the 1950s with that of the CEECs in the 1990s, some questions should be raised. Why should the CEECs have behaved differently from Western European countries 50 years ago? Was their economic situation different? Was the general economic climate different? Or, did the political and economic doctrines differ in the two periods?

In the 1950s, there was a different climate of opinion in both economic theory and policy, a hyper-sensitivity to unemployment, different perceptions about the role of government in the economy, distaste for floating exchange rates, all aspects that are mentioned by Cooper. Moreover, the international trade regime was much less liberal than the current regime, and Europe was divided. In the 1990s, in addition to the changed international environment, there has been a desire for greater freedom after the collapse of communism, and greater acceptance of liberalisation. Moreover, the CEECs severed their post-second World War economic linkages with the "East" and have aimed at a rapid integration with the "West". No wonder that under these conditions they were more inclined to harmonise their trade and exchange rate regimes with those of the "West".

But there are no convincing economic arguments (and indeed, Cooper finds none) to support quick liberalisation and convertibility in the transition economies, if the associated costs are taken into account as well. After considering all these differences in the economic environment, the early introduction of convertibility in the CEECs was certainly not a mistake (in fact, there was no other option) but, with the benefit of hindsight, the initial extreme undervaluation and the extent of trade liberalisation appear to have been a problem.

Note

[1] The ERDI for Austria and Germany was about 0.8 (i.e. overvaluation) throughout the first half of the 1990s.

Daniel Gros

My comments will focus on the issues raised by the two contributions that deal with the exchange rate regime. The historically-orientated study by Cooper seems to show a certain sympathy for early convertibility. I would go further and say that early external trade liberalisation is a key element of a successful reform programme, and current account convertibility is one of its indispensable components. Cooper, on the other hand, does not emphasize enough that convertibility alone does not guarantee a liberal external trade regime. As Russia's experience in 1992 shows, *de facto* convertibility coupled with a peculiar trade regime involving heavy export taxes and high selective import subsidies can have disastrous results (see Gros and Steinherr, 1995). My own research on the causes of output decline and the subsequent recovery (see Brenton, Gros and Vandille, 1996) shows that the correlation of output recovery with an external liberalisation indicator is stronger than with domestic liberalisation indicators, such as privatisation.

Moreover, it can be argued that, among the FSU countries, those that were more advanced in external trade liberalisation had a better record in terms of some social indicators. Another piece of evidence is drawn from a sectoral analysis: the sectors which were more open to trade with OECD countries experienced a smaller output decline than the others.

Hence, my first point is that current account convertibility is part and parcel of an overall package of external trade liberalisation. After the second World War, most European countries were slow both in re-establishing free trade and in making their currencies convertible. In this respect, it should be noted that these European countries represented a large portion of the world economy (the EPU countries covered 70 per cent of world trade), while at present the transition countries account for only a very small part of world trade (less than 2 per cent).

The exchange rate regime is another component of the external trade regime. The choice of an exchange rate system has to take into account several considerations. A flexible exchange rate makes it easier to maintain convertibility and free trade, but it would not provide an anchor for domestic prices. Since the latter is particularly important at the outset of reforms, when price liberalisation leads to open inflation, the initial choice of a fixed exchange rate seems sensible.

As the reform process advances, the level of real exchange rate that maintains external equilibrium (at the given supply of external financing) varies considerably. Hence, it is appropriate to have some flexibility in the exchange rate regime. In principle, progress in reform should lead to a period of real appreciation because of large productivity gains. In reality, however, this effect might be overwhelmed by the impact of increased demand for investment goods, which, in my view, should not be financed through an accumulation of external debt.

A final point on the implications for CEECs of membership in the EU. This implies a commitment to EMU, since this is the final goal for EU countries. In this light, Rosati's optimal pattern of exchange rate policies should end with a fixed exchange regime. Would this be justified from the point of view of these economies? When would this regime be justified? These are the key issues that economists and policy-makers in central Europe should consider at the present time.

References

Gros, D. and Steinherr, A., 1995, *Winds of Change: Economic Transition in Central and Eastern Europe*, Longman, London.

Brenton, P., Gros, D and Vandille, G., 1996, "Output Decline and Recovery in the Transition Economies: Causes and Social Consequences", CEPS Working Document No.100, Brussels, March.

Eduard Hochreiter

The empirical evidence provided by Cooper helps us to evaluate whether the move to convertibility was a mistake or not. It may not be very robust, but on balance it is positive. In any event, four CEECs (Czech Republic, Slovakia, Hungary, Poland) have already formally accepted IMF Article VIII convertibility (i.e. current account convertibility) and, in addition, some of them have also taken measures towards achieving full convertibility.[1] I have long advocated an early move to formal Article VIII convertibility, not only for the reasons commonly given (to introduce a rational relative price structure, to support a competitive climate, etc.) but also because this move constitutes an important signal of the commitment of the authorities to pursue open and stability-oriented economic policies. In particular, Article VIII convertibility may be used to enhance the credibility of the monetary policy of central banks, which lack a good track record regarding price stability (Hochreiter, 1996). Judging from the evidence, early convertibility has successfully fulfilled this role in a number of countries. There are also other important factors which prompted Article VIII convertibility. For instance, it can be interpreted as a political signal, i.e. the desire by the reforming countries to (re-)integrate their economies swiftly into the world economy, eventually leading to EU entry for a number of them.

As regards the evolution of convertibility, the direction is clear. I expect a rather rapid move to achieve full (capital account) convertibility, because international organisations are advising these countries to proceed in this direction, and a number of countries, including the Czech Republic, Poland and Hungary, are "suffering" from large capital inflows. These flows are related to the success achieved in reforming these economies and political systems, and in providing good investment opportunities and a healthy growth potential. They may also be the result of "excessive credibility" of monetary policy. Hence, there is a clear rationale for liberalising capital exports. By mid-1996 some of these countries, i.e. the Czech Republic, have actually satisfied the requirements of the OECD to liberalise capital movements. Yet, in contrast to my staunch support of Article VIII convertibility, I tend to see capital account convertibility as a two-edged sword. Capital reacts swiftly to changes in expectations, and capital inflows can quickly turn into massive outflows once speculative attacks strike, as the EMS or Mexican crises have shown.

As far as the exchange rate regime is concerned, I am heavily influenced by the Austrian experience, so I support the fixing of the exchange rate, after the initial devaluation, at a somewhat undervalued level (Hochreiter, 1996) on the grounds that it initially mitigates the cost of transition, while providing a simple and clear anchor for expectations. Nonetheless, I fear that fixing the exchange rate for a period of only six to twelve months, as Rosati suggests, might not be sufficient to enhance the credibility of monetary policy. Afterwards, while Rosati favours a crawling peg (presumably of the exogenous type) to limit the movement of the real exchange rate,

The opinions expressed are those of the author and do not necessarily represent the views of the Oesterreichische Nationalbank.

I would emphasize the overriding role of domestic policies, i.e. fiscal and wage policy (an incomes policy of the Austrian type[2] and not the Anglo-Saxon version of administered wage controls) to limit real exchange rate changes. Rosati, instead, fixes the path of domestic policies, and consequently the exchange rate needs to be used as an adjustment instrument. However, the evidence clearly indicates that the real exchange rate is much more volatile if driven by changes in the nominal exchange rate instead of by the changes in domestic prices. Insufficient flexibility of the domestic economy may result in an unsustainable trend of the real exchange rate. Hence, an understanding of the causes for real exchange rate movements is essential.

In his advocacy of exchange rate flexibility, Rosati holds the view prevailing among OECD countries since the EMS crises of 1992 and 1993, and more recently among CEECs, that flexibility is needed in the presence of large capital movements (Svensson, 1994). In fact, there are very few counterexamples that do not support the prevailing view, among which I would like to mention the Austrian, the Dutch and possibly the Belgian experiences. Yet, exchange rate flexibility raises a problem. In view of the desire of some CEECs to join the EU, including its monetary union, *less* rather than more exchange rate flexibility will be required to satisfy the Maastricht exchange rate criterium.

As regards foreign direct investment, I wish to mention that in 1991 and 1992, Austria supplied some 40 per cent of all FDI to Central and Eastern Europe, focusing particularly on Hungary. The reasons behind these large investment flows are in line with the survey results presented by Lankes and Venables.

As shown by Hunya, the flow of FDI into CEECs is only a small fraction of total investment in these countries. As a consequence, the importance of FDI in *quantitative* terms should not be over-estimated. Its importance in *qualitative* terms should, instead, be stressed, particularly with respect to know-how transfer connected with FDI, as underscored by Fischer *et al.* FDI should also be seen as a useful addition to domestic savings, as a means to raise the growth rate and as a factor contributing to the sustainability of a current account deficit, especially when the exchange rate is pegged.

Looking at the research agenda for the future, subjects which merit further work concern the interlinkage between convertibility and financial sector reform, the credibility effects of convertibility for monetary policy and the relationship between convertibility, the exchange rate regime and FDI. Other important topics for research are related to the preparation of CEECs for EU and EMU membership.

What would the *monetary policy* requirements be in the run-up to EU membership, regarding policy strategy, instruments and implementation? In this context a number of issues need to be examined with the Maastricht convergence criteria in mind, namely the *exchange rate regime* question, the determination of the equilibrium real exchange rate, the question of how to comply with the Maastricht exchange rate criterium, and the *legal framework for monetary policy* with particular reference to the central bank.

Notes

[1] By comparison, Austria unified its exchange rate only in 1953 and completed the liberalisation of capital movements as late as November 1991.

[2] Wage settlements based on productivity advances.

References

Hochreiter, E., 1995, "Central Banking in Economies in Transition", in: T.D. Willett, R.C.K. Burdekin, R.J. Sweeney and C. Whilborg, eds., *Establishing Monetary Stability in Emerging Market Economies*, Westview Press, pp. 127-144 .

Hochreiter, E., 1996, "Necessary Conditions for a Successful Pursuit of a Hard Currency Strategy in an Economy in Transition", in: R.J. Sweeney, C. Whilborg and T.D. Willett, eds., *Exchange Rate Policies in Emerging Market Economies*, Westview Press, in press.

Svensson, L.E.O., 1994, "Fixed Exchange Rates as a Means to Price Stability: What Have We Learned?", CEPR Discussion Paper No. 872, January.

Daniel Daianu

At the outset, I wish to make few comments on some general issues. One of them refers to the classification of CEECs into fast reformers vs. slow reformers. This taxonomy needs some qualification. On the one hand, it obscures important differences between countries which are grouped together; on the other, it downplays the importance of structural factors and of *history* in explaining differing economic performances. It may be the case that culture (the burden of the past), geography and structural factors to a large extent explain why certain policies (like macroeconomic stabilization) were more likely to be undertaken and have been more successful in some countries than in others. Economic recovery in the transition economies may be linked more closely with structural factors (such as the bottoming out of economic activity and the accumulation of a critical mass of organisational and institutional capital) than with macroeconomic stabilization, as some strongly argue. For instance, the fact that Romania's recovery began in 1993, i.e. at the peak of inflation (about 300 per cent) — should be a point for consideration. Macroeconomic stabilization is unquestionably good for growth, but the implied causality is currently overemphasized and structural factors are often underestimated.

If the impact on policies of structural factors and the burden of the past is well considered then one may need to broaden the focus of analysis. It seems to me that those who provide advice to CEECs frequently equate non-adherence to a "first-best" policy package with a lack of political will. One has to ask whether the advocated "first-best" policies are actually realistic, given the circumstances. Some pundits disconnect what is desirable — from a results-oriented perspective — from what is achievable in each transition economy.

By taking these factors and conditions into account, one can identify the sources of policy credibility in these economies. In this respect, there seems to be a "credibility paradox": those who need to be more credible are not (cannot be) because of the magnitude of required resource reallocation and of overall change, and the related costs. In contrast, those who can afford not to undertake similarly painful changes (e.g. Hungary) enjoy more credibility due to the relatively smaller scale of structural adjustment that is necessary. Obviously, a political element has to be factored in as well. Credibility and the boldness of policy approach can be enhanced by political climate and various anchors. The prospect of joining the EU and NATO has provided a powerful policy anchor to most of the countries which signed Association Agreements with the EU. This helps to explain why there have been no major policy reversals in most of the CEECs, in spite of political backlashes.

Due to the persistence of major structural distortions and the *fragility* of their institutions, the transition economies are potentially subject to intense strain. This applies to all CEECs since even the front-runners (except probably Poland) have not made big strides in deeply restructuring their economies. This aspect needs to be emphasized, because the resumption of growth across a large area may have caused more optimism than is actually warranted.

As regards the role of institutions it seems that economists are not very well equipped to analyse such a deep and wide-ranging institutional change as the one experienced by these countries. This is unfortunate since the quality of institutions is what ultimately counts to explain long-term growth differentials across these economies.

Another aspect to be examined is related to the dynamics of wage differentials and income distribution. Price liberalisation can have a strong impact on income distribution by exposing inefficient sectors to intense competition, which can lead to steep declines in wages and the loss of jobs, particularly where subsidies are removed. As the experience of Latin America shows, wide income differences are not conducive to social stability and long-term growth.

As far as exchange rate policy is concerned, I wish to mention some features of the transition economies which would lead to favouring an exchange rate-based stabilization programme: (a) no significant history of open inflation, which reduces the amount of inertia in the system; (b) no long track record of inflation; (c) most of the governments do not face credibility problems linked with a long history of policy reversals; and (d) relatively low capital mobility due to undeveloped financial markets and reduced integration with world capital markets. There are, however, other aspects that do not favour such a stabilization approach, and they include the intensity of *strain* in the system, the fragility of institutions, and the scarcity of international reserves.

Regarding the initial devaluation, it is very hard to judge *ex ante* the required degree of currency undervaluation. The reforming country should not under estimate the importance of having a longer period at its disposal before the exchange rate becomes again overvalued. In this respect, the parallel rate(s) may not move in tandem with the movement of the official rates unless there is a large initial undervaluation, which would add credibility to the government's external policy. In any case, the exchange rate devaluation cannot work unless it is accompanied by a strong and coherent macroeconomic stabilization and reform package. As the experience of Israel and some Latin-American countries in the 1980s shows, this package might have to be imaginative (heterodox) in order to be successful.

As to the equilibrium exchange rate, it is difficult to identify its level in economies undergoing deep transformation. Several factors need to be considered, such as the level of economic activity, potential efficiency gains, and the nature of capital inflows (autonomous vs. compensatory). It would also be useful to distinguish between the long-term equilibrium level and a short-term one.

As an illustration of some of the problems raised by the selection of a foreign exchange regime, I will briefly mention Romania's experience with the "full foreign exchange retention" system which was adopted in early 1992 as a means to stop massive capital flight. This regime helped to create an informal foreign exchange market. The authorities rapidly obtained the results they expected, i.e. the capital outflows were stopped to a large extent and the pressure on the official foreign exchange market subsided. However, the dollarisation process of the economy intensified and other difficulties arose concerning the conduct of monetary policy. Since the central bank allowed the use of foreign currency in some internal transactions, it had to monitor monetary aggregates that included hard currency holdings as well. Furthermore, the negative level of real interest rates on the domestic currency led to a hoarding of foreign currency and provided an incentive to the expansion of arrears; this, in turn, fed inflationary pressures.

At the same time, since most of the foreign exchange reserves were held by commercial banks, the central bank had little leeway for intervening on the market in order to prop up the exchange rate when the latter was under pressure. A substantial loss of foreign exchange reserves by the banking system (including the central bank) could easily trigger a currency crisis and accelerate the depreciation of the exchange rate. This is actually what occurred in the last quarter of 1995. In conclusion, the regime of full retention calls for a cautious macroeconomic policy stance in view of maintaining a sustainable position in the external account and preventing losses of confidence in the domestic currency.

Jim Rollo

The point of contact between the two contributions by Leamer and Inotai is the question of the impact of trade policy.

I will begin by making one comment and raising two questions on the first contribution. When I was a boy I asked my mother how to become rich. She said work hard and always turn out the light when you leave an empty room. So it is nice to have a fully worked out theory to justify my mother's stylised facts. In that sense this is a Filer-type reality check: if it fits the theory, it must be true. However, I noted that my mother worked hard and turned out lights but was not rich — so I became a civil servant.

The anti-Filer reality check, by which I mean confronting the hypothesis with data and amending it if it does not fit, arises on the gravity modelling carried out by Leamer. The final section of the contribution concludes (and I paraphrase) that: (a) distance from markets is bad for trade generally; (b) capital-intensive goods are particularly sensitive to distance; and (c) protectionism is equivalent to distance and hence is bad for trade and industrialisation generally. The contribution, therefore, concludes that protectionism in Western Europe is bad for industrialisation in Eastern Europe.

This is an important result, but one which has been widely recognised without the benefit of Leamer's modelling. The important question is whether, empirically, West European protectionism is a problem for transition economies. Nominal protection of industrial goods in the EU and EFTA is generally low on an MFN basis. The CEECs enjoy free trade areas in industrial goods with the EU and with the remaining EFTA countries. Contingent protection (by which I mean anti-dumping and safeguards clauses) may be important as barriers, may rules of origin, but they are difficult to quantify. In any case, even these will disappear as countries in Central and Eastern Europe join the EU. Even countries which are in the longer term unlikely to become EU members, notably Ukraine, Russia and Kazakstan, are in line for industrial free trade areas with the EU. So again I ask: is this an important issue? I long for data to be brought to bear.

My question is, therefore, how much "distance" does actual protection add? There are, after all, GATT databases of protection levels. They were used in the calculations of the impact of the Uruguay Round and purport to include the impact of anti-dumping (see Baldwin and Francois, 1996).

My second question, and perhaps it is not a serious one, derives from Leamer's Table 7. This shows positive coefficients on cereals and animal products relative to distance. This implies that the greater the distance, the more advantage there is to producing and trading these goods. Since protection is equivalent to distance, this raises the question of whether the Common Agricultural Policy is good for the agricultural sector in the transition countries?

There is much I agree with in Inotai's contribution. In the end, however, I was rather puzzled about how important promotion of CEFTA trade is or is likely to be. We have been around this track a number of times since 1990. Some of the time the lobby for the promotion of CEFTA trade has had the rather cynical intent of diverting attention from EU protection, particularly on agriculture, or from the general question of CEFTA countries' membership in the EU. But it has never had a high priority in the CEFTA countries themselves, and I might — perhaps cruelly — ask whether CEFTA is an answer in search of a question.

As it stands, the Inotai contribution sets out a series of arguments about why subregional trade is important and why the EU association agreements could in principle — via trade diversion — be damaging to it. Inotai gives us some figures on the fall in intra-CEFTA trade shares (extracting the impact of the separation of the Czech Republic and Slovak Republic) and the rise in the EU shares. But surely the question is what shares should we expect? We cannot take it for granted that the pre-1990 shares were the right ones. Indeed, Rosati (1992) suggests that the combination of trade preferences within the CMEA and the highly distorted transferable rouble exchange rates led to too much trade among the CEFTA countries. On the basis of his analysis, we should have expected intra-CEFTA trade shares to fall after 1989. The interesting question then is whether they have fallen further than we should expect, in which case they might be expected to begin to recover, or whether they indeed have further to fall.

Gravity modelling would be helpful here. The latest study of this that I know of is by Hamilton and Winters (1992) which draws on Wang and Winters (1991). The estimates of the former, which are based on 1985 data and are in absolute terms, suggest that the level of intra-CMEA trade (which is admittedly not the same as intra-CEFTA trade shares) was twice as high as their gravity model would lead one to expect. Moreover, the absolute level of total (the sum of intra- and extra-CMEA) trade was predicted to be higher than actual trade. Thus, if total trade was expected to expand after the transition and intra-CMEA trade to fall by half in absolute terms, then the intra-CMEA share should be expected to fall by more than half and the intra-CEFTA share with it. This is broadly what Inotai suggests has happened for intra-CEFTA trade. Thus actual outturns are not necessarily inconsistent with what we would have expected from the early work of Wang and Winters. What is really needed is an updating of the studies of Rosati and Wang and Winters to test where we are now against a gravity model estimated on current GNP numbers. Only then will we begin to come to grips with whether intra-CEFTA trade is too low.

Finally, let me say a few words about enlargement of the EU to the East, because it will deal with some of the problems identified in the two contributions under consideration, but also because it may give rise to a different set of problems for the CEECs. First the upside — EU membership will embed free trade in goods and services with no contingent protection, both between the EU 15 and each of the CEFTA countries, but also between the CEFTA countries as they become members of the EU. Equally, there will be a common regulatory regime leading to eventual deep integration accompanied by freedom of movement of capital and at some time freedom of movement of labour. The interesting research question that comes out of that is about the attitudes of CEFTA members to EU protectionism, once they become members. Will they continue to call for liberalisation or will they try to protect their "sensitive sectors"? Portugal is an interesting precedent. When outside the EU, Portugal wanted liberalisation of the EU's textile policy. Once inside, Portugal has worked to maintain the advantages of trade diversion, since it was and remains the lowest cost producer in the Union.

On the downside of enlargement is the potential macroeconomic impact of the application of EU policies, the CAP and the structural funds in particular. Unreformed, the CAP could transfer around 10 per cent of GNP *per annum* to the Visegrad countries and the structural funds could transfer anywhere between 17 and 24 per cent of GNP *per annum* (Rollo, 1996). Even plausible reform scenarios for these two policies suggest that transfers of 5-10 per cent of GNP are entirely possible. If new member states maintain flexible exchange rates, these transfers year in and year out will raise the real exchange rate along with it. As and when they join EMU, the adjustment process will then take place via real wages. Either way, export competitiveness will decline. The research question here is once more one of exploration of scenarios and quantification of the effects. It is these issues — and not the ones of protection in the EU and the promotion of intra-CEFTA trade — which will confront the countries of Central Europe as they join the EU.

References

Baldwin, R. and Francois, J., 1996, "Transatlantic Free Trade: A quantitative assessment", CEPR, London, [mimeo].

Hamilton, C. and Winters, A., 1992, "Opening up International Trade with Eastern Europe" in *Economic Policy*, April.

Rollo, J., 1996, "Economic Aspects of EU Enlargement to the East", prepared for Ghent Colloquium on EU Enlargement, March, [mimeo].

Rosati, D., 1992, "Problems of Post CMEA Trade and Payments" in Fleming and Rollo (ed.) *Trade Payments and Adjustment in Central and Eastern Europe*, Royal Institute of International Affairs/EBRD, London.

Wang, Z.K. and Winters, A., 1991, "The Trading Potential of Eastern Europe", CEPR Discussion Paper No. 610.

Joaquim Oliveira Martins

I shall focus my comments on some of the issues raised by Leamer and Inotai. The first issue concerns the relationship between the level of human *effort* and wages. Leamer presented an elegant way of extending the traditional Heckscher-Ohlin-Samuelson model to incorporate the human *effort* variable. His formulation aims to show that transition countries have to work "hard" in order to catch up with the productivity levels of the most advanced economies and that a less uniform wage distribution could create the incentives for this to occur. This approach has, however, a somewhat "Stakhanovite"[1] flavour which may not be the most appropriate way to characterise the evolution that would bring the transition economies close to the level of development of the most advanced market economies. Indeed, the problem is not so much to increase the volume of output but rather to create more product variety and to upgrade product quality. These are the features characterising the bulk of competition in modern manufacturing industries. They certainly require human effort but of a different kind, perhaps more related to the stock of human capital. In many of the transition economies the labour force seems to possess the technical skills which are needed to achieve this result. For instance, the sector of industrial and electrical machinery, to which Leamer referred, is a good example to show that the technical ability to differentiate products may be more important than the increase in the volume of output per worker. Along the same lines, the development of service industries (e.g. tourism) could also be viewed as a viable option for the development of foreign trade. I would, therefore, prefer to see the *effort* variable embodied in a model which includes the possibility of product differentiation, instead of the traditional assumption of dealing with homogeneous goods. Under this alternative assumption, I suspect that the results could be quite different from the Stolper-Samuelson effects presented by Leamer.

A second issue that underlies Leamer's idea of a sectoral bifurcation concerns the interaction between *foreign trade* and *economic restructuring*. In some countries, the export boom was based on heavy industrial products produced in large-sized enterprises which, to a large extent, have not yet undergone deep restructuring. In other countries, trade expansion is due to the development of light industries that are essentially characterised by the presence of small- and medium-sized enterprises. I think that in the latter case foreign trade is encouraging more intensively the transformation of the industrial base and the emergence of a new private sector. It would be interesting to examine this question further.

As regards *access to the European market*, using a measure of economic distance, Leamer has made a convincing case to show the importance of the EU, as *the* natural export market for CEECs. The test would be even more convincing if the data were taken from a more recent period, as there have been substantial changes in international transportation costs.

One could draw a parallel here with the Asian NICs and the American market. Indeed, access to this large market has been crucial for export growth and has enabled countries such as Korea and Taiwan to sustain economic growth without being confronted with serious balance of payments imbalances. The EU has already started to play a similar role for the CEECs, allowing a massive trade re-orientation in most of the transition economies since the early 1990s. This has in turn led to the economic recovery in Central and Eastern Europe. A comparison between the Asian NICs and the CEECs may, however, not be completely warranted. In the case of the Asian region, one country — Japan — played the role of a "locomotive". The European Union needs to play for the CEECs the dual role of a large market (like the US) and an industrial "locomotive" (like Japan) because these countries' exports are still largely concentrated in the sector of intermediate goods and raw materials. This is a challenge that the EU will have to face in the coming years. Furthermore, I have some doubts about Inotai's argument that trade between the CEECs and the EU already may be moving towards an intra-industry pattern. To answer this question, the analysis should be carried out at a more disaggregated level than the one-digit sectoral data used by Inotai.

Finally, it seems questionable that there exists a significant potential for developing *regional* trade among Central European countries, as argued by Inotai. According to standard trade theory, the potential should be limited over the short- and medium- term, due to the similarity of CEECs' production structures, as well as to the fact that they have not yet reached the stage of producing a wide range of differentiated products. In this regard, the case of the Czech and the Slovak republics should be viewed, for historical reasons, as an exception.

Note

[1] Aleksei Grigorievitch Stakhanov was the Soviet coal miner who on the night of 31 August 1935 was able to extract 105 tons of coal whereas the average performance on those days was 7 tons of coal per day and per man. Some months later, with the help of some colleagues, he doubled his performance by extracting 227 tons of coal. He died in 1977.

Zdenek Drabek

1. Arguments for subregional co-operation

Inotai provides a good review of virtually all of the arguments that have been presented in favour of regional co-operation. I will mention, however, four points in favour of subregional co-operation, which have not been addressed.

- *Scope of co-operation.* The focus of Inotai's contribution is on trade, but as he recognises, there is much more that can be done at the subregional level, for instance, infrastructural projects which would bring many benefits to transport, border crossings, energy and other sectors.
- *Foreign trade discrimination.* The Association Agreements liberalised trade between the CEECs and the EU, but in the process, policy measures affecting

trade of the CEECs between themselves have been "forgotten". The end result was that in the aftermath of the Europe Agreements, the trade markets in Central and Eastern Europe were discriminated against as compared to EU markets. There is already some fragmentary evidence of this result. The CEFTA-like arrangement had, therefore, to be put in place in order to eliminate this bias or discrimination.

- *Foreign direct investment.* Each of these countries represents too small a market to be able to attract significant foreign investment. It is important that these markets be as closely integrated as possible in order to allow large multinational corporations to benefit from economies of scale. A small market of 4 to 5 million, such as the one in Slovakia, can hardly justify a major investment of a multinational corporation, unless it can use the country as a base for exports to other markets.
- *Political arguments.* Subregional co-operation will demonstrate to the outside world the ability of these countries to co-operate in preparing themselves for EU membership.

2. *Arguments against subregional co-operation*

- Inotai uses basically three counter-arguments. I find one argument not very convincing, another excellent, and the third one unclear.
- *Gravity model.* Inotai's counter-arguments against the "gravity" models are not very convincing. First of all, these models are not always based on the "developed countries" experience. Moreover, they seem to be very useful in the context of the CEECs because they have been used in the past to test the importance of geographical factors during the inter-war period. Interestingly, they provide a certain degree of continuity between the inter-war period and the current period, and their findings are similar to those of Inotai.
- *Global competitiveness.* This is indeed vital as a first step to regional co-operation. The subregional market could hardly provide either the opportunities or the competitive pressures for industries to modernise. For instance, Southeast Asia has become competitive by exporting to Japan, the United States and Europe, before expanding its trade in regional markets.
- *Distorted production structure.* It is not clear why Inotai thinks that the CEECs have a distorted production structure. Does a "distorted" production structure mean that whenever a country is not competitive, (which appears to be the case with many manufacturing industries in the CEECs today), it must have a "distorted" production structure? What would the policy implications be under those circumstances? Does it mean that countries should pursue strategies that are essentially equivalent to "infant industry protection"?

3. *Empirical evidence on interregional trade*

- More work needs to be done on the basis of more disaggregated trade statistics than the ones that are used by Inotai, in order to learn from recent trends and qualitative changes, such as those leading to sub-contracting or to so-called "distress exports".
- *Positive impact of EU.* The problems of statistics become evident in the analysis of the positive impact of the EU. Inotai points out that the main positive impact has initially been on trade. How can we judge its impact if we have limited empirical evidence? A detailed study of trade flows between the EU and the CEECs is needed to examine the important question of trade creation.
- *Negative impact of the European Union.* Where is the evidence that trade with the EU "destroyed production and export capacities for subregional markets"? Moreover, even if it did destroy some of the local production capacities, this destruction was justified if it eliminated inefficient lines of production that, we know, were abundant under central planning! It would also be useful to analyse the impact on agricultural trade and on enterprises which were relocated or displaced.
- *Dual commodity structure.* All CEECs are slowly losing the "dual commodity structure" which they used to have at the time of Comecon. Trade with other formerly socialist countries was dominated by manufacturing products while all countries were in desperate need of various raw materials and agricultural products. In contrast, the commodity structure of exports of these countries to the West was often characterised by a much lower percentage of manufactures, and they tended to export even those commodities that were not in abundance. It appears that this dual commodity structure is being lost in the new economic system in which price relations are becoming more consistent with those prevailing in world markets where government support has been by and large eliminated. In other words, the trade pattern of these countries is becoming more normal.

4. *Other (positive and negative) impacts*

- *Defensive pattern of adjustment to the EU.* It is true that the CEECs have been "reacting" to the EU rather than initiating their own agenda for restructuring and adjustment. However, I doubt that the CEECs position is defensive because the EU would like to impose its own adjustment rules. Many, if not most, of these rules provide a reasonable basis for integrating the CEECs into the EU. Why would the CEECs want to join the EU if they do not think that the EU is "good"? No doubt there is a need for some adjustment in EU policies and institutions (the "two-way adjustment", as the Poles like to call it, for example, in agriculture, budgetary rules, etc.), but, most of the adjustment has to be done by the CEECs and not by the EU.

- *Speed of reform.* According to Inotai, adjustment to EU rules has been too fast, and the adoption of a market system has been too hasty. What is he suggesting — a slower reform? This could obviously mean that our countries might not be, even today, in a position to apply for membership.
- *PHARE.* Inotai's assessment of the PHARE programme is too negative. Once again, there were many programmes under PHARE that have had poor results (for example, on "privatisation"), but there were many other programmes that were important and well executed. Among the latter, I wish to mention assistance for legal harmonisation; the reform of democratic institutions, bank regulation; environmental projects, investment projects funded by IBRD and EBRD.
- *Similarity of European Agreements.* The similarity of European Agreements, as pointed out, is indeed a problem, and Inotai is right to stress it. Since countries' adjustment capacities are likely to differ, it is questionable that the same European Agreements should be applied to all CEECs. Yet, the truth of the matter is that the CEECs were negotiating the European Agreements "en bloc", which means that some countries most likely obtained better conditions of association than others. Clearly this is an important lesson for the future!

5. *Impact of CEECs on the EU*

- *Global competitiveness of the EU.* While Inotai believes, like many others, that enlargement will increase global competitiveness of the EU, I think that this is unlikely. *First*, intra-EU trade today represents the dominant percentage of total EU trade, i.e. there has not been much impetus to trade globally so far. *Second*, the share in EU trade of the CEECs is very small. Furthermore, trade among CEECs has been historically small, i.e. including the communist period and the inter-war period. *Third*, the main motivation of foreign companies to invest in the region is probably not to improve their competitiveness, but to export to the markets of Central and Eastern Europe. *Fourth*, the EU must want to be globally competitive. Right now, this does not seem to be necessarily the case: political pressures have rather pushed EU countries against the search for global competitiveness. The "block mentality", as Inotai calls it, is very much in evidence.
- *Adjustment of the EU.* It is true that CEFTA has progressed further in liberalising agricultural trade than the EU. However, whether this will have an impact on the EU is very doubtful. It seems to me that what will change trade practices in the EU is likely to be the pressure of more powerful partners, as in the negotiations under the WTO Agreement.

6. *Market access*

- *Role of trade.* It is necessary, first, to ascertain whether market access ultimately matters or not. This depends on the importance of international trade for a given country. Large countries may not be concerned too much about their access to other markets, while for small countries market access is vital. CEECs are also concerned about market access for balance of payments reasons.

- *Existing protection.* Unfortunately, market access for the CEECs remains considerably affected by protective measures in major markets including those of the EU. The latter concerns the so-called "sensitive" products, such as steel, textiles, clothing and agricultural products, and includes measures for contingent protection, such as anti-dumping and safeguards measures.

- *The effect of trade barriers.* It is not entirely clear what has been the overall impact of these measures on CEECs exports. For example, the quotas that were imposed on the imports from CEECs of some textiles, clothing and agriculture products have not been fully utilised by these countries. Even though contingent protection measures have been applied in practice to a relatively small extent, the fact that these measures can be used represents a threat to trade expansion. Finally, no firm evidence is available about the trade creation effect resulting from trade liberalisation measures introduced by the CEECs.

János Gács

I find Leamer's theory of pace of operations interesting, and I hope that he develops it further. If he intends to make his theory empirically testable, he has to solve the problem of how to distinguish between different sources of productivity growth, since the pace of operations is only one of them. In the CEECs that went through systemic changes with astonishing speed, the shift in the types of co-ordination (from bureaucratic to market co-ordination, in Kornai's terms) and particularly changes in enterprise management would be expected to be at least as important as the pace of operations. Obviously, efficiency of enterprise management and pace of operations are also interrelated.

Leamer's focus on the distance to markets is fully consistent with one of his earlier contributions that gravity models are unduly neglected by most analysts of international trade (see Leamer and Levinsohn, 1995). Gravity models display good empirical explanatory properties, but lack sound theoretical foundations. In his contribution, Leamer does justice to gravity models, although he is not alone in doing this. The gravity models by Rosati (1992), Winters and Wang (1994), and Baldwin (1994), for example, use distance to markets and GDP of the trading partners as explanatory variables to calculate the expected trade volume and geographical composition of CEECs' trade.

I agree with the conclusion of Leamer's analysis that "Western Europe is pretty much the only prospect for Eastern Europe". His argument, that "because most of the rest of the world's GDP is naturally too far away" is, however, not convincing for me. First, one should keep in mind that most Eastern European countries are small ones, many of them very small. Out of the 10 East European transition economies, eight have a population of less than 11 million, while in the group of the 25 transition economies (including FSU republics) 19 have less than 11 million population, and 11 less than 5 million. Taking these countries individually, most of them do not need very large markets for marketing their additional exports.

Second, the real alternatives to Western Europe (i.e. other naturally close markets with substantial GDP) are not analysed by Leamer. Such alternatives would be the Central and Eastern European markets themselves combined (the subject matter of Inotai's contribution), or the markets of the FSU. Leamer does not list the Soviet Union in his 127 country sample (most probably due to lack of reliable data). This gives rise to the suspicion that this important market was in fact not taken into account when the distance indices were calculated for 1960 and 1990. We know, however, that markets of the FSU used to be relatively close to Eastern Europe and despite recent systemic changes, many of them are potentially important for the CEECs.

Access to markets is an extremely complex phenomenon. The graphical concept of distance to GDP can explain access only to a limited extent. Recent research sponsored by the International Institute for Applied Systems Analysis investigated impediments to exports in eight small East European economies. The results of this analysis show that much of the obstacles to entering external markets can be found within the transition countries themselves and not in trade protectionism. The lack of knowledge of the potential markets (i.e. ignorance concerning potential partners, specificities of market demand, and trade practices abroad) and the lack of infrastructure, especially competitive trade financing and insurance, can primarily explain why in recent years East European countries could not fully reach their trade potential. Blaming distance (in the geographical, or trade or political sense) for these flaws would mislead both analysis and policy advice. Leamer's distance indices seem to give more guidance for long term projections than for the short- and medium-term.

The importance of internal institution building and a trade-promoting environment also seems to be under-estimated by Inotai. His conclusion that trade expansion even within the CEFTA depends on external factors such as EU membership or the activities of foreign direct investors, seems to focus too much on the external environment. There is sufficient evidence that in the CEFTA region the lack of knowledge of each others' markets and inadequate financing and risk sharing have hindered the development of intraregional trade. Third country intermediation is common in international trade but highly uncommon between close or adjacent countries. Intermediation, however, has become very common between close East European countries in recent years. This is the case of Hungary: in 1994, 52 per cent of its exports to Slovenia, 45 per cent of those to Bulgaria and 27 per cent of those to the Czech Republic were managed by third country intermediators (Törzsök, 1995). These intermediators were mostly from Austria and Switzerland. Trade between other countries of the East European region also shows high percentages of intermediation. These can be attributed to some shortcomings, such as the lack of trade financing, high risks that remain uncovered due to inadequacies of the trade insurance system, and insufficient market research by the exporters. East European governments can improve trade infrastructure in their own countries, and this does not need external incentives such as EU membership or deepening of the integration among CEFTA countries.

References

Baldwin, R.E., 1994, *Towards Integrated Europe, Centre for Economic Policy Research*, London.

Leamer, E.E. and Levinsohn, J., 1995, "International Trade Theory: The Evidence", in Grossmann, G. M. and Rogoff, K. (eds.) *Handbook of International Economics* Vol. 3, Elsevier, Amsterdam.

Rosati, D., 1992, "Problems of Post-CMEA Trade and Payments", in *The Economic Consequences of the East*, Centre for Economic Policy Research, London.

Törzsök, É., 1995, *The Foreign Transit Trade and the Hungarian Trade Balance* (in Hungarian), Külgazdaság Vol. XXXIX, No. 10.

Winters, A.L. and Wang, Z.K., 1994, *Eastern Europe's international trade*, Manchester University Press, Manchester.

Hans-Peter Lankes

Venables and I have presented the first results of an on-going study. Its objective is not to develop a theory of foreign direct investment in the transition economies but to contribute survey-based facts where little information has been available, something which should improve our understanding of investor strategies in a transition environment. It uncovers a number of interesting and statistically highly significant patterns, which appear to be specifically linked to the transition process — the correlation between investment function, control mode and progress in transition, to name just these. On the basis of these results, certain conjectures are possible which, while not formally embedded in a theory of foreign investment, do offer some plausible insights into future patterns of FDI. Some of these have powerful implications; for instance, the increasing share of cost-motivated, export-oriented investments as the transition progresses would affect trading patterns, given the different profiles of market-driven and export-oriented investments.

From the survey results it is inferred that contingent protection of EU markets is not an issue for foreign investors. Respondents with investments in Group 1 and Group 2 countries (Central and Eastern Europe) do not report non-tariff barriers of significance when exporting to the EU. According to the Commission's data, contingent protection has decreased considerably vis-a-vis these countries since implementation of the Association Agreements with the EU. However, the situation is different for investors in the CIS (where the incidence of anti-dumping action has increased significantly over the past five years) — 12 per cent report that they perceive obstacles of this nature when exporting to the EU/EEA area. The sample of export-oriented investors in the CIS is too small to draw definitive conclusions. But it is obvious, for instance, that vulnerability to contingent protection is sector-dependent. The share of investors in "sensitive sectors" who might feel threatened by contingent protection is likely to be much higher than 12 per cent.

7

General discussion

The analytical contributions on the theme of "external policies" raised a very diverse set of non-overlapping issues. The ensuing discussion among the experts focused on only a handful of them, most notably optimal exchange rate policy regimes for transition countries and alternative international trade agreements that are currently relevant for CEECs. The second issue generated some corollary debate on non-tariff trade barriers, regionalism versus globalism, the gravity model of trade, the disciplining effects of trade on domestic monopolies, and the implications of greater labour mobility on growth and development of transition economies.

The first major theme of the discussion was a debate on the merits of fixed versus flexible exchange rate regimes during different phases of transition, drawing on the contribution of Rosati. The experts all seemed to be in general agreement about the need for fixed exchange rates in the initial phases of transition. This stated, the optimal post-stabilization currency regime was a highly controversial issue. One group of experts advocated the early move toward flexible rates that was recommended by Rosati, on the basis that fixing the exchange rate for a prolonged period subjected transition countries to serious dangers of currency misalignments as nominal exchange rates became more and more unrealistic and pressures would emerge for sudden, large realignments. Another group of experts, led by Sahay and Hochreiter, advised against any rapid move by transition economies towards abandoning fixed rates once macroeconomic stabilization takes place, on the grounds that transition economies generally lack effective tools for monetary control. Without such tools, monetary policy cannot be conducted effectively and any benefits hoped for from flexible exchange rates will be difficult to realise. Finally, the question was repeatedly raised whether any general conclusion could be reached regarding optimal exchange rate policies, since economic conditions had varied and continue to vary so widely from transition country to transition country.

The second major theme of the discussion was on the merits and political economy of Central European countries joining the European Union common market, compared with deepening the existing CEFTA.

The close geographic proximity of Central European countries was consistently identified as an important factor in the expansion of trade between them. This led some experts, such as Negritoiu, to question the greater relevance of discussing non-regional (globally) based trade arrangements. Others, in minority, raised the question of whether European transition countries should find a slow-growth, high-unemployment Europe worth linking to in a close institutional sense, in spite of its wealth. Most participants seemed, however, to strongly favour closer trade integration between Central Europe and the EU, for reasons that included the discipline of trade on domestic monopolies and the superseding of bilateral CEFTA agreements with the multilateral trade structure of the EU, which was perceived as significantly less distortionary.

The mechanics and implications of closer CEEC integration with the EU raised some debate. Inotai, in his response to points raised by Rollo, defended his emphasis on short-term pre-accession issues instead of examining such questions as potential changes in attitudes of CEFTA members towards protectionism after becoming members of the EU, or what to do about projected post-accession increases in real exchange rates and associated declines in competitiveness of Central European countries' exports. Inotai also reiterated his thesis that the basic engine for growth in trade between Central Europe and Western Europe is intra-industry trade. In response to Oliveira Martins' recommendation that analysis of this question be carried out at a more disaggregated level than was the case in Inotai's contribution, Inotai cited other research work on Hungarian trade with the EU at the six-digit level of disaggregation. This research reportedly showed Hungary's trade with the EU to be characterised much more by intra-industry trade than was the case for trade by e.g. Greece or Finland with the rest of EU.

A closely related and recurring theme was the persistence of non-tariff trade barriers of various types. There was no consensus on how to eliminate such barriers, which are neither easily quantifiable nor unique to transition economies.

Other salient points brought up in the debate included a discussion of the merits of gravity models in predicting trade. Gravity models operate on the principle that size of and distance between economies are good predictors of trade volumes between countries. Doubts were raised about the usefulness of such models in a transition context, where the explanatory effects of, for instance, distance may be swamped by institutional factors. In spite of this criticism, the experts generally agreed that beyond a medium-range time horizon, distance could be an increasingly important determinant of trade. Once the institutional turmoil of transition has passed, gravity models were expected to be useful even for estimating trade expansion between Central European countries.

As regards the relevance of geographic or locational factors in CEECs as sources of future trade expansion, Leamer argued that they are likely to play a more important role in these countries than is the case for Russia and countries in Asia and Latin America. A main reason for this is the proximity of Central Europe to major European markets, which are relatively unsaturated with comparatively labour-intensive products in contrast with the United States market, which is a major outlet for Asian and Latin American producers of these goods. Leamer suspected that Russia was too distant from the economic centres of Europe to benefit as greatly as Central Europe from increased openness to trade with OECD member countries.

In conclusion, the debate was more concerned with identifying the truly controversial transition issues with regard to external policies, rather than with reaching a consensus on a set of questions and conclusions. The questions that seem to persist currently in the minds of many policy-makers and leading researchers are overwhelmingly short to medium term in scope. They deal in the most general sense with two aspects, namely the role of exchange rate policy in promoting balanced macroeconomic development and the political economy of drawing the maximum benefits from foreign trade.

8

Policy conclusions

It is widely recognised that no reform has had farther reaching effects on the transition than the liberalisation of foreign trade together with its corollaries of external currency convertibility and exchange rate adjustment. Trade expansion, in particular, has provided the strongest impulse to economic recovery, has raised the level of competition in the domestic market and has created incentives for economic restructuring and investment. With such a record, these external policies do not seem to require any reorientation, but they need to be fully implemented in the reforming countries that are lagging behind, while in the other transition economies, they should evolve in response to the needs of closer economic integration into a wider market area. In all CEECs, there is still a large potential in foreign trade and investment that has not yet been harnessed for the purpose of accelerating economic growth.

To this end, a first necessary step, namely an effective currency convertibility for current account payments, has not yet been taken in some CEECs. The experience of the transition, however, indicates that convertibility is not out of reach in any of these economies and does not imply severe adjustment costs, provided that an appropriate macroeconomic policy is followed, particularly in the foreign exchange area. Since the slow-reforming countries have already advanced somewhat towards macroeconomic stabilization, a rapid move to convertibility for "current transactions" seems possible and is recommended.

CEECs' record on exchange rate policy appears rather mixed, with a few countries adopting fixed exchange rate regimes with some success and the others allowing different degrees of flexibility without being able to avoid currency crises from time to time. There is no optimal approach that suits all transition economies, since the choice of an exchange rate policy ultimately hinges upon the ability of each country to redress or prevent macroeconomic imbalances and the changes in external competitiveness that result from productivity growth. The presence of both these conditions, more than the availability of an adequate pool of international reserves, can explain why some countries have succeeded in stabilizing their exchange rates, while others have failed. Those countries which have successfully pegged their currencies should now consider retaining a measure of flexibility, since there is less need for a nominal anchor, such as the exchange rate, than in the initial stage of the transition, given that macroeconomic conditions and expectations are much more settled. This flexibility would help to absorb impacts of any macroeconomic policy slippages or external shocks, including sharp swings in capital movements.

Regardless whether limited exchange rate flexibility is obtained through a crawling peg or through a regime of fluctuations within a band, it has to address two requirements. Exchange rates should be broadly in line with trends emerging in the market place (i.e. monetary authorities should not lean against the market winds) and should not be at variance with the objective of maintaining a sustainable balance of payments position on the current account. Targeting an "equilibrium" exchange rate can be left aside as it is difficult to determine this rate, especially in economies that are still undergoing rapid and extensive changes. With these qualifications, a flexible exchange rate regime need not be inconsistent with the authorities' goal of lessening the degree of uncertainty in the business environment.

Less controversy surrounds trade policy, since any alternative to the trade liberalisation that the CEECs have pursued would be harmful to their growth prospects. In some countries questions have, instead, been raised about the speed, extent and sustainability of trade liberalisation that has been implemented, with the result of some backtracking. Raising the level of protection of the domestic market appears, in the current phase of the transition, even less justified than before, despite rising current account deficits, as domestic enterprises are now in a better position to compete in foreign and domestic markets, and higher trade barriers would reduce incentives to restructure. CEECs would draw more benefits from following the general path of world-wide reduction in trade obstacles, as laid out by the Uruguay Round.

In spite of complaints, EU market protection vis-à-vis CEEC exports does not appear to be a major cause for concern. In contrast, CEEC accession into the EU raises a number of issues in connection with policy constraints stemming from membership. For example, CEECs' exchange rate policies would have to be brought into line with the EU monetary integration process, and current liberal attitudes of the CEECs with respect to foreign trade might change once within the EU, as was the case with some recent EU members. By another token, the potential economic benefits from transition economies intensifying economic links among themselves appear limited, since the size of their combined markets does not compare well with the EU area. In this context, the role of the Russian economy remains clouded with uncertainty.

Attracting more investment from abroad is a better response to shortfalls in national savings as compared to investment needs, than increasing trade protection. Promoting higher capital productivity, preserving the current comparative advantage in unit labour costs and stabilizing the tax and regulatory environment, not to mention the socio-political environment, are three main conditions to achieve this goal. These are also major factors to greatly enhance the quality of the transition, something which is still elusive in many CEECs, even though it is the only guarantee of much higher living standards in the coming years.